As one who serves translation consult.   .... .v...gue transiators
in many parts of the world—often in relation to translating biblical poetry,
I highly recommend this work to all who seek to help teams rise to the
challenge of translating the Psalms. Its comprehensive approach combines
the linguistic with the literary, the academic with the practical, the exegetical
with the translational, and the fine details with the big picture. Having just
taught a course on biblical poetry in Jerusalem, Israel, I have now discovered
a most valuable textbook to use next time!

*Murray Salisbury, Ph.D., SIL International translation consultant, adjunct
professor at the Jerusalem Center for Bible Translation, Jerusalem, Israel; and
adjunct professor at Handong Global University, Pohang, South Korea*

As an SIL member for over 20 years, I am pleased to commend this work
to colleagues translating Hebrew poetry. I applied Dr. Wendland's literary-
rhetorical approach to the translation of some praise psalms into isiZulu
(for my Ph.D. thesis), and found the functional emphasis very helpful. Zulu
poets were able to benefit from this methodology to produce some beautiful
and stirring translations of psalms. Dr. Wendland's approach is practical and
helpful and I hope many others will also benefit from his fine work.

*June Dickie, Ph.D., Bible translation consultant with Wycliffe South Africa;
author of forthcoming "Singing the Psalms: Applying Principles of African Music
to Bible Translation", by Scriptura; and a forthcoming monograph based on her
thesis, "Translating Praise Psalms into Zulu Songs"*

The collection of Psalms is quite possibly the most read and most studied
book of the Bible. The Psalms are memorized, they are sung, they are prayed.
But how does one go about translating such a rich and complex book from
Hebrew into English or, indeed, into any other language?

In this sweeping yet very detailed work, Wendland does it again. Like his
outstanding *Prophetic Rhetoric* in this series, this volume presents individual
studies of chosen texts, each Psalm carefully analyzed from a different angle.

These are dense studies, and as I have said elsewhere, "not for the faint-
hearted." But the style is readable, the text furnished with many insightful
diagrams, and the overall message, clear. As Wendland notes, these "worship
texts" are full of beauty, power and sound.

This is not a sit-down, read-your-way-through book, but rather, a sit-down-
and-study one. It is almost a reference work to be opened as needed, accord-
ing to the task or theme under study. Readers need to take away what they
can for a time, and then later, come back for more.

Readers will be introduced to a fascinating combination of theory and methodology relating to Bible translation. They will be challenged by the complexities of structure interweaving with meaning and delighted by the underlying African backdrop, as seen in the many Chewa renderings, which prove that Hebrew poetry can indeed be rendered as poetry in any language.

The book presents solid discourse and rhetoric analyses of selected psalms, but touches the entire translation process, from the establishment of *Skopos* all the way through to the evaluative process.

The author, quoting Benjamin (297), notes that translating poetry is the "renewal of something living." Wendland is clearly enamored with the book of Psalms and thrilled to delve into the intricacies of this poetic collection. Translators, exegetes, and lay readers will each find within these pages help in understanding and rendering these beautiful sacred texts.

Lynell Marchese Zogbo, Ph.D., United Bible Societies translation consultant; research associate at the University of the Free State (South Africa); and research associate at Institut de Linguistique Appliquée at Université d'Abidjan (Côte d'Ivoire)

When fully appreciated, the incredible complexity of faithfully and intelligibly translating an ancient poetic text for a modern audience can seem as impossible as summiting Everest. While never easy, we are greatly aided in the task when we are led by a seasoned guide.

In the face of the peaks and valleys that challenge interpreters and translators of Biblical Hebrew poetry, Professor Wendland does not offer shortcuts, but he does lend his expert guidance and his approach is as rewarding as it is comprehensive.

These studies will cause you to fruitfully reconsider issues you may have already thought of, and think about issues you have may have never considered before. Readers may not come away from this book with an easier vision for analyzing Biblical Hebrew poetry. Indeed, they will likely developed an even keener sense of its enormity. But Professor Wendland offers here a theoretically and practically commendable model of approaching these texts. And the fruits of his labor attest that for all its difficulty, it is well worth it, and the hard climber is rewarded with the beautiful vistas of Scripture's most affective texts.

For students and scholars alike, *Studies in the Psalms* will be a welcome guide in navigating the complexities of interpreting and translating Biblical Hebrew poetry.

Christian Locatell, M.Div.; M.A. in applied linguistics; Ph.D. candidate in Ancient Languages at Stellenbosch University; research assistant in the department of Ancient Studies for Professor Christo van der Merwe; and author of several works on biblical languages, including poetic texts in the Hebrew Bible

Studies in the Psalms

Literary-Structural Analysis with
Application to Translation

Figure 1. David playing the harp.
(https://en.wikipedia.org/wiki/File:David_Playing_the_Harp_1670_Jan_de_Bray.jpg.
Public domain. Accessed September 2, 2017.)

SIL International®
Publications in Translation and Textlinguistics

8

Publications in Translation and Textlinguistics is a peer-reviewed series published by SIL International®. The series is a venue for works concerned with all aspects of translation and textlinguistics, including translation theory, exegesis, pragmatics, and discourse analysis. While most volumes are authored by members of SIL, suitable works by others also form part of the series.

Managing Editor
Eric Kindberg

Volume Editor
George Huttar

Copy Editor
Bonnie Brown

Production Staff
Lois Gourley, Composition Director
Judy Benjamin, Compositor
Barbara Alber, Cover Design

Cover Photograph
Cover image by Pixabay: https://pixabay.com/en/spring-blossom-bloom-white-2171682/. Creative Commons CCO. Public domain.

Studies in the Psalms
Literary-Structural Analysis with
Application to Translation

Ernst R. Wendland

Foreword by Christo van der Merwe

SIL International®
Dallas, Texas

Copies of this and other publications of SIL International® may be obtained through distributors such as Amazon, Barnes & Noble, other worldwide distributors and, for select volumes, www.sil.org/resources/publications:

SIL International Publications
7500 W Camp Wisdom Road
Dallas, TX 75236-5629 USA

General inquiry: publications_intl@sil.org
Pending order inquiry: sales_intl@sil.org

Contents

Dedication

To the memory of Martin Luther, who loved the Psalms, on the 500th anniversary of the Reformation.

Martin Luther, 1528 (Veste Coburg) by Lucas Cranach the Elder, gallerix.ru.
(https://commons.wikimedia.org/wiki/File:Lucas_Cranach_d.Ä._-_Martin_
Luther,_1528_(Veste_Coburg).jpg.
Public domain. Accessed September 2, 2017.)

Foreword

Translating the Bible is a difficult form of secondary communication. Translating the poetry in this ancient sacred text is, without doubt, an even more trying challenge. It is, therefore. no wonder that translation agencies typically expect translation consultants to be both scholars and language practitioners (among other things). Ernst Wendland is, without doubt. one of the most prolific writers in the field of theory and practice of Bible translation. Over the last few decades he has been involved in multiple translation and study Bible projects in Southern Africa and has conducted scores of workshops for mother-tongue translators—that is, apart from his teaching responsibilities at a theological seminary in Lusaka. However, he has also kept his ears to the ground with regard to Bible translation theory and practice and has excelled in researching developments in biblical exegesis, translation studies, and other disciplines relevant for Bible translation. As extra-ordinary professor in the Department of Ancient Studies at Stellenbosch University, during the last fifteen years he (co-)supervised several Ph.D. projects and has stimulated students and colleagues alike with a steady stream of peer-reviewed research outputs.

It is against this background that the width and depth of the present publication must be understood. It includes a careful revision of several articles published within the last two decades and covers nearly the entire continuum of challenges that Bible translators must deal with—from the analysis of the source text to the preparation of acceptable target text translations. At the heart of each article then is the reality exegetes and translators have to face, namely, the ancient source text first has to be well understood. There was a time when I wondered whether all this detail was really necessary. As I grew older (and was involved in more translation projects) I came to realize that there is no short-cut. The benefit for the reader of this work is that Wendland writes from the perspective of a seasoned translator who, in the spirit of Eugene Nida, is also a lifelong student. He does not take himself too seriously, is not afraid to indicate where he is uncertain, and always points to areas where more research is needed.

When he presents his analysis of the source text within the frame of his *LiFE* (Literary Functional Equivalence) approach, he sensitizes his readers concerning all the parameters that need to be taken into account. In this daunting task he points out all the details that need to be accounted for when one tries to understand Biblical Hebrew poetry. What he proposes is not just another "how to" handbook based on his own experiences. When he suggests practical "steps" that may be followed, they are based on insights of how poetry across languages works. When certain formal features are noted, e.g., parallelisms and chiastic structures, the next question is always, what are their semantic or pragmatic functions. He illustrates how such constructions guide readers as "communicative clues" where, for example, breaks, peaks, and the climax of a poem should be distinguished. This is, however, no clinical, or sterile structural study, but a full-blown discourse analysis which takes into account that language is embedded in a culture. The words and expressions used refer to concepts that reflect an ancient conceptual world that differs from that of modern readers. Furthermore, language is always rooted in a specific context and co-text. For Wendland, the world of the text and that behind the text, are equally important.

On the other hand, a *LiFE* translation also requires an expert knowledge and understanding of the target culture; in other words, the world "in front of the text" is equally relevant. In recent years there is a growing interest in the impact of Bible translation on target language cultures and user communities. Sponsors not only want to know whether their money is wisely spent, but translation agencies are also keen to get a better understanding of the effect of published translations—and all that needs to be considered when planning new projects. It might be by chance, but before addressing more target-language-oriented issues in the second half of his book, Wendland provides in chapter 7 what is arguably the heart of this book, the "full monty"—what singing a "new song" to the Lord is all about, from analyzing the source text to evaluating new songs in English and a *LiFE* translation of Psalm 98 in Chewa!

This book represents a collection of valuable studies by a hands-on scholar who explores nearly every dimension of the multifaceted "act of translation." All those who wish to interpret and translate Biblical Hebrew poetry from a fresh perspective will profit much from reading it.

Christo van der Merwe
Professor of Hebrew and Translation Studies
Director of the Centre for Bible Interpretation and Translation in Africa (CEBITA)
Department of Ancient Studies—Stellenbosch University

Introduction

This book is a collection of studies that illustrate a literary-structural (L-S) approach to the analysis of biblical psalmic literature and its subsequent translation into English and a Bantu language. The literary component focuses on the *formal* (artistic) as well as the *functional* (rhetorical) dimensions of analysis, while the structural component incorporates different levels of arrangement within the poetic composition as a whole. Various aspects of an L-S method of text analysis are applied in these studies (with representative psalms chosen for exemplification), and a specific literary functional equivalence *(LiFE)* style of translation is demonstrated, often in comparison with other types. The opening chapters discuss some of the more technical features of Hebrew poetic discourse, in particular, parallelism and its manifestation on the micro- as well as the macro-level of a given psalm. These characteristics and others are further illustrated with regard to form, function, and significance in subsequent studies. By means of a series of distinct but related types of text analysis and methodological application, I hope to present a synoptic vision[1] of the Psalter and selected psalms that will enable readers to:

---

[1] The "power of the synoptic vision [is] the ability to synthesize heterogeneous elements into a unity" (Kevin Vanhoozer, cited in VanGemeren 2013:44). It should be pointed out, however, that often the apparent heterogeneity of a text lies only on its surface or to the untrained eye.

a. better appreciate the *beauty* and *power* of the Psalms, as they come to
    understand how these stylistic features serve to enhance the theological
    and ethical meaning being conveyed;

b. recognize the importance of *sound* in the Psalter—that the phonological
    dimension of the text contributes greatly to its overall oratorical meaning;

c. understand how to develop an explicit, comprehensive *methodology*
    for investigating the original (Hebrew) text of psalmic discourse in the
    light of (a) and (b);

d. be encouraged to actively apply the preceding insights, derived from
    this small corpus of assorted sample studies, in their own Scripture
    analysis and *translation* practice; and

e. be able to more effectively *evaluate* and critique different translations
    and translation techniques as manifested in published versions,
    especially those in their mother tongue.

I might conclude the preceding statement of purpose with the following
important caveat: The "analysis of poetry is helpful and important—but only
if that analysis serves to assist the reader to enter into a poem [psalm] with
greater sensitivity. Analysis is a *servant*. A competent reader analyzes poetry
so that the poetry itself can speak more profoundly.... Analysis is never in any
sense a substitute for the poem" (Jacobson and Jacobson 2013:1). I trust that
the various psalmic analyses of this book will be read in that light as well as
in the more important guiding light of Psalm 119:105.

Chapter 1 proposes a description, or expanded definition, of Biblical Hebrew
poetry, consisting of ten prominent attributes. This is followed by a suggest-
ed ten-step methodology for analyzing Hebrew poetic discourse in terms of
its literary-structural characteristics, using Psalm 24 as an example. Chapter
2 explores the nature of Hebrew poetry further and examines the structur-
al manifestation of continuity and discontinuity in Hebrew poetic texts, as
illustrated by Psalm 30. Chapter 3 investigates Hebrew poetic discourse from
the classificatory perspective of genre criticism, with special reference to the
organization and speech-act dynamics of Psalm 31. Chapter 4 presents an
L-S analysis of Psalm 22, again with special attention being devoted to the
distinctive qualities of Hebrew religious poetry. Chapter 5 offers a critique of
a recent study of Hebrew parallelism as compared with my own approach in
reference to Psalm 103. Chapter 6 examines Psalm 45 with respect to seven
"artistic-rhetorical features," which are then reproduced in a functionally-
equivalent manner in a Chewa oratorical translation. Psalm 98 exemplifies

the study of chapter 7, with special reference to song and the "musical" features of biblical poetry, as compared with its re-expression in a Chewa rendition and several English versions. A musical perspective coupled with a literary-structural analysis is the focus of chapter 8, as illustrated by Moses' "Psalm by the Sea" in Exodus 15 and its translation in English, supplemented by different paratextual devices. Chapter 9 examines the literary qualities of Psalm 85, with special reference to the key topic of peace and its relevance to an African setting. Chapter 10 is a practical study oriented towards the investigation of quality with regard to the short Psalm 134, including a methodology for the audience testing of a poetic translation. Chapter 11 presents a structural description of the Hebrew text of Psalm 73, providing the basis for a comparison of several versions, which review the main principles and procedures of L-S analysis and translation that have been set forth in the various psalmic studies of this book. Finally, the Appendix presents the review of a recent book on Psalm 145 that admirably illustrates my methodology, followed by three reviews of recent book anthologies that feature a variety of approaches to analyzing, interpreting, and applying the diverse prayer-songs of the Psalter; these studies provide a useful hermeneutical frame-of-reference for my own literary-structural perspective.

This collection builds upon several earlier publications (e.g., Wendland 2013a), to further encourage a literary-structural component in our approach to the poetic—specifically psalmic—literature of Scripture. A special focus is upon the sonic component of the Psalter, along with the text's artistry and rhetoric. These are vital dimensions of the original, but ones often ignored (or not fully recognized) in our analysis/exegesis and, consequently, not given sufficient attention in our translation practice. The full meaning of the Scriptures is thus somehow diminished and not sufficiently communicated, whether in the translated text or via its accompanying paratext (e.g., expository footnotes). It is hoped that this book will motivate and encourage a vibrant, sound-sensitive "hearing" of the biblical text—to complement (but not exclude) other, more commonly applied methodologies of analysis and translation.

The primary intended readership for this study of selected psalms encompasses all those engaged in the analysis, translation, and communication of Scripture, the Old Testament, and poetic literature in particular. This target group would include not only practicing translators, but also all Bible students, e.g., students and teachers in theological schools and seminaries, commentators, and those engaged in research and writing on Psalm-related topics. Above all, in these studies the poetic words of Scripture being analyzed are meant to speak to the hearts, minds, and lives of us all. The aim is that "by learning about the psalms [believers] may learn to read, pray, sing, shout, chant, and wonder the psalms" (Jacobson and Jacobson 2013:2). May these worship texts accordingly motivate us to an active response, impelling us "to compose beautiful and sweet psalms [also in translation!], and to sing lovely and joyous songs, both to praise and thank God in his happiness and to serve his fellowmen (sic) by stimulating and teaching them" (Martin Luther, "Treatise on the Last Words of David," in *Luther's Works* 15:192).

As always, this publication would not have been possible without the essential collaboration of many behind-the-scenes specialist-assistants: the editorial and publishing team of SIL International (Eric Kindberg, Lois Gourley, Bonnie Brown, Judy Benjamin, Mike Cahill); Alan and Iris Pickard of MissionAssist, UK, who restyled and formatted the entire text—(without their help, this book would not be here!); my invaluable reviewers, Dr. Dick Kroneman and Dr. Lynell Zogbo, who provided many helpful comments and suggested corrections—(they are not responsible for any errors that remain!); my keen-eyed editor, Dr. George Huttar; finally, my colleague and friend, Prof. Christo van der Merwe, who introduces this collection of psalm studies with a gracious Foreword. Critical responses and suggestions for improvement are always welcome (erwendland@gmail.com), whether in relation to this text or any of my other efforts in, and for, the Word (https://sun.academia.edu/EWENDLAND).

כֹּל הַנְּשָׁמָה תְּהַלֵּל יָהּ הַלְלוּ־יָהּ!
(Psalm 150:6)

Ernst R. Wendland,
Centre for Bible Interpretation and Translation in Africa
Stellenbosch University – *Pentecost,* 2014

1

The Discourse Analysis of Hebrew Poetry: A Procedural Outline, with Special Reference to Psalm 24

Introduction

This study begins with an overview of what constitutes poetry in the Hebrew Bible. Ten flexible features are briefly described which, when considered together in context, help to distinguish more-poetic from less-poetic composition in the Scriptures. This lays the foundation for a proposed step-by-step methodology that aims to analyze poetic texts from a more holistic, discourse-oriented perspective. Ten analytical procedures are summarized and applied by way of exemplification to Psalm 24, a liturgical work that is often viewed by scholars as consisting of disparate elements, but which on closer examination is found to be more cohesive and unified than a superficial reading would suggest. In addition to describing the artistic beauty, rhetorical power, and significant theological message of this psalm, the present study also illustrates a multifaceted approach for more fully revealing the manifold lyrical character of psalmic composition, with implications also for other types of Hebrew poetic discourse. "In order to read the psalms with understanding, a reader needs to grasp the basic governing logic of how Hebrew poetry creates meaning" (Jacobson and

Jacobson 2013:29). In conclusion, several important practical applications of the proposed methodology are noted.

1.1 What is poetry?

"Poetry is the most intense, most highly charged, most artful and complex form of language we have...long associated with the distant origins of music, dance, and religious ritual in early human cultures" (Grossman 2010:93; cf. Genesis 1:27, 2:23, 4:21, 12:1–3, 48:15–16, 49:2–27). The *Concise Oxford Dictionary* defines a poem as "a literary composition that is given intensity by particular attention to diction (sometimes involving rhyme), rhythm, and imagery." One might wonder about the accuracy, or specificity of this definition, especially when considering some moving oration, e.g., a sermon, that may well manifest all three characteristics—elaborate diction, a certain rhythmic cadence, and imagery—to a noticeable degree (is such an effective sermon an instance of poetry?). The preceding notions may be specified like this: "Poetic language [exhibits]...form, style, structure, and contents of cultivated verbal articulation" that together signify "higher levels of organization and meaning" (Gerstenberger 2014:27–28). Poetry is artistically embellished, typically condensed, discourse that appeals to the sense of sound.

The following, more focused perspective, points to a crucial distinctive feature of most poetic traditions in the world: "As soon as we perceive that a verbal sequence has a sustained rhythm, that it is formally structured according to a continuously operating principle of organization...we are in the presence of poetry and we respond to it accordingly, expecting certain effects from it and not others" ("Hebrew Poetry," Spicehandler et al. 2012:601). Thus, poetry involves some type of sustained rhythmic principle that is manifested in measured line-forms as well as in recurrent patterns of larger formal and/or thematic organization. Note also, that poetic forms elicit a particular kind of cognitive and emotive response. "Poetry is the sound of language organized in lines,...[and] poems are poems because we want to listen to them" (Longenbach 2008:120). We will be exploring these notions and the generic features associated with poetry more fully below.

Biblical Hebrew (BH) does not include a generic (emic) word corresponding to English "poem" or "poetry"—only what appear to be more specific sub-categories, e.g., "song," "lament," "proverb," and so forth. As for most languages, the concept of poetry is culturally defined, and in Hebrew there are no sharply-drawn diagnostic boundaries to distinguish such discourse from prose. The different concentrations of linguistic (or literary) features found within a given text must be evaluated in terms of their relative frequency of occurrence, diversity, density, or syntactic position, on the one hand, and with respect to the quality and intensity of their rhetorical effect upon an assumed implied audience, on the other. What we have, therefore, is a variable continuum of literary types (general) and genres (specific) that comprise the Hebrew Scriptures. These range from those that are more, to those that are less poetic (or more prosaic), as determined on the basis of a complex bundle of interrelated stylistic qualities:[1]

Poetry ← = = = = = = | = = = = = = = = = | = = = = = = → Prose
$\qquad$ *prosaic poetry* $\qquad$ *poetic prose*

Thus, every text must be analyzed and assessed on its own terms with regard to its complement of stylistic features (see below) as they interact within the larger book composition in which they are found, e.g., Job, Psalms, Proverbs, Ecclesiastes, Song of Songs, Isaiah, and Malachi. Finally, it may be noted that, after all, the point of any biblical text study is not simply to determine its formal status—whether prose, poetry, or something in-between—but rather, to ascertain how its constituent linguistic-literary characteristics actually function, both individually and together in context, to convey meaning that is semantic content, functional intent, pragmatic implication, structural form (e.g., acrostic poetry), and so forth. In addition to the use of a set of heuristic analytical criteria such as the following, a good deal of scholarly intuition is also involved in any description and interpretation of the posited relationship between form and function in literary texts,[2] especially where more poetic discourse is concerned.

---

[1] A practicing translator and university professor observes: "I have been fascinated to discover that the translation of artful prose and the translation of poetry are comparable in several significant ways. They both presuppose in the original writing an exquisitely thoughtful use of language to create the many effects that the literary arts are capable of: emotional resonance, conceptual engagement, rhythmic pattern, esthetic tension, and sheer gorgeousness of expression. And they both present analogous challenges to the translator's literary sensibilities and our capacity for entering a text as deeply as possible. The experience of translating poetry, with its obligatory attentiveness to the most minute compositional details—linguistic nuance, rhythm. and sound in two languages—enhances immeasurably the approach to the translation of prose, an artistic idiom that has its own nuances, rhythms, and sounds, all of which need to be transferred, their esthetic energy intact, into a second language" (Grossman 2010:92–93). As far as the sacred Scriptures are concerned (whether prose or poetry), the formal beauty and expressive sounds of the original texts (whether Hebrew or Greek) are present to serve the normally preeminent *informative* function of the divine message.

[2] The relationship between form and function may be manifold. Thus, the same form may be used to convey several (even many) different pragmatic functions or semantic senses: for example, the conjunction *kiy* or the so-called construct arrangement between two nouns. The reverse is also true: the same function or sense, e.g., personal possession, may be indicated by a number of different forms. This is true of all texts, not just "literary" ones.

1.2 Ten literary features common in poetic discourse

Generally speaking, poetry is "heightened speech" (Beldman 2012:86). I have selected ten formal features that contribute to such heightening and which, due to their recurrent appearance, seem to be especially representative of poetry in general and the Hebrew corpus in particular.[3] These formal properties become especially important as markers of poetic discourse (and hermeneutical clues to its interpretation) the more frequently they occur within a given text, and also when they are manifested in close conjunction with one another (convergence). Of course, the boundaries of these categories are not fixed, and some of their constituents may be classified as belonging in another group, e.g., so-called word pairs. The ten devices are listed and briefly described below in their approximate order of importance in the Psalter (cf. Wendland 2011:185–220).[4] A prominent example of each feature is given from Psalm 24, an illustration of usage that will be expanded upon in the next section of this study.

1.2.1 Recursion

One of the most important, albeit general characteristics of literary discourse, oral or written, in any language is recursion, a category which includes the exact, partial, or sometimes contrastive reiteration of formal and semantic features within a composition. When the recursion is exact, it may be termed "repetition." As a generic feature, recursion is involved in many of the more specific devices that follow. An obvious instance of repetition occurs in the first (cola) of verses 7 and 9: שְׂאוּ שְׁעָרִים ׀ רָאשֵׁיכֶם 'Lift up, O gates, your heads!'. This also illustrates the text-demarcative function of repetition to help indicate unit boundaries within a poetic composition, e.g., in the preceding case the respective beginnings of distinct strophes (poetic paragraphs, i.e., vv. 7–8 and 9–10).

---

[3] An additional generic feature that distinguishes Hebrew poetry from other ancient Semitic literature, e.g., Ugaritic epics, is that "biblical poetry is characteristically nonnarrative...events are not recounted, but dramatized" (Spicehandler et al. 2012:603).

[4] Beldman identifies these four macrofeatures as characterizing OT poetry: terseness, parallelism, figurative language, and patterns (2012:86–94). The ten poetic features discussed below are particularly characteristic of the Psalter, but they are also found to a greater or lesser extent in the other biblical poetic books, e.g., Job, SoS. "Poetically, the psalms exhibit a higher degree of convention, cliché, and patterning than other genres of biblical poetry" (Hamlin 2012:1124). Note that while "Psalter" is frequently used as a synonym for the Book of Psalms, more technically it refers to "a printed collection of hymns" (deClaissé-Walford 2004:2); I use these expressions interchangeably.

1.2.2 Parallelism

This refers to a composition that is constructed on the basis of recurrent (cf. 1.2.1) line-forms that are relatively limited in length (in comparison with more prosaic discourse) and also typically related to one another in obvious audible ways.[5] In the Hebrew Bible this is realized as the distinctive feature known as parallelism. This normally involves two (sometimes three) cola that are marked by correspondences in vocabulary (e.g., word pairs), morphology (e.g., gender-matching), syntax (e.g., word order), sense (e.g., antithesis), and/or phonology (e.g., alliteration). The last of these, phonology, includes a rhythmic system of stress accents (usually 2–4 units),[6] with a major pause sign *(athnah)* situated at the perceived midpoint of each paired unit (bicolon).[7] Several distinct types of parallelism have

---

[5] Brogan (2012) views the poetic line (which in BH is always closely related, or "parallel," with at least one other line) as being crucial to the definition of poetry: "The concept of the line is fundamental to the concept of poetry, for the line is the differentia between verse and prose.... The sense in prose flows continuously, while in verse, it is *segmented,* so as to increase information density and perceived structure.... It is impossible that there could be poetry not set in lines.... The poetic line...is perceived 'as a unit of rhythm *and* a unit of structure'.... Hierarchically, a line is progressively *formed* of constituent units while simultaneously *informing* higher-level structures" (cited in Fitzgerald 2013:4). Poetry "in its written form is linebound" (Gerstenberger 2014:32); in its oral form, the "lines" are expressed as distinct utterance units, normally marked by one or more phonological features, e.g., rhyme, meter, intonational contour, tone, and/or end pause.

Brogan's assertions regarding the importance of the poetic line (and lineation) is strongly supported by the more in-depth study of Longenbach 2008. For example: "Poetry is the sound of language organized in lines.... [The] line is what distinguishes our experience of poetry as poetry, rather than some other kind of writing.... The line's function is sonic, a way of organizing the sound of language, and only by listening to the effect of a particular line in the context of a particular poem can we come to an understanding of how the line works.... The music of a poem—no matter if metered, syllabic or free—depends on what the syntax is doing when the line ends" (ibid.:xi–xii).

[6] "Hebrew is a language with a strong stress accent that is phonemic" (Spicehandler et al. 2012:603).

[7] I view the "poetic line" as being equivalent to one of the parallel segments that comprise a closely linked set of 2–3 predicational units (a bi-/tri-colon). In this connection, I frequently find that the Masoretic *athnah* breaks are debatable, and therefore, in order to preserve the poetic qualities of the text, I must divide a *long* colon (consisting of more than four "words") into two (occasionally more) shorter ("half") lines. Such a division is confirmed when the segmented portions clearly reveal themselves to be "in parallel" with one another. There will be many examples of this in the Hebrew text displays found in this and subsequent chapters. This modified lineation may be disputed, of course, and often can be defended only on the basis of a complete literary-structural discourse analysis.

been identified (cf. Tucker 2008:585–588), perhaps the most common being synonymous, e.g., v. 1:[8]

> To Yahweh [belongs] the earth and its fullness,   לַיהוָה הָאָרֶץ וּמְלוֹאָהּ
> [also] the world and those dwelling in it.   תֵּבֵל וְיֹשְׁבֵי בָהּ׃

1.2.3 Direct speech

Every psalm is a prayer of some sort in the sense that it presupposes a divine listener or is directed towards God, whether explicitly or implicitly. Explicit prayers are marked by forms such as vocatives (especially directed towards God), exclamations (e.g., to express emotions), and imperatives (e.g., to make appeals or requests): וְהִנָּשְׂאוּ פִּתְחֵי עוֹלָם '…and be uplifted, you eternal doors!' (v. 7b). In some psalms direct quotations, whether real or rhetorical, are incorporated to further dramatize the discourse (e.g., Ps. 73:15[16]). In Psalm 41, the "voice" (Kaiser 2013:131) of the psalmist directed towards God (v. 4) contrasts with those of his enemies taunting him (v. 5, cf. v. 7). Certain segments of Psalm 24 may well have been uttered antiphonally by different speakers, e.g., v. 3 by the priest (presiding liturgist)—v. 4 by the worshiping congregation (or a select chorus).

1.2.4 Contraction

Abbreviation is another feature recognized by scholars as being diagnostic of biblical poetry, the Psalms in particular (Tucker 2008:585), thus contributing to their perceived "terseness" (cf. Berlin 1985:6). Several types of formal and semantic contraction are often found between parallel poetic lines, e.g., ellipsis, especially verb gapping, asyndeton (absence of initial conjunction), and the lack of so-called prose particles, such as the direct object marker, the relative clause marker, the definite article, and frequently also prepositions. An example of ellipsis is evident in v. 1 above, where there is no explicit verb form in either colon. Many interpreters and versions find an ellipsed vocative of the divine name in v. 6b: "…the ones seeking your face, [O God] of Jacob" (e.g., McCann 1996:774).

1.2.5 Sound play

Since they are composed as direct discourse (cf. point 3 above), the Psalms are eminently oral-aural, often oratorical in character. The rhythm of speech is important, as governed by the lineal composition (cf. 2 above), and so is the

---

[8] These lines may be "synonymous," but they are not the same in meaning. Line B represents a *specification* of meaning (i.e., from אֶרֶץ to תֵּבֵל, and from מְלוֹאָהּ to יֹשְׁבֵי בָהּ) that amounts to a pragmatic *intensification* of the overall sense and hence the impact being conveyed by the two lines in sequence.

actual sound of speech as a given psalm is articulated in its natural form—
aloud. Thus, there are many examples of phonological emphasis—no doubt
including many features no longer audibly distinguishable by us today, but
surely including patterns of pleasing, or jarring, alliteration and assonance,
as well as meaning-enhancing paronomasia (purposeful punning). In Psalm
24:3b, for example, an iterative alternation of key consonants (cf. 1 above)
aurally foregrounds the concepts concerned as well as the utterance as a
whole: וּמִי־יָקוּם בִּמְקוֹם קָדְשׁוֹ '...and who may stand in the place of his
holiness'.

1.2.6 Displacement

"Displacement" refers to the non-standard arrangement of syntactic elements
within a single colon or bicolon, including chiasmus (crossed constituents),
enjambment (a run-over line), and anacrusis (initial extra-metrical word),
as well as the deliberate disjunction of terms that normally occur together.
A full noun or noun phrase that appears before the verb of a colon may,
depending on the pre-text, indicate a constituent focus, involving a new or
renewed topic, a contrastive element, a foregrounded predicate, and so forth.
In Psalm 24:2a, for example, the topic "he" (Yahweh) is highlighted along
with the area of "the earth" (v. 1b) that was thought by pagans to be ruled
by dangerous deities, namely, the "seas" (Craigie 1983:212): כִּי־הוּא עַל־יַמִּים
יְסָדָהּ ('For [it is] *he* [who] upon [the] *seas* founded it [earth]').

1.2.7 Evocative language

The descriptive use of picturesque, evocative, visualizable concepts is of
course a hallmark of all poetry around the world, and this is no less true in
the religious-liturgical verse of the Hebrew Bible. "The power of the Psalms
lies first and foremost in its evocative use of language" (deClaissé-Walford
et al. 2014:42). This feature, a psalm's iconic structure (Bullock 2013:58),
interacts with, but is distinct from, figurative language (cf. 1.2.8, below) and
includes the use of explicit or implicit "allusion"—the reference to well-known
persons, events, places, accounts, etc., in the narrative or prophetic traditions
of Israel. There is an obvious allusion, for example, to the dramatic account of
the creation of the "inhabited world" (תֵּבֵל)—its "land" and "waters" (Gen.
1:1-2, 9-10) in Psalm 24:1-2. This perhaps has the added, significantly related
imagery of "founding/building" a city or temple, suggested by the verbs יסד
and כון (e.g., Jos. 6:26b, 2 Chr. 31:7, Ezr. 3:12; Jud. 16:26, 2 Chr. 3:1, Mic. 4:1)
(cf. VanGemeren 1991:221). "Scripture is...a 'vast collection of interwoven
images'...[for example] the wisdom and kingship themes of the Psalter...create
'word pictures' that provide frames of orientation and worldview" (VanGemeren
2013:46), e.g., the evocation of YHWH as the glorious, almighty "warrior king"
in vv. 7-10. Recent advances in cognitive linguistics and conceptual metaphor

theory enable us to discern and interpret such image schemas and related figurative language (see below) much more precisely.[9]

1.2.8 Figurative language

Poetic discourse also features a variety of conventional imagery, or figures of speech—metaphor,[10] simile, metonymy, synecdoche, personification, anthropomorphism, and apostrophe, to list some of the more commonly occurring literary devices within the Psalter (cf. Tucker 2008:588–589; Wendland 2002:139–157). A rather complex instance of combined figurative language appears in v. 7, where the "gates" of the Temple (implied) are commanded by way of personification to "lift up their heads"—presumably their lintels, arches, or something similar (Bratcher and Reyburn 1991:241). This imagery is then clarified by the subsequent order for "the ancient doors to be lifted/opened," no doubt by the Levites, the purpose being for "the King of Glory" to enter the holy premises,[11] or more broadly perhaps the earthly domain of humanity (from the heavenly realm, vv. 1–2).[12] Here we probably have a case of metonymy where the actual reference is to the sacred ark of the covenant, the figurative royal throne of Yahweh and symbol of his presence (Harman 2011a:231).

1.2.9 Rhetorical overlay

This category includes a variety of stylistic devices which serve to strengthen or foreground any concept or assertion that they are associated with, e.g., rhetorical, leading, and deliberative questions, irony, hyperbole, non-figurative idioms, imperative verbs, and intensifiers (exclamations, interjections). These features also naturally heighten the emotive aspect of the (bi)colon in which they occur, for example, in the pair of rhetorical

---

[9] In his detailed examination of concepts of distress in the Hebrew Bible, including many lament psalms, Philip King observes, "that the language of illness, armed conflict, and trial provide salient examples, functioning as prototypes to metonymically structure the experience of a much wider range of distressing situations" (2012:80).

[10] The importance of metaphor in creating and communicating meaning and feeling about the varied spiritual relationships between God and humankind is central in psalmic discourse (as in the Scriptures generally). "Not only are metaphors a characteristic part of Hebrew poetry's stylistics;...metaphor is [also] a way of conceptualizing reality...a matter of thinking" (Pierre van Hecke, cited in Jacobson and Jacobson 2013:119).

[11] "The Psalms are replete with 'images' of God that are powerful, or more so, than brush or paint could ever depict him" (Bullock 2014:59).

[12] "If the second stanza maps the coming of mortals into God's sphere, the final stanza returns the favor by heralding the coming of the King of Glory into the human realm" (deClaissé-Walford et al. 2014:251).

questions that punctuate the concluding, panegyric portions of Psalm 24 (vv. 8, 10): מִי זֶה מֶלֶךְ הַכָּבוֹד (Who [is] this King of Glory?).

1.2.10 Psalmic diction

Many books of the Bible are characterized by their content-specific vocabulary—such that the mention of a single verse allows one to immediately identify the specific text in which it is found, e.g., Genesis, Leviticus, Judges, Jonah, Lamentations, Proverbs, and Song of Songs. The same is true of the Psalms, where we find certain key liturgical terms (e.g., נַפְשִׁי 'my life', v. 4b), formulaic set-phrases (e.g., מִי זֶה 'who is this?', v. 8a), and utterances typical of their genre, e.g., lament psalms versus hymns (e.g., vv. 8b–c, 10b–c). This would also include such features as distinctive poetic accents,[13] conventional word-pairs (e.g., "the earth"—"seas," vv. 1–2), opening or closing discourse formulas (e.g., לְדָוִד מִזְמוֹר, v. 1a; סֶלָה, vv. 6b, 10b), worship motifs (e.g., "pure-of-heart," v. 4a), and frequent reference to and mention of the deity (e.g., "to YHWH" לַיהוָה, v. 1b; "King of Glory" מֶלֶךְ הַכָּבוֹד, vv. 7–10; "YHWH of armies" יְהוָה צְבָאוֹת, v. 10b).

These ten literary features, generally in artistic combination with one another, perform general discourse functions such as the following (cf. Wendland 2011:76, 222):

- *Segmentation*—dividing a text up into discrete structural units of different sizes;
- *Disposition*—organizing and arranging the reiterated elements into significant textual patterns, e.g., chiastic, alternating, overlapping, enveloping;
- *Projection*—giving additional prominence to certain points and portions of a text, which are thereby marked for special attention;
- *Connection*—linking and interrelating one part of the text with another and thus unifying the composition as a whole.

More specific communicative (pragmatic) objectives, e.g., speech acts, will be considered below with particular reference to the analysis of Psalm 24.

1.3 Ten techniques for analyzing poetic discourse

The ten procedural steps suggested below are given roughly in the order in which they *might* be applied when carrying out a discourse analysis of the compositional and stylistic features of a Hebrew poem, a psalm text in

---

[13] "The system of cantillation signs used throughout the Tanakh is replaced by a very different system for [Psalms, Proverbs, and Job]. Many of the signs may *appear* the same or similar at first glance, but most of them serve entirely different functions in these three books" and hence are distinctive. http://en.wikipedia.org/wiki/Cantillation#Psalms.2C_Proverbs_and_Job. Accessed September 2, 2017.

particular. Due to our temporal and conceptual distance from the original communication event (which itself cannot be specified) and its presumed worship setting, these analytical procedures can only give us a partial grasp of the intended lyric (sung, chanted, recited, etc.) form, content, and function of the text as it has been received. But one must begin somewhere and in the end be able to explain and defend the methodology that has been applied to analyze and expound the text (whether the one proposed below, or any alternative). My description of each step and its exemplification in Psalm 24 will necessarily have to be condensed due to the limitations of space (cf. Wendland 2011:126–149).

1.3.1 Delimitation

In conjunction with a study and specification of text-type (genre) with reference to a particular poetic text, an explicit delineation of its external boundaries needs to be made, unless an entire composition (biblical book) is being considered. The procedures of discourse analysis cannot be regarded as valid unless they are applied to what is generally recognized as a complete, self-contained textual unit (pericope), whose borders can be precisely defined and defended. On the other hand, this may be the purpose of analysis in the first place—namely, to propose and support a specific sectional demarcation in situations where the scholars, commentators, or versions disagree.

Such text delimitation does not pose much of a problem in instances where long-established and universally recognized units are involved, such as individual psalms, or where poetic passages are set within an enveloping prose narrative account, e.g., Exodus 15. The difficulties increase greatly, however, in the prophetic books, especially when seeking to determine the borders of distinct oracles and their internal constituent strophes (cf. Wendland 2011:234–244). This problem of boundary demarcation does not confront us in the case of Psalm 24.

1.3.2 Spatialization

This step provides a way of examining a Hebrew text more closely with reference to its word placement within a text's sequence of (bi)cola. The aim is to more readily discern any standard artistic patterns (e.g., chiasmus) or other special arrangements of form or meaning, including those of a morphological and phonological nature. This exercise consists of a positional vertical (paradigmatic) and horizontal (syntagmatic) display of the discourse on a colon-by-colon basis, with the verb (or its equivalent) being regarded as the nucleus and any fronted pre-verbal elements being of potential added significance. The original text is audibly (re)read while doing this analysis in order to foreground the qualities of sound (as nearly as these can be posited). Different aspects of verbal progression, frequency, and distribution may then be studied with a view towards identifying areas of special interest and possible importance, which will be explored more fully in subsequent steps.

The Hebrew text (MT) of Psalm 24 is reproduced below (from ParaTExt 7.4) along with my own interlinear English translation. The bold letters inserted within the verse-colon (v.co) column on the left side offer a preliminary indication of stanza and strophe units (e.g., B-1 means "strophe 1 of stanza B"); this segmentation provides the foundation for, and will be supported by, steps 4–6 below. The items shaded in gray, italicized, or text boxed in the following display—and elsewhere throughout the book—indicate repeated sounds and words that are viewed (ideally heard!) as important markers within the text (i.e., potential contextual clues to structure and meaning). The hyphens in the English glosses link words that comprise a single lexical unit in Hebrew, while the equals sign represents a maqqeph; "DO" glosses the direct object marker אֵת.

The following diagram shows the sequential-spatial structure of Psalm 24. Similar diagrams will demonstrate relevant passages in following chapters.

v.co		Post-verb2	Post-verb1	VERBAL	Pre-verb2	Pre-verb1
A						
1.a					מִזְמֹור	לְדָוִד
					a-psalm	to-David
1.b		וּמְלֹואָהּ	הָאָרֶץ	-------		לַיהוָה
		and-its-fulness	the-earth			to-Yahweh
1.c		וְיֹשְׁבֵי בָהּ:	תֵּבֵל	-------		-------
		and-those-living in-it	world			
2.a				יְסָדָהּ	עַל־יַמִּים	כִּי־הוּא
				he-founded-it	upon = seas	for = he
2.b				יְכֹונְנֶהָ:	וְעַל־נְהָרֹות	
				he-estab-lished-it	and-on = rivers	

B-1						
3.a			בְהַר־יְהוָה on-[the] mountain =of-Yahweh	יַעֲלֶה he-will-ascend		מִי־ who =
3.b		קָדְשׁוֹ: his-holiness	בִּמְקוֹם in-[the]-place-of	יָקוּם he-will-stand		וּמִי־ and-who =
4.a		וּבַר־לֵבָב and-pure-of = heart	נְקִי כַפַּיִם one-clean-of hands	-------		
4.b		נַפְשִׁי his-selfhood	לַשָּׁוְא to-worthlessness	נָשָׂא he-lifts-up	לֹא־ ׀ not =	אֲשֶׁר who
4.c			לְמִרְמָה: to-falsehood	נִשְׁבַּע he-swears	וְלֹא and-not	
B-2						
5.a		מֵאֵת יְהוָה from-DO Yahweh	בְרָכָה a-blessing	יִשָּׂא he-will-lift-up		
5.b		מֵאֱלֹהֵי יִשְׁעוֹ: from-God his-deliverer	וּצְדָקָה and-vindication	-------		
6.a	(דֹּרְשָׁיו)	דֹּרְשׁוֹ* ones-pursuing-him	דּוֹר generation-of	-------		זֶה this
6.b		יַעֲקֹב סֶלָה: Jacob (Selah)	מְבַקְשֵׁי פָנֶיךָ from-seekers-of your-face	-------		
C-1						
7.a		רָאשֵׁיכֶם ׀ your-heads	שְׁעָרִים O-gates	שְׂאוּ lift-up		

7.b		עוֹלָם	פִּתְחֵי	וְהִנָּשְׂאוּ		
		eternity	doorways-of	and-be-raised		
7.c		הַכָּבוֹד:	מֶלֶךְ	וְיָבוֹא		
		the-glory	king-of	and-he-will-come		
8.a		הַכָּבוֹד	זֶה מֶלֶךְ	--------		מִי
		the-glory	this king of			who
8.b		עִזּוּז וְגִבּוֹר	יְהוָה	--------		
		strong and-mighty	Yahweh			
8.c	מִלְחָמָה:	גִּבּוֹר	יְהוָה	-------		
	battle	mighty-of	Yahweh			
C-2						
9.a		רָאשֵׁיכֶם ׀	שְׁעָרִים	שְׂאוּ		
		your-heads	O-gates	lift-up		
9.b		עוֹלָם	פִּתְחֵי	וּשְׂאוּ		
		eternity	doorways-of	and-lift-up		
9.c		הַכָּבוֹד:	מֶלֶךְ	וְיָבֹא		
		the-glory	king-of	and-he-will-come		
10.a		הַכָּבוֹד	זֶה מֶלֶךְ	-------	הוּא	מִי
		the-glory	*this king-of*		*he*	*who*
10.b		צְבָאוֹת	יְהוָה	-------		
		armies	Yahweh-of			
10.c	סֶלָה:	הַכָּבוֹד	מֶלֶךְ	-------		הוּא
	(Selah)	the-glory	king-of			he

1.3.3 Text-criticism

This is an important, though often difficult aspect of any analysis; fortunately, it is usually the case that only a few words or phrases of the Hebrew text are in serious doubt over the course of a given composition (psalm). Scholarly resources are readily available to explain the various options in terms of the wording of the original text or its interpretation. An increasing number of modern translations too are including footnotes that either simply list the main alternatives or proceed to explain the differences between them along with evaluative recommendations. One of the most helpful versions in this respect is the *New English Translation* (NET), which is available online (www. netbible.com). The following are several examples of the NET's text critical notes (some no longer on the website) with reference to Psalm 24 (cf. deClaissé-Walford et al. 2014:248–249).

- v. **2b**—Some mss. have a perfect verb [*k-w-n*] 'he established it [i.e., fem. sg. => "earth"?]' instead of MT's imperfect form (יְכוֹנְנֶהָ), which is normally translated by a non-past tense; but the latter is probably correct—an instance of poetic variation since the corresponding verb in line A (2a) is perfect.
- v. **4**—Heb. 'who does not lift up for emptiness my life'. The first person pronoun on נַפְשִׁי (*nafshiy* 'my life') makes little sense here [possibly a reference to Yahweh's name?]. Many medieval Hebrew mss. support the ancient versions in reading a third person pronoun 'his'. The idiom 'lift the life' here means to 'long for' or 'desire strongly'. In this context (note the reference to an oath in the following line) 'emptiness' may refer to speech or to 'idols, idolatry' (see Ps. 12:2).
- v. **6b**—MT reads: 'your face, O Jacob'; my translation assumes the addition of an implicit 'God of' (el), which has limited support from several Hebrew and LXX mss.; cf. Psalm 75:9 (10), but may be suggested by the suffix 'him' at end of 6a and the explicit reference to 'God' in 5b. Note also the two readings for the participle in 6a: דֹּרְשָׁיו* (דֹּרְשָׁיו).
- v. **9b**—MT reads: 'and lift up!' (an active imperative, as in 9a) instead of the corresponding passive as in v. 7b; emending the passive to an active verb is supported by several Heb. mss. and all the ancient versions; cf. NET/MT: 'Rise up, you eternal doors!' Hebrew poetic usage would support not only the graphic personification here but also the stylistic variation in the verb forms. *Note: In Heb., 'lift up the head' can also mean 'rejoice'.*

1.3.4 Segmentation

In step 2, the text of Psalm 24 was "spatialized" as a means of revealing some of its verbal patterns based on recursion—phonological, morphological, lexical, and syntactic reiteration. Now we wish to take a closer look to try and detect some of the more significant instances of such recursion which help to determine the structural contours of the discourse as it develops from beginning to end. This procedure is carried out together with identifying probable points of disjunction within the text—points where it presents a break due to a noteworthy shift in form or content, e.g., a change of topic, speaker-addressee, pragmatic function, emotive tone, and so forth. Below is a summary of the principal boundary-marking disjunctive cola of Psalm 24, which help to justify the stanza-strophe divisions that are shown on the chart of step 2:

- Stanza/strophe **A** (vv. 1a–2b): the psalm's *title,* followed in 1b by a *verbless clause* and an *initial* reference to *YHWH* that duplicates the syntactic structure of the first line (the title).
- Stanza **B**₁ (vv. 3a–4c): *shift in topic* (from YHWH to his people)—but *continuity* is also indicated by repeated mention of the divine name (anaphora); the *rhetorical question* acts as a "leading question," i.e., one that introduces the main topic or theme of the following discourse unit—the attributes of the "who" being asked about; the frame of reference narrows from the cosmic dimension of divine creation to a local setting of human worship.
- Stanza **B**₂ (vv. 5a–6b): *asyndeton; shift* from specification of moral character (Law) to that of divine blessing (Gospel); a shift to direct address marks a strong *closure* at 6b (after the psalm's lexical midpoint in 6a).
- Stanza **C**₁ (vv. 7a–8c): *shift in topic* (from the genuine, sincere worshiper back to his/her God—YHWH); *imperative* form—the first in this psalm, plus a *personified vocative* ("you gates"); to whom does this refer? Either (a) the *people* who are fit to dwell in the holy city/place of Yahweh, i.e., those specified in stanza B—or more likely, (b) the religious gatekeepers of Israel, namely, the *priests,* who represent the people/worshipers on the one hand, and their King, Yahweh, on the other.
- Stanza **C**² (vv. 9a–10c): exact *repetition* of v. 7a (anaphora). Verses 9–10 constitute the second strophe of stanza C.
- Thus, in summary, Psalm 24 consists of three stanzas (A–C): a creedal Introduction, **A** (1–2); a central wisdom-style didactic stanza, **B**, comprising two strophes (3–4, 5–6); and a final liturgical stanza, **C**, also comprising two strophes (7–8, 9–10).

The following then are some of the more prominent *patterns of repetition* found in Psalm 24:

- The repeated synonymous *constituent focus* (fronted) constructions of 2a–b help, in part, to distinguish the *closure* of the psalm's short initial stanza/strophe (A).
- A pair of synonymous rhetorical questions (each beginning with "who?") in 3a–b mark the *onset* of stanza B. They resonate with the non-adjacent reiterated rhetorical questions of 8a and 10a, which constitute strong thematic assertions to mark closure in strophes C–1 and C–2.

- Strophes C–1 and C–2 are almost, but significantly not quite, identical (all verses are tri-cola), which suggest that they serve as psalmic "set pieces" of some sort in a patterned worship liturgy (e.g., leader > choral/congregational response). Note the material (variation in content) that falls outside the panels of repetition (in vv. 8, 10), which is thereby foregrounded.

This procedure is important in terms of demarcating a composition's strophic, poetic paragraph structure (note the diversity among the standard English versions, which indicates why this step is necessary). This sequence of disjunctions and recursion patterns serves as opening markers for an overall [A-B-A'] "ring structure" in which stanzas A and A' (stanza C) focus on *Yahweh,* while the inner stanza B describes those *people* who worship him aright.

1.3.5 Confirmation

This step provides a more detailed linguistic analysis of the text under consideration in order to check and confirm the segmentation exercise that was carried out above. At the same time, additional issues that pertain to its micro- and macrocontent are investigated for immediate or future reference. The following is a sample listing of observations that seem relevant to the understanding, interpretation, and translation of Psalm 24:

- Verse 1b is a verbless predication (an acclamation), emphatically leading off with the divine name—with YHWH obviously being the topical focus of this psalm (cf. הוּא in v. 2a).
- 1c is a parallel verbless utterance with another implied existential predicate ("to be") + ellipsis (to YHWH belong). These verbless assertions in v. 1 seem to reflect a formulaic creedal statement that may have been regularly used during meetings for worship in Israel.
- 2a: כִּי + the personal pronoun again foregrounds "YHWH," with additional constituent focus by means of fronting the locus of his creative activities—the "seas," which were feared by Israel and regarded as divinities by many early ANE peoples (this focused element is reiterated in v. 2b).
- The prefixed verb of 2b (יְכוֹנְנֶהָ) is construed as a "completive" (past) form to match the verb of the preceding colon, 2a (יְסָדָהּ).
- The prefixed verbs of 3a–b are probably "modal" in implication, expressing potential or permission, e.g., "Who is allowed to/may ascend Yahweh's hill?"
- The verbless predication of 4a not only makes explicit the answer to the preceding rhetorical questions (v. 3), but it also foregrounds the ethical qualities (not only the ritual requirements) of the person

thus designated as fit for worship (i.e., holy in hands and heart—
in deed and motive!). This same basic structure, coupled with the
initial deictic "this" (זֶ֫ה) reinforced by asyndeton, is found in v. 6
with corresponding rhetorical effect.

- The key verb נשׂא (lit. 'lift up') in vv. 4–5 has different senses, and
  though serving a cohesive function (cf. also vv. 7, 9), cannot be
  translated the same way in many languages.
- The asyndeton of 5a helps to mark the topical shift from personal
  characteristics (v. 4) to consequent blessings from Yahweh (v.5),
  i.e., Grounds/Conclusion (or Reason/Result). The singular pronoun
  "he" is representative, as v. 6 makes clear, e.g., "Such godly people"
  (NET). Accordingly, the prefixed verb (יִשָּׂ֫א) is generalizing, "they
  are blessed." How צְדָקָה relates to יֵ֫שַׁע is an ethical connection that
  may need to be made explicit in translation.
- Deliberate (or poetic) ellipsis in 6b, i.e., "O [God of] Jacob," marks
  strophic closure (B). Some versions (NET) and commentators (e.g.,
  Goldingay 2006:360; Harman 2011a:231) claim that there is no
  ellipsis, but rather that "Jacob" corresponds with "this generation"
  in 6a in a chiastic arrangement.
- The asyndeton of 7a combined with an imperative form signals a
  textual aperture and a new strophe. The vocabulary, repetition,
  and tight parallelism of vv. 7–10 would suggest that this section
  (stanza C) represents a liturgical dialogue.
- Repetition of the phrase "the King of glory" in vv. 7c and 8a
  foregrounds the referent, which is then specified by the repeated
  mention of YHWH in 8b and 8c. The prefixed verb (וְיָבוֹא) following
  an imperative indicates result, e.g., "...so that the majestic King
  may enter" (cf. 9b).
- Asyndeton and clause initial placement in vv. 8b–c further
  spotlights the divine referent—"Yahweh" and the character of this
  verse as panegyric poetry.
- The inserted independent personal pronoun (הוּא) in vv. 10a and
  10c (cf. also 2a—*inclusio*) again serves to draw attention to the
  divine referent, "the King of glory," who is identified specifically
  in 10b as "the LORD of Armies." This shortened medial line 10b is
  thereby also emphasized.
- The pair of poetic selah's at the end of vv. 6 and 10 further mark
  these as points of strophic closure.

1.3.6 Distinction

The preceding linguistic analysis of the pericope at hand is profitably
followed by another examination of the same text from a more focused
literary (artistic and rhetorical) perspective. The objective is to locate

areas of special significance that may, in conjunction with the content being expressed, suggest a particular communicative function, for example, to help mark a unit boundary (aperture or closure) or a point of prominence, whether emotive ("climax") or thematic ("peak"). The following is a simple listing of the main literary features exhibited in Psalm 24:

- Lineal *parallelism*—tight *bi-* and *tri-cola* (vv. 4, 7–10)
- A possible *chiasmus* in v. 6: (A) such a generation, (B) the ones pursuing Him [YHWH], (B′) the ones seeking your [YHWH's] faces, (A′) [they are of] Jacob [= true "Israel"]
- Lexical *balance*—43 words before/after the significant midpoint in 6a—only Yahweh's "generation" of upright folk (can "stand" in his holy place, 3b)
- Poetic *word pairs*, e.g., v. 1 (polemical: earth/world), v. 5 (promotional: blessing/vindication-deliverance)
- Lexical *repetition*—other than that constituted by parallelism, e.g., (not) "lift up" [*n-s-'*] in 4b/5a and 7, 9, thus forming a *cohesive link* between sections B and A′
- *Figurative* language, e.g., v. 3—*metonymy:* "mountain," referring to Zion or the Temple; 8—*metaphor:* Yahweh, the warrior King; 7/9— *personified apostrophe:* command to the "gates" to "lift up the[ir] heads" (open the Temple doors!)
- *Idiomatic* language, e.g., v. 6b—to "seek Yahweh's face" is to request his favor/blessing through prayer and worship (cf. 2 Sam. 21:1; Pss. 27:8, 105:4)
- Strophic structure with *refrains,* e.g., vv. 7–8/9–10 (exemplifies Kugel's dictum: "A and what's more, B" parallelism; i.e., "more" in terms of poetic beauty and intensity)
- Ellipsis/*gapping*, e.g., vv. 1c, 5b
- *Thematic questions*—"Who..." is God (vv. 8a, 10a—A, A′); who is the God-fearing (wo)man (3a–b—B)? The characterizing questions and answers of 3/4, 8, 10 may be uttered by different liturgical groups of speakers.
- *Intertextual* (psalmic and historical) and *extratextual* (mythic, royal) *allusions,* e.g., YHWH as the Warrior King, Deliverer of his people (Exo. 15:6–12; 1 Sam. 17:45); paraphrases of precepts of the Mosaic Covenant ("emptiness" v. 4—idolatry, Exo. 20:7; cf. Pss. 31:6, 73:1, 13; Jer. 18:15; "generation" v. 6, cf. 73:15). Note also the textually-related *expansion* of B in Psalm 15. These significant conceptual associations, if strongly supported by scholarly commentaries (e.g., Craigie

1983:212–213; McCann 1996:772–774) may be referenced in paratextual study notes.[14]
- *Alliteration/assonance,* e.g., vv. 3b–4, 7/9
- Utterance *rhythm,* e.g., v. 9, with a break in the pattern at 10b with emphasis on YHWH *Tsebaoth* (possibly the "throne name" of YHWH, cf. Isa. 6:5; Pss. 84:1, 3; 89:5–14)

As suggested above, these literary features, especially the points of convergence, primarily serve to help mark strophic boundaries (aperture/ closure) and peak or climax, especially when they co-occur with significant elements of linguistic form (cf. §1.3). For example, in v. 7 we have: asyndeton + imperative + vocative + personification + alliteration. Also note the reduction in literary impact and appeal when the significance of these poetic features is removed in translation without effective functional replacement (see examples of this in the CEV).

The results of the distinct analyses of each strophe (which combine to form stanzas) may be then combined in synthesis to reveal a unified structure for the text as a whole. In this case, the evidence mutually supports the hypothesis of Psalm 24 as consisting of three stanzas (A: 1–2, B: 3–6, C: 7–10). Stanzas **A** and **C** (= A′) have the same theme and purpose (praise Yahweh for his creative greatness and magnificent majesty),[15] while the middle stanza **B** presents a thematic counter-point, i.e., designating *WHO* is worthy enough to worship such a wonderful God—to be citizens of ("stand in") the Kingdom of the "glorious King?" (ANSWER: those who serve Him with pure hearts and righteous lives, not dishonoring the LORD through idolatry or false speaking.)

Verses 1–2 thus establish a conceptual frame of reference for the entire psalm: The focus is fixed upon Yahweh—who he is and what he has done/does. This segment of a "Creation Hymn" evokes (by metonymic [part-whole] association) the entire genre and sets the semantic stage, so to speak, for what follows in the text. This hymn is at once universal in scope, but also individual, or personal, in application. Yahweh, the glorious Creator-Warrior of his people [transcendence], wants to come close

---

[14] McCann is especially helpful in pointing out intertextual correspondences and allusions and their significance for the interpretation of Psalm 24. For example: "The words translated [in v. 1] as 'world' (...tebel) and 'established' (...yasad) also occur together in Pss. 93:1 and 96:10, both of which explicitly affirm, 'the LORD reigns'. Thus vv. 1–2 anticipate vv. 7–10, where God is addressed five times as 'the King of glory'.... It is significant that the idiom 'to lift up the soul' [v. 4] occurs again in Ps. 25:1. In this case, and the other two cases where the psalmist lifts her or his soul to God, the word 'trust' occurs in the immediate context (see Pss. 25:1–2; 86:2, 4; 143:8)" (1996:772–773).

[15] "The King of Glory of vv. 8–10 is the same Lord who first established his kingship by creating and founding the world (vv. 1–2)" (deClaissé-Walford et al. 2014:248).

to minister to them [immanence] in the twofold blessing of "deliverance" and "vindication." However, the psalmist also reminds listeners of their moral and religious responsibility in their Covenantal relationship with the LORD, namely, to "seek after" Him in purity of heart, life ("hands"), lips (no "deceit"), and worship (no "nothingness"—i.e., idolatry; cf. Ps. 31:7; Jer. 18:5). The relational attributes of a glorious, holy, life-giving God (YHWH) must be duplicated in the characteristics of his holy, life-offering people so that he can "come in" and reside in fellowship with them.

1.3.7 Contextualization

In this step we investigate the possible situational context of use of the composition under consideration as well as any clear intertextual influence that may be posited.

The three clear-cut sections of Psalm 24 (A: 1–2, B: 3–6, C: 7–10) seem to point to a composite piece. In other words, the psalm was composed by the author from several other extant liturgical pieces in order to formulate this unified hymn in praise of the royal Lordship of Yahweh (A + C), now including a distinctive stanza in the middle which describes those who alone are fit to worship such a great Creator-King (B). Form critics often designate section B as a liturgical entrance hymn for pilgrims and C as a corresponding entrance hymn invoking or inviting the Ark/YHWH to enter the Temple (2 Sam. 6:12–19). But Psalm 24 as it has been incorporated into the Hebrew Bible is now a coherent poetic composition and has been used as such by the Jews in their regular worship on the day after the Sabbath (Sunday) (Craigie 1983:211).

Within the Psalter, Psalm 24 appears to follow topically from Psalm 23 since it elaborates on the theme of YHWH's earthly abode ("the house of the LORD") introduced at the end of Psalm 23 (v. 6b). Psalm 23 focuses upon Yahweh as the personal Protector of his people and the various blessings that they receive from his hand (vv. 5–6; cf. 24:5a), while Psalm 24 features Yahweh as their glorious, all-powerful Creator and Warrior-King and summarizes the characteristics of those who are "righteous" before him (23:3/24:5). The following Psalm 25 is another psalm of trust (like Ps. 23) based on the theological assumptions of Psalm 24 (cf. 24:4–25:1).

At this point we might raise the question: To what extent is the extra-textual (including the canonical) "context" an essential part of the current "meaning" of a biblical text, in this case a psalm? Can the significance of the biblical poet's theological message and communicative purpose be sufficiently understood on the basis of the translation alone, that is, without a supplied cognitive context (frame of reference) which can facilitate its interpretation? Of course, the answer depends on many different factors, which cannot be discussed here (cf. Wendland 2011:355–405). But surely the case can be made for the provision of para-textual descriptive and explanatory notes (as in a study Bible) which might serve to cue readers (in modified form, even hearers) in to selected background information that would enable them to better understand and appreciate the text of Scripture at hand. The following, for example, is a summary reflection on Psalm 24 as a whole that might be effective either as an introduction or a conclusion to the text (based on Broyles 1999:131):

- Psalm 24 has much to contribute theologically as well as ethically. One of the principal ideas is that our worship of God (Yahweh) does not take place solely in a religious realm—"in church." Rather, it is—or should be—integrally connected with our everyday social behavior (vv. 3–6) and in our relationship with the entire divinely established cosmic order (vv. 1–2, 7–10). "Yahweh of hosts" (v. 10), "the hero in war" (v. 8), and "the king of glory" (vv. 7–10) surely rules the universe, but he is also the "God of Jacob" (that is, of his faithful people, vv. 3–6) and the deliverer-protector of every individual believer (v. 5). More specifically, Psalm 24 also implicitly calls for worship that is ecologically aware. This happens when we view the cosmos as operating effectively under God's kingship and, on the other hand, when we respond appropriately by reflecting the harmonious created order in all of our human relations as well as in our equitable management of our world environment.

1.3.8 Conversation

This step involves construing the text as a conversation first of all between the implied author and his originally intended implied audience. This issue would be considered initially when the matter of text-type (genre) is considered (step 1), but it needs to be given further attention again at a later stage in one's analysis. On the broader level of message composition and transmission, what was the author seeking to do through his poetic discourse: How did he intend his text to affect his listeners, or what impact did he expect his words to have upon them, e.g., to instruct, warn, rebuke, entreat, console, encourage, or inspire them? On a text-internal level, what are the speakers within the discourse doing, or hoping to accomplish, with their utterances, e.g., the psalmist, Yahweh, God's worshiping community, or their enemies?

For this type of study, a speech-act analysis is helpful, that is, an investigation of implied illocution (purpose) and supposed perlocution (outcome) of the textual locution (e.g., a psalmic [bi]colon), as well as grouped sets or sequences of these utterances within a composition. In the case of Psalm 24, the following general communicative functions can be proposed:

- 1–2: *informative:* a confessional assertion or declaration of what Yahweh has done—creation (*panegyric* with *polemical*-imperative undertones: versus ancient Near Eastern pagan Canaanite cosmology and mythology, e.g., the adversarial chaos of "sea/rivers").
- 3–6: *imperative:* exhortation to worship Yahweh aright (holy thoughts and lives) plus motivation (blessing-vindication)— (an implicit *didactic*-informative function in that v. 4b refers to commandments of the Decalogue, namely, 1/2 and 8[9]). Christ may have had v. 4 in mind as he uttered the Beatitudes, especially the key terms "blessing" and "righteousness" (cf. Mt. 5:6, 10).
- 7–10: *expressive:* joyously emotive words of praise for Yahweh, the mighty King of glory!

In terms of more specific speech acts then, we observe the following for example in vv. 3–6 (stanza B), which is a pastoral *description* of + *exhortation* for Yahweh's people: *interrogation* (or attention-getter, 3) + *information* (identification, 4) + *promise* (blessings, 5) + *confirmation* (encouragement, 6).

Verse 10, on the other hand, is clearly a final act of *proclamation* + *praise,* that is, lauding the people's Great King Yahweh! This passage perhaps functions as the text's "macro"-speech act, being formally marked by means of full pronouns and the divine name. We also note the complex figurative (metonymic) communicative cycle of 7–8 (9–10): "gates"—probably the gatekeepers, or Temple religious ministers of Yahweh (priests/Levites). "Lift up..." would appear to be words communally declared (shouted?) by the people/pilgrims/worshipers), to which the priests respond in unison, "Who is...?" The people then conclude by proclaiming the name of the LORD in praise: "[To] YHWH of Armies...[be all] glory!"

1.3.9 Summarization

During this step a topical-thematic outline is constructed as a way of organizing the major religious ideas of a composition in relation to its principal structural units. This exercise is based on the preceding analysis, with additional studies prepared as needed, for example, a more precise examination of the text's key terms. The latter are determined on the basis of quantity (i.e., the density, diversity, and distribution of selected lexical items) and/or quality (i.e., the theological or ethical significance of the terms with respect to the text's overall architectural design, theme, or pragmatic function).

An even more detailed exposition of compositional content may be carried out by means of a propositional analysis of the text's sequence of poetic lines. This results in a structural diagram that reveals the semantic relationships between cola as well as their differing levels of dependence (cf. Wendland 2011:271–273), for example, Psalm 24:1–2:

1b to-YHWH [is] the-earth and-its-fullness—*BASE*
1c and-those-living in-it—*ADDITION*- - - - - - - - - - - - -*CONCLUSION*
2a for = he upon-seas he-founded-it—*BASE* - - - - - - - - -*GROUNDS*
2b and-upon-rivers he-established-it—*SYNONYMY*

To explain: colon 1c is linked to 1b by the semantic relation of Base-Addition, while colon 2b is linked to 2a by the relation of Base-Synonymy; 2a + b in turn is linked to 1b + c by the relation of Conclusion-Grounds (or Result-Means). Of course, there is admittedly a certain degree of ambiguity and arbitrariness involved with this type of analysis, but it does provide at least one way of explicitly linking all of the psalm's cola and cola-clusters (strophes, stanzas) to each other to form a representation of its semantic content.

The following then are two possible topical outlines that summarize the content of Psalm 24, one with special reference to its expository theme and the second in terms of its hortatory message.[16] Either one or both (modified as desired) could be included as part of an introduction to the psalm (in a study Bible, for example), or utilized to indicate section headings within a contemporary translation.

Psalm 24

Expository theme:

YAHWEH rules as King,

As shown by:
A. *His mighty works (vv. 1–2); [transcendence]*

B. *His worshipful community (vv. 3–6); [obedience]*
C. *His glorious character (vv. 7–10). [immanence]*

Hortatory theme:

Praise YAHWEH the king of glory

On account of:
A. *His wonderful creation (vv. 1–2);*

B. *His holy people (vv. 3–6);*
C. *His victorious power (vv. 7–10)!*

1.3.10 Translation and testing

This final step offers an excellent way of focusing one's analysis of the Hebrew text, namely, by seeking to express its content in another language, whether more or less literally (correspondently) or in an idiomatic manner. This is especially challenging when rendering the text in a non-Western language

---

[16] Compare these outlines with McCann's handy summary: "…those who enter God's reign [as proclaimed in Ps. 24]—those who know that 'the earth is the LORD's' (v. 1)—will discover what it means to live in harmony with God, with other people, and with the whole creation. This is the ultimate blessing for those 'who seek the face of the God of Jacob' (v. 6; see Ps. 11:7)" (1996:774).

that has few available versions to refer to.[17] The interlingual transformation process should again include an oral reading of the text in the original in comparison with successive translation drafts—both to discern (detect) the phonological qualities (beauty, impact, appeal) of the Hebrew original and their intended reproduction with equivalent sonic effect in the TL.[18] The following is an example for critical examination from a poetic rendering of the first four verses of Psalm 24 in Chewa, a major African Bantu language, along with an English back-translation:

Salmo limeneli n'la Davide mfumu ija.	*This psalm is one of David the king.*
Chauta ndiye adalenga dziko lapansi	1 Chauta (Yahweh) is the one who created the earth
pamodzi n'zonse zam'menemo, inde,	along with everything in it, yes indeed,
anthu onse okhalamo nawonso ndi ake.	all those who live in it are his as well.
Ndiye amene adaika dzikoli pa nyanja,	2 He's the one who set that earth upon the sea,
adalikhazika pamtsinje wozama ndithu.	he established it upon the very deep river surely.
Ndani kodi angalimbe mtima kukwera,	3 Just who can get up the courage to climb up,
kufika paphiri la Chauta, m'malo oyera,	to reach the peak of Chauta, the holy place,
ndikumupembedza moyenera kumeneko?	and to worship him properly there?
Ndi amene amachita zabwinotu m'manja,	4 It is someone who does good deeds with his hands,

---

[17] "The confluence of sound, sense, and form in a poem presents an especially difficult problem in parsing for the translator. How can you separate the inseparable? The simultaneous, indissoluble components of a poetic statement have to be re-created in another language without violating them beyond recognition.... In many consequential and meaningful ways the translator continues the process initiated by the poet, searching for the ideal words, the pefect mode of expression needed to create a poem...the language of the poem, its syntax, lexicon, and structures by definition have to be altered drastically, even though the work's statement [i.e., referential content] and intention, its emotive content and imagery, must remain the same" (Grossman 2010:95).

[18] TL = "target language", SL = "source language"

amene amaganiza zoyera zokha m'mtima.	who thinks only pure things in his heart.
Ndiye amene sakonda kulingalira zoipa;	It is the person who doesn't like to ponder evil;
sanama kapenanso kulumbira monyenga.	he does not lie nor does he swear falsely.

The production of any translation draft must include explicit provision for its testing and subsequent revision where necessary. The following is a simple model that indicates the main elements of such an assessment procedure (cf. Wendland 2004:338–344; 10.2.1):

Focus	Meaning		Form	
Source language	*Fidelity*	↓1	↑4	*Closeness*
Target language	*Intelligibility*	2 ⟶	3	*Naturalness*

Model of an assessment procedure.

We may distinguish four key criteria of **quality**, two that have to do with the source language and two that have to do with the target language (ranked in rough order below):

1. **Fidelity** *(with a focus on the **meaning of the SL text**):* A Bible translation should accurately transmit what we presume (based on a thorough prior text analysis) the original author (or implied author) intended to communicate to his (implied) readers/hearers. This includes emotive impact/response as well as content.

2. **Intelligibility** *(with a focus on **meaningfulness of the TL text**):* The original message must be conveyed in such a way that it is understandable to average listeners, as they hear the text being read, without causing undue difficulty or confusion because of its special style and diction.

3. **Naturalness** *(with a focus on the **naturalness of the TL text**):* Ideally, the translated text should not sound strange, like some foreign document (except for certain aspects of its content and terminology). Whenever possible, it should be idiomatic, relatively easy to read aloud, well-sounding in the vernacular, and manifesting language that is as beautiful and powerful as that of the original text.

4. **Closeness** *(with a focus on the **form of the SL text**):* It is important to remain faithful, that is, as proximate as possible to the historical context and culture of the Bible, in one way or another, i.e., either within the translation itself or without, that is, through the use of supplementary helps like footnotes, good cross-references, and a complete glossary.

No single factor can be considered in isolation. Thus, where any two of these criteria are in conflict, SL text fidelity is of utmost importance, followed by intelligibility; naturalness in the TL takes the third place, and last, but not least (nor to be ignored) comes closeness. The overall aim is to produce a translation that is acceptable in all relevant respects by the intended target audience and one that will be readily, even eagerly, used—ideally sung!—by them.

1.4 Conclusion: Proposed applications of the preceding methodology

The ten distinctive features of Hebrew poetry and the ten-step analytical methodology suggested above can easily be modified to suit one's own academic background, translation philosophy, communicative objectives, and/or cultural frame of reference. I have found these to be pedagogically helpful when working with more advanced students of BH, even those at the dissertation level. They may serve to enable one to "see" the text more clearly and/or deeply. Three more specific applications may be noted in closing; thus, the proposed framework might be used to enrich the

- *Interpretation* of the poetic texts of Scripture—from personal study to the preparation of scholarly articles, resources, and commentaries, a diverse discourse-oriented approach is essential.
- *Transmission* of poetic texts—with an emphasis now on their dynamic oral-aural character, for example, when preparing Bible studies, sermons, or presentations via the public media.
- *Translation* of poetic texts—that is, how to more fully and effectively reproduce their inscribed content, intent, and effect in another language and sociocultural setting.

One thing that we all have undoubtedly experienced when studying the different passages of the Scriptures, particularly those of a poetic nature: There is always more there than meets the eye and the ear at first reading. Therefore, a more comprehensive method of examining and reflecting upon the original text, when carried out carefully and consistently, will always bring results in terms of a greater understanding of and appreciation for what is, after all, the Word of God. As for the chief lesson of Psalm 24, I could not state it any more clearly and correctly (to my mind) than James Mays (1994a:123–124, original boldface):

> The three parts of the psalm concern the central elements of faith, life, and worship. The psalm gives the inhabitant of the world a confession with which we may acknowledge how the world came to exist and whose we are. Existence in the world is possible because of the existence of the world.... The confession calls for a life that is itself ordered by the sovereignty on which it depends.... It is a life founded and established by the blessing and righteousness of the LORD in the midst of the chaos of evil.... He comes as the victor who has prevailed against the chaos of unbeing and so is able to prevail against the chaos of evil.... **Our existence depends on his creation; our blessing and righteousness depend on his coming.**

2

Continuity and Discontinuity in Hebrew Poetic Design, with Special Reference to Psalm 30

Introduction: When "and" is "but"

There is a major turning point that occurs near the middle of Psalm 30 (verse 6a; Hebrew v. 7). It is marked in the original by the emphatic initial pronoun "I" (אֲנִי), which is preceded by the common transitional conjunction "and" *(waw)*. In its present location, however, as on many other occasions in the Hebrew Bible, this inseparable particle is best translated, not by its dictionary gloss, "and," but rather according to its contextual function in the discourse. The composite form that results from the linkage of this conjunction with the foregrounded personal pronoun represents a paradoxical point of progression in the text ("and"), coupled with an obvious interruption ("as for me"). The development of the prayer-poem is carried forward, but a new and unexpected stage in the author's argument commences at this juncture (cf. the following analysis). In order to highlight this important transition, Craigie renders it as follows: "But I—I (said in my security)" (1983:250). Thus, in this textual setting "and" is equivalent to "but." Surprisingly, many of the major English versions leave this *waw* untranslated, e.g., GNT: "I felt secure and said..." (also NIV, NET, etc.).

The purpose of this study is to explore other prominent instances of such continuity and discontinuity within the text of Psalm 30, generally following the methodology that was outlined in chapter 1. We will observe how these complementary principles of composition act in tandem to organize this particular poetic discourse formally and semantically, as well as pragmatically, and arguably, many others like it in the literary-religious tradition of ancient Israel. Then in conclusion, several possible theological implications of this prominent stylistic feature will be briefly considered.

It should be noted at the outset that these two compositional strategies are certainly not the only ones that affect or influence literary creation. But they do seem to be especially important with regard to Hebrew poetic discourse in general and Psalm 30 in particular, and so my discussion will be more or less restricted to them. In addition to calling attention to their complementary literary-structural interaction within this text, I will also evaluate the effect of these devices in terms of their general communicative significance, especially when realized in a more natural medium of transmission, that is, an oral recital or even a musical rendition.

2.1 Continuity and discontinuity in poetry

> The poetic function [of literature] projects the principle of equivalence from the axis of [verbal] selection into the axis of combination. (Jakobson 1960:358)

For over a half century now this well-known poetic dictum has engaged a host of literary scholars in the effort both to interpret and also to apply it in the analysis of specific works, as well as to assess its suitability and relevance as a characterization of poetry. One of the most useful of such studies is Adele Berlin's investigation of the nature and operation of parallelism in biblical poetry (1985:7–17). My purpose here is not to make a review of the extensive scholarly literature on this subject (for that, see chapter 5), but rather to suggest an elaboration of the principle in the light of the theme of continuity and discontinuity, and then to apply this modification in my attempt to explore certain prominent aspects of the organizational structure and communicative dynamics of Psalm 30.

The term "equivalence" has often been limited in reference only to linguistic similarities (e.g., Berlin 1985:11), and Jakobson himself seemed to emphasize this dimension in his various analyses. However, in its original context (1960:358), it is clear that he meant to include the opposing notion of dissimilarity as well (cf. Berry 2012:1056). The notion of equivalence may thus imply the apparent antithetical characteristics of similarity and difference, correspondence and contrast, for one idea implicitly conveys an awareness of its opposite with respect to quantity, quality, form, content, or function. Correspondences establish patterns of resemblance and continuity in verbal discourse, while contrasts involve points of difference and discontinuity. Psalm 30 is a text that is rich in poetic contrasts—with numerous antithetical pairings peppering the prayer from beginning to end. Furthermore, these correlative literary-linguistic strategies operate on both a conceptually vertical plane (the paradigmatic "axis of [lexical] selection") and also a horizontal plane (the syntagmatic "axis of [syntactic] combination") to constitute a complete text.[1]

For a simple example of these distinctions (anticipating the full analysis of Ps. 30 below), we might briefly consider v. 6; the Hebrew text reads as follows:

$$\text{A} \quad \text{כִּי רֶגַע בְּאַפּוֹ // חַיִּים בִּרְצוֹנוֹ}$$

$$\text{B} \quad \text{בָּעֶרֶב יָלִין בֶּכִי // וְלַבֹּקֶר רִנָּה}$$

In this case both similarity and difference are superimposed upon each other within each half-line (colon) as well as between the two cola; thus in literal translation:

A: For moment (a) in-his-anger (b) // lifetimes (a′) in-his-favor (b′);
B: in-the-evening (c) it-overnights weeping (d) // and-to-the morning (c′) rejoicing (d′).

Semantically, (a) and (c) contrast with (a′) and (c′), while (b) and (d) contrast with (b′) and (d′). On the other hand, (a) and (a′) correspond with (c) and (c′), while (b) and (b′) correspond with (d) and (d′). Morphologically and phonologically, the final contrastive lexical units in colon A match: (b) בְּאַפּוֹ and (b′) בִּרְצוֹנוֹ, while in colon B the initial contrastive units (c) and (c′) match morphologically, but phonologically exhibit a reversal in two noun consonants: לַבֹּקֶר and בָּעֶרֶב. The more such linguistic mixing and matching is manifested, the greater the overall poetic perception and impact.

Poetry is therefore distinct from prose (i.e., to a greater or lesser extent, depending on the nature of the language and literary genre involved) in this fundamental respect: In poetry, the anaphoric principle of equivalence (potential substitutability), e.g., רֶגַע and עֶרֶב in 30:6 above, is superimposed upon the cataphoric principle of combination (realized sequence), e.g., to such a degree that it becomes equal if not greater as a significant structuring force within the discourse. In other words, "the elements of a

---

[1] "Where the poetic function is predominant, the words present in the text will have the same kinds of linguistic relations to each other as they do to the words from among which they were chosen. These relations include phonological identity (whence meter and rhyme), grammatical parallelism, and semantic synonymy or antithesis" (Berry 2012:1056).

text, which of necessity occur in linear sequence (contiguity), are then perceived as equivalent or contrasted (similarity)" (Berlin 1985:138). This dynamic is especially perceptible when it coincides, as in Hebrew poetry, with the formal compositional feature of parallelism (two or more sentences or utterances regarded as being closely linked together for the purposes of interpretation). The matter of relative concentration is also a factor: the various equivalences of sound, sense, and syntax which are manifested between adjacent lines of poetry are considerably more numerous than one normally finds in prose. This characteristic not only draws attention to the special formal nature of poetic discourse, but it also contributes to the higher degree of unity and organization which is typical or indicative of poetry—that is, in addition to its greater semantic density and emotive depth.

The critical linguistic features which, by their recursion in a text, serve to establish such poetic, parallelistic equivalence—whether analogous or antithetical in nature—may incorporate all four basic types of discourse organization. These linguistic levels may be ranked according to their putative degree of perceptibility and perhaps also translatability in written (read) discourse as follows: phonological (e.g., alliteration, punning, intonation); lexical-semantic (e.g., use of synonyms and antonyms); syntactic (e.g., the phrasal order of clause constituents); morphological (e.g., the progression of tense, number, gender, etc.). Jakobson's abstract axiom—sameness superimposed upon the sequence of form and meaning—is reflected more concretely then in the device of poetic parallelism, which in one verbal manner and means or another characterizes more from less poetic works (oral or written) in every language. In Hebrew poetry, for example, this is normally manifested in the series of coupled lines, or cola, which comprise a given text.

It is important to recognize that a poetic couplet, whether consisting of the usual two, three, or sometimes more lines, may be contiguous (adjacent) or detached (distant, or displaced) in nature, as illustrated in the hypothetical (and greatly simplified) diagram below. In this figure **W**, **X**, **Y**, and **Z** symbolize individual words (accent-units) or phrases that exhibit one or more reiterated and equivalent linguistic features (i.e., phonological, morphemic-affixal, syntactic, or lexical-semantic); an O refers to a word having no significant feature that either corresponds or contrasts with those just mentioned; [/] indicates a colon-half line boundary and [//] a verse (bi-/tri-colon) boundary:

1. **W X Y Z** / **Z W X** / **X Y** O // 2. O O O / O O // 3. O O O / O O O // 4. **Y Z W** //
5. O **X Z W** / O O O // 6. O O / O O O // 7. O O / O O O // 8. O O **Z** / O **W X** //

This formulaic sequence would indicate a poem of 8 verses and 16 poetic lines. It leads off with a repetitious 4:3:3 tricolon and ends with a 3:3 bicolon that features three elements, Z, W, and X, which correspond to those occurring initially in the text (i.e., an inclusio). The discourse appears to be divided up into two equal parts (stanzas) of 8 lines and 4 verses each, with the final monocolon of part one (YZW) also constituting an inclusio through verbal resonance with its beginning. In addition, the first line of stanza 2 (OXZW) illustrates another important area of equivalence in the form of detached parallelism with the initial line of the poem (i.e., similar unit openings = anaphora), as well as the feature of a hinge, or overlap construction (anadiplosis) with the immediately preceding line (i.e., in the repeated Z and W elements). However, one would expect that at least one significant element in the line which leads off the second strophe (OXZ) should indicate a semantic break at that point, e.g., a new topic-focused item (O, e.g., "Hear!"). Finally, the endings of both stanzas have similarities too (i.e., YZW and Z/OWX), a structural correspondence termed epiphora (for all of these designations, see Wendland 2004:127). In order to display the various distinctions discussed above more simply, the following diagram substitutes some typical psalmic lexical sets (each one hypothetically including several synonyms/antonyms or word pairs): W = "save," X = "God," Y = "people," Z = "righteous."

	1a	**save-God-people-righteous**
	1b	**righteous-save-God**
	1c	**God-people-O**
//		
	2a	OOO
	2b	OO
//		
	3a	OOO
	3b	OOO
//		
	4a	**people-righteous-save (inclusio, v. 1)**
//		
	5a	**O-God-righteous-save (anaphora, v. 1; anadiplosis, v. 4b)**
	5b	OOO
//		
	6a	OO
	6b	OOO

//

    7a   OO

    7b   OOO

//

    8a   **OO-righteous**

    8b   **O-save-God (inclusio, vv. 1, 5a, epiphora, v. 4a)**

In the case of most poetry, the factor of equivalence also governs the mode of syntagmatic combination with respect to the principle of relatively balanced lineation. Thus, there appears to be a phonological (rhythmic-lexical, or metrical-syllabic) constraint that operates in a more or less rigorous fashion to determine the syntactic limits of line length. Biblical verse is somewhat fluid in this respect, the average colon ranging between two and five accent units (the average is three "phonic words" of this nature). The regularity manifested in the Hebrew poetic tradition is not as tightly symmetrical nor as rigidly controlled as in other literatures. But this is a significant feature nevertheless, for such freedom allows for the interruption of established linguistic patterns, in effect creating a break or point of meaningful discontinuity within the text. Furthermore, the relative brevity of line length accounts for another typical characteristic of such poetic composition, namely, its conciseness or terseness. The result in terms of style is a formally and semantically condensed mode of expression in which each word, indeed every single morpheme, is carefully (often sonically) positioned to play an essential part in generating the concentrated, semantically resonant message that the poet (psalmist, prophet) wishes to convey— whether directly by word, or indirectly by allusion.[2]

The typical psalm, in its canonical context, thus embodies a dense and dynamic communication network, in which associative (connotative, expressive, aesthetic) meaning also plays a crucial role. It is a complete, unified verbal composition consisting of many overlapping syntagmatic (forward moving) and paradigmatic (backward referencing) linguistic connections. These textual linkages manifest an unfolding, progressively amplified, yet closely integrated system of semantic representation and pragmatic function. The individual text also resonates intertextually with other psalms in the tradition (e.g., the Psalter's corpus of five "books") as well as extratextually (canonically) with the entire cultural-religious framework of Israel,

---

[2] On the notion of style, Grossman astutely observes: "Translators need to develop a keen sense of style in both languages [SL/TL], honing and expanding [a] critical awareness of the emotional impact of words, the social aura that surrounds them, the setting and mood that informs them, the atmosphere they create," as well as a clear "perception of the connotations and implications behind [their] denotative meaning" (2010:7).

as represented in the Hebrew Bible (e.g., the concepts of law, covenant, prophecy, and YHWH). Individual instances of continuity and discontinuity tend to permeate an entire poetic piece, variously combining and interrelating with each other to structure and shape the discourse more intricately by means of prominent patterns and points of significance. Such an artistically embellished form serves in turn to magnify a given work's overall communicative potential—cognitively, emotively, and volitionally. Both compositional forces are necessary, for patterns cannot be created without points to establish limits and boundaries, while points have no meaning in isolation from larger patterns of linguistic organization. This chapter will illustrate the interactive compositional operation of the poetic principles of continuity and discontinuity, with special reference to the major global strategies of verbal selection and textual arrangement in Psalm 30.

2.2 Continuity—carrying a text forward and tying it together

The principle of continuity is reflected in the tendency of a well-formed verbal composition to manifest the essential properties of progression and coherence. "Progression" refers to the sense of organized forward movement and direction that a coherent text exhibits. The discourse "goes" somewhere, from A to B and even on to Z, in a manner that continually advances, unfolds, and/or develops the author's message. This movement may not be evident immediately, but as the discourse proceeds (or after another more careful reading/hearing), it should become apparent to the majority of respondents. Progression may be syntagmatic (temporal, consequential) or paradigmatic (analogical, associative) in nature, and this tendency is normally perceived or experienced in some tangible way as one advances through the text. Thus, one ought to be able to discern that the message is being meaningfully composed and progressing to a point of completion and/or culmination, for example, in the form of a narrative, exposition, exhortation, argument, depiction, or some type of poetic expression.

The primary ways of organizing a progression in discourse are based on relations of class, time, space, cause-effect, and so forth. These may include various subcategories that intersect or coincide in their textual realization, e.g., with regard to rank (greater to lesser, generic to specific) or co-relations such as positive-negative, question-answer, or text-intertext (allusion, quotation). The more complex the verbal creation, the more numerous the distinct but interrelated patterns and sequences that are conjoined on different levels of structural organization. Poetry generally exemplifies a relatively complex (linguistically) or concentrated (conceptually) type of composition that leaves connections and transitions implicit, less apparent, or expressed in figurative terms.

"Coherence," then, refers to the characteristics of connectivity, conjunction, and congruence that a text displays with respect to form, content, and function. The result is an impression of unity and harmony in which the whole is perceived to be greater than, distinct from, or not immediately derivable from the sum of its individual parts. And yet all the constituent elements fit together appropriately to comprise the composition in its entirety. Coherence may be viewed from both a textual and also an extratextual perspective. The textual aspect may be either formal or semantic in nature, i.e., exhibiting cohesion (verbal linkage) and congruence (meaningful connection), respectively. In all artistic works both of these dimensions are present, but one tendency may be marked more clearly (overtly) or emphasized more strongly than its counterpart on different levels of discourse structure, e.g., between the lines of a poetic bicolon as distinct from the coherent relations between two adjacent strophes/stanzas.

The extratextual component of coherence pertains to the real or imagined conceptual world, or cognitive environment, that is both presupposed and evoked by a particular discourse. Of special importance is the perceived relationship (suitability, relevance, applicability, etc.) of the text with its situational setting and the conditions under which it was originally composed, then subsequently conveyed and received by hearing or reading. In contrast to the initial event, which is (or was) unique, the context of subsequent transmission events is obviously flexible and disparate in nature. These divergences may be comparatively investigated and described with respect to nature and scope, quality and quantity by means of a "frames of reference" analytical methodology (e.g., Wendland 2011:29–60). In cases where the contemporary cognitive, sociocultural, and environmental setting of reception differs appreciably from the situation and circumstances that first prevailed, problems of perception, understanding, appreciation, evaluation, and application necessarily increase, sometimes to the point where a successful act of communication cannot take place at all without additional extratextual supplementation (instruction, explanation, description, etc.). On the other hand, some biblical texts, like individual psalms, may be sufficiently contextualized by the immediate cotextual (Psalter) and wider (TaNaKh) canonical setting in which they are placed to allow adequate understanding and interpretation to occur.

A crucial technique in the creation of textual coherence, or continuity in discourse, is recursion of one sort or another. As noted in chapter 1, such reiteration may be exact (repetition) or recognizably similar with regard to form and corresponding or contrastive in terms of meaning (content, intent). Recursion is a compositional strategy that is especially prominent in poetry, as the subsequent analysis of Psalm 30 will demonstrate. The scope of replication may be restricted to the individual bi- or tri-colon, which is the normal focus of study; alternatively and more significantly perhaps, a much larger structural design may take shape due to linguistic duplication—one which encompasses the entire poem/psalm as well as major sections within it.

Furthermore, as a result of the operation of recursion, there is a strong tendency for a poetic discourse to be constructed in the form of patterns, that is, functionally significant arrangements of distinct elements, on all levels of linguistic organization—sound, sense, syntax, and oftentimes, textual shape as well (e.g., chiastic or terraced constructions). Phonological patterns are perhaps the most immediately noticeable when it comes to poetry, above all, in some manner of metrical textual articulation, but also in the form of assonance, alliteration, paronomasia (punning), onomatopoeia, and rhyme. Indeed, the demarcation of a literary text into discrete coupled lines (cola) that are closely related to one another in multiple ways (i.e., parallelism), and which evince a perceptible equivalence of sound-sequencing by means of a regular rhythmic progression of word-accent units, is one of the principal characteristics that distinguishes poetic from less poetic (prosaic) discourse in the Hebrew Bible.

But the patterned recursion of other features that are formally or semantically related to one another also contributes to the overall effect and identification, such as word endings (e.g., masculine vs. feminine endings, singular vs. plural forms), lexical stems (including merisms and conventionally associated word pairs), phrases (especially those containing key theological motifs and thematic concepts), and syntactic constructions (such as the non-standard order of syntactic units within the clause to reveal instances of topic focus or constituent focus). Such meaningful (aesthetic, rhetorical) patterns, which often incorporate important intertextual correspondences, frequently traverse an entire poem or larger constituents within it. Taken together then, which is how they must always be interpreted, all of these instances of recursion function both to segment the discourse and also to synthesize it, with the borders of primary units and sub-units being indicated through the reiteration of significant elements within a coherent, overarching textual framework of recurrent and interrelated form and meaning.

In this artistic way, yet one that retains the decorum of the sacred tradition, the principle of continuity establishes the essential fabric of a unified lyric composition. It thereby contributes greatly also to a biblical poem's general level of impact and appeal, especially when perceived via its natural medium of sound. The overlapping, multilayered sequences and sets of patterned discourse serve to constitute the structural foundation upon which other, more elaborate stylistic features may be fashioned. The latter thus form the relief—the figures that stand out from their background to create crucial supplementary special effects, such as the marking of internal points of high emotion (climax) or thematic importance (peak). The cumulative interpersonal effect of these continuative techniques in biblical poetry is to establish and maintain a dynamic interaction between a psalmist (liturgical leader) and his communal worship audience, on the one hand,[3] and the ultimate object of their prayerful utterances on the other—namely, Yahweh, God of the eternal, living Word.

2.3 Discontinuity—breaking up a text and highlighting its contents

The various structural and stylistic features that promote formal and semantic continuity within a literary text are normally accompanied in a poetic work by some manifestation of the opposing, yet complementary compositional principle of discontinuity. This procedure creates a certain conceptual surprise (semantic and/or syntactic in nature), hence creating a perceptible artistic tension within the work, which prevents it from becoming predictable or commonplace with regard to form, content, purpose, and/or psychological effect. The cohesive, forward-moving progression of formal similarities and cognitive correspondences needs to be distinguished by being played against periodic differences in order to achieve a certain balance of literary forces, the ultimate aim of which is to facilitate a communication (sharing) of the author's projected meaning. In sum, it is a fine line that the poet must follow: too much continuity, and his (her) work becomes banal—predictable and hence probably boring; too much discontinuity, on the other hand, and the text fragments and begins to disintegrate. In either case, the result is an inevitable decrease, or even a complete disruption in the process of cognitive comprehension and aesthetic appreciation on the part of the intended audience/readership/user constituency.

The poet has a variety of rhetorical devices at his disposal in order to inject points of discontinuity within a developing discourse. Their main purpose is to highlight certain prominent aspects of thematic content and to augment the communicative impact which his poem has upon listeners. In general, these literary techniques all involve the interruption of an established pattern and/or the introduction of novelty (surprise) within the text—some overt addition, omission, or shift in expectancy, whether formal or semantic. In Hebrew poetic discourse, the principal stylistic strategies that are employed to introduce such discontinuity are *figurative language* (e.g., simile, metaphor, metonymy, hyperbole, personification) and *formal alteration* (e.g., a shift in the normal word order, tense sequence, verbal voice, addressee, line length, vocabulary). As far as the Psalms are concerned, the

---

[3] Of course, the psalms may also be prayed individually, silently, and directed to personal needs. This changes the dynamic nature of the prevailing direct discourse in which they are composed, but God (YHWH) remains as the primary addressee, and the community of faith are often assumed to be in the audible background as the implied hearers of the speaker's prayer (whether a lament, petition, warning, exhortation, encouragement, or whatever).

effect of these figures of speech and structural modifications is often due to relatively slight variations in what is normally rather conventional religious diction. Similarly, it should be noted that these linguistic devices frequently sound more jarring (conceptually discontinuous) in a literal translation than they actually are in the original Hebrew. A prominent point of discontinuity in Psalm 30 is obvious as one moves from v. 10 to v. 11 (English text, literally):

> 10: Hear O-Yahweh / and-be-gracious-[to]-me / O-Yahweh a-helper be for-me!
> 11: You-have-turned my-wailing into-dancing for-me / you-have-taken-off my-sackcloth / and-you-have-clothed-me [with]-joy!

The three perfective verbs of v. 11 contrast markedly with the three imperatives of v. 10; the longer, picturesque semi-narrative sequence of v. 11 reflects a calm, grateful attitude as opposed to the clipped, urgent appeals of the preceding verse, intensified as they are by the double divine vocatives. There is no doubt then that v. 11 initiates a new and distinct section of this thanksgiving psalm.

Other common semantic, syntactic, and/or sonic features that may be employed to "defamiliarize" the discourse and create a motivated discontinuity include the following: the insertion of intensive, imperative, or exclamatory utterances; extended plays on local topical or global thematic meaning; shifts among direct, indirect, and embedded speech (quotation and dequotation); rhetorical, leading, and deliberative questions; asyndeton and ellipsis; irony and paradox; an additional or deleted word or line (colon); a direct appeal (vocative address) or descriptive reference to Yahweh; mention of one's enemies or a self-reference to the psalmist himself. There is a notable tendency in Hebrew poetic parallelism for such rhetorical devices to be incorporated in the second (B) line of a bicolon, to give it that heightened or sharpened effect that many scholars have called attention to in recent years. We note this, for example, in the verses cited above, each of which moves to a peak of intensity, specificity, and/or graphicity: "...O-Yahweh a-helper be for-me!" (10, including the reference to YHWH as a עֹזֵר)—"...and-you-have-clothed-me [with]-joy!" (11, "girding" the psalmist with the abstract feeling of שִׂמְחָה).

Poets normally aim to achieve some manner of embellishing what would otherwise be a more prosaic text as a means of enhancing the impact and appeal—hence also the perceived relevance—of their message. With respect to the technique of continuity as earlier described, this will often take the form of a deliberate expansion or elaboration of the content being conveyed, with the feature of parallelism itself being a prime example of this. In the case of discontinuity, on the other hand, we often find a marked concentration or convergence of stylistic features which often function to distinguish areas of extra importance in relation to a work's poetic structure or principal subject. These devices operate together to perform a pragmatic purpose by facilitating the functional dimension of communication, which in Hebrew texts, as in all literature, includes expressive, interpersonal (phatic), informative, imperative, performative, and esthetic motivations (cf. Wendland 2011:146–147).

We turn now to an examination of the various dimensions of discourse presented by Psalm 30 with specific reference to its various patterns of continuity and points of discontinuity. We will see how these complementary poetic principles interact to express the essential message of the psalmist, who speaks both for himself as well as on behalf of the community of God's people. We will pay special attention to the outstanding oral-aural features of the poetic text, on the assumption that this vital audio dimension makes a distinct contribution—not only to the manner of communicating this hymnic prayer to Yahweh, but also to the overall meaning experience that participants (should) derive from its singing, reciting, chanting, and musical performance in communal worship.

Psalm 30 was chosen as the object of this analysis and exemplification for several reasons: It is not featured in many scholarly studies of the Psalter; it is relatively short and seemingly rather simple, appearing to consist of a rather straightforward string of conventional psalmic expressions. But what lies beneath the textual surface of this individual *song of thanksgiving* (on the genre, see Gerstenberger 1988:133; Wendland 2002:38–40)?[4] Which important topical elements of continuity and discontinuity are reflected in the content of this psalm—between the psalmist and his enemies (v. 1b) or the dead (v. 3b), on the one hand, and his fellow worshippers (vv. 4, 12) on the other; or between the psalmist and his God in good times (vv. 6–7a, 11) and bad (vv. 3a, 7b)? How do the analysis procedures outlined in chapter 1 help us to perceive and evaluate some additional, less apparent aspects of its technical artistry and moving evocative effect? Finally, what are some modern modes of communication that may be pressed into service to transmit more of the flavor and essence of this ancient expression of deeply personal faith in Yahweh and joyous commitment to one's fellow "saints" (v. 4) of today?

2.4 Continuity and discontinuity in the discourse design of Psalm 30

> There is little agreement on the structure of the psalm. The parts follow closely on one another without clearly defined literary markers (VanGemeren 1991:257–258).

The author of the preceding rather pessimistic assessment of the discourse structure of Psalm 30 is certainly correct in calling attention

---

[4] Diagnostic verbs expressing "thanks" to Yahweh recur throughout Psalm 30, from the beginning in v. 1 (Hebrew v. 2) (רום) to the very end, vv. 4 (5), 9 (10), and 12 (13) (ידה).

to the widespread disagreement manifested by the different versions and scholarly commentaries with respect to this text. Terrien, for example, feels that "the poet who composed Psalm 30 seems to have put together disparate psalms of thankfulness" (2003:281), thus perhaps fashioning a literary unity out of disunity. But any implication that this psalm is ill-defined or poorly constructed is disproved by a more detailed compositional analysis, which reveals that the present text has in fact been very skillfully put together. Problems of discernment and assessment arise because not just one poetic structure is concerned, but several— each neatly superimposed upon the others to embellish the artistry of artistic form and hence also to increase both the semantic richness and the emotive depth of the work as an instance of profound human-theological communication. Thus, simultaneously operating patterns of continuity and points of discontinuity have been expertly blended and balanced in order to effect the psalmist's larger communicative purpose. That is to sing a song of grateful thanksgiving and praise to a God who has mercifully delivered him from his own pride and prosperity (v. 6) as well as from the malicious tongues of his foes (v. 1) and the very jaws of death (v. 3). A number of distinct discourse perspectives are therefore necessary to reveal the intricacies of this formally manifold, rhetorically motivated poetic configuration.

2.4.1 Linear surface structure

We will begin by documenting the structural organization which is the most obvious, namely, that of the diachronic progression of poetic lines. This exercise will follow the model of text spatialization suggested in chapter 1. An interlinear English translation is incorporated, and table notes are introduced to comment on selected aspects of the Hebrew text on a section by section basis. These highlight selected aspects of the Hebrew text with respect to problematic forms, alternative readings, proposed emendations, interpretive challenges, poetic demarcation, and basic translational issues. Topics of special literary-rhetorical relevance will be more fully considered in the sections that follow.

v.co	Post-verb2	Post-verb1	VERBAL	Pre-verb2	Pre-Verb1
A[a]					
0.1	הַבַּ֫יִת[b]	שִׁיר־חֲנֻכַּת	-----		מִזְמ֫וֹר
	the-house	a-song-of = dedication-of			a-psalm
0.2					לְדָוִד
					to/of-David

	A	B	C	D	E
1.1		יְהוָה	אֲרוֹמִמְךָ		
		O-Yahweh	I-will-exalt-you		
			דִלִּיתָנִי [d]		כִּי
			you-extract-ed-me		for
1.2	לִי	אֹיְבַי	שִׂמַּחְתָּ		וְלֹא־
	to/over-me	my-enemies	you-caused-to-rejoice		and-not =
2.1			------	אֱלֹהַי	יְהוָה
				My-God	O-Yahweh
2.2		אֵלֶיךָ	שִׁוַּעְתִּי [e]		
		unto-you	I-cried-for-help		
			וַתִּרְפָּאֵנִי		
			and-you-healed-me		
3.1	נַפְשִׁי	מִן־שְׁאוֹל	הֶעֱלִיתָ		יְהוָה
	my-life	from = Sheol	you-raised-up		O-Yahweh
3.2	בוֹר	מִיּוֹרְדִי־ (מִיָּרְדִי) [f]	חִיִּיתַנִי		
	a-pit	from-going-down-into =	you-restored-me-to-life		

[a] Every verse in this initial strophe expressing praise (1.1a) plus its reasons (כִּי) (1.1b–3.2) leads off with the covenantal divine name (יְהוָה). These Yahwistic vocatives thus give strong cohesion to the three verses (bicola) that constitute this poetic paragraph, which effectively summarizes the message of the entire psalm. After the psalmist's call for an appropriate response from the community of faith ("saints") in strophe B, the remaining three strophes reiterate the essence of strophe A in greater detail.

[b] "The psalm became associated with the feast of Hanukkah, commemorating the [re-]dedication of the temple in 165 B.C." (VanGemeren 1991:257; cf. Bratcher and Reyburn 1991:283). Many canonical critics give special hermeneutical attention to all historical references to the life of David in these psalmic superscriptions: "If the reader is going to take seriously the canonical form of [the] text...the superscriptions have to be more than an interesting canonical note. The superscriptions should find a place within the interpretation of the psalm" (Wallace 2014:198).

[c] "The 'I' immediately marks the psalm as a thanksgiving rather than a hymn, because its distinctive nature will be to give personal testimony to what Yhwh has done for an individual. 'I' has little place in a hymn, which focuses resolutely

on Yhwh" (Goldingay 2006:425–426). However, the psalmist apparently elicits a hymn from the worshiping congregation in strophe B (vv. 4–5). The verb רום "extol/lift up" sets the thematic tone for the first strophe, as well as the psalm as a whole (cf. v. 9.2), for the LORD "lifts" those who trust him in life, and they in turn "lift" him up in praise (a rhetorically-motivated lexical pun). The verb אֲרוֹמִמְךָ is complemented by אוֹדֶךָ at the very end (12.4) to form a panegyric inclusio.

[d] "Elsewhere the verb דָּלָה (dalah) is used of drawing water from a well (Ex 2:16, Ex 2:19; Pr 20:5). The psalmist was trapped in the pit leading to Sheol (see v. 3), but the LORD hoisted him up. The Piel stem is used here, perhaps suggesting special exertion on the LORD's part" (NET note). Images of the Lord bringing the psalmist "up" from going "down" to the pit of Sheol give this opening strophe some strong visual cohesion. "The suppliant was as good as dead—was standing in the doorway of Sheol..." (Goldingay 2006:427; cf. VanGemeren 1991:258). "The metaphorical polarity of *going down to the pit*/being *drawn up* mirrors the more realistic polarity of being in distress/experiencing deliverance at God's hand" (deClaissé-Walford et al. 2014:293).

[e] This is an unusually structured bicolon: the first colon is apparently verbless, while the second includes two finite verbs. The two lines are connected by the similarly sounding divine references: אֱלֹהַי and אֵלֶיךָ. Harman suggests that "the anguish on the part of the psalmist is reflected in [his] poetry, especially that the rhythmic patterns of the Hebrew text are very irregular. The staccato effect accentuates the distress of heart" (2011a:261). Terrien too feels that "irregularities of rhythm abound," which he documents (2003:281).

[f] "*Heb* 'you kept me alive from those descending into the pit'. The Hebrew noun בּוֹר (*bor,* 'pit, cistern') is sometimes used of the grave and/or the realm of the dead. The translation follows the consonantal Hebrew text *(Kethiv);* the marginal reading *(Qere)* has, 'you kept me alive so that I did not go down into the pit'" (NET note). "It is preferable to accept the MT without emendation" (VanGemeren 1991:259). Craigie, too, supports the *kethiv,* noting that "the normal infinitive construct form occurs in v 10," and therefore, "an alternative form, as implied by *Qere,* is unlikely" (1983:251). Goldingay, on the other hand, argues for the *qere* (2006:423).

B[a]				
4.1	חֲסִידָיו	לַיהוָה	זַמְּרוּ	
	his-faithful-ones	unto-Yahweh	sing-praise	
4.2	קָדְשׁוֹ[b]	לְזֵכֶר	וְהוֹדוּ	
	his-holiness	for-remembrance-of	and-give-thanks	
5.1		בְּאַפּוֹ	-----	רֶגַע[c]	כִּי[d]
		in-his-anger		a-moment	for

5.2		בִּרְצוֹנוֹ	-----	חַיִּים	
		in-his-favor		lifetimes	
5.3		בְּכִי [e]	יָלִין		בָּעֶרֶב
		weeping	it-spends-the-night		in-the-evening
5.4		רִנָּה	-----		וְלַבֹּקֶר
		rejoicing			and-in-the-morn

[a] There is a decided shift from singular to plural references and from visual to auditory images in the hymnic (panegyric) strophe B (vv. 4–5). The contrastive imagery also lends conceptual coherence to this strophe. The emphasis on the need for God's people to "praise the LORD" reflects the beginning of the preceding strophe (A), i.e., similar unit beginnings (structural anaphora; cf. Wendland 2004:127).

[b] "*Heb* 'to his holy remembrance'. The noun זֵכֶר (*zekher* 'remembrance') here refers to the name of the LORD as invoked in liturgy and praise. Cf. Ps. 6:5; Ps. 97:12. The LORD's 'name' is 'holy' in the sense that it is a reminder of his uniqueness and greatness" (NET note). The noun *zekher* (related to the verb 'remember' *z-k-r*) is found in parallel with *shem* 'name' elsewhere, e.g., Psalm 135:13 (Craigie 1983:251). "The word is not *shem* but *zeker*—the name as something people make mention of and thus celebrate in worship (cf. 6:5 [6])" (Goldingay 2006:428; cf. also Exo. 3:15). "It signifies the proclamation of God's [remembered] acts in the history of redemption associated with the name Yahweh (cf. 111:2–4, 122:4, 145...)" (VanGemeren 1991:260).

[c] "The context here shows a contrast between death and life, and the idea that the Hebrew word *rega'* (NIV 'moment') means 'death' has had advocates both among older commentators and those in recent time. This idea receives support, moreover, by the fact that the Hebrew word for 'life' *(chayyîm)* is never used to refer to a 'lifetime'. Rather, it appears in contrast to death" (Harman 2011a:263; cf. Craigie 1983:250–251, VanGemeren 1991:261). Bratcher and Reyburn, however, support the traditional reading: "The psalmist contrasts the Lord's short-lived anger (for a moment) with his permanent favor (for a lifetime)" (1991:285).

"*Heb* 'for [there is] a moment in his anger, [but] life in his favor'. Because of the parallelism with 'moment', some understand חַיִּים *(khayyim)* in a quantitative sense: 'lifetime' (cf. NIV, NRSV). However, the immediate context, which emphasizes deliverance from death (see v. 3), suggests that חַיִּים has a qualitative sense: 'physical life' or even 'prosperous life' (cf. NEB 'in his favour there is life')" (NET note).

[d] As in strophe A, the reason (כִּי) for praise is given after an initial appeal.

[e] Here is a unique personification: "Weeping lodges overnight" (i.e., sorrow lasts but a short time—when one is being kept by Yahweh. Note the elaborate double contrast that highlights the theme of this second strophe, namely, Yahweh's covenantal relationship with the faithful (vv. 5–6): *time*: short (instant/evening)—long (lifetime/morning); *circumstances*: sad (anger/weeping)—glad (favor/rejoicing). "God's favor is longer and stronger than God's anger [towards his sinful saints]—God's favor suffices both to give life and to last a lifetime" (deClaissé-Walford et al. 2014:294).

C					
6.1[a]		בְשַׁלְוִי[b]	אָמַרְתִּי		וַאֲנִי
		in-my-prosperity	I-said		and-I
6.2		לְעוֹלָם	אֶמּוֹט		בַּל-
		forever	I-will-be-tripped-up		not-at-all =
7.1	עֹז	לְהַרְרִי[c]	הֶעֱמַדְתָּה[d]	בִּרְצוֹנְךָ	יְהוָה
	strong	for-my-mountain	you-caused-to-stand	in-your-favor	O-Yahweh
7.2		פָּנֶיךָ	הִסְתַּרְתָּ		
		your-faces	you-hid		
7.3		נִבְהָל[e]	הָיִיתִי		
		dismayed	I-became		

[a] An initial emphatic topic shift (full pronoun with disjunctive *waw*) back to the psalmist marks the onset of a new strophe (C), which appears to be the onset of a flashback that occupies the rest of the psalm (strophes C-E). The praise-leader now goes into poetic descriptive detail concerning his initial thanksgiving of strophe A.

Goldingay feels that the lines of strophe C "abandon parallelism and subordinate poetic form to the telling of a disquieting story...in linear fashion" (2006:429). However, this depends on one's definition of parallelism, and another could readily argue that while the content may be "linear" (or sequential) in nature, the form of parallelism continues in the poetic structure of these connected lines, as delineated by short combinations of 2–3 lexical units.

[b] "The word translated 'prosperity' is found only here; it means quietness, ease" (Bratcher and Reyburn 1991:286). Goldingay suggests that there is no reason to conclude that "the suppliant had lapsed into false self-confidence" or of "wrongful complacency" with the result that his "God has become inaccessible" (2006:430). However, one wonders about the thematic purpose of strophe C if the psalmist had been completely innocent: why this apparent confession? One's construal of the speaker's former situation and his relationship with Yahweh naturally colors the communicative character and aim of the entire psalm; cf. Harman: "the psalmist realizes that in his health he had been complacent and self-sufficient" (2011a:263)—guilty of egocentric hubris (Terrien 2003:282), "a haughty, independent spirit" (VanGemeren 1991:260; Ross 2013:142; deClaissé-Walford et al. 2014:295).

[c] "*Heb* 'in your good favor you caused to stand for my mountain strength'. Apparently this means 'you established strength for my mountain' ('mountain' in this case representing his rule, which would be centered on Mt. Zion) or 'you established strength as my mountain' ('mountain' in this case being a metaphor for security)" (NET note). "Apparently this is a way of saying, 'You established me with the strength of a mountain'" (Goldingay 2006:424). GNT has "you protected me like a mountain fortress"—which reflects the psalmist's past sense of security, when he apparently felt that he was strong enough to "stand" on his

own, without the LORD's help. "The word you established [הֶעֱמַדְתָּה] is another play on the vertical 'go down'/'draw up' metaphor of the psalm…[it] means literally 'you caused me to stand'" (deClaissé-Walford et al. 2014:295).

[d] This key term "in your favor" (taken for granted, or casually assumed to apply), in constituent focus syntactic position, contrastively echoes its correspondent "in his favor" in 5.2 (בִּרְצוֹנוֹ).

[e] The psalmist's long (proud) expression of self-confidence (7.3) contrasts with the short (swift) response of YHWH (7.2) and the poet's immediate dismay (7.3).

D[a]					
8.1			[b]אֶקְרָא	יְהוָה	אֵלֶיךָ
			I-called	O-Yahweh	unto-you
8.2			אֶתְחַנָּן	אֲדֹנָי	וְאֶל־
			I-prayed-for-mercy	my-Lord	and-unto =
9.1			[c]בְּדָמִי	בֶּצַע	[d]מַה־
			in-myblood	benefit	what =
9.2		[e]אֶל־שַׁחַת	בְּרִדְתִּי		
		unto = a-pit	in-my-going-down		
9.3		[f]עָפָר	הֲיוֹדְךָ		
		dust	will-it-praise-you		
9.4		[g]אֲמִתֶּךָ	הֲיַגִּיד		
		your-faithfulness	will-it-recount		
10.1		יְהוָה	שְׁמַע־		
		O-Yahweh	hear =		
			[h]וְחָנֵּנִי		
			and-mercy-me		
10.2	לִי	[i]עֹזֵר	הָיָה־		יְהוָה
	for-me	a-helper	be =		O-Yahweh

[a] From "I" (וַאֲנִי) in 6.1 to "you" (אֵלֶיךָ), the contrastive constituent topic shift announces the onset of strophe D and an apparent embedded direct quotation (vv. 9–10) of his prior prayer for mercy "to you [YHWH]" (8.1), "my Lord" (8.2). This strophe is topically arranged in chiastic form: A + A′ = appeal to God for help; B + B′ = the psalmist's rationale stated as rhetorical questions.

[b] "The imperfect of the Hebrew verbs [in v. 8] may be better translated as a frequentative action: 'I keep on calling…I keep on crying for mercy' (cf. 28:1; 142:2;

Joel 1:19)…. This is an expression of true repentance: concern for God's name" (VanGemeren 1991:261)—cf. לְזֵכֶר קָדְשׁוֹ in 4.2. The shift from direct speech in 8.1 to a 3rd person reference to Yahweh in 8.2 (enallage, in constituent focus position) helps to signal the onset of the incorporated direct quotation in vv. 9–10. The vocative expression "Unto you, O LORD" recalls vv. 1–3, especially "*my God*" (v. 2a); it is significant that even in his deepest distress the psalmist never doubted his personal relationship with the only One who could deliver him.
^c In this case, the nominal construction "in my blood" (בְּדָמִי) is construed as a metonymic reference to one's death (cf. Bratcher and Reyburn 1991:287), hence functioning in place of a verbal within the A colon, in parallel with the rhyming infinitive construct "in my going down [to the grave]" (בְּרִדְתִּי), which functions as the verbal core of the parallel B colon. Some scholars propose an emendation from MT's *dammî* to *dommî* 'my weeping' from d-m-m II (also in v. 12; VanGemeren 1991:262).
^d A pair of short rhetorical questions in the form of matched bicola highlight the rationale for the plaintiff's urgent appeal, one that is based on the LORD's manifest past covenantal "faithfulness" (אֲמִתֶּךָ). The reiterated negative responses expected highlight the somewhat ironic pathos of the psalmist's pleas: only YHWH in his relational faithfulness can help in this dire situation!
^e "The Hebrew term שַׁחַת (*shakhat*, 'pit') is often used as a title for Sheol (see Ps. 16:10; Ps. 49:9; Ps. 55:24; Ps. 103:4)" (NET note).
^f This is a vivid personification: "Can the dust (i.e., a dead person) praise you, (LORD)?" Obviously not! (cf. 88:10).
^g "According to the OT, those who descend into the realm of death/Sheol are cut off from God's mighty deeds and from the worshiping covenant community that experiences divine intervention (Ps. 6:5; Ps. 88:10–12; Is. 38:18). In his effort to elicit a positive divine response, the psalmist reminds God that he will receive no praise or glory if he allows the psalmist to die. Dead men do not praise God!" (NET note). But the psalmist's apparent self-centered appeal to God's self-interest is too limited a perspective, for "the psalmist's question about praise is a question about life, since for the psalmist to live is to praise God [no matter what their circumstances] and to praise God is to live" (McCann 1996:796). The expression "your faithfulness" (אֲמִתֶּךָ) refers to Yahweh's unfailing covenantal loyalty to his people; sooner or later he will deliver them (him or her).

In commenting on this verse, Alter astutely writes: "The language of his appeal takes us right back to the thematic foreground of language…. It is perhaps not so surprising to find in a poem that the whole argument is tilted along the bias of the poem's medium, language. It is through language that God must be approached, must be reminded that, since His greatness needs language in order to be made known to men, He cannot dispense with the living user of language for the consummation of that end" (1985:135).
^h This verb complements its correspondent אֶתְחַנָּן at the beginning of the strophe (8.2) and thus underscores the urgency of the psalmist's appeal. Colon 10.1 also features a double verb construction that further intensifies the psalmist's plea for "grace," one that is emphasized still more by the two vocatives of this verse.
ⁱ The noun "helper" (עֹזֵר) phonologically matches the adjective "strong" (עָז) at the end of the preceding strophe (7.2); note also the corresponding verbs הֱיִיתִ 1l (7.4) and הֱיֵה (10.2)—a case of structural epiphora, parallel unit endings. In terms of meaning, the term עֹזֵר "is equivalent to 'savior'" (Bratcher and Reyburn 1991:287).

E					
11.1	לְמָחוֹל לִי	מִסְפְּדִי[a]	הָפַכְתָּ[b]		
	to-dancing for-me	my-wailing	turn		
11.2		שַׂקִּי	פִּתַּחְתָּ		
		my-sackcloth	you-removed		
11.3		שִׂמְחָה[c]	וַתְּאַזְּרֵנִי		
		(with)—joy	and-you-clothed-me		
12.1		כָּבוֹד[d]	יְזַמֶּרְךָ[e]		לְמַעַן |
		(my)-glory/ self	it-might-sing-to-you		in-order-that
12.2			יִדֹּם		וְלֹא
			it-might-be-silent		and-not
12.3			אוֹדֶךָּ[g]	לְעוֹלָם[h]	יְהוָה אֱלֹהַי
			I-will-thank-you	to/until-forever	O-Yahweh my God

[a] "The *mispêd* is the dirge sung over the dead" (deClaissé-Walford et al. 2014:297)—hence rather more than just "mourning." The pronominal reference "*my* mourning" could be subjective, objective, or probably both: the psalmist grieving over his immanent demise and others mourning his loss.

[b] Strophe E reverses the order of pragmatic elements from that of strophe A, i.e., from praise-reason (1.1) to reason-praise (12.4) and perhaps serves to mark the complete reversal in the psalmist's physical (and spiritual?) circumstances. Asyndeton marks the onset of this strophe, which is distinguished by the rhymed verbs הָפַכְתָּ and פִּתַּחְתָּ. The "mourning" and "sackcloth" (12.1–2) correspond to "Sheol" and the "pit" of 3.1–2.

[c] Contrast the enemies' "gloating" (שִׂמְחָה) in 1.2, and note the correspondence with the community's praise, in v. 4.

[d] "*Heb* 'glory'. Some view כָּבוֹד (*khavod*, 'glory') here as a metonymy for man's inner being (see BDB 459 s.v. II כָּבוֹד 5), but it is preferable to emend the form to כְּבֵדִי (*k'evediy*, 'my liver'). [This is supported by Craigie, based on *G* (1983:251).] Like the heart, the liver is viewed as the seat of one's emotions. See also Ps. 16:9; Ps. 57:9; Ps. 108:1, as well as H. W. Wolff, *Anthropology of the Old Testament*, 64, and M. Dahood, *Psalms* (AB), 1:90. For an Ugaritic example of the heart/liver as the source of joy, see G. R. Driver, *Canaanite Myths and Legends*, 47–48: 'her [Anat's] liver swelled with laughter, her heart was filled with joy, the liver of Anat with triumph'. 'Heart' is used in the translation above for the sake of English idiom; the expression 'my liver sings' would seem odd indeed to the modern reader" (NET note). "For 'my heart' the Hebrew has 'glory'. For this as a term of self-reference, see...Psalm 7:5" (Harman 2011a:264; cf. Bratcher and Reyburn 1991:288); Terrien suggests "my passion" (2003:283).

Goldingay feels that the pronoun "my" may be readily implied from the context (2006:424; it is added in the LXX).

ᵉ The psalmist reiterates his strong desire to "sing praise" *(z-m-r)* to Yahweh as expressed at the beginning of the psalm in v. 1 (also note *mizmor* in the heading), and as he encouraged the "faithful ones" to do in v. 4 (cf. Hezekiah's prayer in Isa. 38:20). This verb thus helps to demarcate the boundaries of this song of thanksgiving.

ᶠ The notion of purpose applies to both the positive-negative cola of 12.1–2. "Music and confession become natural. This last line [12.3–4] also holds together the nature of the psalm as thanksgiving and testimony. It addresses Yhwh, which makes it thanksgiving. But it does so aloud, because the thanksgiving is also a testimony or confession designed to glorify Yhwh in such a way that other people can hear..." (Goldingay 2006:432). This last observation needs a slight correction: Many "laments" also address Yhwh by name, e.g., Psalms 28, 31, and the psalm, like all psalms would have been uttered/prayed aloud in any case, whether individual or communal in nature. The public character of Psalm 30 is clearly indicated by its second strophe (B).

ᵍ The same verbs "laud" (ידה) and "sing praise" (זמר) are found at the beginning of strophe B (4.1–2). Indeed, to some ears strophe B would sound more appropriate coming at the end, after the present strophe E, and hence the more detailed expression of the message, strophes C-E following immediately after its generalized expression at the beginning (strophe A). But the present arrangement of strophes creates a special impact and pragmatic effect, with the worshiping congregation getting actively involved much sooner in the prayer-praise.

ʰ The prayer's pious reference to "forever" (לְעוֹלָם), here in constituent focus position, contrasts markedly with his proud usage at the psalm's midpoint in v. 6.2. In the meantime, he had been brought back to life from the brink of death (vv. 3.2, 9.2).

2.4.2 Semantic-structural summary

Psalm 30 is a prayer of thanksgiving that has a communal (vv. 4–5) as well as an individual (vv. 1–3) perspective. The primary focus is on the psalmist himself (vv. 1, 12) and his desire to praise and thank God for a deliverance that had brought him to the brink of death (v. 9) as well as a laughing stock (v. 1b). He feels chagrined that perhaps it was his own pride that had alienated him from his personal relationship with God (vv. 6–7), and he fervently pleads for mercy (vv. 8, 10) so that he can once again praise the Lord along with the fellowship of the faithful (vv. 11–12). Thus, this is also "a psalm *about praise*" (deClaissé-Walford et al. 2014:290, original italics). As Alter observes, this psalm is fashioned in the form of a poetic narrative, with "a good deal of narrative movement between versets...a poem that celebrates not only God's saving power but the efficacy of speech—both speech to God in prayer and praise of God in thanksgiving" (1985:134).[5]

---

[5] While certain psalms are explicitly narrative in nature (e.g., Pss. 105–106), many lament psalms reflect an implicit underlying narrative movement that proceeds from a time of crisis and concern, through a sudden turning point or peak point when Yahweh

Four principal breaks in the discourse are indicated, that is, after verses 3, 5, 7, and 10. These represent points of significant disjunction, or discontinuity, within the text, which is thereby divided into five poetic segments or "strophes": (A) 1–3, (B) 4–5, (C) 6–7, (D) 8–10, and (E) 11–12. As noted in the text diagram above, there are clear formal and semantic markers that serve to delineate the beginning (i.e., aperture, *Ap.*) and/or ending (i.e., closure, *Cl.*) of each sub-unit. These are summarized on the chart below (only some of the main cohesive devices of continuity are listed):

A

Ap.   The psalm text begins; we have an initial summons to praise God along with a specification of the reason, which suggests a thanksgiving psalm.

Cl.   The motivation for thanking God (three vocatives) progresses to a conclusion in a series of relatively long cola that features synonymous references to the grave/death and first person pronominal references.

B

Ap.   Imperative + vocative opener; a shift in addressees—to "his saints," while Yahweh is referred to in the third person throughout; nevertheless, the content of the initial strophe is similar to that of v. 1a (structural anaphora).

Cl.   A pair of contrasting bicola marks the close in a [b + r] alliterative sequence; there is a condensed, climactic ending ("a-joyous-shout").

C

Ap.   Emphatic, contrastive, opening pronoun + *waw* ("But-I..."); shift in topical focus to the psalmist-self as speaker; beginning of internal quotation (vv. 6b–7a).

Cl.   There is a sudden change in mood/emotive tone (from optimistic to pessimistic), accented by asyndeton and the final, auto-referential word 'dismayed'.

---

suddenly acts (or is predicted to act) on behalf of the psalmist (or the people of God), to conclude in a resolution of praise and promise of worship (e.g., Ps. 18:3–19). Some canonical critics go even further to posit a macronarrative conceptual framework that encompasses the whole Psalter—a grand vision of varied thematic elements that cluster around the central idealized character of "David," in a conceptual development that proceeds from the historical personage (Books 1–2), progresses through the crisis of Exile (Books 3–4), and finally culminates in prophetic glimpses of David's Royal-Messianic anti-type (Book 5) (see the discussion in Wallace 2014, Magonet 2014:162–163).

D

Ap.   Front-shifted topic pronoun with vocative ("Unto-you, O-YHWH..."); change in the tense-aspect to imperfect/prefix verbs; a sequence of shorter cola begins; internal rhetorical questions (v. 9).

Cl.   The closing content mirrors that of the psalm's beginning in an A-B-A' structure, including a double reference to Yahweh.

E

Ap.   Shift back to perfect/suffix verbs; transition in mood from sorrow to joy and in speech illocution from appeal (v. 10) to praise (v. 11); average colon length increases.

Cl.   Final emphatic assertion with asyndeton—a vow to thank God-Yahweh (double vocative) forever; the initial colon (v. 11) echoes that at the beginning (v.1, inclusio); the psalm ends.

This psalm is therefore comprised of five strophes (poetic paragraphs) whose topical constitution may be briefly described as follows:[6]

A (1–3): The psalmist begins by continually asserting his praise for Yahweh and gives the reason why, namely, for preserving his life and hence saving him from the mockery of enemies. This strophe both opens and summarizes the content of this thanksgiving psalm, which features many polarities.

B (4–5): An appeal to the congregation of worshipers begins this strophe, which declares that Yahweh's mercy is dependable despite one's circumstances.

C (6–7): The focus shifts suddenly to the psalmist as he begins a series of three strophes that present his crisis and Yahweh's deliverance in more detail. In this strophe the psalmist confesses his former pride which led him to take Yahweh for granted.

D (8–10): The psalmist reveals that he turned to the Lord in a prayer for mercy, which he summarizes as an embedded speech.

E (11–12): The psalmist's concluding profession of thanks and promise of ongoing worship brings this psalm to an end.

This strophic sequence guides speakers through the various speech acts and attitudes that structure and coherently develop the psalmist's prayer.

---

[6] Compare VanGemeren's less precise structure: A (vv. 1–3), B (vv. 4–7), A' (vv. 8–12) (1991:258). Several potential strophic (paragraph) breaks are thus missed (i.e., at vv. 6, 11), which has implications for formatting the text of this psalm in print.

A corresponding compositional arrangement should therefore be evident in any translation. Any major change in pattern will affect one's understanding and interpretation of the text's content.

Terrien, for example, posits two major sections (vv. 1–9 and 10–12) that express "thankfulness for the healing of a mortal malady"—with the second portion perhaps implying "the fear of a relapse" (2003:281). Such an interpretation completely skews the break that I have indicated between verses 10 and 11 (v. 10 begins Terrien's final strophe). He further suggests (ibid.:280) that verses 1–9 are constructed in the form of an extended chiasmus, with its center (and presumably focal core) being v. 5. However, this arrangement obscures the communally-oriented second strophe as a whole and perhaps deflects the emphasis from what is arguably the psalm's main theme as expressed in v. 5b, which lauds the "remembrance of [Yahweh's] holiness," i.e., his constant covenant faithfulness to his people (cf. vv. 9b, 12). This is a vital theological subject that is here "formally framed by the self-conscious marking of the language of praise" (Alter 1985:134).

The essential unity of Psalm 30 is further indicated by the following analytical charts, which offer several different perspectives on the overall thematic continuity (focused on Yahweh) that serves to tie the topically discontinuous stanza units (which reflect the psalmist's changing psychological states) into a cohesive whole.

2.4.3 Syntagmatic-relational structure

The figure on the following page presents a display of the basic semantic propositions that comprise Psalm 30 according to its five principal discourse divisions (strophes) as noted above.[7] These sequential units are designated by verse numbers with decimals along the right side of the diagram. Observe first of all that these individual event-/state-oriented segments are distinct from the poetic lines (cola) which demarcate the composition according to rhythmic and/or syntactic criteria (as indicated on the earlier spatialization chart). A second important feature of the diagram is that it gives a literal wording of the Hebrew surface structure.

---

[7] For an explanation and illustration of this methodology, see Wendland 2002:98–106.

I-will-exalt-you, Yahweh,	[A]	1.1
for you-lifted-me-out,		.2
and-not-did-you-let-rejoice		.3
my-enemies over-me.		.4
Yahweh, my-God, I-cried-for-help to-you		2.1
and-you-healed-me.		.2
Yahweh, you-brought-up from-sheol my-soul.		3.1
you-kept-me-alive		.2
from-those-descending-into the-pit.		.3
Sing-praise to-Yahweh,	[B]	4.1
his-pious-ones,		.2
and-give-thanks		.3
for-the-memory-of his-holiness.		.4
For-a-moment [is] in-his-anger,		5.1
life [is] in-his-favor.		.2
In-the-evening it-endures weeping,		.3
and-at-the-morning [is] a-joyous-shout.		.4
and-I I-said	[C]	6.1
in-my-security,		.2
"Not-shall-I-be-moved forever!		.3
Yahweh, in-your-favor		7.1
you-made-[it]-stand for-my-mountain strength!"		.2
You-hid your-face,		.3
I-was dismayed!		.4
Unto-you, Yahweh, I-will-call,	[D]	8.1
and-unto-my-Lord I-will-plead-		.2
for-mercy.		.3
"What-profit [is]		9.1
in-my-blood,		.2
in-my-descending into-destruction?		.3
Will-it-thank-you		.4
the-dust?		.5
will-it-proclaim		.6
your-faithfulness?		.7
Hear-O-Yahweh		10.1
and-show-mercy-to-me!		.2
O-Yahweh, be a-helper for-me!"		.3
You-turned my-wailing	[E]	11.1
into-dancing for-me;		.2
you-removed my-sackcloth,		.3
and-you-clothed-me-with joy.		.4
so-that it-may-sing-praise-to-you glory		12.1
and-not it-will-be-silent.		.2
Yahweh, my-God, forever I-will-thank-you!		.3

The propositions are not restated in a simplified semantic form as is the usual practice in such analyses (cf. Banker 1987:2), e.g., "for-mercy" [8.3] = "that you might have mercy on me;" "the-dust" [9.5] = "if I die" (de-metaphorization). This has been done in order to facilitate a comparison between this and subsequent charts of the text. Moreover, in some instances a more precise semantic breakdown could have been made, especially in the case of delimitive or qualificational propositions (ibid.:112), e.g., "his holiness" [4.4] = "he is holy." The detail was spared so as to render the display more manageable and readable as well.

The hierarchical syntagmatic network of inter-propositional connections is shown by the solid lines along the left side of the preceding diagram. The associated series of individual (small) letters refers to the various paired semantic relationships that link the propositional couplets (bi-/tri-cola) and clusters on different levels of the structural hierarchy. These relations are listed below in ordered pairs according to their respective designative letters, within the propositional display (adapted from Beekman et al. 1981:ch. 8).

Sequence of Propositional Paired Semantic Relationships

a implication-grounds	o base-restatement	c′ consequence-condition
b base-addition	p grounds-implication	d′ base-restatement
c orienter-content	q base-circumstance	e′ orienter-content
d base-amplification	r orienter-content	f′ grounds-implication
e means-result	s base-restatement	g′ reason-result
f base-restatement	t means-result	h′ base-addition
g means-result	u concession-contraexpectation	i′ grounds-implication
h concept-description	v reason-result	j′ base-contrast
i base-addition	w base-equivalent	k′ base-restatement
j implication-grounds	x orienter-content	l′ means-purpose
k base-contrast	y orienter-content	m′ base-contrast
l base-addition	z consequence-condition	n′ base-progression
m base-contrast	a′ base-equivalent	o′ base-restatement
n implication-grounds	b′ base-restatement	

Note also that the different degrees of indentation on the above chart mark what appear to be five principal levels of thematic dependency within the discourse as a whole.

The results of a syntagmatic-relational (or semantic-structural) analysis of Psalm 30 clearly indicate that the traditional system of designating the meaningful relations between poetic cola (e.g., "synonymous," "antithetical," "synthetic," etc.) is totally inadequate. It can tell us relatively little about how the poet has constructed his message, either on the micro- or on the macrolevel of the discourse. In order to gain such information, a much finer and more systematically organized semantic grid is needed, such as that illustrated above (alternative analytical inventories and schema are of course possible).

A careful examination of the preceding syntagmatic structure reveals that there are five major clusters of propositions which are conjoined to form the complete composition, i.e., verses 1–3 (a–g), vv. 4–5 (h–m), vv. 6–7 (q–v), vv. 8–10 (w–h′), and vv. 11–12 (i′–n′). These correspond with stanza divisions A–E posited earlier for the linear surface structure on the basis of the formal and semantic markers that highlight points of aperture and closure within the text. Of special significance are the larger-level relations that serve to link the five stanzas to each other and also cumulatively to the discourse in its entirety. These logical connections represent essential patterns of meaning continuity that override, as it were, the internal areas of disjunction and stanza delineation. The macrolinks establish the psalm as an integrated aesthetic and thematic whole—a unified artistic and theological *hosanna* emanating from the LORD's *chasidim* (v. 4).

Beginning with the most closely connected stanzas, C (6–7) is joined to D (8–10) by the semantic relationship of reason-result (g′). In other words, the poet's pride (or overconfidence) and subsequent sudden downfall (C) motivated him (i.e., cause-effect) to call upon his God, Yahweh—a plea recorded in stanza D. The outcome of combined C and D is then lauded in E, a base-progression relationship (n′). This set of three stanzas would be a good example of what Robert Alter terms the "narrative movement" that characterizes the development of many psalms—"a dynamic process moving toward some culmination" (1987:620). In the case of Psalm 30, this movement begins with some "steady state," a stage of spiritual equilibrium, followed by a personal crisis (C) of body and/or mind, which is an intensification that leads to an emotive climax (D), then a divinely initiated turning point or reversal and a final resolution (E).

The key to understanding the overall organization of this psalm lies in a recognition of the next crucial relationship, namely, one that links the first stanza (A) to the final three (C–E). In essence, the former (A) acts as the semantic foundation for the latter triad, i.e., base-restatement (o). After a general iterative assertion of the song's content and intent (A), the psalmist goes on to artistically elaborate on this theme in the second half of his thanksgiving song (C–E)—a poetic instance of semantic recycling, or we could say, A–B parallelism, on the discourse level of composition.

Only stanza B remains, forming the psalm's principal point of disjunction, as the poet unexpectedly (at first impression) breaks off from his line of thought to urge his fellow saints to join in a paean of praise to the Lord. Thus, after the initial stanza, he steps outside his poetic text as it were to address his situational setting in a personal appeal to those who were seemingly present with him on the scene of worship and prayer. And yet, set within the discourse as a whole, the apparent discontinuity is smoothed over—or better, skillfully blended into the compositional structure in its entirety. Stanza B therefore forms a fitting response, i.e., grounds-implication (p) to both stanza A on the one hand, and also to its recapitulation and expansion on the other (stanzas C–E). The chorus of B forms a general communal exhortation to the pious people of God that is based on the poet's individual relationship of faith and personal experience with Yahweh, his/their covenant Lord.

As so composed then, B acts as the structural pivot that bridges the prayer's two unequal portions, but it may have been the psalmist's intention that this vital stanza would actually be repeated after stanza E to conclude the larger second half as well. In any case, even if it is not reiterated as a corporate refrain at the end, stanza B is certainly not misplaced or superfluous when considered in relation to the cotext of its surrounding semantic totality. This will become even more evident as we consider the results of a more synchronically oriented overview of Psalm 30.

2.4.4 Topical-paradigmatic structure

We may begin a closer investigation of the mutually inclusive discourse (speech) patterns that organize Psalm 30 by referring once again to the five horizontal levels of structure that are indicated on the preceding semantic display. These indented variations, with "1" indicating the most general level of discourse and "5" the most embedded material, visually group the song's sequence of propositions according to the following spatial arrangement of communicative functions:

> *Level 1*—utterances invoking **praise**/thanksgiving to Yahweh[8]
> > *Level 2*—**prayer**/appeal to Yahweh for help
> > > *Level 3*—**proclamation** of Yahweh's timely deliverance
> > > > *Level 4*—lament over the Lord's **punishment**
> > > > > *Level 5*—personal expression of **pride**

Several salient observations can now be made. The psalm begins and ends (level 1) with a forceful utterance that expresses its dominant illocutionary force and hence establishes its basic quality and general emotive tone as a panegyric poem: thanksgiving and praise (1.1/12.3, i.e., a text-functional inclusio).

This joyful note of celebration is reiterated at two other points in the discourse. These appear in significantly different modes of formal expression, but in places that similarly balance one another in the structure as

---

[8] There may be an underlying antithetical element (polarity) that further highlights the first verse: The psalmist's praise stands in implicit opposition to his enemies' desire to "praise" (i.e., gloat over) his impending plight or former predicament. The latter also contrasts with the thankful praise of the faithful congregation, which is recalled in v. 4.

a whole: 4.1–4 (hortatory plural imperatives) and 9.1–7 (a series of three rhetorical questions that highlight the positive event by suggesting the possibility of its negative counterpart). The latter segment (a plea) contrasts in functional intent with the former (praise), and together with its continuation in v. 10, this entreaty may have formed part of a conventional prayer that the psalmist (or anyone else) spoke as part of the temple ritual undertaken during a particular time of trial (cf. Pss. 6:5; 28:1; 88:10–12; 115:17; 142:1; Craigie 1983:254). It should be noted that the concluding v. 12.3 is actually the climax of a triad of functionally equivalent expressions—this independent assertion being preceded by an antithetically stated dependent bicolon of purpose (12.1–2). The major propositions comprising this preeminent paradigmatic strand, which is marked by a repetition of the thematic verb *yadah* 'praise', are set off in bold type in the preceding figure.

Turning then to level 2 in the arrangement of utterances, we observe that these are propositions in which, first of all, the psalmist directs various petitions to Yahweh in his hour of need. In relation to level 1, they represent several steps back in time (flashback), referring to that dark, troubled period in his life when all seemed lost, when he was seemingly about ready to "descend into Sheol" (9.3). This motif is only briefly articulated in the first half of the psalm (2.1), but it reaches a much fuller level of expression in the second half, i.e., 8.1–3 and 10.1–3 (the pertinent material is indicated by italics in the propositional diagram above). Notice that the final pair of propositions (10.2–3) reiterates semantic elements from the preceding two (2.1/8.3), excluding the repeated vocative of address to the LORD. Within the framework of this interpretation, it is proposed that verses 9 and 10 should be construed as an actual (quoted) verbalization of the poet's appeal. "The quotation from the earlier prayer fits perfectly with the poetics and rhetoric of the current psalm of praise" (deClaissé-Walford et al. 2014:296), for the central up/down polarity is again prominent in relation to the psalmist's need to proclaim the faithfulness *(emet)* of his God. It is helpful, therefore, to distinguish these words of (internal) direct speech, at least typographically, by means of quotation marks (cf. GNT, NIV, NET). We find here in these verses an instance of thematic overlapping, as levels 1 (praise) and 2 (prayer) merge with one another in the psalmist's coherent discourse.

Internal levels 3 (proclamation) and 4 (punishment) may be considered together, since they are contrastive in nature and are frequently conjoined within the text of Psalm 30 (as well as in other thanksgiving psalms, e.g., Ps. 22). Thus, the prayer-singer offers these assertions almost like a confession of faith as the grounds for his discourse-framing words of praise (level 1). Yahweh in his mercy delivered the psalmist from sickness, danger, and death, thereby also preserving him from the mockery of their common enemies (i.e., the theologically impious or ethically unrighteous). The grateful poet's testimony of trust is proclaimed most strongly in the first and last stanzas (A/E), while the matter of God's prior chastisement is broached only indirectly by way of contrast, especially through several descriptive references to mourning and the grave. This antithesis is foregrounded also in the two internal stanzas (B/D). Yahweh has graciously preserved the poet from what might have been—from an angry (but just) judgment and consequent "weeping" (v. 5), from blood, destruction, and dust, i.e., the grave (v. 9). The psalm's central life–death polarity is figuratively reinforced by its pervasive positively inclined, uplifting imagery: from down to up, sickness to health, night to day, and sorrow to joy (Craghan 1985:178).

We arrive finally at stanza C (6.1–7.4) and the structural center of Psalm 30, where we encounter a point of sudden reversal—a dramatic shift with respect to both form and content. Indeed, there is also a certain measure of dramatic irony here as the psalmist initiates a word of praise to himself and even cites Yahweh in support of his psychologically secure position (7.1–2, at inclusion level 3). He confidently views his future as being "immoveable" on account of the assumed inalienable "favor" of God (a blatant expression of pride, level 5). This particular segment of the discourse exhibits another interesting feature, one that is in fact crucial to an understanding of the psalm's larger form and content. Thus, we have here also an instance of structural irony since this compositional core of the text, a location that normally reveals its thematic peak, now represents its spiritual pit and emotional "pit" of "destruction" (בּוֹר, שַׁחַת vv. 3, 9; cf. the concentric figure to follow). We hear the poet condemn himself in his own words as he boasts of his safe and sure earthly situation, with nary a care for any potential adversary or adversity. This prideful attitude and manifestation of self-sufficiency in the very presence of Yahweh served to precipitate a major catastrophe in his life.

According to this interpretation then, the segment of direct (embedded) discourse begun at 6.3 does not end there (as all English versions indicate), but rather continues through 7.2 (for a similar literary citation of a misguided and self-serving prayer, see Hosea 6:1–3). This self-confident and banal speech directed to Yahweh contrasts sharply with its penitent counterpart in verses 9 and 10. There we hear a chastened appellant fervently and rhetorically plead his case before a God whom he once regarded as sort of a benign benefactor, a divine guarantor of personal peace and prosperity, but whom he now acknowledges as a righteous judge and the sovereign ruler of life and death. This is a God whose "mercy" *(chanan)* he completely depends on for "help" *('-z-r)* of every kind.

Whether one considers 7.1–2 to be a quotative continuation of 6.3 or not, it is clear that the psalm's focal contrast occurs in 7.3–4, that is, immediately after the central core, thus dramatizing its thematic antitype. In the experience of the psalmist, his pride certainly marched before a great personal fall—one occasioned by Yahweh himself![9] This was so serious a calamity that it pushed him physically to the very brink of death and the grave (i.e., punishment, level 4), as reflected in stanzas A and D. But worse, his present state at that time threatened to separate him spiritually from his God, and by implication also from fellow members of the covenant community. This conceit, a self-centered dependence on one's own resources—or assumed religious standing before God—was regarded as being one of the most destructive sins in Israel, whether on the individual or the national level (and hence the burden of many prophetic messages). Proud self-confidence stood as a barrier to a proper acceptance of the gracious protection and provision of Yahweh. This was, in fact, the polar opposite of a complete devotion to and dependence upon him, as expressed, for example, in verse 10.

At this critical juncture, however, the psalmist's supreme crisis of body and soul is but indirectly referred to, and only in the briefest, most figurative and allusive manner: "You-hid your-face *(reason);* I-was dismayed *(result)*" (7.3–4, just four words in Hebrew, but drawn out at the emotive end by a periphrastic construction; cf. Num. 6:26; Deut. 31:17). His technical skill as a lyric composer is demonstrated by the way in which he carefully positions this short poetic line in the structural nucleus of the discourse—indeed, at its very climax at the end of stanza C. The importance of this utterance is further reinforced by being situated at a point with strongly contrastive content on either side. It is also important to note that the psalmist's confession of vv. 6–7 is uttered in the hearing of his fellow believers (cf. vv. 4–5); he thus "refers to his own [pitiful] experience in order to offer a lesson to the community" (deClaissé-Walford et al. 2014:295). Had these rhetorical devices not been employed here or in this captivating manner, the theological and ethical significance of this colon, whether for the original auditors or for readers today, could have been easily missed, or at least deprived of much of its emotive impact. The implication for any contemporary translation is obvious.

2.4.5 Concentric thematic structure

There is yet another way of viewing the overall formal and topical congruence and coherence of Psalm 30. It provides one more hypothetical perspective that might explain how the several primary discontinuities embedded within the text are resolved by a larger pattern of continuity. This takes the form of an extended structural introversion consisting of

---

[9] Martin Luther referred to the punitive divine agency in such cases as "God's alien work": "By manifesting these works He aims to humble us that we might regard Him as our Lord and obey his will...for the purpose of accomplishing God's proper work, which is to save, bless, and be gracious" (ML, cited in deClaissé-Walford et al. 2014:299).

closely paired, but not conjoined passages that manifest a basic equivalence in their respective contents (see a display of this concentric construction on the next page; cf. Alden 1974:22–23; Bratcher and Reyburn 1991:282; Lund 1930:304). Most of these disjunctive parallels are characterized by semantic similarity, but several also feature a prominent contrast in their correlation.

This integrated series of meaningful associations is another illustration of Jakobson's "poetic principle" discussed in slightly different terms in 2.1 (cf. 3.3, 4.2). As the second series of seven structural constituents unfolds, it simultaneously reflects back thematically upon itself in a progressive and systematic reiteration of corresponding elements that have already appeared in the discourse. In other words, there is a syntagmatic (progressive) and paradigmatic (retrospective) convergence of form and content as these two types of literary-rhetorical composition overlay—or merge, depending on how one views this interaction. The principal points of similarity or contrast are highlighted in boldfaced type on the following diagram, while matching compositional units are marked by the same capital letters and vertical broken lines. It is interesting to observe that the verbal midpoint of the psalm in terms of physical mass (individual Hebrew accent groups) corresponds with the center of the synchronic arrangement of topical elements, i.e., between (G) and (G')—44 versus 45 "words" (including the title).

A more general patterned sequence, less obvious perhaps, is also manifested by the distinct utterances that constitute the poetic text of Psalm 30. This is the series of shifting speech interactions which represents the dynamic interpersonal movement of the prayer-poem from beginning to end. As the psalmist joyfully, but reverently engages Yahweh in thanksgiving and praise, he appears to follow a symmetrical ordering of basic illocutions, or conversational goals. In essence this consists of just two alternating macrofunctions that are linked in a cause-effect, logical-semantic relationship, namely, grounds (G), or motivation, and implication (I), i.e., praise/appeal. These are shown forming a vertical string along the figure's right-hand margin; this is just an approximate, generalized visualization.

A   I-will-**exalt-you**, Yahweh, for you-lifted-me-out,   1   *I*

                                                                       G

B   and-not-did-you-**let-rejoice** my-enemies over-me.

C   Yahweh, my-God, **I-cried-for-help to-you**   2
           and-**you-healed-me.**

D   Yahweh, **you-brought-up** from-sheol my-soul.   3
              You-kept-me-alive from-those-**descending-into the-pit.**

E   **Sing-praise to-Yahweh**, his-pious-ones,   4   *I*
                 and-**give-thanks** for-the-memory-of his-holiness.

F   For-a-moment [is] in-**his-anger**,   5   *G*
                    life [is] in-his-favor.
                    In-the-evening **it-endures weeping,**
                    and-at-the-morning [is] a-joyous-shout.

G   And-I I-said **in-my-security,**   6   *I*
                       "**Not-shall-I-be-moved** forever!

G′   Yahweh, in-your-favor you-caused-[it]-to-   7   *G*
                       take-a-stand on-my-mountain [namely] **strength!**"

F′   **You-hid your-face**, I-was **dismayed!**   *G*

E′   **Unto-you, Yahweh, I-will-call,**   8   *I*
                 and-unto-my-Lord **I-will-plead-for-mercy.**

D′   What-profit [is] in-**my-blood,**   9   *G*
              in-**my-descending into-destruction?**
              Will-it-thank-you **the-dust,**
              will-it-proclaim your-faithfulness?

C′   **Hear-O-Yahweh** and-**show-mercy-to-me!**   10   *I*
            O-Yahweh, **be a-helper for-me!**

B′   You-turned my-wailing into-dancing for-me;   11   *G*
         you-removed my-sackcloth, and-you-clothed-me-with joy

A′   so-that it-may-**sing-praise-to-you** [my]-glory,   12   *I*
      and-not it-will-be-silent.
      Yahweh, my-God, forever I-will-thank-you!

To further explain several notable aspects of the preceding diagram: The functional backbone of Psalm 30 is established by the poet's citation of one or more actions on the part of Yahweh that move(d) him to make a verbal response—an expression of appreciation and/or acclaim, for example, at the very beginning: "I will exalt you (I), O Yahweh, for you lifted me out (G)!" Generally, these reactions are positive in connotation, but as was pointed out earlier, in the center of the psalm some contrasting notions are highlighted, as the psalmist recalls his deviation from Yahweh to self. Thus, another structural introversion of parallel elements is created—this one of a pragmatic character that complements the semantic construction outlined earlier. Here, too, the virtual "turning point" occurs immediately after the crucial middle segment, i.e., from $I \rightarrow G$ to $G \rightarrow I$ in the middle of verse 7 (G'—F').

It is also worth noting in general that from an abstract perspective, most psalms manifest just two basic grounds and two corresponding implications, though these can be realized textually by diverse semantic constituents and in various combinations or proportions. Accordingly, the psalmist may be motivated by either some imminent threat/lack in his life (especially enmity or illness)—or by a certain blessing from God, which often includes divine deliverance from one of the preceding maladies. He then makes an appropriate religious response, either a complaint (normally with an accompanying petition) or an expression of praise, based on Yahweh's covenantal attributes, which may be reinforced by a word/vow of thanksgiving or a profession of faith. Thus, the two fundamental psalm types, lament and eulogy (cf. chapter 3), are actualized in a poetic verbal dramatization of the relationship between the faithful singer/pray-er and his covenant Lord and Savior (Protector, Provider).

Once again we have an illustration of discontinuity being swallowed up or overshadowed by continuity in Hebrew religious discourse. The successive points of apparent dissimilarity or disjunction, when viewed from the perspective of the surface level of the text, are progressively incorporated within a larger and deeper structure of meaning and a broader frame of reference, both expressed and implied—one that spans the entire composition. With reference to Psalm 30, this process of poetic and conceptual fusion may be construed as a structural metaphor that effectively mirrors the central theme of this prayerful song. It is in essence an artistic, but reverent reflection upon, coupled with an extolling of, the individual and corporate position of "faithful followers" of Yahweh, the *Chasidim* (חֲסִידָיו) (v. 4) in relation to their mutual trials and pressing problems in this world, on the one hand, and their mighty, merciful Lord, on the other. Thus, in the battles of everyday existence, when temporal discontinuities confront the everlasting continuity of their covenant God, Yahweh is always triumphant—and they with him. He will in time, sooner or later according to his plan, intervene to eliminate earthly disjunctions and surely deliver his godly people from the inevitable vicissitudes of life!

2.5 Continuity and discontinuity in the medium of psalmic transmission

We turn in conclusion to an issue that illustrates the well-known "elephant in the room" adage—an important and influential aspect of our subject that has yet to be considered. This concerns one more major discontinuity that needs to be factored into any discussion of the analysis, translation, and transmission of Psalm 30. This matter is one which, for the most part, has not always been adequately dealt with in the communication history of biblical literature, and that is the medium, or vehicle, of message delivery. This question requires a full-length study of its own (cf. Wendland 2013b), and at this juncture I can simply call attention to a number of crucial factors that need to be more thoroughly investigated in this regard.

In brief, the problem, or special challenge is this: In the case of Psalm 30 we have another outstanding instance of where an originally vibrant oral text has been visually fixed for the sake of ecclesiastical preservation and transmission within the primary medium of print (preceded by a long scribal and manuscript tradition). Many scholars now believe that virtually all of the psalms were either *orally* composed in the original act of creation, or they were verbalized in writing (perhaps with the aid of a scribe) with an oral-aural presentation in mind—via prayerful proclamation, recitation, chanting, or song (with or without instrumental accompaniment). "The Psalter was meant for singing, or reciting to the accompaniment of musical instruments, or chanting" (Bullock 2013:56). This fact is clearly evidenced by the nature and purpose of the discourse itself, which is that of a prayer or a thanksgiving hymn encoded completely in the mode of direct speech— whether uttered by the individual or a corporate congregation.

Many formal features of the Hebrew text testify to its oral-aural potential—a reflection of the original composition that facilitates and enhances its articulation aloud in the presence of an audience. These stylistic attributes would include the text's fundamental lineal structure, an alternating rhythmic cadence, a distinctive tone-accentual system, incorporation of phonological embellishment, multileveled parallel patterns, extensive reiteration of form and content, including many vocatives, rhetorical questions, emotive diction, graphic figurative language, and so forth. Much of this meaning—the sonic dimension at least—is either not fully known (e.g., the ancient, pre-Masoretic system of cantillation), or it gets left behind in any written/printed translation. As a result, the basic quality of communication is significantly altered—in short, we experience a great discontinuity with the original (cf. Wendland 2013b).

In the preceding analysis, we have seen evidence that the poet-psalmist or a worship team[10] utilized a rather large and diverse number of stylistic

---

[10] It is impossible to say how much oral pre-editing based on practice and performance was done before a given psalm was deemed ready for inclusion in one of the

techniques (given the relatively short length of the text) either to harmonize or to bridge over various areas of formal and semantic discontinuity and to knit them together using the available strategies of poetic composition. The question is, how can this be done today using the different tools of communication which are at our disposal? The most obvious need, if possible, is to restore the text to its original medium of transmission, that is, the oral-aural channel. That would be a good beginning, but this solution does not really go far enough, for we are not dealing with the initial Hebrew text, but with a modern linguistic transformation of it. Thus, the ideal would be to have a version prepared in the target language that is as close as possible to a functionally-equivalent rendering of the source text. This would be an artistic composition—a poetic recreation—that conveys the critical content and intent of the original message using verbal forms that are stylistically natural, even idiomatic where appropriate, with respect to the particular literary genre that has been chosen in the TL (cf. Wendland 2011:95–148).

Where biblical poetry is concerned, to be conveyed via an audible text, much more attention and effort must be devoted to the qualities of linguistic and literary form. This is to ensure the greatest degree of equivalence and acceptance with respect to functional purpose across the twin barriers of language and culture. In such situations, one goal might be to replace one oratorical and rhetorical form with another—a TL correspondent to a SL poem—while still preserving the fundamental attributes of the latter's total inventory of cognitive (religious/theological) content. The following for example, is a poetic translation of Psalm 30 by Brenda Boerger (2009:52), one that features a reordering of the content (shown by the verse numbers) to reflect a presumed chronological development of the text. Different line indentations along with boldface and italic print serve to indicate various semantic correspondences and contrasts:

DELIVERANCE DANCE

6	I said when I was feeling ***secure,***
	*"I'll **never be moved** or shaken."*
7	Yahweh, when I received your favor
	I was as ***steady*** as a mountain.
	But when you held back the blessings river,
	My courage failed, I was ***panic-stricken.***
8	So Yahweh, I made my pleading cry,
	For ***mercy,*** Lord, I made my petition.

constituent collections of the Psalter, nor is it possible to know the extent to which any psalm was the product of an individual or a corporate compositional procedure (e.g., by "the sons of Korah," Pss. 42–72). I can only state my belief that, in any case, this was essentially a divinely initiated and inspired process (Lk. 20:42, 24:44; Acts 1:20, 13:33; cf. Bullock 2001:23–25).

9   *"Will my bones' dust **praise** you when I die?*
       *Is there profit in my **destruction?***
     Who will preach your fidelity,
10 *Unless you're gracious now and answer me;*
     And your timely help is my remedy?"
2   Yahweh, to you I cried and appealed,
     And then I found I was completely **healed.**
3   You kept me from resting in the **grave**
       When I wasn't far from death.
4   So all you saints, **praise** his holy name,
       Giving thanks for every breath.
5   Because his anger lasts just a moment,
       But with his **favor** comes life that's permanent.
         All may seem dark, as eyes fill with **tears,**
         But when God's light dawns, what joyful cheers!
1   *I exalt you,* Yahweh, for my salvation,
   Which kept my enemies from jubilation.
11   Lord, you created **dancing** out of all my woes;
      Changed mourning garb to victory clothes,
12 making my heart sing to Yahweh, my Savior.
   So I won't quit or be quiet, nor sit and be silent,
   But Yahweh, my God, I'll shout **"thank you"** forever.

Where a different audience and aim is concerned, on the other hand—a chorused hymn for public worship, for example—translators might be allowed a greater level of freedom with respect to the parameters of form and content, as long as the essence of the original is not lost, unduly distorted, or compromised in the process. The following is a Tonga hymn based on Psalm 30 that might illustrate this;[11] admittedly, however, linguistic-cultural distance and the absence of an actual audio rendition may make this text rather difficult to evaluate.

Lwiimbo lwakulumbaizya Leza	*Song for praising God*
1. Basinkondoma wagwisya,	*You've taken away my enemies,*
Mucuumbwe wangwisya,	*You've taken me out of the grave.*
Mucilindi nsikanjili.	*I will not enter the pit.*
Ngu Leza nteembula!	*It's God whom I praise!*

---

[11] Composed by Mr. Joseph Mwanamulela as part of a senior Psalms exegetical class at Lusaka Lutheran Seminary in 1991.

Ngu Leza nteembula,	*It's God whom I praise, (CHORUS)*
Mwami wangu nduwe!	*You are my king!*
Ninsilikwe ninkwiilila,	*Let me be healed when I call,*
Ngu Leza nteembula!	*It's God whom I praise!*
2. Basalali bamwiimbile,	*The holy ones sing to him,*
Aliimbilwe zyina lyakwe!	*May his name be sung to!*
Nkasyoonto kakukalala,	*His time of being angry is short,*
Ngu Leza nteembula!	*It's God whom I praise!*
3. Kulila nee, nkondwa lyoonse.	*As for weeping, no, I'm always happy.*
Nindiiba mukwaamba,	*When feeling secure I say,*
Nkazungaani nenzi mebo?	*What could ever shake me up?*
Ngu Leza nteembula!	*It's God whom I praise!*
4. Mwami ncilundu, nkwiindi nji!	*My King's a rock, I'm standing firm!*
Busyu bwasiswa, me mpenga.	*When he hides his face, I suffer.*
Nduwe lili witwa ambe?	*How could you not be called to by me?*
Ngu Leza ntembula!	*It's God whom I praise!*
5. Ndili dindi lumba nduwe?	*Which ditch is it that praises you?*
Mwami, mvwa siluse ambe!	*O King, may your mercy be felt by me!*
Mbuvubinzi bwa cilindi?	*What profit is there in the pit?*
Ngu Leza nteembula!	*It's God whom I praise!*
6. Ndila luse lwako, Mwami,	*I cry for your mercy, O King,*
Lugwasyo ngu Leza wangu!	*My help is my God!*
Nendila kwako, nzyanabuya,	*When I cry to you, I'll dance,*
Ngu Leza nteembula!	*It's God whom I praise!*

7. Zyakulizya mpya! Ndukondo.	*Mourning clothes away! I put on joy.*
Moyo wangu nkukwiimbila,	*My heart is singing to you,*
Lyoonse nku Mwami nkwindumba,	*I always give thanks to my King,*
Ngu Leza nteembula!	*It's God whom I praise!*

Another step that can be taken in the direction of re-oralizing the biblical text in translation can often be taken visually with respect to the printed-published version itself. The Scriptures can be presented on the page in a more legible—and hence normally also a more recitable form—by means of a judicious use of the typography and format design. This is especially important where a poetic passage, such as a psalm, is concerned, because most people, no matter what their language, expect poetry (however it is defined in the TL) to manifest a distinctive style and sound. Frequently, traditional publishing conventions and economics get in the way, but it is at least worth a try on the part of a translation committee to do something more to aid readers—and hearers—in their audible reception of the text, hence also their conception of its meaning as well. The figure below offers a sample of some of the features that might be included in such a venture—one that again seeks to overcome certain discontinuities that may arise in transmission in order to produce a textual continuity and consequent communication experience that more closely matches that of the biblical original.

Psalm 30: A song of David for the dedication of the temple

1. **I will exalt you, O LORD,**
      for you lifted me out from the depths of despair
      and did not allow my enemies to gloat over me.
2. O LORD my God, I called to you for help
      and you healed me completely.
3. O LORD, you brought me up from the grave;
      you spared me from descending into that pit.

4. Sing to the LORD, you saints of his;
    indeed, praise his most holy name!
5.   For his anger is momentary,
      but his favor lasts a lifetime.
          Weeping may extend overnight,
      but rejoicing comes in the morning.

6.   When I felt safe and secure, I said to myself,
          "I will never be shaken.

7.   *O how you've favored me, LORD—*
                You made my mountain so strong."
                BUT WHEN YOU HID YOUR FACE FROM ME,
                I BECAME COMPLETELY DISCOURAGED.

8.   To you, O LORD, I called out,
                yes, to my God I cried for mercy:
9.   *"What gain is there in my demise,*
                    In my going down into the pit?
10.   *Can my dust praise you there?*
                    Will it proclaim your faithfulness?"

11.   But you turned my sad wailing into dancing.
            You removed my mourning rags and clothed me with joy,
12.   so that my heart may sing out to you and not be silent—
            O LORD my God, I will give you thanks forever!

The display above is a reformatted and somewhat modified version of the NIV translation of Psalm 30, reproduced in what is hopefully a more readable and hearable English text. This is merely a suggestion as to how the sharp disjunction created by the visual medium of transmission might be compensated for through the application of a more dynamic approach in the area of graphic design (Wendland 2004:350–351).[12] The aim is to produce a version that is not only easier to articulate aloud (in public perhaps), but one that more effectively displays the various patterns and potential pause points within the text, thus encouraging a more intelligent reading, e.g., correct intonational contours. Does such a format help a lector to make the original discourse structure more discernible orally as well as visually? If not, where does it fail (introducing unnatural discontinuities!), and how can the text be revised with regard to the text or its context to accomplish these important communicative objectives? In view of the vast numbers of the world's population who are unable to read convincingly, or even to listen effectively, it must certainly be a high priority for translation agencies to publish biblical texts specifically designed for oral-aural transmission in the form of audio Scriptures (cf. Sogaard 1991).

Is it really feasible to transform the all-too-frequent silence of the written Word, and of biblical poetry in particular, into a more dynamic and meaningful sonic "singing" in thankful praise of Yahweh (v. 12)? It is hoped that the present study might contribute to a more convincing, committed,

---

[12] Many creative examples of such discourse-oriented and reader/hearer-sensitive formatting may be found in the version known as *God's Word Translation*. (For some background, see https://en.wikipedia.org/wiki/God%27s_Word_Translation/. Accessed September 2, 2017.)

and contextualized response to these and related issues as they pertain to the worldwide endeavor to transcend diverse discontinuities in the continued cross-cultural communication of the sacred Scriptures.

3

Genre Criticism and the Psalms, with Special Reference to Psalm 31

Introduction

How do we read and interpret biblical texts? In this study a literary-structural methodology is applied within the framework of a genre-based typological approach to offer one way to answer that question, with reference to the religious-poetic literature of the Psalter, and to Psalm 31 in particular. After a survey of the notion of genre criticism in relation to biblical poetry, two major psalmic macrogenres are described—the *lament* and the *eulogy*. Their complex structural and functional interaction within Psalm 31 is then examined in terms of the composition as a whole and its central theme, which revolves around the covenantal *chesed* relationship between Yahweh and his faithful people. Several alternative discourse formats are evaluated, and the hermeneutical importance of adopting such a generic, text-stylistic and functionally-oriented perspective is pointed out.

In the latter half of the 20th century, a significant "quiet revolution" (Ryken 1984:11) took place in biblical studies, as an increasing number of scholars and commentators came to an ever greater awareness of the many diverse literary features of the Christian Scriptures, and of the important implications of this reality for interpretation. As Ryken states, "the methods of literary scholarship are [now] a necessary part of any complete study of the Bible" (ibid.; cf. Wendland 2004). A problem exists, however, in the application of this insight in the wider field of biblical studies. As Wiklander observes, although "few scholars—if any—would seriously deny this basic premise...the extent to which it is allowed to shape exegetical [and I might add, also Bible translation] work varies considerably" (1984:2).

Thus, the present study is intended to introduce and to illustrate several possible uses of a literary-oriented approach to the text of the Old Testament, whether viewed in its entirety or only with respect to that familiar portion which is the special focus of this investigation, the Book of Psalms. A discourse-centered generic (genre-based) perspective forms the crucial first step in the literary examination of any biblical pericope—large or small, whether in Hebrew or Greek. Such a comprehensive textual "frame of reference" (Wendland 2008:110–111) then serves both to inform and to guide the analytical process as major and minor discourse constituents are considered in relation to one another and the whole of which they are a part.[1] This viewpoint facilitates a number of other, related methodologies that can give us greater insights into the impressive richness and depth of the manifold literature of Scripture.

3.1 Interpreting the Bible as literature

One's understanding of the concept of literature will, to some extent, determine the nature and scope of one's investigation. For some, it is restricted to "something written," as the Bible is basically a "book" (Maier and Tollers 1979:3); thus, "a text is a written work, in contrast to an oral performance" (Scharlemann 1987:7). However, analysts must also take into serious consideration the so-called oral overlay (Achtemeier 1990:3) or "auditory aura" (Silberman 1987:3) of ancient written documents. This would suggest that the distinction between the two modes of communication in these texts is not very easy to maintain (Wendland 2013b:18–28) since "in practice, interaction between oral and written forms is extremely common" (Finnegan 1977:160)—in classical as well as contemporary literature (Finnegan 1970:18). On the other hand, some scholars would limit the notion

---

[1] As the hermeneutical school of canonical criticism has taught us, the Scriptures themselves, the Psalter in particular, provide a vital intertextual frame of reference that must guide the interpretive process with regard to any biblical text. For example, "The canonical placement of Pss. 2 and 149 in the Psalter's introduction (Pss. 1–2) and conclusion (Pss. 146–150) is significant...as 'strategic locations' that provide...a 'hermeneutical horizon' for the interpretation of the Psalter." This exemplifies "the primacy effect...a phenomenon in which material appearing at the beginning of a text creates in the reader a tendency to interpret the text in the light of that material for as long as such an interpretation can be maintained...[as well as] the recency effect, whereby readers of a text tend to revise their readings on the basis of material presented last" (Wittman 2014:57–58).

of literature to "imaginative" or "creative" works "in contrast to expository writing," and therefore, by this definition, "some parts of the Bible are more literary and other parts are less literary" (Ryken 1984:12). I would prefer rather to operate with a broader, yet still qualitative definition of the subject: literature would thus include "all writings (regardless of the degree of oral influence)...considered as having permanent [social] value, excellence of form, great emotional effect, etc." (Agnes 2006:838)—that is, over and above the recognized salience and significance of their thematic content.

What then are the implications of such a literary perspective for biblical interpretation? The case has been well stated in general terms by one who ought to know—the great author and critic C. S. Lewis: "There is a...sense in which the Bible, since it is after all literature, cannot be properly read except as literature, and the different parts of it as the different sorts of literature that they are" (1958:3). Thus, "every aspect of the hermeneutical process [with respect to Scripture] is infused and enriched with literary theory" (Osborne 2008:18). But what does it mean to read the Scriptures "as literature?" How does literature per se affect one's reading and interpretation? In short, it means to approach a biblical text, within its presumed situational setting and canonical context, with a conscious awareness of the expressive and affective (including the emotive and esthetic) dimensions of semantically and pragmatically shaped verbal discourse.[2] This is in addition to being critically aware of the central, cognitively based information (theology, etc.) that such writing conveys. When dealing with the Word of God, one would not wish to overemphasize the imaginative or psychological aspect of the human source or author. But Ryken calls attention to a valid implication with respect to all perceptive text consumers (readers, hearers): "[Good literature] constantly appeals to our imagination...[it] *images* some aspect of reality" (1984:14) that derives from and is relevant to the sociocultural context in which it is originally composed.[3] While this attention to personal, subjective reactions to

[2] "Without denying for one moment that the OT is part of the canon of Scripture, the Word of God, it is equally true that the OT is literature that can be read and studied *as literature*" (Snyman 2008:57, original italics). As the various psalmic prayer-songs of Israel were collected into related groupings (like the "Songs of Ascent," Pss. 120–134), "books," and the complete canonical collection we call the Psalms, from one perspective, it may be true to say that they "underwent a transformation from being the words of humankind into being scriptural words of God to humankind" (deClaissé-Walford 2004:5). On the other hand, even when acknowledged as sacred Scripture, these psalms never ceased being used as the prayerful words of humankind to God.

[3] Of course, the assessment of literary quality is inevitably a subjective exercise to varying degrees, depending on the credibility and sufficiency of concrete evidence adduced by evaluators to support their conclusions. In support of my own estimation of the excellence of the Psalms (among other biblical books, cf. Wendland 2004), Philip King reckons that "the surviving texts [of the Hebrew Bible] are explicitly of a high literary caliber" (2012:96).

the text (as in some forms of reader-response criticism) is helpful, it is more important for biblical interpreters to take into consideration those rhetorical devices, such as irony and sarcasm—even vivid metaphor and metonymy—which serve as triggers to stimulate or appeal to one's impressions, feelings, moods, and attitudes, whether positive or negative. These literary techniques are usually intended to highlight or reinforce key aspects of an author's primary theme or purpose of writing.

Many other, more detailed definitions and descriptions of literature and its various aims are readily available in standard textbooks on the subject in relation to a particular language or corpus. It suffices here to simply point out what would appear to be its central characteristic from the standpoint of discourse analysis, namely, the predominant focus upon linguistic *form* that is typical of a superior, highly acclaimed literary work. In other words, there is a special emphasis upon the artistic dimension of discourse—or what Jakobson termed the "poetic function" of the text (see ch. 2). According to this principle, "the two basic modes of arrangement used in verbal behavior, selection and combination" (Jakobson 1972:95; cf. "paradigmatic" and "syntagmatic" in 2.1) are maximized in order to foreground crucial aspects of the message and to heighten its interest value, level of conceptual engagement, emotive impact, and persuasive appeal. Verbal artists, including the various biblical authors, the poets in particular, typically use a diversity of artistic devices in order to exploit the creative, metaphoric potential of language, thus evoking what Paul Ricoeur calls a "re-description" of reality (1975:88), "in which the world is not so much replicated as transfigured in the vision that poet and audience come to share" (Davis 1992:95). This metaphoric (and metonymic) visualization is especially prominent in the prophetic literature (e.g., Joel), but it is an evocative feature that appears frequently also in the so-called poetic books (e.g., SoS), including Psalm 31 (e.g., vv. 9–13).

The result of this poetic process—the syntagmatic elaboration of diverse paradigmatic parameters—is typically a text that is heavily figured (with many different rhetorical tropes coinciding), strongly patterned (concentric and linear), and permeated by recursive structures of all sorts (lexical, phonological, syntactic, semantic, pragmatic). This occurs on all levels of organization, from the individual colon to the composition as a whole. Literature (or "orature" for an oral-aural equivalent) thus maximizes the "how" (or style) of the text in order to highlight selected aspects of the "what" (content) and the "why" (intent). This is accomplished by means of artistic techniques such as "pattern or design, theme or central focus, organic unity (also called unity in variety, or theme and variation), coherence, balance, contrast, symmetry, repetition or recurrence, variation, and unified progression" (Ryken 1984:23–24).

It is this formal, but fluid quality of literary-oratorical creativity that we wish to explore more fully in relation to the Hebrew lyric-liturgical poem of Psalm 31.[4] We will gradually proceed from the generic to a more specific plane during the process of *analysis* in order to forge an interpretive *synthesis* that results in a better understanding of the intended meaning of this plaintive prayer-song. The aim is to demonstrate how distinct rhetorical structures and strategies function in concert to progressively shape the readers/listeners' expectations and to focus their individual interpretive activities towards a unified comprehension of the poetic text, one that God's people of every age can appreciate, apprehend, and apply in life.

3.2 What is genre criticism, and why is it necessary?

Genre criticism is a type of literary-structural analysis that pays special attention to the distinct compositional forms, or genres, found in a given corpus of literature. The term *genre* refers to "a group of texts similar in their mood, content, structure or phraseology" (Longman 1988:20). From a contextual perspective, "genres are the conventional and repeatable patterns of oral and written speech, which facilitate interaction among people in specific social situations" (Bailey 1995:200). Such standardized discourse templates, or characteristic feature-sets, tend to "reflect the functions and goals involved in particular social occasions as well as the purposes of the participants in them" (Hatim and Mason 1990:69). Every oral or written genre observes its own rules or modes of construction (more or less) and may therefore be classified on the basis of its distinctive stylistic, semantic, and pragmatic features. Thus, these attributes pertain primarily to linguistic organization, but topical content, such as typical themes and motifs, as well as a progressive functional configuration, or "format" (ibid.:171), are also involved. As socially shared patterns of communication, genres serve to alert hearers and readers "as to how a text or speech is to be interpreted or understood" (Kaiser 2013:127; cf. Jacobson and Jacobson 2013:37), and we might add, *analyzed* and *translated* as well.

Genre criticism developed from biblical form criticism (Bailey 1995:198–199), which is literary category analysis with a diachronic dimension. In other words, form criticism…

> analyzes the formal features of a text, including its unique
> syntactical and semantic form or literary structure and its
> typical linguistic genres that give shape to the text and

---

[4] An awareness of the oral-aural—oratorical—dimension of the biblical text must always be kept in the forefront of any analysis, for that is how the original text originated, was transmitted and received, and that is how the Scriptures are most frequently accessed in the world today. "Attention to the literary dimension is a vital component of hearing the kerygma of the Old Testament: to experience its overwhelming provocations and to heed its summons—in other words, to hear God's address in the Old Testament" (Beldman 2012:95).

function within it to facilitate its expression. Form criticism
functions both synchronically to analyze the present literary
form of the text and diachronically to ascertain and examine
its compositional history in relation to its postulated written
and oral stages.... Thus, the social, literary, and historical
settings of a text are key factors in influencing both its com-
position and its function or interpretation in the contexts in
which it is employed and read (Sweeney 2008:227–228).

Genre criticism differs from form criticism in its holistic (canonical)
perspective that does not delve into the compositional history of a text or
seek to identify the supposed sources, oral or written, that allegedly com-
prise it.[5]

A major problem in genre criticism is one of definition in relation to
scope. Simply put, how generic can a genre be? A lyric poem, novel, letter,
newspaper, recipe, written sermon, and essay are certainly different kinds
of literature, but do these constitute different genres on the same level of
classification? Gerstenberger (1988:243), for example, appends a glossary
of poetic genres that range from the highly abstract "accusation" *(Anklage)*
to the very specific "Zion hymn" *(Zionshymnus)*. Closely related to this is the
question of who sets the standard or defines the parameters for categoriza-
tion. With respect to genre-defining criteria, there are two principal per-
spectives. One is the alien outsider's *etic* point of view—a classification that
purports to be universal, or largely so, which may propose a cross-cultural
scheme or taxonomy defined and described with reference to some behav-
ioral feature that is supposedly typical of any human society (see Pike and
Pike 1977:484). The second is the native insider's *emic* viewpoint, in which
"an entity is seen from the perspective of the internal "logic" or structure of
its containing systems, with contrastive identificational features, variants,
and distribution in class, sequence, and system of a universe of discourse"
(ibid.:483).

The Pikes' linguistically focused etic/emic dichotomy corresponds in
part to what the well-known literary critic E. D. Hirsch terms "extrinsic"
and "intrinsic" genres. The latter he defines from the standpoint of oral or
written discourse as "that sense of the whole by means of which an inter-
preter can correctly understand any part in its determinancy" (1967:86).
An intrinsic (emic) genre is situated within a particular system of litera-
ture, for it is grounded in actual usage and related to shared experiences,
on the one hand, and meaning-based expectations and evaluations, on the
other—all of which evoke "a generic conception which controls [one's]
utterance" (ibid.:80). By way of contrast then, an extrinsic genre is "a
generic sense of the whole different from the speaker's...a [partially] wrong

---

[5] Consult Sweeny (2008) for a good overview of form criticism—its history, meth-
odology, and sample applications.

guess" (ibid.:88). In Hirsch's terms, an etic conception would be "a prelimi-
nary genre idea that is vague and broad...a preliminary heuristic tool that
must be further sharpened before it can discriminate the functions of the
partial meanings in their determinacy" (ibid.)—that is, with reference to a
particular literary or oratorical production in a given language and litera-
ture (i.e., an emic conception; cf. Osborne 2006:182; Brown 2008:133).

One way of differentiating these two perspectives—the local (emic) and
the global (etic)—would be to use the expression "discourse type" for the
latter, universal classes of literature, such as poetry and prose on the highest
level, or for more specific classes, designations such as narrative, procedural,
hortatory, expository, juridicial, and predictive (cf. Longacre 1989). The term
"genre" would then be reserved for intrinsic, literature- and language-specific
categories (Wendland 1985:82–83), such as the ancient system of classifica-
tion reflected in the superscriptions found in many psalms, for example:

> (1) *mizmor* ("psalm");[6] (2) *shiggaion* [probably a literary or
> musical term]; (3) *miktam* [another literary/musical term];
> (4) *shir* ("song"); (5) *maskil* [literary/musical term]; (6)
> *tephillah* ("prayer"); (7) *tehillah* ("praise"); (8) *lehazkir* ("for
> being remembered"—i.e., before God, a petition); (9) *leto-
> dah* ("for praising" or "for giving thanks"); (10) *lelammed*
> ("for teaching"); and (11) *shir yedidot* ("song of loves"—i.e.,
> a wedding song). (Barker 1985:782)

The problem is that these terms cannot be determined with any preci-
sion on the basis of available evidence. Indeed, there is much overlapping
in the categories as they are commonly outlined in scholarly literature, e.g.,
shir "lyric song, love song, religious song, pilgrim song, song with musi-
cal accompaniment" (Brown, Driver, Briggs). Therefore, these terms are
not very useful as analytical designations. A comparative terminological
approach carried out in the light of other ancient Near Eastern (ANE) liter-
ary traditions is helpful to a certain extent but certainly not definitive.[7] This
is because these genre systems too have not been clearly specified, their
possible communicative interactions with Hebrew literature have not been
fully established, and it is likely that the categories of sacred literature of
Israel have been defined in distinctive, monotheistic (Yahwistic) ways (cf.
Brown 2008:129; Sandy and Giese 1995:41).

For practical purposes then in our study of the Psalter, we may have to
rely on a combined etic-emic framework for description. This would utilize

---

[6] This is the most common Hebrew term for "psalm" and denotes "a song sung to
musical accompaniment" (Alter and Greenstein 2012:1123).

[7] It should be noted that the Psalms were not unique to Hebrew literature: "Often
associated with ritual, the psalm was an important literary medium in Mesopota-
mia, Egypt, Hatti (Asia Minor), Ugarit (northern Syria), and...Canaan" (Alter and
Greenstein 2012:1123).

more or less general category terms to establish a broad literary frame of reference, coupled with corpus-specific descriptions of the primary formal, semantic, and pragmatic features of the several genres and sub-genres of psalms that can be reasonably identified.[8] This sort of descriptive analysis will be carried out below by way of illustration with respect to Psalm 31.

But a preliminary question first needs to be answered: Of what value are such structural category distinctions in the process of a literary-structural analysis? Hirsch puts the case unequivocally: "All understanding of verbal meaning is necessarily genre-bound" (1967:76). He elaborates (ibid.:75):

> An interpreter's notion of the type of meaning he [*sic*] confronts will powerfully influence his understanding of details...at every level of sophistication.... Thus an interpretation is helplessly dependent on the generic conception with which the interpreter happens to start.

This procedure is simply an instance of the Gestalt principle of figure and ground: One's notion of the meaning potential of the whole (the discourse type or genre) helps to guide one's identification and understanding of the text-related parts (the specific details which constitute any given instance or example of the whole). The converse is also true, thus completing this discourse-level application of the so-called hermeneutical circle (Hirsch 1967:76).

"Genre functions as a valuable link between the text and the reader" (Osborne 2006:182), and hence "an understanding of literary forms is crucial to correct biblical interpretation" (Klein et al. 1993:261). More specifically, "genre is a socially-defined constellation of typified formal and thematic features in a group of literary works, which authors use in individual ways to accomplish specific communicative purposes" (Brown 2008:122). "Genre criticism" then "helps readers to see the similarities among various texts within the genre and the differences among various genres, thereby alerting readers [and hearers] to important considerations in interpretation," including certain literary structures and formal relationships as well as crucial rhetorical (pragmatic) purposes "that would not be noticed as long as there were no context established for them" (Sandy and Giese 1995:36).[9]

---

[8] This diagnostic work would of course be carried out with reference to the work of other recognized scholars in the field, e.g., Gerstenberger 1988 (cf. Bergen 1987:335).

[9] In other words, "To read generically is to sign a rhetorical contract with the author to understand his work in the terms he shared with his intended audience.... Genre study helps to clarify conventions in a culture's literature, defining the rhetorical interplay between an author and his intended audience," thus helping "to clarify proper understanding of a given text" and enabling a reader "to appreciate the idiosyncratic features of a text" (Sandy and Giese 1995:38, 40)—including its beauty, impact, and emotive appeal.

All text processors (readers, listeners) approach a given text in their language and sociocultural setting with a certain literary—over and above a linguistic—competence, based on learning and past verbal experience. This enables them to recognize and properly interpret the various macro- and microstylistic features that are present in the text (Barton 1984:11–19). The more sophisticated the audience, the greater their latent literary awareness and rhetorical expectation, i.e., their hermeneutical proficiency and capability. Thus, the typical conventions associated with a particular genre provide a specific interpretive facility and set of strategies that guide them through the composition at hand (being heard)—informing, enlightening, inspiring, motivating, and often also surprising them along the way (that is, when the expected norms, forms, and structures are deliberately or unexpectedly flouted, altered, or ignored). Genre in effect acts like a "program" that gives artistic shape to a literary text and conceptually arranges its constituent details into an identifiable, more readily processed arrangement. This often turns out to be a complex *system* of linear, concentric, and hierarchically organized patterns which interact with, complement, and reinforce one another to encompass the unified whole.

The diverse codes and conventions that are evoked or elicited by distinct genres "are capable of different kinds of meaning and offer different kinds of information to a reader" (Tate 1991:64). However, such a significant meaning potential exists only as a virtual reality until it is actualized by a person who is familiar with the formal system of linguistic and literary signals (the "communicative clues" of relevance theory) of the principal genre of an oral or written composition, along with the related sub-genres and rhetorical tropes that have been incorporated into the text by the original author. Robert Alter (1981:47) describes this process as follows:

> A coherent reading of any art work, whatever the medium, requires some detailed awareness of the grid of conventions upon which, and against which, the individual work operates.... An elaborate set of tacit agreements about the ordering of the art work is at all times the enabling context in which the complex communication of art occurs. Through our awareness of convention we can recognize significant or simply pleasing patterns of repetition, symmetry, contrast; we can discriminate between the verisimilar and the fabulous, pick up directional clues in a [poetic] work, see what is innovative and what is deliberately traditional at each nexus of the artistic creation.

Furthermore, an explicit or implicit knowledge of generic organization and its contextualized interpretation can lessen the likelihood of one's misconstruing the artistic and rhetorical devices used in a literary work—for example, the pragmatic use of word order or the subtle influence of irony and hyperbole.

On the other hand, ignorance or unawareness of the formal and semantic norms and interpretive conventions that are implicit in a given genre, such as a so-called imprecatory psalm, can lead the reader or listener into what James Barr (1973:125) calls a "literary category mistake," which he explains as follows:

> Failures to comprehend the literary genre lead to a use of the biblical assertions [whether in prose or poetry] with a wrong function.... Genre mistakes cause the wrong kind of truth values to be attached to biblical sentences. Literary embellishments then come to be regarded as scientifically [or historically] true assertions [e.g., the psalmist's lament in 31:9–13].

One must be careful, however, not to push this notion too far in the direction of a denial of the Scripture's capacity to set forth propositional truth as well as historically accurate facts concerning the nation of Israel or the lives of its biblical authors. In any case, genre recognition is an integral part of an evangelical grammatical-historical method of exegesis.[10] As Vanhoozer writes (1986:80):

> The genre provides the literary context for a given sentence [or text of Scripture] and, therefore, partly determines what the sentence [text] means and how it should be taken.... Genre thus enables the reader [or hearer] to interpret meaning and to recognize what kinds of truth claims are being made in and by a text.

The current study is intended to encourage an informed and focused approach that is devoted to both generic and specific artistic-rhetorical forms in the analysis of BH poetry. Such a methodology can lead one more confidently and correctly along the path of a meaningful interpretation

---

[10] For a valuable overview of the maximalist scholarly position on the reliability of biblical historicity in relation to its diverse literary genres, see Mykytiuk 2013 (cf. Kofoed 2005, ch. 5). Such a position includes the assumption of a relatively stable history of oral-and-written textual transmission due to the very nature of the Scriptures as socio-culturally foundational sacred literature (Kofoed 2007:283–284; cf. Wendland 2013b: ch. 3). Furthermore, we note that "Meir Sternberg...in his *Poetics of Biblical Narrative* argues that the biblical narrative should be seen as a literary 'complex' with a multifaceted nature. The *function* of Biblical narrative, according to Sternberg, must be described in terms of three regulating principles, namely ideological, aesthetic, and historiographical" (2007:289). With respect to the Psalter then, I would correspondingly argue that these texts must be analyzed and interpreted from an integrated ideological (theological), aesthetic (literary-poetic), and liturgical (prayer/praise) perspective.

of such attractively and at the same time forcefully composed theological literature. Thus, a literary-structural examination of the original text aims to reveal in clearer degree and to a greater measure both *how* (stylistically) and *why* (functionally) the biblical author conveyed a determinative theological-ethical message with decided affective vigor and aesthetic appeal—not only to the initially intended constituency, but also to countless audiences in subsequent ages, right up to the present day.

The preceding introductory discussion will hopefully provide an adequate orientation for the several remaining investigative aspects of this essay. We will proceed from more generic typological observations to a specific textual examination with the following objectives:

1. Propose a set of criteria for determining the relative degree of poetry (lyricalness) that is manifested by a given pericope of the Hebrew Bible;

2. Describe the two principal genres of lyric poetry to be found in the Psalter, together with several of their major subcategories;

3. Outline a rhetorical, discourse-oriented method of text analysis (i.e., holistic, contextualized, structure-functional, oral-aurally sensitive);

4. Apply these procedures in an integrated analysis of Psalm 31 as a way of illustrating the methodology and its potential value;

5. Summarize the main hermeneutical and practical implications of this approach for biblical studies in general and translation studies in particular.

3.3 The nature of Biblical Hebrew poetry— ten characteristics

Before one can effectively investigate the genres of poetry in the Hebrew Scriptures, that of the Psalter in particular, it is helpful to know something about the poetic resources available for this type of discourse. What are the distinctive features that mark a text as being poetic as opposed to prosaic in nature (more or less)? This distinction between prose and poetry is important, for it affects how the process of understanding and interpreting a given text is carried out, for example, more or less literally or with a greater or lesser emphasis on formal patterning. However, as in much of art, so also in literary discourse, rather than either-or we have a continuum of possibilities to consider—a range of options or characteristics that move between the putative poles of pure poetry and prose. The proportion displayed in a given text varies according to its communicative purpose in relation to both its linguistic cotext and also its extralinguistic, or situational context.

As an introduction then to the subsequent presentation of a lyric functional typology, ten of the most important features of psalmic language are listed below (a fuller description was given in 1.2 above). Used in conjunction with one another, these ten literary-oratorical techniques enable the analyst to propose an initial type-setting of a pericope under consideration as being more or less poetic in quality. If it is very similar to the psalms in form, a biblical text (e.g., Genesis 49, Exodus 15) may accordingly be expected to operate in a corresponding manner, namely, as some type of individual or communal expression of petition, thanksgiving, and/or praise. These ten stylistic attributes, found also in other Hebrew poetic books, will be selectively illustrated in the analysis of Psalm 31 to follow later.

1. *Parallelism*: The Psalms manifest Hebrew parallelism to the maximum. Thus, poetic lines (cola) typically occur in matching, parallel pairs (i.e., line B complements line A), averaging six lexical units ("words") per couplet. These normally resonate with one another through various correspondences in linguistic quality such as rhythm (accent-word meter), phonological properties, morphosyntactic structure/patterning, propositional relations, and interactive-conjoined meaning.

2. *Condensation*: Parallelism is accompanied by a pronounced brevity of expression. This may be occasioned by apocopation or various forms of shortening, ellipsis (especially verb gapping), semantic laconicity (a penchant for implicitness), the absence of prose particles (the definite article, sign of the direct object, relative pronoun, inseparable prepositions), as well as in the incidence of conjunctive particles such as a clause-initial *waw* (especially in the first, or A colon).

3. *Figuration*: Psalmic poetry is characterized by a high concentration of distinctly religious imagery, symbolism, and allusion (including polemical anti-mythological language), accompanied by figures of speech of all sorts—simile, metaphor, metonymy, synecdoche, merism, apostrophe, personification, and (overlapping with the next category) irony or sarcasm (depending on one's interpretation).

4. *Intensification*: Poetic figuration (3) is frequently heightened both emotively and attitudinally by means of emphatic devices such as exclamations, intensified terminology, hyperbole, reiteration, rhetorical or leading questions, cohortative and jussive verbal forms.

5. *Transposition*: One often finds a shift or displacement in the normal (prosaic) order of syntactic clausal and even phrasal constituents to mark topic or focus and to form chiastic, terraced, and other arrangements. These serve to foreground salient items of information and to allow the parallel lines to reflect upon one another semantically and pragmatically (while disrupting normal narrative usage with respect to verbal *wayyiqtol* sequences).

6. *Phonesthetic appeal*: The oral-aural qualities of the psalmic text are maximized through the utilization of recursive auditory patterns, resulting in assonance, alliteration, rhythm, rhyme, and other sound-based rhetorical techniques, such as paronomasia (punning) as well as pure euphony or even dissonant cacophony at times.

7. *Dramatization*: Poetry prefers direct discourse, and this is especially evident in the prayer-praises that constitute the Psalter. There is a prevailing inclination towards "I/we-you" divine-human verbal interaction—a personalized orientation that is accentuated by means of vocatives, (separable) personal pronouns, imperatives, exclamations, embedded quotations, and other oral-oriented intensifiers (see #4).

8. *Lexical distinction*: The religious poetry of the Psalms is typified by a conventional, readily recognizable liturgical-cultic diction that is appropriate for personal as well as communal worship, including certain formulaic phrases, archaic forms, and familiar traditional terminology—coupled with many intertextual quotations, correspondences, re-creations, and re-applications.

9. *Accentual uniqueness*: Within the Tiberian tradition, at least, the Psalter, along with Job and Proverbs, manifests a system of accentuation or cantillation consisting of seven supra- and sub-signs which differ from that of the rest of the Hebrew Bible (Wheeler 1989a:15), though the musical significance of this phonological overlay is no longer entirely clear to us today.

10. *Strophic structuration*: The universal application of Jakobson's "poetic principle" (1972:93) of correspondence (similarity) superimposed upon sequence (contiguity) results in the formation of additional compositional structures (over and above the staple of paired line forms) on the macrolevel of textual organization. This greatly increases the semantic density of poetic discourse in the Psalms and also serves to segment the text into distinct units (strophes/stanzas) and patterns through the strategic positioning of repeated elements, including complete utterances (i.e., refrains).

3.4 Two basic psalmic genres: lament and eulogy

The initial question "Why classify?" has already been addressed: The typological investigation of literature is a proven means of investigating a poetic text more perceptively and comprehensively with regard to its thematic and structural organization—from top-to-bottom, so to speak. This preliminary procedure in turn provides some important insights into the rhetorical significance of specific stylistic forms and the possible communicative function(s) of the discourse as a whole in its presumed historical and sociological setting. This is not mere background information and hence analytically optional. Rather, this overall classification exercise is an essential part of discerning the total meaning package of the text under consideration, which is therefore relevant also in its ongoing transmission via translation in different languages today.

Before we turn to an examination of the two prominent psalm genres that arguably underlie all of the others,[11] it is necessary to take note of a certain ambiguity that is connected with their own wider literary classification. Are the Psalms lyric praise "songs" (Berry 1993:107), religious "prayers" (Balentine 1993:13), whether liturgical or devotional, a mixture of both, or something else? The terms "psalm" and "psalter" come from Greek and refer to a song accompanied by some musical instrument(s) (typically a stringed instrument of some kind), which is apparently what the Hebrew word mizmôr (57x) also refers to. Furthermore, "the common Hebrew designation for the collection of psalms is tehillîm, from the verbal root hll, meaning 'praise'" (Tucker 2008:578). Thus, the Psalter could be classified as a collection of sacred praise songs. On the other hand, many of the psalms are also designated as "prayers" (tephillôt), including the one that concludes Book II ("the prayers of David, son of Jesse," Ps. 72:20). Perhaps we could then combine concepts and call the psalms "prayerful praise songs," but that would seem to blur an essential distinction between the two types that are the focus of our discussion here.

This dynamic, functionally fluid equivocality then, a notable aspect of the Hebrew system of worship in general, is admirably reflected in the two principal psalmic genres of lament and eulogy. The former, based on petition, is more prayerlike; the latter, expressing such emotions as praise and thanksgiving, have a more lyric, hymnic character. And yet, as we shall see, these fundamental communicative purposes in worship—and the linguistic forms that realize them in Hebrew poetic discourse—are very closely related in the Psalter (Westermann 1980:59),

---

[11] "The two predominant genres are praise and supplication... Together these make up more than two-thirds of the Book of Psalms. Many psalms, however, are of mixed genre and treat diverse situations" (Alter and Greenstein 2012:1124).

even as they have been closely associated in earlier ANE literature.[12] Therefore, they are best studied in conjunction with one another, not as rigidly defined structural categories, but as rather flexible and over-lapping sets of formal and functional features. These stylistic attributes are rhetorically and artistically varied according to the particular life situation as the psalmist freely moves between the poles of petition and praise (generally moving from the former to the latter) in order to give voice to the pair of preeminent religious "tonalities" that encompass the totality of human experience—namely, the "rhythm of joy and sor-row" (ibid.:25). This creative freedom of spiritual expression, a genuine "lyric impulse" (Beckson and Ganz 1975:135), is well illustrated in the compositional warp and woof of Psalm 31.

3.4.1 The LAMENT

A generic form-functional typology is most clearly and extensively exhibited in the frequent "psalms of lament," in which there is a decided emphasis upon the element of petition. This prayer designates the central "text act," that is, "the predominant illocutionary force [which characterizes] a series of speech acts" (Hatim and Mason 1990:78). Closely associated with a particular text act is its interpretive frame, a contextualizing cognitive schema or common "body of knowledge that is evoked in order to provide an inferential base for the understanding of an utterance" (Levinsohn 1983:281), or a related set of them (cf. Wendland 2008:1–16). This would correspond to the characteristic life setting *(Sitz im Leben)* for the work as posited in form-critical studies. The theory of speech acts (S-A) thus provides a useful basis for discerning and describing the sequence of functional stages that a lament psalm in its idealized, prototypical form comprises (cf. Briggs 2008). According to the pragmatic, discourse-based perspective of S-A analysis, any utterance or utterance set, whether literary/oratorical or not, consists of a tightly knit cluster of four dynamic elements:

1. *Locutionary act*: the formal linguistic (phonological, lexical, morphosyntactic) features of a given utterance.

2. *Paralocutionary act*: the significant non-verbal signs that accompany an utterance, whether oral (e.g., gestures, facial expressions, body stance) or written (e.g., typography, format, significant space on the page).[13]

---

[12] "Praise and lament belong to the oldest cultic phenomena and literary genres in the ancient Near East and in the Bible. Furthermore, they have existed side by side since the earliest times" (Nõmmik 2014:103).

[13] I have not noted this important fourth component in other S-A analytical proposals.

3. *Illocutionary act:* the conventional communicative force, or function, that is conveyed by a given locution and paralocution, including general categories, such as assertives, directives, commissives, expressives, performatives, etc. (Searle 1979:viii), or those that are more specific, e.g., promise, warning, denial, concession, rebuke, confession, plea (Wendland 2008:97).

4. *Perlocutionary act:* encompasses all those perceptible effects, intended or unintended, that result from the expression of a certain utterance (or speech) in a specific social situation.

For obvious reasons, namely, our lack of access to the original communication event, elements 2 and 4 play only a minor role in contemporary analyses of the Psalter. They factor in only where explicitly specified or clearly implied by the text itself, an example being the ritual action connected with a certain psalm (e.g., 66:13–15).

The individual (as distinct from the communal) lament may be typologically defined in terms of seven functional, or illocutionary, steps, some of which are classified as distinct genres by Form Critical analysts (e.g., Gerstenberger 1988:143ff.). Each step, or stage, which may occur more than once, is realized by one or both of a pair of sub-constituents that more precisely describe the type of religious interaction posited as taking place through the speech act. Only one stage is really obligatory, namely, the central petition;[14] but most of the others are normally found in a psalm of average length, though not necessarily in the order of the sequence given below. It should be noted that these are not rigid categories; rather, they may overlap in their realization, and often a given psalm verse may be classified in more than one way.

I will describe each stage of the seven possible compositional units of the lament psalm with reference to two of their common constituents (cf. Kaiser 2013:128). These will be illustrated in turn by one or more of the formulaic or typical expressions that are frequently found in the Psalter (all quotations are from the NIV). Any psalm categorized as a lament (containing a prayer-petition to God) may be more specifically described on the basis of these constituents and the particular manner in which they are manifested, that is, with regard to form, content, function—as well as with respect to their occurrence (i.e., which of the stages appear) and their distribution or sequential order.

1. **Invocation**
 a. Divine address or appellation, usually by means of a vocative, with or without a short epithetic description or characterization of God:

---

[14] From this perspective, it might be advantageous to term these "Prayers for Help" (Jacobson and Jacobson 2013:39), rather than the traditional "lament."

"Hear us, O Shepherd of Israel, you who lead Joseph like a flock" (80:1); "Surely God is good to Israel" (73:1).

b. An initial general appeal in the form of an imperative and vocative, with or without some expression of hope or motivation: "Answer me when I call you, O my righteous God" (4:1); "O LORD my God, I take refuge in you; save and deliver me" (7:1).

2. **Complaint**
   a. A conventional description of the problem or plight of the psalmist that occasioned his prayer: "...for the godly are no more" (12:1); "How many are my foes, how many rise up against me" (3:1).
   b. A more specific expression of grievance concerning the situation of his suffering or trial, the enemies or opponents, or even God himself for his apparent delay in responding to the psalmist's need: "Many are saying of me, 'God will not deliver him!'" (3:2); "Why have you forsaken me? Why are you so far from saving me?" (22:1).

3. **Petition**
   a. The central plea or prayer to God for help, articulating the central purpose of the psalm in a further description or explanation of the difficulty that the psalmist is facing: "Arise, O LORD, in your anger; rise up against the rage of my enemies...; decree justice!" (7:6); "Hide me in the shadow of your wing from the wicked who assail me" (17:8–9).
   b. The motivation for divine action, the reason why God should intervene to help the psalmist: "Show the wonder of your great love, you who save by your right hand" (17:7); "...or I will sleep in death; my enemy will say, 'I have overcome him!'" (13:3–4).

4. **Confession**
   a. An admission of personal sin, moral weakness, or negligence: "I confess my iniquity; I am troubled by my sin" (38:18); "Remember not the sins of my youth and my rebellious ways" (25:7).
   b. In contrast to the preceding, an assertion of innocence and righteous behavior before God and man: "I do not sit with deceitful men...I proclaim your praise" (26:4, 7); "Though you test me, you will find nothing; I have resolved that my mouth will not sin" (17:3).

5. **Profession**[15]
   a. Affirmation of trust and confidence in Yahweh and in his power to save: "My eyes are ever on the LORD, for only he will release my

---

[15] Estes suggests that "the psalmic songs of trust are closely related to the lament psalms, because they speak of confidence in the face of conflict" (2013:160).

feet from the snare" (25:15); "In God I trust, I will not be afraid; what can man do to me?" (56:11).

   b. Verbal recognition of God"s deliverance in the past and/or fervent hope of a future positive divine response: "In you our fathers put their trust...and you delivered them" (22:4); "[God] will sustain you; he will never let the righteous fall" (55:22).

6. **Imprecation**[16]
   a. Accusation against the wicked and/or pernicious enemies: "Not a word from their mouth can be trusted; with their tongue they speak deceit" (5:9); "They persecute those you wound and talk about the pain of those you hurt" (69:26).
   b. A call for just recompense or retribution upon all evildoers or a particular group: "Let their intrigues be their downfall; banish them for their many sins" (5:10); "Charge them with crime upon crime; do not let them share in your salvation" (69:27).

7. **Praise**
   a. Solemn promise or vow to personally thank and praise God, with or without accompanying ritual action: "I will give thanks to the LORD because of his righteousness" (7:17); "I will present my thank offering to you" (56:12).
   b. A call, with or without motivation, for the congregation of God's people to thank and praise him: "Sing praises to the LORD en-throned in Zion...[for] what he has done" (9:11); "You who fear

---

[16] These often misunderstood "imprecatory" passages, and even entire psalms (e.g., Pss. 12, 35, 58, 59, 69, 70, 83, 109, 137, 140) are perhaps more appropriately termed "justitiary": appeals that justice would be carried out (by God) against evil and enemies (cf. Wanke 2014:116). "Justice is different from vengeance, and when the former fails, the latter must be left in God's hands" (Bullock 2013:50). "These Psalms are not an expression of a malevolent search for revenge, but of a situation in which the psalmist is defenseless, terribly fearful and calls on God to defend him by destroying his enemies;" in other words, the psalmist "in a liberating act of faith places the matter before God, the judge par excellence—God will decide, and the Psalm pleads for God to decide against enemies" (Wanke 2014:107–108). In highly emotive, usually hyperbolic language (hence, not to be taken literally) "the topic of experienced violence is focused on by the psychological terror exerted by violent language" (Hausmann 2014:87). It is important to observe that "the plea for God's intervention against the enemies is often, as in Psalm 58 [cf. also Ps. 31:17–18], a request to destroy the tools of speech. There is no doubt that the aim is not to destroy the enemy itself but to make sure that with God's help, the enemy can no longer harm the psalmist by his/her language" (ibid.), for in ANE times (as in many parts of the world yet today), language was/is regarded as a highly potent force, capable of doing serious psychological—even physical—damage.

the LORD, praise him...for he has not despised...the suffering of the afflicted one" (22:23–24).

The so-called communal laments are much less common than the individual prayers (Klein et al. 1993:285),[17] at least in the Psalter (examples appear also in the OT prophetic books, e.g., Hosea 6:1–3). It is generally assumed that the individual lament form was derived or adapted from the communal one (Westermann 1980:30–31),[18] but this cannot be determined with certainty. In any case, the same basic inventory of functional stages may be found in corporate complaints (cf. Kaiser 2014:129), although, as would be expected, the general orientation is usually national in scope, dealing with some widespread drought or plague, enemy invasion or military defeat. In such petitions, "the anxiety, humiliation, pain, and suffering are those of the community" (Hayes 1976:118). Thus, the psalmist typically incorporates the entire congregation of Israel ("we-our-us" focus) in a public expression of corporate repentance, such as a fast, a summons to sacrifice, and/or an exhortation to a revival of hope for God's future deliverance or blessing (as in the book of Joel). Some representative communal laments are Psalms 44, 58, 60, 74, 80, and 83.

3.4.2 The EULOGY

The eulogy, or song of praise, is distinct from, yet clearly related to, the lament prayer. The most obvious correspondence lies in the final functional unit of the lament sequence—step 7: "praise," which forms the foundation for the eulogy as a whole in its initial stage. But there are other similarities too, as we see in the generalized set of eulogy elements listed below. For example, several components correspond with those found in the lament's stage 5: "profession."

The eulogy is also associated with the lament in terms of the basic two-fold motivation for which the psalm is sung or prayed—namely, distress/problem and deliverance/solution. In the case of a lament, the individual or group confronted with some major crisis or calamity appeals to Yahweh for relief and rescue. In a eulogy, on the other hand, the psalmist or the worship community reflects retrospectively in gratitude upon some serious predicament from which the LORD has saved him/them in his covenantal mercy *(chesed)*. The two genres overlap at the affirmation of faith and/or

---

[17] Kaiser posits that 62 of the 150 psalms are laments; he compares them to those found in Lamentations (2013:127).

[18] Bullock notes that "there has been a tendency in scholarship to deemphasize the place of the individual in the OT preexilic world.... Individuals were central to early OT history, and not an idealization of the community, as the early form critics supposed.... Rather, human personhood was much more a balance between the individual and the group, the private and the corporate" (2013:55).

the (anticipated) act of thanksgiving and praise that marks the major turning point of the typical lament. Thus, it is essentially a matter of perspective: with the lament, the petitioner requests and looks forward in faith to Yahweh's gracious deliverance; in the eulogy he faithfully looks back upon such divine deliverance already received. Another point of correspondence lies in the frequent call to the congregation of fellow believers to join the psalmist in lauding their great and glorious God.

The text of lyric praise is generally not as tightly structured as that of the lament, but the following bipartite constituents are frequently, though not always, found (roughly in this order):

1. **Invitation**
   a. A summons to render thanks and praise to Yahweh, directed either to the psalmist himself or his fellow worshipers: "Ascribe to the LORD, O mighty ones...the glory due his name" (29:1–2); "I will exalt you, O LORD" (30:1).
   b. An initial description of Yahweh's praiseworthy attributes: "Worship the LORD in the splendor of his holiness" (29:2); "The LORD is my rock, my fortress and my deliverer" (18:2).

2. **Motivation**
   a. A recounting of the dangerous situation or dire crisis facing either the individual or the nation as a whole: "The cords of the grave coiled around me" (18:5); 'I was overcome by trouble and sorrow' (116:3).
   b. Reference to, or even a reiteration of the past plea to Yahweh for help: "In my distress I called to the LORD" (18:6); "I called,...'What gain is there in my destruction?'..." (30:9).

3. **Proclamation**
   a. Affirmation that Yahweh did respond in an act of deliverance: "You lifted me out of the depths and did not let my enemies gloat over me" (30:1); "You exalted my horn like that of a wild ox; fine oils have been poured upon me" (92:10).
   b. Confident profession of the glorious, merciful attributes of Yahweh: "Out of the brightness of his presence clouds advanced, with hailstones and bolts of lightning" (18:12); "The LORD is gracious and righteous; our God is full of compassion" (92:10).

4. **Promise**
   a. A pledge to continually render thankful praise to Yahweh: "I will lift up the cup of salvation and call upon the name of the LORD" (116:13); "You are my God, and I will give you thanks" (118:28).

    b. A vow to present some concrete evidence of thankfulness: "I will fulfill my vows to the LORD in the presence of all his people" (116:14); "I will sacrifice fat animals to you and an offering of rams" (66:15).

5. **Exhortation**
    a. A call to the congregation of worshipers to offer praise to Yahweh and/or put their trust in him: "It is better to take refuge in the LORD than to trust in man" (118:8); 'Rejoice in the LORD and be glad, you righteous!' (32:11).
    b. A final moving, motivating testimony to the greatness and goodness of Yahweh: "The LORD is upright; he is my rock and there is no wickedness in him" (92:15); "The LORD will fulfill his purpose for me; your love, O LORD, endures forever!" (138:8).

In concluding this categorization, the form-functional diversity and flexibility of the psalmic corpus needs to be emphasized.[19] The several stages, especially their specific sub-sections, may be mixed and matched in various ways within a given psalm text. Selected compositional units may also be omitted, for example, the sacrificial vow of thanksgiving (4b). On the other hand, some modification may be made in the basic sequence, such as the addition of an initial word of reassurance for the righteous, for example: "Blessed is he whose transgressions are forgiven" (32:1). In any case, variety is the unexpected stylistic "spice" of the Psalter. It is amazing to note how much artistic diversity is realized in the composition of so many functionally similar lyric prayer-praises despite a rather limited inventory of conventional liturgical elements of poetic form and religious content from which to choose.

Certain changes in the typical pattern of a lament or a eulogy may occur so frequently as to constitute a distinct subgenre. The "hymn," for example, is a "pure" eulogy (Gerstenberger 1988:15) that omits the closely-related stages of "motivation" (#2) and "proclamation" (#3). Thus, Yahweh is lauded for his glorious attributes and/or his wonderful works in general—not necessarily for a particular act of deliverance, intervention, or blessing, either anticipated or already received. Westermann (1980:25–26) designates these hymns as psalms of "descriptive praise," whereas those that refer to some past event in the psalmist's life are psalms of "narrative praise." Form critics have posited

---

[19] Many other types of classification are available in the literature. Jacobson and Jacobson categorize psalm genres according to FORM (Prayers for Help, Hymns of Praise, Trust Psalms, Songs of Thanksgiving) and CONTENT, or Themes (Royal, Enthronement, Wisdom, Creation, Historical, Zion, Imprecatory, Penitential, Liturgical) (2013:60, 64). Wendland discerns five MAJOR functions (Petition, Thanksgiving, Praise, Instruction, Profession [trust]) and five MINOR functions (repentance, remembrance, retribution, royalty, liturgy) (2002:34, 46).

anywhere from half to a full dozen or more additional (sub)genres of Hebrew psalmic poetry (for an extensive listing, see Gerstenberger 1988:243–258). However, a literary-structural comparison will suggest that most if not all of these may be generated or adapted from the two basic forms of lament and eulogy. In other words, each sub-type probably arose as a result of the creative process of specification from one or more of the principal stages of the eulogy or lament as contextualized according to the particular socioreligious situation and historical setting that pertained at the time of composition.

3.5 A discourse-oriented, structure-functional, literary-oratorical analysis

Traditional form-critical or generic text analysis does not take us far enough. The linguistic diversity, literary complexity, rhetorical dynamics, and indeed the esthetic excellence of the corpus of psalms in the Psalter require a more comprehensive methodology. An analysis is needed that will enable us to more fully (albeit never completely due to our ignorance of the original sound dimension) discern and describe the biblical text, as well as to transmit it meaningfully in translation via different media today. Any specific psalm must be viewed not only as a general type (or combination of subtypes), but as a unique artistic and purposeful creation. Such poetic individuality may be revealed by a literary approach that is holistic (discourse-based), discerning (structure-functional), and sound-sensitive (oratorical) in nature. The biblical scholar James Muilenburg was one of the first to recognize the need for this broader and at the same time more refined hermeneutical perspective in his speeches and writings, beginning with his Presidential address at the 1968 meeting of the Society of Biblical Literature, "Form Criticism and Beyond":[20]

> To state our criticism in another way, form criticism by its very nature is bound to generalize because it is concerned with what is common to all the representatives of a genre, and therefore applies an external measure to the individual pericopes. It does not focus sufficient attention upon what is unique and unrepeatable, upon the particularity of the formulation. Moreover, form and content are inextricably related. They form an integral whole. The two are one. Exclusive attention to the *Gattung* may actually obscure the thought and intention of the writer or speaker. The passage must be read and heard precisely as it is spoken. It is the creative

---

[20] This quote was taken from the following website: http://conversationaltheology. wordpress.com/2008/02/16/james-muilenburg-and-the-rise-of-rhetorical-criticism/. Accessed on August 10, 2013 (no longer active).

synthesis of the particular formulation of the pericope with the content that makes it the distinctive composition that it is.

In the following section I will overview some of Muilenburg's methodological insights, which he termed "rhetorical criticism," and then, in the remainder of this chapter, apply these within the framework of my own analytical approach to a close textual study of Psalm 31.[21]

3.6 Muilenburg's method elaborated

Muilenburg built upon the foundation laid by the form critics to investigate "the literary unit in its precise and unique formulation" (1992:55). His specific aim was to use a careful text analysis as the basis for "understanding the nature of Hebrew literary composition, in exhibiting the structural patterns that are employed for the fashioning of a literary unit, whether in poetry or in prose, and in discerning the many and various devices by which predications are formulated and ordered into a unified whole" (ibid.:57). His methodology of rhetorical criticism featured two principal steps: delimitation of the scope, or boundaries of the particular unit under analysis, and delineation of the constituent structure of its internal development as a purposeful whole—a composition shaped by the creative intention of the biblical poet.[22] To accomplish his objectives, Muilenburg paid special attention to the diverse "rhetorical devices" that indicate "sequence and movement" within the composition, on the one hand, and "shifts or breaks" in thought, on the other (1992:59). Among such stylistic features, he especially noted the inclusio, metrical variations, clusters of bi- and tri-cola, strophes, refrains, key-word reiteration, particles, vocatives, rhetorical questions, and general repetition. He also drew attention to the need for a functional perspective to get "a grasp of the writer's intent and meaning" (ibid.:57).

My analysis of Psalm 31, undertaken below, is a more text-focused, functionally-motivated version of Muilenburg's approach. This literary-structural method examines the biblical text for coherent stretches of

---

[21] My approach generally incorporates the "seven standards of textuality" of Cotterell (1997) and discussed in Lama (2013:46–49): cohesion of grammar and syntax, coherence, intentionality, acceptability, informativity, situationality, and intertextuality.

[22] Thus, "...the more deeply [the analyst] penetrates the formulations as they have been transmitted to us, the more sensitive he is to the roles which words and motifs play in a composition; the more he concentrates on the ways in which thought has been woven into linguistic patterns, the better able he is to think the thoughts of the biblical writer after him" (James Muilenburg, http://conversationaltheology. wordpress.com/2008/02/16/james-muilenburg-and-the-rise-of-rhetorical-criticism/). Accessed October 8, 2013 (website no longer available).

continuity coupled with disjunctive points of discontinuity within the discourse (cf. 2.4 above, also Wendland 1993:138–140). These two compositional principles govern the generation, organization, and operation of any literary text. However, the various stylistic techniques that realize or effect such objectives tend to be more intricately patterned, artistically crafted, copiously manifested, and strategically positioned in works that are more poetic than prosaic in nature.

Discourse continuity, whether manifested in longer or shorter spans, is primarily fashioned by the diverse modes of repetition that are built into any poetic composition. Such repetition may be either exact (reiteration) or correspondent (recursion) in character, involving phonological, lexical, morphosyntactic, semantic, and/or pragmatic (i.e., illocutionary) elements. Poetic progression in Hebrew verse is typically generated on both the micro- and also the macrolevels of text structure by contiguous or removed parallelism respectively, that is, coupled lines of a synonymous, contrastive, or additive (e.g., consequential) variety.

Discontinuity, on the other hand, is manifested by some break in an established discourse pattern, involving a shift or change in topic, addressee, speaker, purpose, referent, etc. Frequently, such a disjunction is accompanied by a convergence or concentration of special poetic features, as outlined earlier. This may occur at some significant juncture in the development of the discourse, helping to demarcate the boundaries of constituent units—the beginning (aperture) or ending (closure) of a discrete literary unit (e.g., strophe, stanza). Alternatively, the conjunction of stylistic devices appears at a thematic summit (peak) or an emotive high point (climax) of some type, whether affirmative or adverse qualitatively in relation to the text's primary participants (speaker-addressee, agent-recipient, etc.).

The compositional forces of continuity and discontinuity thus complement each other to define the discourse arrangement and operation of a literary text with respect to four major structure-functional properties: segmentation, connectivity, progression, and prominence (Wendland 2004:125). *Segmentation* deals with the delineation of the different compositional units of a text and their main syntagmatic and paradigmatic relationships and patterns of arrangement. *Connectivity* concerns the manner in which the individual poetic units are linked together through interlocking techniques of formal "cohesion" and semantic "coherence" to create a unified text. *Progression* involves the built-in features of a text that move it forward towards some sort of termination, conclusion, or resolution—such as the seven typical (hence expected) stages of a lament psalm. *Prominence,* finally, is realized by devices that rhetorically mark or foreground certain places within the discourse for special attention, such as topical focus (peak) or affective emphasis (climax).

This type of holistic approach to text analysis attaches great importance to the relative linguistic diversity, density, and distribution of the inventory of poetic features and rhetorical strategies that are found in the pericope under consideration. Their unique deployment and textual interaction are the basis for discovering not only the foundational structural design of the poetic work but also its dominant communicative objective(s) plus any associated special effects (e.g., heightened emotion), as presumably intended by the psalmist in the originally envisioned setting of use (whether private devotion or public worship). Any application of the methodology outlined here of course presupposes a prior text-critical study, a thorough microexegesis, literal and/or free translation, and a repeated oral reading of the biblical text in order to aurally internalize the discourse and its expressed meaning.

3.7 Application to Psalm 31

Psalm 31 is a good candidate for a practical application of the analytical procedures outlined above for several reasons. In the first place, it is a discrete and complete poetic pericope of relatively limited length; there is no controversy over the exact delimitation of the discourse. Second, it is a rather problematic text—both structurally with respect to its demarcation of constituents and also functionally with regard to its generic classification as well as its internal sequence of pragmatic, illocutionary elements. These difficulties and the consequent scholarly debates that they occasion present a challenge to the practicality and interpretive capacity of the methodology being proposed in this investigation. Finally and most important, Psalm 31 is a worthy object of study in its own right on account of the significant message that it poetically proclaims. This is a strongly moving expression of personal commitment to, and confidence in Yahweh, the all-powerful, ever-present covenant Lord, who upholds his faithful people even at times when there appears to be "terror on every side" (Ps. 31:13). I will preface this analysis by citing the text from the *New English Translation* (NET):[23]

> **31:1** For the music director; a psalm of David.
> In you, O Lord, I have taken shelter!
> Never let me be humiliated!
> Vindicate me by rescuing me!
> **31:2** Listen to me!
> Quickly deliver me!
> Be my protector and refuge,
> a stronghold where I can be safe!
> **31:3** For you are my high ridge and my stronghold;
> for the sake of your own reputation you lead me and guide me.

---

[23] Used by permission; cited from https://net.bible.org/#!bible/Psalms+31:20. Accessed September 2, 2017.

31:4 You will free me from the net they hid for me,
for you are my place of refuge.
31:5 Into your hand I entrust my life;
you will rescue me, O Lord, the faithful God.
31:6 I hate those who serve worthless idols,
but I trust in the Lord.
31:7 I will be happy and rejoice in your faithfulness,
because you notice my pain
and you are aware of how distressed I am.
31:8 You do not deliver me over to the power of the enemy;
you enable me to stand in a wide open place.
31:9 Have mercy on me, for I am in distress!
My eyes grow dim from suffering.
I have lost my strength.
31:10 For my life nears its end in pain;
my years draw to a close as I groan.
My strength fails me because of my sin,
and my bones become brittle.
31:11 Because of all my enemies, people disdain me;
my neighbors are appalled by my suffering–
those who know me are horrified by my condition;
those who see me in the street run away from me.
31:12 I am forgotten, like a dead man no one thinks about;
I am regarded as worthless, like a broken jar.
31:13 For I hear what so many are saying,
the terrifying news that comes from every direction.
When they plot together against me,
they figure out how they can take my life.
31:14 But I trust in you, O Lord!
I declare, "You are my God!"
31:15 You determine my destiny!
Rescue me from the power of my enemies and those who
chase me.
31:16 Smile on your servant!
Deliver me because of your faithfulness!
31:17 O Lord, do not let me be humiliated,
for I call out to you!
May evil men be humiliated!
May they go wailing to the grave!
31:18 May lying lips be silenced–
lips that speak defiantly against the innocent
with arrogance and contempt!

31:19 How great is your favor,
which you store up for your loyal followers!
In plain sight of everyone you bestow it on those who take
shelter in you.
31:20 You hide them with you, where they are safe from the
attacks of men;
you conceal them in a shelter, where they are safe from slan-
derous attacks.
31:21 The Lord deserves praise
for he demonstrated his amazing faithfulness to me when I
was besieged by enemies.
31:22 I jumped to conclusions and said,
"I am cut off from your presence!"
But you heard my plea for mercy when I cried out to you for
help.
31:23 Love the Lord, all you faithful followers of his!
The Lord protects those who have integrity,
but he pays back in full the one who acts arrogantly.
31:24 Be strong and confident,
all you who wait on the Lord!

3.7.1 A form-functional analysis

A number of studies have drawn attention to the problems posed when one
seeks to analyze the structure of this psalm. Gerstenberger concludes: "All
commentators agree that Psalm 31 shows neither logical nor literary order"
(1988:137). As a result, "there is no firm agreement amongst scholars
as to the correct [constituent] analysis" (Craigie 1983:259). Moreover,
"the difficulty in determining the literary genre of this psalm has led
many scholars to view it as a composite work from anonymous authors"
(VanGemeren 1991:262).

Bratcher and Reyburn point out the emotive and motivational diversity
of Psalm 31: it "combines elements of sorrow (vv. 9–13), statements of con-
fidence (vv. 3, 4, 14–15), thanksgiving (vv. 7–8, 19–20), and pleas for pun-
ishment of enemies (vv. 4, 17–18)" (1991:289). They further analyze the
text as an alternating series of affirmations of trust (T) and petitions (P) for
deliverance, accompanied by occasional reasons (R) for the two preceding
types of discourse. Their analytical perspective is charted as follows (ibid.):

Text (verses)	**Type** (function)
1a	T
1b–2d	P
3a	T
3b–4b	P + R

5a–8b	T + R
9a–13	P + R
14	T
15b–17a	P + R
17b	T + R
17c–18	P
19–22	T + R
23–24	Command to T

Structurally significant in their scheme is the concluding double command to "trust" (i.e., "love the LORD" and "be strong"). One could quibble over some of the details of this analysis. For example, it would be equally possible to construe v. 3a as a "reason" (R) like 4b, which it parallels in content and form. And why is the expression of "hatred" in v. 6a considered to be an assertion of "trust" (T) such as we have in 6b? Should a clear panegyric "blessing" be categorized as a T statement, or rather, as a distinct utterance of "praise" (Pr)? Again, why is v. 15a excluded from the sequence? Perhaps because it is too ambiguous, i.e., either T or R ("My times are in your hands..."). In any case, the proposed framework is helpful in giving one a general overview of the undulating form-functional progression of this lyric personal prayer.

Gerstenberger offers the following as the structure of Psalm 31 from a typical form-critical perspective (1988:136–137):

PSALM 31
COMPLAINT OF THE INDIVIDUAL
Structure

	MT	RSV
1. Superscription	1	—
2. Initial Plea	2–3	1–2
3. Affirmation of confidence	4–7	3–6
a. Confessional statements	4a, 5b	3a, 4b
b. Petitions	4b, 5a	3b, 4a
c. Self-dedication	6a	5a
d. Affirmation of confidence	6b	5b
e. Confession to community	7	6
i. Protestation of innocence	7a	6a
ii. Affirmation of confidence	7b	6b
4. Thanksgiving	8–9	7–8

5.	Complaint		10–14	9–13
6.	Petition		15–19	14–18
	a.	Affirmation of confidence	15–16a	14–15a
	b.	Petition	16b–18a	15b–17a
	c.	Imprecation	18b–19	17b–18
7.	Personal hymn		20–22	19–21
	a.	Communal adoration	20–21	19–20
	b.	Personal blessing (praise)	22	21
8.	Thanksgiving		23	22
9.	Exhortation, blessing		24–25	23–24

This analytical scheme illustrates both the strengths and the weaknesses of a strict form-critical approach. On the positive side, it treats the text as "a liturgical unit" (ibid.:137) and takes seriously the interaction of structure and function within the composition as a whole. On the other hand, the overemphasis upon seeking a precise generic categorization for every utterance soon loses the uninitiated reader in a forest of detail, not all of which is helpful or even correct. For example, the entire psalm is typed as a "complaint of the individual," but this is contradicted by the opening line of v. 23: "Love Yahweh, all you his saints!" Furthermore, the classification "affirmation of confidence" is reiterated on three different levels of the proposed unit covering vv. 3–6 (i.e., III, D, and 2), which is a textual span that is actually broken structurally at v. 6. The petition genre of vv. 14–18 is allegedly composed of three quite diverse constituents, namely, "affirmation of confidence" (once again!), "petition" (thus included within itself), and "imprecation" (which would seem to be a distinct structural unit). The so-called *"personal"* hymn (VII) leads off with a *communal* adoration (A). Finally, vv. 23–24 supposedly contain a blessing, but if such an element is indeed present, it is very different from the literal one that initiates v. 21, which is somehow connected in the classification with a communal adoration (vv. 19–20).

But perhaps the greatest weakness of the preceding form-critical analysis is that it misses the fundamental structural symmetry which arises out of the psalmist's artistic play upon the standard inventory of functional elements (the 7 stages) of the lament genre. Thus, a distinct compositional pattern is formed by his distinctive selection and arrangement of illocutionary aims within the text of his prayer to the Lord. This may not be logical or literary from a contemporary western perspective (e.g., Gerstenberger 1998:137), but the sequence is arguably very effective—once it is recognized for what it is—in terms of communicative strategy and technique, even today. In essence, what we appear to have is an instance of functional recycling on the generic level of poetic discourse. Two distinguishable cycles of the lament series of constituents divide Psalm 31 into two unequal "halves," as indicated in the following table.[24] It should be noted that within each cycle there may be an overlapping or a convergence of functional elements, as well as passages that may be classified in more than one way (several examples are shown in parentheses):

Stage	Cycle I: General vv. 1–8	Cycle II: Specific vv. 9–24
Invocation	1, 2a	9a
Complaint	4a, 7bc, 8a	9b–13, 22a
Petition	3b, 4a, 2b	15b, 16, 17a
Confession	5a	19–20
Profession	1a, 2b, 3a, 4b, 5b, 6b, (7b–8)	14, 15a, 17b, 19–20, (23b–24)
Imprecation	6a	17c–18
Praise	7a, (7b–8)	21, 22b, (23b–24)

The foregoing list is not intended to represent a precise delineation of the illocutionary structure of this lament. That would require a more detailed discussion of each component (plus each of its two possible realizations) within its textual setting and in relationship to each one of the other stages in both cycles. However, the chart does serve to indicate that the functional "alternation" pointed out by Bratcher and Reyburn (1991:289) may be rather more intricate and patterned than first indicated on the surface of the psalm. Moreover, virtually every one of the stages is closely associated with a particular "reason," whether expressed or implied in the text—a motivation that is in some way "related to the notion of trusting" (ibid.). For example, the very use of the covenant name of God, "Yahweh," underlies the opening appeal of the "invocation" in v. 1.

The preceding functional overview (to be demonstrated further below) clearly demonstrates both the logical order as well as the exquisite literary qualities of Psalm 31. My study indicates that what we have here is a skillfully amalgamated "lament-eulogy" hybrid genre. Thus, we find the complaint-problem expressed in vv. 2, 9, and 22b (the last being a flashback in direct speech), while praise is featured in vv. 7–8 and 21–22. There is a predominant focus, however, upon utterances of profession. Such affirmation of complete trust in, and dedication to Yahweh is the dominant

---

[24] I note that this binary structural arrangement of Psalm 31 has also been proposed in the recent book by deClaissé-Walford et al. 2014:300, though not with the same degree of detail.

functional constituent within both cycles in terms of both quantity and qual-
ity (i.e., not only the amount of text, but also the diversity and intensity of
poetic expression that is devoted to it). The foregrounded faith of the psalm-
ist—articulated in such a lyric, perhaps also musical mode—clearly sets the
tone for the prayer-poem as a whole and characterizes its entire structural
development.[25] The shifting back-and-forth between complaint-petition and
profession, a feature which has caused interpretive problems for source- and
form-critics alike, is simply, but significantly, a mark of the creative artistry
that gives Psalm 31 its unique rhetorical force and religious flavor.[26] Its
ongoing progression throughout the discourse has a cumulative effect that
ultimately breaks forth in the concluding communal call to universal confi-
dent praise in vv. 23–24, which in itself is an implicit cry of victorious trust,
uttered on behalf of "all you who hope in the LORD!"

3.7.2 Annotated diagram of the text's sequential-spatial structure

Below we will examine the actual Hebrew text of Psalm 31 in order to
illustrate one possible discourse-oriented methodology and also to lay the
foundation for the literary-structural commentary and comparison that
follows thereafter. As in the case of Psalm 30, I have included an interlinear
English translation which may also serve as a point of reference for readers
not familiar with Hebrew. The Hebrew textual display follows the same
section-based annotated model that was presented in chapter 2; this
allows for a number of additional scholarly perspectives on the original
composition.

v.co	Post-Verb2	Post-Verb1	VERBAL	Pre-Verb2	Pre-Verb1
A[a]					
0.1	לְדָוִ֑ד	מִזְמֹ֥ור[b]	-----		לַמְנַצֵּ֗חַ
	of/to-David	a-psalm			to-the-director
1.1			חָסִ֗יתִי[c]	יְהוָ֥ה	בְּךָ֣[d]
			I-took-refuge	O-Yahweh	in-you

---

[25] The communal, musical character of the psalms is a vital aspect of their com-
municative character. "The Psalms are not simply an expression of faith; they make
the experience of faith possible" (Körting 2014:70).

[26] Such sudden shifts in topic and tone do not surprise serious psalms students
and must not be attributed either to multiple sources or to poor compositional
competence. As in all great literary works, artistic moves are not predictable: "Any
attempt to explain the surprising shifts in these [psalms] must be done on a case-
by-case basis" (Jacobson 2014:234).

1.2		לְעוֹלָם	אֵבוֹשָׁה		אַל־
		forever	let-me-be-shamed		not =
1.3			פַּלְּטֵנִי		בְּצִדְקָתְךָ [e]
			rescue-me		in-your-justice
2.1	אָזְנְךָ	אֵלַי ׀	הַטֵּה		
	your-ear	unto-me	stretch-out		
2.2			הַצִּילֵנִי		מְהֵרָה
			rescue-me		quickly
2.3	לְצוּר־מָעוֹז	לִי ׀	הֱיֵה		
	as-a-rock-of = refuge	for-me	be		
2.4			לְהוֹשִׁיעֵנִי	מְצוּדוֹת	לְבֵית
			to-save-me	fortresses	as-a-house-of
3.1		אַתָּה	-------	וּמְצוּדָתִי	כִּי־סַלְעִי
		you		and-my-fortress	indeed = my-rock
3.2			תַּנְחֵנִי	שִׁמְךָ [g]	וּלְמַעַן
			you-lead-me	your-name	and-because-of
			וּתְנַהֲלֵנִי [h]		
			and-you-guide-me		
4.1		מֵרֶשֶׁת [i]	תּוֹצִיאֵנִי		
		from-the-net	you-bring-me-out		
4.2		לִי	טָמְנוּ		זוּ
		for-me	they-fix		which
4.3		מָעוּזִּי	-------	אַתָּה	כִּי־
		my-refuge		you	Because =
5.1		רוּחִי [j]	אַפְקִיד		בְּיָדְךָ
		my-spirit	I-entrust		into-your-hand
5.2	יהוה אֵל אֱמֶת	אוֹתִי	פָּדִיתָה [k]		
	O-Yahweh God-of *truth*	me	you-have-redeemed		

[a] Stanza A of Psalm 31 (vv. 1–5) is arranged in a rough concentric pattern: vv. 1/5—*General appeal* for refuge/safety to the LORD (YHWH) of the covenant ("righteousness" and "truth"); vv. 2/4—*Specific appeal* for defense against the attacks of enemies; v. 3—*Basis* for the psalmist's trust: Yahweh is a "rock" of protection, his "name" is reliable. It is possible, as Terrien suggests (2003:285), to divide this stanza into two "strophes" at v. 3, despite the strong lexical overlap between vv. 2 and 3 (e.g., the "rocky" imagery). The initial כִּי in v. 3 could be construed as asseverative, "Indeed…" to provide the confident basis for the following confident assertions.

[b] "This psalm cannot easily be identified with any one type, since it combines elements of sorrow (verses 9–13), statements of confidence (verses 3, 4, 14–15), thanksgiving (verses 7–8, 19–20), and pleas for punishment of enemies (verses 4, 17–18). Some see it as a composite work" (Bratcher and Reyburn 1991:289). Though it may be composite in its pragmatic-functional constituents, this does not necessarily mean that it is a compound composition; a single author could have put all the pieces together into the coherent form that we have it. As Craigie argues: "The structure [of the psalm] suggests unity, as does the use of common terminology, repeated words and phrases extending throughout the psalm, and providing a framework of coherence" (1983:259; cf. VanGemeren 1994:831). Terrien lists the main correspondences as follows: "The unity of the entire composition may also be conjectured from the repetition of several motifs: refuge (vv. 2 and 20 [1, 19]); confidence (vv. 7, 15, and 24 [6, 14, 23]); shame (vv. 2 and 18 [1, 17]); and fidelity (vv. 5 and 17 [4, 16])" (2003:288). There are lexical and conceptual links between Psalm 31 and Psalms 4, 7, 18, 22, 28, and 71 (Goldingay 2006:437).

[c] "Such a declaration of reliance is a standard way to begin a prayer psalm" (cf. 7:1; Goldingay 2006:438). Perhaps "a stylized expression" associated with psalms of lament (Harman 2011a:265).

[d] Examples of topic focus (as here, "in you"—YHWH!) abound in this psalm; instances of constituent focus are less common, but also present, e.g., 1.3 (בְּצִדְקָתְךָ); 3.1—Yahweh's "rocky," "fortress-like" (protective) character.

[e] " 'Righteousness' is not a reference to God's justice, but rather to his power to save" (Harman 2011a:266). But this perspective seems overly analytical. In typical OT covenant-oriented thought and terminology, Yahweh's "righteousness" could involve his "justice" in the sense that he would fulfil his promise to "deliver" his faithful people in their time of need, whether communally or, as here, on an individual basis. That is the basis for the psalmist's prayer. God's covenantal righteousness is manifested in his "faithfulness" (v. 5) and "love" (vv. 7, 16, 21).

[f] A cohesive series of metaphoric references (vv. 2–3) to God's sure power and unfailing protection under the figures of high cliffs and rocky fortresses evokes some impressive local imagery that would be especially moving for the inhabitants of Israel (see VanGemeren 1991:264 for a chart of the lexical patterning here).

[g] The "name" being referred to (3.2) is "Yahweh" (YHWH)—the divine "you" אַתָּה (3.1) of the psalms and the covenant Lord of the people of Israel. "The Lord identified with his people by covenant; his honor is at stake when his people hurt" or are oppressed (VanGemeren 1991:263).

[h] "*Heb* 'bring me out'. The translation assumes that the imperfect verbal form expresses the psalmist's confidence about the future. Another option is to take the form as expressing a prayer, 'free me' " (NET note). The same exegetical option

applies to the next verb in 4.1 (תּוֹצִיאֵ֑נִי). The three verbs in sequence here form an alliterative pattern that highlights the appeal being expressed: *tanicheniy—tinahileniy—totsiy'eniy* (3.2–4.1).

[i] Craigie observes that "the meter of this verse is difficult," but agrees that it is 2 + 2 + 2 (1983:258). Harman hears "overtones of the Exodus" in these verses, "with the expression 'free me' being one of the common expressions to describe God's bringing his people out of Egypt (see Exo. 13:3, 9, 14, 16; 20:2)" (2011a:266–267). McCann too observes strong links with the Exodus tradition in these verses (1996:800–801).

[j] "In the Greek text of Luke 9:31 the word for 'departure' is *exodus*.... It is also interesting to consider the way in which Jesus quotes on the cross [Luke 23:46] from a psalm that is replete with Exodus terminology" (Harman 2011a:267). Note the topic-reinforcing stanza inclusio formed by בְּיָדְךָ here and בְּךָ in the *kiy* clause of 1:1. "The translation of 'spirit' should be avoided because in Hebrew culture the spirit was not separable from the physical body" (deClaissé-Walford et al. 2014:301)—hence "my life;" in Lk. 23:46 the Greek sense "my spirit"—"the very thing that transcends physical life" (ibid.:304) is intended.

[k] "You have redeemed:" "The perfect verbal form is understood here as anticipatory, indicating rhetorically the psalmist's certitude and confidence that God will intervene. The psalmist is so confident of God's positive response to his prayer that he can describe his deliverance as if it had already happened. Another option is to take the perfect as precative, expressing a wish or request ("rescue me;" cf. NIV [supported by Bratcher and Reyburn 1991:292]). See *IBHS* 494–95 §30.5.4 c, d. However, not all grammarians are convinced that the perfect is used as a precative in Biblical Hebrew" (NET note; cf. Goldingay 2006:440). In any case, the perfect verb in 5.2 anticipates those of v. 6. There is an analogous use of a section-final "perfect of closure" in Psalm 22:21, 31. The final clause constituent, יְהוָה אֵל אֱמֶת (end focus), prefigures the theme of "trust" that pervades the next stanza.

B[a]				
6.1	הַבְלֵי־שָׁוְא[b]	הַשֹּׁמְרִים	שָׂנֵאתִי[c]	
	idols-of = worthlessness	those-devoting-themselves-to	I-hate	
6.2			בָּטָחְתִּי	אֶל־יְהוָה[d]	וַאֲנִ֗י
			I-trust	upon = Yahweh	and-I
7.1			אָגִילָה		
			I-will-be-glad		
		בְּחַסְדֶּךָ[e]	וְאֶשְׂמְחָה[f]		
		in-your-faithful-love	and-I-will-rejoice		

7.2		אֶת־עָנְיִי	רָאִיתָ		אֲשֶׁר
		DO = my-miseries	you-saw		which/for
7.3	נַפְשִׁי	בְּצָרוֹת	8 יָדַעְתָּ		
	my-life	troubles-of	you-know		
8.1		בְּיַד־אוֹיֵב h	הִסְגַּרְתַּנִי		וְלֹא
		in-hand-of = my-enemy	you-delivered-me		and-not
8.2	ii רַגְלָי	בַּמֶּרְחָב	הֶעֱמַדְתָּ		
	my-foot	in-the-wide-place	you-put-down		

[a] The shorter, second stanza (B), is a declaration of covenantal trust in Yahweh, who is mentioned just once (6.2), but who is not appealed/prayed to as in stanza A. The LORD's affirmative, salvific response is here assumed. The onset of this stanza is marked by a contrastive, chiastically-arranged expression of topic: A: "I-hate (repudiate)," B: idol (worshipers), B′: "in-YHWH," A′: "I-trust."

[b] Lit. 'the-empty-things-of falsehood'—a pejorative expression referring to "idols" or "false gods" (cf. Jon. 2:9, Isa. 56:1, Hos. 12:6). "The translation of *vain idols* will depend upon the way in which this Hebrew expression is to be interpreted. If it is taken in the sense of 'empty vanities', it may be rendered in some languages as 'things that have no worth' or 'worthless things in which people cannot put their trust'. If it is taken in the more traditional sense of idols, one may say, for example, 'idols that have no value'" (Bratcher and Reyburn 1991:293).

[c] "The LXX and Syriac read 'you hate' for 'I hate'…on the basis of the contrastive use of the *waw* before I [in 6.2]: 'you…, but I'…In favor of the MT (and NIV), it is likely that the psalmist sets up a contrast between his hatred of idolatry and his trust in the Lord. Moreover, the contrast between Yahweh and idolatry and the contrastive inclusion of the verbs in the perfect at the beginning and end in the MT ('I hate'…, but 'I trust') argue in favor of the MT" (VanGemeren 1991:266)—which is as much a literary argument as a purely linguistic one.

[d] The sharp contrast here motivates a chiastic construction in 6.2 that is initiated by the subject-speaker (וַאֲנִי) and which places the divine object of his trust (אֶל־יְהוָה) into focused position.

[e] Some commentators draw attention to what they view as a break-up of the "stereo-typed" pairing of "truth" (5.2) and "covenantal love" (7.1), which are often found as a "fixed pair" (e.g., 25:10, 61:7, 86:15, 89:14) (VanGemeren 1991:265). The disjunction in this case serves to conjoin stanzas A and B, which are topically quite distinct. The "truth/fidelity" of Yahweh also contrasts with "vain uselessness" of idols (6.1).

[f] The paired jussive verbs of this colon (7.1) underscore the psalmist's trustful determination and optimistic outlook.

[g] The psalmist's trust is based on an immanent God who is near enough to "see" and "know" his plight; thus, he could "rejoice"—"in anticipation of God's act of deliverance" (VanGemeren 1994:832). The initial relative pronoun (אֲשֶׁר)

technically placed the subsequent parallel cola (7.2–3) into a syntactically dependent position, but by being directly associated with God's "steadfast faithfulness" (בְּחַסְדֶּךָ) they are at the same time thematically highlighted.

[h] The contrastive metonymic senses of "hand," i.e., "protection" (5.1) and "power" (8.1) help mark the close of the first two stanzas (structural epiphora).

[i] "My feet" stands in contrast with the "hand of the enemies," for the psalmist has been made to stand [strong] by Yahweh "in a broad [safe] place" (בַמֶּרְחָב)—constituent focus.

Cᵃ					
9.1			יְהוָה[b] O-Yahweh	חָנֵּנִי mercy-me	
			צַר־לִי[c] distress = to-me		כִּי for
9.2	עֵינִי my-eye	בְּכַעַס with-vexation	עָשְׁשָׁה[d] it-grows-weak		
9.3	וּבִטְנִי and-my-stomach	נַפְשִׁי my-life	-------- 		
10.1	חַיַּי my-lives	בְיָגוֹן in-sorrow	כָלוּ they-come-to-an-end		כִּי for
10.2	בַּאֲנָחָה in-groaning	וּשְׁנוֹתַי and-my-years	[e]_____		
10.3	כֹּחִי[f] my-strength	בַּעֲוֹנִי[g] in-my-guilt	כָּשַׁל it-fails		
10.4			עָשֵׁשׁוּ they-grow-weak		וַעֲצָמַי[h] and-my-bones
11.1		חֶרְפָּה a-disgrace	הָיִיתִי I-became	צֹרְרַי[i] my-foes	מִכָּל־ from-all =
11.2			------- 	מְאֹד[j] very-much	וְלִשְׁכֵנַי ׀ and/even-to-my-neighbors
11.3		לִמְיֻדָּעַי to-those-who-know-me	[k]_____		וּפַחַד and-dread

11.4		מִמֶּנִּי	נָדְדוּ	ᶫבַּחוּץ	רֹאַי
		from-me	they-flee	in-the-street	the-ones-seeing-me
12.1	ᵐמִלֵּב	כְּמֵת	נִשְׁכַּחְתִּי		
	from-heart	like-a-dead-person	I-became-forgotten		
12.2	אֹבֵד	כִּכְלִי	הָיִיתִי		
	being-broken	like-pottery	I-became		
13.1	²רַבִּים	דִּבַּת	שָׁמַעְתִּי |		ⁿכִּי
	many-people	report-of	I-heard		for
13.2	ᵒמִסָּבִיב	מָגוֹר	-------		
	all-around	terror			
13.3	עָלַי	יַחַד	בְּהִוָּסְדָם		
	against-me	together	in-their-conspiring		
13.4			זָמְמוּ	ᵖנַפְשִׁי	לָקַחַת
			they-plot	my-life	to-take

ᵃ This single initial call for help dominates stanza C (two strophes—vv. 9–10 and 11–13), the remainder of which details the various afflictions caused by the psalmist's enemies. "Verses 9–13 continue to provide reasons why the psalmist petitions the Lord. Unlike the other reasons given, all of which have to do with trust in God, this section is a personal lament.... From a statement of serene confidence and trust (verses 7 *[add v. 6]*–8), the psalmist now turns to a description of his pitiable condition and an urgent plea for Yahweh to save him" (Bratcher and Reyburn 1991:294; cf. Craigie 1983:261).

ᵇ There is no other reference to Yahweh in this stanza after the initial appeal; the psalmist fully focuses on the dangerous and distressful situation that existed between him (I/me) and his enemies (צֹרְרָי), 11.1. The preceding verb "be merciful to me" (חָנֵּנִי) is common stock in lament psalms (e.g., 6:9, 30:10, 51:1, 56:1, 123:3).

ᶜ The second prayer-cycle of Psalm 31 begins with a plea (9.1), as in v. 1. The confined and constrained "narrowness" implied in the noun צָרָה (cf. its plural form in 7.3) contrasts with being set in the "wide places" (בַּמֶּרְחָב) of the preceding colon (8.2). The extra-long colon here underscores the psalmist's plight.

ᵈ "*Heb* 'my breath and my stomach [grow weak]'. The Hebrew term נפש can mean 'life', or, more specifically, 'throat, breath'. The psalmist seems to be lamenting that his breathing is impaired because of the physical and emotional suffering he is forced to endure" (NET note). His whole being—body and soul—has been affected (VanGemeren 1994:832); cf. vv. 5.1, 7.3. The coupling of נֶפֶשׁ and בֶּטֶן occurs also in Psalm 44:25[26], seemingly also with the sense of "soul" and "body" (cf. BDB), although normally the latter refers to the "insides" (17:14), and especially the "womb" (22:9–10; Goldingay 2006:442).

[e] In 10.2 the verb of the preceding colon (כָלוּ) is interpreted to apply here too: "and my years [are consumed] by groaning" (an instance of affective hyperbole).
[f] A vivid personification: "My strength stumbles in [on account of] my sin-guilt."
[g] "My iniquity" (deClaissé-Walford et al. 2014:302). Certain ancient versions read בַּעֲנִי 'in my affliction/distress/trouble', which is followed by many modern translations, e.g., GNT; this is supported by Craigie (1983:258); Goldingay suggests "weakness" (2006:443). According to Harman, "the Hebrew word *'avon* can carry ideas both of a misdeed ['guilt'] and its punishment ['affliction']" (2011a:268; cf. also VanGemeren 1991:267), which would be a significant play on these two senses.
[h] Perhaps in summary of the poet's dire circumstances, the object (וַעֲצָמַי) is front-shifted (climactic focus).
[i] Here is another instance of topic focus as the psalmist's "enemies" are placed into the discourse spotlight.
[j] "*Heb* 'and to my neighbors, exceedingly'. If the MT is retained, then these words probably go with what precedes [i.e., with הָיִיתִי חֶרְפָּה implied from the preceding colon—EW]. However the syntactical awkwardness of the text suggests it is textually corrupt. P. C. Craigie (Ps. 1–50 [WBC], 258) proposes that the initial *mem* (מ) on מְאֹד (*me'od* 'exceedingly') be understood as an enclitic *mem* (ם) which was originally suffixed to the preceding form and then later misinterpreted. The resulting form אֵד (*'ed*) can then be taken as a defectively written form of אֵיד (*'ed* 'calamity'). If one follows this emendation, then the text reads literally, 'and to my neighbors [I am one who experiences] calamity'. The noun פַּחַד (*fakhad,* '[object of] horror') occurs in the next line; אֵיד and פַּחַד appear in parallelism elsewhere (see Pr 1:26–27)" (NET note). The MT could be understood and rendered as "I am insulted (or: 'looked on with contempt') by all my adversaries, even more so by my neighbors" (cf. TOB, GNT; deClaissé-Walford et al. 2014:302). With reference to the many proposed emendations (cf. VanGemeren 1991:267), Harman argues that "the uniformity of the MT reading suggests that alteration of the text is not an option" (2011a:269).
[k] The verb הָיִיתִי from 11.1 (cf. 12.2) seems to be implied here: '[I am/have become] a dread (or "dreadful") to my friends'. The *athnah* in the following line (11.4) appears to be misplaced—undoubtedly due to the difficulty that one encounters in construing this verse.
[l] The psalmist's predicament is rhetorically heightened by constituent focus (רֹאַי בַּחוּץ) and by the bookend pronominal suffixes referring to himself ('my...').
[m] "*Heb* 'I am forgotten, like a dead man, from [the] heart'. The 'heart' is here viewed as the center of one's thoughts" (NET note; Craigie 1983:258). "I am forgotten by them as though I were dead" (NIV; cf. VanGemeren 1991:267, deClaissé-Walford et al. 2014:302). Goldingay renders: "I am disregarded like a dead person—out of [their] mind," with כְּמֵת and מִלֵב being in apposition (2006:444).
[n] This final כִּי (cf. 9.1, 10.1) may be a marker of climax in this stanza ('Yes indeed...'): the psalmist's series of complaints appears to culminate in this verse. The following verb too may be significant: The previous complaints might be regarded as a figment of the psalmist's paranoia; but here he gives evidence that he has "heard" (שָׁמַעְתִּי).
[o] "In line *b terror on every side!* may be taken as what the *many* of line *a* are *whispering;* so, in different ways.... Or else it may be the psalmist's own perception of his situation: he is surrounded by frightful enemies, who fill him with dread. The expression [perhaps 'a common saying, or cliché' (Craigie 1983:261;

Goldingay 2006:445)] occurs frequently in Jeremiah (as in Jer 20.3,10 [cf. also 6:25, 46:5, 49:29; Lam. 2:22]). Lines *c* and *d* are parallel and nearly synonymous; line *d* makes clear what his enemies are planning to do, that is, to kill him" (Bratcher and Reyburn 1991:296). McCann lists the correspondences between Psalm 31:10–13 and Jer. 20 (1996:801).

[p] Note the contrasting setting involved in the use of this term in v. 7.3.

D[a]					
14.1		יְהוָה	בָטַחְתִּי	עָלֶיךָ [b]	וַאֲנִי |
		O-Yahweh	I-trust	upon-you	and-I
14.2	אַתָּה	אֱלֹהַי	אָמַרְתִּי		
	you	My-God	I-said		
15.1		עִתֹּתַי	-------		בְּיָדְךָ
		my-times			in-your-hand
15.2	וּמֵרֹדְפָי	מִיַּד־אֹיְבַי [c]	הַצִּילֵנִי		
	and-from-those-pursuing-me	from-hand-of = my-enemies	deliver-me		
16.1	עַל־עַבְדֶּךָ	פָּנֶיךָ [d]	הָאִירָה		
	upon = your-servant	your-face	make-shine		
16.2		בְּחַסְדֶּךָ [e]	הוֹשִׁיעֵנִי		
		in-your-faithful-love	save-me		
17.1			אֵבוֹשָׁה [f]	אַל־	יְהוָה
			let-me-be-shamed	not =	O-Yahweh
17.2			קְרָאתִיךָ		כִּי
			I-cried-out-to-you		for
17.3		רְשָׁעִים	יֵבֹשׁוּ		
		wicked-ones	let-them-be-shamed		
17.4		לִשְׁאוֹל	יִדְּמוּ [g]		
		in-Sheol	let-them-wail		
18.1	שָׁקֶר	שִׂפְתֵי	תֵּאָלַמְנָה		
	lie	lips-of	let-them-be-silenced		

18.2	עָתָק	עַל־צַדִּיק	הַדֹּבְרוֹת		
	arrogance	against = righteous-one	the-ones-speaking		
18.3	וָבוּז	בְּגַאֲוָה	h_____		
	and-contempt	in-pride			

[a] In another stanza consisting of two shorter strophes (vv. 14–16, 17–18), the psalmist reiterates his confidence in the LORD and repeats his calls for deliverance coupled with retribution upon his enemies. These expressions of trust and prayer parallel those heard earlier in stanzas A and B; compare on trust (6.2/14.1)—prayer (1.2/17.1). I have divided this stanza formally into two smaller strophes of similar pragmatic (appellant) content at v. 17, as marked by the initial divine vocatives (יְהֹוָה) in vv. 14 and 17 (structural anaphora). VanGemeren provides a listing of the various lexical elements of vv. 14–18 that have already been introduced in the psalm (1991:268).

Verse 14 + 15.1 is arguably the central thematic assertion of this psalm, being marked by key terms (two divine names), rhyming central verbs, and a pronominal inclusio—beginning with the juxtaposed "I—on you" and ending with "you" (the God in whom "I," the psalmist, "trust"). The first (verbless) colon of v. 15 continues this threefold confession of confidence, with a reversal in pronominal reference: "in *your* hand [are] *my* times" ("You determine my destiny"). This strophe ends with an appeal based on Yahweh's "covenantal love" (חַסְדֶּךָ) in 16.2.

[b] Here is another example of a contrastive front-shift ("and/but-I") that is strategically coupled with constituent focus ("on-you")—once again linking the psalmist with the God in whom he trusts (cf. 6.2). Note how this covenantal relationship his emphasized by pronominal placement, with וַאֲנִי at the beginning and אַתָּה at the end.

[c] Contrastive pronominal references form the foundation of the psalmist's prayer: I am "in [your] hand" (בְּיָד)—deliver me "from [their] hand" (מִיַּד)!

[d] "The plea in verse 16a, *let thy face shine,* is similar to the expression in 4:6, which is used also in 67:1; 80:3, 7, 19; 119:135 [cf. Num. 6:25]; it means to look on someone with favor, mercy, kindness" (Bratcher and Reyburn 1991:297).

[e] The psalmist's request "is doubly based on the covenant: he is the LORD's servant *('avdekâ),* and he pleads on the basis of the LORD's unfailing covenant love *(chasdekâ)*" (Harman 2011a:271).

[f] An emphatic contrast in the psalmist's plea to Yahweh (vocative) marks the onset of the second strophe in stanza D (vv. 17–18): "let me not be put to shame" (אֵבוֹשָׁה)—but instead, "let them be shamed" (יֵבֹשׁוּ)!

[g] "The verb יִדְּמוּ (yiddymu) is understood as a form of דָּמַם (damam, 'wail, lament'). Another option is to take the verb from דָּמַם ('be quiet'; see BDB 198–99 s.v. I דָּמַם), in which case one might translate, 'May they lie silent in the grave'" (NET note). The notion of "silence" is continued by the verb in 18.1.

[h] The preceding participle from 18.2 (הַדֹּבְרוֹת) is assumed to function here implicitly, also as a verbal. Thus, each successive line in this stanza/strophe-concluding tricolon qualifies the preceding one. "In addition to recalling the petition with which the psalm began (see v. 1), vv. 17–18 juxtapose the contrasting

alternatives that are present in Psalm 1 and throughout the Psalter: 'the wicked' (v. 17) and 'the righteous' (v. 18)" (McCann 1996:802).

E[a]					
19.1			b_____	טוּבְךָ֨	מָה רַב־
				your-goodness	how much =
19.2		לִירֵאֶ֗יךָ	צָפַ֣נְתָּ		אֲשֶׁר־
		for-those-fearing-you	you-have-stored-up		which =
19.3	בָּ֑ךְ	לַחֹסִ֣ים	פָּ֭עַלְתָּ		
	in-you	for-those-taking-refuge	you-have-accomplished		
19.4	בְּנֵ֥י אָדָֽם	נֶ֝֗גֶד	d_____		
	sons-of humanity	before			
20.1	מֵֽרֻכְסֵ֫י אִ֥ישׁ	בְּסֵ֥תֶר פָּנֶ֗יךָ	תַּסְתִּירֵ֨ם ׀		
	from-plots-of man	in-shelter-of your-face	you-hide-them		
20.2	מֵרִ֥יב לְשֹׁנֽוֹת	בְּסֻכָּ֑ה	תִּצְפְּנֵ֥ם		
	from-strife-of tongues	in-a-booth	you-shelter-them		

[a] As in the case of stanza B, a shorter unit expressing trust in Yahweh (E) follows his fervent appeals for help (D). The NET notes: "The psalmist confidently asks the Lord to protect him. Enemies threaten him and even his friends have abandoned him, but he looks to the Lord for vindication. In vv. 19–24, which were apparently written after the Lord answered the prayer of vv. 1–18, the psalmist thanks the Lord for delivering him." However, it is not necessary to conclude that this final section was composed at a later date. This is a common feature of Hebrew lament prayers: the psalmist in confident trust anticipates the LORD's deliverance even before it happens, e.g., Psalm 22:22–31; 73:13–28.

[b] A verbless exclamation of praise initiates this new stanza (E), which is followed by a dependent bicolon of explanation, in which the second, parallel line is led off by an implicit אֲשֶׁר־. The "goodness" *(tub/tob)* being referred to here is covenantal in nature, based on the "faithful love" *(chesed)* of YHWH (cf. v. 22.2), and manifested (lit. 'worked'—implicit from 19.3) "before [in the sight of] the sons of mankind," i.e., the ungodly, as in Psalm 23:5–6.

[c] Literally, 'you work [your favor] for the ones seeking shelter in you before humanity'. "'Taking shelter" in the LORD is an idiom for seeking his protection. Seeking his protection presupposes and even demonstrates the subject's loyalty to the LORD. In the psalms those who 'take shelter' in the LORD are contrasted

with the wicked and equated with those who love, fear, and serve the LORD (Ps. 2:12; Ps. 5:11–12; Ps. 34:21–22)' (NET note).

ᵈ The exclamation of 19.1 ("How great [is] your goodness") seems to be applied here in 19.4 as well, to form a structural inclusio.

ᵉ "The noun רֹכֶס (rokhes) occurs only here. Its meaning is debated; some suggest 'snare', while others propose 'slander' or 'conspiracy' " (NET). Note that the reference to Yahweh's silencing the psalmist's enemies (20.4) corresponds to his appeal at the close of the preceding stanza (v. 18), an instance of structural epiphora (similar unit endings).

ᶠ "In line *a* the Hebrew is 'you hide them in the hiding place of your face'—the word 'face' here meaning, as often, 'presence'. For the same sentiment, expressed in similar language, see 27.5" (Bratcher and Reyburn 1991:298). The two lines of v. 20 are closely parallel in structure and longer than the norm, perhaps to signal stanzaic closure.

ᵍ "Just as God 'stores up' love for his people (v. 19), so he stores them up (using the same Hebrew verb) in a secure place, and so protects them against the slander of men" (Harman 2011a:272). This repeated verb (צפן) in its complex figurative senses in these verses (vv. 19–20) also serves as an inclusio for the strophe. "The author uses verbs expressing the 'hidden' but full enjoyment of God's benefits by repeating the roots ts-p-n ('hide', 'store') and s-t-r ('hide', 'shelter' [20.1]) in an inclusionary way" (VanGemeren 1991:269)—thus formally reflecting their content.

Fᵃ				
21.1		יְהוָהᵇ	בָּרוּךְ	
		Yahweh	be-praised	
21.2	לִּי	חַסְדּוֹ	הִפְלִיאᶜ	כִּי
	to-me	his-loyal-love	he-showed-wonderfully	for
21.3	מָצוֹר	בְּעִיר	ᵈ_____	
	siege	in-a-city-of		
22.1		בְחָפְזִיᵉ	אָמַרְתִּי	וַאֲנִיᶠ
		in-my-haste	I-spoke	and-I
22.2	עֵינֶיךָ	מִנֶּגֶד	נִגְרַזְתִּי Iᵍ	
	your-eyes	from-before	I-have-been-cut-off	
22.3	תַּחֲנוּנַי	קוֹל	שָׁמַעְתָּ	אָכֵןʰ
	my-cry-for-mercy	voice-of	you-heard	however
22.4		אֵלֶיךָ	בְּשַׁוְּעִי	
		unto-you	in-my-appealing-for-aid	

[a] A short stanza of thanksgiving (F) expresses the psalmist's gratitude to Yahweh for answering his prayer for help, which is quoted in v. 22.2–4. Craigie lists some of the strong parallels between the psalmist's expressions of thanksgiving/praise in vv. 19–24 and his prior appeals/laments: 19 (1), 20 (16), 21 (16), 22 (2), 23 (6). "In summary, the thanksgiving is directly rooted in answered prayer, or the anticipation of answered prayer, rather than being a general statement of praise" (1983:262). "Thus the psalmist both celebrates deliverance as already having occurred (vv. 5b, 7–8, 21–22) and continues to pray for it (vv. 1b–2, 3b–4a, 9–13, 15b–18). This tension is the persistent reality of the life of faith" (McCann 1996:802). Already, but not yet—and therefore the psalmist's concluding timeless exhortation to all the LORD's "faithful saints" (vv. 23–24).

[b] Yahweh, the covenantal King, should be "praised" whether he has already come to the psalmist's aid (e.g., Ps. 18:46), or whether he is expected, in faith, to do so (e.g., here and in Ps. 28:6). "The expression 'praise' or 'blessed' often comes at the beginning or at the end of a psalm of thanksgiving (cf. 28:6; 66:20; 144:1)" (Harman 2011a:272)—or, as here in Psalm 31, incorporated as the climactic close of a psalm of lament/petition.

[c] Either "he showed in a wonderful way his love to me" or "he showed his wonderful love to me."

[d] The verb "to be" or one of location may be implied here: "[when I was] in a besieged city." "The psalmist probably speaks figuratively here. He compares his crisis to being trapped in a besieged city, but the LORD answered his prayer for help" (NET note; for proposed emendations of 21.3, see VanGemeren 1991:270).

[e] "The psalmist questions his frailty in having questioned God by despairing in his 'alarm' " (VanGemeren 1991:832). His weakness contrasted with the LORD's "steadfast faithfulness" (חַסְדּוֹ) in 21.2.

[f] Another sharply contrastive, emotively toned "but I…" (cf. 6.2, 14.1).

[g] "In verse 22b *I am driven far* translates a Hebrew verb *(garash)* found in two manuscripts (see also Jonah 2.5); the Masoretic text has the verb *garaz*, 'be exterminated', while other Hebrew manuscripts have the verb *gazar,* meaning 'cut, slaughter'. The sense 'to be driven out' seems to fit the context better than 'be slaughtered'. 'To be cut off', meaning 'to be separated', also fits the context. HOTTP says the Masoretic text means 'I found myself left unprovided for' " (Bratcher and Reyburn 1991:300; cf. Craigie 1983:258; Goldingay 2006:448).

[h] A dramatic particle of contra-expectation (אָכֵן) that highlights the psalmist's present dilemma (עֵינֶיךָ) (22.1–2) and his projected deliverance by Yahweh (אֵלֶיךָ) (22.3–4; cf. Pss. 6:8–9, 22:24, 28:6)—again highlighted by corresponding pronominal references ("you" masc. sg.) to disparate situations.

G[a]				
23.1	כָּל־חֲסִידָיו	אֶת־יְהוָה	[b]אֶהֱבוּ	
	all = his-loyal-ones	DO = Yahweh	love	
23.2		יְהוָה	[c]נֹצֵר	[d]אֱמוּנִים
		Yahweh	[is]-keeping	faithful-ones

23.3	עֹשֵׂה גַאֲוָה	עַל־יֶֽתֶר	[e]וּמְשַׁלֵּם		
	doers-of ar-rogance	unto = excess	and-paying-back		
24.1		לְבַבְכֶם	[f]חִזְקוּ וְיַאֲמֵץ		
		your-heart	be-strong and-may-it-be-courageous		
24.2		לַיהוָה	[g]הַֽמְיַחֲלִים		כָּל־
		for-Yahweh	those-awaiting		all =

[a] A final brief stanza (G) calls upon the entire worship community to put their trust in, and remain faithful to the LORD, who always keeps his covenant promises. The sudden shift in address from Yahweh to those who worship him marks this transition. "A 'faithful follower' (חָסִיד, *khasid*) is one who does what is right in God's eyes and remains faithful to God (see Ps. 4:3; Ps. 12:1; Ps. 16:10; Ps. 31:23; Ps. 37:28; Ps. 86:2; Ps. 97:10)" (NET note; "dedicated people"— Goldingay 2006:449).

[b] "The command **Love the LORD** in the Bible refers not so much to the emotion as to the willingness and desire to be faithful to him, to obey him, and to do what he commands" (Bratcher and Reyburn 1991:300).

[c] "The participial forms in the second and third lines characterize the Lord as one who typically protects the faithful and judges the proud" (NET note).

[d] Here is a significant juxtaposition of two crucial covenantal terms—חֲסִידָיו and אֱמוּנִים (23.1–2). "These two words are related to the two fundamental attributes of God celebrated in Psalm 31: steadfast love (vv. 7, 16, 21; 'saints'... *chasîdîm* could be translated 'steadfastly loving ones' or 'steadfastly loved ones') and faithfulness (v. 5). In short, the people of God derive their identity from God's identity..." (McCann 1996:802; VanGemeren 1991:269).

[e] A contrastive chiastic construction may be significant here: object + verbal + subject *(YHWH)* // verbal + [adverb] + object, with the intrusive adverbial phrase (עַל־יֶֽתֶר) highlighting the punishment of the wicked.

[f] The synonymous verbs calling for "strength" of mind and character and attitude naturally underscore the exhortation here—but, as always, "Yahweh is the key to strength and courage of heart" (Goldingay 2006:449). אֱמוּנִים could be rendered "his faithful people" on the basis of "the double-duty suffix" (VanGemeren 1991:270).

[g] Again, the participle here may be construed with an emphasis on its verbal predicative aspect, with concluding end stress upon the psalm's central divine agent (לַיהוָה)!

3.7.3 A structural-thematic summary of Psalm 31

In conjunction with the structure-functional analysis outlined earlier along with the preceding textual display, it is possible to discern some of the main areas of increased expressive (speaker focus) and/or affective (addressee focus) significance within the text of Psalm 31. In addition, several major breakpoints or shifts in thematic emphasis have been noted—namely, at verses 6, 9, 14,

19, 21, and 23 (following the versification of English Bibles). These primary junctures correspond with what have been posited as the psalm's principal structural (stanza-strophe) divisions, as shown in the following outline:

Theme: Commit yourself into the hands of the merciful LORD for refuge from all your enemies!

Cycle One: vv. 1–8
  Stanza 1 (A)—*Petition* (1–5): Deliver me from my enemies (1–2), YHWH, for I trust you (3–5)!
  Stanza 2 (B)—*Profession* [trust] (6–8): The LORD has (already) delivered me from my enemies.

Cycle Two: vv. 9–24
  Stanza 1 (C)—*Lament* (9–13): I am near death (9–10) and surrounded by enemies (11–13).
  Stanza 2 (D)—*Petition* (14–18): Deliver me from my foes and punish them (2x: 14–16, 17–18).
    (E)—*Praise* (19–20): The LORD keeps his people safe.
  Stanza 3 (F)—*Praise, individual* (21–22): YHWH helped me when I was in trouble.
    (G)—*Trust, communal* (23–24): You saints, hope in the LORD, for he will preserve you!

The preceding analysis with respect to the parameter of segmentation was carried out primarily with respect to the psalm's main topical and illocutionary shifts, coupled with features such as the presence of a vocative invoking the divine name, to indicate points of unit aperture, e.g., v. 9.

Note that subdivisions within the stanzas could be designated as internal strophes, e.g., vv. 1–2, 3–5, 9–10, 11–13, 14–16, and 17–18). In my studies, it is rather rare for a stanza unit to go much beyond three verses with respect to form (cohesion), content (coherence), and/or function (communicative goal). Instead, it is usually possible to find a smaller unit—a poetic paragraph (strophe); for example, it is advisable to divide stanza 1 (A) into two sections at v. 3.[27] I recognize that the structure of Psalm 31 is rather more complex than most, but it is certainly not all that exceptional

---

[27] The value of distinguishing these poetic units is not recognized by many commentaries (e.g., Craigie 1983:259) and versions (NIV). One reason for not positing two strophes within stanza A is the common content (e.g., fortress imagery) in vv. 2–3, although this could be interpreted as a case of structural anadiplosis across a (minor) discourse boundary (for a summary description of the main compositional markers, based on repetition, see Wendland 2004:126–128). An argument for a strophic division here is the shift in prevailing verb forms from imperatives (vv. 1–2) to imperfects (vv. 3–5).

for a longer psalm (cf. Ps. 22). McCann suggests that perhaps the alternation of petition, profession (faith), and praise are "an appropriate representation of the psalmist's chaotic life" or "the severity of the psalmist's plight" (1996:799), but in fact, the composer's formidable faith-foundation is foregrounded throughout. The articulation of this psalm in two cycles, with the second expanding upon and intensifying the first, is analogous to typical A—B lineal parallelism, in which the second colon frequently highlights and dynamically develops the first (Bratcher and Reyburn 1991:5–6).

Goldingay is in general support of the preceding bifid structural outline and comments (2006:436–437) as follows:

> Verses 1–8 thus constitute a prayer that could be complete in itself.... Verses 9–24 then go through this sequence again, though with a different profile.... [There is a] parallel with other psalms that go through their "story" twice, not least the immediately preceding one, Ps. 30 (cf. also, e.g., Pss. 42–43, which does that three times; also praise psalms such as Pss. 95 and 100). This suggests that repetition of this kind may simply be part of the rhetoric of prayer. It is natural to go through the "story" more than once.[28]

In his commentary Goldingay makes several larger divisions, i.e., vv. 1–5a, 5b–8, 9–13, 14–20, 21–24, which would correspond with my own, except for the first.[29] Several other discourse arrangements that have been proposed by scholars will be evaluated below.

As far as the compositional principle of connectivity is concerned, unit-internal cohesion is developed largely through referential chains, both positive and negative in connotation. For example, we have the laudatory depictions of Yahweh as a "rock...refuge...fortress" in the first stanza (vv. 1–5) in contrast to the psalmist's plaintive expressions of physical anguish and personal affliction in the opening stanza of cycle II (vv. 9–13). In addition, a number of key terms expressing the principal theme of Psalm 31 appear throughout the text in both cycles: "seek refuge" (1, 19); "be ashamed" (1, 17); "rescue" (2, 15); "deliver" (2, 16); "your hand" (5, 8, 15); "trust" (6, 14); and "mercy" (7, 16, 21). The last-mentioned is of special interest

---

[28] Harman agrees with this twofold division: "This individual lament falls into two parts (vv. 1–8, 9–24) that are more or less parallel, though the second part is more expansive. In both parts the steadfast love of the LORD sustains the psalmist (see vv. 7 and 16)" (2011a:265).

[29] Verse 5.2/5b seems to be clearly associated more with the previous content (vv. 1–5.1/5a), rather than with what follows (vv. 6–8). Furthermore, it may be argued that the expressions "in *you*, O Yahweh, I took refuge" (1.1) and "you redeemed *me*, O Yahweh" (5.2) function as an inclusio for this opening stanza (A). Similarly, stanza C may divide into two strophes on the basis of (a) content: vv. 9–10 deal with the psalmist's internal bodily distress, while vv. 11–13 focus on his external "enemies;" (b) form: an initial inclusio formed by the verb "grow weak" (עֵשֵׁשׁ) in vv. 9.2/10.4.

and importance, חֶסֶד, which denotes a semantic complex that cannot be expressed adequately in English by a single term: "unmitigated mercy," "unfailing faithfulness," "loving loyalty," "continued covenantal commitment." This concept (anthropomorphically) represents the central motivating force behind Yahweh's deliverance of all those who commit themselves in faith to live according to the basic precepts of his gracious covenant. With respect to worship then, "the supreme fact that formed the basis of every liturgical celebration in Israel was the unchanging faithfulness of Yahweh" (Driyvers 1965:42).

Thus, "fidelity" (חֶסֶד), often co-occurring with "truth" (אֱמֶת, v. 5), entails both a socioreligious philosophy, or worldview, as well as a theological orientation and a closely associated code of conduct for the people of God. This mutual interrelationship may be summarized as follows (Bellinger 1984:61):

> [Yahweh] is faithful to his promise to deliver, which means that his commitment to his people does not change as circumstances do...(Ps. 31:6).... This in turn calls for faithfulness from the people in response to this renewed demonstration of Yahweh's hesed to them (31:24...).

The twofold focus of this covenantal relationship (as ideally realized, and faithfully proclaimed by psalmist and prophet alike) may be depicted as follows with reference to its primary expression in Psalm 31:

Yahweh provides	*the covenantal motivation*	*The faithful respond in*
Defense (e.g., 1–5)		Love (23)
Deliverance (15–16,21–22)		Trust (14)
Vindication (17–18)		Joy (7)

This nucleus of focal thematic concepts is articulated progressively as the psalm unfolds. It thus provides yet another testimony to the work's artistic and structural integrity—an overall unity of form, content, function, and ultimately also message. This literary accord needs to be conveyed correspondingly in any translated rendition, oral or written, whether individually or communally expressed and apprehended. From a broader perspective, the crucial covenantal components of חֶסֶד, namely, steadfastness, reliability, constancy, mercy, and so forth, act as the cognitive foundation for the various expressions of certainty and anticipated fulfillment with regard to Yahweh's actions that characterize the lament genre as a whole.

3.7.4 The dilemma of competing discourse designs

One final, more scholarly application of a literary-structural analysis, such as that carried out above, is to provide a means of evaluating other, often competing suggestions in Bible versions and commentaries for demarcating a certain text of Scripture into its constituent parts. Readers are often frustrated or perplexed by the many conflicting proposals that are offered as a compositional outline, reference chart, or theological summary of a given book, portion, or pericope. The discourse outlines of Gerstenberger (1988) and Bratcher and Reyburn (1991) were briefly considered above, but in this section we want to discuss this potential problem in somewhat more detail. In cases where such text structures vary or disagree, how can a student (serious reader) know which scheme is the best? What difference does it make? That is what we hope to demonstrate by examining three additional proposals from commentators for displaying the structural organization of Psalm 31. In each case readers can compare the suggested outline with the original Hebrew text and my exposition above, evaluate the methodology presented and the evidence or arguments given, and then come to their own conclusion.

To begin with, Terrien indicates a strophic division for Psalm 31 that closely matches my structural description; however, he sees a tripartite division within the text rather than a twofold, recycled arrangement (2003:284–286):

I.   My Rock and my Fortress: vv. 1–2, 3–5, 6–8;
II. I am in distress: vv. 9–10, 11–13, 14–18;[30]
III. Love the LORD, all ye his saints: vv. 19–20, 21–22, 23–24.

I would also regard the structure of Psalm 31 to be much more competently composed than consisting of "an anthology of various fragments and confessions," which originally existed in the form of "three psalms of distinct origins" (Terrien 2003:287). Rather: "Psalm 31 is the model of prayer that is confident of being heard—not because the suppliant has such great faith, but because of the One the suppliant trusts in—it is an example of a prayer that needs to be prayed twice" (Goldingay 2006:450), as the consummate poetic structure itself would indicate. The practical faith-implications of this psalm are also most significant: "God's [covenantal] faithfulness and love enable and empower the existence of a people [in essence, a community of faith] who in turn can be faithful and loving to God and to each other" (McCann 1996:803).

Second, VanGemeren comes to the conclusion, as I did, that "the psalm falls into two parts" (1991:263), but his principal divisions, vv. 1–18 and 19–24, are very different. In fact, his proposal seems to be a mirror-image

---

[30] This unit could be divided into two strophes, vv. 14–16, 17–18, based on the initial divine vocatives (YHWH) (structural anaphora)—the first being a profession of trust (14.1), the second a prayer for help (17.1).

of my own in terms of its larger structure, with his smaller "half" occurring second, instead of first:

I.   Prayer (vv. 1–18)
    A   Prayer for Yahweh's Righteousness (vv. 1–5)
       B   Expression of Trust (vv. 6–8)
    A′ Prayer for Yahweh's Favor (vv. 9–13)
       B′ Expression of Trust (vv. 14–18)
II. Thanksgiving (vv. 19–24)

It would appear from the preceding that the formal and functional correspondences between vv. 1–8 and 9–24 have been overlooked in favor of a more logically ordered format. However, there are several problems with this outline. First, the first subtitle "Prayer for Yahweh's Righteousness" (A) is ambiguous. It is also misleading in that Yahweh as a *source* of "refuge" is in focus here. Similarly, the theme suggested for A′ is off the mark since the emphasis of this segment (stanza) is upon the multifaceted affliction being experienced by the psalmist and his lament over this fact. Furthermore, it is debatable to posit the ultimate expression of "Thanksgiving" (II) as beginning at v. 19 rather than at v. 21. It would seem that vv. 19–20 are more an "Expression of Trust" (i.e., still part of B′) than hymnic words of grateful praise. The latter motivation is certainly involved, but with clearly lesser functional priority.

Finally, Craigie's analysis (1983:259) presents several difficulties from a structural perspective. He presents a chiastic framework—logically neat, but not so easy to substantiate on the basis of the Hebrew text:

I.   *Prayer*
    (1) prayer [1–5]   A
    (2) trust [6–8]   B
    (3) lament [9–13]   C
    (4) trust [14]   B′
    (5) prayer [15–18]   A′
         (declaration of oracle between v. 18 and v. 19)
II. *Thanksgiving and Praise* [19–24]

Thus, what I have proposed as the psalm's principal division between v. 8 and v. 9 is not recognized, and as a result undue emphasis is placed upon the final thanksgiving portion, which, as was suggested above, does not begin in v. 19, but rather at v. 21.[31] This section is

---

[31] From a form-critical perspective, Craigie justifies this division as follows: "The transition from v 19 [18] to v 20 [19] appears to presuppose some cultic act, such

thereby detached, as a constituent element, from the lament, which is the psalm's main illocutionary function. Moreover, as was pointed out earlier, the structural components of this lament alternate and inter-act with one another in a much more intricate fashion. As our earlier analysis has shown, expressions of trust permeate the poem and cannot be restricted to vv. 6–8 and 14. The utterance "my times are in your hand" (15a), to be specific, surely conveys as much trust as the words of v. 14, and yet Craigie classifies it as a prayer—along with impreca-tions such as "let the wicked...lie silent in the grave" (17).[32] It is also difficult to see how the final verse of the psalm, "Be strong and take heart, all you who hope in the LORD" (NIV), can be regarded as an in-stance of "thanksgiving and praise." This is obviously a typical lament-concluding communal exhortation to the congregation of believers to celebrate Yahweh's mighty deliverance—whether that of the formerly suffering psalmist in this text or that of the afflicted nation as a whole in some earlier day.

The preceding exercise illustrates both the potential as well as some of the pitfalls of typological analysis—informative and helpful, if done well, along original text-determined lines, but potentially deceptive and distorted when done otherwise. Do such posited structures have any objective basis? (They clearly are not part of the biblical text—not in so many words.) Or do these outlines, like proverbial beauty, exist merely in the eyes (imagination) of the beholder (analyst)? It is hoped that this discourse-centered, structure-functional approach, however biased by the imperfect perspective of its pro-ponent, will have marshalled sufficient evidence to demonstrate the former (a justifiable semblance of objectivity), whether or not one happens to agree with all of its conclusions.

3.8 Some practical implications of this study

This study has shown that use of a literary-structural, artistic-rhetorical based set of analytical procedures to coordinate and supplement a traditional form-critical methodology is recommended for more accurate and defensible results. Only within such a wider textual framework can an adequate typological analysis be carried out on both the macro- and microlevels of literary discourse, poetry in particular, which "is meant

---

as the proclamation of a prophetic or priestly word assuring the suppliant that God has heard and will answer his prayer" (1983:259). But no evidence for assuming such an elaborate intervening scenario is given.

[32] One might thus posit for Ps. 31 the following progressively developed alternating structure with a concluding climax: A (1–8) *trusting prayer;* B (9–13) **lament;** A′ (14–20) *trusting prayer;* B′ (21–24) in dramatic contrast to (B), **joyful praise** and an exhortation to always trust in YHWH.

to engage our memories and our imagination and in that transform our relationship with God" (deClaissé-Walford et al. 2014:305). This manifold approach has several advantages: First of all, it is flexible and able to incorporate diverse methods that can complement one another— as long as the dual focus upon form and function remains. It is also inclusive and comprehensive in scope since only a complete composition or pericope is examined, in the original text, a work considered as a whole along with its constituent parts, as a unified discourse organism, as it were. Furthermore, all procedures are pragmatic, or communication-oriented with respect to both the original context (as nearly as this can be ascertained) and also the contemporary cultural-linguistic and socio-religious settings. This also makes the method effective for traversing the hermeneutical gap that challenges a transmission of the initial, author-intended message by means of translation and often transposition via modern visual and oral-aural media.

A structure-functional perspective can provide some new and valuable insights that can enrich the interpretation of certain familiar passages of Scripture. With reference to Psalm 31, for example, this approach highlights the masterful manner in which the psalmist has interwoven the major elements of the lament and eulogy genres into a tightly integrated network of artistic form and emotive expression. This is a dramatic prayer in which the dynamic motivating force of steadfast trust in Yahweh is renewed and reinforced amidst a succession of diverse appeals, complaints, petitions, and imprecations.[33] This functional complex constitutes the alternating progression that keeps the discourse moving forward from beginning to end, unpredictable in its details, but having a certain beneficial outcome, just like life itself—but only for those who "take refuge" in God (vv. 1, 4, 9). Furthermore, the twofold arrangement of the discourse would suggest the familiar principle of parallelism—"A, and what's more, B"—on the macrolevel of

---

[33] As Jill Carattini ("Telling Limitation" *A Slice of Infinity* [blog], September 3, 2014. http://rzim.org/a-slice-of-infinity/telling-limitation. Accessed September 2, 2017) astutely observes with respect to the pivotal thematic contrast of this psalm: "Significantly, the psalmist presents his list of the various monsters that limit and block his way before the God he seeks. 'Be merciful to me, O Lord', writes the psalmist, 'for I am in distress; my eyes grow weak with sorrow, my soul and my body with grief' (Psalm 31:9). Standing before one who is limitless, the psalmist casts limitation in a wholly different light. The writer powerfully concludes, 'But I trust in you, O Lord, I say, "You are my God." My times are in your hands... Let your face shine on your servant; save me in your unfailing love'. Fixed upon trustworthy hands that hold fleeting days, the psalmist recognizes that, like time itself, all that limits and weakens us will also eventually fade—but God's unfailing love will not."

literary composition, with the B constituent being appropriately magni-
fied and intensified both formally and thematically.[34]

Another aim of a literary (artistic-rhetorical) approach, coupled
with a structural discourse analysis, is to convey in another language-
culture as much as possible of the major themes, patterns, empha-
ses, feelings, aims, and so forth of the original Scripture message in a
functionally equivalent way. This objective thus seeks to express the
essential communicative goals of the biblical author in a dynamic and
relevant manner that corresponds to the needs, wishes, and abilities
of a present-day Bible consumer community. The total, faultless com-
munication of any great literary work, let alone the Word of God, in a
completely different life-setting is, admittedly, an impossibility: *tradut-
tore, traditore*—"the translator [is] a traitor," whether s/he realizes it or
not! But it is a legitimate, responsible goal to try and come as close to
the inscribed meaning—now transferred—as linguistic science, biblical
knowledge, cross-cultural studies, new communication strategies, and
modern media transmission techniques will allow.[35]

The limits of the present investigation tend to point in the direction
of some important future research. A detailed computer/database-aided
text-type analysis of the Psalms and other poetic literature is needed to
provide a more linguistically precise functional typology that is oriented
towards the speech acts (illocutions), both apparent and implicit, found in
the Hebrew text. Similar computer-generated information can give more
concrete insights also with respect to the pragmatics of word-order varia-
tions in Hebrew poetry (e.g., Lunn 2006). A cognitive-linguistic approach
(e.g., van Wolde 2009) may be applied to the key terms and concepts of the
psalmic literature to aid in the comparative specification and differentiation
of closely related semantic-thematic sets (e.g., אֱמֶת and חֶסֶד). All of these
studies may be necessarily enriched by updated pragmatic descriptions of
the formal linguistic markers (e.g., conjunctions and other particles) that
are typically associated with certain functional categories of communica-
tion, e.g., invocation, appeal, imprecation, vow, thanksgiving, etc. (e.g., van
der Merwe 2011).

Similar form-function-ideational studies also need to be undertaken in
target/consumer languages all over the world—wherever a meaning-cen-
tered, popular-language Bible translation is envisaged, planned, or actually
in progress. Ideally, the form-critical concern for describing and categoriz-
ing indigenous genres (text-types) in relation to their primary social settings

---

[34] "Psalm 31 seems to conclude at v. 8, only to offer another set of cries for aid that
are more desperate than the first, followed again by [more extensive] declarations
of trust" (deClaissé-Walford et al. 2014:305).

[35] And more than one attempt at a particular text—trying to get it "right"—is inevi-
tably necessary. As one translator put it: " 'Next time I'll have to fail better'. That is
all any of us can do" (Grossman 2010:88).

of use should be completed *before* a translation project gets underway, but even later in the life of a particular rendition is always better than never. Such comparative research would include oral verbal art forms as well as any written literature that has been published in the language (e.g., Wendland 1993). The goal would be to establish accurate emic TL typologies that could provide an abundant inventory of literary-oratorical resources available for potential use as functional equivalents in the translation process. It is hoped that the present study will serve to encourage ("strengthen the hearts"—Ps. 31:24a) all those engaged in this never-ending task of communicating the "wonderful love" of the LORD (חֶסֶד, v. 21a, NIV) to the multitudes seeking "hope" (יחל, v. 24b) today in an often seemingly hopeless world.

4

A Literary-Structural
Analysis of Psalm 22

Introduction

Hebrew poetic discourse—specifically, the precatory texts found in the collection known as the Psalter (the Book of "Praises" תְּהִלּוֹת, cf. Ps. 22:3)—features a layered type of structural organization consisting of several closely related levels. These are all integrated into a hierarchically arranged unit which provides the basic framework for a given poem's content, its major topics and thematic elements in particular, as well as its expression of communicative purpose. In order then to correctly understand and interpret the meaning of a given psalm, one must be prepared to progressively uncover the overlapping strata of structure in order to discern how the different levels are related to one another and to the ideational and emotive core of sense and significance that they convey.

A discourse analysis of this nature (cf. Wendland 2013a) will be concerned, therefore, with the composition of the whole along with its parts—the macro- as well as the microstructure. First of all, this will involve determining the significant units of construction and their manifold interrelationships. One must observe how the various segments are arranged with respect to one another—either paradigmatically (by semantic analogy) and/or syntagmatically (by syntactic association)—in the development of the essential message of the text. Once this crucial task has been satisfactorily accomplished, the analyst will be in a position to provide some insight into the communicative function(s) of the text, which may be investigated in terms of two key questions: What effects did the original author, whether known or posited (the implied author) intend his literary work to achieve in the initial setting of performance,[1] which would normally be oral-aural in nature? Second, how will the sacred poem in translation communicate in a completely new setting of worship involving some contemporary society and a very different socio-cultural milieu?

The main purpose of this chapter is to illustrate a method of systematic text analysis, with special reference to Psalm 22[2] and featuring a literary-structural approach. This seeks to delineate the overall organization of the poetic composition (its macrostructure) in an effort to determine how the Hebrew author shaped his God-addressed message so as to accomplish certain basic worship-oriented objectives, frequently on behalf of the corporate community of faith. Larger constructions, as has been suggested, are verbally built up out of smaller ones, and therefore it is also important to take into consideration the finer aspects of literary creation (the microstructure). The aim is to produce an objective (testable) exposition of the artistic text—that is, via an explicit set of procedures to cogently and clearly account for the linguistic data recorded in the Masoretic Text (realizing of course that every analysis is only partial at best and inevitably perspectival). Due to limitations of space, a complete microstructural study will not be attempted, excluding, for example, a survey of the psalm's full lexical inventory, most of its phonological features (e.g., poetic accents), and many text-critical issues. I will rather concentrate on giving a broad outline of the poetic arrangement of the text in relation to the psalmist's expression of major theological concepts and personal feelings. It is, after all, a powerful, passionate prayer that conveys an initial complaint and pointed appeal that is later coupled with confident affirmation and praise directed to the merciful "LORD/Lord" (אֲדֹנָי/יְהוָה) of all peoples (22:23, 30; all references are to versification of the English text).

Before beginning our discussion, a few general observations are in order. First, the exposition below, in addition to being partial and selective,

---

[1] I recognize that in the case of the Psalms, a positing of authorship and setting of use is very speculative.

[2] Psalm 22 was chosen for this exercise because of its relative familiarity, its moderate length, its literary quality, and its significant theological content. Some scholars would not agree with this choice: "There is something foolhardy about tackling this Psalm. It is long, complex, and puzzling..." (Magonet 1994:101). On the other hand, all critics recognize that there is something most impressive about this poetic prayer: "The whole psalm has something of this grandiose dimension—the powerful animals that attack [the psalmist], the call to all nations to celebrate God's power. There is a world of belief at stake here" (ibid.:102).

exemplifies just one of many possible methodologies and therefore might be helpfully complemented by other analytical approaches to the text. Second, the Masoretic Text (MT) is presumed formally "innocent" until proven "guilty" (i.e., corrupted, nonsensical, requiring emendation) in view of credible, strongly supported variant options (e.g., LXX, DSS). Finally, once an expressive poem, in any language, has been dissected and lies in pieces, as it were, on the printed page of a silent text, a major portion of its literary, that is, its artistic and rhetorical,[3] vitality has been lost. The communicative value of the whole is undoubtedly greater than the sum of its parts, especially when the latter are presented in a completely different language and medium of message transmission. Thus, my study can offer but a limited, cloudy glimpse of the biblical composition—a tangible *soundscape* that can never be fully comprehended or appreciated due to our present distance from its original context (time, culture, religious tradition, ecological environment, and so forth). Any literary (poetic) work must be emotively and sensorially *experienced,* ideally in a similar setting and circumstances, over and above being cognitively understood. To the extent that I am unable to accomplish these fundamental objectives by bridging the gap, the following description will be that much removed from the full meaning of Psalm 22, whether originally intended or that which has been perceived by competent biblical scholars throughout the ages.

4.1 Patterns of continuity and points of discontinuity in a biblical text[4]

The rationale for my method of discourse analysis finds its basis in the original context of generation and usage of the Psalms—and most of the other Old Testament literature as well. This involved a communication context that featured an oral-aural mode of text composition, transmission, and performance. Whether these religious poems were actually composed

---

[3] I view the "literary" dimension of a text as having a twofold focus on: a) **form**— the "artistry" of how the text is composed; and b) **function**—the "rhetoric" of how the literary forms are employed to carry out general and specific communicative objectives within the text. This analysis is also concerned with "structure" on two levels—the microlevel of the individual poetic colon or bicolon, and the macrolevel, which deals with purposeful combinations and strategic arrangements of poetic lines within the psalmic discourse as a whole (cf. Wendland 2004:1–27). And the poetic "line has a meaningful identity only when we begin to hear its relationship to other elements in the poem" (Longenbach 2008:5), that is, as a holistic rhythmic structure of lineal meaningful development that features a paradigmatic recursion of corresponding verbal elements (e.g., related by analogy and association) within a syntagmatic progression of forward (temporal) movement.

[4] This analytical perspective is based upon the approach presented in chapter 2 of this book.

aloud or not (they probably were), it is undoubtedly true that this was their principal medium of realization, either for personal devotion or, more likely, for public articulation (singing, reciting, chanting, etc.) in some communal ritualized observation or worship setting.[5] It is highly probable, therefore, that the psalms were formulated specifically with oral production in mind—for an audience which did not have immediate access to a written text—and this naturally affected their manner of verbal construction. Thus, these prayers or praises had to be prepared in such a way that they would be memorable, readily expressed, audibly intelligible to, and appreciated by listeners under the normal circumstances of private or group worship. This auditory requirement arguably necessitated a distinct method of sacred, poetic composition, one which was expected to be in harmony with the traditional literary and liturgical norms of that particular ANE age and religious milieu.

The composer could not depend upon standard typographical conventions such as capitalization, punctuation, paragraphing, strategic spacing, and so forth in order to clarify his sequence of words and thoughts or to emphasize the main points of his message. The Hebrew written documents (scrolls) that recorded and preserved these prayer-praise poems did not make such provisions for readers, which meant that the texts were not very legible. Therefore, lectors often had to practice reading, even memorizing them in advance, as part of normal preparation before any public presentation. For his part, the poet would rely upon a cluster of stock oral-based techniques both to shape and to sharpen his key ideas and deeply felt emotions. He utilized such features, generally familiar within the religious tradition, to structure a text so that it would manifest the familiar characteristics of a well-formed discourse, including adaptations made in keeping with current literary criteria, namely, the relevant and appropriate selection, arrangement, progression, cohesion-building, and foregrounding of conceptual content. Furthermore, within this general framework of more or less universal properties, he was able to access and manipulate his repertory of preferred poetic devices in order to achieve a variety of more specific rhetorical and artistic effects (to be illustrated with reference to Psalm 22 below).

The Hebrew poet, like any other, largely accomplished these creative objectives by skillfully playing upon the opposing, but complementary forces of continuity and discontinuity in the formation of his God-focused message (see 2.1 above). Continuity is needed in order to give one's composition a sense of unity, perspective, harmony, purpose, and progression. Discontinuity, on the other hand, provides the text with the necessary

[5] Berlin touches upon this vital aspect of Hebrew poetry in the following comment: "Occasionally provided by the exegete, but often left to the reader, has been the actual [audible] reading of the poem—the making sense and beauty from its sounds, words, and structures, the perception that it is a unified entity with a distinctive message" (1996:314).

variation, novelty, emphasis, prominence, and occasionally also suspense so that its main ideas stand out sufficiently and are not only readily understandable, but esthetically pleasing to the envisioned audience and also emotively moving with respect to particular actions and attitudes.

These are rather basic notions, to be sure, but their realization in literary, especially creative poetic discourse, can assume many different forms—from the most elemental (e.g., overt repetition), to the highly sophisticated (e.g., suggestive allusion), and they may encompass any or all strata of linguistic organization, from elemental sounds to text-spanning chiastic constructions. Thus, the twin forces of conjunction (continuity) and disjunction (discontinuity), which are grounded in one's perception of the essential qualities of similarity and difference, operate in tandem to effect the holistic and harmonious production of an aesthetically, as well as theologically satisfying literary-liturgical work. Correspondingly, these qualities also furnish the principal diagnostic criteria according to which a given poetic text or corpus may be evaluated and judged as being either a relatively outstanding, mediocre, or poor example of a particular genre that may be used in the intended setting of worship.

The normal circumstances of public performance, even in the case of "individual" psalmic compositions, would naturally dictate that the poet should maintain a certain degree of simplicity, directness, and propriety, with special attention being devoted to the medium of sound. But as in the preceding chapters, so also this study will reveal that the typical techniques of biblical lyric composition, though seeming simple on the surface of the text, are not as transparent or unsophisticated as they may at first appear—or sound, on first hearing. This quickly becomes evident as soon as one begins to probe more deeply beneath the outer layers of the literary whole to investigate some of the more intricate instances of continuous and discontinuous construction that are discernable there.

4.2 Poetic parallelism and its prominence in biblical discourse

One of the most prominent and hence widely recognized characteristics of Hebrew poetic discourse is normally referred to by the term "parallelism" (see 1.2.2, above).[6] For hundreds of years now, biblical scholars have made various attempts to describe and define this literary phenomenon, which of course is not limited to the so-called poetic books of Scripture (e.g., Genesis 49, Luke 1, 1 Corinthians 13, Revelation 7). The only real point of agreement

---

[6] "Distinctive of Hebrew literature is parallelism, whether in narrative, prose, or poetry" (VanGemeren 1991:9). The category of prose normally includes narrative, but it is important to observe that parallelism is found also in these types of text, though not of course in the variety, complexity, or density as in poetry (cf. Alter 1981:97).

seems to be that parallelism is typically realized over the space of a pair of adjacent, semantically-related utterances (lines, cola) of comparatively limited length, but generally balanced in relation to each other. "The parts of a verse in the Psalms cohere by the principle of repetition, restatement, differentiation, or progression" (VanGemeren 1991:10)—and no doubt additional such poetic principles could be identified. At times, for rhetorical reasons, three and even four cola combinations occur, as well as monocola. But two lines (a bicolon) is the norm, being phonologically marked in the MT by the minor *athnah* (half-pause) and major *silluq* (full-pause), which often correspond, whether explicitly or implicitly, to two clause units of grammar.

A pair of poetic lines may be linguistically associated with each other in various other ways as a means of specifying the particular type of parallelism involved.[7] Most analysts emphasize the semantic connection between the two cola—from Lowth's familiar tripartite classification into "synonymous," "antithetical," and "synthetic" relations, to Kugel's colloquial condensation of these three into "A is so, and what's more B" (or B "seconds" A) (1981:1–2) and Alter's corollary: "the movement of meaning is one of heightening or intensification" (1985:19). Others, like Collins (1978) and O'Connor (1980), focus strictly upon the syntactic features of the lines and how these match up to constitute greater or lesser degrees of parallelism. However precise the latter, more formalized approaches may seem, I find them, like Alter, "unconvincing" (1985:215). My approach is more simply to take the notion of "parallelism" in its basic etymological sense as being situated, or lying, "side by side"—with reference to clearly delimited line forms that are regularly placed, primarily in poetic discourse, "alongside each other" in some recognizable and interrelated association involving sound, sense, and/or syntax (Wendland 2007). This would seem to agree with Berlin's definition: "Parallelism may be defined as the repetition of similar or related semantic content or grammatical [formal] structure in adjacent lines or verses" (1996:304). Such a lyric coupling (which may also involve three or four cola) therefore manifests various kinds and degrees of linguistic correspondence between (or among) the lines, ranging from the most subtle phonological similarities to utterances that completely contrast with one another in terms of their overt meaning.

Obviously, the more formal and semantic resemblances or correlations that are found between two (or more) lines, especially those that are audibly perceptible, the greater the sense and awareness of parallelism that results—in Jakobson's terms, the more strongly the "poetic principle" is operating (see 2.1). This refers to a compositional strategy that "projects the

---

[7] Twenty-five binary semantic sets are summarized with reference to the wider notions of similarity, contrast, time, cause-effect, and "completive addition" in Wendland 2002:98–99.

principle of equivalence[8] from the [paradigmatic] axis of selection into the [syntagmatic] axis of combination" (1960:358), in other words, similarity being superimposed upon contiguity within the text.[9] Thus, we are not dealing with an either-or phenomenon with reference to poetry and prose, or the amount of parallelism that is displayed between any two poetic lines. It is rather a matter of relative degrees involving a continuum of stylistic possibilities that forge a dynamic, often implicit connection between the cola. A may be related to B in any one of a number of different ways which may generate a variety of possible artistic impressions and rhetorical effects. It is "a special structuring of language that calls attention to the 'how' of the message as well as to the 'what'" (Berlin 1996:302). This manifold, variable quality greatly enhances the expressive potential of parallelism to serve as a subtle, yet multifaceted communicative tool in any composition in which it predominates.

Most studies of parallelism and/or Hebrew poetry in general limit the scope of their attention to the microstructure of a given text—to the cola sequence of A and B lines as they exist in syntagmatic juxtaposition to one another. From a discourse perspective, however, this is far too restrictive, for parallelism is not only contiguous, or conjunctive, in nature. More importantly for the analysis of complete psalms, such coupling may also be manifested in disjunction, that is, the complementary lines being separated over a much larger span of text. This fact has some very important implications for the holistic study of poetic (and other) compositions as integral artistic-rhetorical units. In fact, the data reveal that colon-pairing is employed as one of the key structural (i.e., structurizing) devices in biblical discourse—parallelism unbound, we might say. In this respect, one of its main macrolevel functions is to demarcate the discourse—that is, to mark boundaries and thereby to help signal and establish the onset, midpoint, and conclusion of discrete, larger structural units.

[8] According to Jakobson, "equivalence in difference is the cardinal problem of language and the pivotal concern of linguists...where the equivalence is a *relational equivalence* based on sameness within a system" (1985:150, original italics). The application to translation can easily be made, which may help resolve some of the confusion concerning the notion of equivalence and how it is used in certain approaches, such as functional equivalence. Thus, there may be various types of relational equivalence between a source text and a translated text, and the relative degree of sameness, or closeness, is an important issue that must be carefully negotiated on the basis of pre-determined principles, including those that pertain to the purpose of the translated text in its new setting of use.

[9] "In poetry, the projection of the principle of equivalence from the axis of selection into the axis of combination means quite simply that such sameness is used as (the major) means of constructing the whole sequence.... Moreover, such parallelisms create a network of internal relations within the poem itself, making the poem into an integrated whole and underlying the poem's relative autonomy" (Jakobson 1985:150).

4.3 Forms and functions of disjunctive parallelism

There are a number of spatial possibilities for realizing the separated, or non-contiguous type of parallelism referred to above—in other words, different ways of manifesting the related elements of an [A—B +/- C] couplet in its role of delimiting and distinguishing poetic compositional units. Thus, the crucial correspondences may appear at any of the following structural combinations (examples from Psalm 22 will be given below):

- the respective beginnings of two (or more) different compositional units (anaphora);[10]
- the respective endings of two (or more) different units (epiphora);
- the beginning and ending of the same unit (inclusio);
- the adjacent ending and beginning of different units (anadiplosis);
- the non-contiguous ending and beginning of different units (exclusio);
- the combination of a beginning and/or ending with the center of the same segment—or of two or more centers of different segments (projection);
- an item-for-item chiastic reversal of two series, or panels, of corresponding elements (introversion, palistrophe).

Several of these patterns of linguistic (formal and/or semantic) association may co-occur within the same area of text (a convergence)—especially anaphora, epiphora, and inclusion—to reinforce an especially prominent structural border. The same compositional features may also operate individually or together to delineate a certain range of text. This delimited span may vary in length from the strophe (analogous to a paragraph in prose), to a stanza (the next larger unit), and on up the hierarchy of discourse organization to enclose an entire poetic work (e.g., a psalm). The question of whether one is dealing with a unit beginning, ending, or central core can often be decided only on the basis of evaluating a diversity of interacting literary (artistic, rhetorical) and structural criteria within the context of the lyric composition as a whole. This integrated process of text analysis and assessment will be illustrated in the subsequent analysis of Psalm 22.

It is clear that verbal recursion plays an important part in the positing (and recognition) of these different kinds of disjunctive poetic coupling. The iteration of linguistic features (phonological, morphological, lexical, syntactic) may assume varying degrees of perceived equivalence according

---

[10] See also §2.1; Wendland 2004:126–128. Adele Berlin refers to the devices of anaphora, epiphora (cataphora), and anadiplosis, but limits their usage to "consecutive lines" and to the individual "word or phrase" (1996:309). I have a much wider scope and broader usage in view.

to whether it is based upon reduplication (an exact repetition of form), resemblance (a partial repetition of form), or correspondence (a similarity of meaning, but not form). Such a correspondence of meaning could be potentially effected by a diversity of close semantic relationships, in addition to synonymy, such as literal-figurative restatement, base-contrast, reason-result, means-purpose, condition-consequence, time-progression, and so forth. The amount and import of any instance of recursion that links a pair (or more) of cola is also quite variable. A minimum of two key (theological) terms would need to be involved, e.g., the names of God, but the more extensive the degree (i.e., repetition) and quantity of equivalent items, the stronger the auditory (visual and conceptual) impression that is made, and hence also the greater its diagnostic and/or functional significance within a given psalm (or portion of one).

As suggested above, in addition to the formative (textual) function, which focuses on linguistic forms, there are also two others of special concern in the analysis of poetic discourse. The designative (semantic) function highlights referential, or ideational content—in particular, the author's specification and elaboration of themes and sub-themes, whether literal, figurative, or symbolic in nature. Any presupposed or intertextually implied information would also need to be investigated, especially with regard to all topically related psalms in the Psalter. This concern overlaps then with the interpersonal, or interactive (pragmatic) function, which takes into special consideration the original posited worship setting of the psalm and the primary purpose for which it was ostensibly used as people communicated with Yahweh, e.g., for petition, thanksgiving, instruction, praise, or profession of faith. Furthermore, one needs to study the presumed expression of emotion on the part of the psalmist or his community during the utterance (recitation, singing, etc.) of a given text (the expressive sub-function), the varied illocutionary force of the cola in sequence (the affective sub-function), and the generation or maintenance of psychological contact with fellow-worshippers (the phatic sub-function). And finally, the interactive function must be related also to the contemporary context of communication—that is, how the poetic message as expressed in translation is intended and designed to engage users today with respect to their attitudes, feelings, and desires. The overall perceived strength of this cognitive, emotive, and/or volitional impression, whether great or small, will obviously impact upon their overt behavior as well.[11]

---

[11] Psalm 22 "is characterized by two types of poetic movement: a series of alternating shifts downward and upward (negative and positive feelings), and a sustained shift from [experiencing] exclusion to inclusion in the final upward swing" (Bratcher and Reyburn 1991:212). The challenge for translators is to duplicate this crucial pragmatic effect in the TL text, for it is part of the overall meaning of the psalm (cf. Wendland 2013:243).

4.4 Further thoughts on methodology

As already suggested, there is no single, correct way of carrying out a comprehensive discourse analysis of a biblical text. To some extent the method chosen will depend on the type or genre of text being investigated—narrative, procedural, judicial, expository, hortatory, etc. The approach selected for illustration in this study concentrates initially on the diverse patterns of continuity and points of discontinuity in the poetic work at hand, namely, Psalm 22 in Hebrew.

The literary device of paralleled coupling, when realized on the macrostructure of a composition (any subsequent instance of significant recursion being analogous to the B element of a bicolon) can produce either one, or both, of these formative techniques involving progression (continuity) or interruption (discontinuity). A displaced (separated) line B, for example, whether it is corresponding, contrastive, or completive with respect to A (Wendland 2002:98), exhibits a perceptible continuation from the latter (its complement) simply by being semantically related to it. But within the textual context of the psalm as a whole, it will generally mark, that is, distinguish, the location of an initial aperture (anaphora), a concluding closure (epiphora), or medial centrum (i.e., the core of a given structural unit). In any of these key structural positions, then, a substantial, non-adjacent type of poetic line pairing (A/B as distinct from adjacent A—B parallelism) manifests both continuity (a connection) and discontinuity (a break) as far as the overall construction of the discourse is concerned.

An accurate perception of such non-contiguous A/B parallelism on the macrolevel of a text is essential for its correct analysis because, more often than not, this feature coincides with some type of thematic disjunction (e.g., the onset of a new topic) or reinforcement (e.g., a special emphasis placed on a crucial motif or some critical accompanying emotion). Thus, such textual highlighting often occurs at the semantic peak and/or the emotive climax of a certain structural unit or sub-section.

While the deliberate pairing of cola, as just described, is perhaps the most important means whereby continuity or discontinuity is forged in Hebrew poetry, it is certainly not the only way. Other devices that often accomplish the same effect, whether individually or in combination, involve the familiar literary techniques of expansion (e.g., non-parallel recursion such as alliteration, word-pairs, syntactic correspondence, metrical patterning),[12] contraction (e.g., ellipsis, asyndeton, the deletion of

---

[12] By "metrical patterning" I am referring to symmetrical or balanced arrangements of lexical units as manifested in a sequence of poetic lines (cola), e.g., a series of 3:2 or 3:3 bicola, to create a certain rhythm of recurrent, stressed (accented) sounds. As Berlin observes, "No one has been able to demonstrate convincingly the existence of a consistently occurring metrical system" in Hebrew poetry, that is, poetic "verse" (1996:302). This is because "strictly speaking, meter requires

"prose particles"), intensification (e.g., vocative, exclamation, insertion of a separable pronoun), transformation (e.g., rhetorical/leading question, enallage, word-order perturbation), and figuration (e.g., metaphor, metonymy, personification, hyperbole). The more features that appear conjoined in a given passage, the more "concentrated" it is poetically, the more noticeable perceptually, and hence also the greater the probability that it signals some prominent structural-thematic node within the text.[13]

One might go further to suggest that this feature of parallelized foregrounding in relation to the A and B components of a disjunctive bicolon (or tri-colon, tetra-colon, etc.) is simply an extension of the corresponding poetic feature noted above on the microlevel of organization, including the attribute of ascensive "seconding" (Kugel 1981:8):

> Now by its very afterwardness, B will have an emphatic character...its very reassertion is a kind of strengthening and reinforcing. But often this feature (found in all apposition) is exploited: the meaning of B is indeed more extreme than A, a definite "going one better."

In a similar vein, Robert Alter defines "semantic parallelism" as a device whereby "the characteristic movement of meaning is one of heightening or intensification...of focusing, specification, concretization, even what could be called dramatization" (1985:19). In the case of disjunctive parallelism then, this heightening of significance engages not merely the two (or more) parallel lines themselves, but the associated meaning in their immediate context is also involved, as a progressive, cumulative accretion of communicative (semantic, emotive, affective, etc.) content is created within the poetic prayer. This effective technique for verbally (audibly) delimiting, developing, as well as reinforcing certain important areas within the discourse will be the focus of the following study of Psalm 22, which must necessarily begin with a careful examination of the original Hebrew (MT—based on the ParaTExt 7.4 version).

---

the recurrence of an element or group of elements with mathematical regularity. The element to be measured may be the syllable (or a certain type or length of syllable), the accent or stress, or the word" (ibid.:308). "Other explanations [of Hebrew meter] have been put forward, but all suffer from the problem of reconstructing the text based on a 'preconceived shape' of Hebrew meter" (VanGemeren 1991:9).

[13] Indeed, it is the combination of these different features that helps to distinguish poetry from prose in biblical texts (or more correctly perhaps, more [or less] poetic from prosaic discourse). Berlin (1996) identifies diagnostic "tropes and figures" such as these: parallelism (which could be viewed as incorporating all of the following), terseness (absence of "prose particles"), rhythm, repetition and patterning (e.g., refrain, inclusio, chiasm), imagery (e.g., metaphor, simile), figures of speech (e.g., allusion, hyperbole, irony, rhetorical questions), and distinctive motifs and themes. She adds, significantly: "Poetry also employs sound and joins it to meaning in interesting ways" (ibid.:302).

4.5 A text-structural display of Psalm 22

The following analytical spreadsheet presents a visual spatialization of the Hebrew text of Psalm 22. The purpose of this exercise is to display the microstructure of this poetic composition in a way that makes its lexical patterning (especially the recursive elements)[14] and significant word orders (topic and focus) more evident (Hebrew word order moves from right to left). Numbering begins after the heading, as in many English translations; each verse is broken down into colon utterance units, as indicated by the number after the decimal point.

The entire text has been divided into putative strophes, which are separated by blank rows and designated by the capital letters in the leftmost margin; each pairing of two strophes represents a poetic stanza (e.g., A + A'). The rationale for these text divisions, moving from the larger to the smaller, will be given in a separate section following the display—in note-like fashion, with each comment identified by a small letter that is also inserted next to the verse/colon (v.co) where it best belongs in the chart. Footnotes are included to provide information on special linguistic problems within the text, exegetical or hermeneutical issues, and literary features of special interest.[15]

I will pause the Hebrew text analysis several times to insert observations that summarize the main items of linguistic-literary[16] evidence which serve to substantiate its proposed strophic segmentation of the text. In one way or another, these features all have to do with the manifestation of varied aspects of continuity and/or discontinuity in the discourse (as described above) to mark the distinct structural boundaries that have been posited.[17] The primary feature of recursion is usually complemented by other poetic devices, as these interact with each other on several levels of verbal organization, from the

---

[14] In this case, since Psalm 22 is fairly well known, no English translation is given at this point. Significant repetitions are highlighted on the chart by gray shading where possible. Note v. 1, for example, where the double vocative suggests urgency and a close personal relationship with "me/my" (-*iy* suffix).

[15] It should be recognized that this "psalm has some of the most significant textual problems in the entire psalter" (deClaissé-Walford et al. 2014:227).

[16] The term "literary" designates those structural elements that involve deliberate patterning, especially those created by significant instances of recursion.

[17] My analysis of Psalm 22 indicates that the text is a structural unity—the literary-poetic product of a single artistic theological composer. This viewpoint would contradict the opinion of a number of modern scholars, for example: "[Psalm 22] consists of several parts that do not originate from the same hand and none of which is likely to date from the pre-exilic period. The second part, occasionally called Psalm 22B, is younger than the first" (Nõmmik 2014:91). Such a pronouncement not only pushes far beyond the available evidence regarding textual dating, but also ignores the typical compositional structure of the psalmic lament, which often shifts suddenly—dramatically towards the end—from sorrowful prayer to joyous praise and thanksgiving (e.g., Ps. 31:19).

largest, most inclusive compositional units of the organizational hierarchy to those which group together the smallest set of poetic lines above the verse/bicolon level, i.e., poetic paragraphs, or strophes.

We will see that Psalm 22, over and above its prominent theological content, is a literary masterpiece—an artistically interwoven composite of the four foundational types of liturgical material found in the Psalter: complaint (lament), petition (prayer), profession of trust (creed), and praise (with or without included thanksgiving). The most obvious and principal break in the text occurs between verses 21 and 22. Here we intuitively experience a fundamental shift in psychological orientation, from an introverted mournful lament over surrounding enemies to a joyous communal celebration of the righteous rule of Yahweh, which embraces all people and extends over the entire earth. This dramatic alteration in perspective is highlighted by a number of important poetic techniques, thus evincing a notable instance of stylistic convergence.

v.co	Post-Verb2	Post-Verb1	VERBAL	Pre-Verb2	Pre-Verb1
0.1				עַל־אַיֶּלֶת הַשַּׁחַר[a]	לַמְנַצֵּחַ
				on = doe-of the-morning	for-the-director
0.2				לְדָוִד:	מִזְמוֹר
				to/of-David	a-psalm
A[b]					
1.1			עֲזַבְתָּנִי	לָמָה[c]	אֵלִי[d] אֵלִי
			you-have-forsaken-me	why	my-God, my-God
1.2[e]		מִישׁוּעָתִי	----------	רָחוֹק	(לָמָה)
		from-my-deliverance		far-away	(why)
1.3	שַׁאֲגָתִי:	(מִ) דִּבְרֵי	----------	(רָחוֹק)	(לָמָה)
	my-groaning	(from) words-of		(far-away)	(why)
2.1		יוֹמָם	אֶקְרָא		אֱלֹהַי
		daily	I-call-out		my-God
2.2			תַעֲנֶה		וְלֹא
			you-answer		and-not
2.3	לִי:	דוּמִיָּה	[g]----------	וְלֹא־	וְלַיְלָה
	for-me	silence		and-not =	and-nightly

A′				
3.1		קָדוֹשׁ holy-one	h_____	וְאַתָּה[i] and-you
3.2	יִשְׂרָאֵל: Israel	תְּהִלּוֹת[j] praises-of	יוֹשֵׁב[k] one-dwelling	
4.1[l]		אֲבֹתֵינוּ our-fathers	בָּטְחוּ they-trusted	בְּךָ in-you
4.2[m]			בָּטְחוּ they-trusted	
			וַתְּפַלְּטֵמוֹ: and-you-rescued-them	
5.1			זָעֲקוּ they-cried	אֵלֶיךָ unto-you
			וְנִמְלָטוּ and-they-were-saved	
5.2			בָּטְחוּ[n] they-trusted	בְּךָ in-you
			בוֹשׁוּ: they-were-ashamed	וְלֹא־ and-not=

[a] Alter has this note: *"ayeleth hashahar.* The name elsewhere meaning 'morning star' (or, literally, 'dawn doe'). One assumes it refers to a musical instrument of some sort or, alternatively, to a melody" (2007:71; cf. v. 19.2). Goldingay observes: "…LXX, Tg make sense in inferring a reference to help here. Dawn is then the moment when help may arrive or the moment when one offers prayer and praise…" (2006:324).

[b] A classical Christian perspective on this psalm by some early Church Fathers teaches us to read it anew in the light of its NT fulfillment: "The psalm is sung by Christ as in the person of all humanity…that when troubles are near, we may pray that he help us" (Pseudo Athanasius). "The words of this psalm are spoken in the person of the crucified one…. He speaks consistently in the character of our old self, whose mortality he bore and that was nailed to the cross with him" (Athanasius) (Blaising and Hardin 2008:168).

[c] "The *lâmah (why)* appears to govern all three subsequent phrases…" (deClaissé-Walford et al. 2014:228).

[d] "The repeated cry, 'Eli, Eli', shows the intense quality of the bond which heretofore united this devotee of Yahweh to his Creator" (Terrien 2003:230). There is bitter irony in the fact that "the psalmist complains of being forsaken, yet still addresses God as 'my God'" (McCann 1996:762). But others would view this as an

instance of residual faith in God's power to act—to deliver—despite God's apparent distance (Ross 2013:140). Ross lists four types of God's apparent "negligence" that the Psalmists lament about, moving from the least to the most disturbing: God hides himself, God has forgotten, God has forsaken, and God is hostile (ibid.:136–141).

[e] Line 1.2 is semantically very complex on account of an increasing amount of implicit information. Thus, the rhetorical question "Why…" is actually expressed two more times: "Why (are you) so far from saving me?"—"Why (are you so far from hearing) the words of my groaning?" I have indicated the implicit elements on the chart in parentheses.

A greater number of long cola appear in the eulogy of Part Two, e.g., in stanza E. These differences may reflect the change in psychological tone as one moves from the psalmist's agitated mental state in Part One (vv. 1–21) to a calm (albeit jubilant) expression of praise and thanks in Part Two (vv. 22–31).

[f] The verb "means roar like a lion or to scream…this is not groaning or complaining or whining" (deClaissé-Walford et al. 2014:228, 233).

[g] The gapped verb "I call out" (plus alliteration in לְ) accentuates both the time frame: "day" and "night" (i.e., constantly—a merism), as well as the lack of a response ("silence, quietness") from "my God" (cf. Ps. 62:1). "Psalm 22 concerns the theological mystery of 'the deaf God'" (Goldingay 2006:327).

[h] The apparent lack of a verb in 3.1 highlights the attributive quality of "holiness" (in this context perhaps also "separateness"—transcendence) being attributed to "you" (God) (cf. Exodus 15:11). On the other hand, it would be possible, along with the LXX, to construe the verbal יוֹשֵׁב as part of line one, i.e., "and you sit (as the) holy one," though this construal (e.g., Goldingay 2006:327–328) would detract somewhat from the vivid, highly expressive style.

[i] The initial conjunction plus a separable pronoun indicates a constituent (referential) contrast and marks the onset of a new strophe, as also in 6.1, 9.1, and 19.1. This focus upon "you" (YHWH) continues throughout the strophe (4.1, 5.1, 5.2). Such usage reflects the separation, or distance, that the psalmist perceives between him and his God.

[j] The noun "praises" (תְּהִלּוֹת) anticipates the occurrence of this root (halal) in the psalm's praise portion in Part Two (vv. 22, 23, 25, 26).

[k] God's "sitting" here refers to his universal "enthronement," or righteous royal rule (cf. vv. 28, 31), for which he deserves the highest praise, not only from "Israel," but from all "nations" (v. 27).

[l] The allusions to Moses' song at the sea in praise of Yahweh's mighty deliverance of Israel during the Exodus (ch. 15) grow stronger in vv. 4–5; the crucial concept of "trust" is foregrounded by a chiastic construction in v. 4. Once again, there is a double contrast implied: the psalmist's present isolation versus the corporate unity of Israel in the past; their deliverance by Yahweh versus only "disappointment" for him.

[m] The strong parallelism of vv. 4–5, coupled with the distinctive opening bicolon (v. 3), formally reinforces the content of strophe A', continuing the "intensity and inclusiveness that sets Psalm 22 apart" (McCann 1996:762).

[n] "The threefold reference to the 'trust' of the fathers is symmetric with the threefold statement of [the psalmist's] personal trust in the Lord in the phrase 'my God'. The faith of the ancestors and the faith of the psalmist are one, but their experience is far different" (VanGemeren 1991:201)—or so the singer

sadly concludes. However, "crying out in pain and expressing trust are not incompatible" (deClaissé-Walford et al. 2014:233).

B				
6.1	תּוֹלַעַת	ª----------		וְאָנֹכִי
	a-worm			and-I
	אִישׁ			וְלֹא־
	a-man			and-not =
6.2	חֶרְפַּת אָדָם	----------		
	a-disgrace-of humanity			
	וּבְזוּי עָם׃			
	and-one-despised-of people			
7.1	לִי	יַלְעִגוּ	רֹאַי	כָּל־
	at-me	they-mock	those-seeing-me	all =
7.2	בְשָׂפָה ᵇ	יַפְטִירוּ		
	their-lips	they-open-widely		
7.3	רֹאשׁ׃	יָנִיעוּ		
	head	they-shake		
8.1	אֶל־יְהוָה	גֹּל ᶜ		
	unto = Yahweh	roll/commit		
		יְפַלְטֵהוּ ᵈ		
		let-him-rescue-him		
8.2		יַצִּילֵהוּ		
		let-him-liberate-him		
	בּוֹ׃	חָפֵץ ᵉ		כִּי
	in-him	he-delights		since

[a] The sense and imagery of this colon reflect and form a dramatic thematic contrast with the beginning of the preceding strophe (3.1), one that is reinforced by the verbless syntactic structure that matches the divine "Holy One" with a worthless "worm!" "God's absence dwarfs his self-image...he feels less than

human" (VanGemeren 1994:821). This reading would also support the interpretation of the colonic constituents of v. 3. The psalmist's vivid expressions of personal shame (vv. 6ff.) contrast markedly with the experience of his ancestral saints (v. 5.2).

[b] The graphic antagonistic interpersonal references here anticipate the heightened bestial images in v. 14. "Sticking out the lip" is "obviously a gesture of scorn, although its exact nature is unknown" (Bratcher and Reyburn 1991:216). The people's disparagement of the psalmist contrasts with their praise of Yahweh, in whom they all rely upon for deliverance in times of trouble. They make the same wrong conclusion as Job's three friends.

[c] The imperative form (often too quickly emended, e.g., Craigie 1983:196; VanGemeren 1991:203; NIV) suggests a sarcastic insertion of direct speech, aimed emphatically by the enemies (like weapons) directly at the psalmist: "[Go ahead and] trust in Yahweh [i.e., and see what good it does you]!" The literal sense of the verb is "to roll (something: your cause/burden) onto the Lord."

[d] This verb (יְפַלְּטֵהוּ), used sarcastically by the psalmist's enemies here, ironically recalls his own reflection concerning Yahweh's "deliverance" (וַתְּפַלְּטֵמוֹ) of his people in v. 4.2, thus reinforcing his sense of alienation.

[e] Here we have another case of ironic intertextuality (or intertextual irony): In other usages of this verb, God "delights in" a person or group in a positive, beneficent sense, e.g., Num. 14:8, 2 Sm. 22:20, 1 Kgs. 10:9, Psalms 18:19, 41:11. This verb supplies the derisive reason for the three preceding exhortations. "The psalmist's enemies sarcastically appeal to God to help him, because he claims to be an object of divine favor. However, they probably doubted the reality of his claim" (NET note; cf. Bratcher and Reyburn 1991:217).

B′					
9.1	מִבֶּטֶן	גֹחִי	----------	אַתָּה	כִּי־
	from-abdomen	one-drawing-me-out		you	For =
9.2	עַל־שְׁדֵי אִמִּי:	מַבְטִיחִי[a]	----------		
	on = breasts-of my-mother	one-making-me-trust			
10.1		מֵרֶחֶם	הִשְׁלַכְתִּי		עָלֶיךָ
		from-womb	I-was-thrown		upon-you
10.2	אָתָּה:	אֵלִי	[b]----------	אִמִּי	מִבֶּטֶן
	you	my-God		my-mother	from-abdo-men-of

[a] The *hiphil* participle 'You caused me to trust' (מַבְטִיחִי) or "inspired trust" (VanGemeren 1991:204) plaintively recalls the psalmist's repeated assertion "they (our fathers) trusted" (בָּטְחוּ) in v. 4.

[b] This short strophe (B′) is almost entirely verbless and features a cohesive chiastic arrangement: "you" + ref. to God + "my mother" – "my mother" + ref. to God + "you" (אַתָּה begins and ends this unit). Just as Yahweh brought Israel

forth figuratively as a nation at the Exodus (vv. 4–5, strophe A′), so he gave birth physically to the psalmist by "bringing him out" from his mother (vv. 9–10, strophe B′). Note that vv. 9–10 clearly express the psalmist's (early/initial) trust in Yahweh, so it is not quite accurate to say that "Psalm 23's words of trust [serve as] the 'missing' *Expression of Trust* of Psalm 22" (deClaissé-Walford 2004:39).

Colon 10.2 is designated as the close of cycle one, stanza B′ because of the repetition of the crucial reference to deity, "my God" (אֵלִי), followed by the emphatic pronoun "you" (אַתָּה) in utterance-final position (1.1/10.2, inclusio). This feature calls attention to another important methodological procedure: The diverse units of discourse must never be analyzed in isolation from one another. Instead, there should be a constant interplay—a continual shifting of one's analytical attention back and forth between the different levels of structure and their respective constituents. The external boundaries of one segment tend to harmonize with those postulated for another, whether the latter happens to be an internal, an incorporating, or a syntagmatically adjacent or parallel unit. In addition, we normally find that the end, or closing boundary of unit A will coincide with the beginning or onset of unit B, the two borders thus reinforcing one another. At the end of a careful literary-structural analysis then, we observe that a widely recognized biblical pericope, such as a psalm, generally turns out to be a unified, well-integrated whole—not a mélange of textual bits and pieces, all rather clumsily cobbled together by some incompetent scribe or redactor from a collection or assortment of "sources."

Turning to verse 11, a closer examination reveals an important correspondence, one that also in Janus, hinge-like fashion has links in both textual directions (i.e., anaphorically and cataphorically).[18] This mournful plea, "Do not be far from me!" (11.1) clearly reflects the psalmist's initial moan שַׁאֲגָתִי (lit. 'roar'):[19] 11–2, "My God, my God, why...are you so far from my deliverance?" (יְשׁוּעָתִי) (i.e., anaphora, note also the phonological rhyme). But there is also a connection with the psalmist's final, extended appeal which begins at 19.1: "But you, O Yahweh, do not stay far away!" (אַל־תִּרְחָק; i.e., an instance of structural anaphora, which distinguishes the two complementary prayers from the included lamentation of

[18] Indeed, in many translations (e.g., NIV) and commentaries (e.g., Bratcher and Reyburn 1994:212), v. 11 is construed as the close of Cycle 1 (stanzas A + B), rather than the beginning of Cycle 2 (stanzas C + D), for example: "The prayer moves through two cycles (vv. 1–11 and 12–19), each concluding in the petition, 'be not far' (vv. 11, 19)" (Mays 1994a:107). I am construing the notion of the psalmist being "far away" from God as marking the onset of three major units, stanza A (v. 1), stanza C (v. 11), and stanza D′ (v. 19). Even in Mays' analysis, v. 19 is not a "concluding" verse (ibid.:110). Bratcher and Reyburn regard v. 11 as a "transition" within the text (1994:213).

[19] "[The] cry of supplication, 'Do not stay far away from me!'...is no longer the question of 'Why?' but the cry of a child who still hopes" (Terrien 2003:232). "The word 'far'...helps to maintain the sense of isolation throughout the psalm" (Harman 2011a:216)—to be more specific, within Part One.

vv. 12–18). Yet another reinforcing link between the two strophe-initial verses 11 and 19, the second "half" of Part One, is manifested by the connotatively contrastive references to the concept "help": "Indeed, there is no *helper!*" (עֹזֵר—11.3), a complaint and "O my Strength, hurry *to help me!*" (לְעֶזְרָתִי—19.2), an appeal.

There is another, somewhat less significant piece of evidence to support the positing of a major division between verses 10 and 11. This is debatable because it is based on my construal of the organization of the cola of Psalm 22, namely, the number of poetic lines that constitute a given section. It is interesting to observe that the total for each "third" of the whole composition (including the heading), verses 1–10, 11–21, and 22–32, turns out to be roughly the same: 24, 28, and 25 lines, or cola respectively. The number of constituent words per cycle gradually increases in size, approximately (depending on how one counts lexical units) 79, 83, and 91 words. Structurally, then, the three sections rather closely approximate one another with respect to poetic length, thus giving an impression of balance as the psalmist develops his heart-felt thoughts in prayer to the Lord. All of the strophes of Part One begin with some sort of a conjunctive particle except the two that comprise stanza C, both of which are asyndetic.

C					
11.1		מֶמֶּנִּי	תִּרְחַק		אַל־
		from-me	may-you-be-far		not =
11.2		קְרוֹבָה[a]	----------	צָרָה	כִּי־
		nearby		trouble	since =
11.3		עֹזֵר׃	אֵין		כִּי[b]
		one-helping	there-is-no		since =
12.1		פָּרִים רַבִּים	סְבָבוּנִי		
		many bulls	they-surrounded-me		
12.2			כִּתְּרוּנִי׃[c]		אַבִּירֵי בָשָׁן
			they-encircled-me		beasts-of Bashan
13.1	פִּיהֶם	עָלַי	פָּצוּ		
	their-mouth	at-me	they-open		
13.2			טֹרֵף וְשֹׁאֵג׃		אַרְיֵה[d]
			tearing and-roaring		a-lion

[a] Similar, but inverted consonants help to foreground the contrast in concepts "far away" (רחק) versus "nearby" (קָרוֹב) in v. 11.

[b] This second *kiy* is arguably asseverative (emphatic), "Surely..." (cf. Craigie 1983:196).

[c] In contrast to the strict parallelism of v. 11, v. 12 features a chiastic construction, with the two verbs including reference to the psalmist ('me') being the outer elements. This descriptive assertion is formally and semantically paralleled at the beginning of the next stanza (D) in v. 16, where the same verb form is found (סְבָבוּנִי).

[d] Literally, v. 13 reads: "They gaped against me their mouth—a lion tearing and roaring!" The poet dramatically visualizes the terrifying scene as he personally experienced it, and his syntax seems to reflect this. "To the modern eye, this might look like a contradictory image. But the sequence works as follows: First the crowd of enemies is likened to a herd of brawny bulls; then the poet focuses on the gaping mouths, presumably imagined as human mouths.... In the final step, these rapacious men ready to swallow him are likened to lions" (Alter 2007:73). "The description of the lions is more moving in the MT by its brevity and use of participles: 'tearing' and 'roaring'" (VanGemeren 1991:205).

C′					
14.1			נִשְׁפַּכְתִּי		[a]כַּמַּיִם
			I-am-poured-out		like-the-waters
14.2		כָּל־עַצְמוֹתָי	וְהִתְפָּרְדוּ		
		all = my-bones	and-they-are-dislocated		
14.3		כַּדּוֹנָג	לִבִּי	הָיָה	
		like-beeswax	my-heart	it-has-become	
14.4		[b]מֵעָי	בְּתוֹךְ	נָמֵס	
		my-insides	within	it-has-been-melted	
15.1		[c]כֹּחִי	[d]כַּחֶרֶשׂ	יָבֵשׁ	
		my-strength	like-the-potsherd	it-is-dry	
15.2		מַלְקוֹחָי	מֻדְבָּק		וּלְשׁוֹנִי
		roof-of-my-mouth	being-stuck-to		and-my-tongue

15.3			‎תִּשְׁפְּתֵנִי:	‎מָוֶת	‎וְלַעֲפַר־
			you-lay-me-down	death	and-to-the-dust-of =

[a] Strophe C′ is given internal cohesion by a triad of similes, each marked by the inseparable preposition *k-*.

[b] "The psalmist feels the impact of [his] alienation deep within his inner being. Great fear is likened to 'water' (cf. Jos 7:5; Eze 7:17; 21:7) and to 'wax' (2Sa 17:10). These express formlessness and bring out the feelings of an anguished man. He can no longer function as a human being. The 'bones', 'heart', 'strength', and 'tongue' fail him…because of a traumatic response to being hated and alienated" (VanGemeren 1994:821–822). These anatomical terms in vv. 14–15 and 16–18 suggest that the psalmist is having a near-death experience (McCann 1996:763).

[c] At this point, it may be advisable to adopt "an emendation proposed by many interpreters, medieval and modern, reading *hhiki*, 'my palate', for the Masoretic *kohhi*, 'my vigor' (a simple reversal of letters in the consonantal text). Palate and tongue recur as parallel terms in Hebrew poetry" (Alter 2007:73; cf. Craigie 1983:196). GNT has "my throat" although "there is no ancient witness in support of" this interpretation (Bratcher and Reyburn 1991:220).

[d] Just like a piece of broken pottery, the psalmist feels like a completely broken man, in body and spirit.

[e] "You" (2nd-sg.) in the verb clearly refers to God (cf. vv. 9–11): "The enemies are vexing, but the center of this one's distress is the feeling of separation from God to the point that here God is seen as actively participating in this one's suffering" (deClaissé-Walford et al. 2014:235).

We note that verses 14–15 represent a deliberate alternation in the psalm's established pattern. Here the expected appeal is replaced by another complaint, one that is foregrounded by the psalmist's graphic description of his physical and mental anguish that is coupled with a stark depiction of his felt proximity to death. One senses a note of hopeless resignation in his words, especially in the final climactic utterance: "Surely (*waw*-emphatic), to the very dust of death you are depositing me!" (‎וְלַעֲפַר־מָוֶת תִּשְׁפְּתֵנִי) (15.3). There is a certain irony here: the God whom the psalmist feels is too far away (v. 11) is close enough to lay him in the grave! The actual position of this exclamation may be significant by virtue of its position within the psalm, viz., at its virtual midpoint with three stanzas (36 versus 39 cola) on either side.

The fact that structural centers are often important in Hebrew poetic construction would lead one to check to see whether there might be any special communicative significance at this juncture in the text. In relation to its cotext, it may be suggested that these two verses (14–15) represent the emotive and spiritual nadir of Psalm 22. As reflected in the intense physically based imagery, the poet was almost completely played out at this point (though he could at least still verbalize his feelings despite his tongue sticking to the roof of his mouth!). He suddenly turns upon Yahweh in direct address, seemingly accusing him of permanently sealing his fate on account of his failure to act in his behalf. The general complaint that "There is surely no helper!" at the end of the preceding stanza (כִּי־אֵין עֹזֵר—11.3, i.e., structural epiphora), is here bitterly sharpened into a specific charge against Yahweh—that his God was laying him in the grave! The psalmist could descend no lower in his faith, either for the present or for any possible future; all hope was seemingly gone. Perhaps it was in order to distinguish this crucial segment in his lament that the pray-er decided to alter its regular thematic arrangement, shifting from the expected plea for help to the expression of a grievance that is Job-like in its grim pessimism (cf. Job 10:9; 30:23).

D					
16.1		כְּלָבִים	סְבָבוּנִי		כִּי
		dogs	they-surrounded-me		indeed
16.2			הִקִּיפוּנִי	מְרֵעִים	עֲדַת
			they-encircled-me	evil-men	a-company-of
16.3				יָדַי וְרַגְלָי:	ᵃכָּאֲרִי
				my-hand and-my-foot	like-the-lion
17.1		כָּל־עַצְמוֹתַי	ᵇאֲסַפֵּר		
		all = my-bones	I-count		
17.2			יַבִּיטוּ		הֵמָּה
			they-stare		they
			יִרְאוּ־בִי:		
			and-they-look = on-me		
18.1	לָהֶם	בְּגָדַי	יְחַלְּקוּ		
	for-themselves	my-garments	they-divide-up		
18.2		ᶜגוֹרָל:	יַפִּילוּ	לְבוּשִׁי	וְעַל־
		a-lot	they-cast	my-clothes	and-for =
D′					
19.1			אַל־תִּרְחָק	ᵈיְהוָה	וְאַתָּה

			not = you-should-be-distant	O-Yahweh	and-you
19.2			חוּשָׁה:	לְעֶזְרָתִי	אֱיָלוּתִי[e]
			rush	to-aid-me	my-strength
20.1	נַפְשִׁי	מֵחֶרֶב	הַצִּילָה		
	my-life	from-sword	rescue		
20.2	יְחִידָתִי:[f]	מִיַּד־כֶּלֶב	----------		
	my-only-one	from-hand-of = dog			
21.1	אַרְיֵה	מִפִּי	הוֹשִׁיעֵנִי		
	lion	from-mouth-of	save-me		
21.2	רֵמִים	וּמִקַּרְנֵי	----------		
	buffaloes	and-from-horns-of			
21.3			עֲנִיתָנִי:[g]		
			you-have-answered-me		

[a] "*Heb* 'like a lion, my hands and my feet'—The Hebrew manuscript evidence is almost without exception supportive of the reading 'like a lion'" (Harman 2011a:220). However, this reading is often emended because it is grammatically awkward [e.g., "it can scarcely be correct," Craigie 1983:196], but perhaps this obvious awkwardness is by rhetorical design. "Its broken syntax may be intended to convey the panic and terror felt by the psalmist. The psalmist may envision a lion pinning the hands and feet of its victim to the ground with its paws (a scene depicted in ancient Near Eastern art), or a lion biting the hands and feet" (NET footnote; cf. Goldingay 2006:321). Such "broken syntax" aimed at verbally evoking the psalmist's awful predicament is employed elsewhere in this section (see at v. 13).

Some versions attempt to supply an implicit verb: "Like lions [they maul] my hands and feet" (NJV). Based on the tendency for a certain word in the first line of a bicolon to be necessary for the interpretation of the second line, e.g., 'Why?' in 1.1–2 and 'to Yahweh' in 28.1–2, Magonet proposes a similar phenomenon in v. 16: "…a company of evildoers has enclosed me, *(they have enclosed)* like a lion my hands and feet" (1994:107; cf. deClaissé-Walford et al. 2014:230). "The point of mentioning hands and feet is that 'hands' form the means of defense against the enemy, the 'feet' the means of escape" (Harman 2011a:220).

[b] The unexpected insertion of a 1st person singular verb interrupts the sequence of 3rd plurals (the enemies), thus grammatically highlighting the surrounded psalmist's predicament.

[c] As in the case at the close of the preceding strophe (v. 15), the psalmist concludes here with a definite anticipation of imminent death (structural epiphora).

[d] Another dramatic shift foregrounds the covenantal name of Israel's "Holy God"—YHWH! (cf. v. 3a). This is the first time that the psalmist appeals to this divine name in his plight. It was mentioned earlier, but sarcastically by his adversaries (v. 8a). The psalmist next praises the LORD's "name" in vv. 21–22. Already at this point in the psalm, a change in thematic direction is subtly intimated: "Whereas the psalmist had concluded that there was no one to help (v. 11), here [he] addresses God as 'my help' or 'my strength' (v. 19)" (McCann 1996:763). Further evidence of the transitional nature of strophe D' is the fact that the three verbs of final appeal in vv. 20–21 (deliver, rescue, answer) occur with a negative sense in vv. 1–10 (vv. 8, 1, 2, respectively), while the mention of "my helper" in 20.2 contrasts with "there is no one helping" in v. 11.3.

[e] "The Hebrew term *'eyalut* ['Strength'] is an unusual epithet for the deity [in fact, a hapax legomenon]. Some have argued that it brings out the etymology of the ordinary word for God, *'el.* It has even been suggested that the term may play on *ayeleth* in the superscription of this psalm" (Alter 2007:74; cf. Craigie 1983:197).

[f] "My only one" (or "my precious one"—in contrast to death) is an adjective used as a noun, "which in parallel with 'my *nefesh*' always refers to something like 'the only life I will ever have'" (Bratcher and Reyburn 1991:222). Alternatively, "the idea here may be to call on God to realize the precious resource God has made [i.e., created—the psalmist!] as a motivation for God to act" (deClaissé-Walford et al. 2014:231).

[g] "*You answered me.* This is how the received text reads…. Because the rest of the psalm is devoted to praising rather than imploring God, perhaps the verb in the past tense is intended as a compact turning point: God has indeed answered the speaker's prayer" (Alter 2007:75). "The structure of the psalm as a whole implies that the text and meaning of MT should be retained" (Craigie 1983:197). "God's help arrives while the person is still crying out" (deClaissé-Walford et al. 2014:236)—*in medias res,* as it were, to vindicate the psalmist's implicit trust.

"The psalmist, perhaps in response to an oracle of salvation, affirms confidently that God has answered him, assuring him that deliverance is on the way…. 'You have answered me' is understood as a triumphant shout which marks a sudden shift in tone and introduces the next major section of the psalm. By isolating the statement syntactically, the psalmist highlights the declaration" (NET note). The detailed *HOTTP* textual commentary agrees with this decision (Bratcher and Reyburn 1991:223). "You have answered me" (עֲנִיתָנִי) triumphantly responds to "you do not answer [me]" (לֹא תַעֲנֶה) in 2.2 (a sub-inclusio); it corresponds to the synonymous verb "he heard" (שָׁמַע) at the end of the next strophe in 24.2 (structural epiphora).

The most prominent structural marker of the major division is the emphatic monocolon of closure in 21.3: "You have answered me!"[20] This

---

[20] This interpretation and the consequent effect on translation is in dispute. It is supported by Craigie, among others: "The perfect tense (of the verb עֲנִיתָנִי) expresses the worshiper's confidence…based on his faith that God would answer his prayers…" (1983:200).

is a cry of faith which so strongly anticipates a positive response from the
LORD to the preceding pleas (especially those expressed in vv. 19–21)
that one can assume that the deed is already done![21] This forward-looking
affirmation also acts as a transitional bridge or structural hinge between
what we might (for lack of a better poetic term) simply call "parts" One
and Two of the psalm. It thus initiates the song of thanksgiving in which
the singer-prayer, together with his fellow-worshipers, commemorates
some gracious act of deliverance of Yahweh on behalf of his people,
whether an individual or a group.

The exclamation "You have answered me!" (21.3) also links up with
the other principal borders of Psalm 22.[22] This occurs by way of contrast
with its beginning, "you have abandoned me!" (עֲזַבְתָּנִי, 1.1, i.e., inclusio)
and "you do not answer" (וְלֹא תַעֲנֶה, 2.2, another inclusio). There is a cor-
responding connection with the onset of cycle one, stanza C: "Indeed (cli-
mactic כִּי), there is no helper!" (11.3, i.e., anaphoric aperture). On the other
hand, an idea similar to 21.3 is reaffirmed at the very end of the psalm in
the words, "For/indeed (כִּי), he has done [it]!" (31.2, i.e., structural epi-
phora). Another inclusion between the onset and conclusion of Part One is
formed through repetition of the key verb 'deliver': "from my deliverance"
(מִישׁוּעָתִי) in 1.2 and "deliver me" (הוֹשִׁיעֵנִי) in 21.1.

One will notice that what has been posited as the two main parts of
Psalm 22 are unbalanced in terms of length—the first "half" roughly twice
as long as the second in terms of lexical units (see below). This would lead
us to look for an appropriate break in the initial section—not that another
major division has to be there (i.e., for the sake of structural balance), but
simply as a check to make sure one way or the other. In this case we might
apply the phonemic principle of "pressure toward symmetry in the system."
Thus, a potential place to consider as a possible boundary would be the
section-initial passage that has already been shown to have a connection
with the principal break between verses 21 and 22, namely, the beginning
of stanza C in v. 11.

---

[21] Craigie offers a liturgical explanation for this unusual structure: The assertion
"You have answered me," "was elicited by the oracular statement declared by a
priest (or perhaps by a prophet) that God would answer. The oracular proclamation
presupposed by this statement of confidence is implied, not stated; presumably it
could not be stated in the text of the liturgy, for the officiating priest (or prophet)
would be waiting for the divine word and would proclaim only the divine word that
was given to him" (1983:200).

[22] "The whole psalm pivots on this one word" (deClaissé-Walford et al. 2014:236)—
in Hebrew: 'you-answered-me!'

E					
22.1	לְאֶחַי	שִׁמְךָ	אֲסַפְּרָה^a		
	to-my-brothers	your-name	I-will-declare		
22.2			אֲהַלְלֶךָּ:^b	קָהָל^c	בְּתוֹךְ
			I-will-praise-you	congregation	inside
23.1			הַלְלוּהוּ ו	יְהוָה	יִרְאֵי^d
			praise-him	Yahweh	fearers-of
23.2			כַּבְּדוּהוּ	יַעֲקֹב	כָּל־זֶרַע
			glorify-him	Jacob	all=seed-of
23.3	כָּל־זֶרַע יִשְׂרָאֵל:	מִמֶּנּוּ	וְגוּרוּ		
	all=seed-of Israel	from-before-him	and-be-awed		
24.1			בָזָה	לֹא־	כִּי^e
			he-despised	not=	for
24.2	עָנִי	עֱנוּת^f	שִׁקַּץ	וְלֹא	
	an-afflicted-one	affliction-of	he-abhorred	and-not	
24.3	מִמֶּנּוּ	פָּנָיו	הִסְתִּיר	וְלֹא־	
	from-him	his-faces	he-hid	and-not=	
24.4			שָׁמֵעַ:	אֵלָיו	וּבְשַׁוְּעוֹ
			he-heard	unto-him	and-[in]-his-cry
E'					
25.1	רָב	בְּקָהָל	----------	תְהִלָּתִי	מֵאִתְּךָ^g
	great	in-congregation		my-praise	from-with-you
25.2	יְרֵאָיו:	נֶגֶד	אֲשַׁלֵּם		נְדָרַי
	those-fearing-him	in-the-presence-of	I-will-pay		my-vows
26.1		עֲנָוִים ו	יֹאכְלוּ^h		
		afflicted-ones	they-will-eat		

			וְיִשְׂבָּֽעוּ		
			and-they-will-be sated		
26.2	דֹּרְשָׁיו	יְהוָה	יְהַֽלְלוּ		
	those-seeking-him	Yahweh	they-will-praise		
26.3	לָעַֽד:	לְבַבְכֶם	יְחִי		
	forever	your-heart	may-they-live		

[a] "'Let me sing' is a cohortative intensive in the singular, still the style of a personal prayer. 'I shall celebrate thy name' is an indicative future with a *daghesh energeticus*, which indicates an emphasis of the will in making such a decision" (Terrien 2003:233).

[b] The verb "praise (Yahweh)" (הלל) occurs cohesively in every verse of stanza E (vv. 21–26) except v. 25, where the negative-positive reasons for praise are given. "The taunts of the mockers are thus drowned out by the songs of the faithful" (VanGemeren 1991:209).

[c] "The 'congregation' [GK 7702] is here a technical term for the congregation of the righteous, which excludes that of ungodly and mocking Israelites (cf. vv. 7–8). They are further identified as 'you who fear the LORD'....The taunts of the mockers are now drowned out by the songs of the faithful" (VanGemeren 1994:822). The community of the godly (vv. 21–22) will always ultimately triumph over the diabolical forces of evil (vv. 12–18).

[d] The translation "fear" for this Hebrew verb is often misunderstood in English. Here the psalmist addresses fellow 'devoted ones'—"Human fear brings forth not praise but abuse, but fear of the Lord is just and right, and so it begets praise, confesses love, fires the flames of charity" (Cassiodorus) (Blaising and Hardin 2008:175). "The verbs 'praise', 'honor', and 'revere' form the outward expression of the fear of the Lord" (VanGemeren 1994:823).

[e] Strophe E climaxes with an emphatic assertion of the "reason for praise" (כִּי) here in v. 24. "This may be the most powerful verse in the whole psalm," as the psalmist publicly testifies that "even in the lowest moments when the feelings of fear and shame surround, God did not abandon" him (deClaissé-Walford et al. 2014:236)—and that contrary to his own agonized cry of initial accusation (v. 1).

[f] The noun-adjective (used as a noun) combination based on the same root underscores the psalmist's prior dilemma—that is, before the Lord intervened in deliverance (cf. v. 26.1 below).

[g] Yahweh is both the source and the object of the psalmist's "praise" (Bratcher and Reyburn 1991:225); God is also the object of the psalmist's prior vows, that is, of thanksgiving for anticipated deliverance. The noun תְהִלָּתִי serves as the action word of this emphatic, strophe-initial verbless construction. The psalmist now joins the community of Israel in their heartfelt "praises" of Yahweh (cf. v. 4.2).

[h] Apparently, in a meaningful play on words, the psalmist promises that as part of his votive thank offering (Lev. 7:16–21), he will have a fellowship meal to which he will invite (formerly) afflicted folk (like him, v. 24.2), who will be able to eat their fill in honor of Yahweh (Bratcher and Reyburn 1991:226; VanGemeren 1991:210).

[i] The strophe (and stanza E) concludes with a dramatic insertion of direct speech: "The psalmist wishes health, prosperity, happiness, for all his guests" (Bratcher

and Reyburn 1991:226). This wish may be a conventional expression that was used during the making of a vow—or during the meal celebrating its successful completion. In any case, "other similar statements without any introductory comment or explanation, that are in effect exclamations, occur in Psalms 31:14a; 45:6a; and 87:6b.... Here the use of the jussive form (*yechiy*, 'may [your hearts] live') may be an intentional use in order to vary the verb sequences, addressing directly the persons who have just been spoken of [to or about] in the preceding context" (Harman 2011a:223)—namely, v. 25 (cf. 22–23).

The two binary stanzas that constitute the strongly optimistic Part Two of Psalm 22 are likewise quite clearly demarcated, namely, vv. 22–26 (E + E′) and 27–31 (F + F′). The ethnic vision of worshipful commendation of the LORD that is expressed in stanza E is progressively amplified in order to accommodate the whole world in stanza F. Thus, references to "my brothers in the congregation [of]...the seed of Jacob/Israel" (vv. 22–23) lead off the former unit, while the onset of the latter section is distinguished by a greatly expanded human scope, including "all the ends of the earth" and "all the families of the nations" (v. 27, i.e., structural anaphora with vv. 22 and 25). Correspondingly, the joyous, exclamatory wish that concludes stanza E: "May your hearts live forever!" (יְחִי לְבַבְכֶם לָעַד) (26.3) is complemented by an enthusiastic affirmation of a divine response at the close of stanza F: "Indeed, he has done [it]!" (כִּי עָשָׂה) (31.2, i.e., structural epiphora). In this connection, it is interesting to observe that each of the six stanzas seems to end on an emphatic note; in addition to E and F just mentioned, there is A: "...and they were not ashamed!" (5.2); B: "Indeed, there is no helper!" (11.3); C: "Yes, in the dust of death you are depositing me!" (15.3); D: "You have answered me!" (21.3).

F					
27.1			יִזְכְּרוּ		
			they-will-remember		
	כָּל־אַפְסֵי־אָרֶץ	אֶל־יְהוָה	[a] וְיָשֻׁבוּ ǀ		
	all = ends-of = earth	unto = Yahweh	and-they-will-turn		
27.2[b]	כָּל־מִשְׁפְּחוֹת גּוֹיִם:	לְפָנֶיךָ[c]	וְיִשְׁתַּחֲווּ		
	all = clans-of nations	to-your-faces	and-they-will-worship		
28.1		הַמְּלוּכָה	----------	לַיהוָה	כִּי[d]
		the-kingship		to-Yahweh	because

28.2		בַּגּוֹיִם:	וּמֹשֵׁל		
		over-the-nations	and-[he is]-ruling		
F′					
29.1			אָכְלוּ[e]		
			they-will-eat		
	אֶרֶץ	כָּל־דִּשְׁנֵי־[f]	וַיִּשְׁתַּחֲווּ ׀		
	earth	all = fat-ones-of =	and-they-will-worship		
29.2	עָפָר[g]	כָּל־יוֹרְדֵי	יִכְרְעוּ		לְפָנָיו
	dust	all = going-down	they-will-kneel		to-his-faces
29.3			חִיָּה:	לֹא	וְנַפְשׁוֹ
			he-keeps-alive	not	and-his-life
30.1			יַעַבְדֶנּוּ		זֶרַע[h]
			it-will-serve-him		a-seed
30.2	לְדוֹר:	לַאדֹנָי	יְסֻפַּר		
	to-the-[next]-generation	to/about-the-Lord	it-will-be-declared		
31.1			יָבֹאוּ		
			they-will-come		
		צִדְקָתוֹ[i]	וְיַגִּידוּ		
		his-righteousness	and-they-will-proclaim		
31.2				נוֹלָד	לְעָם
				being-born	to-a-people
			עָשָׂה:[j]		כִּי
			he-did-[it]		that

[a] The prefixed verbal forms of v. 27 may be understood as jussives, as in the NET: "Let all the peoples of the earth acknowledge the LORD and turn to him!"—with v. 28 then providing the reason (כִּי).

[b] The bicolon of v. 27 represents the longest poetic lines of the psalm—perhaps a phonological isomorphic equivalent that reflects the content being expressed, with reference to "the ends of the earth!" "The nations—included in the Abrahamic covenant as "all the families of the nations" (Ge 12:3;

Ps. 96:7)—will "remember"...the Lord. The act of remembrance is an act of obeisance and worship" (VanGemeren 1994:823).

ᶜ Most versions render "before him" to stay consistent with the preceding colon's "to Yahweh;" however, an emendation is not needed to support this translation since pronominal interchange, especially between different cola, is quite common in Hebrew poetry (enallage). Thus, just as there is a direct address to the assembled congregation at worship in v. 26, so also in v 27 their God, Yahweh, is addressed directly (Harman 2011a:223).

ᵈ As in the case of strophe E, so also here in strophe F, the unit concludes with a focus on the "reason for praise" (כִּי), cf. 24.1, i.e., structural epiphora.

ᵉ This verse is typically heavily emended by scholars (e.g., Broyles 1999:122), for example, the first word from *'okhlû* 'they shall eat' to *'ak lô* 'indeed, to him,' cf. BHS, RSV; VanGemeren 1991:211). However, "if this suggestion is followed, then a further emendation is required to change the following verb from being a *vav* consecutive to a simple future by deleting the initial *vav*. As eating has already been mentioned in verse 26, it seems best to retain the MT, avoiding... word division, revocalisation, and deletion" (Harman 2011a:224; deClaissé-Walford et al. 2014:232).

With regard to the unusual verb usage, "eat and worship [lit. 'bow down']": "The verb forms (a perfect followed by a prefixed form with *vav* [וֹ] consecutive) are normally used in narrative to relate completed actions. Here the psalmist uses the forms rhetorically as he envisions a time when the LORD will receive universal worship" (NET note; cf. 27.1). This is just one example of how the microsyntax of this psalm (over and above the normal poetic lexicon) is used functionally—to serve a literary-structural purpose, hence enhancing the text's communicative quality and effectiveness.

ᶠ Some commentators emend the first consonant of the verb form from *dalet* (d) to *yod* (y)—from "the fat ones" to "the sleeping ones," thus providing a close semantic and literary (i.e., phonological) parallel with the verb in the next line, "those who descend" (e.g., Craigie 1983:197); however, there is little manuscript or versional support for this change (cf. VanGemeren 1991:211 and the *Logos Lexham Interlinear Bible*).

Furthermore, we note what appears to be a strongly contrastive reference in the next line to the dead, which may have sounded strange, perhaps even shocking to most Jewish hearers. "This inclusion of the dead among God's worshipful subjects is unusual because a reiterated theme in Psalms is that the dead, mute forever, cannot praise God. Perhaps the poet, having imagined God's dominion extending to the far ends of the earth, also wants to extend it downward—against common usage—into the very underworld" (Alter 2007:76). The antithetical usage here (29.1 vs. 29.2–3) might be interpreted as an all-inclusive merism, which is quite appropriate for this climactic point in the psalmist's praise (cf. deClaissé-Walford et al. 2014:232).

In favor of the MT, the NET (footnote) offers a reasonable explanation, which is always better than an emendation: "*Heb* 'fat [ones]'. This apparently refers to those who are healthy and robust, i.e., thriving. In light of the parallelism, some prefer to emend the form to...*y'esheney*, 'those who sleep [in the earth]'; cf. NAB, NRSV, but...*dishney*, 'fat [ones]') seems to form a merism with 'all who descend into the grave' in the following line.

The psalmist envisions all people, whether healthy or dying, joining in worship of the LORD."

[g] The expression "all those descending [into the] dust" recalls the psalmist's own sad situation (v. 15.3)—an amazing reversal, but with the same God in sovereign control.

[h] Future generations join the fathers (v. 4) as the psalm draws to an all-inclusive close. "As in a medieval ballad [the final verses] sum up the poem and become the equivalent of a musical 'fugue'" (Terrien 2003:235). "Each generation will join in with the telling of the story of God's kingship (cf. vv. 3–5) and will add what God has done for them. This is the essence of redemptive history" (VanGemeren 1994:823)—one that climaxes at the Cross (cf. Mt. 27:39–46; Mk. 15:29–34).

[i] "In this context 'righteousness' has the idea of 'salvation', 'deliverance'" (Harman 2011a:224; cf. VanGemeren 1994:823).

[j] "Neither the subject nor the object are expressed in the Hebrew text, but the preceding references to the way in which the Lord heard the cry of the psalmist makes it plain that it is the deliverance by the LORD that is in view" (Harman 2011a:224; cf. deClaissé-Walford et al. 2014:233). *"For he has done.* The abruptness reflects the Hebrew. What God has done, in any case, would have to be His bounty or kindnesses (Hebrew *tsedaqot*) to those who fear Him" (Alter 2007:77)—more specifically, "his deliverance/righteousness" in v. 31.1—with reference to Yahweh's saving actions that vindicate his people, the oppressed in particular. The LXX makes the subject explicit, viz. "what *the Lord* has done" (Craigie 1983:197). GNT reflects the concluding emphasis of the Hebrew by rendering the final clause in direct speech: "The LORD saved his people," which would certainly be appropriate in this context (strophe F′).

4.6 Summary

Part One of Psalm 22 is segmented into what we might term cycles (for lack of a better term)—that is, a pairing of related stanzas, designated as (A—A′) + (B—B′) // (C—C′) + (D—D′) on the structural chart above. Part Two of the psalm consists of cycle 3: (E—E′) + (F—F′). Cycle 2 of Part One, as we will see, represents a thematic and emotive intensification of cycle 1, in several ways: the human source of the poet's grief is more graphically described (vv. 12–13, 16–18); the expression of his own physical and psychological reactions is magnified (vv. 14–15); his personal appeal to Yahweh is made more verbally concrete and concentrated (vv. 19–21). The explicit heightening observed in cycle 2 thus follows the general tendency of Hebrew verse to manifest a sharpening of semantic focus and/or a strengthening in the affective impression that is conveyed by the (B) half of a parallel bicolon (Alter 1985:615).

Moving down to the next lower level of poetic organization, we come to the stanza unit of structure. A consideration of the content as well as the form of Psalm 22 indicates a very symmetrical manner of construction. There are six compound stanzas in all, four in Part One (two per cycle), and another pair in the Part Two. Each stanza consists of two strophes, e.g., A +

A′, B + B′, etc.[23] With one significant exception, the sequence of stanzas in Part One reveals an alternating illocutionary movement, which produces a doubly twofold pattern that relates to the author's primary communicative intentions and associated personal feelings. Thus, there is an initial complaint describing his desperate situation followed by either an implicit or explicit appeal (based on trust) to Yahweh for deliverance. This pragmatic framework of Part One may be summarized as follows:

Stanza/Cycle	Complaint	Appeal
A + A′	1–2	3–5
B + B′	6–8	9–10
C + C′	11–13	
	14–15	
D + D′	16–18	19–21

This succession of strophes may also reflect a subtly alternating shift in perspective, that is, from an inward to an outward point of view, thus, internal: strophes A, B′, C′, D′; external: strophes A′, B, C, D. The proposed boundaries for these four stanzas and their constituent strophes will be further justified when the psalm's microstructure is examined more closely below.

4.7 A further review of the structural evidence

As suggested above, each of the six putative stanzas that have been delineated may be further segmented into strophes, or poetic paragraphs, which are the smallest structural division above the colon complex, or poetic line (consisting of a bi-/tri-colon). Psalm 22 is thus composed of twelve strophes which function in a dual capacity, namely, to mutually define one another within the wider discourse and hence also to help demarcate the larger units (e.g., stanzas) into which they have been incorporated. A number of the key strophic signals in this psalm have already been pointed out. The remaining structural markers are summarized below in the sequential order in which they appear. Not every literary (artistic-rhetorical) feature in the text is included in this description—only those which are most prominent and have greater significance with reference to the overall compositional organization.

---

[23] Terrien, too, finds an artistic balance that runs throughout Psalm 22: "Structural analysis...reveals a remarkable symmetry of strophic continuity.... The strophic analysis appears to support the unity of composition for the whole psalm" (2003:229–230).

It is important to recognize the linguistic diversity that is revealed in this overview, a literary phenomenon that has two major implications— one extrinsic and the other intrinsic to the biblical text. The first principle pertains to procedure, suggesting the unreliability of any approach which depends largely upon a single literary feature or diagnostic technique (e.g., meter, repetition, inclusio, etc.) to describe the intricacies of the discourse structure of a poetic work. Rather, all of the rhetorical devices found to be present in the text must be interpreted together, in relation to one another, in order to offer a balanced and mutually corrective perspective on the whole. And secondly with respect to appreciation or assessment, we observe that the essential unity of an admirable literary work, like Psalm 22, is realized on all layers of verbal composition by its varied combination of artistic qualities, which manifests different aspects of formal as well as semantic continuity and/or discontinuity (see 4.1 above). This is yet another fact that attests to the exceptional literary expertise of its original author. He (presumably, in view of the culture and age concerned) was not only a perceptive theologian and a sincere worshiper of Yahweh; indeed, it is evident that he was also one of ancient Israel's most eloquent poets.

4.7.1 *Psalm 22: PART ONE*

Stanza/Strophe   *Structural Markers*

A   Throughout Part One of the psalm, the strophes correspond to the pragmatic divisions presented above; that is, they match the alternating units of complaint and appeal. The beginning of this poetic prayer is announced in dramatic fashion by the reiterated, hence intensively personified vocative call, "My God!" (אֵלִי).[24] This introduces a rhetorical question which dramatizes the issue of theodicy that dominates the first half of the psalm: "Why have you abandoned me?" (i.e., *you should not have treated your servant so!*). The pronominal ending *-iy* (ִי- 'me/my') sound appears eight times in the initial strophe to give it phonological cohesion as well as to accentuate the pathetic plight of the poet. These reiterated first-person references also highlight the irony of the situation: how could such an afflicted individual presume to call out, "*my* God?" After yet another resounding vocative, אֱלֹהַי, the crucial notion of separation is continued, with the addition of the concept of time (v. 2, a merism) to that of space (v. 1) to reinforce the idea of completeness—the gap was indeed great! This, in turn, underscores the "no-answer" (a repeated

---

[24] A double vocative like this indicates a close personal relationship, e.g., Genesis 22:11 (Abraham), Exodus 3:4 (Moses), 2 Samuel 19:4 (Absalom), 2 Kings 2:12 (Elijah). "Notice that in declaring his right to say 'my God', the figure speaks not of his own acts or character or status but only of God and what God has done" (Mays 1994a:109).

"no!" לֹא) which is the only response that the non-silent suppliant receives to the many pleas to his God (לִי... אֵלַי—phonic inclusio).

A′ The topical focus suddenly shifts by way of contrast from the first to the second person singular pronoun to signal the onset of the second strophe: וְאַתָּה 'But you...' (3.1). This emphasis upon the sovereign, divine "you" continues, as three more lines in succession are initiated with a pronominal reference to the trustworthy Lord, Yahweh: בְּךָ (4.1). אֵלֶיךָ (5.1). בְּךָ (5.2). These assertions are further conjoined by a common syntactic pattern: Adjunct (prep./"you") + Verb (reason) + Verb (result). A final switch from the prevailing optimistic pattern to a negative (yet still connotatively positive) with the last verb indicates a closure of the strophe as well as the stanza (A): "...and they were not ashamed/disappointed," which reflects, but this time in topical contrast with, the negatives that conclude the preceding strophe. This final verb, בוֹשׁוּ, phonologically recalls the initial description of Yahweh: קָדוֹשׁ יוֹשֵׁב '(you are) holy, seated/enthroned' (inclusio). Three repetitions of the key verb/concept "they trusted," בָּטְחוּ, along with the recurrent word-final pronominal marker 'they' (וּ-) contributes to this strophe an additional correspondence in both sense and sound. The prayerful "cry" of Israel's fathers was based on 'trust' and it resulted in "deliverance"—not "shame!" "Having God as 'my God' rests first of all on belonging to a community for whom the center of all reality is 'the holy one' who is enthroned as king in heavenly and earthly temple...and whose acts of salvation are the content of Israel's hymns of praise" (Mays 1994a:108).

B Another emphatic pronoun, וְאָנֹכִי 'I/me' (6.1) announces the onset of the initial strophe of a new stanza. This contrasts with the divine 'you' of 3.1 (anaphora) and coincides with a temporal shift back to the present time of praying. This self-reference is pejoratively heightened by means of a syntactic juxtaposition with the connotatively opposing nouns "worm" and "man." Conceptual coherence for this unit is provided by a string of terms selected from the semantic field of denigration: "reproach," "despised," "mocked," etc. A profound sense of self-rejection (v. 6), exacerbated by social rejection (vv. 7–8), is the apparent consequence of divine rejection (v. 1)—or so the psalmist perceives his situation. This depreciatory sequence reaches its emotive climax in the concluding segment of direct speech, provocatively set in the mouths of his enemies (v. 9). This utterance features a chiastic verbal pattern that divides the quotation and foregrounds the two focal participants:

a *he* relied on **Yahweh** (motivation)
　b let **Him** deliver *him* (invocation)
　b′ let **Him** rescue *him* (invocation)
a′ for **He** delights in *him* (motivation)

These strophe-final references to "reliance" and "rescue" constitute an ironic echo of the corresponding notions found at the close of the preceding unit (v. 6, i.e., contrastive epiphora). In this case, the actual "trust" (expectation) is that Yahweh will *not* act to deliver the believer. Nevertheless, these words of the enemies, whether real or conjectured, do in fact bear negative testimony to the psalmist's close relationship to his God.

B′　A striking pronominal switch coupled with an asseverative conjunction, "Surely you..." (כִּי־אַתָּה), again leads the new strophe off with a contrastive personal reference (9.1, anaphora). An extended lexical introversion, which includes some consonance (i.e., *m/b/t* sounds) and assonance (in *–iy*), forms the conceptual backbone of this unit. The carefully constructed sequence also accents the closeness of the fatherly, yet also the "motherly" (covenantal) relationship that once existed between the plaintiff-psalmist and his (lit. "my") "God" (cf. 1.1):[25]

a Surely **you**
　b the one who drew me forth
　　c from the womb
　　　d the one giving me assurance
　　　　e upon the breasts of *my mother*
　　　　e′ upon **you**
　　　d′ I was cast (i.e., in trust)
　　c′ from the womb, from the womb of *my mother*
　b′ my God
a′ (are) **you**!

The repetition of 'you' (2ⁿᵈ masc. sg.) at the beginning, middle, and end of this construction creates a thematic projection that focuses again upon the divine addressee of the psalmist's prayer. The psalmist's fervent "statements about God are confessions of faith, of confidence in God. But in the prayer they serve also as complaints, as panels of contrast to the figure's present situation" (Mays 1994a:109).

---

[25] "This individual relationship is described by the use of a metaphor that portrays God in the role of a human father who takes the child as it comes from the womb, lays it on its mother's breast to be nursed, and thereafter furnishes the environment of provision and security in which life is lived" (Mays 1994a:109).

C   However, with a further touch of pathetic irony, the preceding
     positive affirmation of faith leads directly back to the central
     notion of perceived separation and the appellant's grave per-
     plexity concerning a God who is "far away" when trouble is
     "nearby" (v. 11; cf. v. 1, anaphora). Thus, the opening staccato
     tricolon (11.1–2–3) contrasts in form (2 + 2 + 2, three "words"
     per colon) as well as in content with the preceding poetic mate-
     rial. Several other prominent markers of aperture that converge
     to clearly indicate the beginning of this new strophe/stanza/
     cycle have already been pointed out.
         A shocking new image in rhyme then confronts the poet and
     his audience alike to develop the theme that "trouble is near": the
     psalmist is "surrounded" by פָּרִים רַבִּים 'many bulls' (12.1; cf. 16.1,
     anaphora).[26] The author's human enemies (vv. 6–7) are thus meta-
     phorically transformed into raging beasts as they suddenly appear
     on the lyric scene to attack him with increased ferocity.[27] Another
     structural reversal highlights this structural aperture:[28]

         a they have surrounded me
             b many bulls
             b' the strong ones (i.e., bulls) of Bashan
         a' they have encircled me.

     The strophe closes with an even more vicious scene, one that is
     augmented by vocal assonance: אַרְיֵה טֹרֵף וְשֹׁאֵג 'a lion ripping and
     roaring' (13.2). The strophe-final verb 'roar' recalls the psalmist's
     own "roaring" (שַׁאֲגָתִי) in response to his dire predicament (1.2, i.e.,
     a paronomastic inclusio).

---

[26] The pairing of oxen and lions is a conventional pairing that represents the epito-
me of brute force and fearsomeness, while "hounds and hunters (vv. 16, 20) evoke
the helpless prey.... Perhaps the metaphors give these enemies a demonic cast;
in the ancient Near Eastern religions, demons and divine figures often appear as
animals" (Mays 1994a:110). "Such metaphors...serve to engage the mind and to
stir emotions" (Harman 2011a:219). They also suggest that "the powers of evil are
unleashed against the psalmist so as to make it appear that the only possible con-
sequence is death" (McCann 1996:763).
[27] In the laments such as Ps. 22, "the enemies are described in rather general ways
and are thus difficult to identify with any specificity. In additions, the identity of
the enemies varies from psalm to psalm" (Bellinger 1990:53). This generality of ref-
erence makes it possible for believers of every age to imagine their own particular
foes as they pray the words of this psalm.
[28] "Chiasmus is one of the syntactic techniques in Hebrew poetry for marking stan-
za boundaries" (Bratcher and Reyburn 1991:219).

C′   The preceding external, bestial imagery is unexpectedly altered to that depicting the internal distress that is seemingly associated with a severe physical ailment. Thus, the psalmist turns from the threatening enemy without to that within as he introspectively struggles to deal with his own inner physical pain and psychological stress (vv. 14–15). Matters appear to get even worse as liquid images ("water" and "wax") paradoxically merge with those of extreme dryness and thirst, which reach their emotive peak (his mental cellar) in the "dust of death" (וְלַעֲפַר־מָוֶת) at the close of the strophe/stanza (15.3). Another prominent lexical string that lends supportive cohesion to this segment involves various references to the sufferer's internal organs: "my bones...heart...bowels...tongue...palate." The pointed juxtaposition of the pronouns "you—subject," i.e., Yahweh, and "me—object" (תִּשְׁפְּתֵנִי) as the strophe terminates brings together the central protagonists in this deeply religious drama of life and death. The psalmist echoes Job as he appears to hold God responsible for his perilous plight!

D   This fourth stanza begins in almost the same way as the preceding one, namely, with a vivid portrayal of the enemies "surrounding" the suppliant (16.1–2; cf. 12.1–2, i.e., structural anaphora). But this time the horror of the psalmist's situation is intensified (including an initial כִּי 'Yes, indeed...') as the adversaries are referred to as spatially near, but ritually impure "dogs" (כְּלָבִים). Another chiasmus, exactly parallel to that of 12.1–2, serves to reinforce the drama of this scene:

>   a they have surrounded me
>   b dogs
>   b′ a pack of wicked ones
>   a′ they have hemmed me in.

A corresponding circular construction concludes the strophe (18.1–2) with a description of the enemy now shamefully invading the psalmist's very person. This may in fact be a gloomy allusion to his own imminent demise, which he thus views as having already taken place:

>   a they divide
>   b my garments among them
>   b′ and for my clothing
>   a′ they cast a lot.

At the midpoint of the strophe (17.1) there is a brief and unexpected shift in the grammatical subject sequence from "they" to "I (count)" (אֲסַפֵּר), as the poet sadly contemplates his miserable condition. Supportive phonological connectivity within this unit is maintained by the continual alternation between *-uw* 'they' and *-i/-ay* 'me/my' inseparable pronouns, a combination that mimics the pathetic participant who is being poetically depicted.

D′ An emphatic shift to "you-sg." (וְאַתָּה) with reference to Yahweh, coupled with the central motif of separation, recalls the first strophe of Part One (cf. v. 11, inclusio) and here also begins its final strophe (אַל־תִּרְחָק/רָחוֹק מִישׁוּעָתִי, vv. 1.2/19.1, i.e., anaphora). This contrastive aperture initiates a series of petitionary verbs that plead to the LORD for "help" (לְעֶזְרָתִי, 19.2; cf. עוֹזֵר, 11.3): "do not be distant...hurry... deliver...save me." The extended prayer sequence is forcefully and somewhat surprisingly concluded (as noted earlier) by the plaintiff's proclamation: "you have answered me" (עֲנִיתָנִי) in v. 21.3 (cf. 2.2, a perfect tense of anticipated prophetic fulfillment).[29] This verb thus foregrounds in an extraordinary way the onset of the psalm's second "half" (Part Two) through a clear foreshadowing of its second thematic division (cf. 24.4, 31.1, i.e., corresponding epiphora).

To further underscore the significance of this conclusion, the psalmist makes mention again of the human "beasts" from whom he is requesting his God for deliverance: the "dog" (כֶּלֶב), the "lion" (אַרְיֵה), and the "wild oxen" (רֵמִים)[30]—in reverse order now from their introduction earlier in this cycle (20.2, 21.1–2; cf. 12.1, 13.2, 16.1). In this final strophe, the poetic appellant masterfully fuses together the two principal themes of his petition, namely, his separation from a God who seems far away in contrast to his proximity to a multitude of formidable foes. On the other hand, the seed of his hoped-for salvation has been planted in the very verbs that he prays, confidently trusting now that his God would "come quickly" to "deliver" him (1.2, 2.2 // 19.2, 20.1), thus not "despising" his

---

[29] This interpretation is supported by Magonet; also, "despite the abruptness, this [verb] effectively forms a bridge to the third part of the psalm which is a hymn of praise to God" (1994:108). And this section (Part Two) does not appear to be a separate psalm that has simply been scribally cobbled on to the close of the preceding unit (v. 21), for "there are again a number of linkages with earlier parts of the Psalm.... [For example], in verse 18 [17] he 'counted' his bones, in verse 23 [22] he will 'recount' God's name, i.e., praise God, and this will happen in future generations as well (v. 31 [30]), 'it will be told', *y'suppar*" (Magonet 1994:109).

[30] "The Hebrew term רֵמִים (*remim*) appears to be an alternate spelling of רְאֵמִים (*rǝ'emim*, 'wild oxen'; see **BDB** 910 s.v. רְאֵם)"—NET footnote.

"afflicted one" (vv. 6, 8; cf. 24). This implicit faith provides an impressive close to a powerfully expressed lament to the LORD. In the great conceptual gap between verses 21 and 22, then, the psalmist either assumes a scenario in which Yahweh actually did come to his aid or he strongly anticipates such a saving outcome, which in turn motivates his thankful response in Part Two.

4.7.2 Psalm 22: PART TWO

Stanza/Strophe   *Structural Markers*

E This second major portion of the psalm leads off with an intensive form that introduces a new poetic genre and sets the tone for all of the words that follow.[31] It is a cohortative verb (אֲסַפְּרָה) that emphasizes the speaker's determination or resolution to perform the action expressed. Thus, in sharp contrast to the mournful complaints and desperate appeals that characterize Part One, here the psalmist starts off with an optimistic assertion: "Let me proclaim (or, 'I will surely declare') your name to my brothers..." (22.1). This self-imperative to praise Yahweh is reiterated in chiastic form to suggest the completeness of the verbal action involved, as well as the corporate solidarity and full participation of all those concerned:[32]

a Let me proclaim your name
    b to my brothers
    b' among the assembly
a' I will praise you!

The circle of agents who are active in this acclaim is then widened considerably in the subsequent chiasmus, which features a reversal

---

[31] The sudden, commentator-confounding shift in topic and tone that occurs here at the onset of Part Two (stanza E) is not an uncommon feature of lament psalms. This conceptual gap-spanning movement significantly illustrates the *chesed*-based covenantal *(birith)* relationship that binds believers with their LORD. Thus, there is "the emergence of a remarkable outburst of praise from a covenantal appeal as though the prayer were already answered (see Pss. 6, 13, 22, 28, 31, 54, 56, 57, 69, 71, 85, 109). It is not however, that the circumstance has changed [not necessarily—not unless prayed retrospectively]; the individual has changed. The prayer of faith has brought him [her] into an experiential connection with God's love *[chesed]*, and it is here that faith blossoms into joy, irrespective of what the prevailing circumstances might be" (Jacoby 2013:78; material in brackets added).

[32] "The group who celebrate [the psalmist's] deliverance with him have a theological spiritual identity. They are not simply family, friends, and neighbors, a company constituted by natural and accidental relations. They are brothers (v. 22) in a religious sense" (Mays 1994a:111).

in the structural position of the doers and their deeds, thereby reinforcing the implication of total harmony and mutual engagement:

    a all the seed of Jacob
       b glorify him
       b' and reverence him
    a' all the seed of Israel!

A series of verbs from the semantic set of commendation (giving vocal expression to the "fear of the LORD" [יִרְאֵי יְהוָה], 23.1) lends cohesion to the initial part of the strophe. This same compositional function is performed in the latter portion by a similar negative (לֹא)-punctuated progression that enunciates the reason for such an enthusiastic celebration of Yahweh: "he has *not* despised...he has *not* hated...he has *not* hidden from...but he has heard (the suffering afflicted ones)" (v. 24).[33] It almost sounds as if the poet wishes to contradict all of the pessimistic assumptions that he uttered at this psalm's beginning (vv. 1–2). A switch to an affirmative assertion at the very end (שָׁמֵעַ) draws the intensive sequence, as well as the strophe itself, to a satisfying close (24.4, a relatively rare tetracolon). This verb synonymously echoes both the climactic resolution of Part One (21.3, i.e., epiphora) and also reaffirms a corresponding set of historically based actions at the end of stanza 1 (A', vv. 4–5, but with an inverted pattern of negative and positive verbs).

E'   Another emphatic "you-sg." form (וְאַתָּה) in reference to Yahweh (topic focus) marks the commencement of the second strophe of this stanza (25.1, i.e., anaphora with 3.1, 9.1, 19.1). The initial line continues with strong anaphoric links to the preceding strophe: "my praise in the great assembly" (22.2) and "his fearers/those fearing him" (23.1). The psalmist's own worship now blends in with the congregation of "Israel" as a whole (cf. 3.2). Following the topical pattern of strophe E, a further reference to the downtrodden is made in an apparent play on two possible senses of the same root: "the humble ones" (עֲנָוִים) of 26.1 and "the afflicted ones" (עָנִי) of 24.2. The strophe/stanza comes to a rousing close in a double expression of rejoicing: First, the pious are exhorted to "praise Yahweh" (יְהַלְלוּ יְהוָה, 26.2), a phrase that recalls similar words at the stanza's beginning (22.2–23.1, i.e., inclusio). This is followed by an

---

[33] The psalmist "is by self-understanding and confession one of the lowly, an '*ani*. It is not his affliction that has made him a lowly one; rather, he has undergone his affliction as one of the lowly" (Mays 1994a:112)—one of the God-"fearers" (25.2). It is possible, as in GNT, to construe vv. 23–24 as the content of the psalmist's "praise" (Bratcher and Reyburn 1991:224).

optative exclamation—a distinctive monocolon—that invokes Yahweh's eternal blessings upon his people: "May your (pl.) hearts live forever!" (26.3; cf. the other concluding monocolon in 21.3 and 31.2). This entire stanza (E), with its stress on lauding the LORD for deliverance received, stands in joyous contrast to the psalm's opening strophe (A), where the poet was contemplating his personal crisis from the opposite side of the fence, as it were.

F   A double verb construction announces the onset of this new strophe and stanza: "They will *remember* and they will *return*..." (27.1). The subject, initially presumed to be the faithful of Israel "seeking (Yahweh)" from 26.2, remarkably turns out to be "all the ends of the earth," that is, "all of the families of nations" (27.1–2). This represents a considerable expansion of thematic scope, implying a mass conversion (lit. "turning") to Yahweh from among the Gentile (non-Jewish) nations.[34] An inclusio demarcates the boundaries of this short panegyric unit, which ends with a verbless emphatic assertion in v. 28.1–2: "Truly (כִּי), to Yahweh (belongs) the dominion—(he is the) one ruling over the nations!"

F'   As in the case of v. 27, so also in v. 29 (an instance of structural anaphora) a double-verb linkage opens this new strophe, literally: "They have eaten and they have bowed down..."[35] Yahweh's worshipers will include the rich (lit., "all [the] fat ones of [the] earth") as well as the poor (lit., "all [the] ones going down [into the] dust"), which constitutes a figurative merism that embraces all people. The latter expression is expanded by "even (someone who) is not able to keep (himself) alive" (29.3), i.e., the materially most wretched people in society.[36] This recalls a similar description that the psalmist used with reference to himself in Part One (v. 15.3), but the respective situations have been dramatically reversed. The morbid pessimism of the earlier passage is here transformed into a glorious hope

---

[34] "This last panel of the psalm identifies [the poet-prayer] as the one whose suffering and salvation are proclaimed to the world as a call to repent (notice *shub* in v. 27...) and believe in the kingdom of God, the dominion of the LORD" (Mays 1994a:112).

[35] These two verbs are interpreted as "predictive perfects" with reference to a future fulfillment, i.e., they will eat (i.e., participate in a ritual feast) and bow down (i.e., worship). The action of religious "eating" (אָכְלוּ) in 29.1 echoes the same verb and sense in v. 26.1 (יֹאכְלוּ), thus forming an exclusio around strophe F.

[36] "To praise the LORD in the throes of death means that some profound change has taken place because of the salvation of the afflicted one that brings dying itself within the sphere of the LORD's reign. The reach of the LORD's righteousness is pressing on the limits of Israel's view of the possible" (Mays 1994a:113).

for the future through the implied agency of Yahweh, the Life-Giver (cf. v. 28). The 'seed' (זֶרַע) of this future generation (30.1) significantly broadens the scope of the poet's prior reference to the 'seed' of Jacob/Israel (v. 23). Another bonding element within Part Two is the summons to 'proclaim' (אֲסַפְּרָה/יְסַפֵּר) the name of Yahweh (22.1/30.2, inclusio). The importance of such public testimony concerning Yahweh's 'righteousness' (צִדְקָתוֹ) is underscored through a reiteration of similar concepts in v. 31: 'they will declare (it) to a people (about) to be born'.[37] On a number of occasions in the Hebrew Bible, the notion of 'righteousness' is connected with that of 'salvation' (e.g., Isa. 46:13, 56:1). Thus, the LORD's covenant justice is overtly manifested in his mighty acts of delivering his people in their time of need, an expectation which the dire straits of the psalmist had almost led him to 'abandon' as he took up his lament (v. 1; cf. v. 11).[38]

A final word of exaltation brings Psalm 22 to a close: "Indeed, (Yahweh) has done (it, i.e., deliver me/us)!" (31.2), and this declaration forges a final contrast with the prayer's downcast beginning: "My God…why have you abandoned me…!" (1.1). This brief utterance also forms the reason portion in an alternating pattern of praise and thanksgiving that runs throughout each of the strophes of Part Two. This sequence is analogous to the interchange of lament and appeal which typifies Part One.

stanza/strophe	*verses: call to praise*	*: reasons for praise*
E	22–23	24
E′	25.1–2, 26.2–3	26.1
F	27	28
F′	29–31.1	31.2

In three of the four reasons (or grounds) sections (the exception being 26.1), the initial colon begins with the ambiguous conjunction כִּי: 'for/because/that', but in these instances probably also asseverative:

---

[37] "Finally, in contrast to the images of death that have so dominated the Psalm, [the poet] talks of future generations, linking verse 24 [23] that speaks of the 'seed' (*zéra*) of Jacob and the 'seed' of Israel with the 'seed' (v. 31 [30]) of a people yet to be born" (Magonet 1994:110).

[38] "The vision of this hymn [stanza F′] is prophetic in character and eschatological in scope. Its place at the conclusion of Psalm 22 connects a vision of the universal, comprehensive, everlasting kingdom of God to what the LORD has wrought in the life of this afflicted one whose prayer and praise the psalm expresses,… In its present form the figure in the psalm shares in the corporate vocation of Israel and the messianic role of David" (Mays 1994a:113)—as, indeed, its superscription would also imply.

"truly/indeed!" The theological point of Psalm 22 thus seems to be that the LORD graciously cares and provides for his own, sooner or later—those who worship him from every people-group on earth as well as from each generation, station, and situation in life.

It may be helpful at this point to summarize the "finely wrought compositional design" (Bratcher and Reyburn 1991:108) of Psalm 22 by means of the following chart, which indicates the various layers of organization:

Psalm 22

PART	ONE (1–21)				TWO (22–31)	
Cycle	A (1–11)		B (12–21)		C (22–31)	

STANZA	A	A′	B	B′	C	C′	D	D′	E	E′	F	F′
Strophe	1–2	3–5	6–8	9–11	12–13	14–15	16–18	19–21	22–24	25–26	27–28	29–31

The preceding strictly linear structure may be complemented and hence compacted by a thematic concentric arrangement, as proposed by Dorsey (1999:178):[39]

A *Introductory Complaint:* God does not hear my cry for help! (1–8)
  B *Specific Appeal* for Help (9–11)
    "Do not be far away (אַל־תִּרְחָק) from me...for there is no helper (עוֹזֵר)!"—v. 11
      C *Description of Dire Situation:* the pit of despair (12–18)
      "Do not be far away (אַל־תִּרְחָק) from me...hasten to help (לְעֶזְרָתִי)!"—v. 19[40]
  B′ *Specific Appeal* for Help (19–21)
A′ *Concluding Praise:* God has heard my cry for help! (22–31)

This proposal rather generalizes the interpersonal dynamics of Psalm 22, but it does provide another formally defensible perspective on the text's expert literary construction.

---

[39] This may be compared with VanGemeren's rather artificial chiastic arrangement: A (1–5), B (6–8), C (9–11), C′ (12–21), B′ (22–24), A′ (25–31), the segments of which do not cohere very well either formally or semantically, for example, with respect to the center: C—"God's Covenantal Responsibilities;" C′—"Abandonment and Prayer for Covenantal Favor" (1991:199).

[40] The parallel pleas of vv. 11 and 19 constitute an exclusio, a structural frame around the central core (vv. 12–18). The repeated notion of being "far away" (רחק) is present to mark the onset of distinct poetic units (i.e., structural anaphora) in vv. 1.2, 11.1, and 19.1.

As I have tried to demonstrate in the preceding discussion, the symmetrical arrangement of this poetic composition is not the superficial product of an artificially contrived and externally imposed desire to achieve harmony or symmetry of form. On the contrary, this framework is eminently functional, being confirmed by the corresponding theologically focused content of the text itself and the proficient manner in which the psalmist has exploited the traditional literary (artistic-rhetorical) devices at his disposal to fashion his heartfelt message for oral-aural proclamation (prayer, recitation, cantillation, etc.) in the most compelling and appealing way.

4.8 On the interaction of topic and type

What happens in this psalm is, in its basic plot, a case of the experience through which the believing Israelite passed in praying in tribulation, using prayers for help and then later, when delivered, praising God with a company of friends. Here the two are joined, intensified, and magnified in a scenario that identifies the combination as the way in which God manifests and discloses his universal eternal reign. (Mays 1994a:108)

Whatever the language, any significant piece of literature maximizes the artistic form in which it has been constructed on both the macro- as well as the microlevel of discourse in order to enhance the communication of its authorial content and intent. These latter two aspects are also closely interconnected with one another in the compositional process, for the subject matter of a text must somehow be related to the writer's perceived objective(s), or his (her) message may be judged by readers to be inappropriate or irrelevant to the situation in which it is transmitted, or the setting to which it is to be applied. We see this felicitous integration of thought, word, and purpose in Psalm 22. To be sure, we are very much removed from the original worship venue for which this liturgical prayer was first created as an individual lament, and in which it was subsequently articulated on innumerable occasions in Israel's history of public prayer. Nevertheless, it is still possible to advance a few general hypotheses which would account for the final shape and substance of the text.

To begin with, one cannot deny the possibility that certain segments of this psalm may have existed elsewhere as part of the Hebrew corpus of religious literature, whether oral or written. In this connection, one might compare verses 6 and 7 with Psalm 44:13–14; verses 11, 13, 19, 22, and 25 with Psalm 35:18, 22–24; and verses 6–8, 22, 26–27 with Psalm 69:16–19, 30,

32, 34—as being possible manifestations of literary intertextuality (though the diachronic direction of influence cannot be determined).[41] However, it is the canonical, received form of the message (essentially the Masoretic Text) that we are concerned with in our analysis and which forms the basis for any type of translation today, whether more or less form-based/meaning-oriented. As has been validated in the preceding text study—and contrary to the opinion of some scholars (e.g., Westermann 1989:82–83)—Psalm 22 is demonstrably a complete whole, structurally as well as rhetorically,[42] and it is on this basis that we might make some tentative observations with regard to its overall communicative function.

With respect to its semantic organization, it may be argued that this psalm's two principal thematic constituents are introduced together in the opening stanza. The first notion, which maintains its prominence throughout Part One is that of divine separation: "Why have you abandoned me?" A transcendent Yahweh seems to be both spatially and temporally remote (vv. 1–2), which are of course conceptual metaphors suggesting the great psychological barrier that seemingly blocks the alienated psalmist from access to his God. Closely associated with the idea of separation is that of silence and the communication breakdown that has occurred: "You do not answer me!" This sovereign quiescence, in an apparent pun on two possible senses of the noun דּוּמִיָּה, has resulted in the poet's restless condition (2.3).

The second topical core is then introduced by way of contrast. The second strophe of stanza A celebrates the solidarity that an imminent Yahweh maintains with his people "Israel." This involves an affinity and a fidelity that manifests itself in action: time and again in the past he answered their "trust" with "deliverance" in the day of trouble (v. 4). His proximity to hear their "cries" for help led in turn to their "praise" of him (3.2, 5.1). Here we have abundant speech, or sound, set in opposition to the above-mentioned quiet that confounded the psalmist, who perceived his "crying," even "roaring," to go unanswered (1.2–2.1). His consequent mental disorientation, occasioned by the apparent aloofness of the "Holy One" upon whom he and his "fathers" depended (3.1, 4.1), is highlighted by his initial plea: Why has *my* God chosen to ignore *me,* in contrast to his merciful dealings with fellow members of the covenant community? He is shocked and dismayed by this

---

[41] Broyles calls attention to the many similarities in structure and theme between Psalms 22 and 69 (1999:121). Holladay calls attention to certain notable parallels in Jeremiah (1996:42).

[42] There is a critical "difficulty of classification inherent in form criticism, namely that lament and praise are often found in one psalm: *praise is frequently the fruit of a transformation in outlook which the psalmist embraces in the midst of crisis or difficulty*" (Hutchinson 2005:95, original italics). It is almost as if this transformation is intended to occur, by faith in the mercy and power of the God being addressed, during the very articulation of the prayer in corporate worship.

supposed contradiction between established theology and his own personal experience (Craigie 1983:199).

The psychological correlates of the spatial metaphors of separation versus proximity may be designated by an antithetical pair of religious terms: estrangement versus fellowship. These concepts, along with the corresponding negative/positive feelings and attitudes that they are associated with, combine to form the connotative background which the psalmist blends into his prayer-song to add emotive richness and resonance to the thematic melody that he is playing, be that largely dissonant (Part One) or harmonious (Part Two). Moreover, it may be that his extreme mental agitation finds its structural reflection in the rapidly shifting topics and perspectives (i.e., alternating from strophe to strophe) which typify the first major portion of Psalm 22 in comparison with the second.

These two discordant themes are appropriately treated in two distinct, but closely interrelated types of poetic composition—the lament (sad) and the eulogy (glad), the first featuring in Part One (1–21), the second in Part Two (22–31) (cf. the discussion in ch. 3). The former manifests illocutionary functions such as complaint, protest, and appeal, while the latter conveys the positive pragmatic notions of praise, thanksgiving, and profession (of faith).[43] We are not dealing, however, with two independent psalmic compositions, rather artificially patched together in their present unified form. Instead, abundant evidence from the Psalter itself would indicate that the lament and the eulogy (thanksgiving) were very often conjoined in the corpus of Hebrew hymnody, e.g., Psalms 10, 13, 28, 41, 55, 64, 69, and many more.

Two pairs of fundamental presuppositions underlie and coalesce in what on the textual surface appear to be two antithetical literary impulses: The first concerns the character of the primary addressee (who he is); the second relates to this individual's activities (what he does/has done). The personage involved here of course is Yahweh, the covenant God of Israel— the nation as a whole, but in particular all those who have accepted his lordship and live accordingly. A pair of fundamental assumptions that pertains to the lament may be expressed as follows: Yahweh has not acted in a crisis situation where he might have been expected to do something on behalf of his believer. Nevertheless, it is worthwhile for the troubled person to address his God in prayer under such circumstances, no matter how seemingly hopeless his situation. The second pair of presuppositions follows from the first: Yahweh has indeed demonstrated his willingness to act in behalf of those who found themselves in a most difficult and

---

[43] Stanza F (vv. 27–31) further exemplifies certain features of the so-called royal (or kingship) sub-type (Broyles 1999:120; cf. Wendland 2002:51–52). Note that expressions of trust are, almost paradoxically, interwoven within the lament proper of Part One, e.g., vv. 3–5, 9–10.

dangerous predicament; in fact, he does so on a regular basis as their history has borne out. Therefore, he is most worthy of praise—not only the acclaim rendered by his pious people, but surprisingly, also that offered by heathen nations found all over the world (v. 27). From this transactional perspective we see that the two principal parts of Psalm 22 are not unrelated at all. On the contrary, they readily complement each other (thematically and literarily) in an ongoing tradition of faith that God's faithful community sought to affirm and articulate in their public as well as private liturgical expression. Estes offers the following rationale for the close relationship between the two major pragmatic portions of the typical lament psalm (2013:162):

> The praise of the psalmists may be better explained by their internal process of mediation, as they reflect upon the significance for their experience of what Yahweh is like, how Yahweh rules over his world, how Yahweh cares for his people, what Yahweh has done and said in the past, and the abiding presence of Yahweh with them. As the psalmists contemplate these theological truths, their view of their adversities is altered as the process of mediation causes them to perceive their experience through the lens of Yahweh's attributes and activity.

The two different poetic types (genres) that comprise Psalm 22 evince a number of formal similarities, held in common with many similar lament-eulogies in the Psalter. Among the more prominent artistic-rhetorical features of Hebrew lyric poetry, as illustrated in the preceding analysis, are the following:

- use of a cola-level chiasmus (inverted parallelism) to introduce or conclude a text unit;
- foregrounding the central topic through its expression in the form of a larger introverted or some other symmetrical construction;
- the repetition and strategic placement of key terms;
- various figures of speech and vivid imagery;
- emphatic, often contrastive personal pronouns;
- intensive vocative openers;
- frequent direct address to Yahweh;
- phonological (including rhythmic) patterning for reinforcing certain key concepts.

Governing this entire poetic compositional process is the application of a comprehensive strategy of balanced structuration. This features the artistic positioning of corresponding semantic elements, both analogous and antithetical, on all levels of linguistic organization to give a sense of unity and harmony to the whole lyric-liturgical composition, as well as to highlight the important disjunctions or thematic peaks within it.[44]

Nevertheless, there are also some important communicative differences between Parts One and Two. The chief of these pertain to the divergence in their respective illocutionary functions, as well as to the more obvious matters of topic and tone. These variations would seem to be significant enough to substantiate our initial inclination to distinguish the two sections as being representative of distinct poetic category types. The major dissimilarities as they apply specifically to Psalm 22 (not the complete Psalter) are listed for comparative purposes below:

Lament	**Eulogy**
personal focus	communal focus
introverted perspective	extroverted perspective
connotatively sad	connotatively glad
sudden contrasts	smooth progression of ideas
subject matter differences:	
affliction from Yahweh	*blessing from Yahweh*
Yahweh as adversary	*Yahweh as deliverer-vindicator*
(but his aid is possible)	*(his aid has been demonstrated)*
constant attack by enemies	*surrounding fellowship of friends*
pain and perceived affliction	*health and total well-being*
typical imagery reflects:	
persecution and suffering	*peace and tranquility*
great disappointment	*complete satisfaction*
continual conflict	*constant unity*
interpersonal disjunction	*interpersonal harmony*
emotive climax:	
individual descent	*universal ascent*
down to the grave	*forward to a new generation*

We also note an interesting contrast in the respective relationships involving the principal cast of characters (or participants) in this psalm. They correspond as shown on the diagram below with reference to the divine center of thematic "gravity":

---

[44] The unity and message of Psalm 22 would be severely diminished if it were limited to the first 21 (22) verses. Thus, many commentators view the subsequent text is post-exilic in origin (e.g., Holladay 1996:43). Besides having no manuscript evidence for such a proposal, we have on the other hand many laments that manifest a medial break as radical and significant as we find in Psalm 22 (vv. 21/22), for example, Ps. 73:14/15.

| Lament: | *enemies* ← (supports) | ---- YAHWEH ---- (disappoints) | → *me* |
| Eulogy: | *enemies* ← (destroys) | ---- YAHWEH ---- (delivers) | → *me* |

4.9 The thematic flow of Psalm 22

The dynamic movement of semantic progression, or thematic development proceeds in the main along an axis which begins from the key concept of separation in Part One and extends to that of solidarity in Part Two. However, allusions to the opposing notion are found at the end of each progression, for example, a passing reference to the unified "praises of Israel" in stanza A (v. 3.2) in contrast to mortuary "dust" in stanza F (v. 29.2). The theme of alienation is gradually intensified in both time and psychological immediacy—from the distant ancestral past (stanza A), through the trials of the psalmist's birth (B), and finally to the persecution of the immediate present (C–D). As part of his general isolation, the poet's links with his own society are perceived to grow ever more tenuous. This begins with an ostracism occasioned by widespread verbal abuse (B) that is later exacerbated by the infliction of severe physical punishment (C). This anti-personal movement descends finally to his enemies' determination to get rid of him for good (D).

In vivid contrast to this connotatively negative movement, the positive concept of community is progressively strengthened in Part Two.[45] This extends ever outward from the familiar circle of family, friends, and fellow-countrymen (E) to encompass a future world fellowship which even includes all foreigners (F). This all-inclusive company constituted for the pious Israelite quite an unexpected group of individuals, for it incorporated the dead, the dregs of society, as well as the yet unborn. As was observed during the earlier structural analysis, the climactic peak/pit of each Part occurs at an important boundary, namely, the psalm's virtual midpoint (death/the grave, v. 15.3) and its compositional conclusion (life/the coming generation, v. 31.2).

A cluster of related motifs, which revolve around another polarity, namely, that of silence as opposed to speech, may be viewed as functioning in contrastive fashion to coordinate, or mediate between, the two central ideas of separation versus solidarity. Thus, Yahweh's apparent lack of response to the poet's pleas (stanza A) is highlighted by example with reference to the garrulous mob of the sufferer's surrounding enemies (B). The deafening divine silence that accompanies his socially ascribed status as a religious outcast returns to the fore in stanzas C–D, and he is forced to withdraw even deeper within himself to contemplate his miserable condition

---

[45] This dynamic movement, or "healthy turn" (Longman 2013:220), from prayer to praise is typical of the lament psalms and the Psalter in general.

width:1091px; height:1537px;

in utter loneliness, seemingly forsaken by God as well as man. It is rather surprising then at the close of the prayer's first half (strophe D′) to hear the psalmist break out of his introspective state in words that resolutely ring out once more in a final appeal to the LORD for deliverance.

In extended contrast to the preceding, the sound of worship and praise animates the eulogue of Part Two. The mass chorus of the godly (stanza E) takes up the "cries" of their ancestors (v. 5), growing louder and louder as ever more of the representative segments of humanity, especially those whom one would not expect to be present, are progressively integrated into this joyous throng. So great is the acclamation of Yahweh's glorious rule that even voices that would normally be completely silent, i.e., the deceased as well as the unconceived, are compelled to join in to swell the eschatological anthem of thanksgiving (F). Whether this last all-encompassing vision is an instance of poetic hyperbole or a divinely inspired prophetic prediction cannot be determined with certainty, but I favor the latter (cf. Harman 2011a:224; Mays 1994a:113; VanGemeren 1991:211).

A third noteworthy polarity parallels and complements the other two—that of strength as opposed to weakness. The alternating and interchanging pattern formed by this thematic contrast is not difficult to discern as it proceeds from one end of Psalm 22 to the other. The total supremacy of Yahweh (though distant) and the increasingly violent hostility of the poet's nearby adversaries contrast markedly with his own lack of power and apparent inability to do anything to improve his dreadful situation. It is a perceptible personal deficiency that grows progressively worse in images of abject frailty as his lament unfolds (especially stanzas C–D). The "afflicted one" (v. 24) never abandons his hope entirely, however, and at the very brink of death, with only his clothing left as the evidence of his demise (v. 18), he makes a final attempt (strophe D′) to renew his physical and spiritual vitality by appealing to the LORD, his "strength" (v. 19).

The mighty power of Yahweh, which operates on behalf of his oppressed people, then is a prominent thought that runs throughout the last "half" of Psalm 22. The thematic development proceeds from individual and communal (Israel-oriented) acts of deliverance (stanza E) and peaks out in a description of the LORD's universal kingdom.[46] This theological realm is quite unexpectedly, given the ethnic prejudice often manifested in this nation (e.g., Jonah), expanded to embrace all peoples (F). Here we

---

[46] It is important to note both the individual as well as the communal reference and application, not only of Psalm 22 but also the Psalter as a whole. "God addresses both the individual and the community. Old Testament scholars have been guilty of emphasizing Israel's collective experience as a worshiping community to the virtual exclusion of the individual use...the Psalms contain evidence of Israel's private devotional experience (*'Sicut Cervus'*), as individuals call on the Lord to deliver them from adversity, long for his presence, and are involved in dialogue with the Lord (Pss. 73, 139 [+ 22!])" (VanGemeren 1991:7).

have a godly dominion in which, according to the divine order of things and contrary to all human notions of greatness, "right makes might!"—and a vindicating "salvation" ultimately comes to those who don't even know it (v. 31). The only response to such a paradoxical outcome is expressed in the poem's final utterance: כִּי (יְהוָה) עָשָׂה!

4.10 The literary-structural analysis of Psalm 22—a brief retrospect and prospect

In conclusion, we may note several benefits that may be derived from a literary-structural analysis of a given biblical discourse, in its entirety, integrity, and originality (i.e., the Hebrew text in relation to its assumed context of use), whether this involves an entire book or a constituent pericope. A comprehensive, discourse-oriented approach can provide analysts with a vigorous new perspective on the intricate design and personal implications of theological literature of the Scriptures. It is a methodology that not only restores confidence in the reliability of the particular text that one is examining, but one which at the same time can awaken one to some novel insights into its compositional and thematic dynamics—as well as its transferred relevance in application to a contemporary setting. This is especially true in the case of a literary masterpiece having a message as significant as that of Psalm 22 for the people of God, believers of every age, language, and culture.[47] The New Testament writers set the tone and gave direction to this inscribed hermeneutical course by fully drawing out the Messianic implications of both the initial lament as well as the concluding eulogy—that is, by ascribing these to the life, death, and resurrection of Jesus the Christ (e.g., Mt. 27, Jn. 19, Hb. 2). These inspired interpreters thereby added a whole new dimension to this psalm's central thematic emphases concerning solidarity, strength, and speech in relation to divine salvation history.

---

[47] This is not to claim that scholars and versions agree on the internal structure of a unified biblical pericope like Psalm 22—far from it. My strophic structure that was outlined earlier agrees exactly with that proposed by the ESV and very closely with the NIV. However, it differs significantly with the strophes/stanzas indicated in the *Tanakh* Jewish translation, for example, which appears to make the major break of Ps. 22 at v. 24, or the NRSV, which segments even more strangely at the midpoint of v. 21.

Similarly, Terrien's commentary, which pays special attention to the "strophic structure" of the Psalms, begins its third principal division at v. 24 rather than v. 22, as proposed above (2003:205). Such differences naturally affect the reader-hearer's understanding of the text, both as a whole and in terms of its constituent parts. In these cases, serious Bible readers and scholars alike must carefully exam-ine the literary-structural evidence (whatever has been provided in the paratext) and then come to their own conclusion and construal of the psalm.

A careful, reflective reading of Psalm 22 can lead readers (or listeners) today to an ever greater awareness of, and appreciation for, this prayer-song's artistic beauty, emotive power, theological richness, and hence also its pragmatic significance with reference to their own everyday existence. Thus we, too, encounter similar situations in life—being more or less down and out in the surroundings of an increasingly hostile secular society, whether overtly antagonistic or insidiously apathetic to matters of a spiritual nature. Yet we also possess the same invigorating hope as that offered here—in a righteous, almighty God, who has already provided deliverance for all people in the One prefigured in this psalm, who has led the way and is even now controlling the events of history in preparation for an ultimate salvation to come (vv. 24, 28; cf. Hb. 2:9–15). So in the "fear of the LORD" (v. 23.1) we, too, are summoned to make the same joyous response to the call of the psalmist—hopefully in the words of a poetic translation that captures at least some of the artistic beauty and rhetorical power of the original text. We might then articulate (ideally orally) a universal, timeless paean of praise and thanks to a God who cares, in unison with a fellowship that embraces the whole of humanity (vv. 22–23, 27):

אֲסַפְּרָה שִׁמְךָ לְאֶחָי

יְהַלְלוּ יְהוָה דֹּרְשָׁיו

יְחִי לְבַבְכֶם לָעַד׃

5

Aspects of the Principle of Parallelism in Hebrew Poetry

Introduction

This selective overview of parallelism has been stimulated by the discussion of this subject in the excellent study of *Word-Order Variation in Biblical Hebrew Poetry* by Nicholas Lunn (2006). The description of this distinctive compositional feature of poetry in the Old Testament is not a major aspect of Lunn's ground-breaking exposition of the pragmatic dimension of lexical positioning in poetic lines (i.e., to mark topic and focus), but several issues were raised by his discussion of the phenomenon that I would like to explore further from a literary-structural perspective. My treatment begins with an examination of some classic scholarly definitions of parallelism. This lays the groundwork for my specific interaction with Lunn, which leads then to a brief discussion of my notion of "extended parallelism," as illustrated with reference to Psalm 103. My cursory analysis may serve to stimulate others to take up a more detailed exploration of this important subject which, though very well-known and well-worn (documented) by past studies, is not without its lingering ambiguities and points of controversy,[1] which at times significantly affect Bible interpretation and translation as well.

---

[1] Cf. the overly general definition offered in a recent major commentary on the Psalms: Parallelism is "the juxtaposition of two or more balanced grammatical

5.1 Some standard definitions

Any serious consideration of biblical parallelism stands upon the collective work of a host of past and present scholars in the field and must therefore begin with what has already been written, or said, on the subject. Space prevents a thorough treatment here, so I will simply cite a selection of several well-known commentators in order to establish a framework for the more specific discussion to follow in subsequent sections (see also 1.2.2 above).

One of the clearest descriptions of "parallelistic lines" in the Hebrew Bible is that of James Kugel, who does not limit his attention to the traditional poetic texts of Scripture, but includes the heightened passages of direct speech in narrative prose:

> The basic feature of biblical...[articulated discourse]...is the recurrent use of a relatively short sentence-form that consists of two brief clauses.... The clauses are regularly separated by a slight pause—slight because the second is...a continuation of the first and not a wholly new beginning. By contrast, the second ends in a full pause.... Often, the clauses have some element in common, so that the second half seems to echo, answer, or otherwise correspond to the first.... The medial pause all too often has been understood to represent a kind of "equals" sign. It is not; it is a pause, a comma, and the unity of the two parts should not be lost for their division.... It is the dual nature of B both to come *after* A and thus add to it, often particularizing, defining, expanding the meaning, and yet also to hearken back to A and in an obvious way connect to it. One might say that B has both *retrospective* (looking back to A) and *prospective* (looking beyond it) qualities. Now by its very afterwardness, B will have an emphatic character... (Kugel 1981:1–2, 8; original italics)

In an earlier study Geller observes that the pressure of patterning in poetry brings even non-synonymous lines into a parallel relationship of close correspondence—a parallelism of proximity that is forged by the essentially binary poetic principle itself as it is regularly realized in Hebrew verse: [2]

---

elements" (deClaissé-Walford et al. 2014:39). This definition might be applied to most of the sentences of the Hebrew Bible, depending on one's definition of "balanced" and "grammatical element."

[2] The priority of syntax over semantics, of form over meaning, in the constitution of parallelism is stressed by Michael O'Connor: "PARALLELISM.... The repetition of identical or similar syntactic patterns in adjacent phrases, clauses, or sentences; the matching patterns are usually doubled, but more extensive iteration is not rare. The core of a [parallelism] is syntactic; when syntactic frames are set in equivalence

> The couplet is the indispensable and necessary unit of com-position for parallel verse and is, of course, isolated by semantic parallelism or repetition. The couplet itself must, of necessity, be composed of A and B lines. Non-parallel lines and couplets also occur, and are forced into the pattern of parallel verse by their relative infrequency and tendency to correspond generally to the syllable length of parallel units in their environment within a poem. (Geller 1979:6)

Among other important observations (which we cannot consider in this context), Kugel highlights the semantic distinctiveness as well as the inter-connectedness of *any* two conjoined poetic lines, or cola.[3] This is a signifi-cant difference from Lunn's notion of parallelism, which is summarized in 5.2 below.

Robert Alter adopts the proposal of Benjamin Hrushovsky (1971) for his own definition of what he terms the "principle of parallelism" in bibli-cal poetry, that is, "a 'semantic-syntactic-accentual rhythm' as the basis of Hebrew verse":

> In most cases…there is an overlapping of several such heter-ogeneous parallelisms [that is, semantic, syntactic, prosodic, morphological, phonetic, and so on] with a mutual rein-forcement so that no single element—meaning, syntax, or stress—may be considered as purely dominant or as purely concomitant…a "free rhythm…based on a cluster of chang-ing principles."… Like rhyme, regular meter, and alliteration on other poetic systems, it is a convention of linguistic "cou-pling" that contributes to the special unity and to the memo-rability (literal and figurative) of the utterances, to the sense that they are an emphatic, balanced, and elevated kind of discourse… (Alter 1985:8–9)[4]

---

by [parallelism], the elements filling those frames are brought into alignment as well, esp. on the lexical level (thus the term 'semantic p'.)" (1993:877). Thus, the Hebrew psalmists had a formal structure of poetic organization ready at hand (including many variable options), and into this they poured their diverse theologi-cal concepts, religious motivations, and expressions of emotion.

[3] For the purposes of this study, I will focus on the predominant manifestation of lineal parallelism in the biblical poetry, that is, as a pair of short poetic lines (a bi-colon), thus largely ignoring mono- and tri-cola, etc. The importance of regular line forms in poetry is that this feature not only serves as the basic foundation for a text's sonic rhythmic impression, but also "the lines organize the syntax in a way that feels [sounds!] balanced and coherent" (Longenbach 2008:9, word in brackets added).

[4] The notion of free rhythm is defined more precisely by Korpel and de Moor: "All ancient Oriental poetry was meant to be sung or recited to the accompaniment of music. This music was of a type characterized by a so-called free rhythm. This

Alter goes on to point out the singular character of "semantic parallelism" in terms similar to those of Kugel: "...the movement of meaning is one of heightening or intensification...of focusing, specification, concretization, even what could be called dramatization" (1985:19).

For Adele Berlin, parallelism "combined with terseness...marks the poetic expression of the Bible" (1985:5). More specifically, it is the "parallelism of consecutive lines" that creates a distinctive "paratactic style" (1985:4, 6):

> The lines are placed one after another with no connective or with the common multivalent conjunction waw; rarely is a subordinate relationship indicated on the surface of the text. ... The lines, by virtue of their contiguity, are perceived as connected, while the exact relationship between them is left unspecified. (1985:6)[5]

Thus, whether explicitly marked or not, the juxtaposition of two (or three) lines gives the impression, whether orally/audibly or in print, that

---

means that stressed syllables could be combined with a considerable number of unstressed syllables or could be drawn out at will to make one word sound as long as a whole phrase.... [There is] a tendency to keep the number of stressed syllables per colon approximately the same throughout.... Because of its average length of three words it is likely that the colon is the unit that could be recited or sung in one breath" (1988:2–4; cf. Berlin 1985:142–143). "The length of the line establishes a relationship to the syntax, and that relationship is guided by the author's sense of how the syntax should be paced—how the given syllables of the words should be organized so that we hear the pattern of their stresses in one way rather than another way" (Longenbach 2008:32).

[5] One wonders whether Berlin was considering participle- and infinitive-based predications as being in such "a subordinate relationship." The importance of examining these clause types is also noted by Lunn (2006:279). In any case, Berlin's emphasis on "contiguity" as well as "equivalence" (1985:2) reminds one of Roman Jakobson's familiar, albeit rather enigmatic description of the essential parallelism of all poetry: "The poetic function projects the principle of equivalence from the axis of selection into the axis of combination. Equivalence is promoted to the constitutive device of the sequence" (1960:358; cf. 2.1 above). Hence, "pervasive parallelism inevitably activates all the levels of [poetic] language" (1966:423). In short, where there is poetry, linguistic correspondence is concentrated: similarity is superimposed upon sequence. In other words, multiple formal and semantic resemblances are packed within standard poetic units (bicola, strophes). Thus, manifold recurrence—prosodic, morphological, lexical, syntactic, strophic reiteration—of various sorts is artfully selected and harmoniously combined or condensed into line-forms and patterned sets of them. The more distinct correspondences there are between the A and B lines, the more poetic the couplet normally sounds, and the more marked it is in terms of semantic and/or pragmatic significance. This is the creative motivation and compositional manner for all well-formed poetic matter, in BH at any rate.

the "two statements are made as if they were connected, so the reader [or hearer] cannot avoid considering their relationship" (1985:6). The nature of this constitutive connection, which brings one poetic line into some manner of close linguistic and/or literary correlation with another,[6] will be examined from somewhat different viewpoints in the next two sections (5.2–3).

I will close this overview with a more abstract, theoretical reflection on the subject of parallelism in literature—and "orature" (the oral equivalent) too:

> Language seeks to express this plurality or this continuum [of perception] by dividing and putting it together again. It divides the continuum and then rebuilds its unity. Parallelism is part of the most basic operation of language, that of "articulation." There is articulation of sound, syntactic articulation, articulation of semantic fields, of rhythm. By articulation the continuum is divided into pieces which can be put together again. The continuum is thus more precisely perceived, more genuinely presented, and can be simplified in some of its elements; above all, the elements can be combined in different groups, producing flexibility of language, the great richness of poetic language.... The simplest kind of articulation is binary parallelism, so common in Hebrew poetry. (Schoekel 1988:51)[7]

Although we are dealing here with written texts from a rather visual, analytical perspective, it is important always to keep in mind the essential oral/aural character of poetic parallelism—that it was normally composed, presented (or performed), and memorized aloud in the form of a chant, recitation, or song. The phonological factor is thus of critical concern when studying the manifold nature of parallelism as it is manifested in any given instance of biblical poetry, wherever it happens to appear in the Scriptures,

---

[6] "Literary" is a subtype of "linguistic" verbal phenomena, used to designate some of the distinctive stylistic devices or techniques that are employed in the production of literature in a given language, i.e., various artistic (formal) and rhetorical (pragmatic) features. The term "correspondence" is perhaps preferable to "equivalence" (e.g., Berlin 1985:27), for it may be more easily used to refer to various types and degrees of similarity as well as contrast when making a comparison of two or more texts. Watson does not seem to get much further in his description of parallelism than a discussion of different aspects of "symmetry" (1984:114–117), though he does proceed more helpfully to delineate several abstract types that frequently occur in biblical poetry (1984:118–119).

[7] Schoekel proposes a set of criteria that are "used to classify parallelism" in Hebrew poetry (1988:52–57): (a) number of parallel lines, (b) quantity of text involved in any given instance, (c) the relationship of contents ("synonymous... antithetic...synthetic"), (d) the correspondence of components within a colon, and (e) twofold and threefold articulation with respect to the A and B lines.

or in translated representations of the Word of God in languages throughout the world today.

5.2 Lunn's description of parallelism

Lunn devotes much of chapter 2 of his book to this topic, "the organisation of bicola into two related parallel lines," which is regarded as "a characteristic feature of Hebrew verse" and "a basic structuring principle" (2006:14). His initial description of the phenomenon summarizes a number of approaches essentially similar to those outlined above:

> The two lines of a poetic parallelism may resemble each oth-
> er in one or more different ways. Parallelism may exist on
> the level of semantics, syntax, morphology, lexis, phonology,
> or rhythm. It may be total, with respect to all the elements
> in both lines, or partial, only respecting some. Principally
> parallelism is seen as a semantic relationship.... But this
> parallelism of meaning is often accompanied by parallelism
> of form.... Where two lines are related in meaning there is
> usually also a relationship of syntax, though by no means
> necessarily so... (2006:15)

Later, however, the importance of *syntactic* parallelism is underscored:

> Parallelism in biblical poetry, though predominantly
> existing at the semantic level, need not do so at all. Paral-
> lelism may apply, for example, solely with respect to the
> syntax.... The same holds true for the other forms of paral-
> lelism – grammatical, morphological, lexical, phonological,
> etc., – though typically these are found combined with a
> correspondence of meaning also. (2006:16)

It is somewhat surprising then that later in this same chapter (and then throughout the rest of the book), when discussing "intercolon relations," Lunn appears to narrow his definition of parallelism quite considerably:

> We have previously considered the construction of parallel
> lines. These may be denoted as:
>
> **HEAD + Parallel**
>
> where "HEAD" indicates the main proposition or base line.
> While the B-line of the parallelism is invariably co-ordinate
> with and may be grammatically independent of this base-
> line, semantic dependence is shown where gapping occurs, in
> that the preceding line provides information necessary to the
> full understanding of the B-line. (2006:22; boldface added)

All other types of poetic bicola are regarded as "those not exhibiting parallelism," and these may be classified into three categories: (a) HEAD-1 + HEAD-2, (b) HEAD + Subordinate, and (c) HEAD [Phrase-1 + Phrase-2 ...] (2006:22).[8] The following couplet from Psalm 103, for example, is thus considered to be non-parallel in nature—verse 16:

כִּי רוּחַ עָבְרָה־בּוֹ וְאֵינֶנּוּ
וְלֹא־יַכִּירֶנּוּ עוֹד מְקוֹמוֹ׃

> The wind blows over it and it is gone,
>   and its place remembers it no more.

Lunn comments:

> There can therefore be seen to be some semantic overlap between the final word of line A and the meaning of line B, but as the major part of the first line concerns the passing over of the wind itself rather than its effects, there is *strictly no parallelism, either in form or in overall meaning*, between the two cola. (2006:206; italics added)

On the contrary, there does seem to be a considerable degree of parallelism demonstrated here in terms of both form (e.g., in the four repetitions of the 3rd masc. sg. pronominal suffix, two per colon) and also meaning (i.e., by virtue of the clear MEANS-Result relationship that closely links up the three clauses of this bicolon).[9]

Apparently, Lunn regards true "parallelism" tc be present only in lines which exhibit syntactic coordination plus a perceptible degree of synonymy—that is, "a close enough correspondence in meaning" (2006:207). But such a narrow conception of this primary poetic feature would seem to run counter to the mainstream of Hebrew biblical scholarship as well as Lunn's own definition that was initially offered above. In any case, it must be stressed that any flaw in this minor aspect of Lunn's presentation does not seriously detract from the main object of his study, which is to explore

---

[8]Lunn defines these three categories as follows (2006:22–23; my addition in italics): "(a) **HEAD-1 + HEAD-2** consists of a bicolon containing two grammatically independent clauses. They offer two semantically distinct, that is, non-parallel *[i.e., non-synonymous?]* propositions, which, while independent with respect to grammar, may relate to each other on a logico-semantic level... (b) **HEAD + Subordinate**. In this category are included all those B-lines that show either semantic or grammatical dependence upon the first line of the pair.... (c) **HEAD [Phrase-1 + Phrase-2...]**. Here each colon contains a phrase or phrases (NP, VP, PP, or Adv) which, when the two cola are taken together, form a complete sentence." In contrast, I do not feel that these formal sub-types, assuming their validity, automatically "fall outside of the category of parallelism" (2006:26, material in brackets added).

[9]One could also argue that "its place remembers it no more" [RESULT-1] in line B is a synonymous expansion, or amplification, of "it is gone" [RESULT-2] at the end of line A. Lunn himself notes this semantic overlap.

and explain the intricacies of word-order variation in Hebrew poetry. It merely presents the reader with some occasional confusion when a pair of obviously related lines, like Psalm 103:16, is classified as being "non-parallel" in nature.[10]

5.3 Another perspective on parallelism

In this section I will set forth a few thoughts of my own on the subject of parallelism in Hebrew poetry: first, with regard to its definition; then, concerning an extension of the principle of parallelism to the discourse level of poetic organization; and finally, with respect to the visual-spatial representation of poetic parallel structures for analytical purposes. These reflections stem from my studies of the biblical text from a literary-rhetorical perspective (e.g., 2004), an approach which may contribute a few additional insights concerning the dynamic, multifaceted character of Hebrew poetic composition, specifically its preferred parallelistic mode of religious expression.

5.3.1 Definition

Lunn correctly calls attention to my earlier, inadequate and misleading description of the operation of parallelism: "Such a coupling of poetic lines is effected by formal as well as semantic repetition" (2006:25).[11] I would therefore revise this to read as follows, with special reference now to Hebrew poetic discourse: *Parallelism involves the recurrent compositional coupling of relatively short (terse) poetic lines, which* ipso facto *manifest a close semantic relationship between them; this binary linkage of cola is normally marked by some manner of formal linguistic correspondence—phonological, morphological, lexical, syntactic, and/or structural.*[12] The connection between

---

[10] Cf. also the examples in ch. 4 dealing with "Non-Parallel Lines," e.g., Pss. 37:9, 2; 51:6; 78:20; 91:8.

[11] The page cited for this quotation (p. 58) (i.e., in Wendland 1998) is now page 62 in Wendland 2002.

[12] Thus, the biblical poet typically composed his text in chunks according to a recurrent lineal grid of 2–3 short predicative units that are somehow related in meaning. Their correspondence may be based on similarity, contrast, or some other basic semantic association, e.g., cause-effect, condition-consequence, etc. As Kugel observed some time ago: "Parallelistic lines appear throughout the Bible, not only in 'poetic' parts, but in the midst of narratives (especially in direct discourse)" (1981:3). There is thus a gradient in literary character, ranging between prose and poetry such that any text may be classified as being more (less) prosaic or poetic in nature. A poetic text will manifest not only recurrent A + B (+/– C) lined parallelism, but also a large variety of stylistic features that are frequently associated with parallel cola (cf. Wendland 1994:3–5; Berlin 1996:302–314), such as: the lack

the two lines may be synonymy, some variant of this, or virtually any other type of meaningful correlation (cf. Wendland 2002:98–99). Furthermore, "in Hebrew parallelism, the norm is that the second element [B line/colon] is usually both echoing and extending the primary [A] element in some fashion" (Jacobson and Jacobson 2013:19). According to the principle of parallelism then, it is not the semantic quality of interlineal similarity that creates or initiates parallelism, but the purely syntactic factor of juxtaposing the two (or more) lines within a poetic format (including genre). The relatively restricted length and concise construction of these lines is an outcome of the pressure towards symmetry principle in language systems, applied in accordance with the implicit phonological norms of Hebrew poetry in general (e.g., lines that average three accent/word-units) and specific artistic creativity or authorial preference.[13]

To conclude: the *semantic* relationship that is established between Hebrew contiguous poetic lines is a function of their juxtaposition, B to A.[14] The *formal* arrangement of these sequential cola thus leads the listener to search also for a meaningful connection between them. Thus, from another perspective, "parallelism can be defined as the repetition of elements within a grammatical unit" (Jacobson and Jacobson 2013:9)—which in Hebrew poetry is normally constituted by two short, sequential utterances. In most cases, this is quite obvious—provided one knows the socio-religious background plus any important theological assumptions that are relevant to the present text in its context. But such clarity does not always apply to the relation that links one bicolon, or a set of them (strophe), with another in the discourse at large, e.g., verses 5b and 6a of Psalm 103 ("...so that your youth is renewed like the eagle. YHWH works righteousness..."). In such cases, a higher-level principle of poetic organization is normally operative, e.g., 103:6 being the onset of a new strophe. This may be distinguished from the broader function of poetic discourse—parallelism and all that goes along with it—which is to imbue a text with special communicative significance

---

of certain "prose particles," phonological play, stress rhythm, imagery, linguistic condensation, and as Lunn has so well documented, a higher incidence of "defamiliarised" word orders (2006:276–277).

[13] For some documentation regarding the phonological data, see Korpel and de Moor 1988:1–6. In view of the preceding discussion, I am not quite convinced of the following conclusion: "...Wendland is mistaken when he defines all of the bicola he analyses as 'parallelisms'" (2006:25). My particular analyses may well be mistaken, but that does not affect the parallel status of the lines being analyzed in the sense that line B does manifest a very close (definable) semantic relationship with line A as part of a deliberate poetic compositional strategy by the psalmist.

[14] The relationship between non-contiguous parallel lines is just the reverse—that is, where some prominent correspondence in meaning serves to signal, hence also to forge a formal link between the A and B cola, e.g., as in the case of an inclusio (e.g., Psa 103:1a and 22c; see Extension below).

(e.g., rhetorical impact, aesthetic appeal, emotive expressiveness, memorability, fluency, etc.).

5.3.2 Extension

Lunn applies the term "extending" to one of three "additional features of parallelism" that he calls attention to (the other two being "gapping" and "embedding;" 2006:18–20). Thus, "a parallelism can extend beyond the confines of the basic bicolon," with particular reference to the occurrence of tricola and, rarely, longer sequences of poetic lines (2006:20).[15] However, this attribute may be stretched even further to include non-contiguous sets of cola, a characteristic of Hebrew poetry that I call "distant parallelism" (Wendland 2002:ch. 3). Such parallel couplets are marked or manifested by some patent semantic relationship (usually synonymy, but also antithesis or correlation), which is often, but not always, accompanied by certain formal similarities. These separated, even textually remote, correspondents based on linguistic recursion normally perform higher discourse functions such as thematic realization or reinforcement,[16] topical cohesion, strophic boundary demarcation, and the foregrounding of peak points within a poem. Here we observe the importance not only of word placement within the (bi)colon, as studied by Lunn, but also of colon placement within the complete poetic text as an essential facet of the overall principle of parallelism.

For example, non-adjacent poetic lines may be used to signal the beginning (aperture) or ending (closure) of a poetic paragraph (strophe) of some larger unit of discourse (Wendland 2002:108–117; cf. 2004:126–127). This demarcating function is evident in the sequence of YHWH characterizations that appear at the onset of most strophes within the thematic "body" of Psalm 103, that is, verses 6a, 8a, 17a, and 19a,[17] each of which includes the divine name (יְהוָה) itself (see the Hebrew text in §4 below). Such boundary-marking cola do not operate in isolation; rather, they are normally supported by a convergence of other literary devices to help mark the spot as it were, for example: a preceding or subsequent discontinuity, or break, within the text (e.g., a shift of major topic, setting, genre, etc.), a rhetorical question, vocative (+ /- imperative or exclamation), embedded segment of direct speech, prominent intertextual allusion, concatenation of figurative language (Wendland

---

[15] The parallelism of constitutents may also be manifested *within* the poetic line, for example Psalm 145:8:
    A: The LORD is *gracious* and *merciful,*
    B: slow to anger and abounding in steadfast love.

[16] We see this exemplified in so-called twin psalms, such as Pss. 42–43, 103–104, 105–106, 111–112, 113–114.

[17] Verse 19 may be construed either as a distinct (Body) concluding strophe or as the close of the psalm's Peak, the strophe covering vv. 17–19. The divine name appears to mark strophic closure also in v. 13b.

1994:3, 32–34), or a "poetically defamiliarised constituent [word] order" (Lunn 2006:110).[18] A selection of these features is seen, for example, in Psalm 103:5b at the close of the opening section and also in 17a to mark the beginning of this praise poem's thematic peak.

5.3.3 Representation

What is the most accurate and informative way to represent the semantic relationship of one colon to another (or a related set of "parallelisms containing five, six, or even seven cola"—Lunn 2006:20)? Indeed, is it possible, or even helpful, to try to depict the relations between adjacent bi-cola and conjoined sets of cola (strophes)? Lunn suggests a method based on the "semantic structure analysis" technique pioneered by Wycliffe Bible Translators (Beekman and Callow 1974: chs. 17–19; cf. Deibler 1998:9–13),[19] and I have made an attempt to apply this to complete poetic texts (e.g., 1994:50–54; 2002:98–107). Thus, as the poet adds one bicolon to another, he automatically places the sequence of couplets into varied semantic relationships that need to be investigated both internally, one line with reference to its parallel, and also externally, one bicolon and cluster in relation to another, as part of a systematic exegetical-thematic study of the entire discourse as an integrated literary unit.

As noted above, most of the logical linkages are not explicitly marked in the original text, so this necessitates a certain amount of reading between the lines of the individual bicola (and sets of them) in order to posit a reasonable hypothesis as to how they are conjoined and interrelated to form a hierarchically arranged poetic whole. On the other hand, as one proceeds beyond the level of the poetic couplet and colon clusters, one often finds unit A joined to unit B by a simple additive or restated relationship, especially in the lyric poetry of Psalms, Proverbs, and Song of Songs (see the example below).[20] In any case, despite the periodic indeterminacy of its

---

[18] For me, this was one of the highlights of Lunn's informative study of word-order variation, namely, an explicit set of rules for differentiating between pragmatically and poetically marked cola in the strictly parallel lines of Hebrew verse (see §2). "We can conclude as a general rule in Biblical Hebrew poetry that the ordering of clause constituents in B-lines of parallel cola is not something governed by linguistic rules relating to pragmatic functions.... This variability of word order in parallel lines is to be classed as one particular manifestation of the previously mentioned 'defamiliarisation of language' characteristic of Biblical Hebrew poetry" (2006:105, 110). As noted above, my only quibble is what I perceive to be Lunn's overly restrictive definition of "parallel lines."

[19] However, Lunn does not apply or display this methodology beyond the scope of the bicolon, e.g., 2006:24–25, for that was the primary focus of his study.

[20] The argumentative poetry of Job and the prophets naturally differs, being distinguished by many more cause-effect type relational complexes also at the upper levels of discourse structure.

object of study and the somewhat debatable nature of the results obtained from it, this analytical method does provide another focused viewpoint on the organization of poetic texts, sometimes offering a valuable insight that would escape the scope of a normal critical study.

The following is a sample discourse representation of the interlocking structure of parallelisms that span Psalm 103:17–19, which I posit as being the thematic peak strophe of the prayer as a whole. Since the Hebrew text is given below, I will use a literal English translation in the following display (see 1.3.2 for conventions used in English translations—cf. Wendland 1994:51–52):

and-the-steadfast-love of-YHWH [is] from-everlasting____
and-unto = everlasting unto = the-ones-fearing-him____ a————————d
and-his-righteousness to-the-children of-children _____
                                                                c
to-the-ones-keeping-of his-covenant_____
and-to-the-ones-remembering-of his-precepts to-perform-them_b—   —f

YHWH in-the-heavens he-has-established his-throne__
and-his-kingdom over-all it-rules_____ e

The binary intercolon connections (a–f) may be specified as shown below:[21]

a: base (A)-amplification (B)   d: base-amplification

b: base-amplification   e: base-amplification

c: generic-specific   f: base-addition

Most of the semantic relations listed above (a–e) are variants of the basic *synonymous* type, while just one (f) involves a less closely linked augmentative *correlation*. This particular colonic grouping might well be expected in the climactic strophe of an essentially panegyric psalm, the purpose of which is to render manifold praise to the LORD God from diverse perspectives and for many different reasons:

> To the praise of His goodness is now finally added praise
> of His majesty, seen in His all-embracing kingly rule.... No
> one can ever understand God's universal reign, it cannot be
> comprehended intellectually. It can only be spoken of as the

---

[21] Whether the lines joined by (a) should be two or one is debated (see below). The abstract base-addition relation that links vv. 17+18 to 19 (f) may indicate the latter's status as a separate mini-strophe.

author of this psalm speaks of it, in terms of awe and praise. (Westermann 1989:243)

This thematically focal strophe (vv. 17–19), which introduces the key notion of covenant (בְּרִיתוֹ), is also distinguished at its beginning by an implicit contrastive relationship "but" (Heb, *waw*) with the preceding strophe (vv. 15–16). This is the only antithetical linkage of the entire psalm, which is another indication of the potential value of plotting such relations up to the discourse level of poetic organization.

5.4 An application to Psalm 103

The following is a cursory (selective, incomplete, condensed, etc.) commentary on several interesting literary-rhetorical features of Psalm 103,[22] "a meditation on the *hesed* of the Lord" (deClaissé-Walford et al. 2014:759), which accordingly articulates "the favored praise of sinners" (Mays 1994b:326; vv. 3–18) in juxtaposition with joyous verbal applause for the universal supremacy of YHWH (vv. 19–22). After my own literal translation of the Hebrew text (in italics), I will make special reference to some of the issues pertaining to the multileveled poetic principle of parallelism (both adjacent and distant) that have been raised in the preceding sections of this study (gray shading of a verse number marks the onset of a new strophe at that point and is also used to highlight selected reiterated features in the text):

Poetic features involving Parallelism	Psalm 103
The individual call to praise the LORD (vv. 1–2) for his blessings (3–5) is expanded to a communal perspective in vv. 6–7, and finally rendered universal in the cosmic acclaim of vv. 20–22b, thus dividing the text into 3 major portions: **Introduction** (vv. 1–5), **Body** (6–19), **Conclusion** (20–22).[a]	

---

[22] Space limits my discussion of this psalm to the text itself. Its many formal (lexical) and semantic (thematic) connections with adjacent psalms (possibly a larger mini-collection incorporating Psalms 101–110 or a smaller praise set of 103–107) cannot be considered. I will simply note the importance of such intertextual parallels within the Psalter as a whole and point to one prominent example in Ps. 103, namely, the divine attribute formula of v. 8—cf. Exodus 34:6–7; Pss. 86:15 and 145:8 (for many other examples, see McCann 1996:1090–1093). For a short but thorough overview of text-critical and genre-related issues pertaining to this psalm plus a summary of its colon structure, see Allen 1983:17–21. Virtually all form-critics classify Ps. 103 as a "hymn" (cf. Firth and Johnston 2005:299). "Psalm 103 is a wide-ranging hymn of praise that reaches out and touches most of the great issues of the life of faith.... Given the nearly universal scope of the psalm's praise, one might well consider it the most soaring lyric in the psalter" (deClaissé-Walford et al. 2014:759).

Of David	לְדָוִד ׀ [1]

Perhaps this title is intended to link Psalm 103, in which the Lord's royal rule is praised (vv. 6, 19), with Psalm 101, in which "David" apparently reflects on his just kingship (v. 1).

O my life, praise Yahweh;	בָּרֲכִי נַפְשִׁי אֶת־יְהוָה

The opening invocation of v. 1a exactly matches the coda at the close of the psalm (22c—a perfect *inclusio*). The pair of closely parallel bicola in v. 1 announces the onset of the discourse as well as the personal side of this psalm-hymn's theme.

and all my inner-being, (praise) his holy name!	וְכָל־קְרָבַי אֶת־שֵׁם קָדְשׁוֹ׃
O my life, praise Yahweh;	בָּרֲכִי נַפְשִׁי אֶת־יְהוָה [2]
and do not forget all his benefits.	וְאַל־תִּשְׁכְּחִי כָּל־גְּמוּלָיו׃

The parallel chain of participles dependent upon יְהוָה (in 2a) lends formal cohesion to the opening poetic unit, while at the same time dividing it into two poetic clusters (strophes), i.e., 1–2 and 3–5. The repeated כִ- f.sg. suffix (7x, with reference to "self" *nephesh*) links the two strophes phonologically.

He forgives all your iniquity;	הַסֹּלֵחַ לְכָל־עֲוֺנֵכִי [3]

Verses 3–5 enunciate the reasons or motivation for the psalmist's praise of vv. 1–2.[b]

he heals all your diseases.	הָרֹפֵא לְכָל־תַּחֲלֻאָיְכִי׃
He redeems your life from the pit;	הַגּוֹאֵל מִשַּׁחַת חַיָּיְכִי [4]
he crowns you (with) loyal love and compassion.	הַמְעַטְּרֵכִי חֶסֶד וְרַחֲמִים׃
He satisfies your desire/life with good;	הַמַּשְׂבִּיעַ בַּטּוֹב עֶדְיֵךְ[c] [5]
your youthfulness renews itself like the eagle.	תִּתְחַדֵּשׁ כַּנֶּשֶׁר נְעוּרָיְכִי׃

A new explicit subject in 5b plus a break in the prevailing syntactic pattern (disjunction), i.e., from a series of participles to an imperfect tense verb, marks a closure in the psalm's Introduction. Figurative language (simile) in the B line highlights the strophe-concluding logical result relation that is found here.

///

The psalm's personal focus now shifts in v. 6 from the individual to a communal perspective (1/2 sg. => 1/3 pl.).[d] The mention of YHWH as explicit subject initiates the Body of Psalm 103.[e] The divine name also helps to mark the aperture of new strophes at vv. 8a, 17a, and 20a, while it forms an *inclusio* for the Body section at 19a.[f] Key divine attributes occur at the beginning of several of the Body's constituent strophes: 6–7, 8–10, 17–18 + 19—e.g., at v.6: "righteousness" + "(just) judgments."[g]

Yahweh is working righteousness,	עֹשֵׂה צְדָקוֹת יְהוָה 6
and full justice for all the oppressed.	וּמִשְׁפָּטִים לְכָל־עֲשׁוּקִים:
He made known his ways to Moses;	יוֹדִיעַ דְּרָכָיו לְמֹשֶׁה 7
all his deeds to the sons of Israel.	לִבְנֵי יִשְׂרָאֵל עֲלִילוֹתָיו:

A chiastic parallel helps mark strophic closure: "his ways + to Moses" (7a) – "to the sons of Israel + his deeds" (7b). A new strophe then begins in v. 8 (aperture): YHWH + "compassionate and gracious, slow to anger, and abounding in steadfast love" (a citation of Yahweh's crucial covenantal proclamation of Exo. 34:6–7).[h] The strophic onset is accented by sound-play: רַחוּם וְחַנּוּן.

A sequence of לֹא־initial clauses, highlighting God's *chesed* via the negative, gives cohesion to this new strophe (vv. 8–10), while the last occurrence (10b) marks its close (v. 9b parallels Ps. 30:5a). The pair of bicola spanning vv. 9–10 displays internal syntactic parallelism, and v. 10 also incorporates some internal rhyming to distinguish strophic closure (contra deClaissé-Walford et al. 2014:765).

Yahweh is compassionate and gracious;	רַחוּם וְחַנּוּן יְהוָה 8
slow to anger and abundant in loyal love.	אֶרֶךְ אַפַּיִם וְרַב־חָסֶד:
He does not persist in making accusations,	לֹא־לָנֶצַח יָרִיב 9
and he does not stay angry forever.	וְלֹא לְעוֹלָם יִטּוֹר:
He does not do to us as our sins (deserve),	לֹא כַחֲטָאֵינוּ עָשָׂה לָנוּ 10
And he does not deal with us as our iniquities (deserve),	וְלֹא כַעֲוֹנֹתֵינוּ גָּמַל עָלֵינוּ:

A new strophe begins in v. 11 (aperture): YHWH is not explicitly mentioned in v. 11, but the core attribute of 'his steadfast love' (חַסְדּוֹ) is. The object of God's mercy ("on those who fear him")[i] is specified at the beginning and ending of this strophe (11b, 13b; cf. 17a). The initial כִּי clause helps mark aperture at 11a ("for" to link up with the preceding strophe, or "indeed!" to announce this new strophe). Verse 11 then begins a parallel set of comparative (כְּ) bicola : 11 + 12 + 13; the pattern is broken at v. 14 with a כִּי asseverative-explanatory clause, which announces the beginning of a new strophe (vv. 14–16; cf. the parallel in v. 11a—anaphora). The ר consonant sounds at the onset of every line of this strophe (except the first, where it appears at the end) is an instance of cohesive phonic parallelism, which complements the syntactic balance of vv. 12–13.

For as high as the heavens are above the earth,	כִּי כִגְבֹהַּ שָׁמַיִם עַל־אָרֶץ 11
so great is his loyal-love to those who revere him.	גָּבַר חַסְדּוֹ עַל־יְרֵאָיו׃
As far as east is from the west,	כִּרְחֹק מִזְרָח מִמַּעֲרָב 12
so far he has removed our transgressions from us.	הִרְחִיק מִמֶּנּוּ אֶת־פְּשָׁעֵינוּ׃
As a father has mercy on his children,	כְּרַחֵם אָב עַל־בָּנִים 13
So Yahweh has mercy on those who fear him.	רִחַם יְהוָה עַל־יְרֵאָיו׃

The emphatic full pronouns, הוּא and אֲנַחְנוּ, placed at opposite ends of v. 14, also distinguish unit aperture.[j] The focus dramatically shifts from YHWH to "our form" (יִצְרֵנוּ) of "dust" (עָפָר, Gen 2:7), "mankind" (אֱנוֹשׁ) in all his (our!) mortality. This new topic is highlighted by asyndeton and an initial noun in *casus pendens*. Verses 14–16 represent a "motif from the psalm of lament" (Westermann 1989:241)—which functions as a contrastive emotive "pit" before the thematic peak of vv. 17–19. The strophe's closure is marked by the conj. כִּי and repeated pronominal reference (3rd m. sg.) to a person's life (lit. "days") and/or to "man" himself, which/who is completely finished and forgotten (as distinct from the God-"fearers" of vv. 13b, 17b)!

For he knows our form (nature),	כִּי־הוּא יָדַע יִצְרֵנוּ 14
he remembers that we are (but) dust.	זָכוּר כִּי־עָפָר אֲנַחְנוּ׃
As for mankind, his days are as grass,	אֱנוֹשׁ כֶּחָצִיר יָמָיו 15
like a flower in the field, so he flourishes.	כְּצִיץ הַשָּׂדֶה כֵּן יָצִיץ׃
For a wind blows upon it and it's gone,	כִּי רוּחַ עָבְרָה־בּוֹ וְאֵינֶנּוּ 16
and its place remembers it no more.	וְלֹא־יַכִּירֶנּוּ עוֹד מְקוֹמוֹ׃

The next strophe leads off (v. 17) with an emphatic announcement of the theme of Psalm 103: וְחֶסֶד יְהוָה ׀ מֵעוֹלָם (aperture). The onset here is further marked by the psalm's first tricolon.[k] Merciful divine disposition is manifested towards: יְרֵאָיו.[l] There is alliteration (עָ לְ) involving both lines, thus accenting the notion of eternity (עוֹלָם). Verses 17–19 realize the PEAK strophe of the psalm in terms of content and form: two verbless bicola lead to one with a highly marked word order (v. 19: S M V O + w-S M V) that delineates the scope of God's rule. Verses 17–18 specify those who are incorporated in his eternal (v. 17), universal (v. 19) kingdom.[m] A sequence of לְ-initial phrases lends cohesion to vv. 17–18. Verse-initial יְהוָה + the mention of "all" (כֹּל) form an inclusio (distant parallel marking) for the Body of Psalm 103—cf. v. 6.[n] A highly alliterative colon helps to signal the Body's closure,[o] which also transitions to the cosmic perspective of vv. 20–22.

But the loyal love of Yahweh is from everlasting,	17 וְחֶ֤סֶד יְהוָ֨ה ׀ מֵעוֹלָ֣ם
and to everlasting (it remains) on those who revere him,	וְעַד־עוֹלָ֭ם עַל־יְרֵאָ֑יו
and his justice (continues) for the children of their children,	וְ֝צִדְקָת֗וֹ לִבְנֵ֥י בָנִֽים׃
and for those who keep his covenant,	18 לְשֹׁמְרֵ֥י בְרִית֑וֹ
and for those who remember to keep his precepts.	וּלְזֹכְרֵ֥י פִ֝קֻּדָ֗יו לַעֲשׂוֹתָֽם׃
Yahweh has established his seat (throne),	19 יְֽהוָ֗ה בַּ֭שָּׁמַיִם הֵכִ֣ין כִּסְא֑וֹ
and his kingdom rules over everything.	וּ֝מַלְכוּת֗וֹ בַּכֹּ֥ל מָשָֽׁלָה׃

The compass of Psalm 103 progressively enlarges, from the individual (Introduction), to the whole community of God's people (Body), to the entire universe (Conclusion, vv. 20–22), with v. 19 being a transitional verse.[p]

///

This concluding paean in praise of YHWH features many parallel elements that stress the common function of the final strophe (20–22). Different fillers for the parallel object and vocative slots create a panoramic range for the reiterated calls to "praise the LORD!"[q] Correspondence of this Conclusion with the psalm's Introduction (1–5) is made concrete by the six morphologically interlocking occurrences of the imperative "bless"—3 sg. (#1, 2, 6) and 3 pl. (#3, 4, 5). The qualifier "all" (כֹּל) too is prominent in both sections, which laud the pervasive, all-sufficient greatness and goodness of YHWH. The thrice-iterated verbal form עֹשֵׂי ('do'), coupled with the synonyms "hear/obey" and "serve," lends cohesion to this final strophe (vv. 20b–22). It is our rightful response to the Lord's "steadfast love" (חֶסֶד—v. 17a; cf. v. 18).

Praise Yahweh, you his angels,	20 בָּרְכ֥וּ יְהוָ֗ה מַלְאָ֫כָ֥יו
you mighty warriors who do his bidding (word),	גִּבֹּ֣רֵי כֹ֖חַ עֹשֵׂ֣י דְבָר֑וֹ
obeying the voice of his word.	לִ֝שְׁמֹ֗עַ בְּק֣וֹל דְּבָרֽוֹ׃
Praise Yahweh, all you his armies,	21 בָּרְכ֣וּ יְ֭הוָה כָּל־צְבָאָ֑יו
those who serve him and do his will.	מְ֝שָׁרְתָ֗יו עֹשֵׂ֥י רְצוֹנֽוֹ׃
Praise Yahweh, all you his works,	22 בָּרְכ֤וּ יְהוָ֨ה ׀ כָּֽל־מַעֲשָׂ֗יו
in all places of his dominion—	בְּכָל־מְקֹמ֥וֹת מֶמְשַׁלְתּ֑וֹ
Praise Yahweh, O my life/soul!	בָּרְכִ֖י נַפְשִׁ֣י אֶת־יְהוָֽה׃

Verse 22b parallels the ending of the psalm's Body portion in v. 19b, one closure thus reinforcing another. A shift in the morphology of the initial imperative (m. pl. → f. sg.), with a singular replacing a plural vocative, marks the ultimate closure in v. 22c, which repeats 1a and 2a to form a perfect inclusio. The psalm concludes as it began with a focus on the wonderful person of יְהוָה—and perhaps also implies that the psalmist's voice (v. 1) is included among those of the heavenly praise-choir (vv. 20–21).

[a] This act of discourse demarcation cannot be taken for granted or assumed to be correct. For example, one structural proposal (deClaissé-Walford et al. 2014:760) begins "stanza 1" at v. 3, which syntactically carries on in a dependent construction from v. 2, and then distinguishes a "community perspective" (vv. 9–16) from that of "humanity" (vv. 17–19), where the latter unit clearly refers to the "covenant" community (v. 18) of "Israel" (v. 7), and the angelic host (vv. 20–22) is seemingly left out of the psalm's thematic scheme.

[b] "Praise exists for the purpose of theological witness. To praise is to recall God's past acts and thus to remember those acts (to recontextualize them) for the present moment" (deClaissé-Walford et al. 2014:762).

[c] "The text as it stands makes little, if any, sense. The translation assumes an emendation of...'ed'ekh, 'your ornaments' to...'odekhiy, 'your duration; your continuance', that is, 'your life'" (NET note).

[d] Contrary to the evidence presented here, deClaissé-Walford et al. include v. 6 with vv. 3–5 (2014:764).

[e] The word order of v. 6a is marked for predicate focus, with YHWH's activity preceding the divine name (cf. 8a). The initial participle has no article, thus distinguishing it from the preceding series.

[f] יְהוָה marks a "mini-break" within the Body at 13b, just before the man-centered strophe (vv. 14–16).

[g] The extensive study by Terrien focuses on the "strophic structure" of the psalms, which is in turn based on the prosodic dimensions of parallelism: "The Hebrew psalmists could express their theology of divine presence with a remarkable familiarity with rhythmic and strophic structure.... The psalmists aimed at mnemonic purposes as well as elegance when they grouped their verses in sections now called 'strophes'. Most often a strophe is composed of two substrophes: one longer and one shorter" (2003:36, 39). Unfortunately, Terrien does not provide us with an explicit methodology for analyzing a given text into strophes, and the results that he arrives at for certain psalms are hard to reconcile with the textual markers actually present—for example, delineating the three final strophes of Psalm 103 as: 15–17, 18–20, and 21–22 (2003:704–705).

[h] "This loyal love [חֶסֶד], the focus of praise at every service of thanksgiving—what was it? The psalmist expounds its significance in the course of vv 9–18" (Allen 1983:22). "In the end...it is not human righteousness, but the abiding *hesed* of Yahweh that matters decisively.... God's *hesed* is everything. That *hesed* overrides, contextualizes, and transforms guilt and finitude" (Brueggeman 1995:201–202). As indicated in my overall structural plan for this psalm, I would include "the heavens" (שָׁמַיִם) within the scope of YHWH's all-encompassing covenantal *chesed,* which along with the other attributes specified in this verse manifest the LORD's "name" to his reverent, obedient people (v. 1a = > vv. 17–18; cf. also vv. 19 and 11). Note that there are other allusions to Exodus 34 in Ps. 103, e.g., the three terms for sin in vv. 10–12 (Exo. 34:7); v. 3 (Exo. 34:9); v. 18 (Exo. 34:10–11) (Allen 1983:18).

[i] "Many scholars regard 'Lord fearers'...(cf. Pss. 115:11; 118:4, etc.) as a term that refers to non-Israelites who worship the Lord" (deClaissé-Walford et al. 2014:767)—thus further extending the salvific scope of Yahweh's *chesed.*

[j] "Since there are no other obvious indications in the context why this subject should be marked, what we are looking at here is probably an instance of the grammatical encoding of an 'evidential', a non-pragmatic phenomenon..." (Lunn 2006:205–206). However, occurrence of this pronoun's referent, יְהוָֹה, just three words earlier at the close of the preceding strophe, supports the supposition that הוּא (argument focus—i.e., "he is the one who...") helps signal a discourse aperture. One could also view v. 14 as a topical-transitional hinge passage that bridges the focus on Yahweh's attributes in vv. 11–13 to the contrastive emphasis upon the mortal frailties of mankind in vv. 15–16. The subject of YHWH's *chesed* manifested towards "those who fear him" (עַל־יְרֵאָיו) resumes in v. 17b (cf. vv. 11b, 13b).

[k] Allen adopts the tricolon here but observes that "the parallelism is suspiciously poor" (1983:19; cf. v. 20 at the onset of the Conclusion). Could it be then that an *extra-long* line initiates the onset of this thematically central strophe? Allen also notes that v 18a is "unusually short" (ibid.)—perhaps (?) similarly to mark the occurrence of the thematic key term "covenant" (בְרִיתוֹ), which appears only here in the psalm.

[l] One normally looks for the topical heading of a discourse within its thematic peak, e.g., "The LORD's steadfast mercy sustains his covenant-keeping people." GNT's "The Love of God" is too general.

[m] The LORD manifests his powerful rule within a covenantal framework by mercifully forgiving the sins of his people (vv. 11–12 => 19). Verses 17–18 may be an echo then of Exo. 20:6, which would of course call to mind the whole of Exo. 20:2–17 and its seminal significance to the nation of Israel.

[n] YHWH, in *casus pendens,* occurs in absolute first colonic position only here in the psalm. "In Ps. 103 the usual praise of God for both his grace and majesty is here developed one-sidedly, but the theme of majesty does finally emerge at this point" (Westermann, cited in Allen 1983:19).

[o] With regard to v. 19, Lunn considers the "motivation for the non-canonical word order" and concludes: "All the English versions make a new section of the psalm at this point and do so upon good grounds" (2006:207). My reading above suggests the converse—that v. 19 marks a closure, not aperture (cf. *The Jewish Study Bible,* Tanakh Translation), though the argument that this is an independent strophe, an instance of hinged, or Janus parallelism (linked to verses on either side), could also be made (cf. NIV).

[p] "The development is an attempt at total praise. How can Yahweh be praised enough?" (Allen 1983:22). This worthy theme is shaped and reinforced by the poetic principle of parallelism in all its diversity. One might distinguish the emotive *climax* of a text (vv. 20–22) from its thematic *peak* (vv. 17–19), though they may, of course, converge within a single strophe.

[q] The universal scope and relevance of this psalm's message is suggested by its appearance in 22 verses, the number of the Hebrew alphabet (Mays 1994b:326).

5.5 Conclusion

The principle of parallelism in poetry, whether in the Hebrew or any other literary tradition, is realized essentially through the laying down of one formal structure alongside another during the generation of text material, normally involving the poetic line (a single clausal utterance bounded by pauses). In Biblical Hebrew, the default system requires two poetic lines or cola, i.e., a bicolon, of similar, but not necessarily equal length (3–5 words or accent units; cf. Geller 1993:510), which are joined together sequentially in more or less related sets or larger segments (strophes) to form rhythmic verse texts. These syntactically coupled cola (as well as bicola and strophes) are also semantically linked to one another (B to A) by means of a variety of logical sense relations—usually some manner of synonymy, but also by various other kinds of temporal or logical connection (contrast, reason-result, condition-consequence, appeal-grounds, unfolding addition, etc.) that frequently includes a noticeable degree of intensification, augmentation, specification, figuration, or dramatization in the B-line.

The text-constitutive, normative template of parallelism attracts, as it were, a number of other stylistic attributes which thus tend to be associated with Hebrew poetry—first and foremost, a perceptible terseness (e.g., ellipsis such as asyndeton, verb gapping, the reduction of modifiers and prose particles, etc.) that exists by virtue of the deliberate brevity that has been determined for the basic utterance units (cola). The defamiliarization (Wendland 2004:424) that serves to further distinguish more from less poetic discourse is effected by the addition of other devices. These include features such as the insertion of a mono- or tri-colon, a concentration of evocative imagery and figurative language, conventionally associated word pairs, patterned repetition, phonic symmetry (alliteration, assonance, paronomasia), rhetorical tropes (irony, questions, hyperbole, allusion, etc.), typical religious-liturgical motifs, diction, and formulas—plus the distinctive word orders so precisely noted by Lunn (e.g., 2006:105–120).[23] As suggested earlier, the parallelism principle is extended in non-contiguous fashion to construct distant salient parallels based primarily on meaning (similarity, antithesis, consequence, purpose, etc.), to a lesser extent also on linguistic form. These intratextual connections function to delineate structural boundaries (aperture, closure) and/or to accentuate thematic peak points within a longer poetic composition. A number of the characteristics just mentioned were pointed out within the text of Psalm 103. Indeed, the many purposeful examples of parallelism (diverse linguistic correspondences concentrated within the individual bicola and their correlates within the discourse) reveal why this thanksgiving hymn in praise of Yahweh's unfailing faithfulness (חֶסֶד) is at the same time also a masterful instance of Hebrew lyric art.[24]

---

[23] Lunn asks why "marked, as distinct from defamiliar, word order is…seen to be more extensive in poetic discourse than in narrative…" In addition to the two reasons proposed by Lunn, namely, "the lack of linearity in poetic discourse" and its encoding in the form of direct speech, giving rise to the need for more new topics and focus constructions (2006:277), the feature of parallelism itself is obviously a factor. Two (+) lines are available for creative religious expression instead of just one.

[24] "The fundamental character of God is boiled down to one word—*hesed*. But *hesed* is a concept so rich and so deep that no amount of words can adequately

There are naturally some important implications here for Scripture exegetes and translators—that is, to correctly perceive and interpret any marked instances of parallelism in poetic as well as prose texts (the latter in the oracular pronouncements or divine decrees that occur in direct speech). Bible translators in particular (who must also be good exegetes!) should strive to replicate at least some of the various rhetorical, as well as pragmatic, functions of *marked* parallelism in their work.[25] These may pertain to foregrounding certain components of the structure and content of the text at hand,[26] or to manifesting its non-tangible but no less vital qualities of beauty, bonding, feeling, and forcefulness (cf. Wendland 2004:260–264). In many of the world's oral and literary traditions (including those of Africa), different types of parallelism already exist so it is not so very difficult also to reproduce some of the formal attributes of this poetic device. But in order to achieve meaningful as well as natural poetry (or some manner of heightened, marked, emphatic, etc. discourse) in the vernacular, a translation approach that aims for a certain measure of functional equivalence (or, relevant similarity in terms of communicative clues)[27] must be applied, namely, through the use of genre-appropriate, idiomatic, oral-aurally sensitive forms in the target language.[28] Only in this way can the great power

---

plumb its depth. And yet, [this] psalm itself is testimony that the *hesed* of the Lord can be communicated through words—through praise" (deClaissé-Walford et al. 2014:768).

[25] The strophe-initial cluster of key covenantal terms in v. 8, for example, would certainly warrant a poetic equivalent in the TL. This is how it might be done in Chewa, for instance (cf. Wendland 2004, Appendix B):

Chifundo amatichitiratu Chauta,	As for mercy, Chauta-God really shows us,
Kutikomera mtima sikutha konse,	(His) heart-favor (for us) never ends at all,
Iyeyu satipsyera mtima msanga,	He does not get heart-burn over us quickly,
Chikondi chake chimatichurukira!	His love always abounds on our behalf!

The "pragmatic functions" of syntactic word-order variations in Hebrew poetry relate to the manifestation of topic in relation to comment and focus in relation to presupposed material.

[26] In addition to helping the analyst to delineate a credible (defensible) structure for a given poetic text, as demonstrated for Ps. 103, a careful literary analysis can also serve to call attention to more/less preferred interpretations of the discourse as a whole. For example, if the reasoning and evidence in favor of positing medial strophes at vv. 11–13 and 14–16 are accepted, then translations that suggest an aperture at v. 15 are misleading, e.g., "*As for man,* his days are like grass" (NIV). It would be better then to indicate a closer connection with v. 14, e.g., "*In our mortality,* the days pass away like grass."

[27] Perhaps it would be helpful to maintain a distinction here: "communicative clues" (or "cues") are specific literary-structural forms that signal particular communicative functions, whether general (expressive, imperative, informative, artistic, etc.) or specific (e.g., the illocutions of speech-acts).

[28] "The activity of praising in the Psalter is essentially vocal...the most appropriate locus of praise is a congregational setting..." (Hutchinson 2005:87–88). The implication

and appeal of parallelism in biblical poetry be reproduced to an appreciable as well as appreciated degree.[29]

To reiterate: the present chapter discusses merely one feature of Lunn's significant book and a rather peripheral subject at that. His primary concern is to present a demonstrable pragmatic theory that deals with word-order variations in Hebrew poetry, and to that end he is quite successful within the limitations that he set for himself (2006:6–10, 279–280).[30] In this respect his careful analysis has also established the foundation for many future studies of the subject of word order in biblical poetry—which is but one aspect of the multifaceted material realization of the poetic principle of parallelism in the literary verse forms of Scripture.

---

for translation is obvious: Why produce a vernacular textual equivalent that is not equally vocal in communal purpose, poetic style, and evocative effect?

[29] This is veritable literary artistry in service of an emotively stimulating and an intellectually satisfying message, as we have seen illustrated in Psalm 103—"an Old Testament *Te Deum*" (Dahood 1970:24). Here the psalmist "has been granted an insight into the heart of the majesty of God, and what he has found there is grace" (Weiser 1962:663).

[30] Several of Lunn's findings stand out for me in this regard: "It is primarily within the B-line of *synonymous* parallelisms that word order variation as a purely stylistic or rhetorical device, i.e., poetic defamiliarisation, is admissible.... Such variation is an optional not obligatory feature, and chiefly occurs where the A-line of a parallelism is canonical [i.e., exhibiting a VSO word order], that is, unmarked.... Where the A-line of a parallelism is marked, the B-line is equally marked.... Gapping of clause constituents mostly occurs in the B-line of *synonymous* parallelisms.... Any departure from the norms described [by Lunn]...is a deliberate literary device which serves to set apart that particular unit as performing some higher text-level function, i.e., aperture, closure, or climax" (2006:275–276; italics added, also the material in brackets). The qualification "synonymous," however, does raise the question: What happens in the case of *non*-synonymous parallelism?

6

'My Tongue is the Stylus of a Skillful Scribe' (Psalm 45:2c): If so in the Scriptures, then why not also in Translation?

Introduction

In this chapter[1] I survey seven characteristics of the poetic style of Psalm 45, with special reference to the "sound effects" (musical phonological features) of the Hebrew original and the importance of this text's manifold literary (artistic-rhetorical) technique in communicating its essential message. This leads to a brief discussion of the translation of this psalm in Chewa, a Bantu language of SE Africa. How "skillful" (מָהִיר, v. 2) does this version sound in the vernacular, and why is this an essential aspect of the translator's task in order to ensure that the "good word" (דָּבָר טוֹב)

---

[1] This is an extensively reworked and greatly expanded version of an earlier analysis published in *Verbum et Ecclesia* 34:1, 2013a. It may be noted that this remains but a partial, selective investigation; due to space limitations, not all of the items of stylistic interest or thematic importance have been referred to, let alone examined in sufficient detail. For additional examples of the type demonstrated in the present study (with variations), see Wendland 2013b.

("beautiful song," v. 2 – NET)[2] of the Bible is transmitted faithfully, as well
as in a lovely and lively manner?[3] Suggestions will be offered to indicate
how current Chewa and English versions might be improved so as to "stir
the heart" (רְחַשׁ לִבִּי) and the mouth (lit. "tongue" לְשׁוֹן) (v. 2)[4] of singers
and listeners also today—to complement an inspired royal, potentially
messianic theme.

6.1 The Hebrew text and two translations

The two English versions of Psalm 45 below provide an initial translational
orientation for the Hebrew text of this psalm (MT, from ParaText 7). In the
left column, a more literal, foreignized rendition (favoring the SL),[5] the *English
Standard Version* (ESV) is given; on the right, a more natural, "domesticated"
rendering (favoring the TL), the *New Living Translation* (NLT):[6]

ESV	NLT
Your Throne, O God, Is Forever. *To the choirmaster: according to Lilies.* *A Maskil of the Sons of Korah; a love* song.	*For the choir director: A love song to* *be sung to the tune "Lilies."* *A psalm of the descendants of* *Korah.*
	1 לַמְנַצֵּחַ עַל־שֹׁשַׁנִּים לִבְנֵי־קֹרַח מַשְׂכִּיל שִׁיר יְדִידֹת׃

---

[2] Verse references are to the Hebrew text (MT) throughout, thus numbering one
more than in English versions.

[3] When stimulated—even inspired—by the original text, translators will seek to
observe its "rhetorical numbers [i.e., oratorical style]," according to the early
French scholar and translator Estienne Dolet, "that is to say, a joining and arrang-
ing of terms [in the TL] with such sweetness that not alone the soul is pleased, but
also the ear is delighted...by such harmony of language" (from "The Way to Trans-
late Well" [1540], cited in Weissbort and Eysteinsson 2006:75).

[4] "The language of this verse [2] is so unusual that some commentators believe
the poet is claiming special inspiration. Herman Gunkel even translated the verse,
Mein Herz wallt ueber von begeisterten Worte ('My heart overflows with inspired
words')" (Boice 1996:382).

[5] Potentially problematic (unnatural, ambiguous, unclear, etc.) expressions in this
version (ESV), which has been reproduced as formatted (namely, the line breaks),
are marked in boldface. Do you agree? If so, propose more naturalized English ren-
derings, perhaps with reference to the NLT. What about the signification of ESV's
published format: how legible is the translation as it has been printed out—how
readily can this text be read aloud?

[6] *English Standard Version* (2001), Wheaton: Crossway Bibles; *New Living Translation*
(2004), Wheaton: Tyndale House Publishers—each text being cited in accordance
with the publisher's blanket permission.

1 **My heart overflows** with a pleasing theme; I address my verses to the king; my tongue is like the pen of a ready scribe.	1 Beautiful words stir my heart. I will recite a lovely poem about the king, for my tongue is like the pen of a skillful poet.

2 רָחַשׁ לִבִּי ׀ דָּבָר טוֹב
אֹמֵר אָנִי מַעֲשַׂי לְמֶלֶךְ
לְשׁוֹנִי עֵט ׀ סוֹפֵר מָהִיר:

2 You are the most handsome of **the sons of men;** **grace is poured upon your lips;** therefore God has blessed you forever.	2 You are the most handsome of all. Gracious words stream from your lips. God himself has blessed you forever.

3 יָפְיָפִיתָ מִבְּנֵי אָדָם
הוּצַק חֵן בְּשְׂפְתוֹתֶיךָ
עַל־כֵּן בֵּרַכְךָ אֱלֹהִים לְעוֹלָם:

3 **Gird** your sword on your thigh, **O mighty one,** **in** your splendor and majesty!	3 Put on your sword, O mighty warrior! You are so glorious, so majestic!

4 חֲגוֹר־חַרְבְּךָ עַל־יָרֵךְ גִּבּוֹר
הוֹדְךָ וַהֲדָרֶךָ:

4 In your majesty ride out victoriously for the cause of truth and **meekness** and righteousness; **let your right hand teach you** awesome deeds!	4 In your majesty, ride out to victory, defending truth, humility, and justice. Go forth to perform awe-inspiring deeds!

5 וַהֲדָרְךָ ׀ צְלַח רְכַב
עַל־דְּבַר־אֱמֶת וְעַנְוָה־צֶדֶק
וְתוֹרְךָ נוֹרָאוֹת יְמִינֶךָ:

5 Your arrows are **sharp** **in the heart** of the king's enemies; the peoples **fall under you.**	5 Your arrows are sharp, piercing your enemies' hearts. The nations fall beneath your feet.

6 חִצֶּיךָ שְׁנוּנִים
עַמִּים תַּחְתֶּיךָ יִפְּלוּ
בְּלֵב אוֹיְבֵי הַמֶּלֶךְ:

6 Your throne, O God, is forever and **ever.** The scepter of your kingdom is a **scepter of uprightness;**	6 Your throne, O God endures for-ever and ever. You rule with a scepter of justice.
	7 כִּסְאֲךָ אֱלֹהִים עוֹלָם וָעֶד שֵׁבֶט מִישֹׁר שֵׁבֶט מַלְכוּתֶךָ׃
7 you have **loved righteousness** and hated wickedness. Therefore God, your God, has anointed you with the **oil of gladness beyond** your companions;	7 You love justice and hate evil. Therefore God, your God, has anointed you, pouring out the oil of joy on you more than on anyone else.
	8 אָהַבְתָּ צֶּדֶק וַתִּשְׂנָא רֶשַׁע עַל־כֵּן ׀ מְשָׁחֲךָ אֱלֹהִים אֱלֹהֶיךָ שֶׁמֶן שָׂשׂוֹן מֵחֲבֵרֶיךָ׃
8 your robes are all fragrant with myrrh and aloes and cassia. **From ivory palaces** stringed instruments make you glad;	8 Myrrh, aloes, and cassia perfume your robes. In ivory palaces the music of strings entertains you.
	9 מֹר־וַאֲהָלוֹת קְצִיעוֹת כָּל־בִּגְדֹתֶיךָ מִן־הֵיכְלֵי שֵׁן מִנִּי שִׂמְּחוּךָ׃
9 daughters of kings are among your ladies of honor; at your right hand stands the queen **in gold of Ophir.**	9 Kings' daughters are among your noble women. At your right side stands the queen, wearing jewelry of finest gold from Ophir!
	10 בְּנוֹת מְלָכִים בְּיִקְּרוֹתֶיךָ נִצְּבָה שֵׁגַל לִימִינְךָ בְּכֶתֶם אוֹפִיר
10 **Hear, O daughter,** and consider, and **incline your ear:** forget your people and your **father's house,**	10 Listen to me, O royal daughter; take to heart what I say. Forget your people and your family far away.
	11 שִׁמְעִי־בַת וּרְאִי וְהַטִּי אָזְנֵךְ וְשִׁכְחִי עַמֵּךְ וּבֵית אָבִיךְ׃

11 **and** the king will **desire** your beauty. Since he is **your lord, bow to** him.	11 For your royal husband delights in your beauty; honor him, for he is your lord.

12 וְיִתְאָו הַמֶּלֶךְ יָפְיֵךְ
כִּי־הוּא אֲדֹנַיִךְ וְהִשְׁתַּחֲוִי־לוֹ׃

12 The people of Tyre will seek your favor with gifts, **the richest of the people.**	12 The princess of Tyre will shower you with gifts. The wealthy will beg your favor.

13 וּבַת־צֹר ׀ בְּמִנְחָה פָּנַיִךְ
יְחַלּוּ עֲשִׁירֵי עָם׃

13 **All glorious is** the princess **in her chamber,** with robes interwoven with gold.[a]	13 The bride, a princess, looks glorious in her golden gown.

14 כָּל־כְּבוּדָּה בַת־מֶלֶךְ פְּנִימָה
מִמִּשְׁבְּצוֹת זָהָב לְבוּשָׁהּ׃

14 In many-colored robes she is led to the king, with **her virgin companions** following behind her.	14 In her beautiful robes, she is led to the king, accompanied by her bridesmaids.

15 לִרְקָמוֹת תּוּבַל לַמֶּלֶךְ
בְּתוּלוֹת אַחֲרֶיהָ רֵעוֹתֶיהָ
מוּבָאוֹת לָךְ׃

15 With joy and gladness **they are led along** as they enter the palace of the king.	15 What a joyful and enthusiastic procession as they enter the king's palace!

16 תּוּבַלְנָה בִּשְׂמָחֹת וָגִיל
תְּבֹאֶינָה בְּהֵיכַל מֶלֶךְ׃

16 **In place of your fathers** shall be your sons; **you will make them princes** in all the earth.	16 Your sons will become kings like their father. You will make them rulers over many lands.

17 תַּחַת אֲבֹתֶיךָ יִהְיוּ בָנֶיךָ
תְּשִׁיתֵמוֹ לְשָׂרִים בְּכָל־הָאָרֶץ׃

17 I will cause your name to be **remembered in all generations;** therefore nations will praise you forever and ever.	17 I will bring honor to your name in every generation. Therefore, the nations will praise you forever and ever.
18 אַזְכִּירָה שִׁמְךָ בְּכָל־דֹּר וָדֹר עַל־כֵּן עַמִּים יְהוֹדֻךָ לְעֹלָם וָעֶד :	

[a] In v. 14a we have a sample of the sort of text critical issues that challenge the translator of Psalm 45: "Heb. 'within, from settings of gold, her clothing'. The Hebrew term פְּנִימָה (pÿnimah 'within'), if retained, would go with the preceding line and perhaps refer to the bride being 'within' the palace or her bridal chamber (cf. NIV, NRSV). Since the next two lines refer to her attire (see also v. 9), it is preferable to emend the form to פְּנִינֶיהָ ('her pearls') or to פְּנִינִים ('pearls'). The *mem* (מ) prefixed to 'settings' is probably dittographic" (NET text note).

6.2 Psalm 45 is unique

"Nearly every study of Psalm 45 contains some variation on the statement 'Psalm 45 is unique'" (Bowen 2003:53). In fact, this psalm seems to be known more for its problematic text and extraordinary theme than for its theological insights and distinctive style. "Many words and word usages are unique to this psalm" (Bowen ibid.; cf. Mulder 1972:113–142). As Craigie observes: "the text is difficult to translate and interpret at many points, and the analysis of the poetic structure is equally uncertain" (1983:337). Its subject matter also presents a bit of a conceptual barrier. This is because "Psalm 45 is unique in the Psalter in that it is a royal marriage psalm" (Day 1992:93) and "focuses on human beings rather than God" (Goldingay 2007:54; cf. McCann 1996:860). "It is also the only psalm where women occupy a central place" (Bowen 2003:53),[7] and "the only instance in the Hebrew Psalter of a poet being self-consciously present in a composition" (deClaissé-Walford et al. 2014:49).[8] With respect to overt content, its setting of normal performance would be the royal court, not the holy Temple (Broyles 1999:206). The spotlight of attention is clearly fixed upon "the king" (הַמֶּלֶךְ—vv. 2, 12, MT) (Mays 1994a:180), who is the primary addressee (v. 3):

Psalm 45, a royal psalm, is unlike any other psalm. Most
psalms praise God (with God as the sentences' grammatical

---

[7] Perhaps as a result of the preceding compositional characteristics, it may also be that this "Psalm is unique in that it seems to have no function of any kind in contemporary communities of faith" (Bowen 2003:55), for example, in hymnbooks or worship liturgies.

[8] "This psalm differs from all others in the canonical collection both rhetorically and stylistically. Only here do we have a poet who begins by celebrating his own art—a gesture that might well be appropriate for a court poet..." (Alter 2007:158). For detailed text-critical notes, see Craigie 1983: 336–337.

subject), but this one praises the king. It opens with, "You (i.e., the king in v. [2]) are the most excellent of men," and closes with, "the nations will praise you (i.e., the king) for ever and ever." (Broyles 1999:206)

However, 'God' (אֱלֹהִים) is not entirely absent, being referred to explicitly twice (vv. 3, 8), and indeed, many commentators, beginning with the Targum (Whybray 1996:91; deClaissé-Walford et al. 2014:416), have seen an underlying, secondary meaning, with reference to the divinely promised Messiah running as a covert theme throughout the psalm (Craigie 1983:340; Harman 2011a:365; Boice, n.d.). But the main thrust of my investigation is not text-critical, exegetical, or theological in nature (as important as such studies may be, cf. Nel 1998), but rather it has a stylistic emphasis, with special reference to the translational transmission of Psalm 45 in a Bantu language, namely, Chewa. I will concentrate therefore on the art and craft of the translator—the person with the 'skillful stylus' (or eloquent voice) today—and how well s/he is able to match something of the beauty of poetic expression as well as the power of the psalmist's persuasive (indeed, 'inspired' רחש—v. 2) rhetoric in a contemporary vernacular.[9] As Wm. A. Smalley stated the case in an earlier age of translation:

> In applying the principles of dynamic equivalence translation to poetry, I think it is essential to expand 'meaning' to be the author's overall purpose in the broadest sense.... Why did the original writer write in poetry? What was the original effect?... To the degree that there is a poem in the original, there should be a poem of nearly equivalent value in the receptor language if the other functions involved are also suitable for verse form in the receptor language. (1974:359, 366)

Among the seven stylistic features identified for discussion, I will pay particular attention to the psalm's *phonic* component because: (a) the oral-aural dimension is explicitly highlighted by the poet himself (v. 1); (b) this is such an essential aspect of poetry in any language; (c) this auditory element is so often neglected in translations, past and present; and (d) more specifically, sound is also a vital facet of the entire Hebrew text of Psalm 45, both in its original form and, ideally, also during its subsequent dynamic oral-aural transmission in another language.[10]

---

[9] The exquisite quality of this composition may also be suggested by its apparent emic genre—a *maskil* (מַשְׂכִּיל): "The word is derived from a verb meaning 'to be prudent; to be wise'. Various options are: 'a contemplative song', 'a song imparting moral wisdom', or 'a skillful [i.e., well-written] song'" (NET text note; cf. LXX εἰς σύνεσιν). The technical term *maskil* suggests "presenting songs and poems in a skilled, intelligent, and artistic way" (Kraus 1993:25)—cf. 2 Chr. 30:22.

[10] A concern for the essential orality of the biblical text and its corresponding echoing in translation practice was the primary emphasis of the early 20th century German

To be sure, the challenge of rendering literary poetry within the framework of a completely different sound system is indeed great. As a practicing translator of Modern Hebrew observes: "Poetic music—the untranslatable sound of a poem that carries and conveys so much of the poem's meaning and essence—is fleeting and changing" (Rachel Tzvia Back 2014) on account of the transient medium of sound via which it is most naturally conveyed. But on the other hand, the joy of (at least partial success in) matching sound effect [TL] for sound effect [SL] (with respect to impact and appeal—not necessarily the linguistic forms!) provides all the encouragement that Bible translators need as they continue their ongoing efforts to pay honest attention to the complementary esthetic-emotive dimension of the original text of Scripture.

6.3 Seven artistic-rhetorical features of Psalm 45

"Psalm 45 is rich in literary features" (Patterson 1985:30). By way of summary, I have selected seven important stylistic, specifically artistic-rhetorical, devices for consideration: patterned organization, sonic effect, dynamic speech, figurative language, contextual reference, semantic density, and pervasive intertextuality. I will not be able to examine any of these poetic characteristics in detail, but can simply point out certain aspects of their purposeful significance (i.e., meaning!) within the Hebrew text of Psalm 45, which implies that they must also be handled with corresponding care and craft in any translation (to be discussed in §3). The attribute "artistic" refers to the original text's attractive formal linguistic features, while "rhetorical" calls attention to their vital functional, or pragmatic, dimension in religious-cultic communication. Thus, in addition to conveying theological and/or ethical content, the sacred text aims to please as well as to persuade with corresponding effect (convincing impact, emotive force, aesthetic appeal, and oral-aural resonance) in its envisioned setting of religious use, whether for praising, instructing, petitioning, warning, encouraging, or simply broadcasting a "remembrance" of God's "name" (אַזְכִּירָה שְׁמֵךְ) (v. 18). This same literary dimension, if granted (whether more or less), should be correspondingly prominent in any contemporary version that aims to be functionally equivalent in nature, that is, in accordance with the project's

translators Martin Buber and Franz Rosenzweig. The latter points out that "the most familiar term denoting the Old Testament [is] *queri'ah*, the 'calling out'. It is in response to this command that in all worship Scripture is customarily read aloud; it is in the service of this command that Luther in his translation has recourse to the spoken language of the people" (from "Scripture and Word" [1925], cited in Weissbort and Eysteinsson 2006:312–313). Rosenzweig also made the important practical observation that "We must free from beneath the logical punctuation that is sometimes its ally and sometimes its foe the fundamental principle of natural, oral punctuation: the act of breathing" (ibid.:313). That is my goal in the utterance-based Chewa samples found below in §4.2–4.3.

overall job description (brief) and primary communicative goal *(Skopos)* (Wendland 2011:95–122).

6.3.1 Patterned organization

"Hebrew poetry is most often organized according to patterns" (Beldman 2012:90; cf. 1.2.1–1.2.2). Although this is not reflected in most (English) translations, the structural organization of Psalm 45 is rather symmetrical and binarily arranged in Hebrew, a feature that would contribute to both its memorizability and oral performance. This structure is summarized in the outline below (cf. VanGemeren 1991:343; Gerstenberger 1988:186).[11] After each descriptive heading, the applicable verses are given in parentheses, followed by the principal text markers indicating the particular rhetorical-poetic devices that help to distinguish the onset (aperture) of a new discourse unit, or strophe (cf. Wendland 2002:118–119). The psalm's superscription is also significant in relation to the text's overall genre and theme (e.g., "song of loves" שִׁיר יְדִידֹת) and has therefore been included in the following architectural overview of the compositional arrangement of Psalm 45:

I. A **Introduction** (1–2): technical poetic-musical information + 1st-person
   authorial (self-) reference announcing *the poet's personal goal of praising
   the king!*
   B **Appeal** to the **king** (3–6): shift to 2nd pers. sing. masc. pronouns
       C **Description** of the **king**'s glory (7–10):[12] vocative opener + shift
          to non-imperatival verbs;
          "God" is the king's personal point of reference

II. B' **Appeal** to the **bride/queen** (11–13): vocative opener + shift to 2nd
    pers.
    sing. fem. pronouns *(the addressee suddenly shifts from the king to his bride)*
       C' **Description** of the **bride**'s glory (14–16): shift to 3rd pers. sing.
       fem. pronouns; *"the king" is the bride's personal point of reference*

---

[11] Harman suggests a more basic structure that is determined by shifts in the primary addressee, which in turn is centered around the king (2011a:365):
The king (vv. 2–5, English versions)
  God (vv. 6–7)
The king (vv. 8–9)
  The bride (vv. 10–15)
The king (vv. 16–17)

[12] DeClaissé-Walford et al. include v. 9 (Heb. 10) as part of "The Praise of the Bride" (2014:417). However, the second person singular pronominal references ("you/r") in this verse are masculine, as in the preceding verses, "The Praise of the Groom;" feminine forms being only in v. 10 (Heb. 11).

A' **Conclusion** (17–18): shift back to 2nd pers. sg. masc. pronouns + a concluding 1st-person authorial (self-) reference announcing *the poet's goal of praising the king (and the King) forever!* (compositional *end stress*)[13]

Thus, personal pronouns are instrumental in guiding the hearer/reader through this psalm's well-crafted organization, that is, along with the distinctive subject matter which is expressed within a given discourse unit (strophe).[14] Poetic symmetry, too, is manifest, as the royal bard (one of "the sons of Korah") begins and ends his lyric with a dramatic declaration of purpose—to praise the king/King. In between, he presents an expressive summary of the wonderful wedding to which he was evidently a specially invited eye-witness and perhaps even an active participant. The psalm is thus divided into two major stanzas—the second being somewhat shorter than the first—and the text is developed around a pair of authorial exhortations: first to the king/groom, second to his queen/bride. The two stanzas are transitioned at their medial border by means of an overlapping lexical link of the key term "daughters/daughter" (בְּנוֹת/בַּת–10a/11a), and each unit may be further segmented into a set of three matching strophes (a semi-chiastic arrangement: A-B-C / B'-C'-A').

In addition to the climactic, text-final promise and vow regarding the king's future blessings (vv. 17–18), there is one sub-strophe of particular thematic import in this royal eulogy, namely, an internal segment that may have implicit Messianic implications (vv. 7–8; I, C, *a*). It appears to be chiastically arranged in order to highlight its semantic prominence within the discourse, that is, with a focus on the "upright" king—whose reign is, in turn, framed by the divine promise that is based upon the premise of righteous ruling (see further below for additional support for this interpretation):[15]

A temporal blessing by "God" (אֱלֹהִים)—king's "eternal" rule [7a]
    B description of the king's ethical 'justice' (מִישֹׁר) [7b]

---

[13] There is also a partial inclusio in vv. 3 and 18 that encloses the song's body: 'therefore...forever' עַל־כֵּן...לְעוֹלָם.

[14] Technically speaking, a discourse is a verbal text, or a segment of one, that derives specifically from direct speech, whether actual (vocal) or represented (written), as in the case of the Psalter.

[15] I therefore interpret these verses as operating according to the covenantal (*Torah*) principle of gracious divine blessing *before* (encouraging) human righteous response (Deut. 17:18–20, 28:12–13). Thus, with reference to the amazing deeds described in v. 5, "God's blessing will mean that the king sees God do them by means of his own deeds as he himself rides out in the cause of truthfulness and faithfulness" (Goldingay 2007:58). Furthermore, Israel's kings were divinely 'anointed' (v. 8b) based "on the supposition that they affirmed that commitment" to righteous behavior, that is, 'faithfulness' to the Mosaic covenant (ibid.:59). "Elsewhere, such as in Psalm 65:5, 'awesome deeds' refers to God's own actions" (Harman 2011a:367).

B′ description of the king's moral "uprightness" (צֶ֫דֶק) [8a]
A′ personal blessing by "God" (אֱלֹהִים) – king's 'superior', regal status [8b]

The covenantal (Yahwistic) vocabulary that permeates this passage (cf. Pss. 2:2, 33:5; Isa. 61:1–3) clearly indicates the importance of these verses, which must also be signaled somehow in a translation (or noted in its paratext with reference to vv. 7–8).[16]

The balanced arrangement of Psalm 45, including it spotlighted strophes in the middle (7–8) and at the end (17–18), would have been made familiar through repeated liturgical choral performances. This communal participatory factor would also be helpful to any audience—that is, to assist them in following along or joining in, in responsive fashion, as the text is being chanted, recited, or probably (given the occasion) sung to the accompaniment of selected musical instruments (cf. v. 9b).[17] A discourse analysis of the entire text gives us a grasp of the poetic whole and its parts; from this viewpoint—and soundscape—we are in a better position to discover and evaluate its microstructural features.

6.3.2 Sonic effect

The predominant phonological quality and identifying characteristic of Hebrew (Semitic) poetry is the familiar (but never to be underestimated!) device of concise, lineal parallelism, a rhythmic, progressive sequence that is delineated into strophes comprised of variable sets of bi- and tri-cola.[18] Bratcher and Reyburn assert that "this psalm has a minimum of semantic parallelism" (1991:420), but this view would have to be understood in a very narrow sense as referring to *synonymous* parallelism (cf. ch. 5). In fact, Psalm 45, like any other, is constituted completely by paralleled poetic line couplets (bi-/tri-cola, cf. Wendland 2007), here primarily of the *additive*

---

[16] Terrien suggests that Psalm 45's "emphasis on the religious, moral, and ethical obligations of royalty" was another reason for its inclusion in the Psalter (2003:365; cf. Deut. 17:18–20 and the category of pervasive intertextuality in 6.3.7 below).

[17] No doubt the type of melody would modulate according to the prevailing subject matter and emotive mood of each strophe, for example (some tentative suggestions), contemplative for the opening and closing authorial reflections; majestically grand for the king's stanza (military, vv. 3–6 + celebratory, vv. 7–10); delicately beautiful for the bride's piece (instructive, vv. 11–13 + triumphant, vv. 11–16).

[18] "The first characteristic of Hebrew poetry, a feature it shares with much poetry throughout history, is its *terseness*. Even in translation the lines of poetry are shorter than those of prose, and in Hebrew this economy of words is even more pronounced.... The second and most distinctive characteristic [then why is it not listed *first*?] is *parallelism*.... There is always a dynamic movement from the first line to the second. This progression or intensification is most significant on the semantic level, increasing the impact of a statement" (Beldman 2012:88; words italicized and in brackets added).

type, including five tricola (vv. 2, 3, 8, 12, 15; Craigie 1983:335–336) and with a prevalent accentual rhythm of 4 + 4 (Goldingay 2007:55).[19] These deliberate poetic line parallels combine to form the text's most prominent sound effect, one that creates an extended cadenced, oft patterned style of composition (cf. 1.2.5). This is a lyric feature that literally calls out for public oral articulation, as indeed, the psalmist himself attests at this song-poem's very beginning. But the phonic frame of Psalm 45 is very much evident (audible) in other ways as well.

For example, sound is referred to at the onset of the poem as the psalm-ist reveals that he "is uttering his (praiseworthy) work to the king (with his) tongue" (אֹמֵר אָנִי מַעֲשַׂי לְמֶלֶךְ לְשׁוֹנִי). The particular type of utterance in this case is undoubtedly a musical piece—a "love lyric" (שִׁיר יְדִידֹת), or "wed-ding song" (NIV), as specified in the text's superscription.[20] The prime sub-ject of the bard's flowing, flowery praise—"the [handsome][21] king"—is also quaintly described as having "lips [speech] poured on with grace" (הוּצַק חֵן בְּשִׂפְתוֹתֶיךָ) (v. 3).[22] The bride/future queen (lit. "daughter") is correspond-ingly exhorted at the onset of the psalm's second half to "listen, and see (visualize?), and give ear" (שִׁמְעִי-בַת וּרְאִי וְהַטִּי אָזְנֵךְ) to what the psalmist has to say to her (v. 11). Sound is also suggested in the "stringed instru-ments" (Craigie 1983:337) of v. 9 and the corresponding voices of "gladness" (שׂמח) emanating from the bridal procession (v. 16). It is further implied in the singer's concluding vow to "perpetuate the (king's) memory" (אַזְכִּירָה שִׁמְךָ), which, quite significantly and perhaps surprisingly, *results in* (עַל-כֵּן) everlasting worldwide acclamation (עַל-כֵּן עַמִּים יְהוֹדֻךָ לְעֹלָם וָעֶד) (v. 18b).

---

[19] Poetic parallelism also creates a certain corresponding conceptual pattern or thought progression to complement the verbal utterance rhythm linking bi-/tri-cola and even larger lyric segments (strophes, stanzas). "Poetry was a welcome aid to memory, for it employed parallel lines that had a certain rhythm of thought, though no set meter" (M. R. Wilson 1989:141).

[20] The vocal lyric nature of this psalm is suggested already by the technical term *shoshanim* (שֹׁשַׁנִּים) in its title: "This is still another unknown musical term, though the literal meaning is 'lilies'" (Alter 2007:158). This term frequently appears—quite significantly for comparative purposes—in the Song of Songs (e.g., 2:1–2, 16; 4:5; 5:13; 6:2–3; 7:2).

[21] Alter renders the superlative descriptive verb יָפְיָפִיתָ as "you are loveliest," which seems rather strange when applied to a man. In any case, he comments: "[This word] is unique to this poem and looks like an elegant stylistic flourish suited to the celebratory language of the psalm" (2007:158). The key question is: How "elegant" (in terms of form) or "celebratory" (with regard to function) does the translation in my/our language sound when enunciated aloud?

[22] "The context of other references to gracious speech...suggests that the king has a way with words, a facility for speaking a winning word (Prov. 22:1; Eccles. 10:12)" (Goldingay 2007:57). "Part of God's gift to the king was loveliness of speech, an indication of his blessing"—"forever," that is, for as long as he lived (Harman 2011a:366).

The preceding colon exhibits some of the resonant, rhythmic alliteration that is heard periodically throughout this psalm. This is evident also in v. 8b–c:[23]

מְשָׁחֲךָ אֱלֹהִים אֱלֹהֶיךָ | עַל־כֵּן – al-kên m'shach°kha °lôhiym elôhekha

שֶׁמֶן שָׂשׂוֹן מֵחֲבֵרֶיךָ –   shemen sâsown mech°bherekha

On the other hand, and by way of contrast (perhaps to signal a final strophic boundary, i.e., closure), we observe a broken, breathless style (asyndetic, perhaps to convey excitement)[24] as the king's wartime exploits are described (v. 6, in literal translation; note the phonological chiasmus, highlighted in gray):

חִצֶּיךָ שְׁנוּנִים   –   [A] your arrows *are* [B] sharpened *(shinûniym)*

עַמִּים תַּחְתֶּיךָ יִפְּלוּ – [B'] peoples *('ammiym)* [A'] under you *they* will fall

בְּלֵב אוֹיְבֵי הַמֶּלֶךְ: – in the heart of the enemies of the king

The verb 'they will fall' (יִפְּלוּ) at the end of the pre-positioned second line appears to do poetically motivated double duty.[25] Thus, as the royal army's arrows rain down upon hostile hearts, the affected enemy peoples correspondingly "drop" beneath the king's control (note the corresponding verse/strophe-final climactic position of "the king").

6.3.3 Dynamic speech

This third poetic feature is closely related to sonic effect (6.3.2; cf. 1.2.3). Thus, Psalm 45 was, like most ancient formal and informal discourse, composed as well as transmitted aloud (cf. Craigie 1983:339; Hilber 2009:357)—in the case of the Psalter also explicitly in the form of direct [prayerful] speech, whether individual or communal in nature.[26] God, or

---

[23] The tricolon of v. 8 is the longest verse of the psalm as well as its physical (lexical) midpoint, viz. vv. 1–8: 77 words, vv. 9–18: 82 words. Often, as here, this location is a point of thematic prominence within a psalm. Note also the corresponding occurrences of the consequential conjunction "therefore" (עַל־כֵּן) at the beginning, middle, and ending of Ps. 45 (vv. 3b, 8b, and 18b).

[24] In contrast, the asyndeton in the tricolon of v. 2 may convey a "sonorous" vocal impression (Goldingay 2007:56).

[25] A similar thing occurs at the close of the next strophe in v. 10, where the verb that begins colon B in the MT, 'she stands' (נִצְּבָה) may be construed as applying also to the preceding verbless line A (despite its plural subject, 'daughters'; cf. Goldingay 2007:60; Craigie 1983:336–337).

[26] As the German translator Martin Buber correctly emphasized: "The Bible is a product of living recitation, and is intended for living recitation; that speech is its

the LORD *(YHWH)*, was normally the primary addressee (in contrast to Ps. 45), while the psalmist and/or the people of God were the usual speaker(s).

Such composition thus lends itself well to a functional (speech-act) analysis: what were the speakers doing through their words; what pragmatic goals were they seeking to accomplish? In general, are the varied cola (poetic utterances) of a given psalm informative, expressive, directive, evocative, eulogistic, relational, performative, and/or artistic in nature?[27] More specifically then, what vocalized communicative intention does a particular colon (bicolon) embody or express, and what is the expected outcome or impact upon the audience or addressee(s)? In short, "the three [speech] acts are '*of* saying' (locution), '*in* saying' (illocution) and '*by* saying' (perlocution)" (Briggs 2008:88, original italics); cf. 1.3.8 and 3.4.1 above.

What can a speech-act (S-A) study tell us about Psalm 45? First of all, we note that related sets of S-As tend to group themselves according to the stanzaic and strophic structure of the text that was outlined above (for two classificatory systems, see Wendland 2011:44, 46; cf. Levine 1995:95). Thus, the psalm leads off with a short strophe consisting of several combined S-As of expressive exaltation and authorial self-affirmation (v. 2).[28] The second strophe of stanza 1 then consists of a sequence of S-As that generally praise and exhort the king/groom in terms of his royal character: commendation, encouragement, and especially an appeal to valor in the face of Israel's enemies (vv. 3–6). This strophe sounds rather militaristic in tone as the psalmist impressively focuses his verbal spotlight upon the royal warrior being displayed on stage:[29]

> He addresses the king directly with verses that sound appropriate to a pre-battle liturgy anticipating victory and that highlight the military accoutrement of this supreme warrior. (Broyles 1999:206)

This leads to the third strophe (vv. 7–10), which begins by describing the king with regard to his benevolent, 'righteous' governance, but then

---

nature, and the written text is only a form for preserving it" (from "A Translation of the Bible" [1927], cited in Weissbort and Eysteinsson 2006:320).

[27] Gerstenberger outlines the structure of Ps. 45 in terms of these functional elements (1988:186).

[28] From a secular perspective, such functional "self-presentation...is necessary whenever a singer performs before an audience, whose benevolence is vital to him;" cf. medieval minstrels (Gerstenberger 1988:187).

[29] "From loveliness and grace, the poem quickly moves on to military might, something the kings of the ancient Near East proverbially needed to exercise in order to maintain securely the grandeur of their courts even in times of peace, such as the wedding occasion of this poem" (Alter 2007:159). Longman feels that the "divine warrior" motif, which first occurs in Exo. 15:4, is a "theme that ties together many of the writings of the Old Testament" (1993:105).

subtly shifts to a portrayal of the extravagant physical setting of the royal wedding.

Stanza 2 begins by offering fatherly counsel, advice, and encouragement to the future bride (first strophe, vv. 11–13),[30] followed by a more physical description of her beautiful person and blissful surroundings (second strophe, vv. 14–16). The psalmist interjects himself again at the end of his song (vv. 17–18) with a benediction-*cum*-prediction concerning future progeny, coupled with a vow to perpetuate the king's glorious memory forever through his poetry. This is an instance of what Patterson calls "rhetorical parallelism that fits the stated needs of lyricism for progression" (1985:31)—a poem with a particular purpose in mind.

In any such classificatory scheme there is of course a considerable amount of interlocking and overlapping, as one S-A meshes with or is molded into another. The drama of direct discourse becomes a challenge for translators as they must seek to convey the same, or similar pragmatic implications—naturally—in their language. Especially difficult are those cases of convergence, where a single utterance (colon or bicolon) appears to express two or more S-As at once, but on different levels of interpretation. For example, a strong case can be made that the apparent (surface level) descriptive and/or predictive praise of the king in vv. 7–8 is simultaneously also an implicit (deep level) exhortation for him to continue to reflect the godly attributes of "justice" (perhaps "truth" and "humility" עֲנָוָה as well, cf. v. 5; Craigie 1983:336; Perowne 1878:376).[31] Such godly behavior must be manifested throughout his current rule for the good of his subjects (the people of God, implied in v. 3) and for the sake of his future reputation (v. 18b).

6.3.4 Figurative language

"Images are the glory, perhaps the essence of poetry" (Schoekel 1988:95; cf. 1.2.7–8)—intended to stimulate the imagination and to generate interest and allure. In terms of its genre, or literary type, Psalm 45 may be classified as a "royal psalm" (Craigie 1983:337; Wendland 2002:51) that functions more specifically as an epithalamium—a marriage hymn and, especially if a public choral arrangement were involved, also as an encomium—a song of communal praise (Alter 2007:17; Gerstenberger 1988:189; Preminger and Brogan 1993:332, 378; Ryken 1992:273, 293;) in honor of the king, the "mighty one" (גִּבּוֹר), an attribute also appropriate for God (Pss. 24:8, 120:4). The elaborate, albeit rather cryptic (to scholars today!) Hebrew

---

[30] These words of admonition to the bride (esp. vv. 11–12) may have formed part of the ritualized bridal instructions delivered as part of the wedding ceremony (Gerstenberger 1988:188).

[31] Similarly, the apparent authorial *wish* of v. 17 may actually serve as a more substantive divine *promise,* declared by the inspired singer (v. 2) (Gerstenberger 1988:189).

title (לַמְנַצֵּחַ עַל־שֹׁשַׁנִּים לִבְנֵי־קֹרַח מַשְׂכִּיל), with its reference to "lilies" (as frequently in the *Song* of Songs, e.g., 2:1), seems to refer to "a popular tune about romantic love" (Terrien 2003:365), or contrastively, to a "hymn tune" (Bullock 2001:30)—in any case, a musical composition of some sort (Craigie 1983:264, 336), which would certainly be suitable for "a love song" (שִׁיר יְדִידֹת) (v. 1).[32] Such a lovely lyric typically features a diversity of picturesque figurative language (especially metaphor) and related imagery that pertains to the personage(s) being praised.[33] This song-poem thus "ties together in a single bunch of many-colored flowers a variety of essential motifs and thoughts associated with the [marriage] feast" (Weiser 1962:362); it thereby depicts the various ceremonies that accompanied the several distinct stages of an ancient Jewish traditional wedding celebration.

Ryken et al. set the scene well in what amounts to a semi-narrative description of the festive communal, double-focused procession, a scenario that abounds in "extravagant joy and sensory richness" (1998:938)—naturally with jubilant sounds implied:

> The poet sets the tone at the outset when he asserts, "My heart overflows with a goodly theme" (Ps. 45:1, RSV). The couple stands at the center of the event, and both appear at their best. The king is "fairest of the sons of men" (Ps. 45:2, RSV), girded with his sword in "glory and majesty" (Ps. 45:3). He is anointed with "the oil of gladness," and his robes "are all fragrant with myrrh and aloes and cassia" (Ps. 45:7–8, RSV). The princess, for her part, "is decked in her chamber with gold-woven robes" (Ps. 45:13) and then led to the king "in many robes...with her virgin companions" (Ps. 45:14, RSV). The whole procession enters the palace of the king "with joy and gladness" (Ps. 45:15, RSV).[34]

---

[32] Note that the inclusion of these psalm titles in the LXX translation indicates their long and close association with the rest of the text; therefore, it is not a wise policy to simply exclude or abbreviate them as some modern versions do (e.g., *Good News Translation*).

[33] In Hebrew poetry generally, "an abundant use of various figures of speech enhanced its liveliness, creativity, and depth of meaning" (M. R. Wilson 1989:141) in relation to the topic at hand. Furthermore, "the nature of Hebrew poetry is to paint pictures with broad strokes of the brush. The Hebrew authors of Scripture were not so much interested in the fine details and harmonious pattern of what they painted as they were in the picture as a whole" (ibid.:145). A good example of this is the overall wedding scenario suggestively sketched in broad, metonymic strokes by the author(s) of Psalm 45. And yet, the descriptive evocations can also be quite specific in nature, such as those "sharp arrows that pierce through the hearts of the king's enemies" (v. 6).

[34] The custom of the husband-to-be awaiting his bride for the imminent wedding ceremony (as depicted in Ps. 45) is also reflected in "the Jewish marriage service" (M. R. Wilson 1989:204).

But although two persons are naturally center-stage in this wedding scene, the main spotlight is undoubtedly fixed upon the regal groom, who is highlighted even when his bride is being described (e.g., vv. 12, 14–15). This picturesque song includes not only rich nuptial images, but it also incorporates, as befits a royal personage, figurative references to the king's outstanding gifts of speech (v. 3b), fighting prowess (vv. 4–5), and ruling capabilities (vv. 7–8a).[35] It is important to note too that, while the imagery of Psalm 45 is patently visual in nature, it further appeals to the sense of smell (e.g., "myrrh and aloes and cassia," v. 9a) and sound as well (e.g., "strings," v. 9b).

6.3.5 Contextual reference

Every text automatically comes with a context—verbal (intra- and intertextual) and nonverbal (sociocultural and environmental)—which is necessary for proper audience understanding and appreciation (cf. 1.3.7).[36] Even the author's opening self-reference as being a "scribe" (סוֹפֵר) cannot be taken for granted or interpreted anachronistically; thus, they were not mere copyists, but "scribes and sages were the official storytellers of the kings of the Ancient Near East" (Walton et al. 2000:528).[37] Some commentators take space to speculate about the historical life-setting of Psalm 45 and who might have been the king and bride concerned, for example: Solomon and the daughter, either of Pharaoh or of Hiram, king of Tyre; Ahab and Jezebel (which would be most ironic in view of the psalm's later typological hermeneutical history, but see Terrien 2003:367–368 and Holladay 1996:28); Joram, son of Jehoshaphat, and Athaliah (also ironic), or most far-fetched, some later Persian king and his wife (or one of them) (Perowne 1878:367).[38] But truth be told, we cannot know for sure, and "all

---

[35] "Descriptive words dominate in the verses, eulogizing the ideal king.... In the highly poetic language of Psalm 45, the psalm-singer addresses the groom-king with a hyperbolic appellation [v. 6] that reflects the ancient Near Eastern culture of which Israel was indisputably a part" (deClaissé-Walford et al. 2014:419–420).

[36] "In order to understand Psalm 45 we need to know something about ancient betrothal and wedding customs" (Boice 1996:381; these are then summarized, ibid.:381–382).

[37] Walton et al. continue (2000:528): "Their command of the traditions and their association with the royal bureaucracy made it appropriate that they perform songs and stories that remind the people of the king's role to feed and protect the land as God's political agent." Traditional royal praise poets and griots perform an analogous role in many African societies.

[38] With reference to the word שֵׁגָל in v. 10b, the NET notes: "This rare Hebrew noun apparently refers to the king's bride, who will soon be queen (see Neh 2:6). The Aramaic cognate is used of royal wives in Dan 5:2–3, 23." Alter adds: "The Hebrew *shegal* is probably an Akkadian loan-word. Other features of the poem's style are also archaic, and some commentators, given the wedding with a Tyrian princess

that can be safely said is that [this psalm] originated during the existence of the [Jewish] monarchy and was probably used [officially] at several royal weddings" (McCann 1996:861, words in brackets added; cf. Day 1992:93). However, it is most probable that Psalm 45 was also used "unofficially" and functionally recontextualized, that is, liturgically for Temple worship, especially in later years, to celebrate the covenantal relationship between Yahweh and his chosen people.[39]

As our preceding survey of the psalm's figurative language would suggest, an awareness of the text's real or assumed extralinguistic setting is a crucial factor in its contemporary interpretation.[40] Such imagery, whether expressed in greater or lesser explicitness, always evokes a richer, often less obvious cognitive environment than more prosaic discourse. Thus, precise knowledge of the ancient Near Eastern (ANE) situational background is essential to reveal this added semantic and connotative significance, hence also to provide some vital contextually-based hermeneutical insight. For example, the customs referred to in verses 8 and 9 (anointing the head, wearing perfumed, gold-embroidered robes, festive stringed music, etc.) could be applied to both a wedding ceremony and also the coronation of a king, two public events that were often combined (Walton et al. 2000:528).

Another important perspective affects the analysis and hence also the translation of verse 13. "A daughter of Tyre" (בַּת־צֹר) might refer to a particular person—some prominent woman (perhaps even the queen herself!) from the Phoenician seaport city of Tyre—but it is more likely a figurative reference to the affluent merchant inhabitants of that location, which "was associated with the epitome of wealth (Ezek. 27:1–33)" (Hilber 2009:359; cf. Goldingay 2007:61; Walton et al. 2000:529; NET study notes).

The psalm's prevailing frame of reference involving ANE marriage ceremonies and associated family traditions is helpful also for understanding the structure as well as the message of Psalm 45. As suggested earlier, this psalm consists of a narrator frame that opens (v. 1) and closes (vv. 17–18) the text as a whole. In between we have two principal poetic units (stanzas) that present a quasi-narrative discourse featuring two central characters, first the groom and then his bride. These stanzas correspond to the two

---

(see verse 13), have been tempted to see the psalm as a product of Solomon's court" (2007:160).

[39] Westermann wrongly concludes that Psalm 45 was "really a completely secular song, which originally had nothing to do with worship" (1980:107).

[40] "This psalm contains language and detail suitable for a marriage anthem or the anointing of a king (Ps. 133:2). In the Ancient Near East these two were combined in the sacred marriage ritual described..." (Walton et al. 2000:528). The scene envisioned includes its general setting, for example, the "ivory palaces" (v. 9), which refers to "the lavish use of ivory to decorate furniture and wall panels.... The wealth of a nation might well be displayed in the king's palace—a sign of power and prestige for the state" (ibid.; cf. Gerstenberger 1988:188; Amos 3:15).

ritualized journeys connected with a typical Jewish wedding celebration: the groom must first travel with his company to the bride's residence (3–10), and then with the addition of her entourage they all move in the opposite direction back to the groom's home (11–16).[41] In the first stanza we hear effusive praise extolling the virtues of the groom—how fitting a person he is (or should be!) in terms of regal character and capacity (performance).[42] The second stanza then features a contrast in both content and tone as the bride-to-be is paternally advised (perhaps with some maternal influence as well), in sapiential fashion (cf. Proverbs 1:8, 3:1, 4:1, 5:1), to adopt a completely new outlook on life (v. 11). This would be in customary submission to her husband, yes (v. 12), but also in the prospect of an optimistic future (v. 16) that promised both public respect (v. 13) and considerable domestic responsibility (implied in v. 17).[43]

6.3.6 Semantic density

The device of semantic density is characteristic of the typical terseness, or formal-semantic condensation, of poetry.[44] It specifically applies to words or phrases that arguably have more than one compatible sense or reference in a given cotextual setting (Wendland 1990:302–304). The qualifier "arguably" is necessary because commentators may disagree on whether or not this literary device is actually present in the biblical text, and whether deliberate authorial intention can be demonstrated in such usage, as distinct from its being a product of the history of Scripture interpretation and/or contemporary scholarly consensus. Such functional semantic ambiguity is a typical characteristic of most, if not all lyrical traditions, and it certainly plays a central role in the poetic books of the Hebrew Bible, especially in texts that are more expressive and panegyric in nature, such as the Canticles and Psalm 45.

We may have an example of such lexical density at the very onset of the psalm, as the composer describes himself as a "scribe" who is מָהִיר. This adjective, derived from the verb "hasten" (מהר), could refer to the writer's actual quickness of composition and/or, metonymically, to his artistic expertise in doing so, as in the case of Ezra; cf. 7:6 (Prov. 22:29;

---

[41] "Wedding processions that mark the transition into another sphere of life are customary in many parts of the world.... The text [of Ps. 45] reflects this 'rite of passage'" (Gerstenberger 1988:188–189).

[42] "This text also supports the view that the royal psalms speak of the royal ideal in ancient Israel, an ideal often unfulfilled" (Bellinger 1990:114).

[43] We find the corresponding didactic-hortatory custom involving the bride and groom in Chewa traditional marriage ceremonies.

[44] In the opinion of Adele Berlin, "it is not parallelism per se, but the predominance of parallelism with terseness, which marks the poetic expression of the Bible" (1985:5).

cf. Harman 2011a:366). The swiftness of the author's skill (v. 2) would then contrast with the potentially long duration of his song's panegyric message (v. 18).[45] On the other hand, the mention of "tongue" in the third colon (v. 2) might also indicate that the term "scribe" (סוֹפֵר) is to be taken figuratively and the reference made (in addition) to his manner of oral delivery, "whose words are fluent and mellifluous" (Goldingay 2007:56).

Along with the abundance of emblematic speech, already noted, hyperbolic exaggeration appears to be an important poetic element in this psalm—that is, if a human personage, even some prominent royal figure (or dynasty), is being so greatly lauded, for example, in the case of statements like "God has blessed you forever" (בֵּרַכְךָ אֱלֹהִים לְעוֹלָם) in v. 3b, or "your throne, O God, will last for ever and ever" (כִּסְאֲךָ אֱלֹהִים עוֹלָם וָעֶד) in v. 7a (cf. 18b).[46] Furthermore, the king is described at times with "characteristics normally reserved for God,

---

[45] "Etymologically 'quick', but Ethiopic suggests 'expert'...which makes better sense esp. in Ezra 7:6; Prov. 22:29" (Goldingay 2007:52).

[46] "Suddenly the psalmist looks beyond the immediate occupant of the throne of David to the kingly glory of the messianic ruler. This is similar to the way in which Isaiah inserts direct address to 'Immanuel' into a passage that is dealing with the impending Assyrian invasion (Isa. 8:8)" (Harman 2011a:367)

Alter translates the latter text somewhat awkwardly as "Your throne of God is forevermore" since he feels that "it would be anomalous to have an address to God in the middle of the poem because the entire psalm is directed to the king or to his bride" (2007:159). However, the deliberately ambiguous vocative "O god [king]" might also be interpreted as another subtle literary-rhetorical device which acts as a hermeneutical key denoting the secondary divine personage ("O God [King YHWH]") that underlies the overt royal referent of this psalm. Broyles suggests that the change of addressee at the onset of v. 7 with the unexpected reference to "God" may indicate a typical psalmic liturgical turn: "If we were to hear [Ps. 45] performed, it may have been obvious [that] these words were directed to God above, not to the king" (1999:207).

The NET text note comments: "Rather than taking the statement at face value, many prefer to emend the text because the concept of deifying the earthly king is foreign to ancient Israelite thinking (cf. NEB: 'your throne is like God's throne, eternal'). However, it is preferable to retain the text and take this statement as another instance of the royal hyperbole that permeates the royal psalms. Because the Davidic king is God's vice-regent on earth, the psalmist addresses him as if he were God incarnate. God energizes the king for battle and accomplishes justice through him." Broyles proposes that vv. 7–8 "thus make the same point as the one made in the longer liturgy of Ps. 89, namely that Yahweh's kingship is the basis for David's...." (1999:207; on the exegetical difficulties of this verse, see Goldingay 2007:53). The LXX supports the reading of the MT: ὁ θρόνος σου, ὁ θεός, εἰς τὸν αἰῶνα τοῦ αἰῶνος....

Another option is to follow Dahood's proposed emendation to *kis'ăká* "[God] has enthroned you" (Holladay 1996:125), which provides a close parallel (and an

namely, 'splendor' and 'majesty' (v 4; cf. Ps. 96:6)" (Craigie 1983:339; cf. also vv. 5–6).[47] In the wider context of Scripture then (see 6.3.7 and 6.4.7 below on intertextuality), early Jewish (and later Christian) commentators began to construe the language of these texts as exceeding poetic license and thus having divine or messianic typological significance (Craghan 1985:91; Hilber 2009:378; Mays 1994a:182; McCann 1996:863; Whybray 1996:91).[48]

A distinct lexical-semantic feature of Psalm 45 that supports this broader interpretive perspective is its use of the term "God" (אֱלֹהִים) to refer figuratively to the king, but within a wider (psalmic-canonical) hermeneutical framework also to its literal divine referent (v. 7a). Such conceptually dense nominal usage is coupled with the associated second person (m.) singular pronoun "you/your" in referential cotexts where, humanly speaking and hyperbole aside, it does not quite belong, for example: "the nations [i.e., the whole wide world!] will praise *you* forever and ever" (עַמִּים יְהוֹדֻךָ לְעֹלָם וָעֶד) (v. 18; cf. also vv. 3, 7–8).[49] This semantic overlay comes to the fore in the conjoined expression "God, your God" (אֱלֹהִים אֱלֹהֶיךָ) in v. 8b: "The person designated as 'God' in the previous verse is now marked off from him by the reference to 'your God'" (Harman 2011a:368). "Thus, vv. 6–7 [7–8] may use a pun to make the point that the enthroned king, while a 'mighty ruler', must acknowledge [*the rule of*] his God above" (Broyles 1999:207).[50]

---

instance of structural anaphora) with "God has blessed you forever" in v. 3b. The potential Messianic implication would nevertheless be the same.

[47] It would be a mistake, however, to conclude that the people of Israel viewed their kings as being endowed with "divine status" (Gillingham 1994:221).

[48] "Either we have here a piece of poetical exaggeration far beyond the limits of poetic license, or a 'greater than Solomon is here'" (Alexander Maclaren, cited in Boice 1996:381).

[49] With reference to v. 18a, Alter comments: "*Let me make your name heard.* Though some interpreters understand 'you' to refer to God and read this final verse as a stock psalmodic ending, it is more plausible to see it as a conclusion of the address to the king. This would be in keeping with our understanding of verse 7, 'Your throne of (sic) God is forevermore', as well as with 'Therefore has God blessed you forever' in verse 3" (2007:161). However, my point is this: why can this not be rather a both-and interpretation, overtly designating the king of Israel, but also having a secondary, canonically shaped reference to the great King, Yahweh, the Lord of all generations and nations? This too would then be an instance of hermeneutical semantic density.

[50] Alter suggests that "this odd phrasing is the result of an editorial substitution of *'elohim 'elohekha* for YHWH *'elohekha*" (2007:158), which would not be an unexpected occurrence in the so-called "Elohistic Psalter" (Pss. 42–83) (Broyles 1999:20; cf. Bellinger 1990:11). Whether this is true or not (one cannot really be as certain as Alter about such textual emendations), it does not change the interpretation being proposed here.

6.3.7 Pervasive intertextuality[51]

As suggested above (cf. also 4.8), the surrounding cotextual setting of the Psalter itself serves to stimulate and to shape our understanding of Psalm 45 with regard to its literal as well as any deeper theological significance. The various individual psalms, though probably composed separately, were normally not meant to be silently read and interpreted in isolation. Rather, they were gathered into smaller compositional groups (e.g., the "Psalms of Ascent"—Pss. 120–134), later into edited "books" (I–V), and finally the Psalms-scroll as a whole so that they might be sung, recited, chanted, or otherwise articulated—whether in familial meditative (but audible!) devotion and prayer—or more frequently, during public worship and communal liturgical expression. The memory of the entire psalmic corpus acted metonymically as a broad conceptual point of reference and an associated hermeneutical guide for the community of faith.[52] This reflective process is well illustrated in the book of Hebrews with respect to the Psalter and, in particular, the passage under consideration: Psalm 45:7–8 > Heb. 1:8–9 (with an emphasis on the text's spoken orality in Heb. 1:6, 2:12, 3:7, 3:15, 4:3, and so on).

The most immediate cotextual grouping for Psalm 45 is that "of/for/ by the sons of Korah" (לִבְנֵי-קֹרַח), a distinct corpus that is divided between Books II (Pss. 42–49) and III (Pss. 84–88).[53] Psalm 45 is most closely related thematically to the Korahite psalms that immediately follow it: "The psalm insists on the close relationship between God and his king and prepares the way for the great affirmations about the reign of God that we find in Psalms 46–48" (Firth 2008:27; cf. Patterson 1985:32). Psalm 48 is especially relevant, as we shall see.

There are a number of other psalms having an explicit reference to the king (or King)—the so-called royal psalms, which according to Gunkel include at least the following: "Psalms 2; 18; 20; 21; 45; 72; 89; 101; 110;

---

[51] For the purposes of this essay, we might adopt the following working definition: "Intertextuality relates various 'texts' to one another in a way that is not concerned with issues of priority or dependence. Instead, it is concerned with the way a text acquires different meanings when it is situated in relationship to other texts" (Bowen 2003:54).

[52] This is analogous to the conceptual relationship viewed as contextualizing and connecting one narrative or poem with the entire oral tradition in which it arose and to which it meaningfully contributes, an analytical notion that was popularized by the early French Structuralist approach to myth (e.g., Lévi-Strauss 1972:174–184).

[53] "The Korahites, like the Asaphites, are described in the Books of Chronicles as Levitical singers established by David to serve in the house of Yahweh (1 Chr. 6.31–37; 16.4–7)" (Wallace 2009:92). Wallace endeavors to show certain semantic-thematic connections between the Korahite collection and King David: "The reference to anointing and victory reminds of Psalm 2, while his handsome features recall the description of David in 1 Sam. 16.12" (ibid.:94).

132; 144:1–11" (Tucker 2008:584; cf. Futato 2008:181; Gerstenberger 1988:188).[54] Psalm 72, which is considered "Messianic" by Jews and Christians alike (M. R. Wilson 1989:182), manifests a number of important correspondences with Psalm 45—for example, the ideal king of Israel defending and delivering his people (72:4; cf. 45:4–6)[55] and ruling over them in 'justice' and righteousness (72:2–3; cf. 45:7–8).[56] The notion of God's kingship may well be regarded as the root metaphor of the entire Psalter: "All subsequent affirmations about the work and activity of Yahweh are predicated upon the assumption that Yahweh reigns as king" (Tucker 2008:591; cf. Bullock 2001:62). In short, "the psalms are the poetry of the reign of the LORD" (Mays 1994b:30).

Such a prevailing intertextual resonance involving this preeminent theme of divine kingship was (and is) bound to affect the understanding of Psalm 45 as it was transmitted, and contextually reinterpreted, both orally and in writing over the ages (Miller 1986:12–13). This would be a natural historical hermeneutical development within a long liturgical tradition, despite the fact that this divine perspective was undoubtedly *not* within the cognitive frame of reference of its original composer and setting (Gerstenberger 1988:189–190). There is thus a marriage of hermeneutical horizons in this distinctive wedding hymn, and we hear, visualize, and mentally merge many thematic parallels like the following:

---

[54] Bowen explores Ps. 45 in intertextual relation to several familiar OT texts from a feminist perspective, e.g., Abigail (1 Sm. 25; "a common vocabulary binds the named and unnamed brides together," 2003:57), Esther, the unfaithful wife of Ezek. 16, the assertive young woman of the Song of Solomon, and Jephthah's daughter (Judg. 11). Bowen recognizes, for example, that "like Ezekiel 16, Psalm 45 can be read as both a tale of human marriage as well as a story of divine-human marriage" (ibid.:66), but unfortunately (in my opinion) concludes that "the problem with Psalm 45 is that the gendered world it wishes for is the very world that feminists critique" (ibid.:71).

[55] In the ANE, a king was ipso facto also a mighty Savior of his subjects (M. R. Wilson 1989:181). Commemorating the wonderful 'name' of the king 'forever' is also enjoined at the close of both psalms (72:17; cf. 45:18). Psalm 72 concludes Book II of the Psalter (a printed collection of hymns), while Psalm 45 occurs near its beginning—the significance being that "the placement of royal psalms...at the 'seams' of the Psalter appears to be intentional" (McCann 2012:281). Thus, "verses 12–14 of Psalm 72 amount to something like a job description for the earthly king in his role as the agent entrusted with the enactment and embodiment of God's will" (ibid.:286)—a role that is clearly celebrated in Psalm 45.

[56] "The words 'justice' and 'righteousness' function as a summary of what God wills in and for the world *(torah)*" (McCann 2012:285)—cf. 45:7–8 and 72:1. "To 'love justice' and to 'hate evil' is a standard requirement for everybody (Amos 5:15; Mic 3:2; Isa 61:8; Pss. 5:5–6; 37:27; 52:5...) but especially for the king (Pss. 72:4; 101:2–8)" (Gerstenberger 1988:188).

> The poet proclaims of his earthly master [the king], "I com-
> memorate your fame of all generations, / so people will
> praise you forever and ever" (Ps. 45:18), just as the psalmist
> praises God, his heavenly lord and master: "Every day will I
> bless You / and praise Your name forever and ever." (145:2)
> (Levine 1995:93–94; words in brackets added)

In an interesting reversal of the anthropopathic theme of "divine suf-
fering in the Psalter" as documented by Gericke (2012), we may have
here in Psalm 45 (among others) a glimpse of manifold divine rejoicing.
"Generation to generation, God celebrates with humanity in their moments
of utter joy and jubilation—a small glimpse, perhaps, into a future of dwell-
ing endlessly in God's presence" (deClaissé-Walford et al. 2014:420). Such
pervasive happiness is elicited, as it were, by the acclamation, honor, devo-
tion, and testimony of God's people (45:2, 4–6, 7, 9, 12)—in the end (v. 18),
a universal mixed multitude embracing members of every epoch, nation,
culture, and language (Rev. 7:9–10).[57] To be sure, this is certainly a "noble
theme" concerning a most praiseworthy royal personage, which therefore
requires the expert "tongue" and "pen" of a "skilled" translator—and song-
ster!—in order to "perpetuate [his] memory through all generations" (Ps.
45:2, 18, NIV).

6.4 A blunt stylus and a dull sound in translation?

Why pay so much attention to the poetic-rhetorical forms and functions
of the original text? Can translators not simply (more quickly and efficient-
ly) access the text via a secondary translation in some language of wider
communication (e.g., English, French, Spanish, Swahili, etc.) and then work
from there into the TL? This of course is the easy way out, and many trans-
lation teams operate that way in order to cut costs and the time needed to
complete their work.[58] But such a policy does not demonstrate what Nord
(1997:125) terms sufficient "loyalty" to—and, we might add, also respect

---

[57] As enjoined also in Ps. 45:18, "the songs of praise regularly invite a world-encom-
passing congregation to praise God" (McCann 2012:288)—a call that occasionally
extends to all creation (e.g., Ps. 98:7–9).

[58] On the other hand, it must certainly be admitted that not every translator or team
is artistically competent enough to translate literature well, poetry in particular.
As John Dryden observed, "A man [sic] should be a nice critic in his mother tongue
before he attempts to translate a foreign language. Neither is it sufficient that he
be able to judge of words and style; but he must be a master of them too. He must
perfectly understand his author's tongue, and absolutely command his own; so that
to be a thorough translator, he must be a thorough poet...to give his author's sense
in good English, in poetical expressions, and in musical numbers [i.e., style]" (from
"Preface" to *Ovid's Epistles* [1680], cited in Weissbort and Eysteinsson 2006:148).

for—the original author-composer of the source text, particularly in the case of a sacred, high value corpus such as the Hebrew Scriptures.

First of all then, translators must convince themselves of this fact—namely, the excellent literary, indeed oratorical, quality of the biblical text (Wendland 2004:272–276). And the only way to do this is by means of a careful linguistic and literary analysis of the source document in order to reveal the diverse artistic, aural, rhetorical, and musical (or melodic) properties of the text which effectively complement its semantic content.[59] Such comprehensive study will both motivate and encourage them to seek to reproduce a stylistically corresponding "transposed" version,[60] that is, an "analogical form"[61] or a *re*-presentation of the original,[62] in their mother tongue (all other conditions being equal—e.g., project funding and support,

---

In my experience I have found that this practical point cannot be taken for granted: an expert source-text analyst (exegete) does not always (or even usually) make a proficient translator, especially in the case of a poetic text.

[59] In this respect, such a TL-oriented procedure would correspond well with the position of the eminent twentieth-century translator and critic, Ezra Pound, who was "one of the most important figures in the history of translation into English" (Weissbort and Eysteinsson 2006:271). Pound renounced the negative translation attitude that "poetry is what is lost in translation." Furthermore, he rejected "a stilted dialect in translation...which imitates the idiom of the ancients" in favor of an approach that gave "care for the beauty of the original...and the meaning" via free verse in modern English (from "Notes on Elizabethan Classics" [1917], cited in Weissbort and Eysteinsson 2006:275). That corresponds to my aim in resorting to Chewa traditional oral and modern written models for use in selected (special audience) translations of Scripture. The American poet W. S. Merwin warns that the "musical [formal] elements" of poetry "embedded in the original language" normally cannot be reproduced in a formally correspondent translation. "You can torment your own language in repeating them, but even if you do, you're not going to get the form doing in your language what it did in the original" (from his "Foreword" to *Selected Translations 1968–1978* [1980], cited in Weissbort and Eysteinsson 2006:466). Only a functionally equivalent rendition will do.

[60] According to Roman Jakobson, "In poetry, verbal equations become a constructive principle of the text.... [Therefore,] poetry by definition is untranslatable. Only *creative transposition* is possible...." (from "On Linguistic Aspects of Translation" [1959], cited in Weissbort and Eysteinsson 2006:335, italics added).

[61] In the usage of James Holmes this is "a form that [fills] a parallel function [as that of the source text within] the poetic tradition of the target language" (cited in Weissbort and Eysteinsson 2006:461).

[62] The latter is the explicit aim of the late Indian poet, A. K. Ramanujan: "One walks a tightrope between the *To-language* and the *From-language*, in a double loyalty. A translator is an 'artist on oath'. Sometimes one may succeed only in *re*-presenting a poem, not in closely representing it" (from *The Collected Essays* [1999], cited in Weissbort and Eysteinsson 2006:479, added italics). Of course, in the case of the Scriptures, the priority must necessarily be fixed upon the essential content (including intent) of the original text over and above its various literary (linguistic)

translator competence and experience, target audience desire and expectations, etc.). This would also be what the Czech Structuralist Jirí Levy figuratively terms an "illusionist version"—namely, one that offers to the intended audience an illusion, or mental image of the original text by retaining its principal aesthetic features through the use of equivalent devices in the target language.[63] And yet this illusion must also be sufficiently phonic in nature—"a new music" that adequately echoes the original (Back 2014).[64]

But what confronts us when we read most versions in the major languages today? Generally speaking, most aurally discerning English-speaking respondents are not very much impressed by the literary (let alone oratorical) properties of the many Bible translations that are available.[65] Even more literary renditions often fall far short of the mark of excellence set by the original—the *Revised English Bible*, for example (v. 2, with several potentially problematic points in bold):

> MY heart is **astir** with a noble theme;
> in honour of **a** king I recite the song I **have** composed,
> **and** my **tongue runs swiftly** like the pen of an expert scribe.

Contemporary readers and especially hearers of the text of Scripture must certainly wonder (if they take the time to reflect about it): precisely where is that skillful tongue that the psalmist lauds here? The translation that they are currently reading (or hearing) certainly does not sound so sweet, at least not in their language. The same sort of reaction is all too common in vernaculars all over the world today—if people are honest enough to admit it. For example, here is how v. 2 sounds in back-translation from the old (1922), but still very popular Chewa (Nyanja) Protestant "missionary version" (formatted below as published):

> *My heart overflows with a lov-*
> *ely thing:*
> *I say (am referring to) what I have composed of/about a chief/king:*
> *My tongue is a 'pen' that is qui-*
> *ck to write.*

forms. For Ps. 45 rendered dynamically and in the form of an English sonnet, see Boerger 2009:73.

[63] From *Umeni precladu* ["The Art of Translation," 1963] cited in Weissbort and Eysteinsson 2006:339.

[64] For a study of the emotive lyrics of the Psalter as compared with those of modern Western rock music, see Goodman 2012, especially ch. 2 in relation to Ps. 45.

[65] The ESV, cited in §1, for example, claims that its highly literal rendition maintains "clarity of expression and literary excellence" (2001:viii). I wonder how many lyric-critical respondents would support that assertion, especially after hearing only an oral articulation of the text.

That rendering is neither "lovely" in terms of Chewa stylistic poetic form nor intelligible with regard to what is meant. The translators were apparently too "quick to write" down what they thought the text should say in the vernacular. In fact, they undoubtedly thought (cf. Wendland 1998:ch.1) that a more formally correspondent, foreignized rendition was more accurate and closer to the "truth" of the original text.[66] The result (in back-translation) indicates that just the opposite is the case.[67]

In this section I will just briefly (due to space restrictions) propose a number of ways[68] in which a contemporary Chewa translation might be fashioned in order to express a closer literary (oratorical) functional equivalent of Psalm 45 (Wendland 2004:12–14).[69] My suggestions will relate to the topics of the

---

[66] The obvious lack of contemporary communicativeness of this older Chewa version (and many others like it in southeastern Africa) would contradict L. Venuti"s promotion of such foreignized versions and their alleged sociocultural value, at least with reference to the reading experience of most Bible users of this region: "Foreignizing translation signifies the difference of the foreign text [i.e., Hebrew], yet only by disrupting the cultural codes that prevail in the target language [i.e., Chewa]. In its efforts to do right abroad, this translation method must do wrong at home [i.e., with reference to Schleiermacher's familiar translation dictum], deviating from native norms to stage an alien reading experience" (Venuti 1993, cited in Weissbort and Eysteinsson 2006:548). It is interesting that Schliermacher himself, when referring to such a translation that "has been bent toward a foreign likeness," must aim "to do this *artfully* and with measure, *without disadvantage* to one's own language or oneself" (from "On the Different Methods of Translating" [1813], cited in Weissbort and Eysteinsson 2006:208, added italics).

[67] King points out an often unrecognized problems with overly literal translations: "Since words, and in particular metaphors, are not understood in isolation but in the context of wider cognitive structures based on conceptual mappings, gestalt experiences, and cultural prototypes, literal translations can lead to unexpected and misleading inferences" (2012:363).

[68] My suggestions in this section may be compared with the more general recommendations concerning how to investigate TL poetic and oratorical forms found in Schrag 2013:140–144.

[69] Having written this proposal, I am reminded of John Dryden's caution: "No man is capable of translating poetry who, besides a genius to that art, is not a master both of his author's language and of his own" (from the "Preface" to *Ovid's Epistles* [1680], cited in Weissbort and Eysteinsson 2006:146; cf. fn. 373). I can consider myself to be a genius neither in the art of poetic discourse nor the mastery of the Hebrew (Ps. 45) and Chewa languages. Therefore, the translation suggestions that follow are very much open to critique and correction. Dryden has many other insightful comments about the craft and qualities of translation. He preferred the method of "paraphrase," which he defined as "translation with latitude, where the author is kept in view by the translator so as never to be lost, but his words are not so strictly followed as his sense, and that too is admitted to be amplified [especially in poetry], but not altered.... [For] the sense of an author, generally speaking, is to be sacred and inviolable.... [On the other hand], a good poet [as in the case of

seven rhetorical-poetic features of the Hebrew text that were outlined in 6.3 above, with special emphasis on those that involve the sound dimension of discourse.[70] When translating the poetry of any language there must be, as Eugene A. Nida pointed out years ago, "obviously a greater focus of attention upon formal [stylistic] elements than one normally finds in prose."[71] If so in secular literature, how much more so in sacred Scripture, such as the Psalter, which is meant to be articulated and accessed aloud, in communal worship. The problem is that most translation teams (projects) have not been constituted or commissioned with this inherent situational requirement in mind.

6.4.1 Patterned organization

The text of the old Chewa translation (*Buku Lopatulika* 'Book Set-apart', 1922) is not subdivided into meaningful paragraph segments at all. Rather, it consists of an intimidating sequence of individual verse units, all confined within a single narrow column of justified print. It is necessary, therefore, to assist readers—and through them hearers as well—to format the text in a way that gives them certain clues concerning the patterned structural organization of the original. In the case of Psalm 45, this would include the major divisions of an introduction (vv. 1–2), two principal stanzas (3–10, 11–16), and a conclusion (17–18). It may be helpful to insert the minor strophic (poetic paragraph) units as well since they reflect some important distinctions with regard to topic, tone, mood, implication, and so forth, e.g., for stanza 1: vv. 3–6 and 7–10.

For certain more sophisticated readers, the format and typography of the text may be modified or enhanced further in order to display significant parallels (whether correspondences or contrasts) and high (peak) points. Indentation (to varying degrees), might be employed, for example,

---

the author of Ps. 45] is no more like himself in a dull translation, than his carcass would be to his living body" (ibid.:145, 147).

[70] For my sound-sensitive revision of *The Voice* translation, a modern version that caters for oral articulation, see Excursus A at the end of this chapter.

[71] Nida 1964, cited in Weissbort and Eysteinsson 2006:347. This is because "the content of a message can never be completely abstracted from the form...[therefore] a lyric poem translated as prose is not an adequate equivalent of the original" in most languages (ibid.). Similarly, but in somewhat more detail, the Victorian translation critic C. S. Blackie observes: "The reader of a translated [poetic] work is entitled to demand a facsimile of the original; but *only in so far as is consistent with the grammatical and rhythmical genius of the language in which the translation is made.* Now what is included in that wide word the GENIUS of a language? It includes two things essentially different...in the first place and principally, whatever belongs organically to the grammatical and metrical *structure* of the language; and in the second place, whatever belongs by use and habit and association to the characteristic *style* and peculiar living expression of the language" (from "A Few Remarks on English Hexameters" [1856], cited in Weissbort and Eysteinsson 2006:223, original italics).

to distinguish this psalm's author-oriented introduction and conclusion, or its chiastically constructed, covenantal thematic core (vv. 7–8), while the use of different typefaces can draw attention to critical utterances in the discourse—boldface print, for example, to highlight the pair of passages that bring "God" into a description of the character of the "king" (and, significantly, are later cited in Hebrew 1:8–9). Most modern versions also feature brief headings, or titles, to indicate a psalm's overall theme and sub-points, in Chewa, for example: "A song for the king/chief's wedding" (*Nyimbo ya pa ukwati wa mfumu),* followed by "Words concerning the king" (*Mau okhudza mfumu,* vv. 3–10), "Words concerning the queen" (*Mau okhudza mfumukazi,* vv. 11–16), and "Concluding words" (*Mau omaliza,* vv. 17–18).

6.4.2 Sonic effect

A few general features involve the poetic phonology in conjunction with the text format referred to above. Thus, in the case of Hebrew poetry it is important to reflect the parallel (half-)lines as clearly as possible.[72] In published versions, this normally requires a single column of unjustified print on the page—not the daunting, double blocks of justified text that characterize most (English) Bibles today. The latter oft-intimidating format frequently results in lines that are broken in awkward (non-meaningful) places along with excessive hyphenation (as illustrated by the Chewa sample given in §6.4 above). These are purely formal, typographical principles that can be applied no matter what the style of translation happens to be, whether more or less literal or idiomatic.

But the sound effects of a given version may be either augmented (to correspond with the Hebrew text) or diminished, depending on the type of the translation (as stipulated by its job description, or brief). In any case, it demands a special effort—and a good deal of poetic expertise!—to render the Psalms in a manner that does justice to their original sonic significance, that is, with rhythmic, euphonious utterances that have aural impact and aesthetic appeal. This phonological feature is what Ezra Pound termed "melopoeia, wherein the words are charged, over and above their plain meaning, with some musical property, which directs the trend or bearing of that meaning."[73] In particular, translators would want to stylistically mark

---

[72] It may be noted that in Chewa poetic discourse, such parallel phrasing is quite natural, even called for, depending on the text's particular theme, mood, medium of transmission, and the sociocultural setting of presentation.

[73] From "How to Read" (1929), cited in Weissbort and Eysteinsson 2006:285. The American poet, critic, publisher, and translator Stanley Burnshaw called a poem "a work of sonal art" (in "The Poem Itself" [1960], cited in Weissbort and Eysteinsson 2006:361). He further proposed providing a literary commentary for a poetic text "aimed at enabling the reader [presumably hearers too!] both to *understand* the poem and to begin to *experience* it as a poem" (ibid., original italics).

those passages that are distinguished somehow in the Hebrew source text, whether in terms of poetic form, thematic content, and/or rhetorical function. The inaugural verse 2 of Psalm 45 is an obvious candidate for such attention, as already noted. The old Chewa version, reproduced in back-translation above, certainly leaves much to be desired. The following is a revised (re-shaped and poetically sharpened) rendition of a more recent popular-language version (*Buku Loyera* 'Holy Book', 1996); in this case, the actual vernacular text is reproduced for verbal (oral-aural) reference and critical evaluation:

> *Wadzazatu mtima wanga ndi nkhani yokomadi.*
> It's filled to the brim my heart with this lovely theme.
> *Nditi ndiimbire mfumu yathu nyimbo yangayi.*
> I propose to sing for our king/chief this song of mine.
> *Lilime langali liri thwa! lofunitsa kulankhula,*
> My own tongue is very-sharp! so eager to speak,
> *Lifanafana ndi katswiri wodziwa kulembadi!*
> It resembles an expert who really knows how to write!

The rhythmic, phonological qualities of this poetically enhanced version should be audible, at least in part, even to those who do not speak Chewa. It is not governed by any sort of fixed metrical scheme based on accents,[74] but depends rather on a lexically constituted utterance rhythm, that is, the sonically shaped, tactically patterned combination of related clauses and phrasal (open) syllable sequences. This is the first step towards an actual musical rendition of Psalm 45, which would match the original even more closely in terms of stylistic form and communicative intent.[75]

6.4.3 Dynamic speech

The first step in creatively dealing with the dynamic speech of the biblical text, once analyzed, in translation is to search for a functionally equivalent, oral-aural genre of discourse in the target language (TL). In Africa this is not usually a problem because most cultures of this continent can boast of an ancient and still vibrant tradition of oral art forms, including folk narratives, histories, myths, legends, riddles, proverbs, songs, and various kinds of poetry, including royal praise verse. Often these traditional oral genres extend their life, albeit in a somewhat modified form, in the extensive

---

[74] "Rhythm in English poetry is based on the varying recurrence of strong and weaker stresses; but Chichewa does not have variable stress, so the achievement of a rhythm effect must be based on different factors, such as a number of syllables, length of words, the penultimate length characteristic of words or groups of words" (Kishindo 2003:351).

[75] For some helpful guidance towards this goal, see Schrag 2013:148–150.

vernacular literatures that have developed both during the colonial age and in post-independence years.

Among the Chewa people, for example, a multifaceted, oral and written genre of lyric poetry *(ndakatulo)* is available for use when translating various types of biblical poetic discourse, including the Psalter.[76] *Ndakatulo* free verse lyrics feature rhythmic lineation, vivid imagery (including emphatic evocative predications, or ideophones), syntactic transposition (for focus and emphasis), phonesthetic appeal (alliteration, punning, rhyme, etc.), deictic specification, formal and semantic condensation or expansion, lexical intensification, rhetorical questions, and synonymous reiteration (Wendland 2004:330–336).[77]

A sample of *ndakatulo* poetry was given above (Ps. 45:2). Another instance is the following rendition of this psalm's final, climactic verse (18):

> *Mbiri yanuyo ndidzaibukitsadi kumibadwo yonse.*
> This reputation of yours I'll surely broadcast it to all generations.
> *Motero azikukumbukirani, inde, amitundu yonse—*
> In this way they must remember you, yes, those of all nations—
> *adzatamande dzina lanu lokomali kwa muyayaya!*
> They will praise your pleasant name (or character) forever-and-ever!

At the very minimum, it would seem appropriate to employ such a manifestly poetic style (assuming functional proximity also in terms of illocutionary force) for the key verses of a given psalm (or any corresponding biblical pericope). This would normally embrace passages that mark major structural boundaries within the text (aperture or closure), those serving to signal a peak point with regard to the psalm's principal theme(s) or theological content, and those that express the psalmist's deepest feelings and attitudes, whether positive or negative in tone (e.g., the strophic aperture of v. 7a). Furthermore, the speaker (author)-intended, pragmatic

---

[76] According to Kishindo (2003:351), "poetry is by far the most popular literary genre in Malawi."

[77] The French poet Yves Bonnefoy emphasized the three important principles that "poetry is form as well as meaning," that this meaning "is already determined" by "the intent of the author," and that "free verse" is a "way of approaching the musicality of language" in the translation of poetry (from "On the Translation of Form in Poetry" [1979], cited in Weissbort and Eysteinsson 2006:467–468). This approach stands in contrast to the procedure of Everett Fox in *The Five Books of Moses* who, while giving "careful attention to rhythm and sound" seeks to "mimic the particular rhetoric of the Hebrew whenever possible" (from the "Translator's Preface" [1995], cited in Weissbort and Eysteinsson 2006:563). My attention too is focused rather on the indigenous Chewa poetic tradition, both oral and written, to serve as a model for a literary re-expression of the original.

implication of the text must always be unambiguously expressed. For example, in the descriptive praise of v. 7b, the implicit imperative needs to be conveyed, in this case, through the use of a habitual present (*-ma-*) tense (*m'ufumu wanuwu mumaweruza molungama*– 'in this kingdom of yours, you [always/regularly] judge justly'), rather than by a more remote future tense ('you will judge…').

6.4.4 Figurative language

In some instances a biblical figure will find a close correspondent in the TL, e.g., the metonymic "tongue" (לְשׁוֹן) in Chewa with reference to "speech" in v. 2. At other times, formally less proximate equivalents will be needed, like the king's "mouth" rather than his literal "lips" (שְׂפָה) in v. 3. The root metaphor of the "king" (chief) and associated imagery, as surveyed above, would naturally be familiar in many regions of Africa, though some ethnic groups (e.g., the Tonga of southern Zambia) do not in fact have a strong royal tradition. In the third strophe of the first stanza, the images shift to those connected with the wedding of some wealthy person, and these too would not be very difficult to convey in a meaning-oriented translation.

The main issue that translators must confront with regard to figurative usage is the degree to which they will use local cultural equivalents for the specific items found in the biblical text. In many cases, the correspondence is rather close, e.g., "long knife" *(lupanga)* for a "sword" (חֶרֶב) in v. 4; "chief's stick" *(ndodo yachifumu)* for "scepter" (שֵׁבֶט) in v. 7; or "[castor-bean] oil" *(mafuta ansatsi)* for the "[olive] oil" (שֶׁמֶן) of ceremonial anointing in v. 8. In other cases, however, either transliterations or indigenous correspondents must be employed. This decision becomes especially important in v. 9, for example, where the imagery also involves olfactory stimulation in the specific aromatic oils that are mentioned, "myrrh and aloes and cassia" (מֹר־וַאֲהָלוֹת קְצִיעוֹת). The old Chewa Bible tried a local substitute for "aloes;" unfortunately, it was the wrong choice, for *khonje* is a homonymic term that refers either to a 'sisal plant' or a 'bunch of bananas'! The new Chewa version made use of three transliterations *(mure, aloe ndi kasiya),* which would be unknown to most listeners, but at least the text has marked the overall sense impression intended by preceding the foreign terms with the generic qualifier *zonunkhira* 'sweet-smelling things'.

6.4.5 Contextual reference

In the case of the final three aspects of the poetic-rhetorical dimension of biblical discourse (in the Psalms and elsewhere), we move from a focus on the translated text to its accompanying paratext and the challenge of constructing a cognitive frame of reference sufficient to guide and enrich the text's interpretation (cf. Wilt and Wendland 2008:23–101). To be sure, there are quite a few contextual correspondences between the content conveyed in Psalm 45 and the worldview and way of life of traditional Africa, e.g., the notion of kingship (chiefdom) and the high honor accorded this social position, including both verbal and ritualized praises. However, as noted above, there also are a number of concepts and customs, either stated explicitly in Psalm 45 or implied within its cognitive background, which are alien or unfamiliar to the Chewa people living in SE Africa today. A few of these notions would be completely foreign and hence unknown, such as the transferred reference (via the king) to God as a militaristic "divine warrior" (vv. 4–6; cf. Ps. 18:14, 77:17; Hilber 2009:358), or the application of the title "God" to earthly rulers (v. 7; cf. Ps. 82:6; Exo. 22:6), or the psalmist's instruction to the bride to "forget your people and your *father's* house" (v. 11; the Chewa are traditionally matrilineal and matrilocal).[78] Other concepts, though initially not understood, might be necessarily clarified through explanation, for example, the king's "riding" in a victory parade (v. 5), the divine covenantal implications of his royal "scepter" (v. 7),[79] the festive wearing of perfumed robes (v. 9), fine gold that originates in "Ophir" (v. 10b),[80] or the significance of the merchant city of 'Tyre' (v. 13, which has nothing to do with today's ubiquitous vehicle tyres!).

In all of these cases of potential ambiguity or obscurity then, the necessary cognitive framework for understanding the text can normally be provided, at least in part, through explicatory and descriptive footnotes, supplemented when and where possible by an occasional illustration, diagram, or photograph, for example, of the "stringed instruments" (מִנִּי $(\square)$) of v. 9b.[81] The process of effective footnoting cannot be taken for granted,

---

[78] In this same sociocultural setting the content of v. 12 might also prove somewhat problematic: "Then the king will be attracted by your beauty. After all, he is your master! Submit to him!" (NET). The difficulty concerns especially the term "master/lord" (אֲדֹנַיִךְ). "This verse offers a capsule version of a royal marriage in a patriarchal society" (Alter 2007:160). The NET provides this short explanatory note: "The poet here makes the point that the young bride is obligated to bring pleasure to her new husband. Though a foreign concept to modern western culture, this was accepted as the cultural norm in the psalmist's day."

[79] For a detailed study of the spiritual significance associated with the שֵׁבֶט, especially when combined with "righteousness" (צֶדֶק), v. 8, see Oliver 1979; Johnson 1967:3–9, 35–37. The corresponding traditional Chewa "royal staff" *(ndodo yachifumu)* was similar in certain respects, but much more magical in its implication and application, that is, according to traditional African religious beliefs.

[80] It is quite possible that the 'gold of Ophir' (בְּכֶתֶם אוֹפִיר) has both a literal as well as a figurative reference here. It is "no doubt decorative, but again the poet has taken the visual element of gold and applied it, by implication, to the inner worth of the princess" (Craigie 1983:340).

[81] Some familiar local "stringed instrument" might well be depicted, especially here where "it is not clear what sort of instrument [the Hebrew term, emended from

however, and often requires just as much scholarly, coupled with solic-
ited community reflection and input as the translation itself (Wendland
2004:370–379). Furthermore, just as in the case of the translation, these
auxiliary materials need to be composed with an ear to how they will sound
aloud. Such an audio-oriented procedure will help to ensure that the text
does not become too complicated for the intended audience to mentally
process, and it may also serve as the basis for an actual oral rendition of the
translation (via CD, MP3, radio, etc.)—that is, the vernacular version sup-
plemented in some discrete way by oralized paratextual helps (e.g., through
vocally distinct asides).

6.4.6 Semantic density

To a certain degree, this poetic feature overlaps with the preceding
one (contextual reference) in terms of the way it might be handled in
a modern translation. Thus, several possible areas of semantic density
were pointed out in Psalm 45 in the earlier discussion of this topic,
most of them having to do with some potential divine implication,
whether in reference to God and Israel, or to the promised Messiah and
the NT people of God. Since this has been such a prominent aspect of
this psalm in the history of the text's interpretation, it is only fair that
readers and hearers today, in whatever language, are made a part of the
ongoing hermeneutical conversation leading to locally contextualized
homiletical insights, theological reflections, and contemporary moral-
ethical applications.

   Most ordinary lay listeners, however, will not discern this interpre-
tive option in the vernacular texts available to them, whether the old-
er or more recent versions. For this reason an annotated study Bible
is being prepared by the Bible Society of Malawi in order to serve this
purpose—first in written form, but with a future audio edition also in
mind. Perhaps the greatest need in Psalm 45 is for the three references to
God to be clarified in verses 7–8, first of all, in terms of the overt mean-
ing of the text as it reads (and is heard), and then also with reference to a
possible "second meaning" (as C. S. Lewis, 1958:101–115, has termed it;
cf. Craigie 1983:340; VanGemeren 1991:45). Such additional theological
significance, for example, applied to praising "your name" (שִׁמְךָ) in v. 18
(the king/God), cannot justifiably be incorporated within the translation,
or even asserted in a note as being actually intended by the original court
poet, but only as a transferred sense that has accumulated for this psalm
by virtue of thematic "attraction" from related passages in the Psalter
(e.g., Pss. 89:26–29) and other books of the Hebrew Scriptures (e.g.,
2 Sam. 7:14–16, 20:8; Isa. 9:6, 11:4–5).

---

minni to minnim, cf. Ps. 150:4] refers to except as a generic term for strings" (Wal-
ton et al. 2000:528).

6.4.7 Pervasive intertextuality

The preceding discussion brings up once again the importance of careful cross-referencing as a supplementary device to aid in the interpretation of any contemporary translation. The aim is to suggest how one text relates to, or depends upon another for its ultimate canonical understanding, both within a given pericope like Psalm 45 and within the sacred corpus of Scripture as a whole, for example, Hebrews 1:8–9 as developed from Psalm 45:7–8 (Eng. 6–7). Especially prominent correspondences like that of v. 8 will probably require more extensive explanation in a footnote—namely, the conjoining of "loving righteousness" (אָהַבְתָּ צֶּדֶק) and "God's anointing you" (מְשָׁחֲךָ אֱלֹהִים), i.e., his royal "son" (Ps. 2:2, 7; cf. Pss. 1:6; 72:1–3;[82] Isa. 61:1–3).[83] Another potential Messianic allusion is discernable in vv. 4–6, which depicts the conquering king riding forth to victory over enemies from all "nations"—a text that is undoubtedly echoed at multiple points in John's apocalyptic vision of the glorious "King of Kings" (Rev. 19:11–16).[84]

A careful, selective, or discriminating referencing procedure is needed, however, so that the paratext is not overburdened with passages, many of which have only a tenuous semantic relationship with the text under scrutiny, for example, the topic of "blessing" (v. 3), "majesty" (v. 4), "right hand" (v. 5), or "the nations" (v. 6). Too many minimal clues and referential red herrings will only result in an overly diffuse, perhaps even misleading interpretation, or they may simply discourage readers from using the cross-reference system at all.

Again, the issue of implementing such intertextual orientation in a non-print, audio version of the Scriptures may be considered. Various potential solutions are available, however, for incorporating such meaningful verbal resonances aurally in a manner that is not disruptive or distracting in relation to a particular verse of the translation. In fact, this supplementary resource may even be easier to include in a purely vocal version due to the flexible signaling value of different features of sound—from distinctive human voices to the use of music, song, or other acoustic indicators (e.g., a gong, chime, cymbal, drum beat, etc.). In an audio-visual presentation of course, even more options are accessible for revealing semantic relevance and the conceptually echoing, richly intertextual nature of the current biblical text.

---

[82] In Ps. 72:1 the verb is "give" (תֵּן) (to) "the king...royal son" (מֶלֶךְ...בֶּן־מֶלֶךְ) instead of "anoint" (מְשָׁחֲךָ) him as in Ps. 45:8, but the sense and significance is the same. In any case, the key verb "anoint" (משׁח) in such contexts (God/YHWH—king) always has Messianic significance in the Psalter (Craghan 1985:91).

[83] Note also the "mighty one/warrior" (גִּבּוֹר) of v. 4b), cf. Isaiah 9:6.

[84] This may be coupled with a corresponding passage that depicts the "all-glorious" (כָּל־כְּבוּדָּה) appearance of the well-dressed royal bride on her wedding day (vv. 14–16), which also bears several interesting similarities with Revelation 19 and the beloved "Bride" of the Messianic Lamb (19:6–9; cf. 21:2).

6.5 Conclusion

"In Psalm 45, the poet likens the composition and oral performance of this song (his 'tongue') to the 'pen' of a skillful scribe, a song of beauty befitting the occasion of the king's wedding" (Hilber 2009:357). That is construing this lyrical piece more or less on its literal face (or ear!) value in relation to its original ANE extralinguistic setting. But as many subsequent commentators have observed, "in the postmonarchical period this 'good saying' for a king's wedding was read by some as a messianic text," while "others likely found in it an allegory of the relation between God and the people of God" (Mays 1994a:181–182; cf. Hos. 1–3, Jer. 2, Ezek. 16, Is. 62:1–5). By the time of the later NT writings (e.g., Heb. 1:8–9) it is clear that the divine-human allegorical reference has been narrowed through intertextual reflection to embrace the relationship between Christ and his Church (Calvin 1949:173; Craigie 1983:341; cf. Whybray 1996:91–92). Attridge (2004:202) notes:

> Heb. 1:8 derives from [a] royal psalm (45:7–8), a celebration of a royal marriage.... Psalm 45 at the very least offers evidence of the superiority of the addressee, anointed with the "oil of gladness beyond your fellows."...The most significant contribution rests on syntactic ambiguity in its reference to God [45:7b]. The nominative form *ho theos* could be used as a vocative, as is frequent in the LXX and New Testament. In fact, there is evidence in Jewish tradition [i.e., the targum on this psalm, Attridge 1989:58, n. 93] that the reference to God was so construed.

The text thus develops a "typological significance" (VanGemeren 1991:343) regarding the Messiah's royal sovereignty and also his loving "truth, humility, and righteousness" (v. 4, NIV).[85] Even in the realm of purely human interpersonal relationships, Psalm 45 held great import for the people of Israel: "Not only the king's prosperity and well-being, but his character and spiritual privileges as well were to be shared by all the community of believers" (Patterson 1985:46).

---

[85] We note here that the key terms "humility" and "righteousness" are actually two nouns in apposition with each other, or in a construct relationship, as indicated by the conjoining hyphen *(maqqêf)* (Harman 2011a:367). "[The people of Israel] understood that the glory of the throne of Israel reflected the glory of God to the world. In this time God's glory does not depend on any earthly throne. However, it is reflected directly in the glory of the messianic throne to which this psalm implicitly and explicitly (in verse 6) refers. The glory of the Messiah is the very glory of God himself, and to praise the Messiah is to praise God. This is what takes place here [in Psalm 45]" (http://www.sonsofkorah.com/ [> Music > Study > Psalm 45]. Accessed September 2, 2017). The challenge of accomplishing this goal in a corresponding musical translation awaits all "sons (and daughters) of Korah" (בְּנֵי־קֹרַח) today (e.g., the Australian CCM band that goes by this name).

Perhaps the conceptual linguistic approach known as mental-space theory might lend some support to our reading more theological meaning into Psalm 45 than the literal surface of the text and its assumed context would allow.[86] I cannot go into detail here on this methodology (cf. Wendland 2011:367–376), but the following is a brief description of its essential components (ibid.:368; cf. de Bruyn 2013:193–194; Grady 2007:190–192, 198–201; Fauconnier 2007:351–354; King 2012:44–45):[87]

> The prototypical cognitive network is composed of four *mental spaces*.... There is one space for each of two "input" domains: The *source* (or base) is "given," or already known information, while the *target* (or focus) is the topic currently being referred to in a verbal text—one that "triggers" an accessing of the source domain. A third, *generic*, space assimilates all of the abstract notions and components of meaning that are common to both source and target domains and conceptually available, or "accessible," in a particular communicative context. Most important is the blend—a "virtual" domain in which the mind selectively "activates," incorporates, and integrates salient information (perceptually relevant cognitive elements and relations) that originated from the two initial input spaces.

Based on the prior analysis of Psalm 45 then, it is possible to identify two major socioreligious target domains, or experience-based frames of reference (Wendland 2008:2–16), that fuel and influence the text's overall content. Both of these involve the conceptual, [human] body-oriented metaphor of SPACE (i.e., AUTHORITY IS UP) as superimposed upon the interrelated sociocultural frames of kingship and marriage. The latter involves an ANE royal wedding with the focal participants being an Israelite/Judean king (higher) and his bride (lower); the other conceptual frame involves the king (a "son," lower) and his God, Yahweh (i.e., "father," higher). The referential source domain, or mental space may be construed (limited, for the purpose of this exercise) as embracing two books, the Psalter and Isaiah (this can be expanded later to the entire Hebrew Bible as well as to extant ANE royal poetry).[88]

---

[86] "Some exegetes and theologians have pointed out that ancient texts (just like modern texts) are often re-contextualized when conditions change or when texts are read in different historical and cultural contexts" (Dick Kroneman, personal correspondence).

[87] Analogous to 'intertextuality' (cf. 3.7), we might term this 'interconceptuality'.

[88] Cf. the much more developed and scholarly methodology described in King 2012. With regard to interpreting the latter corpus, there may be some controversy. For example, one opinion is that "Psalms directed *to the king rather than to the deity* are common in the ancient Near East..." (Walton et al. 2000:528, added italics). On the other hand, one wonders whether this distinction was actually made: "While *other ancient Near Eastern cultures viewed the king as divine,* and while Israel certainly accorded the king special relatedness to God (see Ps. 2:7), it is not

The generic space then encompasses all of the texts in these books that reference or allude to a "king," "kingship/rule," "wedding/marriage," "king/God" ("father/son"), "worship/praise," and "Zion" (the sacred place as well as the people who assemble there).[89] Within this limited corpus we find a number of cognitively "active" passages, which would form close intertextual connections potentially linking propositions such as these (the following representative sample of seven thematic statements is listed merely for the purpose of illustration):

- God/Father installs/anoints his son/Son as king (Pss. 2:2, 6–7; 45:3, 7; 72:1, 18–19; 110:1).
- This kingship is potentially universal in time (Pss. 45:7; 72:5, 17; 110:4) and space, a rule over all earthly nations (Pss. 2:8; 45:6; 72:8–11; 110:6).
- The divinely-appointed/installed king must rule righteously, with perfect covenantal "faithfulness" and "justice" (Pss. 45:5, 7–8; 72:1–4, 7, 12–14; Isa. 9:6–7, 11:1–5).
- Yahweh's chosen king/King will defeat all enemies and deliver his people to live in his upright, peace-filled Kingdom (Pss. 45:5–6; 2:8–12; 46:9, 11; 47:3, 8; 48:4–7; Isa. 2:4; 4:5–6; 9:6–7; 11:4–5; 26:2–3; 49:8–10; 52:7–12).
- God/YHWH chooses faithful people to be his holy "bride" (Ps. 45:10, 15 [implied]; Isa. 41:8–10, 60:7–11); like their Lord, they will serve him faithfully and righteously on earth (Ps. 45:11, 14 [implied]; Isa. 44:1–5, 21–22; 54:1–17; 60:10–11).
- God/YHWH appoints both the royal son/Son as well as his bride to "serve" vicariously as divine agents to bring justice to/on earth,

---

likely that Israelite or Judean kings were viewed as divine..." (McCann 1996:862, added italics). A mediating position might be this: "Although Mesopotamians occasionally depicted their king as a deity, they tended to construe him as a divine representative" (*Archaeological Study Bible* 2005:839). In Israel, however, "Yahweh...placed numerous constraints and moral requirements upon the king, and this is quite different from what we see elsewhere in the ancient Near East" (ibid.). Howard (2013) sets forth a credible canonical argument for a perceptible Messianic implication created by the sequence of royal (kingship) psalms in the Psalter (cf. Snearly 2013:216–217), which would include the seemingly secular Psalm 45

[89] "Zion" (צִיּוֹן) is featured in Psalm 48, another royal praise "song" by "the sons of Korah," one that features a number of key lexical-semantic items in common with Psalm 45 (exact matches and synonyms): universal "praise" for the king/God (45:18/48:1), "king/King" (45:2/48:2), his "beautiful" [bride/Zion] (45:12/48:2), everyone filled with "joy" (45:15/48:2), enemies destroyed (45:6/48:4–7), God has blessed [the king] forever (45:3)/God makes [Zion] secure forever (48:8), "righteousness [in king's/God's] right hand" (45:5/48:10), and the king's/God's throne/rule will last forever (45:7/48:14).

for all peoples (Ps. 45:5, 7–8, 17–18; Isa. 42:1–7; 49:1–7; 52:13–15; 53:11–12 + 54:1–10).
- This faithful, covenant-keeping God—Father, Son, Messiah, King—is surely worthy of our most excellent words of praise! (Pss. 45:2, 7, 17; 47:1–2, 6; 48:1–2; 19:1–4, 14;90 Isa. 12:1–6; 25:1, 9; 26:1–8; 49:13).

Within the blended conceptual space that emerges from the preceding generic mix, some novel propositions would emerge in perceptive minds (i.e., those guided by an active *canonical* consciousness, or frame of reference) and in certain *contextual* (e.g., a Second Temple Jewish worship setting) as well as *cotextual* environments (augmented as more, conceptually relevant Scripture texts are accessed, both verbally and by way of memory):

- God's son, the king, is no ordinary human being, that is, in passages which describe his rule as clearly transcending the earthly and mundane; in such cases, this person may be viewed as the Lord's specially chosen Son-King-Servant—the Messiah.
- Yahweh's metaphorical "wife," his holy people of Zion then, by divine association, may be identified as the Messiah's bride.
- Both entities, in turn, will be distinguished by their "righteous" character and their "just" behavior—in relation both to each other and also to the world at large within which they "serve."
- The appropriate faith-response of God's people to the just and merciful rule of his anointed King is to "glorify" (praise) him— enthusiastically!—in/with their hearts, speech, and lives.

Of course, it is only fair to acknowledge that such a mentally blended, secondary (symbolic) understanding is derived (or downloaded) in accordance with a certain hermeneutical expectation that is based on one's resident theological world view which influences one's interpretation of key thematically related texts in the Psalter (e.g., Pss. 1–2, 72, 87, 110–111),[91] as well as in the Hebrew canon at large (e.g., Isaiah 2:3–4, 4:2–6, 46:12–13, 51:1–8, 52:7–10, 59:18–20, 62:1–12).

Whether the preceding messianic and ecclesiastical interpretation is accepted or not, it is clear that the long history of Jewish and Christian interpretation has plainly answered the crucial question: "Why was this seemingly secular psalm included in the book of Psalms?" (McCann 1996:861; cf. Terrien 2003:367). Moreover, as we have seen, the text

---

[90] Note the connection between "tongue" (45:2) and "mouth" (19:14) as metonymic instruments of the poet's words of praise to Yahweh.

[91] Note in these psalms the focal Father/God—Son/King relationship in/with the "joyful" people of "Zion," coupled with the notion of victory over enemies and an emphasis on "righteous" behavior: 45:5, 7–8, 16 > Pss. 1:6; 2:5–9; 72 ["for/of Solomon"]:1–17; 87:5–7; 110:1–4, 5–6; 111:3, 7–9.

itself literally demands a more dynamic, memorable articulation and rendering, whether in the original or another language (cf. 45:2, 18). Therefore, it also behooves all Bible translators to give this composition the keen attention it deserves and hence to render its message accordingly—that is, not only poetically in terms of an artistic style, and rhetorically with regard to its prominent pragmatic implications, but also oratorically, maybe even musically, in view of how this "song" was originally intended to be verbally expressed and publicly transmitted.

In conclusion: the text of Psalm 45—a "good word" (דָּבָר טוֹב; LXX: λόγον ἀγαθόν) in the widest hermeneutical sense—deserves to be re-created in translation regally, as befitting both its central royal personage and its marriage theme involving a lovely ("lily-like!") "song of loves" (שִׁיר יְדִידֹת).[92] Furthermore, such a grand, emotively moving[93] pericope is undoubtedly meant to be rendered so that it may be communally proclaimed (declaimed, chanted, recited, sung)—perhaps even chorally performed—as would have been the case in the initial event. The goal for today's translator "scribes" would be to joyfully celebrate the marriage of a magnificent, majestic king (or *the* King!) (vv. 3–5) "with speech pouring forth grace" (הוּצַק חֵן בְּשִׂפְתוֹתֶיךָ)—that is, by means of beautiful sound to complement the bountifully beneficent sense of the biblical text. This tangible (language-based), poetic (artistic-rhetorical) dimension too undoubtedly derives from its original divine inspiration (v. 1)![94]

לַמְּדֵנִי ׀ לַעֲשׂוֹת רְצוֹנֶךָ כִּי־אַתָּה אֱלוֹהָי
רוּחֲךָ טוֹבָה תַּנְחֵנִי בְּאֶרֶץ מִישׁוֹר׃
(Psalm 143:10)

רוּחִי אֲשֶׁר עָלֶיךָ וּדְבָרַי אֲשֶׁר־שַׂמְתִּי בְּפִיךָ
לֹא־יָמוּשׁוּ מִפִּיךָ וּמִפִּי זַרְעֲךָ
(Isaiah 59:21)

---

[92] According to the Victorian novelist, critic, and translator George Eliot, "The power required in the translation varies with the power exhibited in the original work;" the considerable semantic and artistic potency manifested in a poem such as Psalm 45 (and most others in the Psalter) therefore requires a corresponding "exceptional faculty and exceptional knowledge" in those who would render it accurately as well as with equivalent effect and artistry in the TL (from Eliot's "Translations and Translators" [1855], cited in Weissbort and Eysteinsson 2006:217).

[93] On the importance of discerning the language of emotions in the biblical text and rendering this effectively in translation, see Bailey 2013. "One of the most celebrated characteristics of artistic communication is its capacity to express and evoke emotion" (Schrag 2013:169).

[94] "The canonical Scriptures bear evidence of their divine origin by their beauty, excellence, and perfection....Obviously, part of the beauty and excellency of a book can be its harmony and unity or even its power and efficacy" (Kruger 2012:127).

6.6 Excursus A: Psalm 45 in *The Voice*

"Today's translations often present the Bible as a reference book filled with facts. *The Voice* expresses Scripture as a narrative with engaging conversations, passionate poetry, and beautiful literature. *The Voice* brings literary art to the Bible. This Bible lends itself to dramatic readings; first, because of the beauty of the language, and second, because of the unique acting-script format. It is the Good Book that reads like a good book....

"By expressing the inspired text in the unique voices of the original biblical authors with all their personality, passion, grit, humor, and beauty, *The Voice* begins to recapture how the first readers would have encountered the Scripture. This results in an amplification of the voice of God so it is more clearly heard by today's readers—almost as clearly as when He first revealed His truth" (from *The Voice* website, http://www.hearthevoice.com/about-the-translation).

Although ostensibly orally-oriented for public proclamation, in my opinion *The Voice* translation[95] might be still further improved in this specific acoustic respect (its exegesis aside!). The following are a few of my suggestions, shown side by side in the chart below with the original published version for comparison. My main modification was an attempt to re-construct more rhythmic, cohesive, aurally-sensitive, and poetic-sounding lines and line-sets (formally "verses;" vocally "utterances"), which I would regard as a distinctive feature for poetry in English and many other languages. Readers (Listeners!) are welcome to improve upon these revisions and to propose their own. Note that *The Voice* italicizes words that are contextually implied; I have not followed this convention. However, I have indicated putative strophic units by inserted line breaks.

The Voice	*A more vocalized "Voice"*
For the worship leader. A contemplative song[a] of the sons of Korah to the tune "The Lilies."[b] A love song.	*For the worship leader. A meditative song, by Korah's composers, set to the tune of "The Lilies." A love song.*
[1] My heart is bursting with a new song; lyrics to my king *erupt like a spring for my king, to my king;* my tongue is the pen of a poet, ready *and willing.*	My heart is stirred with a sweet song— lovely lyrics spring forth for my king; my tongue is the skilled pen of a poet.

[95] *The Voice Bible,* Copyright © 2012 Thomas Nelson, Inc. The Voice™ translation © 2012 Ecclesia Bible Society. All rights reserved. http://www.biblegateway.com/passage/?search=psalm%2045&version=VOICE . Accessed September 2, 2017.

2 Better by far are you than all others, *my king;* gracious words flow from your lips; indeed, God has blessed you forever.	More handsome than all are you, my king. Most eloquent are your words as well. Clearly, our God has blessed you forever!
3 With your sword at your side, you are glorious, majestic, a mighty warrior.	Strap your sword to your side, mighty Warrior! Let your glorious royal majesty appear.
4 Ride on in splendor; ride into battle victorious, for the sake of truth, humility, and justice. *Perform* awesome acts, trained by your *powerful* right hand.	Ride forth majestically—to victory in battle! Your great cause is truth, humility, justice. May your power be seen in awesome deeds!
5 Razor-sharp arrows *leap from your bow* to pierce the heart of the king's foes; they lie, defeated, before you.[a]	Sharp arrows spring from your bow; they pierce the hearts of your enemies. Look! They lie—fallen—at your feet!
6 O God, Your throne is eternal; You will rule your kingdom with a scepter of justice.	O God, your royal throne is everlasting; You rule your kingdom rightly— your scepter is absolute integrity.
7 You have loved what is right and hated what is evil. That is why God, your God, has anointed you with the oil of gladness and lifted you above your companions. [c]	You love justice; all wickedness you hate. That's why God has anointed you with joy. Your God has raised you above all rivals.[b]
8 All of your clothing is drenched in the rich scent of myrrh, aloes, and cassia; In palaces decked out with ivory, beautiful stringed instruments play for your pleasure.	Your robes are perfumed with fragrant oils; your palaces are decked with precious ivory; stringed instruments play for your pleasure.

[9] At a royal wedding with the daughters of kings among the guests of honor, your bride-queen stands at your right, adorned in gold from Ophir.	Princesses are among your guests of honor, your bride stands at your royal right hand; she's a queen adorned in the purest gold.
[10] Hear this, daughter; pay close attention to what I am about to say: you must forget your people and even your father's house.	Listen carefully now, my honored Queen— pay close attention to what I have to say: you must forget your people, your home.
[11] Because the king yearns for your beauty, humble yourself before him, for he is now your lord.	Let the king be captivated by your beauty; respect him, for he alone is now your lord.
[12] The daughter of Tyre arrives with a gift; the wealthy will bow and plead for your favor.	The wealthy of Tyre arrive with rich gifts; they seek your favor with their offerings.
[13] A stunning bride, the king's daughter waits within; her clothing is skillfully woven with gold.	Royal princess, you look so glorious— adorned with pearls and clothed in gold.
[14] She, in her richly embroidered gown, is carried to the king, her virgin companions following close behind.	In queenly robes they escort you to the king; your select maids of honor follow closely after.
[15] They walk in a spirit of celebration and gratefulness. In delight, they enter the palace of the king.	They walk along with the greatest of joy and accompany you into the king's palace.
[16] O king, in this place where your ancestors reigned, you will have sons; you will make them princes throughout all the land.	May your sons, O king, reign like your fathers; may they rule as princes throughout the land!

[17] I will make sure your name is remembered by all future generations so that the people will offer you thanks and praise now and forever.	As for me, I will ensure that your name is ever remembered; future generations will always thank and praise you; with these lyric lines of mine, they will do so forever!

| Footnotes:
[a] 45:title. Hebrew, maskil.
[b] 45:title. Hebrew, shoshannim, white lily-like flowers, perhaps the melody to which the song is sung.
[c] 45:6–7. Hebrews 1:8–9. | |

[a] "The choppy style reflects the poet's excitement" (NET—note at v. 5).
[b] The "oil" of line 2 is left implicit in "anointed." Hebrew "companions" in line 3 is taken to refer to other kings; "this king is distinguished from them by the fact that his character is different" (Harman 2011a:368). Other exegetical options can be footnoted, e.g., "all of your people" or "wedding guests."

What is your conclusion then—with regard to my effort, or indeed, a particular translation that you may have already worked with, or are laboring on now: Given an acceptable rendering of the biblical text's semantic content, how sharp has your stylus been shaping the translation in terms of impact and persuasiveness (rhetoric)—how sweet with respect to beauty and appeal (artistry)? In short, how poetically—even melodically!—has your tongue/voice/text been singing these divine-human songs to or for the King?

7

Sing to the Lord a New Song
(Psalm 98:1)—also in Translation!

Introduction

This study develops the notion of a new song, which is the imperative liturgical headline of Psalm 98.[1] I first present a literary-structural overview of the psalm: What is the meaning of this new song (v. 1)? I will introduce this textual analysis with a brief review of the contextual importance of music and song in the Jewish worship tradition, as suggested by several key passages in the Hebrew Bible. So why is the assumed audience encouraged to sing a new song in corporate worship? The psalmist poetically gives his scripturally based reasons in the three balanced strophes comprising Psalm 98, which praises the LORD, Yahweh, as the mighty Savior (1–3), the great King (4–6), and the righteous Judge (7–9) of his faithful people. During the course of his lyric exposition and exhortation, the psalmist also strongly instructs believers how they are to "sing," or audibly express, this new song—that is, enthusiastically (joyfully, involving our whole being),

---

[1] "The designation "new song" occurs seven times in the OT (Ps. 33:3; 40:3; 96:1; 98:1; 144:9; 149:1; Isa 42:10) and twice in the NT (Rev 5:9; 14:3), each time in a holy war context" (Longman 1984:269) "to celebrate the 'salvation' YHWH has wrought" (Magonet 2014:165).

inclusively (incorporating all of God's creation),[2] and eschatologically (with a trusting view also toward God's saving acts in the future).[3]

In the second portion of this study, I give some thought to how Psalm 98 might be translated as well as transmitted in a similar rhythmical, oratorical, even melodic style in Chewa, a major Bantu language of south-central Africa, as well as in several English versions. In the case of Chewa, this transformation may be accomplished through, for example, the use of a corresponding vernacular lyric genre *(ndakatulo)*, an emphasis upon an oral-aural articulation of the translation, and/or a strategic manner of typographically formatting the text so as to highlight its poetic qualities and to facilitate public elocution. All these strategies, and more, are required in order to effectively convey (often quite newly, or novelly, in the language-culture concerned!) the associated rhetorical impact and aesthetic (including musical) appeal of the original song—performance features which both enhance and embellish its primary theological-religious content.

7.1 Music, lyric, and song in the worship of Israel

> Both the word *Judah* (Hebrew *Yehudah*) and the word *Jew* derive from the verb *yadah*, "to praise" [cf. Gen. 29:35]. The Psalms were poems written to be sung to musical accompaniment. So David writes, "I will give thanks to him *(ahodenu)* in song" (Ps. 28:7). The place of song is crucial to a correct understanding of Jewish prayer.... The essence of prayer is a song, and man cannot live without a song. (M. R. Wilson 1989:308)

Granted, the preceding quote may involve some dubious etymologizing, but the author's point about the importance of song, both verbal (i.e., poetry) and musical, in Israel's worship tradition cannot be denied.[4] In this

---

[2] "Just as a sequence of verbs is used to issue the call to praise..., so another sequence of verbs is used to describe God's actions" that have prompted these words of acclamation (Harman 2011b:711).

[3] From a future perspective, "a 'new song' is one with eschatological overtones, an end-time song" (Harman 2011b:712)—presumably, to celebrate YHWH's final consummation of salvation for the faithful.

[4] In fact, we might include the whole Bible in this assertion concerning the importance of music and song as a medium and mode of divine-human communication: "Plato and Aristotle wrote about the helping, healing power of music 2,500 years ago. But centuries before that, the biblical record was saturated with song. From the first mention of Jubal, 'the father of all those who play the harp and flute' (Gen. 4:21), to those who 'sing the song of Moses, the servant of God and the song of the Lamb' (Rev. 15:3), the pages of the Bible resonate with music. The Psalms, often called 'the Bible's songbook', point us to the love and faithfulness of God.

respect, Israel was no different from other ancient societies (e.g., Greece, Sumeria, Egypt, India, Celtic and Amerindian tribes) for whom "*all* scripture [religious texts] and epic poetry was intended to be *sung*" (Wheeler 1989a:12, original emphasis). The Hebrew hymnal, the Psalter, which occupies such a prominent place in the OT and the Bible as a whole, bears eloquent testimony to that fact, for its constituent texts were undoubtedly "intended...to be *musical works* from [their] beginning" (ibid.). "The Psalms are written renditions of songs...orality in written form" (Schrag 1992:54; cf. Dobbs-Allsopp 2014:89–91). Furthermore, "a great deal of the Psalms' continuing appeal lies in the emotionally satisfying combination of words and music through which they are typically encountered in worship" (Levine 1995:1)—both then and now.[5]

According to the dictionary, music is "the art or science of combining vocal or instrumental sounds (or both) to produce beauty of form, harmony, and expression of emotion" (Soanes and Stevenson 2006:942). More generally, music refers to "any rhythmic sequence of pleasing sounds" (Agnes 2006:950),[6] while "singing is the musical use of the voice" (Stallman 2008:483).[7] Functionally speaking, "most people...use music [and lyric poetry] to enhance and reflect the most important things that ever happen to them" (Sproul 2012:61). "In religion, music plays an important role in communicating both essential ideas and appropriate passions" (Towner 2003:17). But while music may facilitate "the communication of emotions," it does so "only within given cultural contexts" (Schrag 1992:48). The eminent English literature professor and critic Lewis Turco provides a more substantial explanation of the close connection that exists between music

They conclude with an unending call to worship, 'Let everything that has breath praise the Lord. Praise the Lord!' (Ps. 150:6)." https://odb.org/2014/09/06/let-me-be-singing/. Accessed September 2, 2017.

[5] "This appeal to emotion through vividness and artfully designed form holds clear connection to the oral roots of the psalms, since they clearly are a form that communicates immediacy and closeness to body experience" (Schrag 1992:53)—a bodily experience that was probably also manifestly expressed in various forms of dancing (cf. Exo. 15:20; 1 Chr. 15:29; Pss. 149:3, 150:4).

[6] Accordingly, the adjective *musical* refers to any vocal expression that has "the nature of music," i.e., "melodious or harmonious" (Agnes 2006:950)—or more generally still, "pleasant-sounding" (Soanes and Stevenson 2006:942). Music is particularly appropriate for private and especially public worship because it serves as a manifold synergistic "vehicle that unites elements within a person [or a group], simultaneously activating the eye, ear, body, breath and voice in addition to the verbal elements of memory and language" (Stallman 2008:488).

[7] Schrag calls attention to the close relationship between music and language—for example, "music can be described phonologically...all music systems have structure consisting of constituents and relationships between those constituents, just like language does.... Just as language may be described grammatically, so may music," which may also "be described under the rubric of 'discourse'" (1992:47–48).

and lyric poetry in the Western classical tradition, which applies in many respects also to the biblical psalms (Turco 2000:120, original italics):[8]

> Lyrics are *songs*, poems meant to be sung originally, and *melic poetry* was written with the intention that there be flute or lyre accompaniment; the term *lyrics* is still used to designate the words of songs. However, *literary lyrics* carry their own music, and no extraneous musical accompaniment is required.

In the present study, I will not be dealing with the more technical aspects of music and song in Psalm 98,[9] but rather in a broader sense with reference to the biblical text's beautiful verbal form, which in turn involves a harmonious, emotive, pleasing, at times inspiring expression. It is my contention that this sonic dimension is an important aspect of the Scripture's overall meaning—whether syntactic, semantic, connotative, or purely aesthetic[10]—and therefore it is a vital feature that Bible translators ought to

---

[8] "Translation of a text that is sung in vocal music for the purpose of singing in another language…is closely linked to translation of poetry because most vocal music, at least in the Western tradition, is set to verse, especially verse in regular patterns with rhyme" (https://en.wikipedia.org/wiki/Translation/. Accessed September 2, 2017). "As with all poetry of the ancient world, Hebrew poetry was intended not merely for reading but for singing" (Bond 2012:71).

[9] For example, the elaborate system of Masoretic accents, or markers to guide the oral rhythmic recitation, or cantillation, of the Hebrew Psalter. In summary: "A primary purpose of the cantillation signs is to guide the chanting of the sacred texts during public worship. Very roughly speaking, each word of text has a cantillation mark at its primary accent and associated with that mark is a musical phrase that tells how to sing that word. The reality is more complex, with some words having two or no marks and the musical meaning of some marks dependent upon context. There are different sets of musical phrases associated with different sections of the Bible. The music varies with different Jewish traditions and individual cantorial styles. The cantillation signs also provide information on the syntactical structure of the text and some say they are a commentary on the text itself, highlighting important ideas musically. The tropes are not random strings but follow a set and describable grammar. The very word *ta'am* means 'taste' or 'sense', the point being that the pauses and intonation denoted by the accents (with or without formal musical rendition) bring out the sense of the passage" (https://en.wikipedia.org/wiki/Cantillation/. Accessed September 2, 2017).

For more information concerning the potential artistic, musical component of the poetic Masoretic accent system *(te'amim)*, see Haik-Vantoura 1991, McCorkle 2009, and Burns et al. 2011. Wheeler (1989a and 1989b) associates this with cheironomy—the association of musical tones or melodies with "hand signs." I will carry out a strictly linguistic analysis of the Hebrew text of Psalm 98 below, yet one that pays special attention to its musical qualities, such as rhythmic balance, syntactic structure, lexical correspondence, euphony, and sound symmetry.

[10] Our examination of Psalm 98 below will illustrate these three dimensions of sonic significance: aesthetic, in the rhythmic beauty of certain sound sequences and combinations; semantic, in the lexical correspondences that highlight certain

strive to reproduce also in their contemporary renditions, to the extent possible and as the circumstances of production allow (Wendland 2004:ch. 2). This concern applies to the psalm's transmission today as well—how musical (aurally appealing) does the text actually sound via whatever channel of communication is being used, whether the medium is print or non-print in nature?[11] These are some of the issues that will be developed during the course of my exploration of this most exuberant of psalms, which one commentator has termed "one of the most joyful songs in the Bible...a noisy, effervescent song from its beginning to the end" (Boice 1996:796).

A *musical* mode of expression is normally associated with some form of verbal *poetic* communication in the Bible.[12] "Poetry, like music, gains much of its effect from the facile manipulation of sounds and rhythm" (Schrag 1992:52, citing E. A. Nida). Before looking more closely at this phonological feature in relation to a specific text, namely, Psalm 98, it may be helpful to consider it in more general terms with reference to the Hebrew testament as a whole and the Psalter in particular.[13] It is arguable (though not provable) that the first recorded song in the narrative progression of the Scriptures is Adam's joyous lyric exaltation, upon seeing the woman that the LORD God had made from and for him: 'This at last is bone of my bone...' (Gen. 2:23).[14] The first instance of a song composed

---

key thematic terms; syntactic, in the phonic parallelistic phrasing of the text. As Stallman points out, "The practice of musically intoning the text of the Bible is ancient.... This setting of the Bible to chant, though somewhat musical, was not a mere aesthetic ornament; it helped to fix the interpretation of the text by punctuating it into syntactic units" (2008:485).

[11] As the German translators Buber and Rosenzweig observed, "the [biblical] text's abundant alliterations and assonances could not be understood in aesthetic terms alone; often if not always it is passages of religious importance in which assonance and alliteration occur, and both assonance and alliteration thus help make this importance emerge more vividly" (1927:194).

[12] Although I will be dealing exclusively with the Hebrew text in the present study, it is important to recognize that there are a significant number of poetic texts also in the New (Greek) Testament, for example, Mt. 5:3–10; Lk. 1:46–55, 68–79; Jn. 17; Ac. 2:17–21; 1 Cor. 13; Php. 2:6–11; Heb. 1; and of course, Revelation, where the text periodically breaks into passages of dramatic poetry and song, e.g., 5:13b:

...καὶ τὰ ἐν αὐτοῖς πάντα ἤκουσα λέγοντας ("saying" in this context = "singing!"),
Τῷ καθημένῳ ἐπὶ τῷ θρόνῳ καὶ τῷ ἀρνίῳ
ἡ εὐλογία καὶ ἡ τιμὴ καὶ ἡ δόξα καὶ τὸ κράτος
εἰς τοὺς αἰῶνας τῶν αἰώνων.

[13] For a handy summary of the main Bible passages that mention sing(ing), see "Scriptures on Singing" at http://www.losthymnsproject.com/Scriptures_on_Singing.pdf. Accessed September 10, 2013.

[14] The Hebrew text introduces Adam's words simply with 'The man said...' (וַיֹּאמֶר הָאָדָם). The difficulty is that the verb 'say' in Hebrew has a rather wide area of meaning (referring even to one's thoughts on occasion, e.g., Gen. 6:7) such that

for public worship is Moses' well-known hymn by the seaside (Exo. 15), and this poetic discourse is clearly marked as such: "Then Moses and the Israelites sang this song to the LORD" (NIV) אָז יָשִׁיר־מֹשֶׁה וּבְנֵי יִשְׂרָאֵל אֶת־הַשִּׁירָה הַזֹּאת לַיהוָה וַיֹּאמְרוּ לֵאמֹר (v. 1; but notice again the close connection with "speaking"). Varied expressions of lyrical song reappear at several other significant points in the recorded history of Israel, usually in the form of communal praise to Yahweh for his saving or enabling actions on the nation's behalf, e.g., Israel's "song of the well" (Num. 21:17–18); Deborah's victory ode (Judg. 5); David's thanksgiving psalm (1 Chr. 16:8–36); or the people's celebration at the laying of the second Temple's foundation (Ezr. 2:11). There are naturally quite a few historical references to music and song in later times after the religious cult and organization had become more formally established (e.g., 1 Chr. 15:15–16; 16:8–36; 2 Chr. 5:12–13),[15] and then again re-established after the Exile (Ezra 2:41, 70; Neh. 7:1, 44, 73).[16]

To be sure, the individual,[17] familial,[18] and corporate worship life of Israel strongly confirms the proverb's assertion: "A righteous person sings and rejoices" (Prov. 29:6b)[19]—that is, in response to the LORD's great works in the world. "The psalms tell us that worship is the core of everything we do" (Joiner 2012:161). Furthermore, in the case of the psalms, such lyric

---

any idiomatic translation must take into consideration both the textual and the extratextual (situational) context of the biblical usage on the one hand and what is natural in the corresponding target language (TL) sociocultural communication setting on the other. Lamech's cruel boast to his wives (Gen. 4:23–24) is probably another early example of a song introduced by "said."

[15] "The books of Chronicles contain many references to psalm singing, both in the temple and outside it" (Wenham 2012b:14).

[16] What is the "cult?" "The cult is 'the socially established and regulated holy acts and words in which the encounter and communion of the Deity with the congregation [community of faith] is established, developed, and brought to its ultimate goal'.... All of life was punctuated by sacral activity of a communal and ritualistic character" (Creach 2005:122, citing Mowinckel 1962:15). Furthermore, "the psalms represented the lyrical component of the cult...rituals and lyrics were inextricably bound in cultic practice" (Creach 2005:123), even in the case of impromptu rituals of worship (e.g., Exo. 15:1–21).

[17] Even personal psalms of petition (e.g., 5), praise (e.g., 9), or trust (e.g., 23) were undoubtedly uttered (recited, intoned, chanted, sung, etc.) aloud by the individual pray-er, probably from memory, rather than being read silently from a written text (scroll).

[18] The (extended) family would recite/sing the Hallel set of psalms (113–118), for example, during the annual sacred Passover celebration.

[19] There is some doubt about the verbal construction of this line, but it seems best to conclude that "the Hebrew verb rendered 'sings' means to give a shout of rejoicing" (*A Translator's Handbook on the Book of Proverbs*, in the Scripture resources of ParaTExt 7.2); cf. also Isa. 24:14, 35:6.

worship is typically done in joint fellowship with others, whatever the motive or mood might be. Collins makes a strong case for the essentially collective character of the individual psalms comprising the Psalter (2012:18–19):

> The book of Psalms was preserved as the hymns and prayers of a worshipping congregation who would sing, chant, and recite them aloud in their services of public worship. This recognition will have consequences for how we interpret and use the psalms—both in our public worship and in our private devotions.

Collins points to certain titles (e.g., "for the choirmaster"), musical directions, internal expressions that indicate the "aware[ness] of an encircling company of exultant fellow worshippers" (Ps. 32:7), including imperatival direct address in the plural, as well as antiphonal stylistic construction, especially in book five (e.g., Ps. 136).[20] A narrative example of this regular as well as spontaneous practice would be 2 Chronicles 29:30 where, in conjunction with King Hezekiah's rededication service at the temple, we read: "Then Hezekiah and his officials ordered the Levites to sing the songs of praise that David and Asaph the prophet had written. And so they bowed down and joyfully sang praises to the LORD" (CEV).[21] Indeed, the carefully edited nature of the book of Psalms itself as a composite songbook "leads to the conclusion that the Psalter was, from the earliest times, connected with both the local and centralized worship among the people of God" (Collins 2012:23).[22] And these, we must not forget, embraced New Testament saints as well as Old Testament believers.[23]

Such a worshipful singing response by the biblical writers on behalf of (or, along with!) God's people is periodically manifested in the "salvation sections" of the prophetic books (e.g., Hos. 2:15; Zeph. 3:14; Zech. 2:10).

---

[20] The quote here is from Kidner 1973:134; I am summarizing Collins's helpful discussion on pp. 19–21.

[21] This verse would suggest that by this time already in the history of Israel a collection of psalms (the Psalter) was already in existence, that it was well known (the people could sing the psalms), and their melodies were also familiar enough to be played instrumentally and sung communally (cf. 2 Chr. 29:25–29). The Septuagint attributes Psalm 98 "to David" (G. H. Wilson 2005:241).

[22] Longman concurs: "While affirming that the Psalms were used in private worship" as well, "most of the evidence for their primary use points to public worship" (1988:47, cited in Collins 2012:24). Ryken counters: "Even if the psalms were sung at the temple, there is no reason to believe that they were not equally recited and pondered by individuals" (2012:138).

[23] This point, "how the New Testament laid claim to the Psalms," is underscored in Van Neste 2012: "Jesus died with the psalms on his lips, and the early church was birthed making its first key decision by appeal to the psalms, preaching its first sermon from the psalms....The psalms were central to the life of the early church as they—following Jesus—preached, prayed, and sang them" (ibid.:50).

This theme is especially prominent in the oracles of Isaiah, even in the well-known instance where a "love song" (שִׁירַת דּוֹדִי) (5:1) turns out ironically to be a condemning message of "woe" (הוֹי) (5:8, 11, 18, 20, 21, 22).[24] Much more often, however, Isaiah proclaims the same "new song" (שִׁיר חָדָשׁ) in praise of Yahweh's saving intentions and interventions on behalf of "Israel," as we find in Psalm 98 (e.g., Isa. 42:10).[25] The musical expression of such salvation songs, along with other functional types (lament, trust, royal, etc.) reached its peak in the form of the sacred songs (מִזְמוֹר)[26] that were regularly employed in temple worship on various ritually prescribed occasions as set forth in the ceremonial laws of the Pentateuch (cf. Hezekiah's religious revival, 1 Chr. 29–30) as well as at other, unpredictable times of weal (such as a bountiful harvest, Joel 2:23–24) or woe (a drought, Joel 1:13–14). This more formal usage is suggested by the various psalm titles, or superscriptions, 95 of which (out of 116 in total) make mention of an assortment of musical terms and technical references, many of which are no longer fully (or even partially) understood (for a useful summary, see Stallman 2008:485–486). In short, "the book of Psalms is replete with references to the temple and its courts; this testifies to the use of psalms in that setting which was full of music" (ibid.). The diverse psalm texts were by and large composed with this lyric mode of communication in mind and for the ultimate purpose of fervent prayer to, and passionate commendation of the great God, Yahweh. This same motive and method should direct the minds and skills of all translators of the Psalter today. הַלְלוּ יָהּ! (Ps. 150:1, 6).

As the various passages referred to above indicate, there are three principal Hebrew verbs translated by "sing" in English, all three of which are found within Psalm 98: שִׁיר (v. 1, cf. Ps. 33:3), רנן (v. 4, cf. Ps. 95:1), and זמר (v. 4, 5; cf. Ps. 30:4).[27] It is not easy to distinguish these terms be-

---

[24] The Song of Songs (שִׁיר הַשִּׁירִים) is the purest as well as the most intensive and extensive instance of this genre in the entire Bible. It is comprised of a number of individual love songs—a "lyric sequence," or "collocation of lyrics...[that] tend to interact as an organic whole" (Strawn 2008:441). Thus, readers/hearers tend to mentally create cohesion, fashioning the discourse into a semi-narrative progression that reaches its emotive climax at the book's compositional midpoint (4:16–5:1) and its thematic peak in the final chapter (8:6–7; cf. Wendland 2013a:ch. 6).

[25] Albertz calls attention to the "eschatological" character and important structural function of Isa. 42:10–13: "The new song corresponds to the newness of the divine message. The praise of God will begin with the Judean audience...from there it will reach the most remote areas of the Persian empire.... Thus, the audience becomes part of a global setting" (2009:102).

[26] The heading *mizmôr* is used 57 times in the Psalter, but on its own only at the onset of Psalm 98 (the LXX has "To David" Τῷ Δαυιδ), "whence it is called in *B. Aboda Zara*, 24b...the orphan Psalm" (Delitzsch 1869:97). This "may signify that the best of all praise psalms should be like it" (Boice 1996:796).

[27] Corresponding terms for "lament," e.g., ספד (Isa. 32:12; Jer. 4:8) and קִינָה (Jer. 4:8; Ezek. 19:1), do not occur in the Psalter. For a summary of NT terms for worship

cause they often appear as word pairs or corresponding synonyms within the scope of a single bi- or tricolon or in closely related verses in a strophe (e.g., Ps. 95:1–2). Furthermore, the more specific verbs of singing may be paired with others that refer to other types of oral (always!) proclamation, for example, "sing" (שׁיר) and "declare" (בשׂר) in Psalm 96:2. Biblical lexicographers make an attempt to distinguish the three verbs rendered "sing" as follows (and for example): "The vb. *rnn* often indicates a loud, enthusiastic, and joyful shout" directed predominantly towards Yahweh in adoration (VanGemeren 1997b:1129);[28] "the basic meaning of the vb. *(zmr)* is playing a musical instrument in the context of worship, usually a stringed instrument"[29] (VanGemeren 1997a:1116)[30]—by metonymy then to "sing" or "praise."[31] *shîr* is arguably the most prototypical of the activity of singing (cf. SoS 1:1) but is often associated in similar conceptual frames of "worship/praise" with both of the other verbs: "[it] indicates *joyous* singing in *praise* of God, under some circumstances with *musical* accompaniment" (Jenni and Westermann 1997:1320, added italics).[32] In fact, the closest approximation of the concept of poetry in Hebrew may be the term שׁיר (Strawn 2008:439). Due to the limited corpus of ancient Hebrew literature,

---

and song, see Van Neste 2012:49). Gerstenberger includes these three roots in his listing of terms for "praise" in Hebrew and notes: "Ugaritic, Syriac, and Arabic, to name only a few more Semitic languages, all show a similar vocabulary of praise... [with] ties to music, singing, instruments...to the intention to lift up, enhance, and magnifiy the deities" (2014:30).

[28] This is supported by Megahan 2013:170. In addition, "The Hebrew verb translated 'shout for joy' *[rnn]* occurs often in the psalms to denote an activity of public praise, as 'sing or shout for joy' (e.g., Pss. 5:11; 20:5; 32:11)" (Collins 2012:24).

[29] Luther comments: "The stringed instruments of [98:5 and] the following psalms are to help in the singing of this new song.... All pious Christian musicians should let their singing and playing to the praise of the Father of all grace sound forth with joy from their organs and whatever other beloved instruments there are... of which neither David nor Solomon, neither Persia, Greece, nor Rome, knew anything" (cited in Plass 1959:982).

[30] "Musical instruments provide entertainment [also appeal, beauty, etc.] as well as background rhythm for dances and ritual performances, such as processions and cultic dramas" (Walton et al. 2000:559). Most frequently, a "harp" (כִּנּוֹר), v.5, and a "lyre" (נֵבֶל), Ps. 92:3, are mentioned (Gerstenberger 2001:197).

[31] Durham concurs: "*[Z-M-R]* refers to the creation of music in worshipful praise" (1987:201). This verb also forms the basis for the noun מִזְמוֹר, often translated as "psalm" in English or as Ψαλμὸς in the Greek Septuagint, "which refers to the playing of a stringed instrument" (Tucker 2008:578).

[32] For these three verbs, Swanson, n.d., offers the following senses: זמר – 1. sing praises, 2. play notes on instrument (this may be only the accompaniment of an instrument to the main focus of singing words); רנן – 1. shout/sing for joy, 2. cry/call out; שׁיר – sing, i.e., use the voice as an instrument to [vocalize] musical tones, rhythms, and often words.

however, it is difficult to contextually maintain all these distinctions, another example being the verb פצח "break forth [into exuberant praise]" in 98:4b.[33] In any case, it would be ideal if this semantically augmentative diversity of lexical form could be maintained in translation through the use of a similar set of synonymous verbs for "sing" in the target language.

The musical dimension of the psalms is integrally connected with its lyric and vocal form of composition,[34] which is further characterized by "subjectiveness, emotionality, and brevity" (Schrag 1992:52). Comparative literary scholars have noted in various poetic traditions the fact that lyric poetry manifests "most prominently the elements which evidence its origins in musical expression—singing, chanting, and recitation to musical accompaniment...[with] the sound patterns of lyric itself...[being] representative of music" (Johnson 1993:713, 715). "The rhythm and patterns of the poetry went hand in glove with musical expression" (Michalowski 1996:144). Thus, lyric poetry is also amplified by its oral-aurality,[35] for it tends to magnify the "naked properties of language" and the intrinsic musicality of its language as "its basic resource for making meaning" (Dobbs-Allsopp 2002:12). While one might not wish to subscribe completely to the preceding claim, at least not as far as the biblical literature is concerned, the vital contribution of the sonic component to the text's meaning cannot be denied. Therefore, Psalm scholars and translators alike must always take into consideration the close "liaison of poetic literary speech forms with oral performance of the texts" (Gerstenberger 2014:32).

The so-called poetic (or artistic) function of language (Wendland 2004:310) serves to emphasize the stylistic form of a particular text in order to underscore its message, including, not only phonological features (rhythmic parallelism, a balanced cadence, euphony, alliteration, rhyme, paronomasia, and the like) but also a concentration of literary devices, such as: diverse figurative language and graphic imagery, rhetorical or leading questions, emotively expressive utterances,[36] condensation (ellipsis), allusion,

---

[33] Gerstenberger suggests "make merry" for this verb (2001:197).

[34] "*The activity of praising in the Psalter is essentially vocal*...it would not be the norm for Yahweh to be praised silently, in a corner!" (Hutchinson 2005:87, original italics). "Psalms, more than any other group of biblical poems, brings to the fore this consciousness of the linguistic medium of religious experience" (Alter 1985:136).

[35] This would include three primary characteristics of oral communication: redundancy and other mnemonic devices (e.g., rhythm, balance, antithesis), the immediacy of verbal face-to-face communication, and semantic density (e.g., formulaic language, metonymic allusion, references to traditional themes and implicit cultural values) (cf. Schrag 1992:50–51).

[36] All communicators need to keep in mind when conveying the psalmic hymns that "praise has an emotional dimension. This emerges from the poetic character of the psalms and especially from particular devices used to heighten the praise

varied types of reiteration, and a preference for direct ("I—you") discourse (cf. the analysis of Ps. 98 below). These lyric qualities operate in concert to intensify the auditory form of the psalms, whether or not they are actually sung, for they "carry their own music," hence obviating the need for actual musical accompaniment (Turco 2000:120). Thus, poetic discourse of such aesthetic and evocative distinction is thereby made more memorable (and memorizable), on the one hand, and orally articulatable (or "reutterable," Strawn 2008:440), on the other—a most suitable, ever reusable vocal vehicle for proclaiming the Word of the LORD (Ps. 68:11).[37] The two always go together with respect to biblical discourse—memorize *poetry* for *oral* communication: "Son of man, eat [i.e., internalize, memorize] what is before you, eat this scroll; then go and speak [poetically proclaim, recite, sing, etc.] to the house of Israel" (Ezekiel 3:1).[38] The associated religious function of such literature composed for oral proclamation was/is manifold—liturgical, of course, for use in public worship, expressive for prayer and petition, panegyric for praise and thanksgiving, didactic for instruction, ethical for personal as well as communal moral guidance, and so forth.[39]

---

mood" (Hutchinson 2005:91)—thus providing "a socially accepted release for intense feelings" (Schrag 2013:169). The same would be true for the laments, though of course using words, images, and other stylistic features (such as 3:2 *qinah* dirge meter) that connote sadness and a somber mood. The socially acceptable verbal and non-verbal customs for displaying sorrow would of course differ from those involving joy.

[37] "The history of reading the Bible is, in no small measure, the history of (re)uttering and (re)appropriating the words of Scripture. Nowhere is this truer than in the case of the psalms (sic), the Hebrew lyric par excellence" (Strawn 2008:440).

[38] "As a reader memorizes a text, he [*sic*] becomes textualized; that is, he embodies the work he has committed to memory" (Wenham 2012b:22). Add music to the mix and you have a most effective means of accurately transmitting a sacred text: "It is quite likely that much of [the Hebrew testament] was originally handed down by word of mouth. Often the traditions were passed along in a melodious manner—words were chanted or at least rhythmically recited" (M. R. Wilson 1989:303).

[39] Thus, Wenham is correct, but rather too limiting in this assertion: "[the psalms] were intended to be memorized with a view to being publicly recited for the purpose of inculcating the nation's values" (2012a:46). From the beginning of Israel as a nation, these "values" included a public confession of theological (Yahwistic) faith and commitment: "Music can help us recall words and ideas we might otherwise forget. God knew that the Israelites would forget Him when they entered the Promised Land (Deut. 31:20). They would forsake Him, turn to idols, and trouble would follow (vv. 16–18). Because of this, He asked Moses to compose a song and teach it to the Israelites so they could remember their past closeness with Him and the sin that hurt their relationship (31:19–22). Perhaps most important, God wanted His nation to recall His character: '[God] is the Rock, His work is perfect; for all His ways are justice, a God of truth and without injustice; righteous and upright is He' (32:4)" (Schuldt 2013). As far as public worship is concerned, in

In conclusion, it is important to reiterate, first of all, the significance of this panegyric theme and its mode of expression in the Scriptures: "The music of the Psalter is not simply an aesthetic adornment; it is participation in the ongoing musical praise [of God] in the universe; the psalms describe this praise in the widest possible terms" (Stallman 2008:487). "The poetry of David, which had originally been set to instrumental music, brings us to the special knowledge that 'God alone' is God" (Levine 1995:2). The frequent citation of the Psalms in the New Testament attests to this substantial theological and ecclesiastical import. Furthermore, it is helpful to note the close linkage between such poetic discourse and song that appears throughout the Bible (culminating of course in the book of Revelation, e.g., 4:8, 11; 5:9–13; 7:10–12; 19:1–7),[40] with the understanding that the vehicle of vocal "singing" (like "saying" in certain contexts) probably includes other forms of rhythmic, musical, or cadenced utterance. This perspective has important implications then for the practice of translation today in terms of how the biblical text is analyzed, composed, and then also tested for acceptability among its primary responsive audience. We turn now to the consideration of a clear representative psalm of praise, one that emphasizes energetic corporate "song" (שִׁיר, רָנַן), lyrically lauding the LORD YHWH from beginning to end (Pss. 98:1, 9).[41]

7.2 Athanasius—on singing the Psalms[42]

In his *Letter to Marcellinius,* a fourth-century non-Christian Roman historian, the prominent early theologian Athanasius (293–376) vigorously commends singing the Psalter as a vital spiritual practice that promotes one's growth in the life of faith. But why is singing in particular so spiritually beneficial? In the first place, such practice encourages the art of imitation with respect to mimetic impression rather than merely personal expression. As Athanasius puts it: "He who takes up this book [the Psalms]…recognizes [the words] as being his own words. And the one who hears is deeply moved, as though he

---

Temple and later synagogue liturgical worship, Psalm 98 was used at the Feast of the New Moon (Bullock 2001:93).

[40] As already observed with reference to OT texts, so also in certain NT cotexts, it would be appropriate to render the Greek "say, speak" in translation as "sing," e.g., Rev. 4:8 (λέγοντες, Ἅγιος ἅγιος ἅγιος κύριος ὁ θεὸς ὁ παντοκράτωρ…).

[41] Generally speaking, with reference to the book (scroll) as a whole, "the dynamic of the Psalter is its movement between the two poles of revelation and response" (Stallman 2008:487)—of *who* Yahweh is in relation to humanity and *how* they are to react to this revelation in their specific circumstances of faith-life, whether in pedagogy (e.g., Ps. 1), proclamation (e.g., Ps. 2), penitence (e.g., Ps. 6), petition (e.g., Ps. 3), profession (e.g., Ps. 8), and/or praise (e.g., Ps. 9).

[42] The following section is based upon the insightful study by Guthrie 2013; all page references (in parentheses) are to this article.

himself were speaking, and is affected by the words of the songs, as if they were his own songs" (46). Guthrie adds: "For Athanasius, the first virtue of the Psalms is not that they allow me to express my emotions. Rather, singing the Psalms makes it possible for me to express Moses' or David's emotions as my own ('as if they were his own songs')" (46)—hence an act of worshipful imitation. Here is an excellent example of the medium being an essential part of the message, for "inflection, rhythm, and tone of voice matter deeply. They are not [mere] aural decoration.... Song is valuable because it carries the words inside us (impression), and because it carries us inside the words" (ibid.).

And yet vocal expression is also involved since "it is fitting for the divine Scripture [of the Psalter] to praise God not in compressed speech alone, but also in the voice that is richly broadened" (Athanasius 46). Guthrie explains: "In ordinary speech there is intonation and rhythm, but these are 'in close sequence' [i.e., as manifested in prose passages]." However, "when 'things are expressed more broadly'—when we draw out and sustain the tones and rhythms of our speech—we move from prose, to poetry, to song" (46–47). Into this broader, musical space, as it were, "the singer enters in, not only inhabiting [or absorbing] the words...but by filling and animating them with her own strength and passion. We are [thus] invited to pour our hearts into this broad space" of worship in which the central focus is upon God and his grace and glory (for which due thanks and praise are due) rather than self/selves and our personal problems and needs (leading to lament and petition). In either case, "the Psalms are a rich and broad place where all the fullness of one's heart and soul and strength can be given voice" (Guthrie 47).

A final reason that Athanasius suggests for the pairing of words and music in the Psalms is that it stimulates religious reflection: The unity of poetry and melody serves as a "symbol of the spiritual harmony in a soul...the perfect image for the soul's course of life" (47). Guthrie explains that in a world saturated with sin, oppression, confusion, and disorientation, we are easily jolted "out of rhythm with God, out of tune with others, and troubled by jarring dissonances within ourselves. Musical harmony, however, may give us some intimation of a life that is composed" (47). According to Athanasius, "not only is this singing of Psalms an image of the well-ordered soul [the Psalter being 'a mirror in which each man sees the motions of his own soul']; it is also a means by which God brings about this order. As the Christian goes about 'beautifully singing praises, he [she] brings rhythm to his [her] soul and leads it, so to speak, from disproportion to proportion'" (47). This spiritual discipline, coupled with an associated life of discipleship in mutual service and encouragement, reaches its culmination when we sing the words of Scripture in corporate fellowship in the presence of God and in the company of God's people. In sum, "by singing our praises, all the diverse elements of our [common] humanity are drawn together, and then together lifted to God in worship" (47). The Psalter is a unique book of Scripture, divinely composed in word and melody to serve that cohesive, unifying purpose for all the saints "from every nation, from all tribes and peoples and languages" (Rev. 7:9, ESV).

7.3 A literary-structural overview of Psalm 98

We will explore certain aspects of the meaning of the "new song" of Psalm 98 by means of the following literary-structural analysis (cf. Wendland 2004:ch. 7; 2013a:ch. 9). What did the original author-orator presumably wish to communicate in and through this מִזְמוֹר in terms of form, content, and function?[43] How did he in all probability want his primary audience, presumably the worshipful, even currently worshiping, congregation of Israel, to utilize—to utter (sing, recite, chant, proclaim, etc.)—the text of this composition in order to communicate with Yahweh, their God, the King (v. 6)? Of course we cannot know everything that the [implied] author or his audience-turned-re-articulators had in mind as they enunciated these words, but we can come to a credible approximation of their communicative intention on the basis of a careful study of the psalm, and others like it in the Psalter (see further below), with reference to "the historical, social and cultural context in which they originated" (de Lang 2012:120). My own examination of the Hebrew text, though by no means complete, can give some initial direction towards this end—to begin with, by a sequence of

---

[43] One must take care in characterizing one's endeavor to seek out the meaning of the biblical text in this postmodern age, in which "serious objections have been raised against [the] claims of objectivity and neutrality" made by the proponents of "historical criticism" (de Lang 2012:117). I would agree that establishing the original context of author-audience communication is made even more difficult in the case of the psalms, where we have little if any information available regarding this initial compositional setting. However, I start from the presupposition that that original psalmist did indeed intend "to communicate a certain message to [an] audience, and that he intended to provoke a certain response from this audience" (ibid.:119).

I further admit the allegedly "normative or prescriptive intentions" that lead me to reject the following stricture: "Issues such as the special status of the canon, the revealed nature of Scriptures, or the inspiration of the biblical authors should not play a role: the biblical author should not be considered different from any other author, and his book should not receive special status over any other book" (ibid.:120–121, with reference to Räisänen 2000). I do not see how any [Christian] believer and interpreter can plausibly adopt such a hermeneutical platform as the preceding with reference to the Scriptures. In fact, despite the lack of an extensive title, an indirect case for Davidic authorship or association (at least) can be made on the basis of Psalm 98's close relationship with Ps. 96, and the many textual connections that both have with 1 Chr. 16:23–33, which is clearly attributed to David (v. 7) (cf. Lama 2013:219).

expository footnotes and subsequently by a summary thematic overview of Psalm 98. By means of the visual display below, I would also like to reveal certain aspects of the psalm's poetic soundscape, though that goal is admittedly rather difficult to accomplish in the absence of an audio transmission.

7.3.1 A visual display of the Hebrew text

The Hebrew text below has been taken from the ParaTExt 7.2 edition. My arrangement of parallel lines and half-lines (bi-cola) in the Hebrew text below (from ParaTExt 7.2) corresponds with that given in Tate (1990:522).[44] I have also demarcated the text into three, three-verse strophes, or poetic paragraphs (see below for the rationale). The accompanying English translation is that of the "essentially literal" *English Standard Version* (ESV);[45] the text has been shifted occasionally in order to align more closely with the original Hebrew. I have inserted periodic footnotes to call attention to special phonic features (the audible soundscape) and poetic devices (including a visualizable landscape of imagery) in the source text (some of the more prominent of the phonological forms are highlighted in gray).

98: A Psalm[a]	מִזְמֹ֥ור
1. Oh sing to the LORD a new song,[b]	שִׁ֤ירוּ לַֽיהוָ֨ה ׀ שִׁ֣יר חָדָ֗שׁ
for[c] he has done marvelous things!	כִּֽי־נִפְלָא֥וֹת עָשָׂ֑ה
His right hand has worked **salvation** for him[d]	הוֹשִֽׁיעָה־לּ֥וֹ יְמִינ֗וֹ
and[e] his holy arm.[f]	וּזְר֥וֹעַ קָדְשֽׁוֹ׃
2. The LORD has made known his **salvation**;[g] A	הוֹדִ֣יעַ יְהוָה יְשׁוּעָת֑וֹ
in the sight of the nations[h] B	לְעֵינֵ֥י הַ֝גּוֹיִ֗ם
he has revealed his *righteousness*.[i]	גִּלָּ֥ה צִדְקָתֽוֹ׃

---

[44] I have adopted (along with Tate), Peter Craigie's rationale concerning this system of lineation. It seeks lexical and syntactic (sometimes also phonological) balance among adjacent cola, and hypothetical meter is therefore based on lexical units, "which may sometimes be single words, or sometimes compound expressions" (Craigie 1983:38). This is because "any approach to Hebrew meter is essentially descriptive of the phenomenon of line length or relative line lengths, there being no evidence that a theory of system of meter was ever articulated in ancient Israel" (ibid.). At times it is also helpful to compare the relative lengths of adjacent cola with respect to notable correspondences and contrasts in terms of syllable counts since "a basic unit of speech production...[and] speech perception is the syllable... [and] syllables are the basic units of rhythm" (Burton et al. 2012:248–249).

[45] Taken from the open website http://www.esvbible.org/Psalm98/. Accessed September 2, 2017. (Cf. Ryken 2009:189–190.)

3. He has remembered[j] his *steadfast love* and *faithfulness*[k]		זָכַר חַסְדּוֹ ׀ וֶאֱמוּנָתוֹ
to the house of Israel.		לְבֵית יִשְׂרָאֵל
All the ends of the earth[l] have seen	B′	רָאוּ כָל־אַפְסֵי־אָרֶץ
the **salvation** of our God.[m]	A′	אֵת יְשׁוּעַת אֱלֹהֵינוּ׃
- - - - - - - - - - - - - - - -		- - - - - - - - - - - - - - - -
4. **Make a joyful noise** to the LORD, all the earth;[n] A		הָרִיעוּ לַיהֹוָה כָּל־הָאָרֶץ
break forth into joyous song and sing praises![o]		פִּצְחוּ וְרַנְּנוּ וְזַמֵּרוּ׃
5. Sing praises to the LORD with the lyre, A′		זַמְּרוּ לַיהֹוָה בְּכִנּוֹר
with the lyre[p] and the sound of melody! B		בְּכִנּוֹר וְקוֹל זִמְרָה׃
6. With trumpets and the sound of the horn[q] B′		בַּחֲצֹצְרוֹת וְקוֹל שׁוֹפָר
make a joyful noise before the King, the LORD![r] A″		הָרִיעוּ לִפְנֵי ׀ הַמֶּלֶךְ יְהֹוָה׃
- - - - - - - - - - - - - - - -		- - - - - - - - - - - - - - - -
7. Let the sea roar,[s] and all that fills it;		יִרְעַם הַיָּם וּמְלֹאוֹ
the **world**[t] and those who dwell in it![u]		תֵּבֵל וְיֹשְׁבֵי בָהּ׃
8. Let the rivers[v] clap their hands;[w]		נְהָרוֹת יִמְחֲאוּ־כָף
let the hills[x] sing for joy together[y]		יַחַד הָרִים יְרַנֵּנוּ׃
9. before the LORD,[z] for[aa] he comes		לִפְנֵי־יְהֹוָה כִּי בָא
to judge the earth.[ab]		לִשְׁפֹּט הָאָרֶץ
He will judge[ac] the **world** with righteousness,[ad]		יִשְׁפֹּט־תֵּבֵל בְּצֶדֶק
and the peoples with equity.[ae]		וְעַמִּים בְּמֵישָׁרִים׃

[a] As noted, the Septuagint includes as part of the heading τῷ Δαυιδ 'to/for/ by David'. Psalm 98 is the only one of the so-called Enthronement Psalms (93, 95–99; deClaissé-Walford 2004:105) that has any title at all.

[b] Consonance in [שׁ] underscores the notion of 'singing/song'. Emanuel feels that "the preposition לְ could be rendered as 'about', resulting in 'Sing about him', referring to the acts he has performed" (2012:31). However, the corresponding phrase לַיהֹוָה in v. 4a could not be interpreted that way.

[c] The conjunction "for" (כִּי) is normally construed in such contexts as having an explanatory sense, but here an asseverative ("Indeed…") and/or declarative understanding (i.e., introducing direct speech) are also possible as contextually-motivated renderings. The subsequent lines of strophe 1 provide the forceful motivation by reiterating the general reason for this "new song"—namely, the Lord's mighty and universal manifestation of "salvation."

^d Note the prominent assonance in [ô] that audibly links this Hebrew line with the next. This sound—with reference to "him/his" (Yahweh) reverberates thematically throughout Psalm 98 (also Ps. 96).

^e Tate notes "the emphatic *waw* attached to 'arm'" (1990:523); this could also be interpreted as a *waw* of specification and hence another instance of Kugel's well-known characterization of parallelism: "A is so, and what's more, B" (1981:23). As Alter explains: "Semantic parallelism...the characteristic movement of meaning is one of heightening or intensification...of focusing, specification, concretization, even what could be called dramatization" (1985:19), as when there is a shift to direct speech in line B.

^f The right hand and arm are conventional OT synecdoches which symbolize Yahweh's power as a warrior-king; he can "work salvation" to the ends of the earth (v. 2; cf. Ps. 89:10). The key concept of "salvation" (יְשׁוּעָה), or "deliverance, victory, etc.", is reiterated to highlight its thematic nature for the entire psalm. "The polemic of praise consists in the overthrow of Yahweh's rivals" (Hutchinson 2005:98).

^g "The first colon in v. 2 slows down the rhetoric, summing up what preceded" (Goldingay 2008:121).

^h The phrase "to [the] eyes of the nations" (לְעֵינֵי הַגּוֹיִם) could function as an attribute of either colon A or colon C, thus forming a fusing "pivot pattern" within a tricolon (Tate 1990:523).

ⁱ Gerstenberger considers the language of "revelation" here with the verb גלה to be "very unusual" (2001:196), hence presumably—and appropriately—attention-drawing.

^j In the Psalter, the verb "remember" *(z-k-r)* with God as subject is not used in contrast to "forget", but it often has some definite or implied divine act of deliverance—past, present, or future—in view (Ps. 74:2, 89:50, 105:8, 132:1). In this case, the perfect tense זָכַר might suggest "that the psalmist is thinking of some great act of deliverance of the people by God" (Boice 1996:797)—perhaps the Exodus or some subsequent salvation event in the history of God's people. On the other hand, in the light of Psalm 98 as a whole, it is also possible to view God's merciful salvation as encompassing "the whole range of Yahweh's victories" (Tate 1990:524) enacted on behalf of believers during the whole course of human time.

^k "Righteousness" (צְדָקָה), "steadfast love" (חֶסֶד), and "faithfulness" (אֱמוּנָה) (vv. 2b–3a) are the primary covenantal attributes that Yahweh demonstrates through his various acts of "deliverance" (יְשׁוּעָה) on behalf of his people (v. 3d). These qualities also serve as metonymic references to God's eternal "covenant" with his faithful people (not just anyone!). "No real difference exists between the Hebrew expressions 'he remembered his covenant'...and 'he remembered his steadfast love'.... Both speak of the LORD's utter faithfulness in fulfilling his covenant promises" (Harman 2011b:712). However, it may be valid to identify חֶסֶד as the preeminent verbal designation for "the 'faithful love and loyalty' that are present between partners in a covenant" (Magonet 2014:169).

^l I see here a potential convergence rather than a "contrast" involving "the nations and the people of Yahweh" (Gerstenberger 2001:196; cf Magonet 2014:170).

^m A chiastic structure (A – B :: B' – A') encloses verses 2–3 and thus helps to set the boundaries for this psalm's first strophe (vv. 1–3). The final colon (3d) concludes (presumably an instance of end stress) with its theme: A-A', "the

salvation of the LORD our God" (a subjective genitive); B-B′, is manifested/available to "all nations…to the ends of the earth."

[n] "The opening words of verse 4 are the same as Psalm 66:1 (cf. also Ps. 47:1)" (Harman 2011b:713). Tate feels that "the summons to praise is interrupted after 1a and resumed in v4" (1990:524). On the other hand, this is a common structure-marking device in Hebrew poetry, i.e., lexical similarity or lineal correspondence serving to signal the onset of distinct discourse units (anaphora; Wendland 2004:127). In a structural, macrotextual sense, strophes 2–3 heighten and intensify strophe 1 in a way that is analogous to line A-B parallelism, as noted above: "A, and what's more, B." Thus, as expressed in vv. 4–9, "the implications of vv. 1b–3 for the whole world are surprising and breathtaking. The resumptive exhortation and its length reflect this" (Goldingay 2008:121).

[o] This close-knit series of three Hebrew imperatives is as phonologically striking as it is strong in hortative terms. "The Hebrew text uses a cluster of commands to the nations, and in so doing highlights the praise that is expected from them" (Harman 2011b:713). The euphonious sequence and the notion of ongoing praise is continued at the onset of the next line (5a) by means of a repetitive overlapping of the command זַמְּרוּ 'sing a psalm' (Broyles 1999:382), which recalls the psalm's title. For a discussion of the close parallel in Psalm 105:2, see Emanuel 2012:30–31.

[p] Repetition of "with the lyre" (בְּכִנּוֹר) in v. 5a–b forms a terraced construction (technically "anakypdosis;" VanGemeren 1991:629) that carries over with the prepositional (בְּ) phrase "with trumpets" in v. 6a. The specific instruments mentioned in vv. 5–6 evoke concrete images (evoking temple festival scenes) that counterbalance the generic calls to praise. On the commonly-used "lyre," see Walton et al. 2000:559.

[q] Colon 6a may be construed as an instance of "enjambment", a poetic technique whereby a sentence is carried over to the next line without pause, or as the onset of the second half of another chiastic construction (A + A′ – B :: B′ – A″), this one more complex and covering the entire second strophe, thus helping to mark its boundaries (vv. 4–6). To be more specific: "Verses 4–6 are parallel: each of the first two verses begins with an imperative verb, then has 'to Yhwh', then a qualifying phrase, with each second colon expanding on the first. The third then reverses the parallelism, with the qualifying phrases occupying the first colon, the single verb (the same as began v. 4) opening the second, and an alternative expression instead of 'to Yhwh'" (Goldingay 2008:122).

[r] An inclusio involving the verb "shout joyfully" (הָרִיעוּ) coupled with the name of Yahweh (יְהוָה) also serves to clearly demarcate the extremities of strophe 2 and to indicate its closure (vv. 4a and 6b). The fronted and "key word" (Gerstenberger 2001:197) "the King" (הַמֶּלֶךְ) indicates concisely and by implication the reason for praising the LORD with such joy. "What the original order of the words makes more emphatic is God's effective governance of the affairs of this world…" (Leupold 1959:694). "This, then, is really a call for conversion of the nations, and a commitment to the living God" (Harman 2011b:713). The line-final position of "Yahweh" then creates a peak at the end of this strophe; "the [apparent] extrametrical occurrence of 'Yahweh' is not uncommon" (Tate 1990:523). This emphasis upon God's name matches that found at the end of strophe 1 (v. 3d, i.e., structural epiphora; Wendland 2004:127).

[s] The verb forms shift from imperatives to jussives in this third strophe. The verb "roar" (רעם), literally, to "storm/thunder" (Peacock 1981:102), which leads off this poetic

paragraph resembles that which begins the final line of the preceding unit, i.e., "resound" (רוע), thus creating some inter-strophic cohesion with regard to both sound and sense.

[t] Here we have an instance of verb-gapping ("roar" – רעם) which links the two cola of v. 7. These two half-lines also match in their internal alliterative consonance involving voiced bilabial sounds—a liquid (מ) followed by a stop (בּ).

[u] This colon is the same as Psalm 24:1c. "Nature is personified, and rejoices in the coming of the LORD as judge of the earth" (Harman 2011b:713).

[v] The term "rivers" (נְהָרוֹת), coupled with "hills" (הָרִים), may allude to the world's creation—i.e., the seas and the dry land (Gen. 1:9–10; cf. Psalm 24:1–2; Tate 1990:523; cf. Bratcher and Reyburn 1991:844).

[w] This image is not as anthropomorphic as it may seem. "Rivers can clap hands as they tumble over rocks, throwing up spurts of spray that intermingle with one another like hands joining" (Goldingay 2008:123).

[x] "Likewise the mountains resound (cf. 89:12[13]) as the wind roars over them and through their forests (cf. 96:12)..." (Goldingay 2008:123).

[y] The adverb "together" (יַחַד) is Janus-faced syntactically, that is, it could be understood as modifying either colon in v. 8. In the MT it is used with colon B, but in the LXX with colon A (ἐπὶ τὸ αὐτό).

[z] "Before Yahweh" (לִפְנֵי־יְהוָה) may be regarded as another instance of cohesive overlapping enjambment that links the adjacent cola of 8b and 9a. The unusual construction here (with the preceding phrase juxtaposed with the clause "for he comes" – כִּי בָא) functions to highlight the divine name, which occurs only at this medial point in the third strophe. For a different colonic proposal, see Goldingay 2008:119).

[aa] The psalm's two prominent "reason" (כִּי-introduced) sections form an unbalanced alternating structure that overlaps with the linear strophic division: A = Call to Praise (1a, short) + B = Rationale (1b–3, long) :: A′ = Call to Praise (4–9a, long) + B′ = Rationale (9b–d, short) (pace Goldingay 2008:119).

[ab] In Psalm 96:13 the expression "for he comes" (כִּי בָא) is reiterated at the beginning of this line, which is otherwise the same. Some commentators replace it here, claiming a case of haplography (cf. Tate 1990: 523), but there is no reason why these two similar psalms, which differ in other significant respects, could not vary here as well. In Psalm 98 this omission puts the emphasis more forcefully on the notion of "judging."

[ac] Repetition of the verb 'judge' (שׁפט) underscores it audibly as the central action in this strophe. This verb is further implied (gapped) before the psalm's final object "peoples" (עַמִּים). "To 'judge' involves deliverance for [God's] people and destruction for his [and their] enemies" (Harman 2011b:713).

[ad] Reference to the LORD's "righteousness" (צֶדֶק) thus links up the end of Psalm 98 with its beginning (2c). "The revelation of [God's] righteousness in the past (v. 2) foreshadowed a yet greater demonstration in the future (v. 9)" (Harman 2011b:714).

[ae] A relatively rare tetracolon (having a similar lexical accent pattern) begins and ends this psalm in what amounts to a sonic inclusio. There is also a strophic inclusio indicated by the consonance in "m" (מ) sounds—7a/9d (cf. also the end of the first strophe in v. 3. The noun "peoples" (עַמִּים) in v. 9d corresponds with "dwellers" (יֹשְׁבֵי) in v. 7b, thus forming an imperfect inclusio that also delimits the outer bounds of strophe three. Terrien considers v. 9c–d to be a "postlude" which corresponds to a "prelude" in v. 1 such that the internal portion of the psalm consists of "three strophes of three stichoi each" (2003:682). However, such a formal proposal seems artificial and one that contradicts the psalm's semantics.

7.3.2 A strophic summary

I will preface my summary of the semantic sense and pragmatic significance of Psalm 98, based on its structural organization and literary features, by again noting the essential distinction between inscribed meaning and applied or transferred significance. This differentiation was first formulated and subsequently further developed by the secular literary critic and educator E. D. Hirsch, Jr. in two influential books dealing with the interpretation of literature (1967, 1976). In short, Hirsch "distinguished between 'meaning', which is to be located in the text, and 'significance', which he described as the relationship between a text and a reader...[that is] between 'what it meant' and 'what it means'" (de Lang 2012:118–119; cf. Stendahl 2008:2). But more than this, the meaning being referred to here is that intended by the original implied author and inscribed in his (or her) text, from which it may be recovered—never perfectly to be sure, but to a greater or lesser extent.[46] This hermeneutical exercise is carried out with reference to the original text[47] by means of various methods of linguistic and literary investigation (e.g., studies of rhetoric, poetics, genre, speech acts, stylistics, intertextuality, etc.) as well as through scholarly interaction and collaboration over time.

The implication of this pointed interest in meaning concerns not only one's efforts to analyze the text of Psalm 98 (and assert the results), but also one's attempt to translate this text into another language (see below). Indeed, "what is the meaning we translate?" (Gutt 1987) if there is no such thing as meaning recognized to begin with, or if that meaning cannot be reliably ascertained, or if that meaning is relative or idiosyncratic—are we simply left with, *to each his (or her) own?* As suggested above, I have a more optimistic outlook on this interpretive endeavor, and in that perspective then offer the following summary of my construed meaning of Psalm 98's song.

---

[46] "If we remove the author, the text floats in a historical sea of relativity, open to multiple [often competing or contradictory] meanings. The author anchors the text in history [as well as in language and culture] and makes interpretation of its original [intended] meaning possible" (Osborne 2006:497, material in brackets added). The two Appendices in Osborne (2006) are well worth reading by those interested in the meaning of meaning: 1) "The Problem of Meaning: The Issues" (465–499); 2) "Towards a Solution" (500–521).

[47] By "original text" I am of course referring to the Hebrew text as composed by its initial author (+/– any subsequent minor editorial modifications, e.g., lexical updates)—as nearly as this can by posited by the established procedures of modern textual criticism (Hill and Kruger 2012:3–4). "Although recovering the original text faces substantial obstacles (and therefore the results should be qualified), there is little to suggest that it is an illegitimate enterprise" (ibid.:4).

In terms of its wider genre,[48] this is a hymn, or communal psalm of praise (Gerstenberger 2001:197; Wendland 2002:41),[49] that is, a lyric devoted to lauding the LORD for his greatness and majesty, as well as for the covenantal righteousness and steadfast love manifested to his people, Israel.[50] Thus, the praiseworthy divine attributes mentioned are always displayed in action, specifically, in past as well as promised deeds of deliverance. "Praise in the Psalter is both *descriptive* of Yahweh's character and deeds, and *declarative* of his particular acts of deliverance" (Hutchinson 2005:89; cf. Westermann 1981:31). Psalm 98 may also be typed as a "royal" psalm (Wendland 2002:51) because it refers to Yahweh as the great King who not only rules over his people (v. 6), but who also fights on their behalf as their Deliverer (v. 1) and who adjudicates righteously in their best interests as Judge (v. 9).[51] God "comes" to earth "to judge the world with righteousness" (v. 9) through his rule: "justice and righteousness constitute a summary of God's *torah*, 'instruction'—that is, God's will" (McCann 2012:282, cf. 285).[52] "The psalm employs a vocabulary and an idiom that emphasize the Savior and his salvation more than the saved" (Mays 1994a:313).[53] Such panegyric hymns are typically filled with imperatives of praise that call on people,[54] both near (i.e., "Israel", 3b) and far (i.e., "the nations", 3c),[55] as well as all

---

[48] I will not delve deeply or in detail here on the subject of genre classification (cf. Schrag 2013:59–86). This is because "even if scholars could agree on an appropriate taxonomy, the practical problem would still have to be faced that many psalms seem to defy classification" (Hutchinson 2005:94). However, I do not think that the problem has so much to do with a "defiant" classification as it does with coincident classification—that is, many psalms manifest several functional types in harmonious compositional combination.

[49] The command that opens Ps. 98, "Sing to Yahweh" (שִׁירוּ לַיהוָה), is the metonymic equivalent of the other standard summons to praise: "Bless Yahweh" (בָּרְכִי אֶת־יְהוָה), e.g., 103:1, or "Praise Yahweh/Hallelujah!" (הַלְלוּ יָהּ), e.g., Ps. 111:1.

[50] "Psalm 98 shows this grounding of the praise of the people in the steadfast love and faithfulness of God as the summary statement at the conclusion of a description of the Lord's salvific acts" (i.e., in v. 3; Miller 1994:208). We find the same pairing of key covenantal terms coupled with the imperative to 'make music' (*z-m-r*) to the LORD in Ps. 92:1–2.

[51] A case can be made for viewing "Yhwh's royal activity as the reality-defining foundation of the psalmic worldview.... The declaration of *yahwh malak* ['the LORD reigns'] involves a vision of reality that is the theological center of the Psalter.... It does announce a metaphor that...every reader and user of the psalms may know as the code for understanding all of them" (Mays 1994b:15, 22).

[52] The *torah*-foundational roots for "justice" (שפט) and "righteousness" (צדק) are found, significantly, at the climax of the psalm that opens the Psalter (1:5–6).

[53] R.B. Culley (1967) claims that 50% of Psalm 98 consists of "formulaic language" (Gillingham 1994:202).

[54] Thus, Mays classifies Psalm 98 as an "imperative hymn of praise" (1994a:312).

[55] The mission mandate of Psalm 98 is manifold (e.g., vv. 2, 3, 7, 9): "At its highest expression, praise in the psalms becomes the longing for all peoples of all nations

creation (vv. 7–8),[56] to magnify who God is and what he has done. There are ten commands (a symbolically significant number?) that express such acclaim, with rhetorical power as well as aesthetic appeal, within the scope of Psalm 98. On the other hand, some scholars prefer to classify Psalm 98 more specifically as a "divine warrior victory song" because it celebrates the defeat and judgment of Yahweh's enemies (v. 9) and that after such "victory the appropriate response was praise, often musical" (Longman 1984:273; e.g., Pss. 24:7–10, 106:11). Finally, as Magonet observes, the communal worship function of this psalm must not be overlooked: "Ps. 98 turns the whole world into a musical liturgical celebration of YHWH" (2014:170). This observation fits well within an even larger functional perspective: "The Psalter [is analogous to a] 'score', as the musical framework in which the reader [hearer or chorus] may find her [his, their] own voice" in praise (K. N. Jacobson 2014:143).

The structural contours of this eulogy have been outlined above. It consists of three strophes, the first somewhat longer (31 "words") than the latter two, which are relatively balanced in length (20 and 23 words).[57] The same pragmatic (functional) pattern may be observed in each one: a Call to Praise God (1a, 4–6a, 7–9a) is followed by the Reasons based on Yahweh's past/proven actions and divine attributes (1b–3, 6b, 9b). Each strophe then focuses on a somewhat different aspect of Yahweh's commendable character, though these behavioral attributes are all closely related, in fact conceptually integrated: Yahweh is our Divine Warrior (1),[58] King (2), and Judge (3).

---

to enjoy and glorify God. It is a repeated motif throughout the psalms of praise and thanksgiving. The vision of a world united in praise to God is the great vision for which the psalms ultimately reach. This is the synergy of communal enjoyment in its highest form, and it is the goal of human history.... The compulsion to praise God is therefore the underlying motive that compels us to join with God's mission in the world" (Jacoby 2013:173).

[56] "In the hymns that celebrate the rule of God over the earth, the things of nature are summoned to the praise of God along with the human community" (Miller 1994:220). Psalm 98 thus enunciates the two major themes that Parrish discerns as the foundation of Books 4 and 5 of the Psalter: "YHWH creates" and "YHWH reigns" (2003:142; cf. Ps. 98:7–9). Perhaps this royally-toned hymn of nature constitutes a joyful response of the Creation to its Creator (Fisch 1988:166)—as intimated perhaps in the opening verse of Psalm 98 and mention of the "wonderful things" that YHWH has done. All creation too looks forward to a just liberation from the bondage and decay with which man's sin has enslaved it (Bullock 2001:190–191).

[57] Psalm 98 would be a clear exception to the generalization that "the structure of a lyric is frequently disjointed" (Ryken 2012:128).

[58] For a brief survey of the "Divine Warrior" theme and imagery in the Psalter, see VanGemeren 1991:630–635. For more detail on this subject in relation to Psalm 98, see Longman 1984. The various graphic "holy war" images and allusions depict the total "sufficiency and power of Yahweh in all of life's situations" (VanGemeren 1991:631; cf. Alter 2007:344).

In strophe 1 (vv. 1–3), the call to praise in the form of a "new song" of victory[59]—which is really the age-old song of Yahweh's mighty "deliverance" (יֵשַׁע in 1c, 2a, 3d) being articulated anew (cf. Exo. 15:1–18)[60]—is followed by the salient reasons. A cluster of key terms reveals the covenantal commitment that motivates the LORD's diverse saving works on behalf of his people ("our" in v. 3d with immediate reference to Israel): "righteousness" (צְדָקָה), "steadfast love" (חֶסֶד), and "faithfulness" (אֱמוּנָה) (vv. 2c, 3a).

The psalm's compass, or scope, is greatly extended and its manner of singing is significantly intensified through a sequence of imperative commands in the second strophe (vv. 4–6). "The ends of the earth" (people of every tribe everywhere) are encouraged to "rejoice" with all kinds of music and instruments, with an emotive climax being reached with the ritual sounding of the *shofar* (שׁוֹפָר).[61] "The enthusiasm of Israelite worship is illustrated in this passage" (Tate 1990:525). Here the focus of communal attention is directed towards Yahweh the King (6b) and his royal rule over all nations (4a).[62] Longman offers some interesting insights on the royal-military imagery of this psalm and its connection with the prominent musical dimension of its middle strophe (1984:270):

> The musical praise of Yahweh the victorious Divine Warrior further confirms our identification of Psalm 98 as a song of praise

---

[59] "[This] celebration of God's majesty…is a fresh and original composition.… [It] is a weaving together of phrases and whole lines that appear elsewhere…a 'mosaic' of lines drawn from familiar psalms" (Alter 2007:338). "The new song is a celebration of a new realization of the Lord's kingship" (Futato 2008:170).

[60] The opening verse of Ps. 98 is in itself a summary song of praise that harks back to the "old song" of Yahweh's mighty act of deliverance at the Red Sea. "Every major item of vocabulary [in v. 1] recalls Exod 15: 'song' (see Exod 15:1, 21), 'marvelous things' (see Exod 15:11), 'right hand' (see Exod 15:6, 12), 'holy arm' (see Exod 15:11, 16), 'salvation' (see Exod 15:2)…and v. 3 recalls Exod 9:16, which suggests that the ultimate purpose of the exodus was to make God manifest 'through all the earth'" (McCann 1996:1072).

[61] "The psalmist shows his concern for the aesthetic aspect of praise by listing the musical instruments that support the voice and the ritual shouts" (Terrien 2003:683). For some detailed studies of the musical instruments to be found in ancient Israel, see Braun 2002:ch. 1 and Burgh 2006:ch. 2.

[62] In the light of the New Testament and even from the perspective of the canonical shape of the Psalter and the prominence of Psalm 2 (esp. vv. 6–8), it is arguable that Yahweh's Kingship was most concretely and visibly realized in the person of his promised Messiah, Jesus the Christ (cf. Ps. 110:1,4; Acts 4:24–28, 13:32–33; Heb. 1:5). "It does appear that the editors of the Psalter sought to direct their readers to a particular understanding of the future Davidic king by placing some of the royal psalms in a very specific context…to be ultimately reinterpreted eschatologically, creating the expectation of a future king who will live up to the content of these royal psalms (universal rule with complete societal justice, etc.)" (Grant 2005:114; cf. Deut. 17:14–20).

sung by the congregation as it greets the victorious army and its divine commander. Indeed the role of music in holy war passages in the OT shows that its ups and downs comprise an important subtheme to the theme of the Divine Warrior. Simply stated, while the Divine Warrior wars, music languishes (Isa 24:8ff...), and when the Divine Warrior wins, music is taken up again in a paean of praise. This reflects historical custom, since we know that the human war leader and his army were greeted by instrumental music and victory songs upon their return (1 Sam 18:6–7; Judg 11:34).

Interestingly, the reason for praising God in the second strophe is essentially limited to a single word: He is "the King" (הַמֶּלֶךְ)!

In strophe three (vv. 7–9), the vital scope of jubilant song is expanded still further in an "ecology of praise" (Goldingay 2008:124) to incorporate even the inanimate cosmos,[63] which is enjoined, once again along with earth's human inhabitants (7b), to "clap hands" (as a physical sign of acclamation) and "sing together joyously" (8a–b).[64] Along with the natural world,[65] a significant new temporal dimension is then introduced in the psalm's final verse as the scene shifts dramatically to the future *(yiqtol)* and Yahweh's arrival (בָּא) to judge (יִשְׁפֹּט) the world—all peoples (עַמִּים)—"with equity" (בְּמֵישָׁרִים)[66]

---

[63] For this reason some commentators also extend the reference of Yahweh's "deliverance" in 98:1 back to the time of creation and "the primeval combat that led to his victory" (Terrien 2003:683, 684). "In Ancient Near Eastern creation accounts, the sea and the 'floods' represented chaotic forces that oppose in battle the sovereignty of the supreme creator-God (see Ps. 93:3–4). Thus vv. 7–8 call to mind the image of God as divine warrior, who subjected hostile forces to create the world (vv. 7–8) as well as to create and re-create God's people (vv. 1–3)" (McCann 1996:1072). Thus, "Salvation corresponded to and continued creation" (Mays 1994a:313). That the 'heavens' too are invoked in this all-inclusive call to praise is suggested by Ps. 98's parallel in Ps. 96:11—'Let the heavens be glad, and let the earth rejoice...'. That heavenly music and song were involved is further intimated by this reference in Job, when Yahweh himself asks (rhetorically): "Who laid [earth's] cornerstone—when the morning stars sang together, and all the sons of God shouted for joy?" (38:6–7).

[64] The biblical view of creation, though anthropomorphized here, is radically different from that of "modern man." "The world makes either one of two errors where the cosmos is concerned. Either it deifies nature, virtually worshiping it...or the world regards nature as evolving towards perfection, accompanied by the human race, which is also evolving" (Boice 1996:800).

[65] There may be a further connection here with what Longman views as Divine Warrior imagery: "When the Divine Warrior wars, nature droops, withers, languishes (Isa 24:4–13), but when the Divine Warrior wins, nature is revivified and participates in praising Yahweh" (1984:271).

[66] "The term here is comparable to that used in Mesopotamia for the declaration of release from debts. In the ancient Near East the freeing of prisoners (from debtors'

(cf. 96:13).[67] In this strophe "the psalm goes beyond a reflection on the past to a joyful anticipation of the universal restoration of all things in justice (cf. יֵשַׁע vv. 1–3), when God's kingdom will be established..." forever (VanGemeren 1991:627).[68]

Psalm 98 closes by citing yet another reason for this universal ovation— namely, the LORD's "just judgment" (v. 9).[69] On first hearing this last testimony, a person (especially someone unfamiliar with the Hebrew religious and textual tradition) might pause with uncertainty: Who would ever want to by judged by a holy, almighty God? The answer of course lies in the essential nature of the deity being praised, Yahweh, and his notion of "justice" (צֶדֶק) (9c). From a covenantal perspective then, Psalm 98 and similar psalms eschatologically "anticipate the coming of God to judge the nations [the wicked], that is, to decide for the right and against the wrong... [thus] reversing reality and the human situation" (Miller 1986:77).[70] But more than

prison) as an act of justice often occurred in the first or second year of a new king's reign..." (Walton et al. 2000:547). A recontextualized application within the eschatological frame of reference of Ps. 98:9 is not difficult to make.

[67] This promise of God's future "righteous" royal rule (בְּצֶדֶק) over all people/nations could ultimately be "the new song" that the psalmist has in mind as the heart of his lyric, thus forming an implicit thematic inclusio (vv. 2c, 9c). Thus Psalm 98 "claims that Israel's God had been shaping Israel's particular history to establish and reveal his rule over universal history....The righteousness of the LORD shown in the salvation of Israel was the clue to the future of the world" (Mays 1994a:313, 314).

[68] Thus, in one sense it is true to say that "the historical situation was 'dehistoricized', and the psalm now has an eschatological dimension" (VanGemeren 1991:627). But on the other hand, the living memory of Yahweh's mighty acts of deliverance on behalf of Israel, now recorded also in the Scriptures, lend crucial credence to every generation's hope for his ultimate future intervention. "As in the other psalms celebrating God's kingship, the perspective is global, for his reign extends over all the earth" (Alter 2007:345). The OT notion of God's omnipotent, universal, and eternal rule as "King" (Ps. 98:6) is manifestly continued in the NT, often under the epithet "the kingdom of God/heaven" (Mt. 3:2; Mk. 1:15).

[69] The message and mood of Ps. 98 might lead one to question the categorical assertion that "lyric poems are either (a) meditative and reflective or (b) emotional and affective" (Ryken 2012:127). Indeed, Ps. 98 appears to progress from (a), vv. 1–3, to (b), vv. 4–8, and back to (a) again, v. 9. In any case, both the reflective as well as the affective dispositions would seem to be involved.

[70] "In the light of God's coming Psalm 96 [v. 13; and 98:9] exhorts all the earth to acknowledge Yahweh as the only God and to give him praise as the Creator and Lord of all. The means for this to happen, however, is the proclamation of God's people, who are called to proclaim his salvation among the nations and to declare that 'the LORD reigns'. It is interesting to note how this exhortation is so well represented in Jesus' ministry and that of the apostles after him, whose message of salvation focused on the proclamation that 'the Kingdom of God is at hand'. They proclaimed the Lordship of Christ and exhorted people to acknowledge him and come under his rule while the time of amnesty lasted for all those in conflict with God. They were

that, the thematic concept of 'salvation' (יְשׁוּעָה), as the rest of Scripture reveals, includes the LORD's special provision to enable weak and unworthy people to closely fellowship with their mighty Monarch. That is just another instance of the "marvelous things" (נִפְלָאוֹת) (1b)[71] for which he is most deserving of a new song—one that is ever recycled in each new generation.

7.4 The reflected meaning of Psalm 98's new song in the light of similar songs

Psalm 98, though an independent and self-standing lyric composition, does not exist in textual isolation. "Much in this psalm is paralleled in other psalms of Yahweh's kingship" (Broyles 1999:381). Thus, it is linked linguistically with a number of other, topically related psalms within the Psalter itself, both in its immediate cotext and further afar.[72] It manifests many more intertextual links, both generic and lexical, with other portions of the Hebrew Scriptures,[73] as well as the New Testament, only a few of which can be pointed out in the following discussion. In a wider sense then, these complementary passages also form part of that "new song" that Psalm 98 directs us to sing.

Jenni and Westermann (1997:1321–1322) summarize the principal intertextual relationships, a "shared tradition of praise" (Goldingay 2008:120; cf. Broyles 1999:381–382; Gerstenberger 2001:195–196), of the "new song" mentioned in Psalm 98:1 as follows:[74]

> In a series of psalms, an [imperative] call to praise at the beginning of the psalm calls for singing a "new song" *(shir chadash)* to Yahweh (Isa 42:10; Psa 96:1; 98:1; 149:1; cf. Psa 33:3;

doing exactly what Psalm 96 is exhorting us to do" [also 98:9b] (http://www.son sofkorah.com/ [> Music > Study > Psalm 96]. Accessed September 2, 2017).

[71] Mays describes this Hebrew term as referring to "divine interventions that transcended human expectations" (1994a:313). Broyles adds that the word probably refers "not to specific marvelous things, but to all the many instances within Israel's salvation history in a summative fashion" (1999:381). On the other hand, any group of God's people that sings this psalm may rightly apply the concept to the particular instance of the Lord's deliverance that they may have just recently experienced.

[72] "A number of psalms in the Psalter are made up of echoes, phrases, and even whole verses from other psalms.... This phenomenon suggests that a word or idea that was meaningful for one psalmist in a particular context was found to be meaningful by another in a different context" (deClaissé-Walford 2004:94).

[73] Note, for example, the theological significance of the first strophe (vv. 1–3): "The praise here is set within the context of Israel's history, both with broad reference to salvation and reference to 'righteousness, steadfast love, faithfulness' that are central to the covenant tradition" (deClaissé-Walford et al. 2014:727).

[74] The same expression "new song" (שִׁיר חָדָשׁ) is found six times in the Psalter: 33:3, 40:3, 96:1, 98:1, 144:9, and 149:1—most explicitly reflecting a context of deliverance in Ps. 40, and within a more specific setting of divine praise in Ps. 33.

40:4; 144:9...). This new song corresponds to God's new deeds; only a new song can respond to Yahweh's new act.

The preceding characterization is stated rather too generally, however. More specifically, then (VanGemeren 1997b:99):

> Primarily this phrase ["new song"] presupposes a new experience of God in action, which is reflected in thanksgiving (Ps. 40:3[4]; 144:9). It is generally used in eschatological hymns, anticipating by faith the final work of salvation [that] God is to accomplish (96:1; 98:1; 149:1; Isa 42:10; cf. Ps. 33:3 in the light of vv. 20:22; cf. Rev 5:9).[75]

On the other hand, it would be a mistake to view these salvation hymns only in an eschatological light. Rather, history anticipated in Scripture is always based on history fulfilled, namely, how Yahweh has already demonstrated his *chesed* faithfulness to his people in the past, beginning with the Patriarchs (most notably, Abraham, e.g., Ps. 105:6–11, 42), then most mightily (as noted earlier) during the Exodus deliverance from Egypt (Ps. 105:23–41, 43),[76] and continuing even after that greatest of disasters, the Babylonian exile (Isa. 44:28–45:13).[77]

The Divine Warrior language of Psalm 98, especially in strophe 1, and its style as a hymn of triumph are reminiscent of "those which follow the successful completion of Yahweh's action in war (cf. Judg 5:4–5; Deut 33:2–5, 26–29, Pss. 46:9; 68:8–9; 77:17–20; 114:3–6; Nah 1:2–8; Hab 3:3–15...)" (Tate 1990:524).[78] The warrior imagery merges with picturesque concepts

---

[75] So also Bullock: "The 'new' song proclaims Yahweh's sovereignty over the nations, both in judgment and salvation. It announces a new era in history when Yahweh's sovereignty in the world will be finally and universally acclaimed" (2001:192). This would seem best to apply to the future dominion of Yahweh's promised Messiah (Php. 2:10–11). Peacock takes "new song" to refer to the psalm itself (1981:99).

[76] The anthropomorphic reference to Yahweh's powerful "arm" and "right hand" (v. 1c) immediately call to mind the Song of Moses in praise of God's deliverance on the opposite shore of the Red Sea (Exo. 15:6, 12, 16; cf. Deut. 33:2; Pss. 78:54, 118:15–16). For correspondences with Ps. 105, especially singing about God's mighty deeds, see Emanuel 2012:30–31).

[77] "In fact, Ps. 98 can be seen as an actualized version of Ps. 96. Ps. 96.3 commands, 'Tell of his glory among the nations...' and 98.3 claims (in the past): 'All the ends of the earth beheld the victory of our God'" (Berlin and Brettler 2004:1391).

[78] One should not overplay the probable warlike or military topical background here. As Longman points out: "Psalm 98 is a prime example of a tendency that runs through much of the Psalter: the subduing of reference to specific historical events in order to preserve the immediate relevance of the poem in the cult.... Psalm 98 was not recited as a remembrance of an historical deliverance in the hoary past, but was structured in such a way that it could be recited [or sung!] after any of the numerous deliverances that Israel experienced during her history" (1984:272). The same principle applies for God's people today.

of praiseworthy royalty in the second strophe and, indeed, the larger organ-
ization of the Psalter appears to give precedence to this vision—Yahweh as
King (יְהוָה מָלָךְ, v. 6b)—that is, beginning with Psalm 89 and continuing
in the set covering Psalms 93–99.[79] These psalms, which "dramatize more
than any other group of psalms the coming of the King" (Levine 1995:201),
form a prominent "lyric sequence" (Strawn 2008:440), "shift the focus of
the reader [and audience!] away from human kingship to the eternal and
just rule of Yahweh as king" (G. H. Wilson 2005:235). Indeed, Mays argues
that the concept of *Yhwh malak* 'the LORD reigns' is the "root metaphor," or
the theological "organizing center" of the Psalter (1994b:12–13): "Whatever
else is said in the psalms about God and God's way with [the] world and
human beings is rooted in the meaning and truth of this metaphor; it is sys-
temic for psalmic language" (ibid.:6). Mays goes on to summarize the range
of this metaphor in terms of Yahweh's spheres of domination, the institu-
tions of his reign, and various activities involving his sovereignty (ibid.:14–
15), including those psalms in which references or allusions to the Messiah
play "a crucial role in the reign of Yhwh" (ibid.:17).[80] "Repeatedly, God's
future triumphs in these visionary psalms are witnessed by 'all the earth'
(96:1b, 9b)...[by] 'all the ends of the earth' (98:3b)" (Levine 1995:202).

Psalm 98 has an obviously close lexical, structural, and thematic rela-
tionship with Psalm 96, such that "Psalm 98 almost seems to be a variant
of Ps. 96" (Tate 1990:524; cf. Broyles 1999:381; Magonet 2014:169–170).
In fact, what seems to be the first in the set of *Yhwh malak* psalms, Ps. 93,
appears to introduce by way of some common vocabulary and imagery two
pairs of "twin psalms," namely, 96–97 and 98–99, each set of which is simi-
lar in terms of length (96–97 = 29 cola apiece, 98–99 = 24/25 cola) and
content, for example (Tate 1990:508):[81]

---

[79] These psalms, in which kingship is universally ascribed to Yhwh, are sometimes
mislabeled as "enthronement psalms" (Westermann 1980:109). The problem is that
the primary sense of the verb "enthrone" is to *make* someone king, which clearly
does not apply to God. This title applies better to psalms like 45 where the earthly
Davidic king is at least partly in view. Note also the inclusion of other important
"kingship psalms" in the Psalter, such as Ps. 2 and Ps. 47 (Futato 2007:167).

[80] On the translation of "allusions," Back notes (2014): "Once the allusion is
uncovered, the question of how to convey it—through direct insertion into the text,
through notes, or not at all—remains to be answered and carries with it numerous
considerations. As translator, I must follow the sound patterns of the Hebrew origi-
nal and register their effect, then work to create in the English translation 'a new
music', a music that is true in the English..."

[81] Such strategic psalmic placement seems characteristic of the Psalter, where we
can expect to "look for threads running through pairs or groups of psalms which
point to topics that the editors...wished to emphasize.... The seam psalms of Books
I-III take on added editorial significance [which] further accentuates the weight of
the royal psalms within the book as a whole" (Grant 2005:107). For example, we

96	97	98	99
Sing a new song	Yhwh reigns	Sing a new song	Yhwh reigns
earth called to praise Yhwh	thanksgiving to Yhwh	sea and world called to praise Yhwh	exaltation of Yhwh
Yhwh comes to judge the world	Zion...O Yhwh	Yhwh comes to judge the world	Yhwh in Zion
	holy name		holy hill

As suggested by the preceding chart, Psalms 96 and 98 have a great deal of common vocabulary and even some significant structural similarity;[82] thus, "the similar beginnings and endings of these two psalms are well known: 96:1–2 and 98:1–2; 96:13 and 98:9" (Tate 1990:509). With regard to their common theme, Psalms 96 and 98 both consist of "limit language" which expresses "Israel's extremity of hope" that "the creation will be righted by the powerful action of the Creator," thus asserting in turn "YHWH's sovereignty over all centers of power in the world" (Brueggemann 2005:46).[83] Psalm 98 might even be viewed as the ultimate realization of the hortatory imperative of Psalm 96 (e.g., 96:3 < 98:3)—cf. note 520 above. From another perspective, "Between them, the two psalms cover all of nature, both cultivated [96] and uncultivated [98]" (Magonet 2014:170). Generally speaking then, there may be sufficient textual evidence to conclude that "Pss. 96–99 (possibly introduced by Ps. 93) form a single, coherent liturgical unit [within the Psalter], made up of alternating hymns and 'kingship' psalms" (ibid.:173).[84] This is demonstrably a "coherent sequence, one that celebrates...the implications of YHWH's kingship, for Israel and for

observe "the significant placement of Ps. 2 as part of the introduction to the Psalter" (ibid.:115).

[82] Futato suggests this thematic sequence for sermons based on the Psalter: "The series might begin with a sermon on the inauguration of kingship (Ps. 2), followed by sermons on the confirmation of kingship (Ps. 41), the transference of kingship (Ps. 72), the apparent failure of kingship (Ps. 89), the affirmation of kingship (Ps. 96), and the coming of kingship (Ps. 132)" (Futato 2007:184).

[83] Brueggemann regards Ps. 96:10 (cf. 98:9) to be "the quintessential statement of the gospel in all of Old Testament scripture. This is the ground of Israel's hope" (2005:46). This is because "Israel's rhetoric of doxology...puts the Creator at the culmination of well-being" *(shalôm),* and their hope is that "the world will eventually be righted according to the intention of the Creator" (cf. Ps. 98:1–3) (ibid.). For an overview of different themes relating to God's sovereignty in the "Kingship of Yahweh Psalms," including Ps. 98, see Bullock 2001:191–195.

[84] For example, "whereas both Pss. 96 and 98 begin with the call to 'sing to YHWH a new song!' Pss. 97 and 99 begin with the assertion that 'YHWH rules!' thus providing a set of alternating openings and suggesting a deliberate juxtaposition" (Magonet 2014:161).

the peoples of the world, with righteousness [God] and justice [man] being the principle features" (Magonet 2014:176).

In addition to the many intratextual connections that Psalm 98 has with other psalms, the hymns and royal praises in particular, it also has some important links with the prophets, most notably, Isaiah. For example, one commentator asserts that "Isaiah 52:7–10 is the prophetic counterpart of the psalm [98]" (Mays 1994a:313). Other scholars go further, suggesting that there are some significant correspondences between the wording of Psalm 98 and the lyric passages found in the entire second half of Isaiah (e.g., Delitzsch 1869:97; Goldingay 2008:120). For example, in Psalm 98, verse "1b is to be compared with Is. 59:16 and 63:5; v. 2 rests on Is. 52:10; v. 3 on Is. 63:7; v. 6 is reminiscent of Is. 6:5, and v. 8 appears to have Is. 55:12 in mind" (Leupold 1959:691; cf. Broyles 1999:381).[85] More specifically then, with reference to Psalm 98:3b:

> The second line also makes the same point; it almost exactly corresponds to Isa. 52:10b. The acts are *our* God's acts of deliverance. Yet all earth's extremities saw them. And therefore (Isa. 45:22 adds) all earth's extremities can look to Yhwh for deliverance. (Goldingay 2008:121, original italics)

The reflections of Psalm 98 are more abundant and analogous in Isaiah, the prophet of God's "salvation" which encompasses "the ends of the earth" (Ps. 98:3), than in any of the others. But in the latter too, there are a number of lesser correspondences, for example, the call for "Israel" to "sing" with "joy" to "the LORD ... the King" (יְהוָֹה ... מֶלֶךְ) found in the concluding paean of Zephaniah (3:14–15).

"The New Testament shows an extensive use of music, reflecting the same Hebraic tradition" (M. R. Wilson 1989:309; cf. 1 Cor. 14:26; Eph. 5:19).[86] It is no coincidence then to discover the intertextual threads involving the theme of "salvation" that arise from Psalm 98 extending also to the New Testament, in particular to the so-called Magnificat of Mary,[87] the mother of the promised Messiah. In other words, "the New Testament witnesses saw in Jesus a continuation and climax of these salvific comings" (Mays 1994a:314), namely, those mighty acts of deliverance worked

---

[85] Of course, the direction of intertextuality here is very much open to debate. I would reverse the direction of textual influence—that is, the prophet reflecting the words of the psalmist in his oracles. Goldingay points out a number of other such correspondences (2008:120–123).

[86] Music is a vital aspect of worship in the final book of the Bible too: "In Revelation...we return to the Mosaic theme of deliverance (15:3–4). Here John depicts a heavenly scene where, with harps, the Song of Moses (Exo. 15) and the Song of the Lamb [Rev. 15:3]—a single song—are sung" (M. R. Wilson 1989:309).

[87] The title "Magnificat," meaning 'it glorifies', arises from the Latin Vulgate translation where it occurs as the very first word of Mary's praise song.

by Yahweh on behalf of God-fearers. Thus, "in an echo of verse 3, Mary called her unborn child a marvelous deed in which the LORD 'remembered his mercy to Israel' " (ibid.). Could the "striking parallels between the first part of Psalm 98 and Mary's Magnificat (Luke 1:46–55)...mean that the mother of Jesus had the psalm in mind as she composed her hymn..." (Boice 1996:798)?[88] Of course we cannot know for sure. But the prominent notion of transformation and reversal that Mary expresses (Lk. 1:51–53) is surely implicit in the words of the psalmist (98:1–3) as he sketched his grand vision of Yahweh's saving supremacy in a contemporary world where that outlook must have seemed, humanly speaking from the current Jewish perspective, most unlikely, or even a wishful fantasy (cf. 1 Cor. 1:18–19). The hopeful faith that the Lord would indeed come, sooner or (and) later, to "judge the world in righteousness" (98:9) rested on the solid historical evidence of God's past deliverances of his people (98:1; cf. Lk. 1:49–50).[89]

A similar notion appears to be reflected in the thematic passage of the opening of Paul's epistle to the Romans. Thus, the confidence of Paul's assertion in 1:16–17 is reinforced by the echo of Psalm 98:2–3 in these words, especially the key terms "revealed," "salvation," "justice/righteousness," and "nations" (Keesmaat 2004:142). Furthermore, Psalm 98 is not only a psalm of thanksgiving, it is also "a psalm of reorientation...a psalm sung by those for whom the world has been created anew, by those who have experienced a new reality emerging around their God, in the face of what seemed to be a historical ending" (ibid.). And so this psalm can (should) function similarly for God's people of every age and nation as they await his final deliverance at the end of time. This notion is in fact a key theme of the "new song" (ᾠδὴν καινὴν) of thanksgiving mentioned in Revelation 5:9, which "is the response of the redeemed to God's new redemptive acts in Christ in establishing the New Covenant, even as the older song of Moses (Exodus 15) was the response of the redeemed to God's older acts of redemption, associated with the Exodus and the establishment of the Old Covenant" (Gregg 2013:139). It is a song that none but Christ's saints, the "144,000," know how to sing (Rev. 14:1–3).[90]

---

[88] Boice (1996:798) provides a comparative chart in which these correspondences are documented.

[89] "This psalm suggests a new song, which proclaims YHWH's historical work of redemption for Israel as a persuasive testimonial for the world. YHWH's righteousness is revealed in the redemptive history of Israel. Also, YHWH is projected as the coming judge" (Lama 2013:222).

[90] "Psalm 98 is eschatological. Its eschatological orientation...as well as the way it draws an analogy between the exodus and the return from exile, encouraged the people of God to continue to apply it analogically and to use it to profess their conviction that God reigns. For instance, the early Christians, who knew that Jesus proclaimed the reign of God (see Mark 1:14–15), also saw in Jesus the ultimate embodiment of God's reign. They experienced in Jesus a king/messiah, who lovingly and faithfully enacted justice and

7.5 What is the manner of singing the new song of Psalm 98—from then to now?

The manner of singing Psalm 98 would seem all too obvious, at least in its initial setting, where the second and third strophes clearly specify the quality of extreme joy,[91] accompanied and reinforced by all sorts of instrumentation in a corporate worship environment. The equivalent in today's terms depends on the particular culture, age, and Christian tradition concerned.[92] With regard to musical instruments, for example, in the past many African choirs would have used traditional drums and rhythm shakers; nowadays, however, electronic keyboards and guitars are far more common, and the method or fashion of hymn-singing, depending on the occasion, has also changed to a considerable degree.[93]

With reference to the type of translation required, on the other hand, I trust that the earlier literary-structural analysis would have lent sufficient support to an argument in favor of a corresponding poetic-lyric translation of this psalm, indeed the Psalter as a whole. Whether the vernacular version happens to be relatively more literal or idiomatic in nature is not the issue. The point is that the manner of translation, however it is done (see further below), ought to match as closely as possible the original Hebrew text with respect to communicative function and associated generic style in the host language-culture. This would entail a considerable measure of oral-aural sensitivity, emotive expressiveness, rhetorical impact, aesthetic appeal—plus a certain facility or capacity for being re-cast in an appropriate musical mode.[94] And the choice of a suitable melody

---

righteousness for all people; they experienced his ministry as salvation; and they sang psalm 98 as a song about Jesus" (McCann 1996:1073; cf. 98:3 and Luke 1:54, 68–79). Commenting on the "new song" of Rev. 14:4, Beale notes that it is being "sung again, but on an escalated scale and for the last time" in the Scriptures (1999:736; he provides a good discussion of this passage on pp. 735–736).

[91] "The strength and wisdom and love of a leader is magnified in proportion to the diversity of people he can inspire to follow him in joy" (Piper 2010:223; cf. Ps. 98:3–4)—as opposed to the norm, which may range from abject fear to the desire to curry favor.

[92] "In all cultures the meaning of any given musical performance is dependent on cultural conventions...[which may also] reflect the world view of the culture" (Schrag 1992:49).

[93] Longman well summarizes these musical means and their inspiring impact: "The impressive list of musical instruments reminds us that Psalm 150 was sung; indeed, all the Psalms were sung. The Psalms appeal to more than our intellect. They arouse our emotions and stimulate our imaginations as well as appeal to the will. Music involves our emotions, and we can be certain from the list of instruments that the music would have been loud" (2013:223).

[94] Such musical creativity in translation is superbly demonstrated in a Western mode and instrumental key by the Australian band *Sons of Korah*, who remain remarkably close to the original text in their renditions, including corresponding emotive associations and aesthetic effects. These stylistic issues are emphasized also by today's professional secular translators and critics: "Poetry cannot be

is important too, for "the hymn tunes themselves are suggestive of meaning" (Towner 2003:18).[95]

A number of English hymns have attempted to carry out the preceding purpose—that is, in contrast to the standard translations, which typically provide a rather wooden literal rendering of the original (e.g., ESV) or a rather washed-out common-language version of it (e.g., CEV). The issue of lyric Bible translation will be considered further below. As for some examples of hymnody (or psalmody) based on Psalm 98, we have "New Songs of Celebration Render" by Eric Routley; "Come, Let Us Sing unto the Lord" in the Associate Reformed Psalter of 1930; and undoubtedly the best known of all, "Joy to the World" by Isaac Watts (reproduced in Excursus A) (Boice 1996:796).[96] As far as the English language goes, "there is no better way of proving that Psalm 98 is 'An Exuberant Praise Song' than to indicate that Watt's hymn, which is probably the most joyful and exuberant of all our hymns and Christmas carols, is based on it" (ibid.).

The Psalter has played an important role in the New Testament church from the very beginning of its existence.[97] One of the points that I have tried to make in the present study is that verbal "singing" can also be effected metaphorically in the form of beautiful, heart-striking, oral-aurally attuned poetry. A liturgical instance of this (again, in English) would be the *Book of Common Prayer* of the Anglican-Episcopal Church, in which Psalm 98 is known by its Latin title, *Cantate Domino* (Boice 1996:796). Another early example, this time a conflated version comprised of a number of psalmic praise lines is "Antiphon," which was composed by the 17th century Protestant poet, George Herbert. The

---

translated; it can only be recreated in the new language" (Landers 2001:97, citing Clement Wood). "Any translation should—make that must—be read aloud for sonority. Sound is paramount to poets..." (ibid.:100). "Rhythm and other aspects of sound, such as alliteration, assonance, and rhyme, are central to poetry. Often a translator has to give up exact meaning to preserve a sound component" (Wechsler 1998:131). The latter recommendation is unacceptable where the Scriptures are concerned, but the point is well-taken. "What translating comes down to is listening—listening now to what the poet's voice said, now to one's own voice as it finds what to say. Translation is an art of artisanal rhythms" (ibid.:133, 145).

[95] In a Western (English) setting, the answers to questions such as the following need to be tested, as well as expanded upon with reference to a specific audience group: "Is a tune lyrical, written in a major key and with a quick tempo? Then it will support the theme of thanksgiving. Is the melody quiet and gentle? How reinforcing for a song of trust! Perhaps it has the 4/4 march beat of a band of pilgrims or the minor melancholy and largo tempo appropriate to lament" (Towner 2003:18).

[96] For a brief history of Psalmody in the Christian Church, see Leonard 1997.

[97] For a brief but useful survey, see Petersen's *The Psalms in Christian History* (2015).

following excerpt (from Alter 1985:209) well summarizes Psalm 98's call to praise (but not the reason for it):

> Let all the world in ev'ry corner sing (My God and King).
> The heav'ns are not too high,
> His praise may hither flie:
> The earth is not too low,
> His praises there may grow.
> Let all the world in ev'ry corner sing (My God and King).

Alter's reflections on the importance of communicating, via translation, the conceptual essence of such poetry well, in an emotively and esthetically corresponding manner—in many cases as a new song in the local cultural and religious context—also bear repeating (1985:215, 205, material in brackets added):

> Poetry is significant form—which is to say, its depth and precision of statement, like its beauty, inhere in the elaboration of verbal surface. It is to particularly chosen words in a particular order that the reader [especially hearer!] responds.... [There is an] essential connection between poetic form and meaning that for the most part has been neglected by scholarship [and translators alike!].... Poetry is quintessentially the mode of expression in which the surface is the depth, so that through careful scrutiny of the configurations of the surface—the articulation of the line, the movement from line to poem, the imagery, the arabesque [highly decorative interweaving] of syntax and grammar, the design of the poem as a whole—we come to apprehend more fully the depth of the poem's meaning.... The spiritual, intellectual, and emotional values of the Bible that continue to concern us so urgently are inseparable from the form they are given in the poems.

The prior analysis of Psalm 98 hopefully gives credence to Alter's claims, to which I would fully subscribe.

In any case, we come back once again to the issue of meaning and how it may be reflected in the manner whereby it is communicated—via the linguistic forms of the biblical text. The thesis then is simply this: IF literary (artistic, including phonological, and rhetorical) features are part of the meaning of the original text, THEN they must be dealt with in some way or another in translation. Now this may be done—to a certain extent—within the translated text itself, but that is not always, or even usually possible. The source and target languages differ in manifold ways, and so do the respective cultures that cognitively contextualize them. This means that there is no way for the TL text to accurately—let alone poetically or persuasively—express everything, even an appreciable portion, of the total meaning package that is (was) conveyed, either explicitly or implicitly by the SL text. The inevitable loss and/or distortion in content, as well as in communicative intent, will have to be compensated for in some other way. Most Bible translation agencies have come to that sobering conclusion and have learned to depend on various aspects of the paratext to accomplish this—to provide an sufficient and satisfying means of providing a conceptual frame of reference that will allow the primary target audience to understand and interpret their translation adequately, if admittedly still imperfectly in certain respects.[98] These supplementary aids, such as explanatory footnotes, illustrations, cross-references, section headings, etc., would correspond to the different tools and techniques that are available to assist an artist to pleasantly sing this song, including the use of accompanying musical instruments.

Psalm 98 might seem at first reading to be a relatively easy pericope to translate into another language. However, there are a number of potential problem points that lie just beneath the surface of the text that may well complicate or even confound the interpretation process, especially for those who may not be so familiar with the cognitive environment of the ancient Near Eastern world and biblical background in particular. If not addressed, such difficulties can seriously affect the covert quality of the song that is "sung" in translation—namely, its semantic accuracy. Therefore, they will require either some creative "textual engineering" and/or the utilization of some auxiliary paratextual device. The following is just a summary sample of hermeneutical issues to illustrate the diversity that must first be recognized and then dealt with by this twofold, mutually supportive means of establishing a functionally equivalent rendering of the biblical text. Many of these examples are discussed in Bratcher and Reyburn (1991), along with some advice as to how to handle them in translation:

- terms that manifest a rich psalmic cognitive environment, hence a wide area of meaning in Biblical Hebrew, one that may need to be narrowed to fit the current cotext, e.g., "righteousness" (צְדָקָה) (2), "faithfulness" (אֱמוּנָה) (3);
- similar to the preceding, but also abstract terms, often requiring verbalization and/or an explicitation of the subject/agent or object/patient, e.g., "salvation" (יְשׁוּעָה), "covenant love" (חֶסֶד) (3);
- implicit/ambiguous expressions, needing some clarification, e.g., "our God" (אֱלֹהֵינוּ) (3), "all the earth" (כָּל־הָאָרֶץ) (4), "before the King" (לִפְנֵי ׀ הַמֶּלֶךְ) (6);
- synonymous words, e.g., "shout for joy" (רוע), "cry out in jubilant song" (רנן) (4);

---

[98] On the notion of frames of reference (cognitive > sociocultural, organizational, situational, textual), see Wendland 2008. It is not possible to discuss this notion and its implications further here.

- figures of speech, e.g., "holy arm" (זְרוֹעַ קָדְשׁוֹ) (1), "house of Israel" (בֵית יִשְׂרָאֵל) (3); "let rivers clap hands" (נְהָרוֹת יִמְחֲאוּ־כָף) (8);
- culturally specific terms, e.g., "harp" (כִנּוֹר) (5),[99] "trumpets" (חֲצֹצְרוֹת) (6);
- potentially misleading references (if literalized), e.g., "[ram's] horn" (שׁוֹפָר) (6), "he will judge the world in righteousness" (יִשְׁפֹּט־תֵּבֵל בְּצֶדֶק) (9).

As for some sample solutions, we might list the following: the use of an illustration to reveal the difference between the man-made trumpet and the natural ram's horn in v. 6 (Bratcher and Reyburn 1991:846); a suggested rewording for "all the earth" in v. 4, i.e., "all people every-where" (ibid.); and the foundational wording for an explanatory footnote, such as this in the case of "won the victory" (הוֹשִׁיעָה־לּוֹ): "Some think that **the victory** spoken of in verse 1 is a reference to creation, when Yahweh defeated the powers of chaos and destruction...; or else the word may be generic, referring to all the victories won by Yahweh over Israel's enemies..." (ibid.:844).

7.6 Discovering the appropriate genre for a new song in translation

An earlier period of research (Wendland 1993) led me to conclude that the Chewa lyric poetic genre termed *ndakatulo* would be very appropriate to provide an indigenous model for translating biblical poetry in a functionally equivalent manner.[100] The following discussion based on excerpts from practicing Chewa *alakatuli* poets (i.e., poets who produce *ndakatulo*) summarizes some of the major reasons that led me to this conclusion.[101] It also prepares the way for a trial rendering of Psalm 98:1–3 below to illustrate this powerful vernacular mode of oral expression.

Ndakatulo are like songs which a person composes for himself
having personal meanings. In the case of many ndakatulo,

---

[99] For a summary of the importance of the "harp" *(kinnor)* in psalmic worship, see John Wheeler's "Exploring the World of the Harp" at http://www.harpspectrum. org/historical/wheeler_short.shtml/. (Accessed September 2, 2017).

[100] The following notes may be compared with those given by Finnegan for "lyric poetry," which she defines as "a (relatively) short non-narrative poem that is sung" (1992:13; cf. 13–16 and "oral poetry" 16–28). More detailed instructions regarding "how-to" plan and conduct community-based research with respect to "music in an event" are given in Schrag 2013:91–102. In fact, before attempting to translate the Psalter, one should "learn the music system of the receptor culture [and] enlist the help of an indigenous musical expert" (Schrag 1992:56).

[101] I give a small sample of some published secular *ndakatulo* poems in Excursus F; these have been taken from my fuller collection in Wendland 1993:ch. 3. The translations from the original Chewa text are my own.

> the melodies are unknown, but on reading them, whether silently or aloud, one finds that they embellish the language. (Chadza 1967:5)

In the words quoted above, which come from an introduction to a published collection of *ndakatulo,* we find both the general and the specific qualifying characteristics of this genre of Chewa literature. First of all, *ndakatulo* are "like songs" not because they are always sung, or accompanied by musical instrumentation, since that is only an optional feature pertaining to their performance.[102] Instead, the writer seems to be referring to an implicit (i.e., non-lexicalized) distinction which differentiates literary compositions that are relatively more marked by formal stylistic devices from those that are not—or to state this in familiar, but only approximate, terms: poetry versus prose.

More specifically, then, one of the principal diagnostic properties of *ndakatulo* is their capacity to "embellish the language." This alludes to the rhetorical force and the evocative power of the creative style which distinguishes this type of composition where the so-called poetic (or aesthetic) function of communication is maximized—or, in the more picturesque words of an actual practitioner of the art:[103]

> [Lyric poets] know how to flavor *(kutendera)* their work with words that grab the heart *(mau ogwira mtima),* comparisons *(zifanifani)* that bring pictures of what is being spoken about, and other tools *(zipangizo)* of expertise *(luso).* (Sitima 2001:v)

This is literary form drawing attention to itself, not in competition with the message, but as an added complement to it. The latter is an important qualification, for *ndakatulo* poems do not (at least as far as the Chewa

---

[102] There is a basic similarity which underlies the closely related genres of "lyrics" *(ndakatulo)* and "songs" *(nyimbo)* in Chewa with respect to both the language used and also the cultural setting either tacitly assumed or expressly evoked during performance:

"We can find lyric poems in various types of songs. In the village people sing such songs at funerals, while drinking beer, when on a hunt for game, while herding cattle, when pounding out maize meal, at a wedding, when offering sacrifices, during the initiation of matured girls, while rowing a boat, and when doing all sorts of other tasks. These songs are sung to express sorrow, joy, frustration, apology, thanksgiving, rebuke, and instruction. Sometimes songs are sung to help a person forget about the affliction of work in general." (Mvula 1981:v)

[103] Whether sung or orally recited (chanted), *ndakatulo* poems exhibit the essential musical "principles of proportionality, harmony, simplicity, and complexity" (Sproul 2012:61), the last two obviously being held compositionally in a certain tension or balance—sometimes more, sometimes less of one or the other feature. In any case, "part of the reason that we see [or hear!] something as beautiful is that it conforms to some kind of proportional structure" (ibid.).

tradition is concerned) illustrate the familiar principle: "art (or poetry) for its own sake."[104] On the contrary, the highly personalized and deeply felt message articulated by the poet is another crucial aspect of the genre. To this point, a prominent Malawian writer and critic observes:

> Ndakatulo are like magic, riddles, and certain idioms, which cause a person to think more deeply than he does ordinarily. In ndakatulo we find a rich and profound manner of speaking which is closely connected with wise thinking. (Mvula 1981:vi)

There is an obvious and important connection here with biblical wisdom literature, which is also largely poetic in form.

Ndakatulo poets *(andakatuli)* may be described, in the words of one practitioner, as "people who are thrilled by/with words" *(anthu achimkondwa ndi mau),* for "they love beautifully-sounding words which cause the intention of their mind's reflections to quickly overshadow their readers" (Gwengwe 1967:v). The preceding comments refer to the depth of thoughts and feelings which distinguish such lyric compositions, as well as the artistry and innovativeness of the language in which they are conveyed. The authors are known and recognized as skilled wordsmiths in the language— as "word-carvers" *(osema-mau)* or verbal "artists" *(amisiri),* poets who create "ripe lyrics" *(ndakatulo zakupsa),* "digging them out from deep within their necks" *(amafukulira zakukhosi kwake)* (Sitima 2001:1). Their reputation is both enhanced and preserved by another, more recent innovation in the history of African literary development, namely, literacy and the composition of verbal art forms in writing for publication as well as for musical recording and dramatic stage productions. In fact, for some speakers the meaning of the term *ndakatulo* itself has been narrowed to refer specifically to *written* forms of Chewa poetry.

In terms of function, *ndakatulo* are an artistic as well as an emphatic means of externalizing one's emotions, attitudes, opinions, and ideas as they concern virtually any deeply felt situation and circumstance in life. In serving this preeminent expressive purpose, the Chewa lyrics tend to cover a broader range of secular subjects than what we normally find in the biblical literature and are thus applicable to a greater number of ordinary occasions and human situations. However, *ndakatulo* are not composed and performed simply to pass the time of day (though they may indeed also do that) or to give random expression to one's feelings or poetic inclinations. Most of these lyrics manifest an important overt or implicit didactic

---

[104] The same dynamic pertains to the Psalter: "The psalmist's delight in the suppleness and serendipities of poetic form is not a distraction from the spiritual seriousness of the poems but his chief means of realizing his spiritual vision" (Alter 1985:136).

intent—appropriately offering instruction and advice as it applies to every-day experience in central Africa. As one poet defines the genre:

> A lyric poem is an artistic and valuable lesson, a profound skill that concerns especially the behavior of people in all of their diverse experiences. (Gwengwe 1967:v)

Similarly, another artist describes these poems as "the foundation of teaching [appropriate for] human conduct" (Mvula 1981:vii). There may thus be a related ideological, or religious, motivation that is realized at times, especially where ancient, pre-Western customs, mores, and traditions are concerned:

> In his lyric, [the poet] also shows us the faith of our ancestors. Accordingly, he advises the young to go on believing in the clan spirits...[and] he warns them not to act foolishly by despising the words of the elders... (ibid.)

Closely related to the expressive and didactic functions is a certain cathartic, or representative, purpose whereby the poet speaks, or sings, on behalf of Every-(wo)man—to help people work through and give lyric voice to the highs as well as the lows of life:

> When reading these lyrics, you find that the authors touch upon the life of each one of us. They tell about love, envy, death, education, creation, tradition, and similar things (ibid.).

Malunga puts the case in rather more poetic terms as follows (1990:iv):

> As we all know, a person's life does not always follow a straight path, nor is it all pure joy—but often it is a path of mud and stumps. Likewise in [these] lyrics...we find tears, shouts, ululations, laughter, sarcasm, and many other expressions of human experience.

The way in which one personally feels about or deals with such vital emotions and varied life-experiences should not be forgotten or internalized. The *ndakatulo* lyric, whether self-composed or simply appropriated from oral tradition, is an effective means of etching the event upon one's memory for ready recall—and to call it to the attention of the society at large. Thus the performance—recitation, reading, or singing—of poetry effects a mnemonic function for many people. As Mvula explains (1981:vi):

> Perhaps a person has a story that he does not want to be forgotten. In order to preserve that story, he takes its main points and composes a song or a lyric poem. Into such a song he places words appropriate for reaching one's heart with his purpose, yet it must not be too transparent. Since a lyric-song is short and sweet to hear, it is able to quickly spread far and wide.

In a similar vein, Chadza observes (1970:101):

> To store up a lot of things in one's heart alone is difficult
> because there will always be something that is forgotten. For
> this reason, many lyrics help to call certain events to mind
> since people are able to sing them or speak them as if they
> were singing (i e, recited with a rhythmic beat).

At times a certain degree of poetic evasion or indirection is necessary due to a predominant affective or imperative intention. In other words, the poet employs the lyric as an artistic, hence implicit, means of directing or modifying the thinking and behavior of some person or group. What is it, Malunga asks in this regard, that enables these lyrics "to cause people who offend others to cry [due to shame] but to cause people who love peace and justice to rejoice [for being publicly praised]" (1990:13)? Rather than to overtly attack, warn, or rebuke an offender or violator of some sort, a culturally more fitting and effective way of dealing with interpersonal problems is to express one's criticism or censure indirectly, and more palatably, in the words of an appropriate *ndakatulo,* which is—or at least was—typically sung aloud during ordinary community activities. Mvula cites some examples (1981:vi):

> Whether in the village or in town, you find a person either
> resenting or admiring the actions of a certain individual.
> At times then that person [the former] is at a loss for words
> [lit., "dries up in the mouth"] and is unable to speak directly
> about the matter. So what he or she does is to compose a song
> and sing it, perhaps while they are drinking beer together or
> pounding out maize meal. When the offender hears that song
> he [she] either gets the point himself or his friends give him a
> hand and tell him that it means such and such. Just think, how
> often does it happen that women complain about the good or
> bad behavior of their companions at the common pounding
> ground? How often is it that a young man complains to his
> father-in-law by singing a song as together they carve grain
> mortars, cut bamboo strips, or sew sleeping mats? Lyric songs
> are an excellent way of talking about what is really on one's
> mind [lit., "about the things (sticking) in one's neck"].

However, one must not forget the fundamental aesthetic motivation that underlies all of these communicative functions. They are patently poetic compositions and consequently there is always a major emphasis upon the particular artistic form in which the verbal message is cast:

> To lyricize lyrics and to correctly perceive their purpose is
> a very desirable skill...[for] ndakatulo are pleasurable and
> uplifting experiences.... [They] are most attractive to one's
> heart. (Gwengwe 1967:v)

Mvula adds (1981:vii):
> [The poets] try to decorate their writings with idioms as
> well as ideophones. These provide the "spice" for the lyrics
> of our language.

In short, *ndakatulo* poems demonstrate a vital concern for the ears (and other senses) as well as for the hearts and minds of their target constituency. This sensory and emotive inclination does not mean that stylistic mastery is an end in itself or of ultimate concern. Underlying this verbal virtuosity and the playful, often idiosyncratic usages, there is the recognition that all of these poems in one way or another serve a much broader and deeper purpose. In a moving lyric eulogy to a fellow *mlakatuli* poet, one of the pioneers in litericizing the originally oral genre (i.e., the well-known Malawian writer E. J. Chadza), Malunga (1990:41) exclaims:

Mudachikweza pamatanda akukhupuka Chichewa.
You elevated and enriched the Chichewa language.
Mudachikokomeza chikhalidwe chathu.
You embellished our [common] experience!

So even "When they hear his 'psalms' *[masalimo]* so thick with rebuke... his words are like a soothing breeze, in hearts beaten down with affliction" (Malunga 1990:45). Stirring lyrics that either laud or lament the vicissitudes and vagaries of human life in artful, attractive, accented language—that's what the *ndakatulo* genre is all about.

So what are the distinctive poetic devices which by their artful combination serve to characterize the literary process of *kulakatula ndakatulo* "to lyricize lyrics" in Chewa? A survey of the extant published literature reveals a number of typical stylistic markers, which may be organized according to ten general categories summarized as follows: balanced lineation,[105] vivid imagery, phonesthetic appeal, syntactic transposition, concept specification, formal condensation, textual expansion, verbal intensification, direct speech, and discourse design. These generic features were determined on the

---

[105] This refers to a sort of varied sequential parallelism as manifested in line-forms that tend to correspond with respect to syllable counts and breath-groups (brief utterance spans). This is the dominant and most obvious feature of *ndakatulo* poetry—and probably all poetry as well as related song forms (Schrag 2013:148). With respect to parallelism, Finnegan observes, "Many forms of oral poetry make use to some degree of the same principle of parallelism in consecutive stanzas, a literary device which can build up successive layers of insight and meaning around the central theme and manifest a unity as well as an opportunity for development in the poem....The principal of parallelism is often used in music, where it gives scope for unity *and* for variation" (1992:105–106). A good example of such incremental structural and thematic development based on the oratorical principle of parallelism is Ps. 98.

basis of a detailed study of several published booklets of Chewa *ndakatulo*,[106] including a selective corpus of twenty-six individual lyric poems. In view of the sacred text being composed, a somewhat limited number of these artful attributes are employed in the vernacular version used for illustration in the next section.[107]

I have gone into some detail in the preceding survey of *ndakatulo* poems to reveal the great communicative possibilities of this dynamic oratorical art form.[108] They embrace a wide range of topics and themes that encompass the full gamut of human thoughts, attitudes, experiences, and emotions as encountered every day in central Africa. These are expressed in a correspondingly broad assortment of compositional types, each of which in its own way represents a skillful integration of content and form to convey in a highly dramatic style the intended message of the poet for a specific social setting and (inter)personal situation.[109] Thus, we see the potential at least for utilizing the rich poetic structure and style of a Bantu language as a vehicle for transmitting the Word of God through a manifestly literary mode of translation (Wendland 2004).

---

[106] It would appear that a similar set of features could be used to characterize the genre of written lyric poetry in Tonga (another SE Bantu language), known as *kweema*. For example, as described by Shandele, "The lyricist *(weema)* can also employ a fitting word to touch *(-guma)* people. But really it is not the word itself that touches (someone), but the message and how it has been arranged— or the words, or the ideas. When speaking, one does not have a special choice of words *(masalesale)*. But in lyricizing *(kweema)*, that is the essential thing. Often lyricizing is like telling riddles *(maambilambali)*" (2001:v). My ten categories would seem to include all of the specific devices that Sitima then lists as being "tools found in *ndakatulo* lyrics" *(zipangizo zopezeka mndakatulo)*, namely, metaphor, proverbs, similes, symbolism, hyperbole, onomatopoeia, biblical allusion, suspense, euphemism, metre, mood, personification, alliteration, repetition, satire, surface/deep meaning, prefixes, exclamation, and ideophone (following his own listing, 2001:18–19).

[107] For a general survey of some the chief features of African oral poetry, see Finnegan 1992:88–133.

[108] An "oratorical" composition is a literary text (and all that this entails in artistic terms) which is prepared specifically for an overt, oral-aural presentation (or indeed, a public performance). Oratory is meant to be uttered (recited, chanted, sung) aloud—and correspondingly heard, not silently read to oneself from a page of print.

[109] Sitima (2001:3–10) lists the following six "works" *(ntchito)*, or functions, of *ndakatulo* poems: to praise and worship God (note: this was his first function), to teach or reprove someone, to manifest the good or bad character of someone, to express desire and love, to complain or lament about what has happened or will happen, and to describe, request, invite, or report something that has attracted the poet's attention.

7.7 Singing a new song in Chewa and English— samples of lyric translation

What must be said...is that the Psalms are poems,
and poems intended to be sung: not doctrinal treatises, nor even sermons.[110]

It is interesting to observe that a psalm-singing tradition has always been strong among God's people, including the Jewish liturgy and regular usage in the New Testament church—right up until the 20th century.[111] As Brito summarizes:[112]

> Many of us grew up in theological backgrounds where the psalms were known, but not sung. These theological backgrounds are anomalies throughout the history of the Church. E.F. Harrison observed that "Psalmody was a part of the synagogue service that naturally passed over into the life of the church." Calvin Stapert speaks of the fathers' "enthusiastic promotion of psalm-singing" which he says, "reached an unprecedented peak in the fourth century." James McKinnon speaks of "an unprecedented wave of enthusiasm" for the psalms in the second half of the fourth century. Hughes Oliphint Old argued that Calvin appealed to the church historians (e.g. Eusebius, Socrates, Sozomen) as well as the church fathers (e.g. Augustine, Basil, Chrysostom) for the singing of psalms. While the Reformers did not advocate the exclusive singing of Psalms they did express "a partiality for Psalms and hymns drawn from Scripture."

---

[110] Lewis 1958:2.

[111] Some, like the noted Church historian Phillip Schaff, go so far as to assert that "So far as we are able to gather from our sources, nothing, except the Psalms and the New Testament hymns (such as the 'Gloria in Excelsis', the 'Magnificat', the 'Nunc Dimittis', etc.), was as a rule sung in public worship before the fourth century." (Cited by Jeffrey A. Stivason, "Sing Psalms or Hymns," http://www. freechurch.org/index.php/scotland/resources-article/sing_psalms_or_hymns/. Accessed August 8, 2013 [website no longer active.])

[112] Uri Brito, "10 Reasons Why We Should Sing the Psalms," Christian Post Guest Contributor, July 15, 2013, http://www.christianpost.com/news/10-reasons-why-we-should-sing-the-psalms-100031/. Accessed September 2, 2017. The first and most important of Brito's ten reasons is this: "Psalm-singing is an explicit biblical command (Ps. 27:6). The Scriptures encourage us to sing 'psalms and hymns and spiritual songs, with thankfulness in your hearts to God' (Col. 3:16). To have the word of Christ dwell in you richly means to invest in the rich beauty of the Psalter. How can we sing what we do not know? Is there a better way to internalize the word [than] to sing it?" For a study of Col. 3:16 in relation to Ps. 33 and with special reference to singing, see Geiger 2012.

The Reformer Martin Luther urged that Psalms be sung by congregations so that "the Word of God may be among the people also in the form of music." By the end of the 19th century, however, most hymnals produced had limited psalms to a couple of well-known pieces like Old One-Hundredth. Beyond that, scriptural references had all but disappeared.[113]

The question then is: why do so many translations of the Psalter in other languages—the large as well as the small, old versions as well as new—sound so much like prose, so far from poetry, let alone music? And this, despite the fact that "Hebrew poetry was providentially designed to employ parallels of idea rather than of sound, as in English conventional poetry, simplifying its translation to other languages" (Bond 2012:71).[114] One answer to this question might be as follows:

In many ways, translating poetry is like playing music. First, you must be able to read the score to understand the original composition. But if the poet's instrument is language, then each poem is designed specifically for that instrument. Thus converting a poem into another language is like trying to play a piano sonata on a trombone. The melody of the poem may be recognizable in any language, but its sound will be completely different once it's translated. It takes a fine and discerning ear. Often it takes another poet. (Kelly and Zetzsche 2012:106)

"Playing music" indeed—that is an excellent analogy for translating poetry. And why is this so? Because of the emphasis on sound as a vehicle of communicating the essential message of an artistic composition. The

---

[113] Leach adds: "As Christian worship in the West evolved, from the first century's joining the synagogue service of the word with the Lord's Supper, to the elaborate medieval Mass, psalms were the key to its song.... One popular way was responsorial—a soloist singing the psalm text in sections, the people responding to each section with a refrain. The soloist's words would be the biblical text, translated into Latin from Hebrew. The music would be chant—a way to assign notes to syllables regardless of how many or few syllables the line of text to be sung contained" (2001).

[114] In fact, as was shown in the earlier analysis of Psalm 98, this assertion is not completely true: parallels of sound do play a role in Hebrew poetry, though not as prominently perhaps as in other poetic traditions, such as "conventional" English lyrics. Bond goes on to suggest some of the reasons for the demise of poetry in the modern, "image-driven" Western world, which is "postconservative, postmodern, post-Christian, postbiblical, and even postpoetry"—the latter having become a "marginal art form" (2012:66). "Anesthetized as our culture is by amusement technology, our sorrows and joys have become so benumbed, so diluted by virtual distractions, we feel little or no need for such outdated things as poetry...especially high-register poetic words" (ibid.).

sounds of each poetic/musical piece are unique and contribute a great deal to its overall impact and appeal. The same is true for the religious poetry of the Bible, whether this happens to be the totally lyric Song of Songs, the liturgical Psalter, or the pastoral prophetic oracles. "Much of the meaning intended to be communicated by the Psalmist is contained in the form itself" (Schrag 1992:54–55). The Hebrew phonology certainly contributes to the meaning of any pericope or portion of one.[115] But how can this literary effect be duplicated in another language? First, the importance of this dimension of the original text must be clearly recognized and correctly analyzed as part of the exegetical process. This same concern must then be factored into the translators' working procedures as they attempt to re-create the biblical text in their language.[116] In the end, "often [I would say, always] it takes another *(gifted)* poet!" (Kelly and Zetzsche 2012:106)[117]—ideally, one also with musical gifts or sensibilities. The following are some additional insightful comments regarding this challenge

---

[115] In this sense, there is a certain loss in translation when the original Hebrew text is transferred via translation into another language (contra Wright 2013b:2)—namely, certain phonological special effects and emotive accents that simply defy translation and even functional substitution.

[116] The experienced translator-teacher Grossman eloquently describes the process of re-creation in translation as follows: "Our purpose is to re-create as far as possible...and we do this by analogy—that is, by finding comparable, not identical, characteristics, vagaries, quirks, and stylistic peculiarities in the second language....The unique factor in the experience of translators is that we are not only listeners to the text, hearing the author's voice in the mind's ear, but speakers of a second text—the translated work—who repeat what we have heard, though in another language, a language with its own literary tradition, its own cultural accretions, its own lexicon and syntax, its own historical experience, all of which must be treated with as much respect, esteem, and appreciation as we bring to the language of the original writer.... Translators are like actors who speak the lines as the author would if the author could speak English [French, German, Chewa, etc.]" (2010:10–11).

[117] On the other hand, "Where poetry translation is concerned, sometimes two, three, or ten heads are truly better than one. Even if not all those heads can understand the source language, knowing the language of poetry—and having diverse viewpoints involved in the process—is sometimes even more important" (Kelly and Zetzsche 2012:106). In one sense this is true; fixing a number of discerning eyes—and ears (especially in the case of poetry)!—on the task can certainly help to improve and polish up the final poetic product. However, I think that the adage "too many cooks can spoil..." is also true. One creative "head" is needed to compose the initial draft and to act as the final arbiter concerning all proposed revisions from her/his colleagues on the project. The longer the poetic composition, the more important it is to have a single unifying perspective (and audition) on how the text should be expressed. The initial poet-composer need not be an expert in the source language either, for example, Biblical Hebrew in the case of one of the psalms. I would rather have an expert in the target language-literature (including

by Rachel Tzvia Back, a literary critic and practicing translator of Modern Hebrew (2014):

> I offer the following as an articulation of how I see the verse translator's responsibilities and aspirations: the translator of poetry must strive toward loyalty to the original and must also exercise a significant degree of creative freedom in order to convey in translation the poem *as a whole* in the best fashion. The translator of poetry must immerse herself fully in the lexical, linguistic, cultural and musical world of each poem she's translating, and must also, at a certain point, separate herself from that world in order to hear the translated text in its own literary and sound contexts. The translated poem is beholden to and an extension of the original poetic text, just as the translated poem must also stand on its own as a successful poetic entity.... As translator, I must attend religiously to the formal, lexical and syntactic choices [the author] makes (from poem length, length of individual lines, stanzaic structure, to gendered discourses and addresses, inverted syntax, etc.), and strive to be faithful to these elements in my translation choices. However, the issue of "faithfulness" to the original is significantly complicated by the fact that the practical "kinship" between English and Hebrew is a distant one indeed, and the transfer from a highly inflected, gendered and syntactically more flexible language like Hebrew to a weakly inflected, ungendered and syntactically rigid language like English results in countless instances where deviations from the original are not only unavoidable but are in fact essential.

Based on the descriptive background given the earlier sections above, what would the new song of Psalm 98 sound like in Chewa?[118] The first strophe has been rendered below in the modified style of a *ndakatulo* lyric (accompanied by a relatively literal back-translation) to illustrate this vibrant poetic technique.[119] However, this is still a more conservative, colo-

---

poetic and musical forms!) compose the first draft, which may then be corrected or revised with reference to the original text by one or more SL specialists.

[118] "When selecting and writing [and translating!] songs [for prayer, meditation, worship, etc.], we should ask, Is it Psalm-like?" (Bond 2012:78, words in brackets added). The qualifier "Psalm-like" must be further specified with respect to the functionally appropriate musical, religious, and worship tradition of the language and culture for whom the Psalter is being translated.

[119] I prepared the initial draft, which was then corrected in the light of comments from several MT Chewa-speaking students in my seminary Psalms exegesis class.

metric composition,[120] one that would befit a Scripture text intended for liturgical use in formal corporate worship. Thus, certain more dynamic poetic features (e.g., graphic imagery, ideophones, colloquial exclamations) were not utilized lest the translation sound too common or even profane. The Chewa sample is followed by five textually corresponding, but stylistically diverse English poetic versions for the sake of comparison (verses 1–3 only).[121] The aim is to express the biblical text in a euphonious, rhythmic, more literary and lyrically-equivalent manner—one that is amenable to public recitation, oration, chanting, or simply oral elocution in an appropriately reverent mode:[122]

Inu anthu onse, muimbireni pamodzi,[a]	1. All you people, sing to him together,
imbirani Chauta nyimbo yatsopanoyi,	sing to the LORD this new song,
popeza iye anatichitira zodabwitsadi!	because he did for us some most amazing things!
Zoonadi, dzanja lake lamphamvu ndi	Most truly, his right hand and
mkono wake woyera zatipambanitsa.	his holy arm have made us victorious.
Ee, zochita zake zonse zatipulumutsa!	Yea, all his works have delivered us!
Chipulumutsochi Chauta wachionetsa,	2. This deliverance the LORD has shown us,
wavumbulutsanso chilungamo chake—	he has also revealed his justice—

[120] According to the German translator Martin Buber, a colometric translation is one "that gives the text its natural division into lines of meaning as these are determined by the laws of human breathing and human speech, with each line constituting a rhythmic unit" (from "A Translation of the Bible" [1927], cited in Weissbort and Eysteinsson 2006:320).

[121] Ndoga calls attention to the potential problem in translating the expression "YHWH reigns" in Pss. 97:1 and 99:1 (cf. "the King YHWH" in 98:6). "When Scripture uses past, present, and future with regard to God, does the choice of tense have any particular theological meaning?" (2014:153). An equally important question for translators to determine is this: What meaning will most members of our TL audience derive from our particular rendition of this expression? The new Chewa translation translates *Chauta ndiye mfumu* 'the LORD he is king', which is thus not distinguished from 'the King Yahweh'. Perhaps it would be better to maintain the distinction thus: *Chauta amalamulira* 'the LORD is ruling' [continuous tense], or *Chauta ndiye wolamulira* 'the LORD is the one who rules'.

[122] This would be an example of a "literary functional equivalence" *(LiFE)* translation (Wendland 2004:245, 369; cf. Wilt 2005a, 2005b; Wilt's English *LiFE* version of Ps. 98 is reproduced in Excursus C).

izitu waziulula pamaso pa anthu onse.	these things he has disclosed before all people.
Iye sanaiwale konse chipangano chija,	3. He has not forgotten his agreement at all,
chogona pa chikondi chosasinthika.	the one resting upon his unchangeable love.
Wakhala wokhulupirikabe kwa iwo,	He has remained faithful to them,
ndiye kwa anthu ake onse Aisraeli.	that is, to all his people Israel.
Amitundu akumathero apansipano	The peoples at the extremities of the here below
aonadi kuti Mulungu wathu, inde,	have truly seen that our God, yes,
wapulumutsa zedi ife anthu ake!	he has surely delivered us his people!

[a] The Chewa verb *–imba* 'sing' is a relatively close functional equivalent of the Hebrew *z-m-r*. Often musical instruments are used in accompaniment, even drums. One can also 'sing' bells, stories, as well as judicial cases!

I might note here also the importance of the unjustified lineal display of the preceding translation—that is, featuring complete, meaningful utterances, one per line, without breaks. This makes it much easier to read the text rhythmically, especially aloud in public.[123] Such a format is much different from that normally found in published Scriptures, for example, the old Chewa Bible (1922), the first verse of which is closely reproduced below (accompanied by a literal translation), including its style of punctuation and small font—the product of a standard double column of justified print. One might also detect the relative difficulty of this more literalistic rendition, as roughly suggested by the parallel English text:

1 Myimbireni Yehova nyimbo	1 Sing to him, Jehovah, a song
yatsopano;	novel;
Popeza anacita zodabwitsa:	For he did amazing things:
Dzanja lace lamanja, mkono wace	His right hand, his arm
woyera, zinamcitira cipulumu tso.	holy, worked for him salvation.[a]

[a]*In other words, God's own doings delivered him!*

---

[123] "If in oral reading a passage ebbs and flows smoothly, avoids abrupt stops between words and phrases where possible, and provides a sense of continuity, it is rhythmically excellent" (Ryken 2009:154). In the case of a musical version, rhythm would include a pattern of regular (timed) weak and strong beats, or accents, to accompany the basic melody line.

Much more adaptation to the new lyric version above would of course
be needed when composing a musical performance version of this psalm—
that is, if one were to render it as a genuine, naturally-sounding hymn for
local congregational worship.[124] Thus, as Schrag suggests (1992:55–56):

> Though in all cases attention must be paid to both meaning
> and form in translation, those genres whose primary content
> is dynamic may be translated with a great deal more free-
> dom than those whose primary content is propositional....
> For it is the form which creates the desired emotion, sense
> of immediacy, or mnemonic dynamic.[125]

One would need to insert, for example, additional repetition and more
instances of textual relocation, demonstrative marking, line-end rhyme, con-
densation (or implicitization), perhaps also an ideophone,[126] interjection,
nonsense syllable, or two.[127] The following is how the first verse (only) of

---

[124] According to Wikipedia: "Translation of sung texts is generally much more restrictive
than translation of poetry, because in the former there is little or no freedom to choose
between a versified translation and a translation that dispenses with verse structure.
One might modify or omit rhyme in a singing translation, but the assignment of syllables
to specific notes in the original musical setting places great challenges on the translator.
There is the option in prose sung texts, less so in verse, of adding or deleting a syllable
here and there by subdividing or combining notes, respectively, but even with prose the
process is almost like strict verse translation because of the need to stick as closely as
possible to the original prosody of the sung melodic line.
  "Other considerations in writing a singing translation include repetition of
words and phrases, the placement of rests and/or punctuation, the quality of vow-
els sung on high notes, and rhythmic features of the vocal line that may be more
natural to the original language than to the target language. A sung translation
may be considerably or completely different from the original, thus resulting in a
contrafactum" (https://en.wikipedia.org/wiki/Translation/. Accessed September 2,
2017).

[125] However, I don't think that I would go so far as to put "the propositional content
in secondary focus" (Schrag 1992:56) and allow this to "be less strictly adhered to"
(ibid.:60) (or adopt this as a translation principle). Rather, poetic-musical form and
textual meaning must be given equal attention—and where a choice must be made
between the two, propositional content must prevail, especially where key biblical
terms or theological concepts are concerned.

[126] Ideophones are linguistically marked words (phonologically, morpho-
logically, and in syntactic usage) that convey a diversity of sensory imagery
through iconic cognitive mappings of conjoined form and meaning (Dinga-
manse 2012:654, 657–659). They are the ultimate exemplars of orality in
utterance.

[127] The aim is to create a vernacular text having an attractive articulative rhythm.
As Grossman observes: "I think that almost every poem uses rhythmic stress-
es and their effects to create a powerful, frequently subliminal esthetic pull
between the tension of anticipation or expectation and its satisfaction or release.

Psalm 98 might sound then if transposed to form the initial stanza of a typical Chewa hymn (note that such songs are composed in a much more redundant style, necessitating many more vernacular words compared with the original biblical text):

Anthu inu, Chauta muimbireni-ye.	You people, the LORD sing to him.
Nyimbo yatsopanoyi timuimbire.	This new song, let us sing to him.
Zamphamvu zake zaonekadi ee!	His mighty deeds are truly seen, yes!
Chipulumutso chake chiri mbee!	His salvation is visible most clearly!
Zodabwitsa anatichitira ifeee.	Amazing things he's done for us.
Zatipulumutsatu zochita zake!	They've surely saved us, his works!
Zatilanditsa, zatilanditsa tere	They've delivered us, they've delivered us so
Timuimbire M'lungu wathu ife!	Let's sing for our God, let's do!

Turning to some English examples,[128] below we first have the initial strophe of Psalm 98 (vv. 1–3) as lyrically rendered in the "POET" version of the Psalter, composed by Brenda Boerger (2009):[129]

It often seems that this in particular is what people mean when they refer to the music of a verse" (2010:96–97). It is such evocative verbal music that I have endeavored to instill within this initial verse of Psalm 98. See Excursus C for a popular Chewa poetic hymn version of Psalm 98, which is sung according to an indigenous melody.

[128] For a historical survey of translating the Psalter in English—from metrical psalmody to modern hymnody—see Morgan 2014:571–582 (cf. also Hawkins 2014:99–113).

[129] Dr. Boerger comments on her studied poetic translation technique: "A major aim of *POET Psalms* is to convey Hebrew poetry by using verse forms suited to English, together with devices such as rhyme, meter, sonics, and imagery. The expected result is scriptures which can be easily memorized or set to music. This is important because it allows the reader to internalize the Word of God.... *POET* isn't striving for poetic masterpieces per se, but seeks poetry which appeals to the general reader while simultaneously enhancing the semantic content of a psalm and its comprehensibility.... A counterweight to the goal of expressing the psalms poetically in English, is the balancing goal of preserving and drawing attention to some important Hebrew language poetic devices, in hopes that English readers might gain an appreciation of them artistically.... Therefore, an attempt was made to find the English poetic environment which would best capture the Hebrew poetic text, its patterns and devices, and the mood or genre of the psalm" (2009:9–10). The *POET Psalms* well illustrate what it means to "sing a new song to the LORD"—lyrically—in the English language.

Let's sing this new song to Yahweh,
For the marvels he displays:
With sacred power and authority
Victory comes his way.
He showed that he does what's right,
When he saved us by his might.
He didn't hide his love for his people—
Loyal to the Israelite.
The ends of the earth have been shown
Yahweh battles for his own.

Eugene H. Peterson introduces his well-known translation of the Psalter (in *The Message*), by observing that "most Christians for most of the Christian centuries have learned to pray by praying the Psalms" (1994:5). Here then is his colloquial rendition of the opening strophe of Psalm 94 (ibid.:136):[130]

Sing to Yahweh a brand new song.
He's made a world of wonders!
He rolled up his sleeves,
He set things right.
Yahweh made history with salvation,
He showed the world what he could do.
He remembered to love us, a bonus
To his dear family, Israel—indefatigable love.

The Voice is a relatively new Scripture translation in English.[131] It claims to retain "the unique literary perspective of the human writers" (2009:v):

---

[130] Dr. Peterson summarizes his aim with this version of the Psalms as follows: "In my pastoral work of teaching people to pray, I started paraphrasing the Psalms into the rhythms and idiom of contemporary English. I wanted to provide men and women access to the immense range and the terrific energies of prayer in the kind of language that is most immediate to them, which also happens to be the language in which these psalm prayers were first written and expressed by David and his successors" (1994:6). However, I beg to differ with Peterson with regard to his literary assessment that "the Psalms in Hebrew are earthy and rough; they are not genteel" (ibid.). On the contrary, my studies would seem to show that most psalms manifest a high degree of literary polish and sophistication. Of course, the Hebrew language may sound rough to English ears, and the laments (e.g., Pss. 5–6) may indeed express a bitter, mournful tone, in keeping with their theme and life-situation. However, I would venture to say that the thanksgiving psalms (e.g., Pss. 30, 34, 44) and songs like Psalm 98 surely sound sweetly in the original to those who know and have come to appreciate the Hebrew language and its literature.

[131] The *Voice of Psalms*, produced by the Ecclesia Bible Society (2009). This version "uniquely represents collaboration among scholars, pastors, writers, musicians, poets, and other artists" (2009:v). Indeed, quite a cast of translation composers!

The heart of the project is retelling the story of the Bible
in a form as fluid as modern literary works yet remaining
painstakingly true to the original manuscripts...to create an
English rendering that, while of great artistic value, is care-
fully aligned with the original texts.

To what extent has this vision been successfully translated into text—
specifically a version that lends itself to an oral-aural proclamation? The
following sample, again the first three verses of Psalm 98, should provide
some indication (ibid.:171):[132]

Compose a new song, and sing it to the Eternal One
   because of the unbelievable things He has done;
He has won the victory
   with *the skill of* His right hand and *strength* of His holy arm.
The Eternal One has made it clear that he saves,
   and He has shown the nations that He does what is right.
He has been true to His promises; *fresh in His mind* is His
unfailing love for all of Israel.
Even the ends of the earth have witnessed how our God saves.

Next, I have already had occasion to cite the well-known biblical liter-
ary critic Robert Alter. But Alter is a scholar who also practices what he
preaches...in this case, with respect to his own literary translation and com-
mentary on the Psalter (2007). In contrast to the three preceding transla-
tions, Alter aims for a more literal type of lyricism in his renditions. As he
explains (ibid.:xxxi):

What I have aimed at in this translation—inevitably, with im-
perfect success—is to represent Psalms in a kind of English
verse that is readable as poetry yet sounds something like the
Hebrew—emulating its rhythms whenever feasible, reproduc-
ing many of the effects of its expressive poetic syntax, seeking
equivalents for the combination of homespun directness and
archaizing in the original, hewing to the lexical concreteness of
the Hebrew, and making more palatable the force of parallelism
that is at the heart of biblical poetry. The translation is also on
the whole quite literal...in the conviction that the literal sense
has a distinctive poetic force and that it is often possible to pre-
serve it in workable literary English.

---

[132] "**Italic type** indicates words not directly tied to a dynamic translation of the
original language...meant to help the reader better understand the text without
having to stop and read footnotes or a study guide" (2009:v, original boldface). It
seems a bit strange that a version entitled "The Voice" makes no reference to the
hearers of the text.

The main problem in trying to emulate the Hebrew linguistic forms in this way is that such efforts are generally appreciated only by the person who happens to know a bit of Biblical Hebrew to begin with! But Alter is also correctly concerned with conception and how to bring contemporary readers and hearers back to a more original worldview in their understanding of essential biblical vocabulary. Thus, commenting on one of the key terms of Psalm 98, the verb יָשַׁע and its cognate noun יְשׁוּעָה, Alter has this to say (ibid.:xxxiii–xxxiv):

> *Hoshi'a* means to get somebody out of a tight fix, to rescue him. When the tight fix involves enemies on the battlefield, *yeshu'a* can mean "victory," and *hoshi'a* "to make victorious;" more commonly, both the noun and the verb indicate "rescue." It will no doubt take some getting used to for some readers to feel comfortable with "the God of my rescue" instead of "the God of my salvation," but that is precisely the sort of readjustment of mind-set that this translation aims to effect.

In any case, readers can come to their own conclusion with regard to the success of Alter's mission in translation by evaluating his version of Psalm 98:1–3 below in comparison to those given above (2007:344–345).

> Sing to the LORD a new song,
>   For wonders He has done.
> His right hand gave Him victory,
>   and His holy arm.
> The LORD made known His victory,
>   before the nations' eyes He revealed His bounty.[133]
> He recalled His kindness and His faithfulness
>   to the house of Israel.
> All the ends of the earth have seen
>   the victory of our God.[134]

Finally, a rather dated but still impressive rhymed version, *The Psalms in Verse* in King James English (1995:237–238), which may be closely compared to the preceding rendering by Alter:

---

[133] Alter comments that although *tsedaqah* frequently means "righteousness," "it also often has the sense in poetry of 'bounty' or 'beneficent act'" (2007:344).

[134] Alter's version may be compared with that of the ESV given earlier; here is v. 3 again: "He has remembered his steadfast love and faithfulness / to the house of Israel. All the ends of the earth have seen / the salvation of our God." Many would question, among other things, Ryken's claims that an "essentially literal" translation like the ESV exhibits "language as beautiful and sophisticated as the original itself possesses" and "the stylistic range of the original" (2009:191).

> O sing a new song to the Lord,
>   for wonders he hath done:
> His right hand and his holy arm
>   him victory hath won.
> The Lord God his salvation
>   hath caused to be known;
> his justice in the heathen's sight
>   He openly hath shown.

As always, when assessing a particular translation of the Scriptures, it is necessary to keep several important factors in mind as these relate to the version's particular job description, or brief, and its associate principal communicative purpose (or *Skopos*) (Wendland 2004:25–27). Stated as three fundamental diagnostic questions:

a. **For whom** is this translation intended (the primary audience group)?
b. **In which** socio-religious **setting** will it be chiefly used?
c. **What** is the **medium** of transmission that will convey the text?

The answers to these and related queries will serve to guide translators (as well as project organizers, managers, reviewers, and ethnomusicologists) in their efforts to clothe the biblical text in the most appropriate and relevant lyric-stylistic forms.[135] Indeed, the particular genre, style, and mood of the psalm, if that is being rendered, will have to be sensitively matched to the text in order to produce a creative adaptation suitable for vibrant *musical* communication in a context of public—or private—worship.[136] In addition, it may be helpful to keep in mind "two communication principles [that] God uses with song" (King 2001:13, original italics):

---

[135] In the case of musical Scripture translation, specific skills will probably need to be both discovered and developed among the translators: "Ethnodoxology is an application of ethnomusicology, ethnic arts studies, worship studies, missiology, and related disciplines. Those in this field study local musical traditions and work with local musicians and churches to adapt and develop locally created musical forms for Christian worship. Examples of such work include engaging a local praise singer in translating and singing Mary's Magnificat [Wedekind 1975], developing local hymns, leading people in creating localized forms of liturgy, sharing examples of starting points for people interested in utilizing local arts but not knowing where to start" (https://en.wikipedia.org/wiki/Ethnodoxology/. Accessed September 2, 2017).

[136] Towner's study offers some interesting insights regarding the harmonious marriage of original text, translation and music. All too often, he concludes, we must "recognize that the canonical Psalter and the hymnic psalter frequently do not quite convey the same message" (2003:34).

a. "When it comes to song [as for any type of Scripture text], *God wants to be understood....* That means we must use songs that help us to understand what it is that He is saying. Songs should use the language that speaks to us [i.e., the TL community of faith]. They should also use the musical sounds that we know and respond to....
b. "When it comes to song, *God is receptor-oriented....* God, in fact, is the one who enabled peoples from around the world to create their own different musical styles, so why would He want you to sing in someone else's musical style?... [God] communes with us through the music we know and love."

Another principle, often assumed to be a negative, is this: No translation ever reproduces the full communicative value of its source text—there is always some loss in terms of form or meaning. And yet, assuming that the translation does not claim to be the original and always defers in ultimate reference and authority to it, there might be another, more optimistic perspective that we might adopt in the case of excellent TL renditions, as put forth by the translator Rachel Tzvia Back (2014):

But that which is lost is hardly the last word on the translation project (contrary to oft-quoted axioms on the matter). For whatever is lost in the transfer, other attributes and elements are gained. Indeed, the art and act of translating poetry is, finally, an art and act of transformation; as [Walter] Benjamin states, there is "a renewal of something living – the original undergoes a change." Through that renewal, the original gains a new life it might not have had otherwise – a presence in the world that is "...the same – different – the same attributes, / different yet the same as before."

Thus, every meaningful translation of Scripture, especially one that is melodic if not musical (singable) in nature, contributes to that grand chorus of tongues that will one day glorify the King in joyful unison around his heavenly throne (Ps. 98 > Rev. 7).

"Poetry itself is about the impossible. All arts are about doing the impossible. That's their attraction" (Kelly and Zetzsche 2012:107). And poetry coupled with a musical mode of expression is a doubly challenging art form to master. If that is true in the case of secular creations, as referred to in the preceding quote, then what about religious literary artistry? An impossible mode of expression for an equally impossible message? So how is it possible for fallible human beings to communicate the words and ideas of an infallible God? But he gave us his Word to do just that—in terms of form as well as content—as recorded in the sacred Scriptures. However, he would not have given his disciples this assignment (Mt. 28:19) if it were impossible to carry out. Furthermore, we know that "with God's help, everything is possible" (Mk. 10:27)—whether personal salvation itself, or personally communicating the essential Good News about it.[137] That brings all Bible translators into this work-related frame of reference, including their "impossible" (humanly-speaking) task, as it has been, and is being, carried out throughout the ages and in all of the world's many language-cultures.

7.8 Conclusion: Why a lyric, musical translation is an ideal goal

> In Catherine [of Siena]'s prayers...her theology *becomes doxology*. Namely, what Catherine professed to be *true* about God became in her prayers—and arguably in her life—an expression of *praise* to God. It struck me as a beautiful notion—what we *know of* God being something that moves us to *sing to* God. But *shouldn't all theology naturally lead us to doxology?* Throughout Christian story and verse we find lives touched by God's goodness, moved by God's mercy, transformed by God's mighty presence. In these souls we find a profound correlation between profession and praise. This was certainly true of the young peasant girl who was used by God to bring into the world the child who would be named Jesus and called "God with us." In the Gospel of Luke we witness the thoughts of Mary actually erupting into song. In the midst of the uncertainty that must have been running through her mind, she nonetheless praises God for the things she knows to be true, for the promises that have touched her life, and the very character of the one to whom she sings *[Luke 1:46–55, which is clearly influenced by the Psalter]*.... Mary's theology is intertwined in her doxology: God is a God who has acted in history and is present today.[138]

In a sense, the challenge posed in the title of this section is really a sub-point of a more fundamental question: Why "sing to the LORD a new song" (שִׁירוּ לַיהוָה ׀ שִׁיר חָדָשׁ)? And the answer is the same as that of the psalmist: "For he has done marvelous things" (כִּי־נִפְלָאוֹת עָשָׂה) (Ps. 98:1a)—all of which somehow anticipate and activate "the salvation

---

[137] Of course, we must not forget the instructive inspiration of the Holy Spirit in this entire process of translating the Scriptures that he had originally guided human authors to compose (John 14:26, 16:13).

[138] Jill Carattini, Theology As Doxology, online: http://www.rzim.org/a-slice-of-infinity/theology-as-doxology/. Accessed September 2, 2017.

of our God" (יְשׁוּעַת אֱלֹהֵינוּ)! (98:3b). Martin Luther suggested four reasons for singing the Psalms: to follow the example of God's people in the Scriptures, including "kings and prophets;" to thereby become part of that "community of worshiping saints;" to strengthen our faith as needed in any of life's situations; and to allow the music of the Psalter to give emotive expression to our prayer, praise, and thanksgiving to God (Körting 2014:60–62).[139] Therefore, it is appropriate that we do so in the fullest way possible.[140] Artistically composed music and song are the human instruments best suited to serve this panegyric purpose. Matthew Jacoby states the case well:

> The fact that the psalms were written as songs should serve to underline the nature of their purpose. Music is the language of the heart, and it was for this language that the psalms were written. They were written not just to tell us *about* God but to draw us into an encounter *with* God.... The psalms [are] windows into the experiences of people— experiences that exemplify the life of faith from an inside perspective.[141]

Why, then, are the Psalms so lyrical and musical in nature? To be sure, there are many possible answers to this question, from religious reasons (e.g., the Psalter's intended role as "the songbook of the saints"—praise in particular)[142] to more practical purposes, such as was

[139] "The poetic form (with its inherent linkage with music) expresses an immediacy before God via the text which is at root not critical and so is destroyed by critical [analytical] distance"—the Psalms are "poems which make intimate speaking with [God] possible" (Brock 2014:208).

[140] And such fullness of song includes the amount of time devoted to praising the Lord with "new songs"—as the well-organized Hebrew worship practice teaches us (cf. 1 Chr. 9:33).

[141] Jacoby 2013:13, 15. Dr. Matthew Jacoby is an Australian teacher-pastor and leader of the Psalms project band known as the *Sons of Korah*.

[142] Indeed, it is important to note that psalms were intentionally composed to be rhythmically recited and musically sung: "Most, if not all, of the psalms were originally composed to be sung in temple worship, and through the centuries they have continued to be sung in church and synagogue" (Wenham 2012b:13). The traditional Hebrew designation of the Psalter as the "Book of Praises" *(sêper têhillîm)* is attested in the Dead Sea Scrolls, dating back to the later first century BC (Hutchinson 2005:85). In fact, "among the Dead Sea Scrolls, manuscripts of the Psalms are more frequent than any other type, attesting their widespread use among Jews in New Testament times" (Wenham 2012b:15). This practice is reflected in a number of NT passages, notably those of Christ's passion week (e.g., Mk. 11:9; Mt. 26:30) as well as in a number of Paul's exhortations (e.g., Col. 3:16; cf. 1 Cor. 14:26; Eph. 5:19). Already by the onset of "the fourth century the memorization of the Psalms by many Christians and their habitual use as songs in worship by all Christians about whom we know were matters of long-standing tradition" (Holladay 1996:165).

noted earlier: the unifying use of the Psalter in corporate worship,[143] the liturgy in particular:[144]

> The expressive power of music is attested by the way it seems to have such immediate and direct access to our emotions. In a corporate context, moreover, music can draw people together in unified expression. The use of music and song is a wonderful way for a congregation of people to declare something of one accord. Music also holds our attention and enables us to reflect on something [thus expressing the inexpressible—about the Divine] in a way that nothing else can. (Jacoby 2013:171; words in brackets added)

As Richard Leach, a psalmic composer himself (Selah Music), puts it: "I think this three-fold identity is what gives the psalms their special power: Not only do they speak calm belief, desperate need and exuberant joy to God,[145] they do it in words that are also God's word to us. And they do it with the special power of poetry and song" (2001). Arguably then, the Psalms are the perfect mode for articulating what Brueggemann, following Ricoeur, terms "limit expressions," that is, "words and phrases that push one to the extremity of human experience"—speech that "ruptures the tradition and permits a glimpse of

---

[143] Though it is true to say that certain psalms of praise enunciate an individual voice, they regularly incorporate a communal component, e.g., Ps. 144:15. One may justifiably conclude then that "the most appropriate locus of praise is a congregational setting, praise being typically conducted simultaneously on both the horizontal and vertical axes" (Hutchinson 2005:88)—that is, involving the worshipers with one another and the corporate congregation with their God, and indeed, theology in the fullest sense:

"Saint Augustine once called the Psalter 'the Old Testament in microcosm'. All of the riches of the Scriptures filled in the mine of praise, prophecy, and poetry that is the Psalter. These riches, however, need to be brought to the light of day so they might adorn the life of the Christian" (Heath A. Thomas, front-page endorsement in Wells and Van Neste 2012:i).

[144] As C. S. Lewis astutely observes: "Regular church-goers are not surprised by the service—indeed, they know a good deal of it by rote; but it is a language apart. Epic diction, Christmas fare, and the liturgy are all examples of ritual—that is, of something set deliberately apart from daily usage, but wholly familiar within its own sphere" (1942:20–21). The Psalter provides a rich corpus of texts for this purpose.

[145] Singing a "new song" to the LORD, the Great Savior-King, was normally associated with joyful emotions (cf. Ps. 96:1–2, 11–12; Ps. 97:1, 8, 12; Ps. 98:1–3, 4–6). The common connection involving joy in the worship life of Israel is thoroughly documented in Megahan 2013 (e.g., 194–195, 199–200). "All of the lexemes [relating to 'joy'] occur in contexts of Praise-Worship denoting the emotion of the event...all of the collocations of music, singing and shouting, for example, co-occur with all the lexemes denoting JOY..." (ibid.:157).

another world through the cracks" (2005:33).[146] Such ready-made, but ever-realistic expressions encompass the whole gamut of life's events, especially as encountered by God's people. Thus, from their deepest laments (e.g., 88) to their most exuberant hymns (e.g., 150), they were born to be "singers" (שָׁרִים) to and for the Lord (Ps. 87:7). And why? The answer is verbally simple but profound in implication: Because YHWH, our "King" is "so great and praiseworthy" (גָּדוֹל יְהוָה וּמְהֻלָּל מְאֹד) (Ps. 145:3; cf. vv. 1–2; Ps. 18:3)![147] His divine attributes and activities are, therefore, most worthy to be lauded in psalmic song, as in the case of Psalm 98—and many more (e.g., Pss. 145–149). In short, it is most natural to sing the Psalms—how better to articulate them in order to accomplish their intended purpose?[148]

Besides this obvious panegyric purpose and their immediate didactic value, including "some very basic theology about the relationship between God and his people" (Wenham 2012b:23) and "sorting out our worldview" (Wright 2013a:79),[149] there are a number of less frequently cited spiritual

---

[146] "Limit *expression,* says Ricoeur, gives access to limit *experience,* to those dimensions of lived reality that defy our habitual settlements. We experience this daily, but unless we have rhetoric for it [perhaps also lyric/music too?], we cannot fully experience our experience.... The Psalter is the most tried, tested, and true collage of limit expression in the history of humanity" (Brueggemann 2005:34, words in brackets added). Of course, we are here reflecting on the Psalter from our modern, Western perspective. While it may be true to say that psalmic language illustrates "limit expressions" semantically and pragmatically in their original setting, it is not so evident that it does so formally or stylistically in terms of expected Hebrew discourse patterns.

[147] To this vital point, popular Christian singer and songwriter Matt Redman comments: "This mixture of *revering* Him and *celebrating* Him. You find it all over Scripture. Psalm 95: 'Come and *sing joy* to the Lord' (v.1), and in the same psalm, 'Come, let us *bow down* and worship the Lord' (v.6).... You find it in Psalm 25:14: 'The *friendship* of the Lord is reserved for those who *fear* him'.... One of my favorites— back to the idea of being facedown—is in Leviticus 9:24. It says, 'They *shouted for joy* and they *fell facedown*'.... In all these big [musical/worship] gatherings today there are always *shouts of joy* going on, but how much *face to the ground* worship do we see?... Kneeling down—I love to see that in churches. To me that's like the mystery of the universe, these two elements: the *immanence* and *transcendence* of God" (interview in DuRant 2004, added italics).

[148] "The book of Psalms is a song book. Try reading through a book of your favorite songs without singing them and see how dry they are, like cornflakes without milk" (Stutler 2013).

[149] "When we continually pray and sing the Psalms, our worldview will actually reconfigure according to their values, theology, and modes of expression" (Wright 2013a:79). For example: "Praise of God and God's judgment is the ultimate in trust, for it places us squarely in need of salvation"—but "Do we today celebrate God's judgment? Do we dance and sing when we think of what we now call 'judgment day'?" (deClaissé-Walford et al. 2014:728).

benefits to be derived from learning and singing the Psalms.[150] These involve functions such as focused emotive (including deep personal, psychological) expression,[151] communicative facility (i.e., as a ready vehicle of shared expression),[152] their unifying ethos,[153] confessional faith declaration,[154] lasting memorial significance,[155] and transformative character.[156] All of these

---

[150] These may be more specifically categorized in terms of speech acts with reference to a given Psalm text (cf. Wendland 2004:214–218; 2011:146–147), for example: "Save me, O God!" (Ps. 69:1, directive); "I will guard my ways..." (Ps. 39:1, commissive). Thus, "singing them (the Psalms) commits us in attitudes, speech, and actions" (Wenham 2012b:25), that is, to the specific communicative functions that are expressed in the biblical text—often communally uttered by the entire congregation of believers.

[151] "All the griefs, sorrows, fears, misgivings, hopes, cares, anxieties; in short, all the disquieting emotions with which the minds of men are wont to be agitated, the Holy Spirit hath here pictured" (Calvin 1840:vi). "The psalms endorse the notion that the affections have a role to play in the everyday living of the faithful" (Collins 2012:28). In a musical mode of expression, "Language itself is transcended and its delights and power are intensified, and at the same time those who join in are bound together more strongly. So singing is a model of the way praise can take up ordinary life and transpose it to a higher level..." (Ford and Hardy 2005:19).

[152] The Psalms are there, for example, to give worshipful expression to a Christian worldview: "Might not a fully Christian response to insights from biology, chemistry, physics, and astronomy consist not only of the analysis of data, but also a response of wonder (Psalms 8; 19; 33; 104; 139)?" (Witvliet 2012:15). Thus, a biblical response to all the amazing discoveries of science is not, "Is there a God?"—but rather, "How can there *not* be one?"—a God who not only creates, but who also rules over everything! (Ps. 98:7–9).

[153] "Psalmody and classic hymnody serve to unite us with the vast throng of worshippers throughout the ages. The psalms are God-given sung praise that transcends all barriers—ones of race, gender, ethnicity, and geography" (Bond 2012:78). "Churches sing together because it helps to see that our hearts' praises, confessions, and resolutions are shared. We're not alone" (Leeman 2013:18).

[154] "In some ways singing a psalm or hymn is like taking an oath: we are committing ourselves in a binding way to a particular set of beliefs and embracing a lifestyle" (Wenham 2012b:14). The essential truths of Scripture are implicitly inculcated when uttering the Psalms. For example, "Luther scholars think that it was his study of the Psalms that led him to his understanding of justification by faith" (Wenham 2012b:16; cf. Batka 2014:229).

[155] "A psalm, a song, enables us to remember things that we would not remember otherwise. Putting music to something gives it life in a way that prose just does not do" (M. Goetz, in Wells and Van Neste 2012:210).

[156] Wright highlights this transformative feature in his recent book. For example: "All music and poetry regularly have the capacity to transcend ordinary time. They call to the depths of memory and imagination, bringing the past forward into the present (memory) and envisioning the future as well (imagination).... All singers discover that to use the human body as a musical instrument is physically, emotionally, and mentally transformative in a way that nothing else quite is.... To sing

religious motives (and others)[157] coincide in what Gordon Wenham argues is the overall ethical import of the Psalter. For this reason, the Psalms (along with other "wisdom" texts, such as the passages of Proverbs) were no doubt also specifically composed for memorization in order to transmit funda-mental religious and moral values to the pious people of God, young and old alike, both during formal worship and privately in the home (Wenham 2012a:42).[158] Thus, "if you pray ethically, you commit yourself to a path of action" (ibid.:57).

> When you pray a psalm, you are describing the actions you will take and what you will avoid. It is more like taking an oath or making a vow...praying the psalms involves the worshipper in many commissive speech acts: the psalms as prayers are really a series of vows. This is what sets them apart from other biblical texts with an ethical dimension. (Wenham 2012b:27–28)[159]

In short, when "singing the psalms, one is actively committing oneself to following the God-approved life" (Wenham 2012b:35).

---

prayerfully, then, is to invite a physical transformation as well as to stand at the borderlands of time and space. Thus, the mere form of the Psalms—poems meant to be sung—already points powerfully in the direction that...the poems themselves are determined to lead us" (Wright 2013b:27–28).

[157] " 'The psalms,' John Donne once said, are 'the manna of the church.' They provide spiritual nurture throughout the wilderness of life for the people of God, expressing the full range of human hope, despair, confession, praise, and yearning for the living God" (Timothy George, front-page testimonial in Wells and Van Neste 2012:ii). "These sacred hymns express all modes of holy feeling; they are fit both for childhood and old age: they furnish maxims for the entrance of life, and serve as watchwords at the gates of death" (Spurgeon 1882, cited in Wells 2012:205).

[158] "The Psalter is a deliberately organized anthology designed for memorization" (Wenham 2012b:14). The Psalms, both individually, in smaller groupings or collec-tions, and as a whole, feature many literary devices "that may be viewed as aids to memory. Most obvious are the acrostic psalms: working through the alphabet verse by verse would certainly assist memorization. Then there are the verbal linkages between one psalm and the next, grouping of similar themed psalms, and the use of parallelism, alliteration, assonance, chiasms, and rhyme" (ibid.:20). The impli-cations of this pedagogical fact seem to be largely lost even in churches where the Psalms are still regularly sung; how many members other than perhaps the congre-gational choir make this effort?

[159] Commissives, in which the speaker(s) commits himself (themselves) to some definite course of action (e.g., promise, pledge of loyalty, vow), generally alternate in the psalms with expressives, in which speakers articulate their heartfelt feelings and attitudes towards either the addressee or others (e.g., thank, praise, confess, apologize, protest, accuse). We have a commissive combined with an expressive declaration in the following: "I will sing to the LORD all my life; I will sing praise to my God as long as I live!" (Ps. 104:33).

When sung (recited, chanted, reflected upon, etc.) then on a daily basis, especially during corporate worship, as the ancient church father, Ambrose, bishop of Milan, so aptly put it, the Psalter becomes a "gymnasium for the soul."[160] According to Gerhard von Rad (Gerstenberger 2014:36), "Israel's hymnic praise was considered continually necessary for the upkeep of wholesome and blessed life" under the benevolent covenantal governance of Yahweh, their divine Savior, King, and Judge (Ps. 98:3, 6, 9).

In these diverse ways, this select collection of songs and prayers serve to complement, indeed to verbalize a vibrant, communal response to, the Hebrew Bible's set of historical narratives, Torah teachings, ancestral genealogies, ceremonial laws, prophetic sermons, etc. to constitute a vital religious repository for the faithful. The liturgical reiteration of the Psalms in public worship would etch their words into the individual and collective consciousness to act as a verbal memorial of the faith of Israel. The people were (we are) to remember the many saving deeds prompted by Yahweh's own "remembering" (זכר—Ps. 98:3), that is, his repeated decision to act on their behalf. And so, the Psalms were (and are) able to play a formative and sustaining role in the nation's thought, as well as in everyday life, for "as a reader memorizes a text, he becomes *textualized;* that is, he embodies the work that he has committed to memory" (ibid.:53).[161] The biblical text thus acts as an ever-ready guidebook, as it were, lighting up one's daily pathway in life (Ps. 119:105).[162] This textual role relates to one of the *perceived* differences between Psalm verses and other types of Scripture: The primary direction of communication in the case of the latter is from God to man, whereas with the Psalms, this interpersonal interactive trajectory is reversed: "They are placed on worshippers' lips as texts to be prayed—texts that worshippers are challenged to embrace as their own" (Witvliet 2012:7). On the other hand, from another perspective, one might say that in the Psalms God takes the words of humans to him and makes them also his words to humanity (cf. Wolsterstorff 1995:51–54).

---

[160] "Just as a gymnasium creates space for physical exercises that tone muscles and extend flexibility, so too the psalms—when we actually use them and when they subsequently transform us—function to tone and sculpt our souls" (Witvliet 2012:10).

[161] To this point, Luther adds: "It would be well if every Christian used [the Psalter] so diligently and became so well acquainted with it as to know it by heart, word for word, and constantly to have it on his tongue when called on to say or do something" (cited in Plass 1959:1000).

[162] "Music activates the powers of memory and thus endures not only through the day and night but also into times of crisis and trial as well as celebration and thanksgiving. Texts set to music often come to life when they are needed most, seemingly pressed into service by life's circumstances" (Stallman 2008:488).

Several recent commentators on lyric and music in the Hebrew Bible offer some additional insights regarding the particular mode of the Psalter's composition:

> Psalmic poetry through its very lyricism may even inspire us to new ways of seeing and imagining, even to new ways of thinking.... Lyric thinking...is most assuredly a different kind of thinking, a thinking otherwise. (Dobbs-Allsopp 2006:379, cited in Strawn 2008:444)

The manner of thinking may be different—more reflective, insightful, inspired, etc.—but its principal divine object would (should) be the same, namely, the LORD who "has done marvelous things" (Ps. 98:1), both for humankind in general and his people in particular.[163] "Psalm poetry is the God-ordained means of keeping every generation enthralled with the surpassing splendor of biblical truth" (Bond 2012:78). Along these same lines, Stallman observes (2008:488–489, references in brackets added):

> Music is often noted for its emotional effect, but the use of music in praise also tends to focus attention away from oneself to the nature and acts of God, thus functioning to transport one's thoughts to another realm. The act of ("singling") lends artistic expression to truth and thus has a cognitive function that promotes personal appreciation, approval, assent and adoration.... The lyrical music of the Psalter is thus not only a fitting way for the faithful to respond to the Lord's creative and redemptive acts but also an integrated part of the perpetual hymn of praise generated from the entirety of heaven and earth [cf. Rev. 7:9–10, Ps. 98:3].[164]

Indeed, "worship is the highest-register activity a human being can perform, and the content and tone of the psalms wonderfully regulate [and rejuvenate!] our attitude and posture in that worship" (Bond 2012:78, words in brackets added).

---

[163] "Luther said [that] music is theology's handmaiden, leading us to glorify our Lord more fully" (Sproul 2012:62). "I place music next to theology and give it the highest praise" (Luther, cited in Plass 1959:980). The same argument might be made for well-composed lyric-musical translations of the Psalter. "I would gladly see all the arts, especially music, in the service of Him who has given and created them" (Luther, cited in Plass 1959:980).

[164] The frequent psalmic conjunction of notions of creation, music, and praise for the Creator (e.g., Pss. 92:1–3, 95:1–5, 96:1–5, 98, and 100) suggests a further thought—namely, a cognitive linkage between "the image of God" (Gen. 1:26–27) and the creative artistic-aesthetic impulse, capability, and sensitivity in mankind. "Singing is one activity in which God's Word grabs hold of our hearts and aligns our emotions and affections with His" (Leeman 2013:18).

So why translate poetically—and further, musically if possible? The answer would seem to be most obvious and impelling from what has already been said above. An analysis of the form, content, and function of the Hebrew text literally demands such a translation—a rhetorically as well as lyrically powered text:

> The psalms employ *rhetoric* to achieve their end of shaping the worshipper's inner life.... *Singing* is a composition that takes it much further into the heart than merely reading it aloud. And the psalms, as hymns, are to be *sung* (Collins 2012:28–29).

If the original was composed poetically, rhetorically, memorially, even melodically, and the TL has the oratorical resources to match that in terms of both form and function, then why not?[165] How can translators avoid the implication of the panegyric imperative that runs like an intensive chorus throughout Psalm 98? The second strophe should serve as a sufficient reminder of this, as it rings out in our very ears, calling out for worshipful, liturgical, translatorial action[166] (from the NIV, slightly modified):

> *Shout for joy to the LORD, all the earth!*
> *Burst into jubilant song with music!*
> *Make music to the LORD with the harp—*
>   *yes, with the harp and the sound of singing!*
>   *With trumpets and the blast of the ram's horn—*
> *shout with joy before the LORD, the King!*

Alter adds some perceptive comments with reference to both the second and third strophes (2007:345):

> There is a concordance between the human orchestra—in all likelihood, an actual orchestra accompanying the singing of

---

[165] If it is indeed true that "the Hebrew Bible was created and transmitted as 'art song' (compare Psalm 119:54)" (John Wheeler, in review of *The Music of the Bible Revealed,* 1991. https://www.amazon.com/Music-Bible-Revealed-Deciphering-Millenary/dp/094103710X. Accessed September 2, 2017. The "art" of Bible translation seems to have been "lost" in English (David Daniell, cited in Goodwin 2013:15). Accordingly, English versions do not serve as good models for translators who wish to render the Psalms (at least) in an artistically fashioned, poetic manner in their language.

[166] "The translatorial action model proposed by Holz-Mänttäri...takes up concepts from communication theory and action theory with the aim, amongst others, of providing a model and guidelines applicable to a wide range of translation situations. Translatorial action views translation as purpose-driven, outcome-oriented human interaction and focuses on the process of translation as message-transmitter compounds...involving intercultural transfer" (Munday 2008:77). In the case of the Scriptures and the Psalter in particular, such interaction is not only human in nature and object-oriented, but it also has a crucial divine component that reverses the direction of communicative action (e.g., "The LORD has made his salvation known..."—Ps. 98:2a).

this psalm—with its lutes and rams' horns, and the orchestra of nature, both groups providing a grand fanfare for God the king. The thundering of the sea is a percussion section, joined by the clapping hands of the rivers, then the chorus of the mountains. This simple, compact poem...is resonantly expressive: the Israelites chanting the poem's words of exaltation, to the accompaniment of musical instruments, are invited to imagine their musical rite as part of a cosmic performance.

Indeed, as the preceding words themselves would imply, such vivid textual appeals (and their theological implications) literally call out for a corresponding vibrant oral-aural approach to the task, for how can one render such joyous words of praise without actually hearing them?[167] And then—the next essential step: testing the translation aloud, and preferably, as suggested above, in the form of a musical version to match what must have been the case in the original biblical setting of communicative worship.[168] Of course, the initial text might need to be adjusted somewhat in terms of form (not meaning!) to fit an appropriate melody in the musical tradition of the culture concerned, but that normally does not prove to be too difficult of a modification to make (e.g., by means of repeated words, lines, or just extra syllables and sounds)—if a composer familiar with these lyric conventions is consulted.[169]

---

[167] There is also an important spiritual dimension that is active here in such vocal transmission; as C. S. Lewis observed, when praising God one's "inner health [is] made audible" (1958:81).

[168] "It is essential to have the help of a local musician even if the help of a [foreign] ethnomusicologist is available. The semantic and emotional content of the Psalm to be composed should be discussed with [ideally, initiated by] the indigenous composer/musician" (Schrag 1992:59, words in brackets added).

There are of course a number of creative ways in which the Psalms may be vocally performed, most of which date back to early church liturgical practice: "One thing that we know about the use of psalmody in synagogues in the early Christian centuries is that psalms were often sung in alternation between a soloist and the congregation. As this practice was used later in Christian worship, it came to be known as *responsorial* psalmody. Though this was possibly the most common method of delivery, there were other ways of singing the psalms in Jewish liturgy. In one type, which we call *antiphonal* psalmody, alternate verses were sung in turn by two choruses. Another type was characterized by *through-composed* settings of Scripture passages: The texts of the psalm verses were recited or sung from beginning to end without repetition or alternation..." (Montgomery 2000:1). Montgomery gives a helpful summary of "the psalms in chant" (ibid.:2–3). Amzallag (2014) finds many psalms being characterized by one or more of three distinct types of "complex antiphony" as evidenced by patterns of textual symmetry.

[169] Russ Stutler (2013) overviews a number of ways in which the Psalms may be "sung" in English: "In order to sing the Psalms, one has to either edit the words to fit tunes, or create tunes to fit the words. Metrical Psalms are of the first type,

Over and above the issue of fidelity to the linguistic and literary charac-
ter of the original text,[170] which ought to be a priority for every Bible transla-
tor, there is also the matter of what the translation theorist Christiane Nord
terms "loyalty": "In this context, loyalty means that the target text purpose
should be compatible with the original author's intentions" (1997:125). A
professional translator adds: "Intrinsic to the concept of a translator's fidel-
ity to the effect and impact of the original is making the work as close to the
first writer's intention as possible. A good translator's devotion to that goal
is unwavering" (Grossman 2010:31). How then are such intentions to be
ascertained? There may be certain conventional intentions that are as-
sociated with particular literary text types, such as the Psalms—or more
specifically, the royal hymns of the Psalter. "In other cases, the analysis

---

words edited to fit tunes.... Of the three ways to sing Psalms, metrical Psalms are
probably the most familiar to our ears from a musical standpoint....

"The other way to sing Psalms is to keep the words in their original form, and
create tunes to fit the words. Of course, this could result in 150 different tunes with
complex and unpredictable melodies. Fortunately there is another option: chant-
ing. Chanting is a combination of speaking and singing. This is the key to singing
text without rearranging it; most of the words are spoken in a monotone on the
same note, and a small part of the text is sung to specific notes and rhythms, giv-
ing the chant its musical quality. One very old form of chanting is called plainsong,
which has been around since the early centuries of the Christian Church, if not
earlier.... Plainsong is especially suited to individual prayer since there are no har-
monies or instrumental accompaniment, and the range of notes is relatively narrow
and within the range of the average person. You can determine how high or low the
chant will be sung, so no chant is ever outside your singing range....

"Another way of singing Psalms which conforms the music to the text is called
Anglican Chant. This form of chant came from plainsong, and was created to allow
Anglican church choirs to chant the Psalms in four part harmony. It first appeared
around the same time as the first Book of Common Prayer in the 16th century, so
apparently it was intended to be used with the psalter (produced by Miles Cover-
dale) in that prayer book. Plainsong at the time was in Latin while Anglican Chant
was in English."

In the second part of his compact illustrated study, Stulter provides a helpful
review of a number of musical psalters that are currently available for group con-
gregational use or personal oral articulated devotion and meditation.

Here is yet another option—not a "translation" now but a freer "adaptation":
" 'Psalm-based hymns' is what I call a hymn based on a psalm in the way a hymn
may be based on any scripture passage, not directly paraphrasing it but using its
story, images and ideas to proclaim the gospel or to pray. The distinction between
'metrical paraphrase' and 'psalm-based' hymn is blurry, but it can be useful" (Leach
2001).

[170] We are thus dealing with "translation" per se and not "adaptation," which may
involve "deviations from the meaning of the source text," or a "replacement text,"
which presents a functional alternative that may bear little if any semantic relation
to the original text (Low 2013:229).

of extratextual factors such as author, time, place, or medium may shed some light on what may have been the sender's intentions" (ibid.:125–126). However, such a contextual method of investigation is very difficult in the case of most psalms, especially those like Psalm 98 that lack a superscription or any personal information within it. There remains then the application of a methodology that was carried out earlier, where "a thorough analysis of the intratextual function markers helps the translator to find out about the communicative intentions that may have guided the author" (ibid.:126) so that corresponding functions may be activated also in the translation—hopefully with similar effects on the designated audience in terms of informative, expressive, emotive, esthetic, imperative, etc. value.[171] All this would be part and parcel of what we might term the "ethics of translation," which corresponds to a prior ethics of reading (interpreting) the biblical text (cf. Wenham 2012a).[172]

In conclusion, I might underscore the preceding dual ethical imperative by citing the exhortation of a renowned secular translator of (Spanish) literature (Grossman 2010:7, words in brackets added):

> The most fundamental description of what translators do is that we write—or perhaps rewrite—in language B a work of literature originally composed in language A, hoping that the readers [listeners!] of the second language—I mean of course readers of the translation—will perceive the text, emotionally and artistically, in a manner that parallels and

---

[171] The issue of loyalty to original intention also concerns the theological, ethical, and ecclesiastical purpose of the Psalter itself within the community of faith. How prominent are the Psalms in the various forms of public worship today—whether on Sunday or any other day? "Perhaps it is time we organize psalm-praying and psalm-performing communities...and reclaim the art of praying and singing the psalms daily and in corporate worship. Perhaps it is time we actually believe those psalms, and perhaps it is time that, grounded in their great words, we all begin again to perform these psalms, not only in our singing but in our living" (Joiner 2012:166). "Time was," Spurgeon (1882) said, "when the psalms were not only rehearsed in all the churches from day to day, but they were so universally sung that the common people knew them, even if they did not know the letters in which they were written" (Wells 2012:204). On the validity of authorial intention as a hermeneutical principle in literature, see Hirsch 1967.

[172] Wenham adds: "The significance of the Psalms for biblical ethics has been surprisingly overlooked. Their unique character as powerful shapers of individual virtues and social attitudes is largely ignored in books on Old Testament ethics. It is my belief that reciting the psalms, and especially singing them, has profoundly influenced both Jewish and Christian theology and ethics" (2012b:13, added italics).

corresponds to the esthetic experience of the first readers.[173] This is the translator's grand ambition. Good translations approach that purpose. Bad translations never leave the starting line.[174]

Now if that is valid as a goal for composing the poetry of this world,[175] how much more would it be a motivation for persons engaged in Scripture translation, all those who are "shouting for joy before [our] King, the LORD" (הָרִיעוּ לִפְנֵי ׀ הַמֶּלֶךְ יְהוָה) (Ps. 98:6b) in the form of a beautiful "new song", with each being expressed in their own mother tongue?[176] To this end, I might recycle a thought from my earlier study of the book of Psalms (2002:30, slightly adapted):

---

[173] Note the similarity of purpose between this and the oft-maligned notion of dynamic equivalence, which is "defined in terms of the degree to which the receptors of the message in the receptor language respond to it in substantially the same manner as the receptors in the source language" (Nida and Taber 1969:24). However, this guideline must be coupled with the prior definition of "translating," which "consists in reproducing in the receptor language the closest natural equivalent of the source-language message, first in terms of meaning and secondly in terms of style" (ibid.:12). This translatorial intention was later specified as follows: "A Bible translator...is called upon to faithfully reproduce the meaning of the [source] text in a form that will effectively meet the needs and expectations of the [intended] receptors.... The translator [or team!] must strive to identify intellectually and emotionally with the intent and purpose of the original source, but he [they] must also identify with the concerns of his [their] potential receptors" (de Waard and Nida 1986:14, material in brackets added).

[174] Grossman adds perceptively with respect to an oral-oriented translation process: "To my mind, a translator's fidelity is not to lexical pairings but to context—the implications and echoes of the first author's tone, intention, and level of discourse. Good translations are good because they are faithful to this contextual significance. They are not necessarily faithful to words or syntax,... because words do not 'mean' in isolation. Words 'mean' as indispensable parts of a contextual whole that includes the emotional tone and impact, the literary antecedents, the connotative nimbus as well as the denotations of each statement.... We use analogy to recreate significance, searching for the phrasing and style in the second language which *mean* in the same way and *sound* in the same way to the reader [hearer!] of that second language. And this requires all our sensibility and as much sensitivity as we can summon to the workings and nuances of the language we translate into" (2010:70–71, original italics, word in brackets added).

[175] For an interesting and informative study that argues for the importance of translating the poetry of the Bible poetically, especially for the purpose of contextualizing theology in smaller "indigenous" societies, see Morris 2014.

[176] "There is a beauty and power of praise that comes from unity in diversity that is greater than that which comes from unity alone. Psalm 96:3–4 [cf. 98:1–3] connects the evangelizing of the peoples [of this world] with the quality of praise that God deserves" (Piper 2010:222, words in brackets added).

The Psalter provides a psalm for every person and every occasion in life. God intends that it serve that purpose for people of every age, setting, language and culture. That is where the essential activity of context-sensitive Bible translation enters the picture and becomes a primary duty and responsibility for all members of his church world-wide.

As Psalm 98:4 thus declares, joyous lyrics in praise of Yahweh was a distinctive feature of public worship in ancient Israel. May this "(ever-)new song" of salvation (98:1) also resound today among God's people of all nations via a meaningful and musical—most melodious—mother-tongue Bible translation! As one translator-composer asserts (Jacoby 2013:170):

BEYOND WORDS: Joy needs more than words for its expression. The jubilant praise psalms encourage us to go beyond verbal expressions to express our joy. The psalms themselves were never meant to be verbal expressions *alone*. They were written as songs to be *sung* and to be accompanied by musical instruments. We are not just exhorted to praise God in the psalms; we are exhorted again and again to *sing* praise to God, and we are encouraged to use instruments to amplify the expression of our emotions. As Victor Hugo said, Music expresses that which cannot be said and on which it is impossible to remain silent.[177]

And a last word from an ancient Christian commentator and theologian—on the broader, life-related significance of singing a new song (Blaising and Harden 2008:247):

AUGUSTINE, *Expositions of the Psalms:* Strip off your oldness; you know a new song. A new person, a New Covenant, A new song. People stuck in the old life have no business with this new song; only those who are new persons can learn it, renewed by grace and throwing off the old, sharers

---

[177] As already noted, the frequent association of joy with Israel's worship practice is evidenced by Megahan 2013:100–108). Jacoby also makes these important observations about psalmic expression in particular and our worship practice in general: "Even normal verbal communication involves tonality. The words we speak are only half of the communication. Intonation is the other half. The intonations in our voice can change the meaning of words [as well as complete utterances] and amplify [or modify] the force of an act of communication. Music is simply an extension of this aspect of human expression. Singing has always been the most natural thing for people to do. The psalms also encourage us to use musical instruments to stretch the potential for expression [of prayer and praise] as far as it can go. A skilled musician can use an instrument to express something words cannot reach" (2013:171; brackets added). Thus, "sounds, music and instruments as they are mentioned in the Psalter do not just symbolize something, for instance, God's presence, but they (also) evoke it. Instrumental music and singing are media of religious communication" (Körting 2014:69) since the beginning of human history.

already in the New Covenant, which is the kingdom of heaven. All our love yearns toward that, and in its longing our love sings a new song. *Let us sing this new song not with our tongues, but with our lives.*

הָרִיעוּ לַיהוָה כָּל־הָאָרֶץ
פִּצְחוּ וְרַנְּנוּ וְזַמֵּרוּ:

7.9 Excursus A: Psalm 98 (Common Meter: [C.M.])[178]

Praise for the gospel.[179]

To our Almighty Maker, God,
        New honors be addressed;
His great salvation shines abroad,
        And makes the nations blest.
He spake the word to Abraham first;
        His truth fulfils the grace;
The Gentiles make his name their trust,
        And learn his righteousness.
Let the whole earth his love proclaim
        With all her diff'rent tongues,
And spread the honors of his name
        In melody and songs.

The Messiah's coming and kingdom.

---

[178] Watts, Isaac. 1998. *The Psalms and Hymns of Isaac Watts.* Oak Harbor: Logos Research Systems, Inc. Portions of this hymn have been translated and published generally (open source) in the Chewa language under the title *A m'Dziko Akondweretu!* ('May all [people] in the world rejoice greatly').

[179] Obviously, a musical rendition of Psalm 98 should reflect a melody and a rhythm that is socioculturally and religiously appropriate for a song of joyous divine praise. As in the exuberant sound of J. S. Bach's renditions of Scripture: "It is a sin to 'plod'…. The tempo must be bright and fast, and the music 'has to dance'" in accordance with its biblical text. Furthermore, it may be well for today's translator-composers to adopt Bach's perspective on his task, for he "saw both the essence and practice of music as religious, and understood *that the more perfectly a composition is realised, both conceptually and through performance, the more God is immanent in the music*" (Michael O'Donnell, "Book Review: *Bach: Music in the Castle of Heaven* by John Eliot Gardiner," Wall Street Journal Bookshelf (Nov. 22, 2013), http://online.wsj.com/news/article_email/SB10001424052702304527504579169831993833414-lMyQjAxMTAzMDIwNDEyNDQyWj, emphasis added. Accessed September 2, 2017.

Joy to the world! the Lord is come!
    Let earth receive her King;
Let every heart prepare him room,
    And heav'n and nature sing.
Joy to the earth! the Savior reigns!
    Let men their songs employ,
While fields and floods, rocks, hills, and plains,
    Repeat the sounding joy.
No more let sins and sorrows grow,
    Nor thorns infest the ground;
He comes to make his blessings flow
    Far as the curse is found.
He rules the world with truth and grace,
    And makes the nations prove
The glories of his righteousness,
    And wonders of his love.

7.10 Excursus B: Psalm 98 in *The Psalms of David in Metre*[180]

1. O sing a new song to the Lord,
    for wonders he hath done:
    His right hand and his holy arm
    him victory hath won.

2. The Lord God his salvation
    hath caused to be known;
    His justice in the heathen's sight
    he openly hath shown.

3. He mindful of his grace and truth
    to Isr'el's house hath been;
    And the salvation of our God
    all ends of th' earth have seen.

---

[180] Copyright 1991 by Presbyterian Heritage Publications. http://www.swrb.com/newslett/actualNLs/Psalter5.htm/. Accessed September 2, 2017; (cf. Grant 2012:97–101.)

4. Let all the earth unto the Lord
   send forth a joyful noise;
   Lift up your voice aloud to him,
   sing praises, and rejoice.

5. With harp, with harp, and voice of psalms,
   unto Jehovah sing:

6. With trumpets, cornets, gladly sound
   before the Lord the King.

7. Let seas and all their fulness roar;
   the world, and dwellers there;

8. Let floods clap hands, and let the hills
   together joy declare

9. Before the Lord; because he comes,
   to judge the earth comes he:
   He'll judge the world with righteousness,
   his folk with equity.

7.11 Excursus C: Psalm 98 in
Free Church of Scotland Psalter[181]

PSALM 98 (C.M.)

1. O sing a new song to the LORD,
   for wonders he has done;
   His right hand and his holy arm
   the victory have won.

2. The LORD declared his saving work
   and made it to be known;
   To all the nations of the world
   his righteousness is shown.

---

[181] http://www.freechurch.org/2011uploaddirectory/Sing_Psalms_words.pdf. Accessed August 08, 2013 (no longer active; see now http://freechurch.org/assets/documents/2014/Sing_Psalms_words.pdf. Accessed September 2, 2017). The two metrical translations of Appendices B and C may be comparatively evaluated. "A standard metrical Psalm is written in Common Meter (C.M.) which is 8.6.8.6. That means in a four-line phrase, there will be eight syllables, then six syllables, then eight syllables, and then six syllables," e.g., "Amazing Grace" (Stutler 2013).

3. His steadfast love and faithfulness
    he has remembered well—
  The covenant he made with them,
    the house of Israèl.
  And all the nations of the earth
    have seen what God has done—
  Our God who brings deliverance
    by his right hand alone.

4. Acclaim the LORD, O all the earth;
    shout loudly and rejoice.
  Make music and be jubilant;
    to him lift up your voice.

5. With harp make music to the LORD;
    with harp his praises sing.

6. With trumpet and with horn rejoice
    before the LORD, the King.

7. Let earth, the sea and all in them
    rejoice triumphantly.

8. Let streams clap hands and mountains sing
    together joyfully.

9. Now let them sing before the LORD,
    who comes to judge the earth;
  He'll judge the world in righteousness,
    the peoples in his truth.

7.12 Excursus D: Timothy Wilt's *LiFE* rendition[182]

Psalm 98

Sing a new song for Yahweh!
What amazing things he has done!

---

[182] Timothy Wilt, *Praise—The Book of Psalms Translated from the Hebrew* (CreateSpace, 2012; see this text at http://www.amazon.com/Praise-Book-Psalms-Translated-Hebrew/dp/1453730672). The author introduces his translation in general as follows: "PRAISE is a new translation of the book of Psalms. Taking each

His strong, incomparable arm
has assured victory, freedom.

Yahweh has shown the nations
that he is triumphant and just.

He remembered his commitment
to Israel and his reliability.

From all corners of the earth,
the Divine Ones' triumph is seen.

Let the whole world celebrate Yahweh!
Don't hold back: shout and sing praise!
Play songs of praise on the harp!
Play and sing out in praise of Yahweh!
Play the trumpets, blast the shophars,
ululate, in the presence of KING YAHWEH!

The whole ocean roars,
with earth and those on it.
Rivers clap their hands,
mountains celebrate,
in Yahweh's presence.
HE IS COMING
to govern the earth.
He will govern earth and its people
with justice and fairness.

---

psalm, rather than each verse, as the basic translation unit, PRAISE illuminates aspects of the psalms that are often obscured if not hidden in more traditional translations. A variety of styles, innovative formatting, and new renderings of key expressions contribute to appreciating the psalms' different communication situations, genres, moods, thematic concerns, and cultural and religious perspectives." With specific reference to the translation of Ps. 98, Wilt writes: "I translated it as a hymn, with measured verse: in the first part, 7 or 8 syllables to a line (or an average of 8 in a couplet: e.g., 7 + 9), and each line of the couplets has three main beats. The beat changes with the thematic 'Let the whole world celebrate Yahweh'. The last verse changes to 5 syllables/line (2 or 3 main beats). In a few psalms, I do use rhyme but I try to avoid forced rhyme—or forced rhythm. [However], I felt that I could not use rhyme well for Ps. 98, though there is some assonance in the 'Let the whole world...' stanza. KING YAHWEH and HE IS COMING are put in caps to reinforce the thematic link with 96, 97 and 99, which all have 'YAHWEH REIGNS AS KING!' in caps (the first line in 97 and 99). This is one of the few places (maybe the only place) in all 150 psalms where I use caps, but the exultant repetition of this refrain seems to call for their use here" (personal correspondence, 10/02/2013).

7.13 Excursus E: YEHOVA MBUSA WANGADI[183]

1.	Yehova, Mbusa wangadi,	"Jehova," my real Herdsman,
	Ndilibe kusowa.	There's nothing I lack.
	Andigonetsa bwinoli	He makes me lie down very well
	Mu msipu wokoma.[a]	In a pleasant pasture.
2.	Ku madzi ake odikha	To his waters still
	Anditsogolera.	He leads me.
	Ndi moyo wanga wofoka	Even my weak life-force
	Aulimbikitsa.	He strengthens.
3.	Anditsogolera m'njira	He leads me in the way
	Zakulungamazo,	Of righteous (straight) things,
	Chifukwa changa ai, koma	Because of me—no, but
	Cha dzina lakelo.	(Because) of his name.
4.	Ndipyola kodi chikwawa	Should I go through a valley
	Cha mthunzi wa imfa?	Of the shades of death?
	Ndilibe mantha ngati	I have no fear if
	'Nu mundiperekeza.	You are accompanying me.
5.	Chakudya changa chabwino	My good food
	Mwandikonzera pha!	You've prepared for me—all filled up!
	Pa maso pa adaniwo	Before the eyes of those enemies
	Mudyetsa mtimanga.	You feed my heart.
6.	Mwadzoza mutu wanga ndi	You have anointed my head with
	Mafuta okoma.	Wonderful oil.
	Mwadzaza chikho changadi,	You have surely filled my cup,

[183] *Nyimbo za Mpingo wa Lutheran* [Hymns/Songs of the Lutheran Church], Lusaka: Lutheran Press, 1982, Number 110—based on Psalm 23.

Inde, chisefuka.	Yes, it overflows.
7.	Zokoma ndi zakuyanja	Pleasant and suitable things
	Zidzanditsatako.	Will follow after me there.
	Ndikhala m'nyumba ya M'lungu	I dwell in the house of God
	Ku nthawi zonsezo!	For all times!

[a]The fourth line is repeated three times in the sung version of this psalm, that is, according to the melody, and then the final two lines are repeated once more to conclude the stanza.

7.14 Excursus F: Sample *Ndakatulo* lyrics

Moto,[a]	Fire,
Woononga,	Ravaging,
Wochokera ku Madzulo,	Rising from the West,
Unadza usiku	It came at night
Titagona tonse	After we were all asleep
Nyumba yathu nkuotcha.	And burned up our house.
Kalanga ine katundu wanga!	Mercy me, all my belongings!
Kaligo,	Flute,
Msansi,	Finger xylophone,
Limba,	Rhythm bass,
Zeze,	Banjo,
Mbalure,	Kettle drum,
Mphulusa lokhalokha.	Burnt to ashes.
M'phunzitsa bwanji ana?	How will I teach my kids?
Ndikapeza kuti kamsompho	Where'll I find an adze
Ndisemere zina zoimbira?	So I can carve some more instruments?
Nkumbukira pamene munkandisisita[b]	I remember when you used to stroke me
Pamsana, ine chimwemwe mumtima.	Lying on my back, me, with joy in my heart.

Inu munali woyamba kundipsyompsona,	You were the first ever to kiss me,
M'dziko lapansi pano Amayi.	In this whole wide world, Mother.
Mwazi wanu unali kudya kwanga,	Your blood was my food,
Msana wanu unali chikwa changa.	Your back was my cocoon.
Miyendo yanu inali chikochikale,	Your legs were a Scotch cart,
Ndipo mokokeri munali inu Mayi.	And its puller was you, Mom.
Likongolerenji bokosi[c]	Why is the box so beautiful?
Monga losekeretsa?	As if it's so amusing?
Wolipanga analipanga,	The maker, he made it—
Kulipangira misozi.	He made it with tears.
Akonzeranji cosakondweretsaco?	Why did he prepare something so displeasing?
Wocilandirayo naye sacikana.	The recipient likewise does not refuse it.
Likomeranji bokosi	Why is the box so attractive
Monga losangalatsa?	As if it's so entertaining?
Wolipangayo salifuna	The one who made it doesn't want it
Koma analipangiranji?	But then why did he make it?
Wokhalamo salidziwa,	The inhabitant does not know it,
Nanga acitamonji?	So what's he doing in there?
Wolinyamula sakondwera nalo,	The one who carries it is not happy with it,
Tsono alinyamuliranji?	Well why then is he carrying it?
Olitsata liwalititsa misozi,	It provokes those following it to tears,
Nanga alitsatiranji?	So why are they following after it?
Wocipanga sacifuna,	Its maker does not want it,
Wokhalamo sacidziwa,	Its inhabitant does not know it,

Ocinyamula sakondwera naco,	Its carriers are not happy with it,
Ocitsata ciwalirita—Bokosi la maliro!	It makes its followers weep—a Coffin!
Mwana wamasiye[d]	The orphan child
Milomo yake sendekesendeke!	His lips—all peeled, full of sores,
Pamimba pali pefu!	His stomach—panting for breath,
Maso ali mbuu! ndi njala.	His eyes—all cloudy, with hunger.
Msana uli pamtunda,	His back[bone] protrudes,
Kabudula ndi msanza zokhazokha.	His shorts are just rags.
Uku ndi uko amwaza maso ake,	Here and there he casts his eyes,
Kufuna woti ampatse katambala	Looking for someone to give him a half-penny
Kogulira gaga ndi utaka.	To buy a meal of cheap maize and minnows.
Akalandira kanthu,	When he receives anything at all,
Nkhope yake iwala.	His whole face lights up.
Akanyozedwa, agwetsa nkhope	When scorned, his face falls
Nang'ung'udza:	And he mutters to himself:
"Kodi nkufuna kwanga?"	"Well, can I help it?"
Lero kapena mawa tisiniza,[e]	Today or tomorrow we'll press our eyelids shut,
Mudzatiperekeza kumbiya zodooka.	You will escort us to the place of broken pots.
Ananu, kuti mudzaone imbvi,	You children, if you want to see gray hair,
Kuti kumanda kudzakutalikireni,	If you want the grave to stay far away,
Sungani miyambo yathu.	Keep our ancestral customs.
Azimu akakufulatirani, fululani mowa.	When the spirits turn their backs on you, brew them some beer.

Awa ndi mawu wa tsabola wakale.	These are the words of an old chili pepper.
Mtendere alibe, chimwemwe alije. [f]	He has no peace, he has no joy.
Funso la Chilope: "Udandipheranji iwe?"	The Avenging-spirit asks: "Then why did you kill me?"

[a] *Moto Woononga* [Ravaging Fire], the entire poem—Mvula 1981:69. The English translations are my own.

[b] *Kalata kwa Amayi* [A Letter to Mother], lines 13–20—Mvula 1981:22–23.

[c] *Likongolerenji Bokosi?* [Why Is the Box so Beautiful?], the entire poem—Chadza 1967:22–23.

[d] *Masiye* [Orphan], the entire poem—Mvula 1981:72–73.

[e] *Akoma Akagonera* [Advice Appeals a Day Later], lines 8–14, Mvula 1981:77.

[f] *Chimlanga Chilope* [The Avenging-spirit Punishes Him], lines 7–8, Chadza 1970:109.

8

Psalm by the Sea: A Study of Israel's Thanksgiving Song (Exodus 15:1–21) and its Significance for Translation

Introduction

The song (psalm of praise) attributed to Moses in Exodus 15:1–18 is a most important text of Scripture in terms of form, content, and implication. My study will explore some of the reasons for this by means of a multifaceted analysis that focuses on selected organizational, stylistic, and performative aspects of this ancient Hebrew poem as it is situated within its textual context. Particular emphasis will be devoted to crucial artistic and rhetorical features of the original composition because these serve to structure and shape the lyric text as well as to give it added impact and appeal. The methodology applied in this analysis might serve as a basis for critical discussion with reference to possible application when carrying out a functionally equivalent Bible translation.

Of special interest in this study is the challenge of evaluating among a number of possible ways of displaying the macro- and micropoetic arrangement of this pericope. Which discourse model is most defensible, and on what basis can we come to such a decision? Although it is assumed here that a meaning-based rendition will be produced, how can translators determine how far to go in their language to generate a text that will be acceptable to their primary target audience, especially if an oral-aural-oriented, hymnic version is being contemplated? Several different English translations will be compared in this regard with reference to the initial stanza (vv. 1b–6) of this laudatory victory psalm in honor of Yahweh, who "is my strength and my song" (2a). Following an initial overview of the psalm's context, special attention will be devoted to a poetic analysis of the Hebrew text itself, after which some pertinent aspects of its influential intertext, its supplementary paratext, and examples of a translational metatext will be considered.

8.1 Exodus 15—an overview

The "song" (הַשִּׁירָה) recorded in Exodus 15 is undoubtedly a momentous passage of Scripture (Kitchen 2003:244–245).[1] According to many scholars, this is also one of the earliest examples of classical Hebrew poetry (Freedman 1980:176–178). The prominence of this poem is established, in the first place, because it celebrates an event of utmost significance in the history and theology of the people of Israel—their deliverance by Yahweh from certain defeat, slaughter, and enslavement by the Egyptian army, an event that is continually memorialized by direct reference and allusion throughout the Hebrew Bible and on into the New Testament.[2] The significance of this song's content is enhanced by its masterful mode of construction, despite its apparent spontaneity (Exo. 15:1). On the other hand, the text manifests a certain degree of mystery, or ambiguity as well because it allows for a number of different, but complementary analytical outlines and proposals regarding its overall poetic structure (to be summarized below). The formal beauty and powerful rhetoric of this poem argues for the devotion of due diligence in any translated rendition today; a flat reproduction of content

---

[1] "…References to the exodus (episodic and occasional) [are] scattered through all types and dates (however construed) of the biblical writings" (Kitchen 2003:244; this is followed by a long list of OT references broken down into five "congruent groups" of texts). "Late Bronze Age literature from both Mesopotamia and Egypt includes poetic narratives of royal exploits alongside prose accounts of the same events, all written shortly after they took place. They are thus comparable with the Song of Moses in Exodus 15…" (Millard 2003:910). The song of Moses "at the Sea" recorded in Exo. 15 is to be distinguished from that recorded in Deut. 32.

[2] For example: Deut. 11:3–4, Josh. 24:6–7, Judg. 11:16, Neh. 9:9–11, Pss. 66:6, 74:13, 78:13, 106:9–12, 136:13–15, Isa. 43:16–17, 51:10, Nah. 1:4, Hab. 3:8; cf. Acts 7:36, 1 Cor. 10:1–2, Heb. 11:29. Brueggemann offers the following insightful summary: "The Song of Moses is commonly recognized as one of the oldest, most radical, and most important poems in the OT. It not only sounds the crucial themes of Israel's most elemental faith, but it also provides a shape and sequencing of that faith, which we may take as 'canonical'" (1994:799). This pericope, Exo. 15:1–18, forms part of the regular morning worship ritual of devout Jews (Holladay 1996:141).

is completely inadequate and essentially unfaithful to the text's original communicative intention.

Exodus 15:1b–18 may be generally classified as a song, a psalm, or a lyric poem for reasons that will be more fully explored below under considerations of genre.[3] However, difficulties remain as to how to label this text in terms of its title—problems that pertain to hermeneutical issues involving authorship and cotextual relationship. There is some ambiguity, for example, as to who actually composed this poetic piece: was it Moses alone, or did he create it somehow in conjunction with his sister Miriam (vv. 20–21)? Though other interpretations are possible, I feel that the most likely is that, based on the singular verb "he sang" (יָשִׁיר) in 15:1a coupled with the situational unlikelihood of a joint communal composition, the principal author was indeed Moses.[4] I further assume that the text does give an accurate record concerning the utterance, or corporate singing, of this song—that is, in the immediate vicinity of the "lip of the sea" (עַל־שְׂפַת הַיָּם) of Reeds (14:30), soon after the historical events recorded in Exodus 14.[5] I will survey the compositional placement of this song within the book of Exodus more fully below when discussing its situational setting (context). At the outset, however, it is important to note that in any study of the song per se (1b–18) it is necessary to include also a consideration of its immediate cotext, both before (1a) and after (19–21). The relevance of this inclusion is signaled by a literary inclusio itself, namely, a pair of synonymous verbs for 'sing' that are found both at the beginning (1a: יָשִׁיר) as well as the ending (21: תַּעַן) of this thereby conceptually unified pericope.

---

[3] The nature of the discourse is verbally underscored at its onset. Cassuto notes that an initial poetic formula like "I will sing" is "a common feature both of Eastern and Western poesy" (1967:174). The biblical scholar and translator Everett Fox has correctly observed that many portions of Biblical Hebrew prose are "poetic" in character, especially with reference to the text's oral-aural sonic features. This includes Exodus 14, which "demonstrates the Bible's use of an intermediate form between poetry and prose, a form designed to instruct as well as to inspire" ("Translator's Preface" to *The Schocken Bible,* cited in Weissbort and Eysteinsson 2006:567). For this reason Fox also recommends "laying out the text in 'cola' or lines meant to facilitate reading aloud" (ibid.).

[4] Admittedly, when sung, as intended, publicly in unison the "I" of the song becomes, in effect, "the whole community of Israel" (Brueggemann 1994:799). For a survey of various possible titles, or headings, for this text, see McCabe 1981:13–14.

[5] How could the large company of Israel—the adults at least—learn this song so soon, quickly enough to sing it along the banks of the Red Sea (Exo. 15:1)? John Wheeler suggests, by using a method of hand signals (cheironomy) that was well-known and practiced in ancient Egypt: "By the time of the crossing of the Red Sea, Moses was able, using this system, to create and then teach his 'Song of the Sea'... to large crowds of people on short notice...using hand-signs representing notes of the scale" (1989b:115; cf. expressions such as 'by the hand of...' בְּיַד־אָסָף or 'on the hands of' עַל־יְדֵי, e.g., 1 Chr. 16:7; 25:2, 6; Ezr. 3:10).

8.2 The situational setting (context)

The compositional position of chapters 14–15 is pivotal within the book of Exodus as a whole.[6] The poetic reflection, Moses' Psalm at the Sea "provides a natural boundary in the book of Exodus" because it "sets off the Egypt traditions from those of Sinai and the wilderness and brings to a spectacular close the saga of liberation" (Fox 1995:334). Fox also provides an excellent thematic and pragmatic (rhetorical) description of the prominent relevance of this paired set of chapters where they are situated in Exodus (ibid.):

> A poem is necessary at this point in the story, to provide emotional exaltation and a needed break before the next phase of Israel's journey in the book. The Song manages to focus the Israelites' (the audience's?) intense feelings in a way that neither the ritual of Chaps. 12–13 nor even the semipoetic description of God's miraculous intervention in Chap. 14 can do. Only poetry is capable of expressing the full range of the people's emotions about what has happened....
>
> A major concern of the poet is God's kingship.... This is no accident, nor is it inappropriate; since Chaps. 4 and 5 the story of Exodus has revolved around just who shall be king (God or Pharaoh) and just who shall be served. By the end of Chap. 14 this is no longer an issue. The victorious YHWH can now be acclaimed as king, while we hear nothing further of Pharaoh.[7]

Patterson suggests a helpful *narrative* structural perspective on the placement of chapters 14–15 within Exodus (2004:44):

> The narrative of the Re(e)d Sea crossing forms a pivotal part of a larger narrative detailing the Hebrews' journey from Egypt to Sinai (Exo. 12:37–19:2). The major stages of the itinerary are marked structurally by the recurring phrase "and they departed from." The narrative traces the Israelites' movement from Egypt to Succoth (12:37–13:19), from Succoth to the sea (13:20–15:21), from the sea to the oasis at Elim (15:22–27), from Elim to the Desert of Sin (16:1–36), from Sin to Rephidim (17:1–18:27), and from Rephidim to Sinai (19:1–2).

---

[6] I will not propose a hypothetical *Sitz im Leben* for the Song (for a survey, see McCabe 1981:48ff.).

[7] "In Hebrew though the kingdom is where God sovereignly takes charge and rules in human affairs. For example, in the Old Testament God's 'reign' is associated with the crossing of the Red Sea (Exo. 15:18)" (M. R. Wilson 1989:181).

Thus, the people's movement (based on the verb נֹסַע 'pull up tent pegs' > 'set out on a journey') "from Succoth to the Sea (13:20–15:21)" is the second of six recorded travel stages, but if we include a final summary occurrence in 40:36 (highlighted by its negativization in v. 37) the total rounds out to a significant completive number seven. Walter Brueggemann envisions the entire narrative covering Exodus 2–15 to be constituted by the basic shape of "a lament form," including an initial "lament" (2:23), a medial "salvation oracle" (3:7–8), and a culminating word of "thanksgiving" (15:1) (1987:77), which is then elaborated in the following Psalm (15:1b–18).[8]

8.2.1 Pre-text

8.2.1.1 Chapter 14

The natural pre-text and source of inspiration for the Psalm by the Sea is Exodus 14. This too is a skillfully constructed discourse that gives evidence of a number of thematically motivated rhetorical features. It is a dramatic narrative that is driven forward by segments of direct speech with Yahweh as the main character in focus and his foil being the revenge-blinded Egyptian Pharaoh. From one perspective, chapter 14 may be divided into three major sections, each one being introduced by the phrase, "And Yahweh said to Moses..." in 14:1, 15, 26 (...וַיְדַבֵּר יְהֹוָה אֶל־מֹשֶׁה) with a reference to "the sea" (הַיָּם) following soon thereafter in direct speech (14:2, 16, 26b).

In the first section, Israel's problem and the people's complaint is recorded (vv. 1–14); in the second we hear the LORD's proposed solution and initial protection (vv. 15–25); in the third and climactic section Yahweh's great victory and ultimate salvation of his people is described (vv. 26–31). On the other hand, it is also possible to divide chapter 14 roughly in half, with verses 1–14 dealing with the build-up to Israel's crisis largely in direct speech, while verses 15–31 then record the mainly narrative account

---

[8] Commenting then on the theological significance of this strategic shape, Brueggemann observes: "Shaping the exodus in the lament-thanksgiving form gave to biblical faith its most powerful model as a religion of salvation" (1995:77). Miller elaborates: "Outside the Psalter there are other indications of Israel's experience of the continuum of supplication and praise and the movement of faith toward doxology. The heart of the Old Testament story of the people of God is the exodus event recorded in Exodus 1–15. That story is set totally within the movement from the lament of the people under Egyptian slavery and oppression (Exo. 2:23–25; 3:7, 9; 6:5) to the loud and joyous hymns of praise by Moses, Miriam, and the people after God has destroyed the Egyptian army (Exo. 15:1–18, 21)" (Miller 1986:66). The same communicative import applies to the Psalms, for example: "Luther sees the Psalter as a primer in which Christian faith is taught to praise, in so doing exposing anti-doxologies and the ways they obscure the living presence of God's tangible and accessible saving activity" (Brock 2014:203).

of how Yahweh delivered his people on dry land but destroyed the enemy by drowning them in the sea. This second division is supported by the little narrative summary at the end of the chapter (vv. 30–31), which echoes Moses' pep talk to the people at the close of the first half (vv. 13–14).

Patterson provides a convenient summary of some of the main thematic elements that chapters 14 and 15 have generally in common (2004:49; cf. Zogbo and Wendland 2000:3–6):

> The prose and the longer of the two poetic accounts share an essential unity in several matters of theme and vocabulary. Both emphasize the sea and its waters (Exo. 14:2, 9, 16, 21–23, 26–28, 29; 15:4–5, 8, 10) in which the Egyptians perished (14:23, 26–28; 15:1, 4–5, 10, 26). Both mention that the waters were piled up on either side of the path by the breath or wind of God (14:21–22; 15:8). The theme of pursuit also appears in both accounts (14:4, 8, 17, 23; 15:9). Also the two accounts agree on several features: the waters congealed and stood fast like a wall so that the Egyptians unhesitatingly pursued the Israelites into the path that had been established, only to realize too late that Yahweh was returning the waters on them so that they perished in the midst of the sea (14:21–29; 15:8–10).

The fickle, fearful cry (prayer?) of the people for help as the pursuing Egyptian army drew near (14:10–12) echoes ironically in the cognitive background of the Song at the Sea.[9] The hymn thus responds in a way to their lack of faith and amplifies Moses' prior words of encouragement: "Fear not, stand firm, and see the salvation of the LORD, which he will work for you today. For the Egyptians whom you see today, you shall never see again. The LORD will fight for you, and you have only to be silent" (14:13–14; 15:1b–12). The silence of paralyzing terror (14:10) will then befall the inhabitants of the territories that the human lay-army of Israel will pass victoriously through behind King Yahweh on their way to Canaan (15:13–18).

There are also a number of literary lexical links that allow the Song to play off from the preceding narrative account as an excellent instance of embedded poetry—that is, an instance of a poetic text which has been integrally woven into its narrative context in such a way that the two become one composition.[10] For example:

---

[9] The chiastic formation of the people's plea highlights its negative characterizing implication: A: You [Moses] brought us out of Egypt to die in the desert; B: We should have remained in Egypt [rhetorical question]; B′: We should have remained in Egypt, even as slaves [rhetorical question]; A′: You brought us out to die in the desert!

[10] This is exactly what can be said of most (if not all) poetic passages in the narrative prose of the Hebrew Bible, particularly the smaller ones, but this also holds true for the larger compositions. "Poems that are spliced into larger narratives

Some of the links between the Song and the preceding narrative are extraordinarily playful; they exploit the power of pun to make their point. These are easy to miss in translation. For example, the children of Israel leave Egypt with a 'high' *(rmh,* from *rwm)* hand (14:8, 16), but YHWH 'hurls' *(rmh,* from a different root) the Egyptians into the Sea (15:1, 21), for which delivering act the children of Israel 'exalt' *(rwm)* him (15:2). Again, the children of Israel are to 'stand still' *(nsb,* 14:13) and watch YHWH make the waters 'stand' *(nsb)* like a heap (15:8). According to the prose account Moses 'stretches out a hand' *(nth yd)* to divide the Sea and make it return (14:16, 21, 26, 27), whereas in the poem it is YHWH who 'stretches out his right hand' *(nth ymyn)* to make the earth swallow the enemies (15:12). (Steiner 2013:3; cf. Watts 1992:46)

However, one must admit that there are also a number of noteworthy differences between the two chapters, primarily in specifics, for example: the prose narrative, in contrast to the Song, records the details of Pharaoh's preparations to chase after Israel (14:3–9) preceded by Yahweh's prediction of this (14:3–4); Israel's bitter complaint about their situation and Moses' courageous reply (14:10–14); the LORD's response to his people's lament and the special protection provided by "the angel of God" (מַלְאַךְ הָאֱלֹהִים) (14:15–25); the personal role of Moses in holding out his staff over the sea (14:16, 21, 26–27); Israel crossing the sea safely "on dry ground" (14:22, 29). For its part, the Song too has some unique topical elements,[11] for example: the reference to Yahweh as a "warrior" (3) defeating the enemy with his "right hand" (6) in anger (8)—followed

---

typically distill the theological message embedded more subtly in the surrounding prose and give it fresh and emotive expression" (Steiner 2013:7). In my opinion, the difference between an inset poem and an embedded poem is that the former is inserted as a whole secondarily by an author or a later editor into an existing text, while an embedded poem is integrated by the author of the text in question as an essential characteristic of it. Therefore, in my judgment, the term "inset poem" is not suitable for such poetic passages (cf. Labuschagne 2008:1). Ten such "embedded" prayer-hymns outside the Psalms would include: the Song at the Reed Sea in Exodus 15, the Song of Moses in Deuteronomy 32, the Song of Deborah in Judges 5, the Song of Hannah in 1 Samuel 2, the Song of David in 2 Samuel 22, the Letter-Prayer of Hezekiah in Isaiah 38, the Prayer of Jonah in Jonah 2, the Prayer of Habakkuk in Habakkuk 3, Daniel's Song of Praise in Daniel 2, and the Song of Praise Ordained by David in 1 Chronicles 16 (Labuschagne 2008:2).

[11] Yahweh is also foregrounded throughout the psalm: "Moses disappears, and the people are mentioned only in relation to the settlement of the land and the holy mountain, not the sea event. Whereas the interactions between Yahweh, Moses and the people are given considerable space in the prose account, the only humans the

by his gentle, shepherd-like leading his people Israel (13) through hostile lands (14–16) to their new, mountainous (17a) "dwelling place" where his divine "sanctuary" is too located (17b). In any case, it is safe to conclude that "the song of Moses and of Miriam is neither an interlude nor an interruption. Rather, it is the very reason God saved his people: so that he would receive the glory of their praise" (Ryken and Ryken 2007:100).

8.2.1.2 The immediate pre-text

A few other connections between what is reported by way of the narrative in Exodus 14 and the psalm of chapter 15 need to be noted, namely, the summary close of vv. 30–31. This begins with the crucial announcement that also serves as the theme for the following Song: 'And Yahweh delivered Israel on that day from the hand of the Egyptians' (וַיּוֹשַׁע יְהוָה בַּיּוֹם הַהוּא אֶת־יִשְׂרָאֵל מִיַּד מִצְרָיִם). While the LORD's mighty salvation is expressed in different ways throughout the Song, it is set forth explicitly at the beginning of its first strophe in v. 2b:[12] "he has become my salvation/deliverance/victory!" (וַיְהִי־לִי לִישׁוּעָה). The "great power" (lit., 'hand') (הַיָּד הַגְּדֹלָה) that Yahweh put on display (14:31) to defeat the "power" (lit., "hand") of Pharaoh's army (14:30) is reflected in his attribute of "strength" (lit., "my strength" עָזִּי) in 15:2a. The awful outcome for the Egyptians is that their drowned bodies litter the seashore for all Israel to "see" (14:30)—and to celebrate then in song (15:1d). The Israelites not only see, but they also "fear" the LORD and trust him as well as "in his servant Moses" (וּבְמֹשֶׁה עַבְדּוֹ) (14:31). As if there were no gap between chapters then, the account continues "Then Moses sang..." (אָז יָשִׁיר־מֹשֶׁה) (15:1a). The connection between these two texts could not be any closer.[13]

---

psalm depicts in an active role are the Egyptians (15.9), and then only to show the complete reversal of their expectations" (Watts 1992:46).

[12] It is important to remember that the verb *yasha* in most OT contexts does not have a purely, or even a primarily spiritual meaning. "In the Hebrew Bible...the main idea is 'to liberate', 'to deliver from evil', or 'to free from oppression'. Hence the terms safety, welfare, prosperity, and victory are all used to define this saving activity.... The Exodus from Egypt reminds us that 'God's salvation involves a concern for physical as well as spiritual well-being. Exodus is not just a spiritual metaphor. Indeed, it is out of Israel's experience of God's concrete, physical deliverance that a new relationship to God is possible'" (M. R. Wilson 1989:180, citing Birch 1985:47).

[13] The careful literary interlocking of chapters 14 and 15 argue against the view of scholars who see the song of 15:1b–18 as having been only rather later artificially patched into the surrounding narrative text (for a survey of these theories, see Durham 1987:202–205). Thus, this passage is not some later "add-on," pasted into a pre-existing scroll of Exodus by some pious, liturgically minded redactor. Rather, "The smooth flow of the prose narrative from 14:31 to 15:19–21 favors the suggestion

8.2.2 Post-text

Delimiting the text of Exodus 15:1b–18 must also be considered in close relation to vv. 19–21. An obvious inclusio, two passages that are lexically almost exact, demarcates this pericope, i.e., vv. 1b and 21b: "The longer form of this hymn of praise [and thanksgiving, by Moses,] is similar [to that of Miriam], except that it is couched as a first-person, individual declaration of praise, and the elaboration of the reason is extended through many verses" (Miller 1994:210, brackets added). An inclusio which interlocks with the preceding is formed by the close parallels between the narrative accounts of 14:26b–28 and 15:19–20: The LORD brings the waters of the Reed Sea down upon the heads of the Egyptian army after the non-military host of Israel had crossed safely on dry ground. These structural indicators, along with the epilogue-line monocolon of 15:18 (cf. Ps. 29:10; Lam. 5:19), would indicate that verse 19 is not an integral part of the Song (cf. NET), despite its semi-poetic qualities (see further discussion below). Rather, as suggested above, it begins in typical narrative fashion ('When [or, 'Indeed!'] Pharaoh's horse[s] entered...the sea...') and serves as a flashback, as it were, back to the end of ch. 14. It is also an instance of structural anaphora in parallel with v. 1b (similar discourse unit beginnings; cf. Wendland 2004:127).

How does Miriam's hymn of v. 21b fit into the text and relate to the earlier Song-psalm? Most obviously, "the song of Miriam marks the conclusion of the whole Exodus story" (Anderson 1987:285). The following then are several opinions concerning its structural function. According to Patterson (2004:51):

> Perhaps the simplest solution is to view Miriam's song as being sung immediately after the Israelites' safe passage through the sea and the defeat of the Egyptians, while Moses soon afterward composed the poetic masterpiece of Exodus 15:1–18 and led the people in its singing.

Janzen is of the opposite opinion and feels that "the imperative call of Miriam and her sister song-leaders evokes an individualized response in

---

that the poetic piece in 15:1–18 has been inserted into the text to commemorate the grand event" (Patterson 1995:453). Perhaps, not even the term "inserted" is quite accurate. "The poem was not simply inserted as an inset hymn into the existing account of the Reed Sea event, but was woven from the same fabric as the material surrounding it. There is a logical flow of thought from the concluding verse of the Reed Sea story in 14:31 through 15:21. Being in awe of YHWH's saving act, the Israelites put their faith in him and in Moses (14:31) and with a Song of Praise they demonstrate their faith and celebrate YHWH's triumph and his incomparability (15:1–18). In the Epilogue to the Song (v. 19), the author recapitulates the Reed Sea event, significantly in exactly the same way as Deut. 32:44 recapitulates the recital of the Song of Moses. The parashah petuchah (P) after v. 19 in MT is an indication that the Epilogue strictly belongs to the Song,..." (Labuschagne 2007:1).

Moses and the people of Israel" (2003:119–120).[14] Kaiser (1994:92) sees quite a bit more involvement for Miriam (and the women):

> Miriam led the women perhaps in an antiphonal response, repeating the song at the conclusion of each part or strophe, accompanied by timbrels and dancing.[15]

Following Freedman (1980:194–195) and Watts (1992:52), Steiner too feels that Miriam's song served as a communal choral refrain or antiphon, perhaps after every line or stanza of the larger Song (2013:10):

> There we envisioned "cantor Moses" and the congregation leading in the main hymn, with Miriam and the women providing the antiphonal response and rhythmic accompaniment by instrument and dance. In this way all Israel joined in the celebration.

In any case, the onset of a new discourse unit clearly occurs in v. 22, as marked by a new subject ("Moses led"), a shift in genre (from poetry to narrative), as well as a modification in time and place—"into the desert of Shur." This change of scene is accompanied by a new set of vocabulary items, although there is still an emphasis on the water motif—now water to drink instead of a sea to cross.

8.3 The text

In this section I will examine different aspects of the text of Exodus 15:1–21, with special reference to the song of vv. 1b–18. I will consider in turn its genre (8.3.1), different proposals concerning the song's macrostructure (8.3.2), including a detailed poetic-rhetorical analysis of the Hebrew text (8.3.2.3), the song's microstructure, including seven prominent stylistic devices (8.3.3), its main pragmatic features (8.3.4), and finally, a brief thematic overview (8.3.5).

---

[14] Brueggemann agrees, with some added speculation: "The older song is by 'Miriam and all the women'. Thus Moses, the official leader, has taken over and preempted the singing first done by the women" (1994:799; cf. Cole 1973:123).

[15] There may be even greater significance here for the practice of Israel's religious worship: "The text reports that Miriam and the women of the camp danced, played tambourines (v. 20) and praised God...(v. 21b). The fact that other texts portray victory celebrations similarly—women dancing, playing instruments, and singing—shows this type of event had accepted rituals and included music (Judg. 11:34; 1 Sam. 18:6–9)" (Creach 2005:124). Anderson feels that the song and dance of Miriam and her friends "inaugurated a liturgical tradition in which other poets and singers stood, including those who have given us the laments, thanksgivings and hymns of the Psalter" (1987:291).

8.3.1 Genre

"Then Moses and the Israelites sang (יָשִׁיר) this song (הַשִּׁירָה) to the LORD" (15:1a). In this way the focal text under consideration is clearly introduced according to its literary character. The verb שִׁיר and the related noun are generic terms that denote some type of lyric song—the specific nature and type being defined by the social and/or religious setting in which it is sung. In fact, the very declaration "I [will] sing to the LORD..." is a speech act of praise (Miller 1994:211). "*Shîr* 'song', is a general term for any type of voiced melody (e.g., Gen 31:27; Ex 15:1, 21; Judg 5:12), but it may have a more technical meaning in the psalm titles, where it appears to refer to vocal performance with cantillation.... It is most often accompanied by musical instruments" (Brueggeman 2008:618). This musical dimension would certainly fit the situational context of Israel's Song at the Sea (15:20–21). The classification of a biblical text's genre is a critical aspect of analysis, for the outcome provides important clues for its interpretation with regard to structure, style, and communicative aims that relate to a given target audience and contextual setting.

In terms of the various psalm types of the Hebrew Psalter it is rather difficult to classify Israel's Song more precisely. Most scholars feel that this poem is old, "the oldest of all the hymns" (Miller 1994:209), for "the language is full of archaisms" (Cole 1973:123). A survey of literature reveals "varying results as to genre (hymn, hymn and thanksgiving psalm, enthronement psalm, liturgy, and victory song), number of stanzas (whether two, three, or four)" (Patterson 1995:47; cf. McCabe 1981:40–56). However, in terms of its ascribed setting in the book of Exodus, coming after the LORD's miraculous deliverance of his people from the threat of the pursuing Egyptian army, this might be designated first of all as a thanksgiving psalm (or song).[16] "In the psalms of thanksgiving the psalmist offers thanks to Yahweh for deliverance from some form of distress" (Tucker 2008:584). "A declaration of intent to give [praise and] thanks usually comes near the beginning, followed by the account of the distress and the change that has come to the psalmist's life because of the deliverance" (Belcher 2008:805, bracket added; cf. Wendland 2002:38–40). This includes an explicit "confession directed to others that Yahweh was the one who delivered from the distress" (Pss. 18:27–28; 34:6–9) (ibid.). Typical thematic elements would include items such as: descriptions of Yahweh's great power

---

[16] Thus, I do not feel that a strict literary distinction needs to be made between the text of Exo. 15:1b–18 and any of the most closely corresponding psalms in the book of Psalms. In terms of form, content, and function they are essentially the same. McCabe offers a detailed study of possible genres, or *Gattungen,* with reference to this text (1981:40–48). Bullock provides a good overview of some of the main psalms that reflect back on different aspects of the "crossing of the Red Sea" and Exodus 14–15 (2001:106–107).

(vv. 1–6), his proximity to his people (vv. 13, 16–17a), his supremacy over all other powers ("gods," v. 11), and references to his eternal rule (vv. 17b–18) (Miller 1994:211–212). In a very general way, Israel's Song at the Sea could readily be classified in these terms, with the LORD's deliverance, which is clearly proclaimed throughout vv. 1b–12, making possible the momentous change for the people in their journey towards, and settlement in the land of Canaan (vv. 13–17). One optional thanksgiving element that is missing from the Song is reference to either "the thanksgiving sacrifice brought by the worshiper (Ps. 66:13–15)" or "exhortations for others to give thanks (Ps. 118:28–29)" (Belcher 2008:805). On the other hand, these latter features are not present either in Psalm 124, a short communal thanksgiving praise that clearly seems to reflect aspects of the Exodus (vv. 3–5, 7). Other psalms that some scholars classify as being of the "communal thanksgiving" type are 66, 67, and 129 (ibid.:808).

Although not a composite text—that is, comprised of two different songs fused together in Exodus 15 (cf. Durham 1987:202–204), it is clear that this thanksgiving song does include other subsidiary psalmic elements. Aspects of a hymn, or psalm of praise, are obvious, e.g., vv. 3, 11, 13, and 18 (cf. Pss. 96, 98). Several verses also remind one of a historical psalm, e.g., vv. 4–5, 7–10 (cf. Ps. 106:8–12), while the repeated doxologies of verses 1b, 6, 11, and 16b–17 seem to evince a liturgical function (cf. Pss. 41–43, 46–48, 116; Wendland 2002:48–49, 53–54). Rather more specifically, some scholars designate Exodus 15:1b–18 as a subtype of the thanksgiving psalm, namely, a victory song in praise of Yahweh's miraculous deliverance of his people from an imposing enemy (Westermann 1965:91–92). Such a significant poetic discourse, which is found also in Deborah's Song of Judges 5, manifests the following compositional features (Patterson 2004:48; cf. Hauser 1987:280):

> (a) a focusing on the specific name of Israel's God, (b) the application of specific terms or phrases to God and or a description of God's role in the victory, (c) a description of God's use of the forces of nature to give Israel the victory, (d) the mocking of the enemy, and (e) a description of the enemy's fall.[17]

More specifically, we may note the fact that "like many an ancient victory song, it [Exo. 15:1b–18] features both a war cry, 'Yahweh is a man of war' (v. 3), and an exulting in the coming of divine aid during the battle (vv. 4–5)" (Patterson 1995:457).[18]

---

[17] Similarly, the *New English Translation* describes such "declarative praise psalms" as including features such as "the resolve to praise, the power of God, the victory over the enemies, the incomparability of God in his redemption, and the fear of the people" (2003:153).

[18] The NET footnotes point out several of the older poetic features of this psalm, for example, with reference to "majestic" in v. 6a: "The form נֶאְדָּרִי *(ne'dari)* may

Although there are numerous formal and semantic similarities between the songs of Exodus 15 and Judges 5, "two of the oldest pieces of poetry in the Tanak" (Hauser 1987:265), there are also a notable number of differences. "It therefore would not seem appropriate to suggest that there is an established 'form' for victory songs that was followed" in these two pericopes (Hauser ibid.:279). Rather, the general thematic correspondence, having a definite focus on the saving actions of Yahweh on behalf of Israel, was flexibly expressed via a variety of psalmic forms, as noted above with reference to the Song at the Sea.

8.3.2 Macrostructure

Various poetic discourse arrangements have been proposed for the song of Exodus 15:1b–18.[19] This diversity and scholarly disagreement probably stems from the intricate, artistic manner in which the text has been organized.[20] Several overlapping and interacting sub-structures have been incorporated to give the whole an evocatively rich texture and a resonant sound, with certain key lexical items (exact as well as synonymous recurrences) reappearing in similar as well as new positions. Commentators essentially divide the poem into either two or three principal sections; several representative examples of each of these proposals are briefly overviewed below. I will not offer much discussion regarding the internal, strophic sub-units because these present even greater diversity of opinion (cf. McCabe 1981:60). Following this overview of scholarly viewpoints on the macrostructure of the Song, I will give my analytical arrangement in detail, based on the Hebrew text, which forms the basis for the musical-poetic renditions to be considered in §6 below.

8.3.2.1 Two divisions

Durham *(Word Biblical Commentary)*
Durham feels that the Song is "a composite of at least two (vv 1b–12 and vv 13–18) and perhaps three (dividing vv 13–18 into 13a, 14–16 and 13b,

---

be an archaic infinitive with the old ending *i*, used in place of the verb and meaning "awesome." Gesenius says that the vowel ending may be an old case ending" (2003:153; cf. Fox 1995:336; regarding Hebrew archaisms, see Cook 2008:261; regarding the dating of this text, see McCabe 1981:28–39).

[19] Labuschagne summarizes the Song's strophic structure as proposed by thirteen scholars who are recognized for their Hebrew poetic discourse analyses (2007:3).

[20] As Reger astutely observes, "The existence of so numerous delineation proposals does not necessarily confirm the disunity of the song, but rather calls for well-argued methods and conditions of division" (2010:57). That is the aim of this first half of my study, for "a proper articulation of form yields proper articulation of meaning," where the assumption is that "form and content are inseparable" (Trible, with reference to Muilenberg, 1994:91).

17–18) poems…" (1987:205). He feels that "the subject matter and the form of the poem give some support to such a division" (ibid.), but since his structural proposal is ambiguous, he basically leaves it to the reader to discern whether there are two or three parts. This unhelpful outcome is typical of a source-critical approach to the biblical text which often spends more ink on discerning the supposed "sources" for a composition than elucidating its manifest unity.

Brenner *(The Song of the Sea)*

Brenner too applies a source-critical methodology and, like Durham, finds the main division of the Song after v. 12 (so also Fox 1995:334). There are thus two main parts, but in addition he discerns a "formulaic enclosure" comprising verses 1b–3, 18, and 21b. Unlike Durham then, he concludes that "the whole of the liturgical enclosure and part one demonstrates a thematic and linguistic unity" (Brenner 1991:26; cf. McCabe 1981:15–21).[21]

Gispen *(Bible Study Commentary)*

Gispen divides the Song "into two sections according to content: verses 2–12 and verses 13–18" (1982:146). The opening bicolon (v.1b) praises the "exaltedness" of Yahweh, while the "remaining verses elaborated on this exaltedness, which is expressed both in Egypt's defeat (vv. 2–12) and in the favor that had been, and was yet to be, bestowed on His people (vv. 13–18)" (ibid.:147). This division is supported by Cole, with somewhat different themes: "Verses 1–12 deal with the exodus, while 13–18 deal with the future conquest of Canaan" (1973:123).

---

[21] In contrast, Collins feels that "The basic hymn is found in 15:1–12, 18. Verses 13–17 are a later expansion, probably by a Deuteronomic editor, and change the focus of the hymn from the victory over Pharaoh to the triumphal march of Israel into the promised land" (2004:116; similarly Coats 1969:17). In my opinion, the faulty assumption here is twofold regarding (a) the literature (b) of Scripture. Thus, biblical authors are seemingly incapable of composing a unified text that allows for a complex discourse structure or a shift of thematic focus, and second, predictive prophesy in the Bible is an impossibility—or at best, an "improbability." For a brilliant literary-structural counter-explanation for what is going on in the text here, see Alter 1985:52–54. To this point, Cole writes: "Some scholars feel that the second part of Moses' song must have been written after the occupation of Canaan, with which it deals. In particular, some see references in verses 13 and 17 to Mount Zion and Solomon's Temple, but this is not necessary. Both phrases are archaic, and have parallels long before, in the Ras Shamra tablets… [With reference to 'Yahweh will reign' in v. 18]. There are also at least two references in the Pentateuch to the kingship of YHWH in Israel (Nu. 23:21; Dt. 33:5) and indeed the whole concept of covenant probably demands kingship as a necessary corollary" (1973:124, 126).

Labuschagne ("Logotechnical Analysis")
This is one of the most detailed, formal examples of analysis in that it is based largely on lexical word and poetic line counts (2007:8):

> In terms of content, the Song divides into two main parts: vs. 1b–13, dealing with the Exodus event vs. 14–18, the reaction of the nations and the fulfilling of YHWH's intention. The bipartite structure is underscored by the division of the **39** verselines into precisely **26** in vs. 1b–13, and **13** in vs. 14–18, which reflects the YHWH-*'echad* formula: **39 = 26 + 13.** This numerical device buttresses the crucial idea of YHWH's uniqueness which is eloquently expressed in the meaningful centre in v. 11.

> The compositional structure can be outlined as follows:

Canto I, vs. 1b–5	**8 verselines** 42 words	
Strophe 1, vs. 1b–3	5 verselines 26 words	
Strophe 2, vs. 4–5	3 verselines 16 words	
Canto II, vs. 6–10	**12 verselines** 48 words	
Strophe 3, vs. 6–7	4 verselines 16 words	
Strophe 4, vs. 8–10	8 verselines 32 words	
Canto III, vs. 11–13	**6 verselines** 26 words	
Strophe 5, v. 11	3 verselines 12 words	
Strophe 6, vs. 12–13	3 verselines 14 words	**26** verselines total
Canto IV, vs. 14–18	**13 verselines** 52 (2x**26**) words	
Strophe 7, vs. 14–15	5 verselines 19 words	
Strophe 8, 16a–d e–h	4 verselines 17 words	
Strophe 9, vs. 17–18	4 verselines 16 words	**13** verselines total

However, certain aspects of this intricate study cut across a number of other, more prominent and audience-perceptible features of the Song (as discussed below), which raises significant questions about its viability in these areas.

8.3.2.2 Three divisions

Whereas the two-division approach is normally based largely on content, scholars who posit three main sections for the Song tend to do so with reference more to prominent aspects of literary form and structure.

UBS Handbook on Exodus
This tripartite proposal has been adapted from Muilenburg's classic (1966) study (Osborn and Hatton 1999:356; cf. also Berlin and Brettler 2004:136):

Introit (call to worship) 15.1b
   I. Yahweh has defeated the Egyptians. 15.2–6
         Confession 15.2–3
         Narrative 15.4–5
         Response 15.6
   II. Yahweh is greater than all the gods. 15.7–11
         Confession 15.7–8
         Narrative 15.9–10
         Response 15.11
   III. Yahweh will establish his people. 15.12–16
         Confession 15.12–14
         Narrative 15.15–16a
         Response 15.16b–17[22]
   Closing statement of praise 15.18

Patterson (1995/2004)

In two detailed studies, Patterson confirms Muilenburg's strophic division with closing "refrains,"[23] adding the observation "that each refrain proceeds not only on the basis of the prior stanza but points to the one that follows" (1995:455). This creates a threefold "hinged" structure, as above, which furthermore gives the song as a whole a perceptible formal cohesion as well as semantic coherence. Alter too agrees with this three-strophe arrangement, adding that "each strophe then ends with a line celebrating God's [*sic*, why not Yahweh's?] power, and these end lines for a progression: first God's power in battle, then His might over all imagined divine beings for whom men have made claims, and finally, in a kind of envoi [i.e., conclusion], the affirmation of his eternal sovereignty" (1985:52).

---

[22] By interpreting the three "Responses" as "Introits," Kaiser comes up with four stanzas, which he terms "strophes" (1994:90). This is an indication of how differently this poem's structure is viewed by scholars and the consequent dilemma for the translator—and musical composer. Discourse unit endings will need to be crafted rather differently from beginnings with regard to sense as well as sound.

[23] These are not, poetically speaking, refrains because they are not similar enough with regard to form and content. I will therefore term these passages (vv. 6, 11, and 16b–17) "doxologies" since they are the only verses that feature divinely oriented vocatives. A possible refrain for the Song as a whole might have been v. 1b, which is essentially reiterated by Miriam in v. 21. On the other hand, perhaps the designation "refrain" could still be used, in a less strict sense: "The word refrain is not being used in a technical sense, for a refrain is a line of poetry which is repeated periodically in a poem. Actually these refrains [in Exo. 15] are dividers or buffers between the strophes. These refrains or dividers connect what precedes and follows." (McCabe 1981:62).

New English Translation
The NET suggests that Exodus 15:1–18 presents a song of praise sung by Moses and the people right after their deliverance from the pursuing Egyptian army at the Red Sea. This song falls into three sections:
a. Praise to God (1–3)
b. Cause for the praise (4–13)
c. Conclusion (14–18).
However, in the English translation of the text, verse 19 is formatted and punctuated as an integral portion of the poem itself (termed the "coda," according to Steiner 2013:6). The NET comments as follows regarding this division:

> The point of the first section is that God's saving acts inspire praise from his people; the second is that God's powerful acts deliver his people from the forces of evil; and the third section is that God's demonstrations of his sovereignty inspire confidence in him by his people. So the Victory Song is very much like the other declarative praise psalms – the resolve to praise, the power of God, the victory over the enemies, the incomparability of God in his redemption, and the fear of the people.

Steiner ("Celebration in Song and Dance")
In the most recent study of Exodus 15, Steiner views the main body of the Song as consisting of "two strophes/stanzas/paragraphs, with a pivotal centerpiece" (2013:6). However, in effect the division being proposed is tripartite in nature:

> **Retrospect** (1b–10): Celebrating *past* victory at the Sea–with a focus upon YHWH's incredible greatness and power
> > **Pivotal Centerpiece** (11–13): A celebration of *past* and *future* events, centered in YHWH's incomparable being.
> **Prospect** (14–18): Celebrating the *future* conquest in Canaan—with a focus upon YHWH's anticipated earthly residence and eternal rule.

Steiner also feels that "verse 19 functions as a coda, finale, or reprise. It reinforces the occasion and impetus for the Song and provides the upbeat to the explanatory appendix on Miriam's Song (vv. 20–21)" (ibid.).

8.3.3 A "porhetorical" analysis of Exodus 15:1–21

A *porhetorical* analysis of the original is a study that focuses on the poetic, rhetorical, and oral features of the Hebrew text.[24] How is this done?

---

[24] For a more detailed explanation and exemplification of literary-structural analysis techniques—a sequenced methodology and its rationale—with special reference to Hebrew poetry, see Wendland 2004:ch. 7, 2011:126–149.

Essentially, three basic steps are involved: (a) identifying all prominent instances of linguistic *recursion* (phonological, morphological, syntactic, lexical, conceptual) and the resultant *patterns* that are thereby formed; (b) noting all places where a *significant shift* occurs in terms of form or content (e.g., topic, speaker, addressee, type of discourse, etc.); and (c) putting a + b together in an evaluation of pragmatic *function*—whether structural, rhetorical, artistic, and/or performative in nature. These three criteria are combined in the analysis that follows, primarily in the footnotes that accompany the text of Exodus 15:1–21 below as it has been demarcated into poetic units. After the detailed text study, a summary of the discourse structure is presented.

The Hebrew text is given along with a corresponding literal (ESV) translation.[25] The Hebrew is broken down into a sequence of poetic lines (cola), with horizontal spaces indicating minor strophic (---) and major stanza (= = = =) unit boundaries. I have determined poetic lines (cola) on the combined basis of stress and sense—that is, a meaningful unit (normally a syntactic clause or its equivalent) comprised of two to four (on average) word-accent units (i.e., a cluster of syllables having a single major stress).[26] The line length in Hebrew lyric poetry is flexible, i.e., a free rhythm, but often sequences are established throughout a strophe to create a certain rhythmic continuity which may be broken or interrupted at the start of a new strophe.[27] As indicated above, periodic comments on this pericope and the rationale for its poetic organization are offered in footnotes. The reason for doing it this way is that readers can then assess the analytical observations immediately with reference to the original text, rather than having to page back and forth if the analysis were summarized elsewhere.

---

[25] This *English Standard Version* text was obtained from the following open website: http://www.biblestudytools.com/esv/exodus/15.html/. Accessed September 2, 2017 and used by permission.

[26] "A stress (or accent) is a greater amount of force given to one syllable in speaking than is given to another…. When stresses recur at fixed intervals…the result is called a meter" (Kennedy and Gioia 2002:189–190). After his own detailed metrical survey of this psalm, McCabe concludes: "It is…useless to look for a metric system in the Song of the Reed Sea" (1981:76).

[27] I would agree with the poetic rhythmic principles enunciated by Benjamin Hrushovsky (1971), as cited in support by Robert Alter: "[Since] by rule no two stresses are permitted to follow each other,…each [word] stress dominates a group of two, three, four syllables; there are two, three, or four such groups in a verset [i.e., colon]; and two, three, or four parallel versets in a sentence…. It is true that in many poems a particular count of stresses in each of the matched versets tends to predominate, the most common combinations being 3:3 and 3:2, but there is little evidence that the counting of stresses was actually observed as a governing norm for a poem…so the term meter should probably be abandoned for biblical verse" (Alter 1985:8–9).

This is certainly not the only valid discourse arrangement possible, as the previous discussion has indicated (e.g., two versus three stanzas). However, it is a proposal that pays appropriate attention to issues of poetic form, content, and function, and is therefore justifiable as a model that translators might confidently follow in their analysis of the text and in their target language rendition.

1 Then[a] Moses and the people of Israel sang this[b] song to the LORD,	1 אָ֣ז יָשִֽׁיר־מֹשֶׁה֩ וּבְנֵ֨י יִשְׂרָאֵ֜ל אֶת־הַשִּׁירָ֤ה הַזֹּאת֙ לַֽיהוָ֔ה
saying,[c]	וַיֹּאמְר֖וּ לֵאמֹ֑ר
"I will sing to the LORD, for[d] he has triumphed gloriously;	אָשִׁ֤ירָה לַֽיהוָה֙ כִּֽי־גָאֹ֣ה גָּאָ֔ה[e]
the horse and his rider he has thrown into the sea.	ס֥וּס וְרֹכְב֖וֹ רָמָ֥ה בַיָּֽם׃
= = = = = = = = = = = = = =	
2 The LORD is my strength and my song,	2 עָזִּ֤י וְזִמְרָת֙ יָ֔הּ[g]
and he has become my salvation;	וַֽיְהִי־לִ֖י לִֽישׁוּעָ֑ה
this is my God, and I will praise him,	זֶ֤ה אֵלִי֙ וְאַנְוֵ֔הוּ
my father's God, and I will exalt him.	אֱלֹהֵ֥י אָבִ֖י וַאֲרֹמְמֶֽנְהוּ׃[h]
3 The LORD is a man of war;	3 יְהוָ֖ה אִ֣ישׁ מִלְחָמָ֑ה
the LORD is his name.[i]	יְהוָ֖ה שְׁמֽוֹ׃
- - - - - - - - - - - - - - -	
4 "Pharaoh's chariots and his host he cast into the sea,	4 מַרְכְּבֹ֥ת פַּרְעֹ֛ה וְחֵיל֖וֹ יָרָ֣ה בַיָּ֑ם[j]
and his chosen officers were sunk in the Red Sea.[k]	וּמִבְחַ֥ר שָֽׁלִשָׁ֖יו טֻבְּע֥וּ בְיַם־סֽוּף׃
5 The floods covered them;	5 תְּהֹמֹ֖ת יְכַסְיֻ֑מוּ
they went down into the depths	יָרְד֥וּ בִמְצוֹלֹ֖ת[l]
like a stone.	כְּמוֹ־אָֽבֶן׃[m]
- - - - - - - - - - - - - - -	
6 Your right hand, O LORD, glorious in power,	6 יְמִֽינְךָ֣ יְהוָ֔ה נֶאְדָּרִ֖י בַּכֹּ֑חַ
your right hand, O LORD, shatters the enemy.	יְמִֽינְךָ֥ יְהוָ֖ה תִּרְעַ֥ץ אוֹיֵֽב׃[n]

= = = = = = = = = = = = = = = =	
7 In the greatness of your majesty	וּבְרֹב גְּאוֹנְךָ[o]
you overthrow your adversaries;	תַּהֲרֹס קָמֶיךָ
you send out your fury;	תְּשַׁלַּח חֲרֹנְךָ[p]
it consumes them like stubble.	יֹאכְלֵמוֹ כַּקַּשׁ:[q]
8 At the blast of your nostrils	וּבְרוּחַ אַפֶּיךָ 8
the waters piled up;[s]	נֶעֶרְמוּ מַיִם
the floods stood up in a heap;	נִצְּבוּ כְמוֹ־נֵד נֹזְלִים
the deeps congealed in the heart of the sea.	קָפְאוּ תְהֹמֹת בְּלֶב־יָם:[t]
- -	
9 The enemy said,[u] "I will pursue,	אָמַר אוֹיֵב אֶרְדֹּף
I will overtake, I will divide the spoil;	אַשִּׂיג אֲחַלֵּק שָׁלָל
my desire shall have its fill of them.	תִּמְלָאֵמוֹ נַפְשִׁי
I will draw my sword;	אָרִיק חַרְבִּי
my hand shall destroy them."[v]	תּוֹרִישֵׁמוֹ יָדִי:
10 You blew with your wind;[w]	נָשַׁפְתָּ בְרוּחֲךָ 10
the sea covered them;	כִּסָּמוֹ יָם
they sank like lead	צָלֲלוּ[x] כַּעוֹפֶרֶת
in the mighty waters.	בְּמַיִם אַדִּירִים:[y]
- -	
11 "Who is like you, O LORD, among the gods?	מִי־כָמֹכָה בָּאֵלִם יְהוָה 11[z]
Who is like you, majestic in holiness,	מִי כָּמֹכָה נֶאְדָּר בַּקֹּדֶשׁ
awesome in glorious deeds, doing wonders?	נוֹרָא[aa] תְהִלֹּת עֹשֵׂה פֶלֶא:
= = = = = = = = = = = = = = = =	
12 You stretched out your right hand;	נָטִיתָ יְמִינְךָ[ab] 12
the earth swallowed them.[ac]	תִּבְלָעֵמוֹ אָרֶץ:
13 You have led in your steadfast love[ad]	נָחִיתָ בְחַסְדְּךָ 13
the people whom you have redeemed;	עַם־זוּ גָּאָלְתָּ

you have guided them by your strength	נֵהַ֥לְתָּ [ae]בְעָזְּךָ֖
to your holy abode.	אֶל־נְוֵ֥ה קָדְשֶֽׁךָ׃ [af]
---	
14 The peoples[ag] have heard; they tremble;[ah]	14 שָֽׁמְע֥וּ עַמִּ֖ים יִרְגָּז֑וּן
pangs have seized the inhabitants of Philistia.	חִ֣יל אָחַ֔ז יֹשְׁבֵ֖י פְּלָֽשֶׁת׃
15 Now are the chiefs of Edom dismayed;	15 אָ֤ז נִבְהֲלוּ֙ אַלּוּפֵ֣י אֱד֔וֹם
trembling seizes the leaders of Moab;	אֵילֵ֣י מוֹאָ֔ב יֹֽאחֲזֵ֖מוֹ רָ֑עַד
all the inhabitants of Canaan have melted away.	נָמֹ֕גוּ כֹּ֖ל יֹשְׁבֵ֥י כְנָֽעַן׃ [ai]
16 Terror and dread fall upon them;	16 תִּפֹּ֨ל עֲלֵיהֶ֤ם אֵימָ֙תָה֙ וָפַ֔חַד
because of the greatness of your arm,	בִּגְדֹ֥ל זְרוֹעֲךָ֖
they are still as a stone,[aj]	יִדְּמ֣וּ כָּאָ֑בֶן [ak]
---	
till your people, O LORD, pass by [over/through],[al]	עַד־יַעֲבֹ֤ר עַמְּךָ֙ יְהֹוָ֔ה
till the people pass by whom you have purchased.[am]	עַד־יַעֲבֹ֖ר עַם־ז֥וּ קָנִֽיתָ׃ [an]
17 You will bring them in and plant them on your own mountain,	17 תְּבִאֵ֗מוֹ וְתִטָּעֵ֙מוֹ֙ בְּהַ֣ר נַחֲלָֽתְךָ֔
the place, O LORD, which you have made for your abode,	מָכ֧וֹן לְשִׁבְתְּךָ֛ פָּעַ֖לְתָּ יְהֹוָ֑ה
the sanctuary,[ao] O Lord, which your hands have established.[ap]	מִקְּדָ֕שׁ אֲדֹנָ֖י כּוֹנְנ֥וּ יָדֶֽיךָ׃
= = = = = = = = = = = = = = =	
18 The LORD will reign forever and ever."[aq]	18 יְהֹוָ֥ה ׀ יִמְלֹ֖ךְ לְעֹלָ֥ם וָעֶֽד׃
= = = = = = = = = = = = = = =	
19 For when the horses of Pharaoh with his chariots and his horsemen went into the sea,[ar]	19 כִּ֣י [as]בָא֩ ס֨וּס פַּרְעֹ֜ה בְּרִכְבּ֤וֹ וּבְפָרָשָׁיו֙ בַּיָּ֔ם

the LORD brought back the waters of the sea upon them,	וַיָּ֤שֶׁב יְהוָה֙ עֲלֵהֶ֔ם אֶת־מֵ֖י הַיָּ֑ם
but the people of Israel walked on dry ground in the midst of the sea.[at]	וּבְנֵ֧י יִשְׂרָאֵ֛ל הָלְכ֥וּ בַיַּבָּשָׁ֖ה בְּת֥וֹךְ הַיָּֽם׃ [au] פ
20 Then Miriam the prophetess, the sister of Aaron, took a tambourine in her hand,	20 וַתִּקַּח֩ מִרְיָ֨ם הַנְּבִיאָ֜ה אֲח֧וֹת אַהֲרֹ֛ן אֶת־הַתֹּ֖ף בְּיָדָ֑הּ
and all the women went out after her with tambourines and dancing.	וַתֵּצֶ֤אןָ כָל־הַנָּשִׁים֙ אַחֲרֶ֔יהָ בְּתֻפִּ֖ים וּבִמְחֹלֹֽת׃
21 And Miriam sang to them:	21 וַתַּ֥עַן לָהֶ֖ם מִרְיָ֑ם
= = = = = = = = = = = = = = =	
"Sing to the LORD, for he has triumphed gloriously;	שִׁ֤ירוּ[av] לַֽיהוָה֙ כִּֽי־גָאֹ֣ה גָּאָ֔ה
the horse and his rider he has thrown into the sea."	ס֥וּס וְרֹכְב֖וֹ רָמָ֥ה בַיָּֽם׃ ס

[a] The distinctive Hebrew temporal adverb "Then…" (אָז–picking up the "on that day" בַּיּ֣וֹם הַה֔וּא of 14:30) plus the indication of a new genre ("song") coupled with its specified speaker(s) and divine addressee clearly marks the start of a new major discourse division, and yet one that is also closely connected with the narrative account of ch. 14.

[b] The cataphoric (forward-pointing) demonstrative "this" links the "song" referred to in v. 1a with the "sung" text of v. 1bff.

[c] The more expansive Hebrew speech introduction formula announces the onset of direct discourse, and hence a new structural unit.

[d] Craghan offers a somewhat different perspective on the crucial conjunction כִּי in relation to the structure of psalmic praise: "The structure of the psalm of descriptive praise is relatively simple. In the introduction the psalmist expresses his intention to praise God or he may invite others to join in this praise. In the main section the psalmist offers reasons or motives for such praise. They are typically introduced by the conjunction 'for' (*kî* in Hebrew). However, as C. Stuhlmueller (1983) remarks, this conjunction is more like our English exclamation point. The purpose of the main section 'is more to sustain wonder and adoration in God's presence, to involve the worshiping community in God's glorious action'…. For Crüsmann this particle has the function of introducing direct discourse. Hence it is not the reason for the praise but the carrying out of the praise demanded by such imperatives as Exodus 15:21" (Craghan 1985:26). One wonders if aspects of all these elements are not involved here: an exclamative reason in direct discourse.

[e] The perfect form of the verb "rise up loftily/proudly" (גָּאָה) along with its infinitive absolute sonically and semantically emphasize the song's beginning: "[Yahweh] has acted majestically" (active) or "he is highly exalted" (stative)—or possibly both senses might be in mind. The topic of Yahweh's overwhelming defeat of the Egyptian army at the Reed Sea is in focus throughout the Song's first two stanzas (e.g., vv. 4–5, 8, 10).

ᶠ The asyndetic first word (אָשִׁ֣ירָה) echoes two instances of the root "sing" in the preceding verse. Miriam's corresponding song segment in v. 21 differs from the words in v. 1b only at the first verb, which is a direct imperative (שִׁ֤ירוּ) instead of Moses' cohortative form ("Let me sing"). This correspondence would suggest that these two poetic lines function as an initial introit, or call to worship, for the Song of Moses as a whole. It concisely summarized the liturgical action ("sing" = worship) and the twofold reason (כִּֽי) based on Yahweh's character ("greatly exalted") and saving action (defeating Israel's powerful enemies). Janzen observes: "When we see [better: 'hear'!] this verb, "let me sing," sprinkled some ten times throughout the Psalms, and this same cohortative form, "let me," of other verbs likewise so sprinkled, we may conclude that the act of self-encouragement in worship of God, as an internalization of the call from others to such worship, is characteristic of biblical prayer" (2003:120)—and of corporate hymnody too, we might add.

ᵍ Perhaps the shortened form of "Yahweh" (יָֽהּ) is used here (cf. 3a–b) for emphasis and to create a more poetically sounding couplet (v. 2a–b). Scholars debate the meaning of the apparently "archaic" (Cole 1973:123) word "my song" (וְזִמְרָת֙), which "does not occur elsewhere in Hebrew" (ibid.). However, as the NET states the case (supported by the UBS Handbook, Osborn and Hatton 1999:358; Holladay 1996:76), "there is nothing substantially wrong with 'my song' in the line—only that it would be a nicer match if it had something to do with strength."

ʰ The sequence of line-ending "a" assonance suddenly shifts here to "û" (v. 2c–d) to signal the psalmist's personal response to the LORD's mighty works of salvation (לִֽישׁוּעָ֑ה). There is also some notable א consonance in lines 2c–d.

ⁱ The first strophe of stanza 1 progresses to an emotive climax as well as a thematic peak in this short concluding confessional line יְהוָ֣ה שְׁמֽוֹ. The divine name is foregrounded by being syntactically fronted in each of the final four lines of this initial poetic paragraph.

ʲ The final two words of this strophe's first line recall those at the close of the introit (v. 1d).

ᵏ A shift from the direct address to Yahweh in vv. 2–3 to the narrative description of vv. 4–5 would indicate a strophic break at this point. The sudden shift in poetic line length (from short to long) in the bicolon of v. 4 helps to mark this division (cf. 3b).

ˡ A chiastically rhymed (-ôth/-û//-û/-ôth) syntactic arrangement (N + V // V + N) sets off the first two lines of v. 5, leaving the following short climactic non-verbal phrase (a graphic simile) to close out the strophe (end stress). Semantically then, the archaic words for "floods" and "depths" make mournful allusion to cosmic waters (Brueggemann 1994:800).

ᵐ Another short line (2 words) distinguishes the close of this strophe, as in the preceding one (3b).

ⁿ A shift back to direct address in praise of Yahweh coupled with a line-initial "terraced" pattern (in which lexical material from one unit, usually near its end, is repeated in the following unit, usually near its beginning) featuring a repeated phrase with the divine name in vocative form ("your right hand, O LORD") operate together to distinguish the final bicolon of praise that concludes stanza 1 of the Song of Moses. It consists of three strophes: vv. 2–3, 4–5, and 6. The "right hand" (יְמִֽינְךָ) is "Yahweh's most potent capacity for action" (Brueggemann 1994:800), whether for his people or against an enemy.

[o] The noun גְּאוֹן is cognate with the verb גאה in v. 1b—the conceptual correspondence here at the respective beginnings of different discourse units being an instance of structural anaphora.
[p] "The verb is the Piel of שׁלח *(shalakh)*, the same verb used throughout [Exodus] for the demand on Pharaoh to release Israel. Here, in some irony, God released his wrath on them" (NET 2003:153).
[q] The four short lines of v. 7 and the first two of v. 8 are demarcated phonologically by the 2nd sg. pronominal suffix *–châ*.
[r] The first word of v. 8 (וּבְרוּחַ) sonically and syntactically matches the first word of v. 7 (וּבְרֹב), an instance of strophe-internal anaphora. The paired *waw*-initial lines thus serve to link vv. 7–8 even as they seem to distinguish these two from v. 6.
[s] The divine theophanic imagery of hot punitive anger distinguishes the middle of strophe 1 of stanza 2 (vv. 7b–8a). "The poetry here moves well beyond the specific enactment of the Exodus and appeals to the language of the Creator's victory over and administration of chaos" (Brueggemann 1994:800).
[t] The three final lines of this strophe (8b–d) all end in *"-m"* and gradually increase in length. These lines also resound in nasals, acoustically echoing the key terms "sea" *(yam)* and "waters" *(mayim)*.
[u] Roughly in the formal center of this song we hear the only word of "the enemy", a mini-taunt, foregrounded in direct speech. "The heavy threefold beat of this verse [9a–b] is both impressive and primitive in its simplicity" (Cole 1973:124). It is an instance of dramatic irony, for the listening audience already knows the fate of the bragging speakers. This boast features a staccato-like sequence of action verbs that are satirical in their contextual impact and self-indicting implication (note all the 1st sg. pronominal references). Yahweh simply "blows" with his punitive "breath", and they are all gone (v. 10)! "The staccato phrases... almost imitate the heavy, breathless heaving of the Egyptians as, with what reserve of strength they have left, they vow, 'I will..., I will..., I will...'" (NET 2003:154). The final two paired verbs of cruel intention are rhymed and "heavy," manifesting "archaic endings" (Cole 1973:124): I (collective, the army speaking on behalf of Pharaoh) will "get my fill of them" (תִּמְלָאֵמוֹ) and "destroy them" (תּוֹרִישֵׁמוֹ)—with reference to the ostensibly defenseless Israelites.
[v] The rapid-fire series of 1st (sg.) pronominal references (*'aleph*-initial merging into final *–iy* sounds) gives this pseudo-quotation in ridicule of its self-centered ("I/my") speakers (Durham 1987:207) both cohesion and coherence.
[w] All the enemy's arrogant boasts (v. 9) are stopped short by a brief breath of the LORD (נָשַׁפְתָּ בְרוּחֲךָ)—with the form of the text mimicking its pragmatic effect. The contrast is phonically underscored by the pronominal suffixes, which suddenly shift from "my" (ִי) to "your" (ךָ). Asyndeton highlights this divine action and its immediate results upon "them"—the military foes of God's people (v. 10b–d). This bold anthropomorphism poetically recalls the reversal or undoing of 14:21 (cf. vv. 27–28) and anticipates the narrative summary of 15:19.
[x] "The verb may have the idea of sinking with a gurgling sound, like water going into a whirlpool" (NET 2003:154; cf. Cole 1973:124); it echoes the corresponding nominal from v. 5: מְצוֹלָה. "One can hear in the poem the blub, blub, blub of water as bodies disappear into the depths, defeated and helpless" (Brueggemann 1994:799). So from God's punitive "blowing" to the enemy's pathetic "gurgling"—sound amplifies the sense of this text!

ʸ The LORD's inanimate watery agents carry out his swift judgment upon the Egyptian army—the closure of this strophe being highlighted by alliteration in "m," perhaps once again sonically reflecting the "sea" *(yam)* and its "waters" *(mayim)* (cf. vv. 5 and 8—i.e., unit-ending structural epiphora; Wendland 2004:127). Examples like this (and there are more) would contradict Reger's claim that "structural poetic devices on the *phonetic level* like sound repetition, alliteration, assonance or rhyme cannot be observed in the Song of the Sea" (2010:70).

ᶻ Another praise passage (with an audible shift in line length from vv. 9–10) serves to conclude the second stanza, corresponding in form, content, and function to v. 6 (similar end units, structural epiphora). This doxology is more reflective and broader in scope than that of v. 6. The tricolon of v. 11 is distinguished by the divine vocative, an initial terraced pattern, and a double rhetorical question, the second twice as long as the first. The internal strophic structure of stanza 2 (vv. 7–11) thus parallels that of stanza 1: an initial word in praise of Yahweh's great power (vv. 7–8) is followed by a largely narrative strophe that describes the plight of the enemy (vv. 9–10), and the stanza concludes with a final word lauding the LORD in more general terms (v. 11).

ᵃᵃ The phonically paired Niphal participles "majestic" (נֶאְדָּר) and "awesome" (נוֹרָא) foreground the incomparability of Yahweh in relation to other so-called "gods" (i.e., pagan idols). One could argue that the lexical correspondence here acts as an overlapping case of terraced parallelism that serves to highlight and thematically develop the first pairing (מִי כָמֹכָה). Assonance in "ô" and lexical balance (4 + 4) audibly links lines 11b–c.

ᵃᵇ Reappearance of the key term "your right hand" (יְמִינְךָ) from v. 6 serves to enclose the middle stanza (vv. 7–12), an instance of structural exclusio. On the other hand, the narrative confessional tone of vv. 12–13 recalls that of the first strophe of the second stanza (vv. 7–8). The content of v. 12 recalls that of v. 10, though now it is the 'earth' (אֶרֶץ) that swallows the Egyptians to complement the "sea" (יָם).

ᵃᶜ Back-references to the LORD's all-powerful "right hand" (v. 6), conjoined with the enemy's consequently being "covered/swallowed" in death and defeat (vv. 5, 10), are combined in v. 12 at the onset of stanza 3—an audibly perceptible cohesive device that links the Song's three stanzas together. The pronominal reference "them" on the verb (תִּבְלָעֵמוֹ) is ambiguous—perhaps deliberately so, including the Egyptian "enemies" (v. 10) as well as their "gods" (v. 11)!

ᵃᵈ After a brief reminder of the recent past and God's deliverance of Israel at the sea (12a), there is an apparent shift in focus to the "land" (אֶרֶץ) (12b), though the theme of divine punishment continues. Then, a cluster of key covenantal terms, leading off with the foundational חֶסֶד, appears in the text (13) to announce the future-oriented theme of the third strophe. In this prophetic vision (the verbs can be construed as forward-looking "prophetic perfects," as in the NET and NIV; cf. Cole 1973:124), Yahweh will manifest his protective "steadfast love" as his "redeemed" people strike terror into their pagan enemies (vv. 14–16) on their journey to the LORD's "holy abode" in the promised land of Canaan (cf. v. 17). Miller seems to read "the language of creation" into the verb גָּאָלְתָּ (v. 13) (1986:74). More on the mark, he sees "the imagery of the divine shepherd keeping the flock…in relation to the community led into the promised land in the exodus (Exo. 15:13)" (Miller 1986:113).

ᵃᵉ The Piel form of this verb "seems to mean 'to guide to a watering-place' (See Ps. 23:2)" (NET 2003:154)—which would be a fascinating instance of contrastive irony, considering the present ascribed setting of this song! Yahweh's attribute of "strength" (עֹז) ties this latter portion of the Song to its opening (v. 2).

[af] The six poetic lines of the strophe comprised of vv. 12–13 all manifest two lexical units in contrast to the longer lines of v. 11—and vv. 14ff. as well. Each of the three bicola starts off with a verb beginning with the letter נ.

[ag] Reference to the (pagan) "peoples" (עַמִּים) contrasts with "the people (עַם) whom you have redeemed" in the preceding verse, thus highlighting the boundary between strophes.

[ah] Composed in the style of "epic narrative" (Reger 2010:64), caricatures referring to specific members of the pagan "peoples" coupled with various verbs of distress lend topical coherence to vv. 14–16a. A lexical chiastic arrangement also runs through this strophe: general reference "peoples" (עַמִּים) + a region "Philistia" (פְּלָשֶׁת) + specific people "Edom" (אֱדוֹם) // "Moab" (מוֹאָב) + "Canaan" (כְּנַעַן) + "upon them" (עֲלֵיהֶם). "The poem assigns to each of these reluctant witnesses a verb of anxiety and hostility: *seized, dismayed, trembling, melted*" (Brueggemann 1994:801). These nations are all circumscribed as it were by references to God's "people" (עַם) Israel in the surrounding strophes (vv. 13b, 16b). The "Israelites" (בְּנֵי יִשְׂרָאֵל) are not mentioned by name within the Song, only in the initial and final verses as an inclusio (1a, 19b).

[ai] The three lines of this tricolon manifest a chiastic syntactic arrangement: V—S / S'—V' / V"—S".

[aj] The strophic structure of stanza 3 parallels that of the preceding two stanzas. An initial word of direct praise for Yahweh's mighty deliverance of his people (vv. 12–13; note the reiterated 2nd sg. pronominal references) is followed by a descriptive strophe that portrays the fearful plight of the enemy (third person speech)—but now those of the pagan peoples of Canaan that Israel will have to defeat on the way (vv. 14–16c). Each of the three doxologies is preceded by a graphic simile that distinguishes the conclusion of the preceding strophe, thus functioning as instances of unit-closing structural epiphora: v. 5 "like a stone" (כְּמוֹ־אָבֶן); v. 10 "like lead" (כַּעוֹפֶרֶת); v. 16c "as a stone" (כָּאָבֶן). The content of v. 16a–c parallels that of v. 12, thus establishing an inclusio for the first two strophes of stanza 3.

[ak] Paired metonymic references to Yahweh's *powerful* "arm" (זְרוֹעֲךָ) and "right hand" (יְמִינְךָ) in verses 16b and 12a act as a topical inclusio for the first two strophes of stanza 3, which is extended also to encompass the third strophe by "your hands" (יָדֶיךָ) in v. 17c. The climactic simile "as a stone" (כָּאָבֶן) in v. 16c is sonically similar to its referent, the combined heathen peoples of "Canaan" (כְּנַעַן) at the corresponding close of v. 15 (structural epiphora).

[al] The word עבר could be rendered 'pass over', with reference to the Reed Sea of stanzas 1–2, or 'pass through', with reference to stanza 3 and the movement of God's people implied therein. Perhaps the verb is deliberately (poetically) ambiguous. "Your people" manifestly contrasts with "the peoples" mentioned in strophe 2, specifically in 14a (structural anaphora).

[am] The final expression in v. 16e "people whom you purchased" (עַם־זוּ קָנִיתָ) reflects a similar phrase near the beginning of the stanza in v. 13b "people whom you redeemed" (עַם־זוּ גָּאָלְתָּ). The last strophe of stanza 3 is similar to those which end stanzas 1 and 2 in that it features an initial terraced pattern in a bicolon that lauds Yahweh's deliverance of his people (v. 16d–e). This time, however, the word of praise is extended by a verse (17) that functions as an epilogue, highlighting once

again the LORD's name in direct (vocative) address, together with a prophetic promise concerning the new land ("mountain—place—sanctuary") towards which their journey, having safely crossed the Reed Sea, had just begun.

[an] Second person masculine singular pronominal suffixes from vv. 12–13 reappear in vv. 16–17 to enclose the stanza with the thematic spotlight on Yahweh, the Deliverer (vv. 1b–12) and Provider (vv. 13–17) of his people (lit. "your people" עַמְּךָ) Israel, Yahweh"s "redeemed people" (עַם־זוּ גָּאָלְתָּ) (v. 13).

[ao] The mention of "sanctuary" (מִקְּדָשׁ) in v. 17c prefigures the future Temple and reflects a similar reference to "abode of your holiness" (קָדְשֶׁךָ) in v. 13d— an inclusio of sorts for the third stanza.

[ap] In obvious contrast to the pagan place names of vv. 14–15 we have references to Yahweh's "mountain" (הַר), "abode" (יֹשֵׁב), and "sanctuary" (מִקְּדָשׁ) (with increasing specificity!) at the close of stanza 3 in the tricolon of v. 17. These suggest not only a sure place of divine refuge, but also a site for religious worship, with prophetic reference to the future Temple on Mt. Zion, where the LORD will symbolically (and ideally) "reign" among his people as "exalted King" (v. 18, cf. v. 1b).

[aq] This final formulaic royal panegyric utterance (the text's only monocolon) concludes the psalm and corresponds thematically to its initial introit in v. 1c–d (the exalted LORD rules as King forever). "As a concluding affirmation, this colon acknowledges the power and majesty of God as depicted in the song for the past and proclaims it for future times, too" (Reger 2010:66).

[ar] Structurally as well as conceptually it can be argued that verses 19–21 belong logically after v. 31 of chapter 14. It thus serves as a bounding text that highlights the enclosed Victory Song of 15:1b–18. From this perspective, verse 19 summarizes the preceding account (14:26–30), while verses 20–21 (if left in their original position) preview the major song pericope that follows. It may be further conjectured that Miriam may have been the real author of this artful religious poem (cf. Janzen 1992, Anderson 1987:288), being anonymously included among "the Israelites" mentioned in its introduction of 15:1a.

[as] Janzen observes that the opening כִּי performs an important structural function in the discourse as a flashback marker: "Exod 15:19–21 is introduced in Hebrew (and in earlier English translations) by the conjunction 'for,' and functions as an analepsis which belatedly [for the purpose of structurally circumscribing an enclosed passage] gives the reason for the singing in 15:1–18. This analepsis (working like 'for' in Gen 20:18) is obscured in the NRSV [and many other versions] which omits the 'for'" (2003:119, words in brackets added). The initial כִּי in this case could also be interpreted as an instance of climactic asseverative usage, i.e., "Indeed…!"

[at] As already noted, the NET includes v. 19 as part of the Sea Song. The passage does display a number of formal poetic features, such as the repetition of "the sea" at the end of each of three constituent lines and a chiastic (V–S/S—V) syntactic arrangement to highlight the semantic shift that occurs in lines 2–3. However, the length of these lines, along with the initial "When/For/…" (כִּי) and the prosaic character of the first line would suggest that they do not belong to the song per se. Licht (1986:92) also notes the poetic character of v. 19, though he too does not regard it as part of the preceding song.

[au] The Hebrew letter פ irregularly marks an "open portion" (פתוחה, *petuchah*) in the Hebrew Masoretic text, roughly equivalent to a paragraph unit. The appearance of this marker at the end of v. 19 may have been the reason for the

NET's decision to include this verse as part of the preceding poetic text. At the end of verse 21 then we find the corresponding letter ס, which indicates a larger sectional, or "closed portion" (סתומה, *setumah*) of discourse.

[av] As mentioned above, Miriam's words are exactly the same as those found in v. 1b except for this initial imperative form.

8.3.4 Structural summary

The following is an outline of the symmetrically composed structure of Exodus 15:1–21, which was delineated in textual detail above. It supports the overall compositional unity of this Song with respect to form, content, and function:[28]

A **Narrative Frame**—Introduction to the Victory Thanksgiving Song (Moses and the Israelites) (1a)

　B Song's **Opening Introit** (1b)—an exordium (incipit)

　　C **Body** of the Song—three stanzas

　　　1. **Stanza**: Yahweh's defeat of Pharaoh and his army—in general (2–6)[29]

　　　　a) Strophe: Praise the LORD (2–3)

　　　　b) Strophe: What the LORD did (4–5)

　　　　c) Strophe: Praise the LORD (6) (this 3rd strophe may function as a communal doxology throughout the psalm?)[30]

　　　2. **Stanza**: Yahweh's defeat of his enemies[31]—in detail (7–11)

　　　　a) Strophe: Praise the LORD for what He did (7–8)

　　　　b) Strophe: Arrogant boasts of the enemy (9–10)

　　　　c) Strophe: Praise the LORD (11)

---

[28] This conclusion is supported by a number of literary studies of this text, one of the more recent being that of Reger (2010:77): "It forms a unified whole and by its structure composed of introit, stanzas with refrains and coda is shaped as one coherent literary unit. Thematically, its parts are kept together by reappearing motifs and repeated key words."

[29] Strophe a of stanza 1 develops line 1 of the Introit; strophe b develops line 2 of the Introit; strophe c responds to strophes a and b.

[30] Each of the concluding hymnic responses, or doxologies (the vocative praise "c" strophes), serve as the primary organizing devices within the text. They function as thematic hinge verses, reiterating past content and previewing what is to come in the poem. This is true even in the final one (vv. 16b–17), which obviously reviews past content, but also looks forward to the LORD's royal rule over his holy land/place and people (v. 18). In performative terms, the doxologies function like refrains: "Refrains serve to structure a poem or song. They also 'enable people listening (whether as audience or congregation) to join in'" (Reger 2010:69, citing Watson 1984:297).

[31] The enemies are not specified in this second stanza, although the Egyptian army at the Reed Sea is clearly being referred to.

3. **Stanza:** Yahweh *will* defeat Israel's enemies[32] and establish them in their 'land' (12–17)[33]

  a) *Strophe: Praise the LORD for what He did and will do for his people* (12–13)[34]

  b) *Strophe: All Israel's enemies will be terrified* (14–16a)

  c) *Strophe: Praise the LORD for providing his people with a dwelling place* (16b–17)

B' Song's **Concluding Coda** (18)

A' **Narrative Frame**—Introduction to the *Victory Thanksgiving Song* (focus on Miriam) (19–21) (cf. Patterson 2004:51).

The three doxologies are crucial, therefore, not only for delineating the structure of the Song,[35] but also for unfolding its thematic development. The content of the first two stanzas builds up to and culminates in the third: The LORD's ultimate purpose in the Exodus deliverance was to make it possible for Israel to continue their journey, going out from Egypt and through the territories of various tribal enemies in order to reach their divinely appointed homeland (vv. 13, 16b–17). The medial praise verse (v. 11) is of particular importance; its singers are (almost) at a loss for words, as their rhetorical questions imply. Thus, the three lines of verse 11 "express the almost inexpressible: they formulate exactly why God is as peerless as the head sentence 'Who is like You' states, and they formulate it through descriptive terms singing his praise" (Fokkelman, 1998:28). In addition, as pointed out by Freedman (1980:209):[36]

Standing at the center and apex of the poem, it relates equally to both strophes [*sic*]: the God described in vs 11

---

[32] The enemies that Yahweh will defeat on behalf of Israel are no longer the Egyptians—but rather the pagan peoples that they will encounter on the way to Canaan as well as those currently living in the land. Strophes a and b develop line 2 of the Introit, while strophe c develops line 1.

[33] Strophe a of stanza 3 reflects back on the content of the two preceding stanzas and also previews the rest of the Song; strophe b gives the contrastive pagan perspective on these events; strophe c presents a thematic peak from the point of view of God's people: they have reached their goal with Yahweh's help in the land he has chosen for them.

[34] "This strophe is the turning point that leads away from the sea and towards the land" (Reger 2010:64).

[35] "Thus the three refrains or dividers form the skeletal structure on which the poem is built" (Freedman 1974:165).

[36] In terms of form (position within the Song), content (highlighting the supremacy of Yahweh), and pragmatic function (the paired rhetorical questions), Labuschagne too feels that v. 11 stands out as the poem's peak point: "For the gist of the poem, representing its quintessential idea, we have to look for another deliberately designed meaningful centre. This is to be found on the level of the strophic structure: the middle strophe 5, v. 11" (2007:7).

is equally responsible for the victory at the sea and for the triumphant march to the Holy Land. By being less specific than the other refrains, which relate directly to the theme of their respective strophes (i.e., vs 6 focuses on the powerful right hand of Yahweh by which he wreaked destruction on the enemy; vs 16 speaks of the passage of the people of Yahweh into the promised land), vs 11 serves them both as center and fulcrum.

Furthermore, the generalized theological wording of v. 11 at the thematic center of the Song makes it relevant and applicable to virtually any age and human situation—the good times as well as the bad as far as God's people are concerned. Thus, Israel's Song at the Sea is "is more a celebration of Yahweh and the kind of God he is [for all believers] than a celebration of all that Yahweh had done at the sea and would do beyond it" (Durham 1987:210; brackets in original).

If v. 11 is thematically important at the end of the second stanza, then what about v. 12 at the start of the third and final stanza? Robert Alter has an excellent structural explanation for the important topical transition here (1985:53–54):

> A purposeful transition is brilliantly effected at the very beginning of the last strophe with the phrase "the earth swallowed them." This obviously refers to the drowning of the Egyptians, a meaning reinforced...by God's repeating Moses' gesture of stretching out his hand over the sea, and also by the term *'eretz*, which sometimes refers to the underworld rather than to the earth.... One might think of this transition as the application on a larger structural scale of the technique of overlap we have seen used between versets and between lines. God the destroyer of the Egyptians at the Reed Sea becomes in a single, scarcely perceptible step the guide of his people through the wilderness and into the Land...

The third stanza (vv. 12–17) is not simply another poetic composition tacked on to the first two to form a "composite poem" (Durham 1987:207). Rather, the final section presupposes and is built upon what has preceded it in the song. Thus, the act "redemption" (13) that the pagan peoples "hear" about and "tremble" over (14–16) in a cause-effect relationship is nothing other than Yahweh's defeat of the Egyptian hosts at the Reed Sea (1b–11, with v. 12 serving as a transitional link). In ironic hindsight, if the boasting Egyptians had known what awaited them in the great seabed (stanza 2, strophe b), their response would have been like that of their fellow pagan peoples (stanza 3, strophe b). There is also an interesting connective link that ties stanza 3 to stanza 1 via their closing doxologies in v. 6 and v. 16b in particular. Both of these verses are preceded by the pointed simile "like a stone" with reference to Israel's enemies (כְּמוֹ־אָבֶן 5b, כָּאָבֶן 16a). More significantly, the focal verb "pass by" (עבר) of v. 16b could also be rendered "pass over," thus fitting the immediate cotext of v. 16, with reference to the Reed Sea crossing of the people, and the wider context as well, that is, with reference to the great "Passover" event recorded in Exodus 12. Verse 17 then extends the praise passage of Yahweh by foregrounding *what he will do* for his people by virtue of *who he is* (cf. v. 11).

8.3.5 Implications

A description of the discourse structure of a biblical text serves as a roadmap that can guide translators as they render the passage meaningfully in their language in keeping with the genre that has been chosen to model the original in the target language. This is obviously applicable with regard to the text's visual poetic format—that is, how to demarcate the individual lines or where to place the strophe and stanza breaks (even when making the decision to differentiate between these two poetic units). But the discourse organization will also audibly affect the various beginnings, endings, and peak points within the poem with respect to how to distinguish these points of particular structural-thematic—and/or rhetorical significance through the use of corresponding stylistic features in the TL.

In the case of a musical version, the perceived textual arrangement is even more important, for example, in helping composers to lyrically (oral-aurally, melodically) differentiate the initial praise passages (the (a) strophes above) from the semi-narrative portions (b), or whether to highlight the concluding doxologies (c) by means of different, ideally communal/choral, voices. One might further decide to single out the introit (v. 1b) and epilogue (18) passages, through some special, attention-drawing musical technique, or even the centrally-positioned, ironic enemy's taunt-speech (v. 9) in some diagnostic, discordant way that sets this verse off perceptibly from its immediate cotext.

8.4 Microstructure

In this section I draw attention to and exemplify seven primary structure-supporting and discourse-enhancing (artistic/decorative and rhetorical/persuasive) features that are manifested in the Song.[37] Thus, these stylistic literary forms serve to help mark points of special importance in the poem's

---

[37] These are not necessarily the only poetic features that deserve mention in this pericope, but they do include some of the most important ones and sufficiently illustrate why considerable attention must be devoted to these functionally significant devices in the translation process.

organization (especially discourse boundaries and thematic peaks), to heighten the text's oral-aural impact and appeal as well as to enhance its memorability and memorizability. Functionally-equivalent devices will of course have to be sought in the target language in order to duplicate these various communicative goals.

8.4.1 Parallelism

Parallelism, the deliberate pairing of two to three formally and semantically related poetic lines consisting of from two to four "words" each (on average), is of course the defining sine qua non feature of Hebrew poetry. Contiguous parallelism is the most obvious, namely, when the parallel lines are sequentially adjacent to one another in the text in the form of bi- and tri-cola. In this case, any significant variation from the norm is of structural or rhetorical importance, for example, the Song's concluding monocolon (the doxological epilogue), or variations in relative colon length (e.g., stanza 2: strophe 1—long, strophe 2—short, strophe 3—long), or the three strategically placed terraced (overlapping parallel) constructions that seem to function as stanza-concluding, audience-involving doxologies (vv. 6, 11, 16b–17).

Discontinuous parallelism is not as commonly recognized, but it is equally diagnostic and important in Hebrew poetic discourse. This feature manifests itself whenever the semantically-related lines do not appear in adjacent position, but are rather separated within the text, mainly to demarcate discourse boundaries (Wendland 2004:127). Inclusio, where the A-B parallel lines occur at the beginning and ending of a distinct discourse unit, is the best known of these devices, e.g., vv. 1b and 18b to delineate the Song as a whole. But the A-B poetic lines may also occur at: (a) the respective beginnings of different units—aperture (or anaphora)—e.g., vv. 1b–c and 19 to separate the poem from a concluding prose summary; (b) at the respective endings of different units—closure (or epiphora)—e.g., the vocative praises that close each of the Song's three stanzas, vv. 6, 11, and 16b; (c) the end of one unit and the beginning of the next—overlap (or anadiplosis)—e.g., references to "Yahweh" and "Moses" in chiastic order at the end of ch. 14 (31) and beginning of ch. 15 (1); and (d) the ending of one unit and the beginning of another unit, which encloses a distinct unit in between—exclusio—e.g., references to the LORD's "right hand" in vv. 6b and 12a, which circumscribe the second stanza. These different types of structural parallelism are normally confirmed and reinforced by one or more of the following literary features.

8.4.2 Figurative language and graphic imagery

"Imagery…is basic to the genius of poetry. The Song of the Sea offers a veritable goldmine, filled with rich images that evoke sensations with powerful effect" (Steiner 2013:6). In this category we find non-literal devices such as simile, metaphor, metonymy, synecdoche, anthropomorphism, personification, hyperbole, irony, and so forth. Anthropomorphism understandably plays a vital role throughout the Song as Yahweh is the hero and principal agent from beginning ("he has hurled") to the end ("the LORD reigns").[38] The all-powerful "arm/hands" of the LORD feature prominently in the defeat of the Egyptians at the Sea (6, 12), but also when protecting Israel on their way to and establishing them in Canaan (16b–17). Yahweh is also depicted via metonymy as he is "my strength and my song" (2a). Also important structurally in the Song is the set of three conceptually-related similes that are found at the end of the second strophe (marking closure) in each of the three stanzas: "like a stone" (5b), "like lead" (10b), and "as a stone" (16a). Metaphoric-metonymic language denoting divine wrath ("burning anger," "consumed like stubble," "your nostrils") contrasts with the water-sea imagery in the first strophe of stanza 2 (vv. 7–8).

In addition to the imagery inherent in figurative language, the Song presents a sequence of picturesque scenes that naturally reflect back on the dramatic narrative of chapter 14. We can hear and/or visualize the Egyptian "horse and its rider" being "hurled into the sea" (15:1b) by Yahweh the "warrior" (3). In fact, Pharaoh's whole "army," including his "best officers," were drowned in the depths of the "Red Sea" (4–5) by the furious, almighty LORD, who was able to cause the sea waters to stand upright (7–8) [implied: for Israel to pass through safely on dry ground]. The enemy make some vicious threats (9), but they are all are blown down to the veritable sea bed by Yahweh's breath (10). It is as if the *earth* itself has swallowed them all up (12), in contrast to the LORD's quiet leading of his people to their promised *land* (13), while the powerful heathen peoples who inhabit that location can only look on and tremble in fear (14–15) as Israel passes them by in triumph (16a). Finally, in a closing beatific vision God's people are safely planted in their land, where in his holy hilly dwelling the LORD himself lives and reigns forever (16b–18).

8.4.3 Sound stress

This category includes any use of certain phonological features to highlight or emphasize some aspect of semantic content and/or pragmatic effect within the text.[39] For example, line-end rhyme complements lexical repetition to foreground the person of 'Yahweh' at the beginning of the Song (v. 2):

---

[38] This is the first reference to Yahweh "ruling/reigning" (מלך) in the Hebrew Bible and its only occurrence in the Torah. "Such anthropomorphic portrayals as we have in this text belong to the core of biblical faith" (Brueggemann 1994:803) and vividly testify to the constant regnal and covenantal activity of the Lord in world history—past, present, and future. "The anthropomorphisms are part of all poetry" (Cole 1973:124), but especially where Deity is active.

[39] Patterson observes generally that "Alliteration and assonance are frequent, with certain letters being especially common (e.g., ב, כ, and א)" (1995:456).

	2 עָזִּי וְזִמְרָת יָהּ
	וַיְהִי־לִי לִישׁוּעָה
	זֶה אֵלִי וְאַנְוֵהוּ
	אֱלֹהֵי אָבִי וַאֲרֹמְמֶנְהוּ:

Similarly, syllables that sound like the "sea" *(yam)* seem to underscore the concept in the next strophe, thus echoing the Lord's natural agent employed to defeat the Egyptian enemy (vv. 4–5; cf. 8, 10):

	4 מַרְכְּבֹת פַּרְעֹה וְחֵילוֹ יָרָה בַיָּם
	וּמִבְחַר שָׁלִשָׁיו טֻבְּעוּ בְיַם־סוּף:
	5 תְּהֹמֹת יְכַסְיֻמוּ
	יָרְדוּ בִמְצוֹלֹת
	כְּמוֹ־אָבֶן:

In a playful but highly significant sonic reversal, Yahweh's delivered "people" *('am)* are the human objects of his attention at the end of the Song, replacing his inanimate agent, the punitive "sea" *(yam)* at its beginning. Many other instances of this sort of meaningful sound symbolism were pointed out in the earlier text analysis (and other examples can undoubtedly be discovered on further visual examination as well as audio replication).

8.4.4 Lexical (key concept) reiteration

This stylistic feature is closely related to the previous two, but it is distinct and recognizable enough to be worth noting. For example, Yahweh rightfully assumes center stage in the Song at the very beginning, with five nominal references in vv. 2–3: יָהּ, זֶה אֵלִי, אֱלֹהֵי אָבִי, יְהוָה, יְהוָה. In view of the overall topic, there are naturally also many related lexical references to the "sea" (general), "Reed Sea" (specific), and water-associated terms in the first two stanzas of the Song. In several cases, these "sea-lexemes are placed at the end of a colon which gives them a signaling function of definiteness" (Reger 2010:70). Mention of the "land/earth" at the beginning of stanza 3 (v. 12) signals the general shift in reference to the LORD's leading Israel past pagan peoples and places towards their ultimate goal, namely, the "mountain-dwelling-sanctuary" of Yahweh at the climactic close of the unit (v. 17). These notions of Israel's journey form a poetic preview of the next stage of their story and the second half of the book of Exodus (15:22ff.). It is here that the divine laws and ritual regulations that will govern their future wilderness journey (cf. the book of Numbers) are set forth at Mount Sinai.

There are also some significant phonological repetitions that serve to audibly intensify certain semantic concepts on the morphological level within the Song, for example, the second-person masculine pronominal suffixes that foreground Yahweh's contrastive actions of judgment (12) and deliverance (13) in the first strophe of stanza 3. Finally, it is instructive to observe, along with Fox, that the lexical reiteration that is so prominent in this Song extends also to synonymous or topically-related sets (1995:334, 336):

> The vocabulary of the poem is extremely concentrated. Major ideas are expressed by clusters of key verbs. Note, for instance, the grouping of "flung," "hurled," "plunged," "shattered," "smashed," "consumed"—a veritable lexicon of military victory. A number of verbs describe divine leadership ("led," "guided," "brought") and God's establishment of the Israelites in Canaan ("planted," "founded").

8.4.5 Rhetorical questions

Rhetorical and similar leading (topic-introducing) questions are common in the Psalter (e.g., 15:1; 22:1, 25:12, 56:7; 108:10, 116:12). Though not frequent in the Song at the Sea, a prominent pairing is clustered in the doxology that concludes the second stanza in v. 11. The answer to the two "Who...?" questions is emphatically "No one!"—that is, none of the pagan deities, neither those of the defeated Egyptians nor those of the peoples of Canaan, can match the incomparable holiness, glory, and mighty power of Yahweh (the latter divine qualities being made explicit at the close of this pivotal passage).

8.4.6 Direct speech, including vocatives

Israel's Song at the Sea, like most psalms, is composed entirely in the form of direct speech on the part of the community in praise of Yahweh, their triumphant God (1b) and King (18). The LORD is clearly in focus throughout, whether being addressed directly (vv. 6–8, 10–17) or via third-person reference (1b–5, 18) at the beginning and end of the poem. An important alien quotation occurs in the middle of the text (v. 9), that is, a mock-speech put into the mouths of "the enemy" in which they ironically condemn themselves to death as they utter their boastful threats against God's people. There is thus a chiastic arrangement in these different speech types: A. Speech about Yahweh (1b–5), B. Speech to Yahweh (6–8), C. Speech from the enemies (9), B' Speech to Yahweh (10–17), A' Speech about Yahweh (18).

Five vocatives occur in the Song, all of them appropriately within the three doxologies: verse 6 (2), 11 (1), and 16b–17 (2). In this connection, it is important to note the use of the divine name in Hebrew religious poetry; wherever such usage appears, it carries out a pragmatic and often a thematic purpose as well. The OT covenant name "Yahweh" (יְהוָה) occurs a symbolically significant ten times in the psalm (once abbreviated as "Yah" in v. 1b). Reger observes the following with respect to Israel's Song at the Sea (2010:73):

> The *use of the names of Israel's God* is remarkable in its intensity and frequency. The most frequently occurring single word in the Song is the divine name *yhwh*. In addition, different names for God are employed for the sake of variation, but for greater exaltation as well. In the first strophe of the first stanza alone, four different names of God are used *(Yah, Elij, Elohej, Yhwh)*, and a fifth one is added in the Coda *(Adonai, v. 17)*.

8.4.7 Modifications in word order

This feature is undoubtedly the least visible in most versions, perhaps because translators did not recognize or perceive its significance in the original text. The standard word order of finite verb clauses in Hebrew is V—S—O/A (where A = adjunct, some other noun phrase other than object). At times a simple reversal in the basic order to create a chiasmus may be significant. For example, the first line of the Song exhibits an inversion of the key words "sing/song" and "Yahweh," which becomes "Yahweh" and "my song" in v. 1b. The general rule in verbal (or non-verbal) clauses is that any syntactic unit that is moved out of its normal position, either forward (usually) or backwards, may be expected to bear some special semantic or pragmatic significance. Poetic passages are rather more difficult to analyze than prose texts since the influence of artistry (e.g., rhythm, euphony within the bi-colon) cannot be discounted. In any case, scholars recognize two basic functions for units that are front-shifted ahead of their expected clausal position, namely, as topic or focus (Wendland 2011:199).

In the first, topicalization, the fronted element constitutes either a new topic in the discourse, or one that is resumed from a prior discussion in the text, for example, (literally in English): "**horse and-one-riding-him** he-cast into-the-sea" (1d)—this is the first reference to Pharaoh's army in the Song (cf. 4a, where this same topic is resumed after several lines in praise of Yahweh). In cases where a new or resumed topic is not an issue, a fronted syntactic unit may be an instance of focalization, where it is being highlighted because of its important thematic relevance, or to create a little surprise in the discourse, generating additional impact, appeal, and memorability, for example, following up from the preceding topic we have: "**and-choice-of his-officers** they-drowned in-Sea-of Reeds" (4d)—thus, not just any ordinary soldiers or conscripts were lost at sea, but the best of Pharaoh's military men. Furthermore, in the very next line we have "**deep-waters** they-covered-them" (5a)—with ominous allusive reference in the noun תְּהוֹם to the primordial "ocean depths" of the Creation event (Genesis 1:2). As a final, vividly poetic example, we should note the dramatic anthropomorphic expression of v. 8a: "**and-in-breath-of your-nostrils** they-were-piled-up waters"—with compact double reference now to the LORD's anger (7b) as well as to the powerful, divine wind, sent to control the sea-waters (5a, perhaps also another allusion to Genesis 1:2).

8.5 Pragmatic analysis

This aspect of an analysis deals with the varied interactive, communicative (functional) actions of discourse. Thus, the interpersonal dynamics of Israel's Victory Song also need to be clearly conveyed in translation (to the extent possible, perhaps via the paratext), as well as vocally in any audio version or melodically in a musical rendition.

General discourse functions: These would obviously include worshipful praise, profession of faith, promotion of communal solidarity and religious steadfastness. Steiner has some helpful observations regarding the theological-liturgical function of the Song (2013:11):

> The Song supplies Israel's liturgy with a hymn that fulfills the expressed purpose of YHWH's acting against the Egyptians in the manner that he did: so that the Egyptians and the Israelites and the future generations of readers would come to "know that I am YHWH" (cf. 5:2; 6:7; 7:5, 17; 8:10, 22 [MT 6, 18]; 9:14–16, 29; 10:1–2; 11:7; 14:4, 18), that it is I, rather than the Egyptian gods, represented in the anti-God Pharaoh (12:12; 18:10–11; cf. 15:1–18; Num 33:4), who rules the universe as its Creator, whose dominion extends over Israel and the nations, who is able to move heaven and earth to redeem his people. The witness of the Song is unmistakable.

A related perspective on the function of Moses' Song by the Sea, like all psalms, is as follows: "The Old Testament...psalms function as pilgrimage songs, expressing and defining faith for the people of God...[thus reflecting] the practice of the people journeying, going on a pilgrimage to worship in Jerusalem" (Bellinger 1990:2–3). It is this musical testimony that must be accurately conveyed both semantically and poetically with equal feeling and forcefulness in any contemporary translation (*cum* song).[40] A more detailed speech-act analysis (cf. Wendland 2011:43–45, 146–147) is outlined below:

---

[40] The relevance of this Song continues in the Jewish performative worship tradition: "it is no surprise that the *Shirat hayyam* continues to be included in Jewish

Specific speech-act sequence:

1a:	performative declaration ("I will sing"), announcement of theme
2:	profession of faith, performative declaration ("I will praise"), emotive acclamation ("I will exalt him")
3:	confessional acclamation (focus on "the LORD')
4–5:	narrative assertion (focus on watery defeat of Pharaoh's army)
6:	praise affirmation, emphatic thematic reiteration

7–8:	narrative confessional praise, emphatic thematic reiteration
9:	proud boast, threat, prediction
10:	narrative report (focus on watery defeat of Pharaoh's army)
11:	praise affirmation, emphatic thematic reiteration

12:	narrative report (focus on defeat of Pharaoh's army), thematic reiteration
13:	predictive declaration, profession of faith
14–16a:	predictive narrative
16b–17:	predictive promise, profession of faith, personal affirmation
18:	confessional acclamation

A basic set of speech acts (profession, praise, affirmation, assertion) is recycled through the three stanzas to lend pragmatic cohesion to the whole poem. The dramatic pseudo-quotation, ostensibly predicting victory for the Egyptian army (v. 9), is ironically transformed into a set of predictions of victory worked by Yahweh on behalf of Israel (14–16a), as he brings them to the land that he has established for his own 'dwelling' among them (13b, 17b). The dynamic, artfully shaped poetic form of this song, coupled with its stirring heroic content and an exuberant, musical mood serves "the remembrance of the narrated event at the sea and inspires [listeners] to join in the praise to/of God for his saving power and providence" (Reger 2010:67). So it should resonate also in every translated rendition.

8.6 Thematic-conceptual analysis

Most if not all of the main topical and thematic concepts of the Psalm by the Sea have already been considered in the preceding discussion. However, it may be helpful to review several salient and insightful observations by scholars with regard to the central theological notions of this poem. The

prayer books and is recited daily among the praises in the *Shacharit,* or morning service" (Steiner 2013:11).

central, victory-delivering role of Yahweh from beginning to end is one of its outstanding semantic and structural features. "This naming of Yahweh is not only an act of praise, but it is also a polemical act, whereby Israel dismisses and nullifies any rival to Yahweh..." (Brueggemann 1994:799). God is referred to explicitly six times (4x as יְהוָה) in the first three verses to set the stage for his wondrous attributes and activities, which are revealed on a verse by verse basis throughout the text.[41]

In Exodus 15:2 the singer calls him "my refuge"..."my strength"...and "my salvation"...and emphasizes his closeness to God by calling him "my God"...and "God of my father"... In v. 11 the singer asks, "Who is like you among the Gods, O Yahweh?"..., and God is said to be "splendid in holiness"..., "awesome in glorious deeds"..., and a "doer of wonders".... In a more specifically military description, Yahweh is called a "man of war" (v. 3...), and his "right hand"... is said in v. 6 to be "awesome in power"... In v. 16 the greatness of God's "arm"...causes the terrified rulers in Palestine to be still as a stone (cf. Hauser 1987:267).

While the military metaphors "may offend modern sensibilities," it is important to grasp their underlying implications—that "the whole claim of rescue, deliverance, and salvation depends on the reality that God can do for us what we cannot do for ourselves" (Brueggemann 1994:799). Throughout the first two stanzas of the Song, Yahweh's victory over the Egyptian army is described by means of one action-packed scene after another. Then, in the final stanza, the LORD's victories are predicted through ironic depictions of the terror he evokes in the hearts of Israel's future enemies. So overwhelming are Yahweh's deeds and so dominant is his presence in this psalm that the only appropriate ending is the one that is proclaimed: יְהוָה ׀ יִמְלֹךְ לְעֹלָם וָעֶד! (v. 18)

In addition to the overt lexical and conceptual expression of theme, it is also important to note the accompanying, not so evident symbolism (conceptual metaphors) that is involved, for example (cf. Shreckhise 2007):

- The praise of Israel goes UP to Yahweh (1b–2), while Pharaoh's army sinks DOWN in defeat in the deadly SEA (4–5);
- the waters pile UP (8a) along with the enemy's proud boasts (9), but Yahweh blows them DOWN into the SEA (10a);
- Yahweh brings Israel's enemies to a dead, terrifying STOP (also DOWN; 12, 14–16a), while He moves Israel confidently, relentlessly FORWARD, PLANTing them safely in their new LAND (also UP; 13,

---

[41] "Yahweh is described as: most powerful (v. 6), a warrior (3) and king (17f.); glorious and triumphant (1b), most holy (11); holding power over creation (8, 10), the enemies (7), and other gods (11); having chosen Israel, saving and redeeming her, leading and defending her (2, 13, 16, 17); active in history (1b); abiding with Israel in steadfast and zealous love (13); having a place of habitation, the sacred mountain (17), but being mobile, too (13); owner of the mountain of his dwelling (17); ruling with universal reign in time and space (18)" (Reger 2010:80).

16b–17), where He lives and RULES over everything, forever (11, 17–18).

As Reger notes, "All the way through the Song of the Sea, the enemies are thrown into the sea (v. 1), sink in the Sea of Reeds (v. 4), come down into the depth (v. 5), sink in the waters (v. 10), or are swallowed by the earth (v. 12)." (2010:72)—and we might add, experience the fear of the LORD falling upon them (v. 16a).

Steiner (2013:7) offers a good summary of the interrelated double thematic ("Exodus"-related) significance of this pivotal Psalm by the Sea:

> The principal theme of the first part is the victory of Yahweh over the Egyptians at the Reed Sea. The principal theme of the second part is Israel's march through the wilderness and passage into the promised land under the guidance of the same Yahweh. Thus Yahweh the warrior, who annihilates his foes, is identified with Yahweh the redeemer, who saves his people and establishes them in their new homeland. The themes are linked causally. It is the victory at the sea which permits the people of God to escape from bondage; and it is through his devastating display of power that Yahweh overawes the other nations who might otherwise block the passage of the Israelites. Thus the one mighty action produces two notable results: the destruction of the enemy; and the intimidation of the other nations, who are paralyzed by fear and cannot obstruct the victorious march of the Israelites or their successful entry into the Holy Land.

The Song's twofold theme may be stated even more succinctly as follows: "This poem, framed around the crisis of the exodus liberation (vv. 4–10) and sojourn-conquest (vv. 13–17), shapes the credo tradition of Israel…[which] consists in *liberation from* and *entry into*" (Brueggemann 1994:804, original italics).

Brueggemann also suggests the following generalized chiastic arrangement as a thematic synopsis of Moses' Psalm by the Sea (adapted from 1994:802):

A   ***Introduction*** (1–3): The opening announces the essential notion of praise to the LORD for his mighty saving activity.

  B   ***Theme One*** (4–10): God's great victory is proclaimed as evidenced in the Exodus from Egypt and safely out of the Sea.

   C   ***Central Doxology*** (11–12): Offered in praise of Israel's incomparable God, Yahweh!

B′ **Theme Two** (13–17): God's royal triumphal procession leads his people into their new land and holy place of worship.[42]

A′ **Conclusion** (18): A royal enthronement formula predicts Yahweh's rule over his faithful people forever.

"The story of victory and enthronement and the story of liberation and homecoming—are deeply intertwined and cannot be told apart from each other" (ibid.).

8.7 The intertext

For some scholars, the category of intertext in relation to 15:1b–18 would include chapter 14; however, I consider this to be an aspect of the intratext, that is, an integral portion of the discourse structure of the same literary composition.[43] In any case, the lexical and conceptual correspondences (and differences) between these two chapters have already been discussed in §2.1. Therefore, in the present section of this study I will briefly describe how the Psalm by the Sea resonates in terms of form and content with generically similar texts in ANE literature and certain salient portions of the Christian Scriptures.

8.7.1 In ANE literature

Victory songs such as we find in Exodus 15 were common in the oral and written literature of the ancient Near East (ANE—specifically any of the surrounding countries that had anything to do with "Israel"). "The practice of setting forth a historical event in both prose and poetic form occurs with some frequency in Hamito-Semitic literature.... [And] in the Pentateuch there is deliberate placement of poetry after narrative sections and before an epilogue" (Patterson 2004:42–43), for example, also Gen. 49–50, Num. 23–24, Deut. 32–34. Kitchen suggests that the Psalm by the Sea was "the Hebrew counterpart to the Egyptian hymns of triumph by Tuthmosis III, Amenophis III, Ramesses II, and Merenptah" (1966:133; cf. Patterson 2004:43). For example, "The image of an outstretched hand or arm [Exo. 15:6, 12, 16] is common in Egyptian inscriptions to describe the power of

---

[42] Brueggemann proposes a sub-genre here, one that evokes a "victory parade, a triumphal procession, in which the winning God moves in processional splendor to take up his throne" (1994:801). However, the background allusion could just as well refer to some *human* potentate.

[43] Another salient instance of such intratextual reference is the mention of Yahweh's powerful "arm" (זְרוֹעַ) in v. 16, which has just delivered Israel at the Reed Sea and will do the same for them on the way to Canaan—in accordance with the LORD's promise to the people in Exo. 6:6.

Pharaoh" (Walton et al. 2000:547). But there may be a significant difference here:

> It is polemical and ironic that the author of the book of Exodus assigns the same features [as found in ancient Egyptian texts] to Yahweh as he humiliates and destroys Pharaoh and Egypt (Ex. 3:19–20; 6:1; 7:4; 15:6, etc.). James Hoffmeier comments on this parallel, asking, "What better way for the Exodus traditions to describe God's victory over Pharaoh, and as a result his superiority, than to use Hebrew derivations or counterparts to Egyptian expressions that symbolized Egyptian royal power?"... The Hebrew authors use polemic to call into question the power of Pharaoh, and to underscore the true might of Yahweh! (Currid 2013:26–27)

In v. 12 the polemical irony may be even more subtle and at the same time more striking in the anthropomorphic report of the earth swallowing the Egyptian host:

> In Egyptian culture, the act of swallowing was one of great magical importance and significance...in Egyptian magical texts the term "swallow" means to "know" and have power over an object or a person. Therefore, when God had the Red Sea [included by the term "earth"] "swallow" the Egyptian army, it was destroying not only the Egyptian forces; the language of the biblical texts reflects also absorption of their power, authority, and knowledge. (Currid 2013:129)

With reference to "psalm"-like literature in general, although there are some similarities in terms of structural form and literary style, including imagery, "the object of petition and worship is completely different," for Hebrew psalms utilize these compositional features "to worship Yahweh, whom they proclaim as the only legitimate deity in the universe" (Longman 2008:604). This disparity is significant, and thus the songs of Israel, whether of praise or lament, resound in a completely different voice:

> Yahweh is not portrayed as a mythological king, a king of the gods who has subdued the cosmos and reigns over the subordinate gods of the pantheon. Rather he rules in the historical realm over his people, whom he has delivered by means of the forces of nature that he controls. (Walton et al. 2000:91)

Fundamentally then, the Psalm by the Sea does not "exalt his defeat of other gods or of chaotic cosmic forces but his power over historical peoples" (ibid.) on behalf of his covenant people Israel.[44] Furthermore, in contrast to

---

[44] I subscribe to the fundamental historicity and unified literary character of the narrative account of Exodus 14 and its panegyric poetic reflection in Exodus 15,

pagan narrative epics and their associated songs, there is no human hero in the Psalm by the Sea; rather, "the storyteller reserves his praises for God...as an epic warrior: 'The LORD is a man of war' (Exo. 15:3)" (Ryken 1992:134).[45]

8.7.2 Within Exodus

In this psalmic song that celebrates the amazing attributes and miracle-working exploits of Yahweh,[46] the pertinent line appears: 'YHWH is his name' (15:3). This pregnant reference represents "a further commentary on the revelation of YHWH's 'name' (שֵׁם) in Exodus 3 and 6, where, too, the accent falls on God's personal presence with his covenant people, ready to deliver them from bondage and death to life and blessing, even if it means baring his mighty right hand to do so" (cf. v. 6) (Steiner 2013:13).

According to Fretheim, this salvation song relates to all of the events that Yahweh set in motion on behalf of Israel at the Passover when he "struck down the Egyptians" (12:27) (1991:162):

> Verses 1–21 must be seen not as isolated songs from the past but as part of a larger liturgical whole, reflecting a regular dramatization of the crossing.... Hence, 15:1–21 constitutes a parallel to the passover texts, and the two form an inclusio for the larger unit, 12:1–15:21. The stories associated with both passover and sea crossing are thus enclosed within liturgical texts. When such usage is combined with the poetic form, the result is that the images associated with the events are even more impressionistic than those in chapter 14.

Then, from an even broader perspective with regard to the entire book of Exodus (Durham 1987:210):

> The poem of Exod 15 celebrates Yahweh present *with* his people and doing *for* them as no other god anywhere and at

---

which differs from the following assessment: "This vivid account is the culmination of a long process. It should not be viewed as a historical memory but as one of a series of imaginative attempts to give concrete expression to the belief that YHWH had rescued his people and overthrown the Egyptians" (Collins 2004:117–118). The issue of biblical reliability and historicity aside, it does not seem plausible to maintain that the magnificent praise-poem of 15:1b–18 is the product of some evolutionary compositional process.

[45] "Whatever glory there is in the epic belongs to God.... This anti-epic theme reaches its culmination in the song that Moses sings shortly before his death (Deut. 32), a song that praises God's faithfulness and dispraises Israel's waywardness" (Ryken 1992:135).

[46] Exodus records more divine miracles (signs and wonders) than any other Old Testament book, as documented also poetically in the Song at the end of the crucial v. 11 (עֹשֵׂה פֶלֶא).

any time *can* be present to do. As such, it is a kind of summary of the theological base of the whole of the Book of Exodus.

The theme of Yahweh's almighty royal rule of world affairs on behalf of his persecuted people encompasses not only the book of Exodus, but the whole Hebrew Bible (2 Chr. 36:22–23),[47] especially the Psalter (as shown under considerations of genre, 3.1) and the New Testament as well (Rev. 22).

8.7.3 In the Psalter and beyond

The narrative salvific events of Exodus 14 and their poetic memorialization in the psalm of Exodus 15 appear to have influenced the Psalter or Songbook of Israel (and all saints) in various ways and in many places. With regard to the text's central notion of Yahweh's kingship, for example, in relation to Psalm 24:7–10, Craigie notes that "there are few themes more central to Old Testament literature than the kingship of God. It is a concept rooted in creation and elaborated in historical experience, and the presence of the theme in Israel's earliest poetry (Exod 15:18) is indicative of its centrality throughout the history of Israel's religion" (1983:214).[48] Patterson provides a helpful literary overview (1995:459):[49]

> The victory at the Re(e)d Sea, together with the following movements that culminated in the conquest, remained indelibly written in Israel's memory. The song itself was reechoed by many writers in subsequent generations. The opening praise of v. 2 is repeated by the psalmist (Ps. 118:14) and Isaiah (12:2). The song's phraseology and/or imagery is often drawn upon by others. Thus, David in Psalm 18 speaks of God as "my strength" (v. 1), "my fortress" (v. 2), and "my salvation" (v. 46; cf. Hab 3:18), all drawn from Exod 15:2, while "the breath of his nostrils" (Exod 15:8) is found in v. 15. The kindling fire of v. 8 may also stem from Exod 15:7. Psalm 77 appears indebted to Exodus 15, employing the imagery of the right hand, the

---

[47] The combined book of Chronicles ends the Hebrew canon *(Tanakh)*.

[48] Craigie further observes: "The kingship of the Lord is not merely a religious affirmation—it is a basis of worship and praise" (1983:214), just as this is affirmed in Moses' Psalm by the Sea.

[49] Patterson notes the "epic-like" elements in this type of praise poetry: "(1) the account of a perilous journey—from Egypt to Canaan; (2) the surviving of a critical contest—the Re(e)d Sea; (3) the hero's great personal qualities such as magnificence and grandeur, awe-inspiring might, and munificence and concern for others; and (4) the stylistic employment of such literary features as static epithets, set parallel terms, and a lofty tone" (1995:460).

way through the waters, and the divine guiding of God's
people (vv. 17, 19, 20)....[50]

Gillingham notes that "several other psalms on the same theme as Exo. 15
were used in the Temple liturgy" (1994:144), two examples being Psalms 78
and 105, which indicates the substantial intertextual influence of the Mosaic
text.[51] Chisholm suggests that the allusion to "God's battle with the sea" in Psalm
74 (vv. 13–14) has reference to creation as well as the exodus, also serving
polemically to "suppress mythological thinking in Israel" (2013:76–77, 84).
Mays offers a rather detailed description of one psalm, 118, that seems to be
especially indebted to Moses' Psalm by the Sea and concludes: "All these repeti-
tions and relationships can be taken as directives that Psalm 118 is to be read
and understood in light of the situation of Israel and Israel's song in Exodus
14–15" (1994b:141). In the case of Psalm 98, the entire Song of Moses is encap-
sulated within a single verse, its opening tetracolon: "Every major item of vo-
cabulary recalls Exodus 15: "song" (see Exod 15:1, 21), "marvelous things" (see
Exod 15:11), "right hand" (see Exod 15:6, 12), "holy arm" (see Exod 15:11, 16),
"salvation" (see Exod 15:2)" (McCann 1996:1072).[52] In fact, one might argue
that Exodus 15 articulates the "old song" extolling Yahweh's mighty deliverance
of his people that Psalm 98 and others reiterate as a "new song" (v. 1; cf. 96:1).

---

[50] With regard to Psalm 77, T. Longman III observes: "What is it about the Exodus
that so encourages the suffering psalmist and us as we identify with him? Asaph
[cf. title] can't sleep because he can't see any way out of his predicament. There's
nothing he can do to help himself. The only way he could understand his situation
was by comparing it to that of the slaves in Egypt. The Israelites had no escape from
a gruesome fate, an impassable sea before them and Pharaoh charging furiously
behind with '600 of the best chariots, along with all the other chariots of Egypt,
with officers over all of them' (Ex. 14:7). In the face of what looked like certain
destruction, God parted the sea and provided a surprising escape. And in the light
of this event, Asaph remembered that God could continue to rescue his people,
even when redemption seemed impossible" (http://www.christianitytoday.com/
ct/2015/april/getting-brutally-honest-with-god.html?share=zY9sd6MWbTUxvHv7
js68KBXybGXzlFOA/. Accessed September 2, 2017).

[51] M. R. Wilson adds: "Toward the end of the Passover week, the Torah reading in
the synagogue is the Song of Moses (Exo. 15:1–18)" (1989:249). Gillingham feels
that this "raises the question: why has Exo. 15 not been included in the Psalter,
particularly given its close associations with the Passover Festival?" (1994:144).
A counter-query would be: Why reproduce the Psalm by the Sea if it is already
a foundational text for the psalmists? Thus Emanuel more correctly observes:
"Poetic traditions from Deuteronomy 32 and Exodus 15 appear as important to the
psalmists as prose traditions from Exodus 1–14, 16–21, and Numbers 11–14, 16,
20–21, and 25" (2012:243; cf. his study of Ps. 106 in relation to the book of Exodus,
ibid.:32, 63, 97–103).

[52] Furthermore, "Ps. 98:2 is also reminiscent of the Exodus, and v. 3 recalls Exod
9:16, which suggests that the ultimate purpose of the exodus was to make God
manifest 'through all the earth'" (McCann 1996:1072).

Labuschagne (2007:8) summarizes the importance of the "God's salva-
tion" motif and traces its development in the Psalms and a number of other
Old Testament books:

> The first and foremost among these qualities are YHWH's
> saving acts in Israel's history as the redeeming God, the God
> of justice who frees the enslaved and helps the weak and the
> suppressed. In short, his peerlessness emerged through the
> events of the Exodus. This idea permeates the texts relating
> to YHWH's incomparability and reverberates particularly in
> the hymns praising him for this.

> Here is a survey of the relevant texts, starting with the
> three Hymns in the Deuteronomistic History: the Song of
> Moses in Deuteronomy 32 (cf. v. 39), the Song of Hannah in
> 1 Samuel 2 (cf. v. 2) and the Song of David in 2 Samuel 22
> (v. 32—cf. Ps. 18:32). In the Book of Psalms we find: Psalm
> 35 (vs. 9–10), Psalm 40 (v. 6), Psalm 71 (vs. 14–19), Psalm
> 77 (vs. 12–16), Psalm 86 (vs. 8–10), Psalm 89 (vs. 6–15), and
> finally, Psalm 113 (vs. 5, 7–9, compare 1 Sam. 2:2, 5–8, in
> the Song of Hannah!). And elsewhere: Exodus 8 (v. 6/10),
> Exodus 9 (v. 14), Deuteronomy 3 (v. 24), Deuteronomy 4 (vs.
> 32–35), 2 Samuel 7 (v. 22), 1 Kings 8 (v. 23), 2 Chronicles 14
> (v. 10), 2 Chronicles 20 (v. 6), Isaiah 40 (vs. 18 and 25–26),
> Isaiah 44 (vs. 6–8), Isaiah 46 (vs. 5–13), and Micah 7 (v.18).

To the preceding listing we should add pertinent verses from the evoc-
ative epic-sounding prayer of Habakkuk, e.g., 3:13–15. Even Balaam the
pagan prophet had to sing the LORD's praises for his awesome acts on
behalf of Israel (Num. 23:21–23, NIV):

No misfortune is seen in Jacob,
    no misery observed in Israel.
The LORD their God is with them;
    the shout of the King is among them.
God brought them out of Egypt;
    they have the strength of a wild ox.
There is no sorcery against Jacob,
    no divination against Israel.
It will now be said of Jacob
    and of Israel, "See what God has done!"

In short, "the Exodus event became the spiritual basis for all of Israel's
redemptive experience, nationally and individually. As such, it is cited or
alluded to through-out [sic] the pages of the OT" (Patterson 1995:460). It is
arguably the most fundamental orienter of salvation "hyperthemes" in the

Hebrew Bible (Floor 2013). As a final example, it is appropriate to mention that 'mountain of your inheritance' (בְּהַר נַחֲלָתְךָ) appears prophetically toward the very end of Moses' Song:

> The mountain of Sinai/Horeb is often referred to as "the mountain of God" (Ex. 3:1; 4:27; 18:5; 24:13; 1 Kings 19:8), and at least one time as "the mountain of Yahweh" (Num. 10:33). This is the place where God dwells and appears in theophany to his people. Exodus 15:17 anticipates that another mountain will one day become central to the worship of God, and he will dwell there with his people.... The passage [Exo. 15:17] looks ahead to the time when Israel will be established in the land of promise, and Mount Zion in Jerusalem will be the center of worship of Yahweh. Mount Zion is also called "his holy mountain" (Ps. 48:1), and the place where Yahweh "sits enthroned" (Ps. 9:11) and "dwells" (Isa. 8:18; Joel 3:17). (Currid 2013:138)

8.7.4 The New Testament

The theme of God's delivering his people is of course central throughout the newer testament. F. F. Bruce well summarizes this pervading significance (1968:49):

> The presentation of the redemptive work of Christ in terms of the Exodus motif in so many strands of New Testament teaching shows how primitive was the Christian use of this motif—going back, quite probably, to the period of Jesus' ministry. Jesus' contemporaries freely identified Him as a second Moses—the expectation of a second Moses played an important part in popular eschatology at the time—and with the expectation of a second Moses went very naturally the expectation of a second Exodus.

The prominence of singing songs in praise of God's salvation is found at the very beginning of the Gospel accounts—in the Lukan odes, for example, as Mary magnifies the Lord in terms that recall the deliverance of Israel from a proud and powerful enemy at the Red Sea (Lk. 2:51–52, 54–55; cf. Ex. 15:6–7, 9, 12–13).[53] The pervasive influence of Exodus 14–15 comes

---

[53] As Knust and Wasserman observe (2014:343): "Singing was clearly an important feature of earliest Christian worship, as it was in religious settings across the Mediterranean world, including in earlier Jewish liturgical practices. The incorporation of song lyrics within the NT books further confirms the important role of singing in the lives of early Christian assemblies." The evidence suggest that "the songs of praise in the Lukan infancy narrative (1:46b–55, 68–79; 2:14)...may have had their origin in early liturgical practices.... The sheer volume of surviving Psalters, psalm

to the fore, fittingly enough, also in the final book of the Bible (Longman 1984:273). The Song's last verse (18), for example, is clearly echoed in Revelation 11:15—"The kingdom of the world has become the kingdom of our Lord and of his Christ, and *he will reign forever and ever.*"[54] Later, in Rev. 15, the "song of Moses" becomes "the song of the Lamb" (τὴν ᾠδὴν τοῦ ἀρνίου) (v. 3), and God's victory is no longer limited to Israel, but becomes that for believers of "all nations" (πάντα τὰ ἔθνη) (vv. 3–4, NIV):[55]

> Great and marvelous are your deeds,
>> Lord God Almighty.
> Just and true are your ways,
>> King of the ages.
> Who will not fear you, O Lord,
>> and bring glory to your name?
> For you alone are holy.
>> All nations will come
> and worship before you,
>> for your righteous acts have been revealed.

Whereas Yahweh was the "man of war" (אִישׁ מִלְחָמָה) fighting for Israel in Exodus 15 (v. 3), Christ becomes the "Divine Warrior" battling for all

---

commentaries, allusions to psalms, and references to David and his songbook attest to the centrality of the psalms in emerging Christian liturgies, and from the earliest period.... The biblical Odes, a collection of nine to fourteen songs drawn from biblical and apocryphal books that circulated separately from their biblical contexts... appear to have been sung as supplements to the Psalter early on, perhaps from the late second or early third century and perhaps in imitation of a pre-Christian Jewish context. Josephus, for example, mentions the Song of Moses and the songs of David, presumably references to the first biblical Ode (the 'Song of the Sea') and the Psalter" (ibid.:343–345).

[54] The final expression, in particular, (βασιλεύσει εἰς τοὺς αἰῶνας τῶν αἰώνων) is similar to that found in Exodus 15:18 in the LXX: βασιλεύων τὸν αἰῶνα καὶ ἐπ' αἰῶνα καὶ ἔτι.

[55] "The song the redeemed sing is one song, not two. Yet it is called 'the song of Moses...and the song of the Lamb' (v. 3) because the deliverance of God through Moses in the Exodus foreshadowed the salvation accomplished by Christ at the cross" (Gregg 2013:407). Thus, "the continuity of God's saving purpose in both dispensations means that the Old Testament phrases which make up the hymn [in Rev. 15] can be applied to the greater exodus which he accomplished through Christ" (ibid., citing G. B. Wilson 1985:n.p.). An earlier allusion to Exodus 15 in Revelation occurs with reference in 12:16 to the enemies of God's people being "swallowed up" by the Lord in his defense on their behalf (cf. Exo. 15:12; Gregg 2013:329). This may be identified with the "new song" (ᾠδὴν καινὴν) proclaimed by the redeemed in Rev. 14:3.

nations under Satan's ("Babylon's") control in Revelation (chs. 17–19, in particular 17:14):

> They will make war against the Lamb,
> but the Lamb will overcome them
> because he is Lord of lords and King of kings—
> and with him will be his called, chosen and faithful followers.

This passage is then expanded in graphically magnificent apocalyptic detail in John's climactic vision of Christ, the Warrior on the white horse in 19:11ff., who is triumphantly proclaimed 'Βασιλεὺς βασιλέων καὶ κύριος κυρίων!' (19:16).

8.8 Paratext

The biblical text that we seek to interpret must be mentally situated within a related textual context and intertext, but it must also be understood with reference to the correct conceptual frame of reference, or cognitive environment.[56] In this section I will overview four commonly-used supplementary helps that can help to create an expanded conceptual model for better understanding the text of Exodus 15.[57]

8.8.1 Footnotes

Footnotes are probably the most effective paratextual resource available for supplying background information to help readers more fully or correctly understand the biblical text that they are reading in translation (corresponding devices can be employed for audio or audio-visual versions). Such explanatory comments may apply to various aspects of the text: (a) the translation itself, perhaps to clarify some foreign concept (like 'stubble', v. 7b) that would not be very familiar to most members of the primary target audience; (b) certain literary features that are present in the Hebrew original, such as the powerful "right hand" of the LORD (v. 6); other historical, political, geographical, ecological, etc. references that would not be widely understood. The following, for example, is a sample footnote for the prominent natural barrier that made Israel's confrontation with Pharaoh's army inevitable:

> "Re[e]d Sea" (יַם־סוּף): Considerable debate continues down to
> the present day concerning the exact body of water that the
> Israelites crossed on their exodus from Egypt. Most scholars

---

[56] For a description and exemplification of some of the salient conceptual frames of reference that may be applicable during the practice of Bible translating, see Wendland 2008.

[57] For further discussion of these important devices for contextualizing the biblical text in translation, see Wendland 2011:355–405.

feel that the Hebrew word *sûph* refers to "reed" plants that grow in marshy areas since it appears to be derived from the Egyptian word for "reeds" or more specifically "papyrus." The English translation "Red Sea" is based upon the wording of the Septuagint (LXX) version as well as the Vulgate, although it is not known for sure why the Hebrew is rendered thus in these versions. The Greek word translated "sea" *(thalasa)* is similar to the Hebrew in that it designates a general body of water, whether larger ("ocean") or smaller ("lake"). The translation "Reed Sea" or "Lake of Reeds" is considered to be most accurate in the present context.

8.8.2 Section headings

Section headings, major and minor, help to give the reader an initial orientation regarding the main content of the following portion of text—up to the next heading. These titles are helpful for general reference too, for example, when a person is searching for a particular story or subject but does not know exactly where it is found in the book at hand. Section headings do not always correspond with the chapter divisions within a book. For example, it is arguable that the narrative of the Reed Sea crossing actually begins at Exodus 13:17, where the NIV has the heading *Crossing the Sea* because of the reference to the יַם־סוּף in v. 18. On the other hand, perhaps it is more to the point at this stage to see God's leading the people to be of greater significance, hence NET's heading *The Leading of God.* In any case, a minor heading within chapter 15 occurs after the Psalm by the Sea (1b–18) and related passages (19–21). Thus, the NIV has *The Waters of Marah and Elim* at v. 22, in this way maintaining the general topic of "water" (מַיִם) that runs throughout the chapter (vv. 8, 10, 19, 22–23, 25, 27). A completely new subject begins then in chapter 16: *Manna and Quail* (NIV).

8.8.3 Cross-references

The importance of intra- and extra-textual cross-references has already been suggested during the discussion of the intertext above (§8.7). Anyone who is studying (or preaching/teaching on) the Song needs to know, for example, that its keynote theme in v. 2 is cited verbatim in Psalm 118:14 in a similar context referring to Yahweh's help. The theme of joyfully "singing" to the LORD in response to his "salvation" before all the "nations" is prominent also in Isaiah's thanksgiving psalm of chapter 12. A vital intratextual connection that closely links chapters 14 and 15 occurs in the reference to the LORD being a "warrior" in 15:3a, which harks back to Moses' prediction to reassure his fearful followers in 14:14 that "the LORD will fight for you!"

8.8.4 Illustrations

Doré Bible Illustrations • Free to Copy
www.creationism.org/images/

Exo 14:27 And Moses stretched forth his hand over the sea, ...
and the Egyptians fled against it; and the Lord overthrew the
Egyptians in the midst of the sea.

Figure 8.1. The Egyptians drowned in the Red Sea, by Gustave Doré.
(http://www.creationism.org/images/DoreBibleIllus/bExo1427Dore_
TheEgyptiansDrownedInTheRedSea.jpg. Accessed September 2, 2017.
Used with permission.)

The preceding is an example of the potential value of illustrations
for creating a visual hermeneutical frame of reference that can help
readers to better understand a particular passage or scene of Scripture.
Of course, the possible problem with pictures is also exemplified here,
in this case (a) does the artist's depiction actually portray what hap-
pened in the event being referred to? or (b) is it likely that most peo-
ple will correctly interpret the illustration—that is, see what the artist
wants them to see. On both counts there may be some serious reser-
vations with regard to the graphic detail presented in the preceding
picture with reference to 14:27—or to the following one that seeks to
depict the scene of 14:30 and 15:10, 12:

Figure 8.2. Exodus 14:30, 15:10, 12.
(https://commons.wikimedia.org/wiki/File:Foster_Bible_Pictures_0064-1_
The_Water_Came_on_Pharaoh_and_His_Soldiers.jpg.
Public Domain. Accessed September 2, 2017.)

There may be no doubt about the fact that a good illustration can substitute for 1000 (or more) words. Questions may remain, however, as to what those words are actually saying to the average persons as s/he conceptually "hears" them.

8.8.5 Format and typography

An often-neglected formal aspect of the paratext is the visual display of a translation on the printed page. A well-formatted text will not only *read* more easily, it will, as a result, also be *heard* more accurately when the text is publicly uttered or proclaimed aloud. The problem is that the standardized Bible text format does not allow this to happen—not with its rigidly-justified, right-hyphenated, double columns of rather small print. Much more legible would be a single column of lined text that follows the parallelism of the original, including empty lines to show major strophic and stanza divisions as well as horizontal indentations to indicate important lineal patterns and other structural arrangements (cf. Wendland 2008:168–171). The following is an example of the Song's first strophe (15:1b–6), based on the interesting translation of Everett Fox (1995:335–336),[58] but adapted lexically, orthographically, and format-wise—to better display the overall style and structure (with **Yahweh** for "YHWH"):

I will sing to **Yahweh**,
       for He has triumphed, yes, triumphed—
       horses and riders He's flung into the sea!
My strength and the song I sing is **YAH** alone;
He has become my sole salvation.
       This is my God—I always honor him,
       yes, the God of my fathers—I exalt him.
Yahweh is a God of war,
His name is **Yahweh**!
       Pharaoh's chariots and his army
       He hurled into the sea.
       Egypt's choicest chariots
       sank deep into the Sea of Reeds.
       Oceans covered them up,
       they sunk down, down into the deep
       like a stone!
Your right hand, O Yahweh,
    was awesome in power.
You smashed the enemy, Yahweh,
    by the might of your arm.

Of course, the various types of modifications that one employs in this regard and how far one can go in their use, whether in terms of format or orthography, must be determined on the basis of sufficient target-group

---

[58] Fox comments on his (original) rendition: "This translation is guided by the principle that the Hebrew Bible, like much of the literature of antiquity, was meant to be read aloud, and that consequently it must be translated with careful attention to rhythm and sound. The translation therefore tries to mimic the particular rhetoric of the Hebrew Bible whenever possible, preserving such devices as repetition, allusion, alliteration, and wordplay. It is intended to echo the Hebrew, and to lead the reader back to the sound structure and form of the original" (from "Translator's Preface" to *The Schocken Bible* [1995], cited in Weissbort and Eysteinsson 2006:563). While agreeing with Fox with respect to the nature of the BH text, especially its poetic pericopes, I seriously doubt that his translation can accomplish its intended goal—"to lead the reader back..."—except for scholars who already know Biblical Hebrew. Instead, my renditions (as exemplified in Wendland 2004, 2011) are intended to lead *hearers forward* into a sonic correspondent that resonates in a functionally equivalent manner for a specific TL audience.

testing. This must be coupled in turn with instructions to those tested concerning the specific pragmatic meaning that is intended to be conveyed by these formal features of the print medium.

8.9 Metatext: On translating a poetic, musical version

Use of the term "metatext" (Popovich 1976) to denote a translation is appropriate because that is what the latter is—namely, a text that must always be perceived, interpreted, and applied with reference to a primary text, the original, from which it is derived. This is especially true in the case of the Scriptures, which serve as the distinctive, authoritative, directive basis for faith, teaching, and life in relation to a significant religious community. In this section I will not consider the details of actually translating the Psalm by the Sea into another language (for that, see Osborn and Hatton 1999:356–372, Nordley forthcoming) or the theory and practice of literary functional equivalence *(LiFE)* translation (cf. Wendland 2004, 2011), but I will, as a conclusion to this study, offer several examples of a lyric, melopoeic rendition for comparative evaluation.[59] Since a translation can be properly assessed only in terms of its established job commission (brief) and communicative goal(s) *(Skopos;* cf. Wendland 2008:226–239), and because poetry normally involves a significant personal, pragmatic frame of reference, I will not offer many evaluative comments regarding these samples. They are presented simply to suggest some of the daunting challenges that translators must confront when transforming a biblical text into their mother tongue with a higher level of literary artistry and a more dynamic degree of rhetoric in mind.

One poetic model, my adaptation from Fox, has already been given above. The following is Robert Alter's proposal for the first strophe, vv. 1b–6 (1985:50–51, as originally formatted, including type size, but with the verse numbers removed):

Let me sing to the Lord, Who surged, oh surged!	Horse and rider He flung into the sea.
My strength and power is the Lord,	and He became my saving.
This is my Lord, let me extol Him,	my father's God, let me exalt Him.
The Lord is a warrior,	the Lord is his name.
Pharaoh's chariots and his host	He hurled into the sea
And his picked officers	were drowned in the Sea of Reeds.

---

[59] Following Ezra Pound, a "melopoeic" translation focuses on the overall "musical property" of a SL poetic text that conveys certain significant aspects of its connotative, even denotative meaning (from "How to Read" [1929], cited in Weissbort and Eysteinsson 2006:285; see §6.4.2). The aim, then, is to represent this via functionally equivalent musical features in a TL translation.

| The depths covered them, | they went down to the deep like a stone. |
| Your right hand, Lord, is mighty in power. | Your right hand, Lord, smashed the enemy. |

The dual-columned reading format to model the parallel lines is helpful, but the short overlaps are a bit distracting ("sea," "stone," "power," "enemy") since they leave an incomplete colon above. The translation, too, does not seem to be as poetically expressed as the preceding sample of Fox. Eugene Peterson's rather more vibrant rendition follows (2001:121, again as originally displayed on the published page):

I'm singing my heart out to GOD—what a victory!
    He pitched horse and rider into the sea.
GOD is my strength, GOD is my song,
    and, yes! GOD is my salvation.
This is the kind of God I have
    and I'm telling the world!
This is the God of my father—
    I'm spreading the news far and wide!
GOD is a fighter,
    Pure GOD, through and through.
Pharaoh's chariots and army
    he dumped in the sea,
The elite of his officers
    he drowned in the Red Sea.
Wild ocean waters poured over them;
    they sank like a rock in the deep blue sea.
Your strong right hand, GOD, shimmers with power;
    your strong right hand shatters the enemy.

Though quite rhythmic in nature, the preceding translation does raise a few questions with regard to certain expressions—the use of "GOD" to render "Yahweh," for example, or "Pure GOD, through and through" for "Yahweh is his name" (v. 3b).

Somewhat similar to Peterson, the *New Living Translation* (2004) retains a more traditional style of language usage:

I will sing to the LORD,
    for he has triumphed gloriously;
he has hurled both horse and rider
    into the sea.
The LORD is my strength and my song;

he has given me victory.
This is my God, and I will praise him—
  my father's God, and I will exalt him!
The LORD is a warrior;
  Yahweh is his name!
Pharaoh's chariots and army
  he has hurled into the sea.
The finest of Pharaoh's officers
  are drowned in the Red Sea.
The deep waters gushed over them;
  they sank to the bottom like a stone.
Your right hand, O LORD,[60]
  is glorious in power.
Your right hand, O LORD,
  smashes the enemy.

Finally, in keeping with the nature of the original text, I made an effort to work towards an actual musical, sung version of Moses' Song.[61] So that one might better evaluate this rendition, I propose setting it to the tune of the well-known English worship hymn "Praise to the Lord, the Almighty..."[62]—the words of which I have included below to aid in assessing how well my translation fits into the hymn's familiar melody and meter. I have expressed the psalm's first strophe as three hymn stanzas.

Praise	**to**	**the**	**Lord,**	**the**	**Al-might-y,**	**the**	**King**	**of**	**cre-a-tion!**
1. Sing	*to*	*the*	*Lord*	*the*	*tri-um-phant,*	*the*	*Vic-tor*	*in*	*bat-tle!*
2. Sing	*to*	*the*	*Lord,*	*he*	*is my God*	*and*	*I—I*	*will*	*praise him!*
3. Sing	*to*	*the*	*Lord,*	*he*	*cov-ered*	*the*	*ar-my*	*with*	*wa-ter.*

O	**my soul**	**praise**	**Him, for**	**He**	**is**	**thy health**	**and**	**sal-va-tion!**
1. Hor- ses	*and ri-*	*ders*	*he's thrown in*	*the*	*sea*	*all*		*to-ge-ther!*
2. My fa-	*thers too*	*did*	*laud Him*	*for*	*he*	*is*	*a*	*brave war-rior.*
3. All of	*the en-*	*e-*	*my did*	*sink*	*like stones*	*in*		*the great sea.*

---

[60] In the NLT, v. 6 begins a new strophe.

[61] It must be noted that the audience in mind, in this case also the singers of this text, is a traditional evangelical Protestant (Lutheran) community, which of course greatly influences the melody chosen and the proposed wording.

[62] The original version was composed in German by Joachim Neander (ca 1679), translated into English over two centuries later by Catherine Winkworth. For similar examples, see Wells and Van Neste 2012:213–221.

Join	the	full	throng,	wake	harp	and	psal-ter	and song;
1. *He*	*is*	*our*	*might,*	*Yah-*	*weh*	*is*	*al-so*	*our song*
2. *His*	*name,*	*the*	*Lord!* —	*Pha-*	*raoh*	*and*	*all of*	*his men,*
3. *Your*	*right*	*hand*	*Lord,*	*shines*	*glo-*	*r'ous*	*fight-ing*	*in pow'r,*

Sound	forth	in	glad	a-	do-	ra-	tion!
1. *He*	*is*	*our*	*God*	*and*	*we'll*	*praise*	*him!*
2. *in*	*the*	*Red*	*Sea*	*this*	*band*	*di-id*	*end.*
3. *You*	*crush*	*our*	*foes*	*in-*	*to*	*pow-*	*der.*

Obviously, the preceding attempt leaves much to be desired, especially in terms of rhyme. But as one reads it over with a critical eye—and careful ear(!), one's various points of disapproval might be transformed into proposals for modification that will transform this into a revised hymned version that might be sung mightily to the Lord.

8.10 Conclusion: Singing the "Psalm by the Sea" today

On which occasion(s) would a contemporary Christian congregation appropriately sing, recite, or chant the pericope of Exodus 15:1b–18? Steiner offers several helpful suggestions to this point, among them (2013:11–12):

> A Christian reading/singing of the Song, therefore, does not express a triumphant attitude or posture toward the Egyptian people per se ("we do not wrestle against flesh and blood"); rather, it celebrates the Lord's victory over the "spiritual forces of evil in the heavenly places," whose end is determined, en route to the dwelling of God's people in the sanctuary "of God and of the Lamb," where "YHWH will reign forever and ever" as "King of kings and Lord of lords" (Rev 18–22)....
>
> While Exodus 15 is a praise song rather than an invocation, like the imprecatory psalms it offers a dramatically imaged, highly emotive expression on the side of YHWH's righteous vindication against the evil oppression of his people and his purposes. Without gloating in the downfall of those who line up on the wrong side of YHWH's will, when the Church recites the Song it celebrates its own deliverance, collective and individual, from bondage to evil....
>
> "Yahweh now rules; he is being praised by his people. In other words, the poem does not end by defining Israel's role

in the land, but rather by reflecting Israel's function as the worshipping community." (citing Childs 1974:252)

To this same praiseworthy, worshipful effort and end we can dedicate our own ongoing efforts as a distinct community of Bible translators, text consultants, support staff, ethnomusicologists, and hymnic composers:

"I will sing to the LORD for he is highly exalted...
the LORD will reign for ever and ever!" (Exodus 15:1b/18/21b)

אָשִׁירָה לַיהוָה כִּי־גָאֹה גָּאָה
יְהוָה ׀ יִמְלֹךְ לְעֹלָם וָעֶד׃

9

Peace (שָׁלוֹם)—its Prerequisite and Promise: A Poetic Analysis and an Application of Psalm 85 to Africa

Introduction

Psalm 85 gives utterance to a communal appeal to Yahweh for restoration and blessing (peace/well-being). It is a passionate prayer that is based on both the Lord's past gracious dealings with his people and also their own present commitment to remain faithful to Yahweh's covenant principles as expressed in their righteous behavior. Thus, the blessed promise of peace carries with it a divinely established prerequisite, namely, a life-style that is truly in keeping with what the Lord desires for his saints. The admirable manner in which this psalm has been composed in terms of its style and structure serves to highlight the main themes and purpose of its powerful lyric message. As we examine the text of Ps. 85 more carefully in this study, it will become readily apparent that this psalm of/for the sons of Korah (לִבְנֵי־קֹרַח מִזְמוֹר—v. 1, Heb.) has much of importance to say also to the members of God's contemporary Church, no matter where they may live in the world. However, the notion of peace strikes an especially resonant chord in the hearts of all those who live in the continent of Africa. The sense and significance of this psalm is such that it encourages us to seek more dynamic ways of communicating its message of peace via diverse modes and media of transmission today.

9.1 The poetic structure and inscribed message of Psalm 85

Psalm 85 manifests a highly symmetrical formal arrangement which admirably complements its powerful theological and moral message for the "saints" (v. 8b—or forgiven sinners, v. 2) of the Lord. I first outline the psalm's poetic structure on the following chart (minus the musical heading, v.1 in Hebrew; the verse numbers thus refer to those in English translations), which gives the Hebrew text alongside the NIV, and afterwards I endeavor to justify this organization in terms of the prayer's principal stylistic features.[1] As in earlier chapters, I have used several different typographical devices in the English version (capital letters, italics, bold print, underlining, different fonts) in order to indicate some of the primary significant as well as reiterated lexical items. In the Hebrew text different typographical devices, such as gray shading and italics is used to highlight similar sounds or lexical and semantic reiteration, while the two sets of boxes indicate, respectively, a medial pair of fronted syntactic constituents and a final chiastic structure.

I. STROPHE A

1 You showed favor to your land, O LORD;	רָצִיתָ יְהוָה אַרְצֶךָ
you *restored the fortunes* of Jacob.	שַׁבְתָּ *שְׁבוּת* (שְׁבִית) יַעֲקֹב:
2 You forgave the iniquity of your people	נָשָׂאתָ עֲוֹן עַמֶּךָ
and covered all their sins. *Selah*	כִּסִּיתָ כָל ־חַטָּאתָם סֶלָה:
3 You set aside all your wrath	אָסַפְתָּ כָל ־עֶבְרָתֶךָ
and *turned* from your fierce **anger**.	הֱשִׁיבוֹתָ מֵחֲרוֹן אַפֶּךָ:

---

[1] The main text critical issue in Ps. 85 occurs in the second line of v. 1 (Heb. 2) and whether to read the *kethiv* שְׁבִית 'captivity' or the *qere* שְׁבוּת 'turnings/fortunes'. The potential double wordplay of this verse (see below) lends support to the latter reading, which is preferred also by Tate 1990:364 (this is supported also by a NET text note). I also recommend Tate's text-conservative (non-emendative) recommendations for all of the other, lesser issues of this nature that arise in this psalm (ibid.:364–367).

STROPHE B

4 *Restore* us again, O God our *Savior,*

שׁוּבֵנוּ אֱלֹהֵי יִשְׁעֵנוּ

and put away your displeasure toward us.

וְהָפֵר כַּעַסְךָ עִמָּנוּ:

5 Will you **be angry** with us forever?

הַלְעוֹלָם תֶּאֱנַף־בָּנוּ

Will you prolong **your anger** through all generations?

תִּמְשֹׁךְ אַפְּךָ לְדֹר וָדֹר:

6 Will you not *revive* us again,

הֲלֹא אַתָּה תָּשׁוּב תְּחַיֵּנוּ

that your people may rejoice in you?

וְעַמְּךָ יִשְׂמְחוּ־בָךְ:

7 Show us your unfailing love, O LORD,

הַרְאֵנוּ יְהוָה חַסְדֶּךָ

and grant us your *salvation.*

וְיֶשְׁעֲךָ תִּתֶּן־לָנוּ:

STROPHE A'

8 I will listen[a] to what God the LORD will say;

אֶשְׁמְעָה מַה־יְדַבֵּר הָאֵל ׀ יְהוָה

he[b] promises **peace**

כִּי ׀ יְדַבֵּר שָׁלוֹם

to his people, his saints–[c]

אֶל־עַמּוֹ וְאֶל־חֲסִידָיו

but let them not *return* to folly.

וְאַל־יָשׁוּבוּ לְכִסְלָה:

9 Surely his *salvation* is near those who fear him,

אַךְ ׀ קָרוֹב לִירֵאָיו יִשְׁעוֹ

that his glory may dwell in our land.

לִשְׁכֹּן כָּבוֹד בְּאַרְצֵנוּ:

STROPHE B'

10 Love and *faithfulness* meet together;

חֶסֶד־וֶאֱמֶת נִפְגָּשׁוּ

righteousness and **peace** kiss each other.

צֶדֶק וְשָׁלוֹם נָשָׁקוּ:

11 *Faithfulness* springs forth from the earth,

אֱמֶת מֵאֶרֶץ תִּצְמָח

and righteousness looks down from heaven.

וְצֶדֶק מִשָּׁמַיִם נִשְׁקָף:

12 The LORD will indeed give what is good,

גַּם־יְהוָה יִתֵּן הַטּוֹב

and our land will yield its harvest.

וְאַרְצֵנוּ תִּתֵּן יְבוּלָהּ:

13 <u>Righteousness</u> goes before him   צֶדֶק לְפָנָיו יְהַלֵּךְ

and prepares the way for his steps.   וְיָשֵׂם לְדֶרֶךְ פְּעָמָיו׃

[a] The verb (אֶשְׁמְעָה) is clearly a *singular* cohortative and, as such, calls for a stronger translation, e.g., "Let me hear…;" this initial, *waw*-less form helps mark the onset of the psalm's second half.

[b] In this context, the initial כִּי might be rendered as *"Yes, he promises peace…!"*

[c] The line break here is not based on syntax, but rather on phonology—sound and lexical balance.

Psalm 85 offers a condensed poetic "history lesson" on the relationship between God and his people. The text divides itself structurally into two larger stanzas, I = vv. 1–7 (2–8, Heb.) and II = vv. 8–13 (9–14, Heb.), each of which consists of two poetic paragraphs, or strophes: A = 1–3, B = 4–7, A′ = 8–9, and B′ = 10–13.[2] The two stanzas are correspondent in terms of their number of poetic lines (I = 14 cola, II = 14 cola) and word count, as are the constituent strophes: I = 45 words and II = 47, with A = 19, B = 26 and A′ = 22, B′ = 25 words. The obvious symmetry and balance of this liturgical poem not only attests to the skill of the biblical poet, but also suggests the importance of the theologically-focused message being conveyed.[3]

Each strophe embodies a distinct speech act that is nevertheless integrated with the others to form a coherent whole:

A = *profession of forgiveness* (worship leader), B = *appeal* (congregation), A′ = *profession of confidence* (worship leader), B′ = *praise* (congregation).[4]

Furthermore, there are some clear semantic and pragmatic parallels among the four strophes: Thus, the two shorter, initial strophes both refer to Yahweh's merciful acts, A to past forgiveness and A′ to future deliverance, while the two latter, longer strophes suggest a prayer-response sequence, with B articulating a request for restoration and B′ giving joyful expression to a beneficial response or outcome.

A number of topical and lexical ties recur within the text to help demarcate the psalm's four divisions and to lend internal cohesion to each of them. First of all, a reference to "God" (אֵל) or the divine covenantal name "Yahweh" (יְהוָה) occurs in each of the four strophes, notably, in a

---

[2] Most commentators do not break the second half of the psalm into two, but treat verses 8–13 as a single poetic unit (e.g., deClaissé-Walford et al. 2014:656; Goldingay 2007:604; Tate 1990:370; VanGemeren 1991:546–547).

[3] It is not possible to record all of the intertextual links that Ps. 85 has with other OT literature. I might simply note that Goldingay sees connections between vv. 1–7 and Ps. 44 as well as between vv. 8–13 and certain passages in Isa. 40–66 (2007:605–616).

[4] It is very possible that Ps. 85 served in a liturgical setting as an antiphonal communal prayer in which the officiating priest or Levite chanted strophes A and A′, while the congregation responded communally with the words of strophes B and B′ (cf. Goldingay 2007:610).

prominent position either at or near the beginning (vv. 1, 4, 8) or ending (vv. 7, 12) of the poetic unit at hand. In the first strophe (A), the psalmist lists an impressive series of synonymous demonstrations of the LORD's favor towards the people, in spite of their chronic sinfulness—as rendered by the NIV: "showed favor...restored fortunes...forgave iniquity...covered sins...set aside wrath...turned from anger." The final topic of divine anger (v. 3) continues to be in focus in strophe B as the people communally call upon their "Savior God" (v. 4a) to "break off his displeasure"[5] that appeared to be currently afflicting them with some sort of a calamity, possibly a drought in view of the agricultural bounty pictured later in strophe B'.[6] Two sets of rhetorical questions underscore the people's plight in the middle of strophe B—the first rather negative in outlook (v. 5, e.g., "will you be angry with us"—תֶּאֱנַף־בָּנוּ), the second more positive (v. 6, i.e., "will you not return to revive us"—תָּשׁוּב תְּחַיֵּנוּ).[7] The first half of the psalm ends (v. 7) with an appeal which echoes a parallel that initiated the second strophe (v. 4), thus bringing to the fore the divine attributes upon which the people based their hope, namely, his (lit. "your") "steadfast love" (חַסְדֶּךָ) and "salvation" (יִשְׁעֶךָ) (inclusio).

The principal turning point of Ps. 85 occurs at its textual center in v. 8 and the onset of strophe A'. This is marked by an exceptional tetracolon, the first line of which is extra-long, that is, 5 + 3/4/3 words (the norm is 3 to 4 words per colon). The sudden shift from a plaintive plea uttered by the worshiping congregation (v. 7) to the psalmist's expression of patient trust (v. 8) also signals this major juncture in the psalm.[8] Strophe A' then reiterates the people's fervent desire and confident hope that their prayer (strophe A) will be positively answered by linking up the key words "peace" (שָׁלוֹם), "salvation" (יֵשַׁע), and the "glory" (כָּבוֹד) of the Lord. This is the prayer that the psalmist utters vicariously on behalf of "his [Yahweh's] people, his saints" (אֶל־עַמּוֹ וְאֶל־חֲסִידָיו), namely, "those who fear him" (לִירֵאָיו), on behalf of "their (lit. 'our') land" (אַרְצֵנוּ). However, the petitioner's eager expectation is tempered by juxtaposition with an exhortation or warning

---

[5] Some scholars emend the text from "break off" (H-PH-R) to "turn aside" (H-S-R).

[6] "...God bestows the good and makes the land productive (v. 12). The optimum conditions for human life will exist (on the productive land as a feature of salvation prophecies, see Amos 9:13; Hos 2:21–23; Isa 30:23–25; Jer 21:21; Lev 26:3–6)" (Mays 1994a:277).

[7] Thus, the first rhetorical question (v. 5) looks backwards to the divine "displeasure" of v. 4, while the second (v. 6) looks forward to the Lord's "unfailing love" in v. 7. Note the crucial covenant-relational verb "turning" שׁוּב, which occurs throughout the first two strophes, vv. 1b, 3b, 4a, 6a.

[8] Such a sudden and surprising shift from a negative to a positive outlook and tone at some point after the midpoint of the text has been reached is found in many psalms of the lament genre, whether individual (e.g., Ps. 22:22, 77:10) or like this, communal in nature (e.g., Ps. 79:12, 83:9).

concerning his community's present spiritual state. This clearly stands as a pre-condition for divine blessing: "let them *not* 'return' (repeating the key word שׁוּב) to [their] folly" (לְכִסְלָה, i.e., based on the historical and prophetic record, probably a mixture of rampant idolatry, coupled with gross immorality and social oppression).[9]

The fourth and concluding strophe B′ then lauds in vivid abstract personifications the chief ethical qualities that should characterize Yahweh's true covenant community (v. 10): "steadfast love" (חֶסֶד—in effect, mirroring that of Yahweh himself, v. 7!), "faithfulness" (אֱמֶת), "righteousness" (צֶדֶק), and "peace" (שָׁלוֹם).[10] The communal (not just individual) activation of such behavior (cf. נִפְגָּשׁוּ 'they meet together', v. 10a) will, in turn, open the way for Yahweh to put his abundant blessings correspondingly on display in "our land" (אַרְצֵנוּ) (vv. 11–12). In v. 12, the worshipers confidently look into the future by paraphrasing and re-applying the psalm's initial verse, which documents the Lord's past favor upon his (lit. "your") "land" (אַרְצֶךָ). Psalm 85 concludes with an implied reminder that the "righteousness" (צֶדֶק) of Yahweh, that is, his just dealings with his people, must also be reflected in their corresponding interpersonal behavior, even as he himself anthropomorphically "steps forth" (lit., "his footsteps"—פְּעָמָיו) to encourage and empower them towards that same providential ("peace"-full) outcome.

To conclude this cursory text study of Ps. 85, I will briefly highlight a number of poetic features that serve to highlight different dimensions of the Lord's message to his saints. In the preceding structural overview, I called attention to the well-fashioned poetic organisation of this communal prayer in terms of balanced lineation as well as strophic arrangement. The following stylistic devices (communicative clues)[11] function both to establish the internal boundaries of the psalm as a whole and also to foreground certain key aspects of the text's content (principal topics) and function (pragmatic aims):

- Strong alliteration forming a double paronomasia in the first verse underscores the psalm's fundamental presupposition and foundation for the people's confidence in their covenant Lord: 'you favored your

---

[9] "The psalmist may have been thinking of the way God had forgiven them and brought them back to the land after their sin and unfaithfulness had led to the fall of Jerusalem and the destruction of the temple (Isa 40:1–11; Jer 33:7–9)" (Okorocha 2006:692).

[10] "Such keywords as "mercy," "truth," and "trust" appear as mouthpieces for living realities that apply to both the character of God and the hoped-for behavior of renewed man" (Terrien 2003:608).

[11] Stylistic, literary-structural communicative clues are "not just properties of the text, but features built into the text for the purpose of guiding the audience to the intended interpretation" (Hatim 2013:112)—and, we might add, the text's translation as well.

land—you restored [their] fortunes' *(râtsiythâ...'artsecha – shabhtâ shibhuwth)*. The reiterated second person singular subject and possessive suffixes, namely -*thâ* and -*chá* 'you/your', with reference to Yahweh is a prominent reminder of this personal divine thematic focus that runs throughout the first strophe (A). The repeated "all" (כָּל) in vv. 2b and 3a formally links the people's "sins" with God's "wrath"—which now by his "favor" (רצה), v. 1, have been "covered over" and "set aside."

- A repetition of the verbal root "(re)turn" also helps mark the transition from affirmation to petition as strophe A moves into strophe B: "you turned" (הֲשִׁיבֹותָ—v. 3b) ... "turn us!" (שׁוּבֵנוּ—v. 4a) (structural overlap, or *anadiplosis*). Although the 2nd singular pronominal reference to Yahweh continues strongly in strophe B, the 1st-plural suffix "us" (-*nû*) is even more prominent, occurring *seven* times to create significant cohesion throughout the unit.

- A divine vocative begins and ends strophe B: 'O God of our *salvation*' (יִשְׁעֵנוּ—4a) ... "O Lord" (7a), an inclusio that is even more noticeable due to the mention of "your *salvation*" (יֶשְׁעֲךָ) in v. 7b. The close of strophe B is also marked by a chiastic arrangement of the divine actions being requested by the people: "show us— your steadfast love" // "your salvation—give to us!"

- The fronted (constituent focus) personal references of v. 6 "you" (אַתָּה) and "your people" (עַמְּךָ) conjoin the corporate petitioners with the divine object of their prayers.

- A broader chiastic structural formation links the four verses of strophe B: the two outer verses, 4 and 7, present three imperative appeals, while the two inner verses express three negative rhetorical questions.

- In addition to the extended poetic line that introduces the second half of Ps. 85 and strophe A' in v. 8a, this major aperture is distinguished by another divine vocative (הָאֵל | יְהוָה) and שָׁלֹום "peace"—a concept that admirably expresses the result of the covenantal relationship between Yahweh and his people when things are right between them.[12] This applies to "his saints"— perhaps better rendered "his steadfastly faithful ones" (חֲסִידָיו), a term that echoes the people's emotive plea for the LORD's "steadfast faithfulness/love" (חַסְדְּךָ) at the end of strophe B (v. 7).

- The close of strophe A' features a pair of emphatic utterances that contrast with each other—first the negative warning, "but let them

---

[12] "Shalom...is the culmination of God's kingdom, where all have what they need and live in comfort without fear" (deClaissé-Walford et al. 2014:658). Of course, such a peace-filled scenario, whether in this life or the next, can be achieved only in fellowship with the Lord's Messiah-Christ.

not return (אַל־יָשׁוּבוּ) to [their] folly," which is followed by an exclamation of confident trust, "Surely near (אַךְ ׀ קָרוֹב—note also the distinctive word order) to those who fear him [is] his salvation!" The latter line (9a) is a poetic parallel to v. 8b: "peace—salvation;" "his faithful ones—those fearing him." The end of this strophe may also manifest another boundary-marking chiastic structure (as in v. 7): "near to those fearing him—his salvation" // "his glory to dwell—in our land."

- A string of the same or similar-sounding words creates a cohesive chain throughout strophe A': יְדַבֵּר—יְדַבֵּר (v. 8a–b); וְאֵל—אֶל—וְאַל (v. 8c–d); כָּבוֹד—קָרוֹב (v. 9). But there is more than simple phonological similarity here. The first pairing, for example, highlights the verb דבר and the psalmist's resolve to "listen" (שׁמע) to the Word where Yahweh "speaks" (promises) the "restoration/revival" (שׁוּב) that the people prayed for in the preceding strophe (vv. 4, 6). God will manifest his "glory" (כָּבוֹד) by bringing salvation "near" (קָרוֹב) to those who fear him (v. 9).

- The "faithful love" (חֶסֶד) appealed for by the people (v. 7) is linked in turn to a series of covenantal correlates in v. 10, at the onset of the psalm's final strophe (B'). The two poetic lines (cola) of this verse display exceptionally strict parallelism of form and meaning: "faithful-love + and-faithfulness + they-meet-[together]"[13] // "righteousness + and-peace + they-kiss-[each-other]." There is even some significant end rhyme in the two colon-final verbs נִפְגָּשׁוּ and נָשָׁקוּ. Thus the prayer of strophe B' (vv. 4, 7) and the assured hope of strophe A' (v. 9) have seemingly been realized within the very framework of the psalm itself!

- The exact parallelism of v. 10 continues in v. 11, thereby symbolizing within the text's precision of form and content the continual flow of divine blessings being realized. These blessings occur in focal fronted position in each of the poetic lines: "faithfulness + from-[the]-earth + it-springs-forth" // "and-righteousness + from-[the]-heavens + it-looks-down." The key covenantal concepts אֱמֶת and צֶדֶק are reiterated for emphasis in initial colon position (constituent focus).

- The strong expression of trust of v. 12 parallels that of the preceding strophe in v. 9—the "glory" (כָּבוֹד) heightened by "surely" (אַךְ) of the earlier verse being identified with and/or derived from "Yahweh" (יְהוָה) heightened by "yes!" (גַּם) in the later passage.

---

[13] The two verbs of v. 10 are perfect forms, but they are interpreted here as exemplifying a dramatic prophetic usage, thus rhetorically describing what is hoped for as if this has already happened, or is in the process of happening, e.g., "loyal love and faithfulness have met together!" This same vivid poetic verbal style is exhibited in many African languages, e.g., Chewa of Malawi and Zambia.

- The striking personifications of vv. 10 and 11 are transformed into a divine anthropomorphism in the psalm's rather enigmatic final verse. Verse 13 is arranged chiastically, perhaps to verbally announce its conclusive, climactic character: NP (subject) + NP (adjunct) + verb // (and) verb + NP (adjunct) + NP (object).

   The question is: whose "righteousness" (צֶדֶק) is being referred to here, God's or man's—that of Yahweh or that of his covenant people? Most commentators take the different attributes referred to in this strophe (B′) as characteristic of the Lord God, who is explicitly mentioned in v. 12 (cf. v. 7).[14] However, an intratextual case can be made for viewing here also an implicit reference to the covenant community, namely those who have repented (strophe A), begged for forgiveness (strophe B), and explicitly identified themselves as being "his people, his faithful ones...those fearing him [Yahweh]" in vv. 8–9 (strophe A′). They are the living messengers, or heralds, figuratively depicted in v. 13, who prepare the way for their King by reflecting in their very lives his righteous behavior in relationship to one another, thus establishing "peace" (vv. 8b, 10b) and blessings throughout their land. Those who hope for peace from God must in turn allow that same peace to distinguish their own virtuous (peace-promoting) life-style.[15]

- And what preeminent ethical quality is most likely to encourage peace and harmony in the land between distinct individuals and groups? According to Psalm 85 it would seem to be the characteristic of 'righteousness' (צֶדֶק), which runs like a thematic thread through the text's second half (vv. 7, 9, 10, 11, 13).

9.2 Reading and applying Psalm 85 in Africa today

The original setting of Ps. 85 cannot be stated with certainty, and it is therefore surrounded with a considerable amount of speculation, especially on the part of form critics.[16] Most commentators suggest that some time in

---

[14] For example, "The psalm closes with a fine section of poetic depiction of the great qualities of Yahweh's presence and power: Glory, Loyal-Love, Faithfulness, Righteousness, and Well-Being (Peace); all are ready to go forth to participate with Yahweh as he bestows his goodness on the land and its people" (Tate 1990:367).

[15] Some commentators and versions (e.g., NEB) propose "peace" as the implicit subject of the second colon of v. 13, thus paralleling the beginning of strophe B′ in v. 10b (e.g., VanGemeren 1991:551).

[16] Weiser, for example, argues that the principal setting of Ps. 85 is "probably that of a service of supplication of the cult community, held within the framework of the festal cult...celebrated at the autumn feast...when the cult community witnessed at first hand...the *Heilsgeschichte* as the representation of the gracious hand of God's

the post-exilic period, whether earlier or later, seems to fit best.[17] However, there is really nothing in the text itself that would unambiguously point to that particular temporal framework. Rather, as in the case of most psalms (excepting cases like Ps. 137), the wording and references are generalized to the extent that the text may be applied to the religious life of ancient Israel at just about any point in its (post) Davidic history. Indeed, this is the special genius of the Psalter in functioning as the "prayer book of the saints," no matter who they are (what culture, language, etc.), where they happen to live in the world, or in whichever age.

As noted above, the general development of the central petitionary argument of this communal prayer, which borders on that of a standard psalmic lament (vv. 4–8), is quite clear: The faithful community was currently facing a serious threat to their very existence—whether this danger confronted them in the form of a drought, some severe pestilence or pandemic, attack by a foreign army, political, social, and moral disintegration, or some combination of these. In the psalm's second strophe (B), the people attribute the pressing danger to the "anger" of Yahweh in reaction to their persistent sinful behavior, as had happened on numerous occasions in the past history of their nation. They now appeal for "restoration" (v. 4) on the basis of the Lord's manifest "loyal love/steadfast faithfulness" (v. 7), which had always been his gracious covenantal response to their corporate repentance. That historical record becomes a matter of public testimony as the psalm opens (strophe A), and as various expressions documenting Yahweh's forgiveness emphatically follow, one immediately after the other (vv. 1–3).

Psalm 85 then pauses in the middle (v. 8a), as it were, as the psalmist (priest),[18] speaking declaratively on behalf of the prayerful congregation announces his hope (strophe A') for a positive divine reply to the people's plea (strophe B). This is motivated by the promise of "peace" that Yahweh characteristically desires to bestow on his "faithful saints" (8b) by revealing his "glory" among them (in their "land") (9b).[19] This providential "deliverance" is thwarted, however, whenever they move away from their "fear" of

---

guidance (deliverance from Egypt, bestowal of the promised land)" (1962:571–572). This may well be another example of the form-critical fashioning of a wealth of speculative detail from a paucity of actual textual and contextual data.

[17] See, for example, Coetzee (2009:559–560), who feels that "the dynamic in Psalm 85 reflects a struggle towards restoration and maintenance of this three-dimensional relationship," i.e., between "people, God, and land."

[18] With reference to v. 8 in particular, Mays feels that "the singer,…prophet or Levitical priest, rehearses the promises of God before the congregation as reassurance in their time of distress" (1994a:277).

[19] "The expression which encompasses all that Yahweh will do is שָׁלוֹם 'Well-Being/Peace', used in vv 9 and 11" (Tate 1990:372). In most OT occurrences, peace is a corporate, interpersonal, not an individual notion.

him into worldly and religious "folly" (8c–9a). But all doubt is cast aside in the final strophe (B′), which lauds the Lord's wonderful attributes (loyal love, faithfulness, righteousness, peace) as they are assumed to be reflected in the lives of his people (vv. 10–11, 13), and as he correspondingly blesses their land in response (v. 12, cf. 9b).

So what does Ps. 85 say to Africa—to its diverse settings, nations, and peoples, along with their current crises, challenges, opportunities, and resources, especially as occasioned in the religious realm and spiritual sphere?[20] In general, it may well be true to say that "more than any other book in the Christian Scriptures, the Psalms live in the veins of many African Christians to whose lives the Bible is central" (Masenya 2014:233). The special focus of my study is "peace" *(shalom),* so what can this psalm contribute with regard to that subject in relation to African life, past and present, as well as the hopes and aspirations of many people for the future? I will not presume to try to answer in specifics, but will merely offer some rather general personal observations, first arising from the theology of Ps. 85, and then with respect to several, hopefully practical life applications.

It is quite striking that the promise of peace (85:8) comes with a prominent prerequisite, one that looks back into the past and extends its range into the foreseeable future. Indeed, this is a divine requirement that applied not only to ancient Israel, the initial consumers of this psalm, but also concerns people of all nations and of every age, not just those who happen to be living in Africa today. We notice where this pledge to all faithful God-fearers occurs in the text—namely, after completing the first half of the psalm. These two opening strophes emphasize, respectively, former "restoration" that is predicated upon a "forgiveness" and repentance (implied) (vv. 1–3), as well as a present peaceful (non-"angry") relationship between the Lord and his covenant people (vv. 4–7). This relationship involves an implicit trust that is expressed in both word and deed on the part of those who are appealing for restoration and revival in an immanent personal God (Yahweh), whose very nature is characterized by "steadfast faithfulness" and who does, in fact, have the transcendent power to "deliver" his people in their time of need (v. 7).

---

[20] I present my thoughts in this section rather tentatively as a "resident outsider" (or "alien insider")—that is, as someone who has lived, worked, taught, and learned in Africa for most of my life (since 1962). In more ways than one, my most meaningful education really began when I entered this cross-cultural, multilingual learning environment and encountered the many African teachers, both professional, and lay, whom I have personally benefitted from in various respects along my journey. I also realize that "Africa" covers a large expanse manifesting great differences among diverse peoples and places. Therefore, I will discuss the subject of peace in Africa more in general terms and from my limited perspective of the south-central region—Zambia, Malawi, and Zimbabwe.

In the second place, the central pronouncement and promise of peace is closely attached to an explicit warning by the psalmist with regard to the future: If people expect Yahweh to "return" to them in forgiveness and favor, then they, on the other hand, must not "return" to their former life of "foolishness" (v. 8c), which in a biblical sense refers not to some mental incapacity, but rather to a deliberate rejection of God and his ways. The Lord in his "glory" chooses to live only among God-fearing folk (v. 9). While the divine presence may be demonstrated in agricultural bounty and general economic prosperity (v. 12), such *physical* peace is rarely found generally in any earthly society and even less so for any length of time. In the context of the Scriptures as a whole, therefore, I feel that these agrarian references are better interpreted as figurative depictions of essentially *spiritual* realities that are—or ought to be—displayed in abundance among God's people. Thus, in v. 10 the covenantal qualities of "loyal love," "faithfulness," "righteousness," and "peace" (in this context, probably peace-'makers'; Ps. 34:14, 37:37, 120:7; Matt. 5:9) may well refer either to Yahweh or to those who revere him (v. 9)—or, in my opinion, to both. The ambiguity of the psalm's final strophe (B′) then is deliberate: The Lord's righteousness becomes visible only in the lives of his people (v. 13)!

What might be the point in terms of a practical application? Africa is a continent that has been longing for peace and security for a long time. The end of the colonial age (we might just begin at that point) ushered in an era of abundant optimism. But in all too many countries—east, west, north, and south—the hopes of the proverbial common man (*bantu balya maila*—'the millet eaters' in Tonga) were soon dashed, and they often found themselves no better off than before independence. They continued to suffer similar sorts of social and economic oppression, but now, however, this was at the hands of different masters—frequently from among their own countrymen (and the male gender here is significant!). The sad irony was that during these same early independence years (and thereafter) the Christian church was growing faster than ever before in virtually every quarter of the continent. New, non-European/mission-based churches (the so-called African Independent Churches, AIC's) were springing up everywhere, as were splinter groups, those that had broken away from long-established and often missionary-dominated denominations. In many countries of Africa, Christianity (consisting of a multitude of different churches) soon became the dominant religion, and in some nations over 75 percent of the population claimed to be Christian. However, the peace and associated freedoms that the masses had so fervently hoped for—political, economic, social, and religious—never quite seemed to materialize, at least not with the same quality or intensity of vision that their leaders had originally promised. Instead, the old adage appeared to keep repeating itself: "The rich (and powerful) just keep getting richer (more powerful)." This all too often applied to the leadership of the churches as well.

Does Ps. 85 offer any solutions? Two preliminary points should be noted to begin with: Corrupt and oppressive leadership is a problem not only in Africa, but is common throughout the world—in so-called developed as well as in developing nations (though the former may be more sophisticated in concealing their dishonesty and wrongdoing).[21] The second thing is that the agricultural imagery of bountiful blessing found in the final strophe (B') should not be construed in an overly literal, materialistic manner. In other words, the God-fearing, righteous nation (on the whole) will not necessarily be prosperous in every possible respect, nor will it always be able to avoid the different crises and calamities that regularly befall this earth—wars, plagues, famines, floods, earthquakes, hurricanes, and other environmental disasters. To adopt such a *do ut des* religious philosophy ("I give that you [God] may give [me]")[22] means that one has more or less subscribed to the same sort of faulty mechanical reasoning as did Job's false comforters, who thought that every worldly misfortune must be the automatic result of human sin and divine judgment—and vice-versa (e.g., Job 11:13–17). The experiences of life, including man's relationships with God, with each other, and with nature, are much more complicated and unpredictable than that!

In contrast, the truths or teachings of Ps. 85 are relatively straightforward when interpreted in a spiritual, ecclesiastical sense, which is the primary hermeneutical level, I believe, whereby the text is intended to be understood. The Lord's offer of "peace" (v. 8b) is his default desire, not only as exhibited between him and "his people," the God-fearers, but also as this harmonious well-being is realized among his covenant community in all of their relationships with each other as individuals and ideally also as corporate Christian religious groups.[23] The chief behavioral demonstrations of covenantal peace (in general, 8b) are clearly specified as involving a complex of characteristics: implicit trust (v. 9), loyal love, faithfulness, righteousness, and the activity of peace-making (specific *shalom*, v. 10). One African commentator explains it this way (Okorocha 2006:693; material in brackets added):

> True righteousness and real peace belong together as God's
> gifts, in the lives of individuals or nations. One cannot exist

---

[21] The greedy, cut-throat banking system in most Western nations is a prominent case in point. It is important, too, not to overgeneralize: there are certainly exceptions in the broad area of civic righteousness, but such notable national states and internal governmental departments simply prove the rule.

[22] The corresponding saying in Chewa is: *kupatsa ndi kuika* 'to give [to someone, including God] is to deposit [for a future repayment]'.

[23] The quality of concordant communal vertical and horizontal relationships is a vital dimension of biblical *shalom* (cf. Leiter 2007:ch. 1).

without the other. The life that results is what the Igbo of Nigeria describe as *Ezi-ndu,* a life that involves total well-being as well as the fullness of justice and moral upright-ness…. It is when we order our lives along these "paths of righteousness" [Ps. 23:3; cf. 85:13] under the guidance of the word of God that we can enjoy "blessings" or lasting suc-cess, God's shalom (Josh 1:8).

On the other hand, the *failure* to achieve this godly concord and orderli-ness within the community is dealt with in the first half of the psalm. Quite simply, all expressions of conflict and hostility are the inevitable result of human iniquity and sinfulness (v. 2)—chronic sins that are left unrepented and unforgiven, hence also punishable by the Lord (v. 3). Such communal discord and wickedness within the fellowship of God's people may be cou-pled with widespread evil in the nation as a whole and thus provoke his wrath in the form of adverse political, social, economic, and physical con-sequences for them all. How can there be any peace if there is no righteous-ness in the land?[24] And how can there be righteousness in society if there is no real repentance? Finally, how can there be genuine repentance if peo-ple habitually return to their former folly—their diverse forms of ungodly behavior (v. 8c)? Any hope of restoration and revival is quickly extinguished in a prevailing climate of sin and injustice, whether on the national or local level, or indeed, within the church itself. In such a corrupt environment, only the wrath of God may be expected (v. 5).

But as in the case of Ps. 85 itself, it is good to end on a positive note. No matter what happens in contemporary society and the nation at large, when the "saints" actively fellowship with their Lord of "loyal love" (vv. 7–8), they are united by a bond that can never be broken. Then they will experience the matchless "peace that surpasses all understanding" (Phil. 4:7, 9)—a pervasive sense of spiritual well-being, which begins in this life but comes to full fruition only in the next, when God's peace and "glory" will be manifested among his people forever (v. 9; cf. Ezek. 36:26–28, 43:4–7). And how can a person become more firmly con-vinced of this encouraging message, such that s/he applies it more ful-ly to all aspects of life? The psalmist himself gives us the key in the middle of his prayer: "*I will listen* (אֶשְׁמְעָה) to what God the Lord will say" (v. 8a). We do that by immersing ourselves in his Word and by correspondingly putting it into daily practice. As another psalm-writer poetically puts it: "Great [better: "abundant"] peace (שָׁלוֹם רָב) have

---

[24] And it starts from the top: "Zambia's new President [as of 20/09/2011] Michael Sata, the first elected Catholic head of state and a devout believer, said on Sun-day his government would follow the tenets of the 10 Biblical Commandments" (News24, "10 Commandments for Zambia," http://www.news24.com/Africa/News/10-Commandments-for-Zambia-20110925/. Accessed September 2, 2017.)

they who love your Law...I obey your statutes for I love them greatly"
(Ps. 119:165a, 167, NIV).[25]

9.3 Towards an oratorical equivalent of Psalm 85

The importance of studying the Scriptures for spiritual growth and
development leads to our final topic for consideration, namely, how we
might better communicate God's message concerning the peace that we
have in Christ, as prefigured in Ps. 85, to a contemporary audience. The
term "audience" is used deliberately, for research has shown that most
people today, especially in Africa, actually hear the Word rather than
read it silently in print for themselves. This raises the question of media
compatibility: How accommodating are the published Bible translations
that we are most familiar with to transmitting the text via oral-aural means?
In other words, are our local Bibles generally easy to read (are they clear
and readable) as well as being easy to listen to (idiomatic and natural
sounding)? In my experience, this is normally *not* the case—for various
reasons, for example, the primary vernacular Bible is an old, rather literal
version, a translation that was dominated by non-mother-tongue speakers, a
version containing errors, a poorly formatted text, one that uses the wrong
dialect of a language, and so forth.

In contrast, the Scriptures are, by and large, comprised of excel-
lent "literature," that is, texts that have been composed in an artful
manner in terms of structure and style to complement the crucial theo-
logical messages being conveyed. I cannot argue the case for this con-
clusion here (cf. Wendland 2004), but our brief survey of the superb,

---

[25] Immersion in the Word means just that—a rigorous daily study of Scripture at
the comparative worldview level, individually and in community, followed by a
corresponding thorough application in one's everyday life. As one African apolo-
gist-theologian has recently noted: "Simply stated, the version of Christianity that
was planted in Africa was largely divorced from the intellectual legacy of Christen-
dom that had produced first-rate Christian scientists, moral philosophers, political
thinkers, artists, business entrepreneurs, etc. It was instead the product of a pietis-
tic strain of evangelicalism which was already in intellectual retreat in the West
by the time it was coming to maturity in Africa. In short, since the advent of the
missionary movement in the latter eighteenth century, the Judeo-Christian tradi-
tion has never been rooted in Africa as it had once been in the West. The West may
presently be busy hacking away at the root of its moral foundations, but Africa in
one sense has yet even to break ground in order to lay down a strong biblical foun-
dation within its many cultures" (Njoroge 2009:12). It is not incidental, I believe,
that the "peace" (εἰρήνη) that Christ promises his disciples is intimately associated
with the "teachings" (διδάσκω) of Jesus, as imparted by his Spirit through the Word
(John 14:26–27; cf. Matt 11:28–29, where "learning" [μανθάνω] from/about Jesus
is linked with "rest" [ἀνάπαυσις], which is the equivalent of peace).

literary-fashioned discourse of Ps. 85 is just another supporting example, as are the literary-structural analyses of other psalms throughout this book. The various biblical books, the Psalter in particular, were both created orally and ideally also intended for aural reception. But that is not how many of the current translations into African languages read or sound. On the contrary, due to a sight-focused, print-based translation technique, these versions often seem to reflect a language style that is as far-away and foreign as the divine concepts being conveyed. This state of affairs is of special concern in Africa whose societies are still characterized by the dynamics of orality and also reflect a wonderfully rich oral artistic tradition that is still very much alive and well in many respects.[26]

How, then, can the vibrant orality of African languages be revealed more fully in Bible translations—that is, in oratorical renditions that idiomatically capture the essence of the original message of Scripture in a functionally equivalent manner, which is faithful to its semantic content and pragmatic intent as well as its primary medium of transmission? In short, how can we pray for peace more poetically and potently in the vernacular? I will conclude with a short example that will hopefully illustrate some of the important issues involved here and also encourage such community-based experimentation in other African languages and cultures. The following is the dramatic central portion of Ps. 85 (vv. 4–9), rendered in a way that reflects a traditional *ndakatulo* genre of Chewa poetry, which is well-suited for re-oralizing the text for a contemporary listening audience. This version has been formatted for easier oral articulation and is accompanied by a relatively literal English back-translation:

Inu Mulungu, ndinu Mpulumutsi wathu.	4. O God, you are our Deliverer.
Mutibwezerenso ife anthuanu mwakale;	Restore us, your very people, as in the past;
mutichotsere mkwiyo wanu, inu Ambuye!	remove from us your wrath, O Lord!
Kodi mudzakhalabe wakupya-mtima mpaka muyaya?	5. Will you remain being hot in the heart as long as forever?
Mudzapitiriza kutikalipira kwa mibadwo yonse?	Will you continue to be angry with us through all generations?

---

[26] For a recent survey of African orality in relation to the religion, performing arts, and verbal art forms of a selection of published traditions, see Draper and Mtata, n.d.

Nanga simudzatipatsanso ife moyotu,

6. Well, will you not give us again real life,

kuti tikondwere mwa Inu ife anthuanu?

so that we might rejoice in you, we your people?

Tiwonetseni chikondi chosasinthikadi,

7. Reveal to us [your] love that never-ever changes,

Inu Chauta, choonde mutipulumutse ife!

Oh Lord, please deliver us!

Hah! Koma ndimve zimene Chauta adzanene,

8. Ha! Just let me hear what the Lord will say,

popeza amalonjeza mtendere kwa anthu ake,

since he promises peace to his people,

indedi, ndife anthu oyera-mtima okhulupirika.

yes indeed, we are the clean-hearted, faithful people.

Koma zedi, ife tisabwererenso kuzopusa zathuzo!

But surely, let us not revert to that foolishness of ours!

Zoona, Mulungu ali wokonzekera nthawi zonse,

9. Truly, God is prepared at all times

kuti anthu amene amamuwopa awapulumutsewo,

those people who always fear him to deliver,

kuti Ulemerero wake m'dziko lathu uzikhalebe.

so that his Glory in our land might ever remain.

I cannot detail all of the various stylistic features that distinguish this poetic, oral-oriented Chewa translation. I will simply point out a few of its principal characteristics in summary fashion:
- The text has been composed with prominent rhythmic lineation, including typical lyric alliteration, assonance, rhyme, and euphony in general.
- An additional vocative is inserted (4c) along with vocative pronouns on every occurrence, as would be natural in direct discourse (e.g., *inu Ambuye*).
- The prolonged lines of v. 5 constitute an isomorphic image of the content, which refers to an extreme length of time—forever in fact!

- A number of emotive emphasizers have been incorporated into the text, also as a way of naturalizing it for orality, for example *Hah!* and *indedi* in v. 8a, c.
- A shift has been made from the third to second person plural in v. 8c–d so that the text sounds more personal and immediate, more typical of vernacular prayer.
- Several word order changes were effected for rhythmic purposes and also to reflect the apparent focus of the original, for example 9b–c, where the verbs appear in colon-final position.
- Expressive, idiomatic figures involving the "heart" *(mtima)* were added in vv. 5a and 8c.

The artistic and rhetorical devices just listed exemplify the way in which a dynamic translation may be fashioned in order to render it more amenable to oral articulation, as in the case of a congregational gathering for worship or a group Bible study. Such an oratorical version would also be suitable for a dramatic, enacted performance of the biblical text, or for use as the basis for a musical sung composition. Presentations of this nature, if done well, would be especially effective in societies where an active tradition of vibrant oral art forms is still in force. Even in cases where this performance convention has diminished in the face of the present decade's electronic media revolution, enough people would no doubt be familiar with such ancient artistry to be able to appreciate alternative versions of their vernacular Scriptures communicated to them in this audible way.

An innovative sound-sensitive strategy would be beneficial not only to offer more variety in terms of Bible products, or to provide the basis for novel comparative studies of the text, but it would also give people the opportunity to sense the beauty and power of God's Word in a manner that offers them a new perspective on—indeed, hearing of—familiar Bible texts. Surely the poetic message of Ps. 85 concerning the "peace of God" (v. 8) is one that has ongoing relevance and unremitting urgency in today's world—not only for Africa. (See the figure, below, which summarizes the current Bible translation status in relation to the world's 7000 + languages.) [27] This expressive prayer-poem should therefore be transmitted verbally via those communication media that have been carefully selected as being most suitable for especially receptive segments within the society at large. But above all, it must also be *lived ethically in community* as the text further implies, that is, with conjoined loyal love, faithfulness, righteousness, and personal efforts continuously

---

[27] Wycliffe Global Alliance presentation of Scripture and Language Statistics is compiled from data provided by Wycliffe Organizations, SIL International, and other partners. Data is current as of October 1, 2016. (Source: ©Wycliffe Global Alliance, http://www.wycliffe.net/statistics. Accessed September 2, 2017. Used by permission.)

and vigorously directed towards the promotion of interpersonal and inter-ethnic *peace* (v. 10).

Figure 9.1 Global Bible translation status.

10

Aspects of Quality and Quality Control in Bible Translation, with Reference to Psalm 134[1]

Introduction

This study begins with a survey of six salient factors involved in the discernment and assessment of quality as it applies to the practice of Bible translation. Three of these variables pertain with special reference to the

---

[1] This chapter has been written in honor of Dr. Eugene A. Nida, whose teachings, writings, and personal correspondence have greatly influenced my thinking about the theory and practice of Bible translation. Practice of course includes a concern for both quality and quality control which are features that Dr. Nida has also stressed from the very beginning of his new "dynamic equivalence" approach to the task. For example, "Three fundamental criteria are basic to the evaluation of all translating, and in different ways help to determine the relative merit of particular translations. These are: (1) general efficiency of the communication process, (2) comprehension of intent, and (3) equivalence of response" (1964:182). "The ultimate test of a translation must be based on three major factors: (1) the correctness with which receptors understand the message of the original (that is to say, its 'faithfulness to the original' as determined by the extent to which people really comprehend the meaning), (2) the ease of comprehension, and (3) the involvement a person experiences as a result of the adequacy of the form of the translation"

source language (SL) text (accuracy, proximity, authenticity), and the other three to the target language (TL) text (clarity, idiomaticity, relevancy). To further develop this evaluative framework, I also explore a number of essential control measures that must be implemented in order to help ensure that the quality of a translation is maintained on the one hand and will ultimately prove both appropriate for and acceptable to its designated target audience on the other. These qualitative concerns need to be directed first towards the text of the translation itself and, increasingly nowadays, also to the auxiliary paratext that accompanies it, as well as to any available extratextual materials and techniques designed to expand or enhance the cognitive processing capacity of text consumers.

To illustrate the procedure, I present a summary of the results of a limited testing exercise involving a liturgical and relatively literal version as compared with several innovative literary English translations of Psalm 134, plus or minus accompanying explanatory notes and other supplementary helps. The aim of this little case study is to call attention to some relevant methodological principles, procedures, and problems (!) when evaluating the quality of a translated text, and also to emphasize the importance of such audience-oriented considerations when carrying out any Bible translation program today, no matter what its overall sociocultural and organizational frames of reference might be. In Excursus A I cite a selection of insights from Katharina Reiss (2000) on the subject of translation criticism and related issues; in Excursus B I list some key parameters and principles of quality control proposed by Brian Mossop (2001).

10.1 Defining quality and quality control

All translations aim to achieve a certain measure of quality in terms of their production. No translation is easy to produce, and therefore those who carry out this work normally expect that the resulting text will not only prove to be worth their effort but will also be recognized as worthy by others, namely, those for whom the version has been prepared.

What then do we mean by the key characteristic of quality—and if the concept can be satisfactorily defined, is it something that can be credibly "controlled?" If so, to what extent and by what means? Since quality is a variable attribute, having to do with the relative excellence (or lack thereof) in certain relevant respects in terms of some object or activity (*Webster*, sense 3), how can it be measured, and who is qualified to carry out such an exercise? Some of the primarily practical issues that arise from theoretical questions such as these form the subject of this chapter. In other words, this is not a technical or philosophical discussion of quality in the

(1974:173). It is this last-mentioned feature, namely, a concern for literary form, on which I am especially focusing in this chapter.

abstract; rather, it is very much text- and task-related, namely, to the mission of Bible translation and presentation. Obviously, where the Scriptures are concerned, we want to carry out the work in the best possible way—that is, with the highest level of quality attainable. How can that be done and the progress of a given project evaluated, from the period of pre-translation planning to the time of final publication—and beyond, when the completed Scripture product is actually used in various socio-religious settings?

The goal of quality assessment (critique) and management (control) is not easy to accomplish; it is a complex, continual process that requires a great deal of audience research and text testing, along with subsequent revision and more testing. This entire cycle must be repeated, on any number of occasions, until the necessary degree of quality has been achieved, as determined by the appropriate evaluators using suitable methods. But who are these value judges, and what gives them the right or authority to make these decisions? I certainly do not have all the answers to the questions I am raising here, but I hope that a consideration of the issues presented here will serve to clarify some of the main factors involved in the quest for quality and its measurement as well as management. I also have several suggestions to offer, based on a limited amount of experience in a small area of the world, which may generate further interest in the development of a more comprehensive framework for a broad intercultural study in which the data, conclusions, implications, and recommendations of other researchers in the field may be comparatively examined and evaluated with regard to the variable of quality as it concerns the entire multifaceted process of Bible translation: analysis, composition, testing, publication, and usage.

As suggested by the definition above, the feature of quality in relation to a given object, being, event, or state may be highly positive or negative in nature—moving from either pole in varying degrees towards mediocrity. With regard to the field of translation, it would perhaps be much easier to evaluate an initial draft, a trial portion, a completed publication, or indeed, an entire project with an emphasis upon the opposite of what we are actually looking for, that is, with respect to its relative *inferiority*. Thus, it is often easier to perceive and point out the various exegetical or stylistic errors, deficiencies, and failures of a published translation, or the apparent reasons for its inability to satisfy and gain acceptance among its intended target audience. But in this paper I will adopt a generally optimistic outlook and attempt to overview some of the chief factors that are involved in determining and improving the relative superior quality of a given draft or published version. The term "relative" is essential because, like the related notion of style, so also quality is never absolute (e.g., complete "perfection"), but is always based on some sort of comparative analysis, whether implicit or explicit, formal or informal, consciously designed or completely intuitive.

I begin this experimental study with an overview of six proposed perspectives on quality as they might hypothetically apply to translation, a rendering of the Scriptures in particular. This general orienting framework is briefly described in relation to an evaluative consideration of the text, paratext, and extratext of any given Bible translation. Certain aspects of this tentative model are then more specifically illustrated and assessed by means of a limited testing exercise that involved several different translations of Psalm 134 as judged with regard to their relative acceptability by several distinct African audiences. My focus will be upon the formal (literary, stylistic) qualities of these versions, rather than upon the perceived accuracy of their expression of content. An explanatory overview of the testing process and its rationale is first preceded by a brief examination of some of the prominent artistic and rhetorical features of this short, but well-fashioned Hebrew hymn. A selective review of the test results forms the basis for some final observations pertaining to the different dimensions of quality that may be displayed in a particular Bible translation and how these might be more explicitly evaluated in the effort to prepare the best possible hypertext-like "Scripture package" for a specified consumer group and setting of use.

10.2 Perspectives on quality in relation to Bible translation

In order to broaden the usual scope of this exercise in evaluation, I propose that there are three different *fields* (text, paratext, extratext) and three interrelated *dimensions* (form, content, function) that need to be considered. Each of these has many overlapping facets that are pertinent in the qualitative assessment and/or improvement of a specific Bible translation (or a draft version). However, there would appear to be just two distinct viewpoints involved in the personal appraisal process. This pair of essential perspectives focuses upon the translated text in relation to (a) the original SL document on the one hand, and (b) its primary target audience on the other. Keeping these two factors in proper balance during a translation project is quite a challenge, if the participants are serious about dealing with all of the interrelated variables concerned. It is my contention that the principal TL audience must first be clearly identified in the first place, and then be made aware of these different options, to the extent possible under the circumstances, in order for a successful, plausible assessment to be made. How can this best be done? There are a number of possibilities in this endeavor, each involving a great deal of preparatory as well as ongoing research, testing, education, and explanation. These are outlined in 10.2.1 and then experimentally applied in 10.2.2.

10.2.1 An etic qualitative framework aimed at audience acceptability

The following (cf. 1.3.10) is a translational grid comprised of six qualitative factors that pertain selectively to the form, content, or function of a text (vertical aspect) as manifested in either the source language (SL) or the target language (TL) (horizontal aspect). These criteria (or similar features) need to be considered when directly evaluating the compositional quality of the translated text and at the same time when implementing a pre-determined set of quality-control measures aimed at ensuring, to the extent possible, a translation's future acceptability among its main constituency after it is ultimately published. The six variables are given a hypothetical priority rating (1–6) in terms of how important each one is assumed to be in relation to most target audiences and a Bible that is intended for use in public worship. Change the primary purpose, and the priority rating will naturally shift as well, say, for a version like the *Good News Bible* that is intended for non-native speakers of English (the ratings for the SL and TL columns would probably then shift places, that is, 5–6–2 on the left and 3–4–1 on the right side of the diagram). Other audiences, historical settings, and situations of use would produce different configurations.

Focus→	Source Language	Target Language
↓	accuracy	intent
Content	3. **FIDELITY** < reliability	5. **INTELLIGIBILITY** < content
		+
	microstructure	written
Form	4. **PROXIMITY** < macrostructure	6. **IDIOMATICITY** < oral-aural
	↓	↓
	form	processing cost
Function	1. **AUTHENTICITY** < meaning	2. **RELEVANCY** < cognitive gain

The primary concern of each of these variables may be briefly described in the form of key investigative questions as suggested in the box below (cf. Wendland 2004:337–347). In this case, the six qualities are to be evaluated by well-trained assessors (text testers) from the perspective of diverse representatives of the primary target audience (e.g., clergy—laity, educated—non-schooled, literate—non-literate, younger—older generation, male—female). A similar appraisal made using different test parameters would probably result in a different overall conclusion. Furthermore, it is obvious that a given translation program cannot satisfy or emphasize all six factors at once. Rather, a set of priorities will have to be established—one that is determined on the basis of various local considerations, e.g., the designated audience group, setting of use, history of Bible translation and usage in the community, available resources, including overall staff competence, and so forth.

FIDELITY
How *accurate* is the translation in terms of analyzing the semantic content of the biblical text (including all explicatures and primary implicatures),[2] and how *reliable* is it in representing (synthesizing) this conceptual inventory in the TL?

PROXIMITY
How closely does the translation reflect the *structural* and *stylistic* forms of the Hebrew or Greek text, that is, with respect to the original's macro- as well as microlevel of compositional organization?

AUTHENTICITY
How authentic do TL speakers perceive the translation to be in terms of *form* (proximity) and/or *meaning* (fidelity); in other words, how trustworthy or credible do they regard their translation in terms of representing the "complete" Word of God in their mother-tongue?

INTELLIGIBILITY
How clear and understandable is the TL text with respect to both *content* and also *intent*—the latter embracing the principal functional aims and accompanying connotative aspects of the original as expressed in the vernacular translation?

IDIOMATICITY
How natural, even idiomatic, is the translation stylistically with respect to its macro- and microforms, both in writing (print) and when heard as the text is being audibly articulated (spoken, recited, chanted, sung)?

RELEVANCY
How difficult is the translated test to handle conceptually (i.e., processing cost, or mental effort) in relation to the beneficial cognitive, emotive, and volitional effects (psychological gains) that a majority of the target audience derive from this hermeneutical activity?

---

[2] The following quote defines the terms in parentheses: "Thus, in the process of inferring meaning, the audience combines the set of utterances from the communicator and the explicatures they yield with additional *contextual assumptions* serving as premises, and draws conclusions, which are called *contextual implications*. Both the premises (contextual assumptions) and the conclusions (contextual implications) are referred to as *implicatures*" (Hill 2004:5 original italics). An effective way of testing different aspects of audience comprehension in terms of their culturally-based cognitive context is described and illustrated in Hill (2003). The semantic content of the biblical text, as near as we can come to the intended meaning

Authenticity is viewed as being the most important qualitative criterion in the majority of situations, being the product, as it were, of a positive evaluation with regard to both semantic fidelity and formal proximity in relation to the biblical text. Similarly, relevance is rated number two because it is the sum of conceptual intelligibility and stylistic idiomaticity, which are the key factors involved when matters of Scripture use, or engagement, are being considered.[3] These six criteria are thus perceived and assessed by members of the user community, with a special focus or emphasis being placed on either the SL text or the TL text as the translation is intended to be utilized in a particular communicative setting (e.g., a liturgical or "pulpit" Bible, common-language translation, youth devotional version, audio-Scriptures, dramatic performance rendition, the basis for a musical composition). Considered and evaluated together in relation to one another (whether consciously or more likely, intuitively), the end result will be a formal or informal determination of relative acceptability on the part of the target constituency.[4] Acceptability, then, is the overall cover term to designate

---

(an inevitably partial, yet ultimately a sufficient, understanding), is ascertained by means of a careful analysis of the original and a study of reliable scholarly commentaries on the passage at hand.

[3] "Scripture use here applies to use of mother-tongue Scriptures in church services and liturgy, various forms of ministry in the church including evangelism, youth and children's meetings as well as family use in family prayers or personal use" (Hill 2005:1).

[4] The evaluative model just described may be compared with that proposed by Williams and Chesterman (2002:8–9; original italics): "We can distinguish three general approaches to quality assessment. One is *source-oriented,* based on the relation between the translation and its source text. Assessment methods of this kind set up definitions of required equivalence and then classify various kinds of deviance from this equivalence.... The second approach is *target-language oriented.* Here, the relation at stake is not with the source text but with the target language.... This approach uses text analysis...in order to assess the differences between the language in question and other comparable texts in the target language. The idea is to measure the translation's degree of naturalness—... The third approach has to do with the assessment of *translation effects*—on clients, teachers, critics and readers.... You might carry out comprehension tests on the translation, to see how well people understood it. Or you might send out a questionnaire to translation teachers.... This approach finds functional and/or communicative theories of translation useful, such as skopos theory...." Thus in terms of my model, fidelity and proximity would fit under a source-oriented approach, intelligibility and idiomaticity under a target-language oriented approach, authenticity and relevancy under a translations effects approach.

a translation that people are generally happy with and consequently make regular beneficial use of.[5]

The various parameters and possibilities that pertain to the composition of a given translation are governed by a project's written job commission, or brief. This essential document, mutually agreed upon by all sponsoring and supporting churches or institutions, specifies in as much detail as possible all the production-related factors that are involved in the project, for example: the primary purpose *(Skopos)* of the translation, its chief intended setting of use, the style of the version (relatively speaking, how foreignized or domesticated it is)[6] and associated general translation principles, qualifications of the translators, their training and job description, the composition and operation of review committees and the project's administrative-management team, a projected schedule of specific completion stages, and its stipulated quality-control measures. The latter are intended to maintain or reinforce a perception of loyalty in relation to the original author and the SL text as well as to achieve the desired level of suitability in relation to the primary target audience and situation of use. This issue of qualitative assessment is the one that we are giving special attention to in this chapter, with reference to the aesthetic dimension in particular.

We are admittedly dealing with a very subjectively perceived and evaluated set of criteria, especially where matters of style are concerned. Those entrusted with making these assessments and acting upon them must be competent to do so in the first place, and secondly, they must be generally agreed as to their understanding of what the different variables represent and how they are to be estimated. For example, idiomaticity covers a broad range of possibility, ranging from a simplified, common-language version to an unrestricted oratorical, popular, or literary, rendition that is free to draw on all the artistic and rhetorical resources of the target language. Furthermore, it is recognized that each term is quite flexible and must

---

[5] The crucial composite quality of acceptability includes a number of other important text-external variables that have not been considered in this paper, for example: a positive or negative perception of one's mother-tongue in relation to languages of wider communication, government educational and communication policy, a target group's perceived ownership of a given translation, their unrealistic expectations of a MT version in relation to some older, long-established translation, the order of books and primary medium for presenting a translation (which involves a speech community's general level of literacy), the degree of multilingualism in churches and the society at large, spiritual problems occasioned by persecution or religious cults, text presentational problems (e.g., cover color, page format), availability—distributional difficulties, the credibility of the translators in terms of their ostensible life-style (for a survey of these and other factors in relation to Bible translation in Africa, see Hill 2005).

[6] More simply, "foreignized": bringing the readers/hearers via a less mediated text towards the original author and setting; "domesticated": bringing the author via a more mediated text towards the current readers/hearers and their setting.

therefore be defined much more closely in actual practice, namely, when a particular translation is being evaluated. This would be done through the use of a more detailed set of queries that are designed to more fully explore the parameters of a given category (see 10.2.2 below).

In any case, it does seem useful to carry out such an evaluative assessment on the basis of more, rather than fewer criteria because, though overlapping, each aims to probe a somewhat different facet of the text under consideration, as noted in the box above. Fidelity, for example, is not the same as intelligibility, for an exegetically weak translation might turn out to be widely used and appreciated by a certain community simply because the text can be easily understood, in contrast to a more obscure, but accurate version on the market. A demonstrable level of public acceptability then is the sum total, so to speak, of all the factors, operating in interaction—some being ranked more highly than others—during any given testing program.

In addition, I might suggest the possibility of a different point of view that could be applied in the process of evaluating a given translation. This alternative perspective would consider not only the perceived acceptability of the version, but in addition (or in distinction) the text's apparent appropriateness for the target constituency. These two criteria are obviously not the same: A translation may on the basis of considerable research and testing be deemed appropriate for a particular audience, but it turns out to be not accepted by them for one reason or another (e.g., perhaps they object to certain illustrations or to the use of explanatory footnotes). Conversely, a widely accepted translation is not necessarily the most appropriate version for the group concerned. For example, a well-known version may be acceptable to a religious community for the wrong reasons, such as prestige, long usage, being a badge of distinction against another church body (e.g., Catholic vs. Protestant)—but it is in fact inappropriate for them because the text no longer communicates effectively to a majority of the people, and it may not incorporate many, or any, paratextual aids to assist poor as well as proficient readers. As will be pointed out below, the feature of appropriateness might be more suitable than acceptability when evaluating paratextual and extratextual aids.

Who then should be the judge of appropriateness? In this case, a deeper, more sophisticated and far-ranging sort of analysis must be implemented, one that investigates the interaction of a variety of sociocultural, religious, and situational factors on a more objective basis than that which is used to define and measure acceptability. My practical survey sample considers the issue of quality mainly from the latter, popular or perceived, perspective. However, the need for a corresponding, but more systematically researched study carried out according to a fuller, more comprehensive methodology as well as from a more neutral, or unbiased viewpoint will no doubt become evident as the nature and results of my modest experiment are reported in §3.

To conclude this section, I will build upon the preceding discussion to answer three pertinent questions that were posed in the call for papers for the Bible Translation—2005 conference at which the material in this chapter was first presented:[7]

- *"How do we define quality, and who is the one who determines what it is?"*

  We need to investigate different aspects of "quality" from the perspective of the original text and its presumed setting of communication as well as from the point of view of the TL text and the opinion of its primary audience in relation to its intended situation of use.

- *"In light of advances in communication theory and cognitive linguistics, what have we learned about quality issues?"*

  "Quality" in the first instance is not a concrete, tangible feature of texts, but rather a relative, conceptual, emotively-influenced attribute that may vary in the mind of the evaluator from one time to the next (e.g., after being educated with regard to the genre of the text being assessed).

- *"How do we really measure accuracy and faithfulness?"*

  We can do so only to a relative degree in relation to clearly defined perspectives and parameters. My proposed grid puts several of these into a conceptual framework, but this is certainly not the only way of carrying out such a qualitative evaluation. There are certain quantitative considerations too, especially with respect to accuracy; thus one can count the number of punctuation errors found in the translation or how many times a certain key term is inconsistently or inappropriately used. On the other hand, quantitative criteria might also be relevant in assessing idiomaticity, e.g., the number of TL figures of speech or local idioms used in the translation.

10.2.2 Applying the evaluative framework to text, paratext, and extratext

The heuristic model proposed above may be applied to the text of a particular translation, and in reduced form also to any accompanying paratextual features as well as auxiliary extratextual aids. The paratext includes all those co-textual features that surround, as it were, the translation and shed light on certain selected aspects of it—devices such as section headings, associated sectional introductions, marginal or footnotes, cross-references, glossary entries, a condensed concordance, illustrations, graphs, tables, and

---

[7] The conference was held at the International Linguistics Center, Dallas, TX, in the second week of October, 2005.

maps.[8] Various illuminating biblical "frames of reference" (cf. Wilt 2003:43–58) can also be created through the use of supplementary publications that explain, describe, illustrate, cross-reference, and perhaps also locally contextualize different aspects of the overall setting of the Scriptures, for example: essential Bible history, a parallel sketch of world history during Bible times, flora and fauna of Palestine, geography and climate of Israel, Jewish culture and customs, key concepts and topics of the Bible (e.g., kings, prophets, parables, miracles of Christ), and so forth. These ancillary extratextual products (i.e., "out-of-text solutions," Hill 2004:10), whether presented in print or an audio or video format, must be carefully geared to the educational level of the primary target audience of the translation that they are intended to accompany. Of course, such subsidiary tools can do little, if any good if people do not know how to use them—or use them properly. These are practical educational matters that also need attention on the part of a translation project's administrative (management) committee.

How then is the six-faceted evaluative framework to be applied in practical terms? In the case of the translated text itself, it would probably be more effective to use it by way of a close comparison so that the differences between two (or more) versions help to focus on the particular dimension being investigated and evaluated, for example, a new translation as compared with an older one. The all-embracing criterion of acceptability is viewed as being a function of the personal perception or experience of the following graded series of audience oriented variables: *authenticity > relevance > fidelity > proximity > intelligibility > idiomaticity* (in relative order of one hypothetical ranking, depending on the type of translation envisioned). The project organizers, under the guidance of technical advisers trained in research sampling techniques, would first want to clearly determine the nature of their target constituency, including an indication of the people's preferences (based on prior instruction concerning these variables) as well as needs in relation to a new translation of the Bible. After that has been done, specific questions or exercises may be composed for assessing the six characteristics in relation to a specific vernacular translation, or translations. A limited proposal for carrying out this sort of exercise for sampling audience opinion is outlined in 10.3.

A modified test would then have to be devised for determining how these factors may be utilized in the qualitative evaluation of a set of paratextual supplements as well as any available extratextual resources. For one thing, three of the original set of six would no longer apply, at least not as directly—namely, those that are oriented towards the biblical (SL) text: authenticity, fidelity, and proximity. It is possible that issues pertaining to the fidelity of

---

[8] Ralph Hill refers to these devices as "in-the-text solutions"—i.e., for solving the problem of an inadequate cognitive contextual background for interpreting a particular text of Scripture (Hill 2003:9).

the biblical text as represented in the wording of certain footnotes, for example, might still arise, but hopefully such instances would turn out to be very much the exception, not an occurrence to be expected. On the other hand, the variables of relevance, intelligibility, and idiomaticity would be of utmost concern in the provision and subsequent appraisal of these paratextual devices—whether a major illustration were involved (e.g., how relevant and visually intelligible is it?) or some minor cross-reference (e.g., does it nevertheless direct the reader to a topically pertinent passage?).

To conclude this section, I might just reemphasize the importance and potentially great value of paratextual and extratextual techniques for increasing the overall communicative quality of a given Bible translation. A few decades ago, less so in many regions of the world, such Bible text supplements were often viewed with suspicion and hence appeared as very much the exception and not the rule; most Scripture translations were presented in the main without editorial note or comment. Nowadays, however, most of us cannot get along without such "contextual adjustment strategies" (Hill 2004) aimed at creating a wider, more accurate conceptual frame of reference, or reservoir of background information, that enables one not only to understand, but also to see the relevance of and hence to personally apply the biblical text at hand. But it is important to point out the need for an adequate amount of prior contextualized research and testing so that our efforts at "communicating context" (Hill 2003) are actually going to serve the purpose for which they are intended in relation to a specific target audience and primary setting of use, whether these be large or small in scope.

In this connection, it is necessary to call attention to the use of somewhat more innovative methods of creating a relevant hermeneutical horizon for a particular target group, thus increasing the effectiveness (i.e., quality) of their interpretation of the Scriptures. For example, Richard Brown makes the following suggestion (2004, slide 41):

> People in oral cultures do not generally use lists or organize things by alphabetical order or define them abstractly, so a traditional glossary may be foreign to their learning style. A more effective approach may be to organize the key terms by semantic domain and then introduce the members of the domain in a concrete, narrative style, such as *A visit to the temple* or *How Romans ruled Judea*. People are more likely to read or listen to this kind of "glossary" than to a list of definitions.

In addition, it is important to recognize that the presence of a communicative translation coupled with various context-building devices does not guarantee the ultimate intelligibility of the Scripture package so produced. The primary target audience (speaking now of a general representative majority) must possess a certain critical mass of basic biblical literacy to begin with—that is, an operational familiarity with important persons and events, political and religious institutions, customs and cultural artifacts, as well as key aspects of the ancient Jewish belief and value system. Without this essential conceptual grid, or mental model, even the most clearly rendered, amply supplemented translation is not going to succeed in conveying the original author's intended sense and with regard to a particular passage. Thus, the people's lack of an adequate cognitive framework, coupled with corresponding interference from their own world view and way of life, may prove to be too formidable a communicative barrier to overcome. In this case, the translated text may still prove to be too difficult to understand, while a copious supply of explanatory notes quickly overloads their text-processing capacity.

How can these contextual gaps be bridged, these cognitive mismatches repaired, so as to improve the quality of message comprehension? Two recent proposals may be briefly noted: Ralph Hill (2004:14, original italics) suggests the possibility of oral or printed "adaptive retellings," which he describes as the

> attempt to retell the text to a new audience in a way that is most accessible to their starting point, which can be quite different from the way the text was delivered to its original audience. Thus, there is at least potentially some trade-off in accuracy in order to achieve clarity. The approach attempts to go *the full distance* in reaching such audiences, either by adding any essential information necessary, or by omitting encumbering detail that is likely to confuse.

On the other hand, Richard Brown makes a pedagogical application of the exegetical principle of the "hermeneutical spiral" (2004:80), recommending the use of a progressive translation (my term) in certain pioneer communication settings. This multi-staged educative program would involve a series of selective translations of Scripture portions, beginning from those that establish the global meta-narrative framework for the Bible and move from that cognitive foundation to incorporate and interrelate the other books according to a scale of increasing difficulty for the audience concerned.

In brief, the method works like this (Brown 2004:85–86):

> Each time the receptors cycle through key portions of the Pentateuch, the Prophets, the Writings, the Gospels, the Epistles and Revelation, they grow in biblical literacy. And with each cycle, [the producers] can expand the selection to include additional portions from each section of Scripture. Thus each cycle builds on the gains of the previous cycle, leading to greater understanding (especially if the receptor has been acquiring additional extra-biblical contextual information each time).

The following, then, is a hypothetical sample[9] of the implementation of this context-building, cognitive-enrichment program, as successive publications of the Bible text appear in four measured stages, progressively adding to what has been already presented and learned (ibid.:100–101, used by permission):

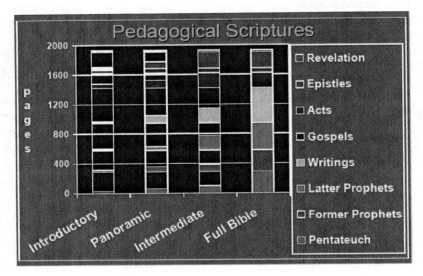

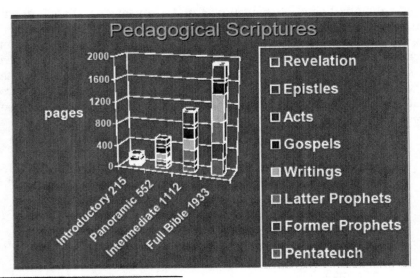

---

[9] This proposal could be modified depending of the setting, that is, according to variables such as the availability of Scriptures (or Scripture portions in major or related languages), the needs and wishes of the TL constituency, the abilities of the translators and their support team, etc. More factors are listed below.

Principles and guidelines regarding the book/pericope selection process and the order of publication must be established locally within the wider framework of the project's job commission (brief), but only after due discussion and the necessary prior audience opinion sampling and need assessment. This planning strategy would focus on the primary criterion of perceived appropriateness with respect to major target audience-related variables such as: the people's average educational level and literacy rate; their sociocultural background, value system, and world view in comparison with that of the ANE (Hebrew-Semitic and Greco-Roman) setting; their degree of familiarity or experience with other, influential translations of the Bible; the genre preferences and specialties of their oral or written tradition; the nature and purpose of the full translation, once completed; the different skills and demonstrated abilities of the translators and reviewers; the spiritual needs of the target constituency; and so forth.

In addition, the project planners would seek to strike a balance in terms of the Scripture's major concepts, themes, and teachings as the contents of the several publication cycles are chosen and composed. The following is one suggested listing (adapted from Brown 2004:110):

- God's holiness, goodness, love, and faithfulness,
- God's kingdom and his good plan and purpose for humanity,
- The hopeless sinfulness of humanity,
- The terrible present and eternal consequences of sin,
- Humanity's need for a perfect substitutionary sacrifice for sin,
- Humanity's need for regeneration by faith through the Holy Spirit,
- Jesus' role as the Redeemer-King, who died for all people and brings believers into God's kingdom,
- The need for the citizens of God's kingdom to serve him in this life, even as they await his establishment of a new and everlasting kingdom.

Paratextual and extratextual tools for relating such crucial biblical notions to the language, thought-world, and life-style of the target culture would again be necessary in order to help increase the effectiveness of the overall, cumulative communication process. It is clear then that the quality-control measures discussed in 10.2.1, especially the audience-oriented triad of idiomaticity < intelligibility < relevance, would have to be applied throughout all the stages of a more elaborate translation and contextualization program such as that proposed above.

10.3 Case study: A qualitative testing of different literary versions of Psalm 134

> Both successful and unsuccessful translations are judged such by indigenous criteria. A good translation vindicates local norms and standards; a bad translation fails for the same reason. Bible translation, thus, has a self-correcting mechanism built into the feedback (Sanneh 2003:127).

The challenge for translators that arises from the preceding observation is threefold: how to reliably obtain such TL audience feedback, how to assess or evaluate these popular results, and finally, how to utilize such knowledge to improve the particular Scripture product at hand. In this section I make an attempt to apply certain aspects of the text (translation) assessment plan discussed above to a selection of English and Chewa versions of Psalm 134. This psalm was chosen because of its brevity, which facilitates the testing process, but also due to the surprising number of artistic and rhetorical features that it manifests. My primary goal was to see how several groups of Bible students react, first of all, to a more poetically composed and formatted rendition, in contrast to a liturgical version. This poetic version would be a text that displays a higher level of quality, as it were, in terms of the target language, i.e., a stylistically more domesticated version. Secondly, I wanted to determine the relative effect of adding certain paratextual supplements to the biblical text (in particular, a section heading, cross-references, and marginal notes). The aim here was to seek the participants' response as to how much these contextualizing devices served to enhance the quality of their interpretation of this psalm. And finally, I wished to get the readers' preference as to the nature and placement of explanatory-descriptive notes in particular—whether as footnotes, side notes, or combined in the form of a sectional introduction.

For the purposes of this restricted experiment then,[10] I was focusing more upon target text style, rather than on source text content and the corresponding factor of fidelity (unless this issue happened to be specifically raised by one of the testees). A more comprehensive, meaning-based and context-oriented investigation would need to be patterned along the lines of that proposed by Harriet Hill (2003). My main purpose was to explore the key features of idiomaticity and intelligibility as they related to the perceived relevance (more specifically, likeability) of one translation over against another. The factors of idiomaticity and

---

[10] The time and resources available for me to carry out this testing process were rather limited; as a result, only several pertinent factors could be investigated and, even then, only in cursory fashion. A much more extensive, systematic, and controlled program of evaluation is therefore required in order to follow up on this very tentative, exploratory beginning.

intelligibility are clearly related, but one quality does not automatically entail the other. Thus, a stylistically natural text may not be understood well, if at all, when respondents are not familiar with the various literary features used, or if they lack the necessary background information to know what is being talked about, especially if certain unexpressed assumptions are involved. On the other hand, a relatively intelligible text may be expressed with different degrees of (un)naturalness as far as TL style is concerned. I am not able to go into details with regard to either of these variables due to (a) the unrefined type of testing procedures being employed (i.e., a simple Q&A technique) and (b) the literarily unsophisticated nature of the audiences being tested.

10.3.1 The text and its meaning

Before we can properly test a biblical text we must first of all understand it—that is, its overall meaning in terms of structure, style, sense, and significance. It is not possible to do all this here, so I will merely summarize some of the salient aspects of these four variables as they relate to Psalm 134. But first, let us have a closer look at the original text (minus the title); this is reproduced below in a poetic line format which is slightly modified from that provided by the Masoretic tradition. The Hebrew text is accompanied by my relatively literal translation, and several different translations are reproduced below in §10.3.2. Noteworthy poetic-rhetorical features are highlighted in gray shading or by enclosure in a box in order to display certain verbal parallels and other structural arrangements:

Listen—praise Yahweh, all (you) servants of Yahweh,	הִנֵּה ׀ בָּרֲכוּ אֶת־יְהוָה כָּל־עַבְדֵי יְהוָה[1]
you who stand in the house of Yahweh by night!	הָעֹמְדִים בְּבֵית־יְהוָה בַּלֵּילוֹת׃
Lift up your hands (in the) sanctuary,	שְׂאוּ־יְדֵכֶם קֹדֶשׁ[2]
and praise Yahweh!	וּבָרֲכוּ אֶת־יְהוָה׃
May Yahweh bless you from Zion,	יְבָרֶכְךָ יְהוָה מִצִּיּוֹן[3]
the Maker of heaven and earth!	עֹשֵׂה שָׁמַיִם וָאָרֶץ׃

10.3.1.1 Structure and style

The basic organization of this deceptively simple psalm[11] manifests a reciprocal call (appeal) and response pattern. The former (vv. 1–2), a

---

[11] Psalm 134, a community hymn, is the last in the collection known as "Songs of the Ascents" (Pss. 120–134).

word of blessing [praise] to God, is apparently uttered (recited, chanted, sung) by the worshiping community and addressed to "all servants of the LORD" (an honorific term)—most likely the priests and Levites currently on duty in the Temple (Goldingay 2008:571–572).[12] The rejoinder (v. 3), a blessing from God to the people (cf. Num. 6:22–26), is directed by these Temple ministers, in turn, to each and every devotee (singular "you") who is now about to depart the sacred premises of worship. "The people acknowledge the presence of God in their lives [1–2]; God acknowledges the presence of the people [3] in a reciprocal relationship" (deClaissé-Walford et al. 2014:941). This psalmic "hymn" (i.e., focused primarily on the praise of Yahweh) is surprisingly poetic for its small size; virtually every word conveys some special literary significance. The song's special stylistic features, including those performing a structural function, are summarized below:

- Key thematic repetition ("[you] bless" + "LORD"/YHWH) gives the text strong cohesion.
- This expression features a semantic reversal on the third occurrence ("may the LORD bless you") to distinguish the second, responsive verse and the probable change of speakers that occurs there.
- This principal break in the psalm is reinforced by a prominent lexical inclusio (בָּרְכוּ אֶת־יְהוָה) that bounds the people's speaking part (vv. 1–2), thus setting off the priest's concluding blessing (v. 3).
- The spotlight is on the LORD throughout, although there are three main participants: the worshipers, temple ministers, and, by invocation, Yahweh as well.
- The psalm is very succinct: only 6 lines and 23 words in Hebrew (ignoring the hyphens and excluding the title); thus every word counts in terms of its form, content, and function within the whole piece.
- There is a single centered line—v. 2a (שְׂאוּ־יְדֵכֶם קֹדֶשׁ), which is preceded by two longer poetic lines and followed by three shorter ones; from a different perspective, eight words (now counting hyphenated terms as one) precede 2a, and eight more follow this central point.
- The core verse 2a, which expresses the psalm's only physical deed, a ritually symbolic act accompanying prayer, is very condensed, lit. "lift-up your (pl.)-hand holy-place." This central utterance may perhaps be deliberately ambiguous or poetically allusive in order to suggest a range of meanings involving a

---

[12] Some commentators interpret "servants of Yahweh" to refer to "the whole community of ancient Israel" (deClaissé-Walford et al. 2014:940; Tate 1993:217). However, the context favors "Temple servants" (cf. Ps. 135:1–2).

"holy" Person (God), a "holy" place (Temple), and/or "holiness" (the forgiven people).

- A probable implicit merism occurs at the end of v. 1b (immediately preceding 2a): "in the night" = "day and night" or better, "all the time." In this case, only one member of the pair (denoting a totality) is cited, i.e., "night;" "day" is implied both from conventional usage of this pair (cf. Ps. 1:2b) and also from contextual usage, i.e., Psalms 134 and 135 are an instance of paired psalms that functioned together in the Jewish liturgical tradition (compare Ps. 134:1–2 and Ps. 135:1–3a).
- The text begins with a prophetic-like attention-getter, "behold" *(hinneh),* and it closes with a liturgical "Maker of heaven and earth", which designates the supreme cosmic rule of Yahweh as well as his immediate saving presence in his "house"—"in Jerusalem" (cf. 135:21).
- The final verse (3) features a concatenation of prominent intertextual expressions from the Ascent collection (Pss. 120–134; cf. 121:2, 124:8, 128:5) that highlights the contrastive spatial-interpersonal realm in which God operates: heaven—Zion—earth, Yahweh—you (sg.)! The term "Zion" is ambiguous, for it could refer figuratively to God's heavenly place, more concretely to his earthly "house" (Temple mount), or in this context probably to both.

10.3.1.2 Sense and Significance

Psalm 134 is a consummate psalm about blessing: the congregation's blessing (= thank + praise) of Yahweh (vv. 1–2), and Yahweh's prior and subsequent blessing (provision, protection, promotion, etc.) of his people. This highly emotive hymn is a powerful joint expression of corporate religious unity among all the worshipers, their leaders, and the God whom they jointly bless because of his wondrous divine attributes and activities (as specified in other psalms, most notably in the very next two, 135:5–18, 136:4–25), including his universal control and governance of the universe. All that remains for his people to do is to offer Yahweh their total praise and worship (cf. 135:1—הַלְלוּ יָהּ) "[day] and night" as members of his faithful worshiping community (the priests and Levites representing the assembly in this unending mediatory capacity).

Being the last in the group of fifteen pilgrim psalms explicitly designated as "Songs of Ascents" (lit. "ascents/steps;" Heb. שִׁיר הַמַּעֲלוֹת),[13]

---

[13] The ParaTExt version of the *UBS Translator's Handbook* notes: "Psalms 120–134 all have a title in the Hebrew text which is translated by RSV as **A Song of Ascents** (TEV does not include this title). The collection is also called "The Book of Pilgrim Songs." The Hebrew word translated **Ascents** comes from the verb "to go up," but

Psalm 134 appropriately concludes the collection while recalling its central themes (as noted above). Some have suggested that it may have been used as part of an "exit liturgy" (cf. Ps. 24, an "entrance liturgy," ch. 1) as "a blessing for the pilgrims in Jerusalem, a brief word of departure as they ready themselves to return to their homes..." (deClaissé-Walford et al. 2014:940).[14] Psalm 134 may have been also used in the evening worship liturgy at the Temple (בַּלֵּילוֹת 'at nights'— v. 1b), thus concluding the day's worship program with a final "praise the LORD" and a word of benediction from him, as mediated by his servants. This short song is also an important reminder that worship is more than mere words; the verbal collocation of the first two verses suggests something else: "lifting up your hands" (שְׂאוּ־יְדֵכֶם) not only in prayer, but also in active "service of the LORD" (עַבְדֵי יְהוָה), which constitutes true "holiness" (קֹדֶשׁ). While the priests and Levites may represent the people before Yahweh, this does not absolve the laity of their responsibility in turn to "minister" (הָעֹמְדִים—always "standing" at the ready) before him—representing their holy God to the world at large:

> Human living is dependent on blessing in its personal, social, and national dimensions. Blessing is the LORD at work in human work (Psalm 127). The family, the community, and the world are brought to life-supporting and life-fulfilling completeness and rightness by the LORD's blessing. (Mays 1994a:415)

The rhetoric of this psalm, bolstered by all those that have preceded it in the Psalter, thus intimately engages and challenges each and every reader and hearer of the text in its final, individualized ("you" sg.) word of blessing (יְבָרֶכְךָ). The Creator God, Lord of the universe, is summoned to bless the individual believer so that s/he might in turn be a blessing to others in his name (cf. Ps. 133:1).

---

other than this there is no agreement as to what the phrase means. Some take it to indicate the return of the Hebrew exiles from Babylonia; others take it to refer to a stylistic feature found in some of the psalms, in which the order of the statement progresses in a step-like fashion from one verse to the other; others take it to refer to the steps in the Temple precincts which led from one court to the other; the majority take it to refer to the ascent up the mountain on which the Temple was built (Mount Moriah, known as Mount Zion). Thus understood, these psalms are songs which the pilgrims sang as they came to Jerusalem for one of the three major annual festivals (see GECL)." This psalm corpus features a general liturgical, emotional, and theological progression from the opening lament in a faraway place (120) to this eulogy in the very courts of the Temple on "Zion."

[14] Similarly, "at the close of each worship service in the Christian tradition, worship leaders utter words of benediction—concluding words that prepare the congregation to leave the sanctuary and return to the world" (deClaissé-Walford et al. 2014:941).

10.3.2 Testing for artistic (poetic) quality in a Bible translation

The principal aim of this simple, informal testing program was to determine whether or not several groups of English speakers preferred a manifestly poetic rendition of Psalm 134 or a traditional, more literal version. If a more dynamic translation was selected, which of several different styles was most appreciated, and for what reasons? Five groups of respondents were tested, totaling some 75 persons in all, consisting mostly of second-language speakers of English, but including several native English speakers as well (members of Group 2 on the table listed in 10.3.2.3 below).[15] A secondary aim was to test as a control two vernacular translations, a literal and a poetic version in Chewa, just to see how the African respondents, most of whom were non-mother-tongue speakers, would react to this text in comparison with the different English versions. A more traditional, formal correspondence version, the NIV, which was the only Bible familiar to all participants, was included as the first item in the line-up of versions to evaluate. However, like all of the other texts, it was not identified in either the oral or the written test lest this information possibly prejudice the choices (e.g., "This is the Bible translation that I own, use, and therefore prefer").

---

[15] One group (#1) consisted of 11 African third-year seminary students (who had completed an exegetical course on the Psalms the preceding year); group #5 was composed of 20 national translators from six projects in Zambia who were attending a workshop at the Lusaka Bible Translation Centre; the other three groups were composed of adult Bible study participants attending different Lutheran congregations in the Lusaka (Zambia) area.

10.3.2.1 The versions tested

1. NIV

> *A song of ascents.*
> [1] Praise the Lord, all you servants of the Lord
>   who minister by night in the house of the Lord.
> [2] Lift up your hands in the sanctuary
>   and praise the Lord.
> [3] May the Lord, the Maker of heaven and earth,
>   bless you from Zion.

2. Boerger[a]

> **GIVE ACCOLADES**
> a pilgrim song of praise
> A Rubliw as a benediction
> tr 2/03 SC, 6/03
> Yahweh's
> Own! Give him praise!
> And spend your nights always
> In prayer to him and turn your face,
> In the temple courts, toward the Holy Place.
> From Zion, may God who creates
> Heaven and earth, show you grace.
> Give accolades
> And praise!

3. *The Psalms in Verse*[b]

> BEHOLD, bless ye the Lord, all ye
>   that his attendants are,
>   ev'n you that in
>   God's temple be,
>   and praise him
>   nightly there.
> Your hands within God's holy place
>   lift up, and praise his name.
> From Zion's hill the Lord thee bless,
>   that heav'n and earth did frame.

4. REB

> *A song of the ascents*
> [1] COME, bless the **Lord,**
>   all you his servants,
>   who minister night after night
>   in the house of the **Lord.**

[2] Lift up your hands towards the sanctuary
and bless the **Lord.**
[3] May the **Lord,** maker of heaven and earth,
bless you from Zion!

5. The Message

A Pilgrim Song
Come, bless God,
       all you servants of God!
You priests of God, posted to the nightwatch
       in God's shrine,
Lift your praising hands to the Holy Place,
       and bless God.
In turn, may God of Zion bless you—
       God who made heaven and earth!

6. ERW

      A closing hymn of worship
      1 Keep praising the Lord, all you who attend him,
           ministering day and night in his holy house!
      2 Lift up your hands in prayer and praise,
           all you who serve in his sacred space.
           Praise the Lord—yes, praise the Lord!
      ----
      3 Now may the Lord, Creator of heaven and earth,
           God of Zion, bless you all as you leave this place!

7. Traditional Chewa

Nyimbo yokwerera	*Song of climbing up [to a place]*
1 Taonani, lemekezani Yehova,	Look, reverence Jehovah,
atumiki a Yehova inu nonse,	all you servants of Jehovah,
Akuimirira m'nyumba ya Yehova	standing in the house of Jehovah
usiku.	at night.
2 Kwezani manja anu ku malo oyera,	Lift up your hands to the holy place,
Nimulemekeze Yehova.	and reverence Jehovah.
3 Yehova, ali m'Zioni akudalitseni;	May Jehovah, he is in Zion, bless you;
Ndiye amene analenga kumwamba ndi dziko lapansi.	he is the one who created heaven and the earth below.

8. Poetic Chewa	
Nyimbo yotsiriza mapemphero	*A song when finishing prayers [i.e., worship]*
1 Tiyeni, yamikani Chauta!	Com'on, give thanks to *Chauta!*
Mutamande Mulungu wathu,	Praise our God,
inu nonse atumiki ake, amene	all you his servants, who—
mumamtumikira mokhulupirika	serve him faithfully
m'Nyumba mwake usana n'usiku.	in his House day n'night.
2 Kwezani manja popempheraku	Lift up your hands when praying here
kwa iye m'malo ake oyerawa,	to him in this holy place of his,
inu nonse, mutamande Chauta!	all of you, praise *Chauta!*
3 Tsopano akudalitseni Chauta,	Now may Chauta bless you,
iye amene amakhala ku Ziyoni,	he who dwells in Zion,
amene adalenga zakumwamba	who created the heavens
pamodzi ndi dziko lonse lapansi!	along with the whole earth below!

[a] This second version of Psalm 134 was kindly provided by Dr. Brenda Higgie Boerger of SIL International (cf. Boerger 2009:208). Dr. Boerger makes this explanatory comment: "the Rubliw form, has identically rhymed lines of 2, 4, 6, 8, 10, 8, 6, 4, and 2, and starts with a vocative" (personal correspondence, 2014).
[b] Re-published (with no indication of editorship) by Barbour and Company, Uhrichsville, Ohio, 1995; this text was originally published over 100 years ago for use in the worship services of the Church of Scotland.

10.3.2.2 Sample questions for hearers and readers

The questions given below were employed to test the respondents both orally and in writing with respect to the six (eight, if they understood Chewa) versions of Psalm 134—particularly in terms of each text's qualities of intelligibility and idiomaticity, or literariness (verbal power, beauty, memorability, poetics, etc.). During the initial oral phase of the testing process, only two samples were considered at a time, in order to try to prevent a confusion of choice. In the first tests conducted, no printed copies were handed out during the oral part of the assessment process, but this procedure was later changed in order to help listeners focus more fully on the two texts being evaluated. The two versions were read twice in sequence, with the first clearly identified as A, the second as B. The more popular of these two (which became A) was then re-tested against another version (B), with the same questions being asked—and so on sequentially throughout the corpus. When giving the very first test, I suspected that an initial brief introduction to the structure and purpose of Psalm 134 would be helpful, and I followed this procedure thereafter as well.

Only the first two questions were given during the oral test; during the subsequent written test, the participants were asked to consider all the queries in relation to the six English test versions. They were given about 15–20 minutes to read the texts again for themselves and to answer the questions on separate, blank sheets of paper. The two Chewa translations (7 and 8) were evaluated separately, first in relation to each other and then, as a final exercise, the favorite English text was tested against the favorite Chewa translation, just to see whether the vernacular would be preferred, at least by mother-tongue speakers of the language. The other respondents did not have to evaluate the two Chewa versions unless they wished to, or wanted to comment on the English back-translations.[16] Along with the individual translations, readers were asked to assess and comment on the different print formats that were used.

1.	Which version did you like the *best?* Give at least one reason why.
2.	Which version did you like the *least?* Give at least one reason why.
3.	Did you notice any possible *mistakes* in any of the versions? Make a list of these.
4.	Are there any words or phrases in these translations that are *difficult* to understand? Underline all of these places.
5.	Which version was the easiest to *understand?* Can you give a reason why?
6.	Which version was the easiest to *read* aloud? Can you give a reason why?
7.	Which version was the most *beautiful* or poetic? Can you give a reason why?
8.	Which version is the best to use in *public worship?* Can you give a reason why?
9.	Which version was the best to use for *Bible study?* Can you give a reason why?
10.	Which *Nyanja*[a] version do you like better? Give reasons why.
11.	Do you prefer the vernacular version over *all* English versions? If so, tell why.
12.	Is there *any* English version that you like better than your preferred Nyanja version? If so, tell why?

---

[16] These questions may be compared with those suggested for a trained translation critic or reviewer (see Excursus B).

13.   Write any other comment that comes to mind with regard to your *favorite* version.

14.   Write any comment that comes to mind with regard to any of the *other* versions.

15.   What do you think about this test: was it too difficult or unclear? Mention any specific problem areas that you recall.

16.   Do you have any additional modifications to propose or questions to suggest regarding the test that you have just completed?

---

[a] The term *Nyanja* is used in this questionnaire (and hence also in the discussion in this chapter) instead of *Chewa* because that is how the language is referred to officially in Zambia, as distinct from Malawi. The preceding translations use the Chewa dialect of the language.

The final questions of this sequence are intended to give the respondents an opportunity to express themselves more freely with respect to the different versions of Psalm 134 as well as the overall testing process itself in the interest of improving future applications.

10.3.2.3 Results

As it turned out, not all of the questions suggested above were equally revealing in terms of evaluating the different translations, e.g., some less revealing ones were those distinguishing between versions more suitable for public worship as distinct from Bible study (Qs 8–9) and those asking for additional comments (Qs 13–16).[17] One question could not be responded to in most cases due to the lack of time (Q 6). A selective summary of the results of the five separate group tests is given below, followed by a few additional comments about what this testing process taught me about consumer preferences regarding the various versions of Psalm 134 that were considered, as well as the informal method of literary qualitative evaluation that was carried out. In some cases, no clear majority opinion was evident in the results; such occasions are noted by the (#) sign.

Category tested ↓ // Group tested →	No. 1	No. 2	No. 3	No. 4	No. 5
Favorite English version (oral test)	6	---	6	6	1
Second favorite (oral)	4	---	1	1	6
Favorite English version (written – Q1)	6	4	4	6	1
Least favorite (2)	2	2	2	2	3

---

[17] In addition, for two groups (2, 5) the oral only test proved to be too difficult to administer due to the relatively large number of people participating.

Easiest version to understand (5)	4	4/6	#	#	1
Most beautiful/poetic version (7)	#	#	6	#	1
Best for worship // Bible study (8–9)	#	1/6	1	1	#
Favorite Nyanja version (10)	8	---	8	8	8
English or Nyanja favorite (11)	N	E	E	#	#

I will first comment briefly on the different versions of Psalm 134 that were tested in this little exercise, and then say a bit more about the method of testing itself, especially with regard to several problems that were noted during the course of this experiment in evaluative assessment. Each one of the versions, except no. 2, was appreciated by the five groups for at least one reason or another. Though technically the most sophisticated in terms of poetic technique (and my personal favorite), version 2 was found to be the most difficult and hence was not appreciated by the majority (mainly non-native speakers of English). Similarly, neither Nyanja version was preferred over any English version by non-mother-tongue speakers; on the other hand, those mother-tongue Nyanja speakers tested did clearly appreciate the modern vernacular translation (8) more than the old one (7).

A relatively high, perhaps unacceptable number of "no clear results" (#) was recorded overall; this was no doubt a result of having too many versions on offer to choose from as well as asking the participants to make too many different choices (see further comments below). Consequently, this test did not turn out to be as informative or diagnostic regarding different aspects of translation quality as had been anticipated. Nevertheless, three English versions—namely, nos. 1, 4, and 6—did emerge as clear favorites, being selected for various characteristics by the different groups considerably more often than the others. This outcome would in turn suggest the need for another, perhaps simplified, text assessment involving just those three versions. Unfortunately, my time constraints did not allow for an additional test of this nature to be carried out, either among the original groups or different ones.

A number of interesting problem areas and translational issues in the various versions were pointed out by the participants, mainly the seminary students and Bible translators, during this text evaluation exercise. These comments, including several direct quotes, are simply listed below as part of my observations on the results:

- *Cultural concerns* may be raised in the most unexpected places. For example, the expression "at night" (v. 1) provoked questions from many respondents: What a strange, in fact unnatural, time to be seemingly serving full-time in the temple, especially "night after night" (#4)! On this point, version 6's "day and night" was appreciated (as also in Nyanja version #8). According to African traditional beliefs and taboos, the night is not a proper time for ordinary human activities, except on the occasion of a death (abnormal), when vigils are customarily held.

- *Connotation*, involving the emotive reactions to certain words and phrases, is an important consideration, and needs to be followed up in more detailed types of text-testing. For example, the older dialect of English in version 3 gave one respondent a "religious feeling;" on the other hand, the iterative expression "Praise the Lord—yes, praise the Lord!" (#6) sounded too "charismatic" to another. The positive connotation of familiarity was undoubtedly a factor for those people who did happen to recognize the NIV (#1— or who checked their evaluation paper with the Bible that they had with them), for as one wrote, "We always use this version in class."
- A slight majority of readers who responded on the separate issue of *format* preferred side- to footnotes (see sample in 10.3.3 below) for being "easier to connect" with the biblical text. However, one perceptive individual pointed out that "the notes must be on the right side of the Bible page because a person first needs to read the text, then look for the notes....Remember, we read from left to right." But another person did question whether the same amount of note material could be included in side notes as in footnotes. The general opinion on note placement was divided: some felt that footnotes were "more familiar" and also necessary to signal this material as being supplementary to the biblical text—"to leave the Scripture stand out more clearly." On the other hand, others suggested that the side notes better attracted readers to actually read them. Another item of format that generated a critical comment concerned the broken and semantically incomplete lines of the Nyanja version 7 (a result of end-line justification); one complained that this artificial printing procedure "cut the message, leaving it to the reader to connect to" the sense again.
- *Poetic form and literary technique* need to be carefully explained first to those who are not used to reading such texts, especially in the Bible. The first line of #2, for example ("Yahweh's...Own!"), was not understood by most, even mother-tongue English speakers. Similarly, others could not see the reason for the dashed line dividing the two portions of Psalm 134 in #6. A few readers did call attention to the creative use of the format, for example with regard to #2, which presents "an image of the text in print."
- The replacement of the specific "LORD" (Yahweh) by a generic "God" in version #5 created the sense of an awkward *stylistic overuse* for some, including the non-mother-tongue speakers. For one person, there was even a theological problem involved here

since instead of a unity, it gave him the conceptual impression of "many gods" in the case of this rendition.

- The matter of *regional dialect* is important in the case of a widely-spoken world language like English. Translators must pay careful attention to local usage and avoid terms that have a different or more limited range of meaning. In south-central Africa, for example, the term "shrine" (#5) is closely associated with the traditional, pre-Christian religion and also denotes a much smaller and less permanent type of structure. The expression "bless the Lord" (#s 3–5) is also problematic since people are expected to be the recipients, not the originators of blessing (even more strongly so in the closest vernacular lexical equivalents). In the case of the vernacular versions, one person noted that the designation for "Yahweh" in version 8—namely, *Chauta*—marked this text as being written in the Chewa (Malawian) dialect of the language.

- *Poetry* speaks to people more clearly and forcefully in their *mother-tongue*. As one respondent put it: "It's easier to tell what is happening [in Nyanja] and why the language is being used as it is." But even for second-language speakers of English, a poetic text does seem to carry a special impact: "It (#6) helps people to hear the voice of God!"

- Several other *difficult expressions* in the English versions were listed in the respondents' comments (in addition to those already mentioned), e.g., "Lift up your hands *towards* the sanctuary" (4); "Give accolades" (2); "posted to the nightwatch" (5); "In turn, may God…" (5—as if the people expect a reward for their service). A number of people appreciated the fact that version #6 mentioned the priests' ministering during the "day" as well as the "night." Nyanja version #7 also manifested a number of phrases and usages that were questioned, e.g., the very first word: *Taonani* "Look!" – which forms an immediate collocational clash with the second word *lemekezani* "praise!"

- With regard to the issue of English versus vernacular usage, an interesting tendency emerged that needs to be confirmed by further testing: Non-mother-tongue Nyanja speakers who knew English quite well preferred the English versions (though they did not say why); on the other hand, those respondents who did not know English very well but could at least read the Nyanja texts preferred the latter. One non-mother-tongue Nyanja participant (the majority in all groups) even commented that he liked "the vernacular because I hear God speaking *my* language," while another preferred Nyanja over English because it was more "idiomatic" to him.

- My testing of the value of added paratextual notes could not be completed with every group due to a lack of time. Clearly, this aspect of a translation needs to be assessed via a separate test that considers both usability and utility—that is, in providing information of interest and applicability to respondents. The participants were unanimous in their desire for such explanatory notes, but it was not possible for me to ascertain how (much) the comments supplied for Psalm 134 actually helped them.

In summary, I might comment on what this little experiment appears to have revealed about the measurement and evaluation of the characteristic of quality in relation to Bible translating and translation(s). In the first place, as the Nyanja proverb put it: *Zikachuluka, sizidyeka* "When there's too much to eat, you get indigestion." Similarly, for ordinary Bible readers, too many detailed questions often lead to confusion, frustration, or both. Thus, my questionnaire undoubtedly attempted to measure too fine a grid, and as a result certain questions seemed to be pretty much the same to people who have not previously thought much about the esthetic and emotive aspects of biblical discourse. This was not as much of a problem for the third-year seminary students or Bible translators, but even several of them remarked that they had difficulty at times making the qualitative choices being asked for. This difficulty was compounded by the number of versions being tested, some of which appeared to be very similar in wording and hence indistinguishable to non-specialists. But at least the testing process did serve to single out the three English versions 1, 4, and 6—which, as suggested above, might be profitably evaluated again with a "short list" of questions, such as the following:

---

1. Which version did you like the *best?* Give at least one reason why.
2. Which version did you like the *least?* Give at least one reason why.
3. Which version was the easiest to *understand?* Can you give a reason why?
4. Are there any words or phrases in these translations that are *difficult* to understand? Underline all of these places.
5. Which version was the most *beautiful* or poetic-sounding in English? Can you give a reason why?
6. Write any other comment that comes to mind with regard to these versions being tested.

Another important requirement surfaced during the course of this investigation, namely, the need for priming the pump, as it were, in order to more adequately prepare ordinary Bible students to respond in a text evaluation of this nature. For example, more time for instruction about poetry in general, biblical poetry in particular, and the challenge of Bible translation may have helped to clarify some of the main issues involved in this study as well as the general purpose of the questionnaire. Such pre-education might possibly change the negative opinion that most respondents had about version 2—though further examination may well reveal that it is not really fair to test this highly poetic piece on non-mother-tongue speakers of English. More background also needs to be given about the nature and purpose of text formatting on the printed page in order to permit a more informed choice to be made among the different options. No clear opinion emerged from this study, although the non-traditional formats of versions 3 and 6 did seem to strike a responsive chord with most respondents. Another option worth exploring with an unsophisticated, vernacular-only group of testees is a general, dialogue-only evaluation process that does not include so many Q&As, but rather allows the discussion to take its own course as each participant expresses his/her own opinion on various issues when interacting with others.

In conclusion, many people did comment that they enjoyed participating in this little testing exercise because, as one person wrote, "It helps me to study my Bible more carefully." Another remarked that she had not thought much before about having different Bible translations to serve the diverse needs of the Church, but now this goal should be given great priority, especially in Africa, which she said is also very "poor" with regard to the variety, quantity, and quality of Scriptures readily available. A current Bible translator remarked that he is now convinced of the benefit of using "*both* vernacular and English versions, because a comparative study of plural versions...sheds more light on my understanding of a particular text." In this connection, the test also sparked requests from several people that multiple versions be prepared and published in their own languages. In particular, a more poetic translation is needed to act as a contrastive complement to what most readers already have at hand, either a standard, relatively literal missionary version or a more recently published "common-language" (simplified, GNB-type) rendition.

Finally, when conducting any research and testing program such as that outlined above, it is important to take factors such as the following into consideration in relation to the methodology itself, the results (data) that are obtained, the conclusions that are drawn from this, and the applications that are made on the basis of those conclusions:[18]

> When we undertake a research project, we develop a complicated relationship with our data. We collect it, check the ethics of using it, manipulate it, store it, share it with others,

---

[18] Abstract for a lecture entitled "Data: Making the right choices" to be delivered by Prof. Stuart Campbell at the University of Manchester on July 7, 2005 (received as an email message from Prof. Mona Baker [translation@monabaker.com] on June 24, 2005).

find new ways to squeeze more knowledge from it, and often worry about it because it is the wrong kind, or there isn't enough of it, or it isn't telling us what we thought it would. Sometimes people even make it up or quietly discard the bits that don't fit. Getting the relationship right can make a project or break it.

But this is a two-way relationship. While we might believe that as translation researchers we are in command of our data, I will assert that each of us is predisposed to choose certain kinds of data because of a complex of factors. At the individual level, these include the researcher's level of training, their beliefs about the nature of enquiry, and their location in the discipline landscape. At the level of the specific project, there will be the issue of the centrality of the data and the degree of reliance placed on it by the researcher. The institutions we work for also shape our relationship with data by way of strategic priorities, ethics policies, and funding opportunities. Next is the influence of the academic publishing industry, which—by reflecting the beliefs and practices of senior researchers through peer review—privileges certain research topics and approaches, and by implication certain types of research data. Finally, there is the discipline of translation studies itself with its dominating ideologies and discourses shaping—and being shaped by—our behaviour as researchers, including our propensity to choose certain kinds of data.

There are some interesting and important implications here for those of us who do from time to time undertake some type of testing program for the Bible translation(s) and/or associated auxiliary aids that we happen to be working on. To adequately explore these issues, however, would take me well beyond the limited scope of the present paper.

10.3.3 Providing a textual frame of reference to facilitate interpretation

The short text of Psalm 134 includes a surprising number of important concepts that are either alien to, or not fully compatible with, a south-central African model of reality—religious reality in particular. In addition, there are certain structural and stylistic features (as outlined in §3.1) that will certainly be missed in any bare translation, English or Chewa, unless pointed out through some paratextual or extratextual devices. Such "contextual adjustment strategies" (Hill 2004) are intended to promote a greater degree of comprehension (or, quality of communicability) with regard to the biblical text. Thus, these auxiliary techniques too need to be evaluated in terms of their relative quality just like the translated text itself. From a cognitive perspective then, the issue is as follows (Brown 2003:53):

> The key technique for assessing and improving communicativeness is to test the translated text and associated contextual helps with the receptors to assess the cognitive effects, and then to revise the text and contextual helps in the light of the deficiencies that are discovered. Again, testers need to give more weight to intended conclusions than to premises, and much less weight to incidental implicatures that arise from the original communication situation but were not part of authorial intent.

I was not in a position to carry out a full testing program of this kind as part of the present study. Thus, I will simply call attention to several important aspects of such an exercise that will need to be more fully explored in future research. This type of investigation may be directed holistically at all of the communicative dimensions of Psalm 134, or it may be restricted, as in the case of my study, more to literary form and the comparative excellence of the stylistic features of various English or vernacular translations.

I might summarize the main potential conceptual problem points regarding the explicatures and principal implicatures of Psalm 134 as follows; these are indicated by the expressions in bold print as they appear in the NIV text:

A song of ascents.
[1] Praise the **Lord,** all you **servants of the Lord**
    who **minister by night** in the **house of the Lord.**
[2] **Lift up your hands** in the **sanctuary**
    and praise the Lord.

[3] May the Lord, the Maker of heaven and earth,
    bless you from **Zion.**

These problems are of three different types, as revealed by the examples in quadrants numbered 2–4, shown on the table of possible conceptual relationships below (adapted from H. Hill's table, "Mutual Cognitive Environment Possibilities and Challenges," 2003:2).

A key biblical concept from the perspective of the **TL audience** → and the **original text** ↓	*Think it is shared*	*Do not think it is shared*
Actually shared	1. e.g., "Lift up your hands"	2. e.g., "ascents"
Not actually shared	3. e.g., "Zion," "Lord," "house of the Lord," "servants"	4. e.g., "sanctuary"

We may start from the shared concepts, that largely overlap in both denotation and connotation and hence cause little problem for a specific target group, e.g., quadrant 1: most African Christians realize that "lifting one's hands" during worship, whether they happen to practice that custom or not, is a significant symbolic action that accompanies individual or corporate prayer and praise of God (cf. Ps. 63:4). However, various difficulties of comprehension and/or communication are presented by many other important concepts contained in Psalm 134, for example, those that people recognize but do not fully or even partially share with the actual biblical cognitive domain (quadrant 3)—such as, "Zion," which people tend to identify only with a particular hill in Jerusalem (cf. Ps. 133:3) or, more distortedly, with a certain type of indigenous African brand of Christianity. Then there are those concepts that people do have in their world of experience but do not realize the correspondence that there is with the biblical notion (quadrant 2), e.g., the term "ascents" as a figurative way of referring to acts of worship that people periodically carry out in a group, e.g., choral singing, while proceeding on the Lord's day to the house of worship ("church," especially during the festivals of Lent and Easter). Most difficult of all are those concepts that are foreign to the target culture and are not even recognized as such (quadrant 4), e.g., the "sanctuary" with reference to a restricted sacred part of the Jewish Temple in Jerusalem; in this case, people understand the vernacular term as simply a synonym for the entire Temple itself, or in transculturated fashion, as a designation for a Christian church building.

What can be done about such communicative gaps? Harriet Hill makes the following suggestion (2003:3):

> To enlarge the mutual cognitive environment so that it replicates the one the first receptors shared with the biblical author, the contextual assumptions of Quadrants 2–4 need to move into Quadrant 1. Then the secondary receptor can process the text in the same way that the first receptor did. This enlargement can take place in two directions:

1) receptors can access more of their cognitive environment by recognizing similarities that are actually present, and 2) they can learn new assumptions from the first receptors' environment. Both processes are necessary to enlarge the mutual cognitive environment. The first allows the biblical message to permeate more of the receptor's cognitive environment. The second serves to expand their cognitive environment.

Whether different cognitive environments can ever be made to fully coincide (made "mutual") in all respects is doubtful, but that does not render the various attempts to do so any less worthwhile, or indeed necessary. A lesser aim would thus be to achieve as large or precise a correspondence as possible in the most communicatively relevant respects, using all the means available, in view of the target audience concerned.

What would be some of the possibilities in relation to Psalm 134? The following is a list of suggestions:

- **Section heading** (e.g., "A psalm for the close of worship")
- **Glossary entries** (e.g., "*sanctuary*—a special sacred room set apart in the tabernacle/temple in which the high priest burned incense on an altar every morning and every evening; the incense symbolized the people's prayers of repentance and worship being lifted up as an offering before the LORD on a daily basis")
- **Cross-references** (e.g., for 'house of the LORD'—see Pss. 135:2; 122:1; 101:2,7; 92:13; 84:4; 69:9; 66:13; 52:8; 42:4; 27:4; 26:8; 23:6; Ezr. 2:1–7; 2 Chr. 2:1–12; 3:1–15; 2 Sam. 7:1–29; Hag. 1:8–9; 2:3, 7, 9)
- **Illustration** (e.g., diagram of the 'holy place' located within the tabernacle/temple building, set off from the general courtyard on the one hand, and from the most holy place, containing the altar of incense, the golden lamp stand, and the table for the consecrated bread, on the other)
- **Introductory note** (e.g., under the section heading noted above: *In this psalm the worshipers first encourage all ministers of the LORD to continue to praise and serve him; these temple servants, in turn, call for God the Creator's blessings upon the people as they leave his house of worship.*)
- **Explanatory note** (e.g., v. 3: *"Maker of heaven and earth"*—This poetic title is both a confession of faith in the one true God and also an encouragement to the people that the LORD who created all things also preserves and protects his faithful people. This added implication is suggested by two earlier psalms in the Ascent corpus that use the same expression for God in key positions within the text, at the beginning [Psa. 121:2] and at the end [Psa. 124:8].

These two psalms deal explicitly with the LORD's protection of his people when they are in danger.)[19]

These paratextual features would then have to be evaluated in terms of their quality: How well do they pass the tests of intelligibility, idiomaticity, relevancy, and fidelity in particular? Other important issues could be assessed at the same time: First of all, do readers really want such helps? Do they even realize that they need them in order to better understand the biblical text? Have they been educated as to how to use these aids to enrich their study of the Scriptures? Is there any other type of background information that they would like to have included with their translation? A (mini-) concordance is often requested, but this would probably add to the cost of any version that included one.

Other practical matters need to be determined as well—for example, where should the explanatory notes be placed: in the foot (the norm), in the margin—right or left (the latter is illustrated below, for Psalm 134:1–3, NIV [reformatted]), or condensed and combined together in a sectional introduction? The visual quality of the printed format should probably be tested several times, based on some prior instruction to readers as to the available options and their typographical significance. One must be relatively sure about this issue *before* a complete Bible or Testament is published.

	Psalm 134 A psalm for the close of worship *(Last of the "Songs of Ascent," 120–134)*

134:1 *"Praise the LORD"*—More literally, "Bless *[barkuw]* the LORD!"; cf. Ps. 135:1, *where Hallelu-Yah is* used.
 	
[OTHER NOTES OMITTED for the sake of this example]
	1 Praise the Lord,
	    all you servants of the Lord
	      who minister by night
	        in the house of the Lord.
	
	2 Lift up your hands
	    in the sanctuary
	      and praise the Lord.

[19] R. Hill distinguishes between an "explanatory" note, which reveals certain important contextual implications along with contextual assumptions, and a "descriptive" note which deals only with the latter type of background information (2004:20–21).

| 134:3 *"Maker of heaven and earth"*—This poetic title is both a confession of faith in the one true God and also an encouragement to the people that the LORD who created all things also preserves and protects his faithful people. This added implication is suggested by two earlier psalms in the "Ascent corpus" that use this same expression for God in key positions within the text, at the beginning [Ps. 121:2] and at the end [Ps. 124:8]. These two psalms deal explicitly with the LORD's protection of his people when they are in danger. | 3 May the Lord,
        the Maker of heaven and earth,
        bless you from Zion |

A thorough evaluation of the different types of *extratextual* supplementation will have to await a separate study, one perhaps carried out in conjunction with those local church bodies that are serious about providing their members with such hermeneutical helps for the Scriptures. Topics of special interest and importance with regard to Psalm 134 would include the following:

- Notes on key aspects of the varied liturgical worship of Israel, including alternating speakers/chanters/singers, as in the case of this psalm
- A biography of King David, especially in relation to the "historical" titles of the Psalms
- An OT historical survey and time-line to show the relatively long period during which psalms were composed in Israel and what was happening in the nation during these years (e.g., from the time of the Judges [Jdg. 5] to the post-exilic period [Psa. 137])
- A survey of the different genres, or literary types, of psalm, e.g., lament, eulogy, thanksgiving, Torah psalm, profession of trust, royal, etc.
- An overview of the typical stylistic features of the psalms, especially those that are often reproduced in a translation, e.g., parallelism, key terms of worship, and figurative references to the LORD God

- A summary of the nature, purpose, and possible contemporary application of the Ascent Psalms (120–134) and related psalms (135–136)
- A context-sensitive and specific topical and thematic study of the Psalms corpus

The discussion of this section has necessarily focused on printed presentations of the biblical text in translation. Corresponding methods for the qualitative testing and assessment of audio, video, and electronic products are also essential. Considering the first possibility, for example: how are paratextual tools (e.g., explanatory notes, section titles, cross-references) most effectively presented via an aural medium of communication (alone)—that is, to clearly distinguish these different verbal devices from each other and from the text of Scripture itself? These are challenges that need to be carefully investigated and resolved from the specific perspective, and with the available resources, of the local TL community of Bible consumers and communicators, including use of some of the modern electronic devices (e.g., ipads) with which they are increasingly becoming quite familiar.

10.4 Enhancing the value of a Bible translation: How is quality created, compromised, encouraged, and/or "controlled?"

Gule aliyense akoma potsiriza 'Every dance is pleasing at the end' (after your troupe has worked hard together to practice and perfect all the synchronized dance movements and steps). This Chewa proverb teaches that every communal effort may be difficult to perform or accomplish at first, but if all participants cooperate on the various details, they will ultimately succeed. So it is also with the task of Bible translation: Many different individuals with their various abilities are needed to carry out all of the diverse aspects of the work program—from the initial sampling and specification of the target audience to the post-publication testing of the results. The greater the competency that can be contributed to the various stages and coordinated towards the common goal, the more satisfying the final outcome, all other things being equal. The converse is just as predictable: the quality of a given Scripture product may be compromised by either incompetence or the lack of sufficient collaboration, organization, management, or motivation at any step along the way. Thus, the end-product will only be as good as the level of quality manifested at each of the essential steps that are involved in the production process. This is a commonplace, to be sure, but it is one often overlooked or neglected by project planners in their eagerness to translate the Scriptures as quickly as possible, without first counting the cost—or being unwilling to pay it in the end.

The following listing summarizes ten components of the Bible translation production process that require the basic minimum (at least) of quality

in terms of competence or excellence as part of an overall coordinated pro-
gram of activities:

1. #1—the sine qua non!—gifted and proficient translators and text
    reviewers (with regard to basic education, translation training, practi-
    cal experience, personal commitment, etc.)

2. #2—a close second!—strong community-based project organization,
    administration, management, local support, and public relations initia-
    tives, carried out according to a clearly defined commission (brief) and goal
    (Skopos)

3. Provision of continued training and ongoing professional development
    of all translation staff

4. Compatibility and a high level of mutual cooperativeness on the part of
    staff members and their supporters (team spirit)

5. Cohesiveness, transparency, and efficiency with regard to the team's
    daily working procedures (drafting, cross-checking, testing, revising,
    mutual assessment, data management, scheduling)

6. Qualified review team composition with a coordinated operation—
    including any special consultants and technical advisers (e.g., how ex-
    perienced, qualified, and available for service are they?)

7. Adequate supply of recommended exegetical and translational resourc-
    es (commentaries, handbooks, dictionaries, target language and cultur-
    al studies, etc.)

8. Integrated electronic text-processing resources and data bases (Para-
    TExt, Translator's Workplace, Stuttgart Study Bible, Logos) along with
    the necessary skill in using them

9. First-rate translation equipment and programs, adequate internet
    access, office facilities, staff accommodation, and conditions of service
    for the various team members

10. Rigorous translation testing methods and quality control procedures
    applied for each mode and medium of text preparation and presenta-
    tion (SL exegesis, TL composition, stylistic polishing, text formatting,
    computer checks, provision of supplementary helps, etc.—print, audio,
    video, mixed or combined format)

The preceding is not necessarily a priority listing, except for the first two items, but it is safe to say that a serious deficiency or malfunction with respect to any one factor might severely cripple a translation project, while a failure in the case of two or more components would probably be fatal as far as the ultimate quality of that project's performance is concerned.

10.5 Conclusion: *Mutu umodzi susenza denga* 'One head cannot raise a roof'

"Raise the roof?"—of a traditional African pole and thatch hut—that is. On the contrary, a coordinated and committed communal effort is required for the job to be done correctly—efficiently and without doing damage to the final product. As was suggested in the previous section, all-around cooperation and competency are needed for such a complex and challenging communicative task as Bible translation to succeed. Many project organizers do not seem to realize this, or perhaps they were not clearly told what sort of sacrifice to achieve the desired quality was required from the outset.

Thus, all stakeholders—or better perhaps, the project's co-owners— must be confronted with the basic test of *commitment*, that they are willing to do everything possible for project success, *before* they actually get into it. The entire community of TL speakers need to be continually educated as well as encouraged to grow in their diverse roles and responsibilities as the project progresses. If they are to be the chief determiners of excellence (or the lack of it) in a translation, as judges of its ultimate acceptability and appropriateness, then they also have to accept the burden of *accountability*, that is, the responsibility for seeing to it that each person or group do their fair share so as to achieve the highest standard in as many aspects of the multifaceted translation process as possible. The ultimate quality of the translation project will be only as good as the weakest link in a long chain of interdependent activities that comprise the production process as a whole. And quality, as we have seen, is a relative attribute—that is, greater or lesser with regard to a desired standard or a pre-determined norm. In the case of Bible translation, the very nature and purpose of the sacred object of our efforts should be motivation enough!

Therefore, my dear brothers, stand firm—let nothing move you. Always give yourselves fully to the work of the Lord, because you know that your labor in the Lord is not in vain! (1 Cor. 15:58, NIV)

10.6 Some final thoughts for consideration

In light of the acceleration worldwide of new translation program starts, what are the concerns about quality which need to be addressed? *Should any new project really be started without carrying out a credible and comprehensive quality assessment study beforehand—or without receiving the necessary level of commitment from project sponsors and potential consumers alike?*

With educational and experience levels varying among translators, what are the concerns and correctives in quality control? *Answer as in the preceding: The factor of quality assessment regarding all translation staff needs to be built explicitly into the project job description (brief) and must be applied in terms of prior qualifications as well as subsequent on-the-job performance ratings.*

How are our training institutions building into the translation students a mindset of quality? *These institutions must include as much actual task-specific practice along with theory, including both problem-solving as well as TL-promoting exercises, and if possible also some apprenticeship training with experienced translation consultants and translators.*

What are the quality issues related to computer adaptation and generation of text? *How can the computer be programmed to assess aspects of literary quality (stylistic excellence) in the TL as well as identifying standard, quantitative features of the translated text (e.g., simple punctuation and compositional errors)?*

What does it mean for a translation consultant to check for quality, and to help the team make needed adjustments? *The responsible* translation consultant *too needs to be evaluated, or graded if you will, as to the level of quality that s/he can contribute to a given project, that is, depending on her/his level of competence in the biblical languages as well as in the verbal art forms of the TL—plus her/his practical experience in checking vernacular translations and managing all aspects of the program.*

What have we learned about quality control from translation arenas outside the Bible translation world? *We have learned the importance of the determinative project Skopos, which needs to be much more target-audience oriented and monitored accordingly from beginning to end. From the business world we learn lessons such as: What product is most likely going to sell (in the case of a literary or advertising translation) and What procedure will probably get the job done most effectively (in the case of a technical or information-oriented translation).*

Excursus A: On Translation Criticism

Some comments from and queries based on Katharina Reiss 2000

After completing most of the preceding study, I came across a little book in my library that seemed most relevant to the topic at hand—Aiming to achieve greater quality in Bible translation production. In fact, I found so many pertinent quotes in this text, which was written in German over 40 years ago, that I thought it would be helpful simply to prepare a series of citations and follow these with my own reflective questions (in italics) aimed at bringing out the possible theoretical implications and practical applications of Prof. Reiss's insights. In some cases too, these questions are intended to update some of the seminal ideas that are contained in this pioneering book on the subject of evaluating translation. The numbers in parentheses after each quotation are the page references to Reiss (italics as in the original; all quotations are used by permission from the publisher).

    a.   Undeniably many poor translations have been made and even published. An interest in better translations could be stimulated by more contextually sensitive principles of criticism. (xi)
           Is the initial assertion true in the case of any Bible translation that you know of? Explain the situation. What do you think Reiss means by "contextually sensitive...criticism?"

    b.   (T)ranslation criticism is possible only by persons who are familiar with both the target and source languages and is accordingly in a position to compare the translation directly with its original. (2–3)
           Is such a strict criterion for criticism (reviewing) possible in your translation setting? If not, what are the main limiting factors, and what might be done to come closer to satisfying this ideal?

    c.   What is meant by *objective* translation criticism? In the present context objectivity means to be verifiable as in contrast to arbitrary and inadequate. This means that every criticism of a translation, whether positive or negative, must be defined explicitly and be verified by examples.... In a negative criticism the critic should try to ascertain what lead [*sic*] the translator to make the (alleged) error.... But then this also raises the challenge of matching any negative criticism with a suggestion for improvement.... When translations are criticized there should always be a proposed remedy. (4–5).
           According to the principle set forth above, how "objective" is the process of translation (draft) criticism in your setting? How might ordinary and experienced reviewers be encouraged and equipped to be more objective in their work, for the benefit of the entire review process? Certainly the

final challenge can be accomplished, at least to a certain degree—how, or by what methods?

d. The criteria and categories for critical evaluation cannot be formulated without a systematic account of the requirements, the presuppositions and the goals, of every translation process. (7)
    Where should one be able to find such a "systematic account of the requirements," etc. of a particular translation project? What other types of information would a translation job commission (or brief) contain?

e. It is generally acknowledged today that a translator should have "a real talent for writing in his [sic] own language" (Sir Stanley Unwin) since "clumsiness in the language of the translation has a certain prejudicial effect on the work as a whole," because "if a translator does not have mastery over his own language and is incapable of writing well, his translation is bound to be poor, however well he may understand the text" (Hillaire Belloc). (11)
    Do you agree with these assertions? If so, what is the implication for the process of Bible translation? How can project organizers discover (or develop) stylistic excellence in their translators? Which is paramount—TL stylistic competence or SL exegetical skills? Tell why.

f. Language serves simultaneously to *represent* (objectively), *express* (subjectively) and *appeal* (persuasively).... Of course the whole of a text will not always be dedicated exclusively to a single function. In actual practice there are constant combinations and overlapping. And yet as one or another of these functions becomes *dominant* in any given text, it becomes evident that distinguishing the three functions is justified: the depictive function is emphasized in *content-focused* texts, the expressive function emphasizing *form-focused* texts, and the persuasive function emphasizing *appeal-focused* texts.... In addition to these three text types based on the functions of language, however, there is a fourth group of texts which may be designated the "audiomedial" type. Such texts are *written* to be *spoken* (or *sung*) and hence are not *read* by their audiences but *heard*, often with the aid of some *extralinguistic medium*, which itself plays a part in the mediation of the complex literary blend. (25, 27)
    What is your opinion of this functional perspective regarding the categorization of literature? What modifications, if any, would you recommend, e.g., the addition of another function? If you agree with this approach, what are the implications for Bible translation? What about the "audiomedial" type of text—how does that relate to the Scriptures and their? translation? Give an example from the Bible of a book that is: content-focused, form-focused, and appeal-focused. Do you know of a book that contains a mixture of all three primary functions? If so, explain how this functional classification applies to

this text. What is the relevance of a functional approach to the assessment of quality in Bible translation?

g. The translator of a form-focused text should also be creative in deviating from the norms of the target language, especially when such "erosions" have an aesthetic purpose.... The most thorough justification of this practice is the statement by W. E. Sueskind...: "The original author wrote with full command of his own language, and he can therefore demand exploitation of the full range of subtle implications peculiar to expressions which our language, and our language alone, can offer." (36–37)

What do you think of this argument—how valid or applicable is it when translating the literature of Scripture? Have you thought about this issue before—or better, applied it in your translation practice? If so, give an example to illustrate the point.

h. So the evaluation of a translation should not focus on some particular aspect or section of it, as is so often done, but it should begin rather with a definition of its text type. Once this has been done and the appropriate translation method has been identified, then the degree to which the translator has met the relevant criteria can be assessed. In other words, in a content-focused text, it is whether *primary* concern has been shown for accuracy of data; in a form-focused text, whether special attention beyond the general concern for accuracy of information has been paid so that rhetorical structures will achieve a comparable esthetic effect; in an appeal-focused text, whether it achieves the purpose intended by the original; in an audio-medial text, whether the relevant media have been accommodated and their contributions duly incorporated. (47)

Have you ever thought about Bible translation, specifically translation criticism, in these terms? Do you think that this is a valid concern— and more, is it a realizable goal to try to achieve? If you have already translated or evaluated a certain text of Scripture according to a functional methodology, describe what you did, how you did it, and what the effect was on your target audience. If you have never considered Bible translation from a functionalist perspective before, do you think that this approach is worth considering? Explain why (or why not).

i. Every translation is a compromise and an accommodation to the larger context of life. But it is a compromise that has to be weighed very carefully. Schadewaldt (1964) calls this "the art of the proper sacrifice," which should be dictated for a text by its type. (47)

Explain the meaning of this assertion that translation is a "compromise" requiring "sacrifice." Should any other determining factor come into consideration here, that is, other than the "text type" of the original?

If so, list this factor(s) and why you think that it (they) need to be included in the translation-planning strategy.

j.　The context determines the meaning. Words qualify each other and are mutually limiting, and the more so if the context is complete. On the other hand, the *extralinguistic* situation plays a critical role in determining the form in the target language. (51)

Give an example of how the extralinguistic situation is operative to determine a certain aspect of the form of a Bible translation that you know of. How does this factor relate to the task of qualitative assessment in the case of a translation of Scripture?

k.　The critic must examine the translation with regard to each of these linguistic elements: the semantic elements for equivalence, the lexical elements for adequacy, the grammatical elements for correctness, and the stylistic elements for correspondence. Attention must be paid to how each of these elements relate not only to each other, but also to the demands of the text type. On the one hand these elements are not independent entities; on the other hand their value differs in each of the various text types. In content-focused texts verbal semantics (the lexical element) and syntactical semantics (the grammatical element) assume priority, while in form- and appeal-focused texts the phonetic, syntactic and lexical elements are especially important. (66)

Have you ever evaluated, or critiqued, a translation in terms of the categories that Reiss sets out above—more or less? Explain. Are the different "linguistic" distinctions and associated criteria that she makes clearly differentiated for you? If so, give an example of each of the four categories; if not, propose a modification of her system. How does her evaluative model relate to the "etic qualitative framework" proposed in §10.2.1 of this chapter?

l.　*Rem tene,* as Cato said, and *verba sequentur* ["Know your subject, and the words follow"].... The subject matter of a text must be well understood and duly recognized by the translator and by the critic as well. (70–71)

Apply this principle to the critical reviewers of a particular Bible translation—how qualified must they be? If not sufficiently so, how can they be trained to do the job required of them?

m.　In order to evaluate a translation objectively—"it is not enough to learn the language. One must study its culture, not just as an interested visitor, but from the ground up, and...systematically." (Georges Mounin, 78)

How does one go about studying a culture "systematically?" Is it necessary for a mother-tongue speaker of the language to do this? Why (or why not)? Give an example of the importance of this principle as applied in Bible translation.

n. The critic should test whether these implications (i.e., affective values) are appropriately echoed in the target language. He should notice whether the linguistic means for expressing humor or irony, scorn or sarcasm, excitement or emphasis in the original have been recognized by the translator and rendered appropriately in the target language. Frequently, the linguistic elements of the original alone do not call sufficient attention to particular affective aspects, so that these must be detected in other ways. Naturally in appeal-focused texts these determinants call for the greatest attention. (83) *Which biblical texts would seem to be especially "appeal-focused" in nature? Give an example or two of "humor or irony, scorn or sarcasm, excitement or emphasis," for example from John 9. Point out the "determinants" of such affective values in the original Greek—and correspondingly, how these sentiments have been rendered in your language.*

o. By the term *translation* we mean here the version of a source text in a target language where the primary effort has been to reproduce in the target language a text corresponding to the original as to its textual type, its linguistic elements, and the non-linguistic determinants affecting it. On the surface this definition excludes any consideration of translations which do not share the purpose of the original or have a purpose other than that of the original author, and are directed to the interests of a special clientele. Such products are better characterized as adaptations, paraphrases, more-or-less free revisions, abstracts, summaries, and the like…. The functional category is the guiding principle for judging renderings which are designed to serve a special purpose and are accordingly intended to fulfill a special function that is not addressed in the original. Under these conditions the appropriateness of a translation method should be judged in the light of the special purpose instead of by text type. … The many kinds of Bible translations provide another example of how the purpose of a translation affects translation methods. (90, 92–93, 95) *Evaluate the definition of "translation" given above: do you have any corrections or modifications to suggest? Do you agree with the author's distinction between translation per se and "adaptations…and the like?" Why or why not? Do you agree with the author's principle for the assessment of what she regards as "adaptations…and the like?" Explain. Do you agree with the final assertion of this section? If not, explain why; if so, make a specific application to a specific Bible translation that you know of, and give an example that illustrates this point.*

p. Both text-oriented and goal-oriented kinds of translation are affected by subjective influences…. A proper translation criticism…is accordingly objective only to the extent that it takes these subjective conditions into consideration. (114)

What do you think are some of the most important "subjective influences" that affect the process of Bible translation? How is it possible to take "these subjective conditions into consideration"—what strategy would you propose? How does the consideration brought up in this proposed principle relate to the "objective" position presented in quotation (c) above?

Finally, in view of the various issues discussed by Prof. Reiss in the preceding citations, make your own application to Bible translation criticism, with special reference to the concern for quality or quality control, by presenting three essential principles that might serve as basic guidelines for translation critics and/or reviewers in the project that you are associated with.

Excursus B: Some Parameters and Principles of Translation Criticism

(Mossop 2001:99, 149)

Assignment: Make an adaptation and application of the following parameters and principles, which have professional secular translators in mind, to the process of Bible translation.

The Revision Parameters

Revision parameters are the things a reviser checks for—the types of error.... In order to think about and discuss revision, it is convenient to have a reasonably short list of error types....

*Group A – Problems of meaning transfer (**Transfer**)*

1. Does the translation reflect the message of the source text? *(Accuracy)*
2. Have any elements of the message been left out? *(Completeness)*

*Group B – Problems of content (**Content**)*

3. Does the sequence of ideas make sense: is there any nonsense or contra-diction? *(Logic)*
4. Are there any factual, conceptual or mathematical errors? *(Facts)*

*Group C – Problems of language and style (**Language**)*

5. Does the text flow: are the connections between sentences clear? Are the relationships among the parts of each sentence clear? Are there any awkward, hard-to-read sentences? *(Smoothness)*
6. Is the language suited to the users of the translation and the use they will make of it? *(Tailoring)*
7. Is the style suited to the genre? Has the correct terminology been used? Does the phraseology match that used in original target-language texts on the same subject? *(Sub-language)*
8. Are all the word combinations idiomatic? Does the translation observe the rhetorical preferences of the target language? *(Idiom)*
9. Have the rules of grammar, spelling, punctuation, house style, and cor-rect usage been observed? *(Mechanics)*

*Group D – Problems of physical presentation (**Presentation**)*

10. Are there any problems in the way the text is arranged on the page: spacing, indentation, margins, etc.? *(Layout)*
11. Are there any problems of text formatting: bolding, underlining, font type, font size, etc.? *(Typography)*
12. Are there any problems in the way the document as a whole is organized: page numbering, headers, footnotes, table of contents, etc.? *(Organization)*

Summary of Revision Principles

1. If you find a very large number of mistakes as you begin revising a translation, consider whether the text should be retranslated rather than revised.
2. If you cannot understand the translation without reading it twice, or without consulting the source text, then a correction is definitely necessary.
3. Do not ask whether a sentence *can* be improved but whether it *needs* to be improved. Make the fewest possible changes, given the users of the translation and the use they will make of it.
4. Make small changes to a sentence rather than rewriting it.
5. Minimize introduction of error by not making changes if in doubt whether to do so.
6. Minimize revision time through unilingual re-reading unless the longer comparative procedure is dictated by the likelihood of mistranslation or omission (difficult text, untried translator, etc.) and by the consequences of such errors.
7. When you make a linguistic correction or stylistic improvement, make sure that you have not introduced a mistranslation.
8. When you make a change, check whether this necessitates a change elsewhere in the sentence or a neighboring sentence.
9. Do not let your attention to microlevel features of the text prevent you from seeing macrolevel errors, and vice-versa.
10. Do not let your attention to the flow of linguistic forms prevent you from seeing errors in meaning (nonsense, contradiction, etc.), and vice-versa.
11. Check numbers as well as words: they are part of the message.
12. Adopt a procedure which maximizes your opportunity to see the text from the point of view of the first-time reader.
13. Adopt a procedure which allows you to strike a suitable balance between the degree of accuracy of the translation and the degree of readability.
14. In the final analysis, give preference to the reader's needs over the client's demands.

15. Avoid creating an immediate bad impression: make sure there are no spelling or typographical errors on the front page of the translation.
16. Do not make changes you cannot justify when revising the work of others.
17. Do not impose your own approach to translating on others.
18. Do not impose your own linguistic idiosyncrasies on others.
19. Make sure that client and reader receive full benefit from revision work: ensure that all handwritten changes are properly input and that all changes are saved before the text is sent to the client.
20. If you have failed to solve a problem, admit it to the client.

11

Psalm 73—Exegesis, Evaluation, Re-Expression

11.1 The Psalter's central Psalm: From heartfelt doubt, to deliberation, to declaration

"Psalm 72 strikes a high note; it is flush with the hopes and dreams for the future. In contrast, Psalm 73 opens Book Three on a note of confusion and doubt" (deClaissé-Walford et al. 2014:584). Psalm 73 is the first of a set of Asaphite Psalms (Pss. 73–83), which introduce Book III of the Psalter.[1]

---

[1] "The Asaph Psalms are located in a pivotal place in the Psalter. Not only are they the first psalms of book 3, the middle of the five-book Psalter, but they are also located in the numeric middle of the Psalter.... Psalm 73 presents the underlying problem of the larger Asaphite collection: life is not as it should be.... Attempts to understand the Psalter as a whole are challenged in the Psalms of Asaph. In these Psalms the role of the Davidic king is greatly diminished when compared to the Psalms before and after them.... God's dominant role in the Psalms of Asaph is judge, an aspect of divine kingship that is not often emphasized in the Psalms" (Jones 2014:71, 78, 82). Walter Brueggemann, too, views Psalm 73 as the center of the Psalms, "transitioning the overall tenor of the Psalter from obedience to praise" (1995:204), in contrast to Snearly, who considers Psalm 89 to function as "the turning point of the message of the Psalter" (2013:210–211).

On the other hand, Cole points out a number of lexical connections between Psalms 72 and 73, thus forming a bridge between Books II and III of the Psalter:

This group includes several communal laments (Pss. 74, 79, 80, 83), and like them Psalm 73 includes a number of this genre's features, with the psalmist initially lamenting his lot in life (e.g., 13–14). On the other hand, according to Bratcher and Reyburn, "like Psalms 37 and 49, this psalm is a wisdom psalm, designed to instruct the reader about certain basic questions relating to belief in God as a God of justice" (1991:632; also VanGemeren 1991:475).[2] In contrast to the orderly moral world depicted in the principles of Proverbs, the "individual lament" of "Psalm 73, along with other biblical wisdom compositions such as the books of Job and Ecclesiastes, addresses the realities of day-to-day living [in which] reward does not always come to the righteous" (deClaissé-Walford 2004:88). With respect to genre, then, the commentators and "form critics have not arrived at a consensus regarding this psalm" (Tate 1990:231; cf. Terrien 2003:526; deClaissé-Walford et al. 2014:584). The location of Psalm 73 at the head of Book III in the Psalter is significant (deClaissé-Walford et al. 2014:592–593):

> Scholars have noted that it shares a great amount of vo-
> cabulary with Psalm 1 and is concerned primarily with the
> dichotomy between the "pure in heart" and the wicked....
> This psalm challenges, and then ultimately accepts the
> premise of Psalm 1. Its placement then is key. Books 1 and
> 2 end with Psalm 72 and the statement that the "prayers of
> David" are ended and the superscription to Solomon places
> it at a very historical juncture.... Psalm 73 opens a collec-
> tion and a book that on the whole will stand beside a specific
> period in Israel's history and will end with the painful ques-
> tions of the exile as a haunting end to psalm 89.

Psalm 73 manifests a prominent personal component in which the psalmist explores his own faith and commitment to Yahweh and finds this wanting (vv. 13–14, 21–22). Apparently, during a period of sacred meditation (v. 17), he comes to a renewed understanding, a paradigm shift in fact[3]—not only of God's transcendent justice (vv. 18–20, 27), but also of his immanent care and concern for the individual believer facing a crisis of conscience (vv. 23–26, 28). In the process, he gives a strong personal testimony of his faith in God. Psalm 73 in the middle of the Psalter is similar

---

"Psalm 73 is a good example of specific questions directed at the words of Psalm 72, as the repeated terms...between each psalm demonstrate" (2013:195).

[2] Psalm 73 manifests a "teaching tone" (often contrastive in nature), "wisdom terminology," and "wisdom questions or topics," in this case: "why evildoers seem to prosper while good people suffer" (Jacobson and Jacobson 2013:72).

[3] "A paradigm shift is a radical change from one system or way of looking at something to another, a change in a person's world view" (Boice 1996:209). In the case of Psalm 73, this worldview shift apparently incorporates life beyond the grave (vv. 23–25).

in some ways to Psalm 1 at the beginning (cf. McCann 1996:967–968). But instead of giving a straightforward, sapiential picture of the "righteous person" as we have there, in Psalm 73 we get a glimpse of a troubled soul who first questions, in Job-like fashion (cf. also Ps. 37), the prevailing justice of God in a world where the wicked seem to prosper, while the righteous must suffer in shame on account of their godly faith and life-style.[4] However, after his re-entry into the "sanctuaries of God" (v. 17)—perhaps the Temple, but arguably the Torah (Word)—the psalmist suddenly realizes his error of superficial judgment and recognizes anew that a genuine fellowship with Yahweh (vv. 23–28) is really what counts both in this life—and "forever" (v. 26.2). Such a lasting peace with God sharply contrasts with the destiny ("terrors") of the wicked (vv. 18–20). Tate classifies Psalm 73 as a "reflective testimony, not directly instructional but certainly intended to function in that mode" (1990:232; cf. Mays 1994a:241).[5]

I have posited a linear literary structure of Psalm 73 in the following constituent listing that consists of seven major poetic units, or stanzas; for each one I have added a topical summary:

- **A** (1–3), main Theme (*God is good*) and initial Problem: *Envying the prosperity of the wicked;*
- **B** (4–12, consisting of three strophes: 4–6, 7–10, 11–12), *Description of the wicked;*
- **C** (13–14), *The psalmist's wrong conclusion;*
- **D** (15–17), *Turning point—paradigm shift;*
- **E** (18–20), *New perspective on the destiny of the wicked;*
- **F** (21–26, consisting of three strophes: 21–22, 23–24, 25–26), *New perspective on his initial problem and its solution in fellowship with God;*
- **G** (27–28), *Contrastive testimony: destruction for the unfaithful—deliverance for the faithful.*[6]

There is an interesting pattern of pronominal references that follows the basic outline of this psalm's thematic development: In the first major section (1–12), the pronoun *they* is predominant, with reference to the well-being of

---

[4] Psalm 73 "has much in common with the questions lifted in the book of Ecclesiastes. The psalm, in essence, presents a hypothesis [1] and questions that hypothesis [2–14], coming finally to a resolution [15–17 > 18–26]" (deClaissé-Walford et al. 2014:584, verse numbers added)—and a godly conclusion (27–28).

[5] Tate, following Murphy, also notes a number of stylistic features that Psalm 73 has in common with Ecclesiastes (1990:231–232). The key word "heart" (לֵבָב), man's volitional center of being, occurs five times in this psalm, beginning in v. 1, thus "leading Buber to call it a 'meditation of the heart'" (ibid.:232).

[6] Terrien (2003:528) proposes a "strophic construction" that is similar to mine, except for the first two units: 1–2, 3–6, 7–10, 11–12, 13–14, 15–17, 18–20, 21–22, 23–24, 25–26, 27–28. In favor of my division is the shift from a first-person (the psalmist) to a third-person (the wicked) orientation at v. 3.

the wicked. This suddenly shifts to *I* in vv. 13–17, as the psalmist articulates his deeply-felt personal response to the prosperity of the ungodly. There is a change again at v. 18, as the psalmist shifts the focus of his attention to *you*—to Yahweh, the God of justice (18–22). And finally, in the psalm's last section (23–28), we note an interesting mixture of *you* and *I* references, as the psalmist testifies to the wonderful fellowship that he enjoys with his God throughout life—unto "glory" (v. 24)!

It is rather important to pay attention to these discourse divisions because they affect how one understands the poet's development of ideas—and hence also their translation into another language, for example, with respect to how one marks the onset of a new stanza (aperture), its ending (closure), its central thematic point (peak) or emotive expression (climax), and possibly any internal divisions within a unit (as in stanza B).

A different structural arrangement will affect one's interpretation. Tate (1990:233–234), for example, seemingly[7] proposes an imperfect chiastic (concentric) pattern as follows:

A (v. 1),
   B (2–3),
      C (4–12),
         D (13–15),
            E (17),
         D′ (18–20),
   B′ (21–26),
      C′ (27–28)
A′ (16)

However, several questions could be raised with respect to this proposal: To begin with, why should vv. 1 and 17 constitute separate units? Verses 1–2 are linked medially by the contrastive "But I..." (וַאֲנִי) just as in the case of verses 27–28. Verse 17, which leads off with "until" (עַד־), appears to be clearly part of the larger stanza of vv. 15–17.[8] Unit C (4–12) does not correspond with C′ (27–28) with respect to either size or theme. Unit D (13–15) with a focus on the psalmist does not match D′ with its emphasis upon the wicked, unit B′ can be divided at least once, e.g., at v. 23,

---

[7] I say "seemingly" because the diagram given on p. 234, which is clear, does not jibe with the structural formula on p. 233, which is confusing as stated: "A-v 1a; B-vv 2–3; C-vv 4–12; D-vv 18–20; E-v 17; D′-vv 18–20; B′-vv 21–26; C′-vv 27–28; A′-v 16 (ABCDED′B′C′A′)."

[8] In contrast also to the linear structure proposed in deClaissé-Walford et al. 2014:587. This is not to deny Brueggemann's observation that "the whole psalm, and in a way the whole psalter, pivots on this verse" (referred to in deClaissé-Walford et al. 2014:591). Such a structural "pivot" does not usually function as an independent poetic unit (strophe).

and for some reason unit A' (16) is out of place syntagmatically as well as thematically at the end of the arrangement. Thus, in terms of pure structure (paragraphs, topical headings, format, etc.) a more logical concentric arrangement might be this: A (1–3), B (4–12), C (13–14), D (15–17), C' (18–20), B' (21–26), A' (27–28). But despite the formal balance, the corresponding units do not match well thematically.[9] Perhaps a simple three-part structure for the psalm as a whole might be proposed, based on the three occurrences of the consequential-emphatic particle אַךְ:[10] I—the psalmist reflects upon (foregrounds) the wicked (1–12); II—the psalmist reflects upon himself (13–17); III—the psalmist reflects upon his God (18–28). Part I presents the psalmist's theological problem; part III gives the divine solution; and part II provides the transition from one spiritual side (psychological state) to the other.

In the following section, I present another annotated diagram of the textual structure of Psalm 73, accompanied by my own interlinear translation (cf. similar charts in chs. 1–4 above). As a practical exercise then, readers might study this psalm in relation to the various textual and exegetical notes provided in order to come to their own conclusion concerning the discourse structure (main constituents) and its key communicative clues—that is, those particular literary (artistic-rhetorical) features that serve to guide them to the text's intended meaning and pragmatic impact. Afterwards, we will consider several proposals for rendering this psalm in a more dynamic, functionally-equivalent manner—in a way that pays special attention to the text's literary (poetic) as well as oral-aural (phonological) features.

---

[9] The same applies to VanGemeren's concentric construction: A (1–3), B (4–12), C (13–17), D (18–20), C' (21–22), B' (23–26), A' (27–28). This proposal also reflects several decisions that could be challenged, e.g., omitting the prominent break at v. 15, and v. 17 from Psalm 73's central core, for example: it does not recognize the strophic unit covering verses 15–17—thus indicating vv. 18–20 as the structural center (designated as "Affirmation of God's Justice") (1991:476).

[10] More specifically, אַךְ is "a 'particle' which sometimes is used to express the certainty of an observation" (Christo van der Merwe, personal correspondence, 2014). DeClaissé-Walford et al. 2014:585 suggest highlighting the thematic development as follows: Surely God is good! (v. 1); Surely I have been good for nothing! (vv. 13–16); and God is good! (v. 28). However, whereas this proposal follows the appearance of אַךְ in the first two divisions, it does not do so in the case of the last (cf. v. 18). The final section is also somewhat mistitled, for v. 28 literally reads: "And/But as for me, it is good to be near God," which is a rather different notion.

11.2 Annotated diagram of the poetic, sequential-spatial structure of Psalm 73

v.co	Post-Verb2	Post-Verb1	VERBAL	Pre-Verb2	Pre-Verb1
I. A					
0.1				לְאָסָף	מִזְמֹור
				of/for-Asaph	a-psalm
1.1		אֱלֹהִים	-------	לְיִשְׂרָאֵל [a]	אַךְ טֹוב
		God		to-Israel	surely good
1.2				לְבָב [b]	לְבָרֵי
				heart	to-those-pure-of
2.1		רַגְלָי	נָטוּי (נָטָיוּ)*	כִּמְעַט	וַאֲנִי [c]
		my-feet	they-slipped	as-little (almost)	and-I
2.2		אֲשֻׁרָי	שֻׁפְּכָה * (שֻׁפְּכוּ) [d]		כְּאַיִן
		my-footsteps	they-slid		as-not (nearly)
3.1		בַּהֹולְלִים	קִנֵּאתִי		כִּי־ [e]
		the-arrogant-people	I-envied		for =
3.2		אֶרְאֶה [f]		רְשָׁעִים	שְׁלֹום
		I-saw		wicked-people	prosperity-of
Ba					
4.1	לְמֹותָם [g]	חַרְצֻבֹּות [h]	אֵין		כִּי
	at-their-death	bonds/struggles	there-is-no		for
4.2		אוּלָם	-------		וּבָרִיא
		their-belly/body			and-fat/healthy
5.1			אֵינֵמֹו	אֱנֹושׁ	בַּעֲמַל
			there-is-not-[for]-them	humanity	in-the-trouble-of

5.2				יְנֻגָּעוּ	לֹא	וְעִם־אָדָם
			they-are-plagued	not	and-with = mankind
6.1		גַּאֲוָה	עֲנָקַתְמוֹ		לָכֵן
		pride	they-put-on		therefore
6.2	לָמוֹ	חָמָס	יַעֲטָף־שִׁית		
	on-them	violence	it-covers = [like-a]-garment		
Bb					
7.1	עֵינֵמוֹ[j]	מֵחֵלֶב	יָצָא		
	their-eyes	with-fat	it-protrudes		
7.2	לֵבָב	מַשְׂכִּיּוֹת	עָבְרוּ		
	[their]-heart	conceits-of	they-overflow		
8.1			יָמִיקוּ ׀		
			they-mock		
	עֹשֶׁק[k]	בְרָע	וִידַבְּרוּ		
	oppression	with-evil-of	and-they-speak		
8.2			יְדַבֵּרוּ		מִמָּרוֹם[l]
			they-speak		from-high-places/positions
9.1	פִּיהֶם	בַשָּׁמַיִם	שַׁתּוּ		
	their-mouth	against-the-heavens	they-set		
9.2		בָּאָרֶץ[m]	תִּהֲלַךְ		וּלְשׁוֹנָם
		on-the-earth	it-moves-about		and-their-tongue
10.1	הֲלֹם	עַמּוֹ	*יָשִׁיב (יָשׁוּב)[n]		לָכֵן ׀
	hither	his-people	it-returns		therefore

10.2		לָמוֹ	יָמְצוּ	מָלֵא	וּמֵי
		for/by-them	they-are-drained	abundance	and-waters-of
Bc					
11.1			וְאָמְרוּ		
			and-they-say		
		אֵל	יָדַע		אֵיכָה
		God	he-knows =		how
11.2		בְּעֶלְיוֹן	דֵּעָה	וְיֵשׁ	
		in-Most-High	knowledge	and-is-there	
12.1		רְשָׁעִים		אֵלֶּה	הִנֵּה
		wicked-people		these	look =
12.2		חָיִל	הִשְׂגּוּ	עוֹלָם	וְשַׁלְוֵי
		wealth	they-increase =	forever [always]	and-care-free-people-of
II. C					
13.1		לְבָבִי	זִכִּיתִי	רִיק	אַךְ
		my-heart	I-have-kept-pure	in-vain	surely =
13.2		כַּפָּי	בְּנִקָּיוֹן	וָאֶרְחַץ	
		my-hands	in-innocence	and-I-washed	
14.1		כָּל־הַיּוֹם	נָגוּעַ		וָאֱהִי
		all = the-day	I-am-being-plagued		and-I
14.2		לַבְּקָרִים	-------		וְתוֹכַחְתִּי
		in-the-morning			and-my-punishment
D					
15.1			אָמַרְתִּי		אִם
			I-said		if =

		כְּמוֹ‎ᵂ	אֲסַפְּרָה		
		like-it [thus]	let-me-declare		
15.2			בָּגַדְתִּי	דוֹר בָּנֶיךָ	הִנֵּה‎ˣ
			I-would-have-betrayed	generation-of-your-children	indeed
16.1	זֹאת	לָדַעַת	וָאֲחַשְּׁבָה		
	this	to-understand	and-I-considered		
16.2	בְּעֵינָי	*הִיא (הוּא)	-------		עָמָל‎ʸ
	in-my-eyes	it			trouble
17.1ᶻ	אֶל	אֶל־מִקְדְּשֵׁי‎ᵃᵃ	אָבוֹא		עַד־
	God	into = sanctuaries-of =	I-enter		until =
17.2		לְאַחֲרִיתָם	אָבִינָה‎ᵃᵇ		
		their-destiny	I-discern		
III. E					
18.1		לָמוֹ	תָּשִׁית‎ᵃᶜ	בַּחֲלָקוֹת‎ᵃᵈ	אַךְ‎ᵃᵉ
		for-them	you-will-set	in-the-slick-places	surely
18.2		לְמַשּׁוּאוֹת‎ᵃᶠ	הִפַּלְתָּם		
		into-ruins	you-cause-them-to-fall		
19.1	כְרֶגַע	לְשַׁמָּה	הָיוּ		אֵיךְ‎ᵃᵍ
	as/in-a-moment	for-desolation	they-have-become		how
19.2		מִן־בַּלָּהוֹת‎ᵃʰ	סָפוּ תַמּוּ		
		from = terrors	they-come-to-an-end they-are-finished		

20.1			מֵהָקֵיץ[ai] from-[their]-arousing		כַּחֲלוֹם like-a-dream
20.2			בָּעִיר ׀ in-[their]-awakening		אֲדֹנָי O-Lord
20.3			תִּבְזֶה you-will-despise		צַלְמָם[aj] their-delusion
Fa					
21.1		לְבָבִי my-heart	יִתְחַמֵּץ[ak] it-is-grieved		כִּי[al] for
21.2			אֶשְׁתּוֹנָן I-am-pierced		וְכִלְיוֹתַי and-my-kidneys
22.1		בַּעַר[am] foolish	------- 		וַאֲנִי and-I=
			אֵדָע I-know		וְלֹא and-not
22.2		עִמָּךְ[an] with/before-you	הָיִיתִי I-was		בְהֵמוֹת[ao] [like]-beasts
Fb					
23.1		עִמָּךְ[ap] with-you	------- 	תָּמִיד continually	וַאֲנִי and-I
23.2		בְּיַד־יְמִינִי by-hand=my-right	אָחַזְתָּ you-have-held		
24.1			תַּנְחֵנִי[aq] you-guide-me		בַּעֲצָתְךָ by-your-counsel

24.2			תִּקָּחֵ֑נִי [ar]	כָּב֣וֹד	וְאַחַ֖ר [as]
			you-will-receive-me	[with]-honor	and-after-ward
Fc					
25.1		בַּשָּׁמָ֑יִם	-------		מִי־לִ֥י
		in-the-heavens			who = for-me
25.2		בָאָ֙רֶץ֙ [at]	חָפַ֣צְתִּי	לֹא־	וְ֝עִמְּךָ֗ [au]
		in-the-earth	I-desire	not =	and-with-you
26.1	וּלְבָבִ֑י	שְׁאֵרִ֪י	כָּלָ֤ה [av]		
	and-my-heart	my-flesh	it-may-perish		
26.2	לְעוֹלָֽם	אֱלֹהִ֣ים	-------	וְחֶלְקִ֥י	צוּר־לְבָבִ֑י [aw]
	forever	O-God	-------	and-my-portion	rock-of = my-heart
G					
27.1			יֹאבֵ֑דוּ	רְחֵקֶ֣יךָ	כִּי־הִנֵּ֣ה [ax]
			they-are-ruined	those-far-from-you	indeed = look
27.2	מִמֶּֽךָּ	כָּל־זוֹנֶ֥ה [ay]	הִ֝צְמַ֗תָּה		
	away-from-you	every = unfaithful-one	you-have-destroyed		
28.1		לִ֫י־ט֥וֹב [az]	-------	אֱלֹהִ֡ים	וַאֲנִ֤י קִֽרֲבַ֥ת [ba]
		to-me = good	-------	God	and-I nearness-of
28.2	מַחְסִ֑י	בַּאדֹנָ֣י יְהוִ֣ה [bb]	שַׁתִּ֖י ׀		
	my-refuge	in-my-Lord Yahweh	I-have-placed		
28.3		כָּל־מַלְאֲכוֹתֶֽיךָ	לְ֝סַפֵּ֗ר [bc]		
		all = your-works	to-declare		

^a To provide a better parallel with the next line, some emend the Hebrew phrase...*lўyisra'el 'elohim,* 'to Israel, God'...to *'elohim* [or *'el*] *lўyyashar,* 'God [is good] to the upright one'. However, "there is no compelling reason to change, especially since MT and LXX agree" and since this verse has the force of a "creedal statement" (deClaissé-Walford et al. 2014:585, 589). Thus, RSV's attempt through emendation to produce "a more satisfying parallelism" in v. 1, or to transform an individual psalm into a collective one (Terrien 2003:527), "is not necessary" (Bratcher and Reyburn 1991:633; cf. also Harman 2011b:552; Tate 1990:228; VanGemeren 1991:477).

^b The emphatic assertion of this confessional or proverbial verse (Broyles 1999:299; cf. Mays 1994a:241), introduced by אַךְ, is highlighted by alliteration in both lines. In addition to the 'heart' (לֵבָב), many other body parts are referenced: "feet" (2), "eyes" (3), "tongues" (9), "hands" (13), "kidneys" (21), "right hand" (23).

^c As distinct from the communal "good" that God showed to the people of "Israel" (v. 2), the psalmist implies that this was not true in his individual case (contrastive topic וַאֲנִי), caused by a flood of doubt concerning God's justice in relation to the "wicked" (v. 3; i.e., the issue of theodicy). He continues this line of thought in vv. 13–14.

^d "The Hebrew verb normally means 'to pour out', but here it must have the nuance 'to slide'. *Study Note: My feet almost slid out from under me.* The language is metaphorical. As the following context makes clear, the psalmist almost "slipped" in a spiritual sense. As he began to question God's justice, the psalmist came close to abandoning his faith" (NET note).

^e The psalmist gives his reason (כִּי) for "slipping" in faith in a chiastically arranged thematic statement that summarizes his former jaundiced perspective over the central issue of "well-being/prosperity" (שָׁלוֹם) in life: V—NP-obj. // NP-obj.—V. "This teacher struggles with the question of the *shalom* of the wicked" (Mays 1994a:243).

^f The imperfect verb here as distinct from the preceding perfect form suggests a continual action (reflective "observation") in the past.

^g "Or 'fat'. The MT of v. 4 reads as follows: "for there are no pains at their death, and fat [is] their body." Since a reference to the death of the wicked seems incongruous in the immediate context (note v. 5) and premature in the argument of the psalm (see vv. 18–20, 27), some prefer to emend the text by redividing it. The term לְמוֹתָם (*l emotam,* 'at their death') is changed to לָמוֹ תָּם (*lamo tam,* '[there are no pains] to them, strong [and fat are their bodies]'). The term תָּם (*tam,* 'complete; sound') is used of physical beauty in Song 5:2; 6:9. This emendation is the basis for the present translation. However, in defense of the MT (the traditional Hebrew text), one may point to an Aramaic inscription from Nerab which views a painful death as a curse and a nonpainful death in one's old age as a sign of divine favor. See *ANET* 661" (NET note). In fact, the painful death of the wicked is referred to several times as this psalm develops (e.g., vv. 18–20, 27).

"The MT is not unintelligible" (Harman 2011b: 553; cf. Tate 1990:228) and may be understood in three ways: (1) "(for there are no bonds) (leading them) to their death;" (2) "(for there are no torments) until their death" (Bratcher and Reyburn 1991:634, following the HOTTP); or (3) "there remains the possibility that this line *does* indicate that their deaths are without struggle" (deClaissé-Walford et al. 2014:586).

^h "In Isa 58:6, the only other occurrence of this word in the OT, the term refers to 'bonds' or 'ropes'. In Ps. 73:4 it is used metaphorically of pain and suffering that restricts one's enjoyment of life" (NET note).

[i] Verse 6 presents the consequences of the untroubled life-setting of the wicked (vv. 4–5): it results in personal pride and belligerent behavior. After observing the good health (v. 4) of the ungodly and their lack of problems (v. 5), the psalmist bitterly comes to the conclusion (לָכֵן) of v. 6. Two metaphors based on the imagery of clothing sharpen the poet's point in this verse: the wicked (רְשָׁעִים), introduced in 3.2, "wear" their "arrogance" like a necklace, and "violence" is their normal everyday garb.

[j] "The MT reads 'it goes out from fatness their eye', which might be paraphrased, 'their eye protrudes [or 'bulges'] because of fatness'. This in turn might refer to their greed; their eyes 'bug out' when they see rich food or produce (the noun חֵלֶב [*khelev*, 'fatness'] sometimes refers to such food or produce). However, when used with the verb יָצָא (*yatsa'*, 'go out') the preposition מִן ('from') more naturally indicates source. For this reason it is preferable to emend עֵינֵמוֹ ('*enemo*, 'their eye') to עֲוֹנָמוֹ, ('*avonamo*, 'their sin') and read, 'and their sin proceeds forth from fatness', that is, their prosperity gives rise to their sinful attitudes. If one follows this textual reading, another interpretive option is to take חֵלֶב ('fatness') in the sense of 'unreceptive, insensitive' (see its use in Ps. 17:10). In this case, the sin of the wicked proceeds forth from their spiritual insensitivity" (NET). Yet another interpretation is this: "The MT reading is used here with the understanding that this is an ancient metaphor, as in v. 4, indicating that these ones are *fat*, meaning wealthy and/or lazy" (deClaissé-Walford et al. 2014:586).

The second line is literally: "the thoughts of [their] heart [i.e., mind] cross over" (i.e., violate God's moral boundary, see Ps. 17:3) (NET note). "Instead of following the Masoretic text 'their eye', TEV follows the Septuagint, Syriac, and Vulgate 'their iniquity'; and the word for 'fatness' is taken in the sense of 'heart' (see its use in 17.10a)" (Bratcher and Reyburn 1991:635). DeClaissé-Walford et al. suggest: "their hearts overflow with delusions" (2014:585; cf. Tate 1990:228; cf. VanGemeren 1991:479); NEB: "…vain fancies pass through their minds."

[k] "*Heb* 'oppression from an elevated place they speak'. The traditional accentuation of the MT places 'oppression' with the preceding line. In this case, one might translate, 'they mock and speak with evil [of] oppression, from an elevated place [i.e., 'proudly'] they speak'. By placing 'oppression' with what follows, one achieves better poetic balance in the parallelism" (NET note).

[l] Literally, "from on high"—that is, proudly, "in their arrogance" (NIV). The notion of highness leads naturally to that of the heavens in 9.1 and the impious, even blasphemous attitude of the wicked.

[m] "*Heb* 'they set in heaven their mouth, and their tongue walks through the earth'. The meaning of the text is uncertain. Perhaps the idea is that they lay claim to heaven (i.e., speak as if they were ruling in heaven) and move through the earth declaring their superiority and exerting their influence. Some take the preposition –בְּ *(bet)* [in] the first line as adversative and translate, 'they set their mouth against heaven', that is, they defy God" (NET note).

[n] NIV's "turn to them" adopts the *qere* reading, "indicating a turning away from God to the prosperity of the wicked" (Harman 2011b:554; cf. Tate, who considers this to be "the most difficult verse in the psalm;" 1990:228). Most scholars suggest that "*his* (meaning God's) people have returned to the [wicked] ones of vv. 3–9" (deClaissé-Walford et al. 2014:586).

[o] Note the initial conjunction (לָכֵן) and the final pronominal form (לָמוֹ), which matches the structure at the end of the preceding strophe, v. 6 (i.e., structural

epiphora—similar unit endings; Wendland 2004:127). The Hebrew text in between is difficult, "quite unintelligible" (Bratcher and Reyburn [who suggest several emendations] 1991:636–637; also Terrien 2003:529). Literally, the MT reads: "'therefore his people return [so *qere* (marginal reading); *kethiv* (consonantal text) has 'he brings back'] to here, and waters of abundance are sucked up by them'. The traditional Hebrew text (MT) defies explanation. The present translation reflects M. Dahood's proposed emendations (*Psalms* [AB], 2:190) and reads the Hebrew text as follows: לָכֵן יִשְׂבְּעוּם לֶחֶם וּמֵי מָלֵא יָמֹצּוּ לָמוֹ ('therefore they are filled with food, and waters of abundance they suck up for themselves'). The reading יִשְׂבְּעוּם לֶחֶם (*yisvÿ'um lekhem*, 'they are filled with food') assumes (1) an emendation of יָשִׁיב עַמּוֹ (*yashyyv*, 'he will bring back his people') to יִשְׂבְּעוּם (*yisvÿ'um*, 'they will be filled'; a Qal imperfect third masculine plural form from שָׂבַע *[sava']* with enclitic *mem* [ם]), and (2) an emendation of הֲלֹם (*halom*, 'to here') to לֶחֶם ('food'). The expression 'be filled/fill with food' appears elsewhere at least ten times (see Ps. 132:15, for example). In the second line the Niphal form יִמָּצוּ (*yimmatsu*, derived from מָצָה, *matsah*, 'drain') is emended to a Qal form יָמֹצּוּ *(yamotsu)*, derived from מָצַץ (*matsats*, 'to suck'). In Is 66:11 the verbs שָׂבַע (*sava';* proposed in Ps. 73:10) and מָצַץ (proposed in Ps. 73:10) are parallel. The point of the emended text is this: Because they are seemingly sovereign (v. 9), they become greedy and grab up everything they need and more" (NET note; cf. Tate 1990:228; VanGemeren 1991:479; deClaissé-Walford et al. 2014:587). The sense of the second colon of v. 10 appears to be reiterated in v. 12 for emphasis.

[p] An embedded quote attributed to the wicked, cast in the form of a double negative rhetorical question, highlights their impiety. They accept the general transcendence of God, but not his immanence or his omniscience. In a sense then they are practical (practicing) atheists—acknowledging divine sovereignty, but denying his power and relevance in their lives (cf. Pss. 10:4, 11; 14:1) (VanGemeren 1991:479).

[q] The emphasized sight of these "wicked folk" in their proud prosperity (cf. v. 3.2, epiphora) is almost too much for the pious psalmist to bear, which leads to the following pessimistic conclusion (strophe C).

[r] Instead of 'wealth' or 'prosperity', deClaissé-Walford et al. feel that חַיִל "has a much broader meaning" and in this context is closer to "power" (2014:587). "The power of the wicked occupies the concerns of vv. 6–11" (ibid.:2014:590).

[s] The psalmist's reflection on keeping the heart clean reflects the precept of v. 1.2 and God's goodness to people who are 'pure in heart' (similar unit beginnings, structural anaphora, cf. v. 7.2; Wendland 2004:127).

[t] The fronted noun "vanity" used adverbially ("in vain") is an instance of (renewed) topic focus—picking up the psalmist's pessimistic sentiments from vv. 2–3. His personal perspective ("I/me/my"), including its transformation in v. 17 and following, is foregrounded throughout the remainder of the psalm, except for a short reversion to the destiny of the wicked in vv. 18–20. The psalmist's words here are echoed by the impious in the prophetic dialogue of Malachi (3:14–15).

[u] The psalmist here directly expresses the spiteful sentiments that he stated he felt back in v. 3: Literally: "'and washed my hands in innocence'. The psalmist uses an image from cultic ritual to picture his moral lifestyle. The reference to 'hands' suggests actions" (NET note)—in parallel with the preceding mention of 'heart' with reference to his thoughts.

[v] The antithetical use of *waw* suddenly introduces the psalmist's contrastive perception of his own situation or circumstances in life, perhaps involving a certain degree

of hyperbole, e.g., כָּל־הַיּוֹם. There is also the implication that God has been treating him unfairly—facing all sorts of problems (vv. 13–14) in contrast to the prosperity of the wicked (v. 12), who have no concern at all about God (v. 11). In effect, the assertion of v. 14 at the close of the first half of Psalm 73 seems to contradict the confident confession at its beginning (v. 1). But the pessimistic conclusion of v. 14 is itself about to be strongly challenged by the very next utterance (אִם־אָמַרְתִּי).

ᵂ What is the antecedent of כְּמוֹ? Bratcher and Reyburn suggest what the wicked say in v. 11 (1991:638); but the reference is more likely to what the psalmist himself thinks (= 'says' in Hebrew) in vv. 13–14.

ˣ Literally, "look, the generation of your sons I would have betrayed." In this case, the initial "hinneh is a discourse marker that draws the attention of the addressee to the unthinkable implications of the protasis" (Christo van der Merwe, personal correspondence, 2014). "The phrase 'generation of your [i.e., God's] sons' occurs only here in the OT. Some equate the phrase with 'generation of the godly' (Ps. 14:5), 'generation of the ones seeking him' (Ps. 24:6), and 'generation of the upright' (Ps. 112:2). In De 14:1 the Israelites are referred to as God's 'sons'. Perhaps the psalmist refers here to those who are 'Israelites' in the true sense because of their loyalty to God (note the juxtaposition of 'Israel' with 'the pure in heart' in v. 1)" (NET note; the final observation is supported by Bratcher and Reyburn 1991:639; cf. Mays 1994a:242).

Five prominent communicative clues highlight v.15 as a special point of emphasis—arguably the key turning point—in this psalm: (a) "it is the actual [structural] mid-point of the psalm" (McCann 1996:968); (b) the introductory hypothetical question that refers back to the preceding negative assertion (15.1); (c) the psalmist's self-quotation, (d) including the first direct address to God (בָנֶיךָ); and (e) the subsequent contrastive conclusion introduced by הִנֵּה (15.2). This structural apex might be extended to include this entire strophe, especially the thematic statement of v. 17, which Harman, along with many others, views as the text's chief "turning point" (2011b:557; cf. Tate 1990:232). The psalmist's entire attitude and perspective on life radically changes after this—vv. 18ff.

ʸ In contrast to the 'troubles' (עָמָל) being viewed by the psalmist, the wicked have none (cf. 5.1).

ᶻ Psalm 73 "pivots on verse 17...a moment of utter inversion" (Jacobson and Jacobson 2013:28).

ᵃᵃ "The plural of the term מִקְדְּשׁ (miqdash) probably refers to the temple precincts (see Ps. 68:35; Je 51:51)" (NET note). "The language suggests a special revelation from God, either in a vision or through the inspired word of a priest" (Bratcher and Reyburn 1991:640). Harman suggests "some specific revelation" or "purposeful mediation," "probably at a local altar" (2011b:555; cf. Terrien 2003:531). However, since this is a wisdom psalm, seemingly alluding to the certainties expressed in Psalm 1, it is quite possible that the psalmist here describes a serious reflective encounter with Yahweh's revealing presence in the Torah as being the basis for his renewed hope (cf. Ps. 1:2).

Broyles points out a number of the "echoes of the psalms of entry" that are found in Psalm 73. For example, "the importance of a 'pure heart' and 'innocent hands' (73:1, 13 // 24:4; 26:6); the description of the wicked as 'arrogant' (73:3 // 5:5; cf. 52:1)... the designation of Yahweh's group of worshipers as a 'generation' (73:15 // 24:6);... the symbolism of Yahweh as 'refuge' (73:28 // 5:11; 36:7).... The liturgies of temple entry make plain the instability and imminent fall of the wicked" (1999:301).

[ab] The cohortative, apparently employed to emphasize the significance of this verb, "carries the idea of 'discernment/understanding/consideration of a matter/ perception'" (Pss. 28:5, 50:22) (Tate 1990:229). Such understanding "means nothing less than the knowledge of faith" (Mays 1994a:243). "Vv. 11 and 16 use a form of *yd'* ('to know'), but v. 17 uses a form of *byn* ('to discern'). This change in pattern is noticeable in a psalm that has used so much repetition in its structure" (deClaissé-Walford et al. 2014:591).

The non-completive (imperfect) verb forms may be employed in these verses for dramatic effect as the psalmist vividly relives his former state and attitude. [ac] "Most translations place these verbs [of v. 18] in the present tense," but the future ('you will set') may be better "because it seems that God will set [things] right, but there is no evidence that this is a reality in the world at the moment" (deClaissé-Walford et al. 2014:591).

[ad] It is possible to understand "the four nouns in the Hebrew text of verses 18–19 [as being] titles for Sheol, the world of the dead: 'Perdition…Desolation… Devastation…Terrors'" (Bratcher and Reyburn 1991:640).

[ae] The emphatic אַךְ here contradicts and thematically counteracts its usage in 13.1 as the psalmist's perspective is transformed from despair and depression to confidence and hope—to coincide with the assertion of 1.1, which is also introduced by this particle to set the structural contours of this entire confessional discourse. The three recurrences at the start of different poetic units constitute another instance of structural anaphora. "The whole psalm may be intended as a confessional address to God" (Mays 1994a:240).

[af] This rare word (cf. Ps. 74:3) seems to combine the notions of "deception" and "ruin" (Tate 1990:229; "fall in ruins," deClaissé-Walford et al. 2014:587)—with the former perhaps viewed as precipitating the latter (cause-effect).

[ag] A paronomastic emphasis may be featured here, with אֵיךְ reflecting the initial אַךְ of the preceding verse, hence reinforcing the descriptive prediction of the demise of the wicked.

[ah] The word 'terrors' might be construed as a euphemism for (violent) death (VanGemeren 1991:481), or perhaps "a note of subtle psychology is quietly but ferociously added…a self-accusing guilt" (Terrien 2003:531).

[ai] "This verse is not very clear in Hebrew, but it seems reasonable to understand it to say '(they are) like a dream after one awakes, O Lord; when you rouse, you despise their shadows'. The meaning is that the wicked will last no longer than the images in a dream (see similar figures in 39.5–6)…" (Bratcher and Reyburn 1991:641; see Tate 1990:229–230 for a more detailed discussion of the textual-exegetical problems involved). The present text lineation of v. 20 is represented in NIV's rendering: "As a dream when one awakes, so when you arise, O Lord, you will despise them as fantasies" (supported by VanGemeren 1991:481). In this case, "the sudden intervention of God in judgment is described…as if he awakens in sleep (35:23; 44:23; 59:4; 78:65)" (Harman 2011b:556).

[aj] Literally, 'you will despise their form' "The Hebrew term צֶלֶם (*tselem*, 'form; image') also suggests their short-lived nature. Rather than having real substance, they are like the mere images that populate one's dreams. Note the similar use of the term in Ps. 39:6" (NET note; deClaissé-Walford et al. 2014:588).

[ak] The Hithpael of the verb *ch-m-ts* (be sour) expresses the great intensity of the psalmist's inner feelings.

[al] The conjunction here is perhaps best rendered as 'When' and seems to introduce a flashback in temporal reference to the setting of v. 16, as the psalmist was undergoing his life-changing experience. The imperfect (prefix) verbs suggest an ongoing psychological event in the past. The embittered ideas being expressed by the psalmist are underscored by a chiastic arrangement of elements: V (being bitter)—N (my heart) // N (my kidneys)—V (being bitter).

[am] Even in his brutish ignorance, the psalmist was "with God"—or more correctly, Yahweh remained with him by "holding him fast by the right hand" (v. 23). Clearly this was divine providence (*shalom*, v. 3) at work!

[an] "This verse contains the psalmist's self-understanding, and the translator must decide whether verse 22b describes God's attitude toward him (NEB 'I was a mere beast in thy sight, O God') or the psalmist's own behavior toward God, 'I behaved like an animal toward you'. The latter seems preferable" (Bratcher and Reyburn 1991:642). Translations like the NIV are ambiguous: "I was a brute beast before you."

[ao] "The whole personality of the psalmist has been shattered [v. 21], and the recognition of this devastating weakness leads him to confess that his sapiential questioning lowered him to the level of a beast. 'I was with thee like a hippopotamus'..." (Terrien 2003:531).

[ap] Pronominal parallelism involving references to the psalmist (וַאֲנִי) and Yahweh (עִמָּךְ) highlights the negative-positive thematic contrast—a sudden epiphany—between vv. 22–23 and the structural border between these two strophes. Bratcher and Reyburn (1991:642) consider this verse to be "the turning point" of Psalm 73. However, as noted above, I would view that shift from a thematic negative to a positive outlook to occur in strophe D, especially vv. 16–17. I interpret v. 23 to be a reversion to the psalmist's optimistic perspective after his flashback in vv. 21–22—as marked by the contrastive use of the emphatic self-reference (וַאֲנִי) in both verses. "The well-known phrase is 'God is with me (or us)', Emmanuel. Here the prayer turns the phrase on its head: *but I am continually with you*" (deClaissé-Walford et al. 2014:592, original italics).

[aq] "Also prominent in the psalms of temple entry and pilgrimage is the assurance that Yahweh 'guide[s]' his pilgrims (Hb. *n-ch-h*: 5:8; 23:3; 43:3; 61:2; cf. 27:11; 31:3; 32:8; 139:24)" (Broyles 1999:302).

[ar] Literally, "and afterward [to] glory you will take me." Some interpreters view this as the psalmist's confidence in being "taken" to an afterlife in heaven and understand כָּבוֹד (*kavod*) as a metonymic reference to God's presence in heaven (e.g., Harman 2011b:557). "But this seems unlikely in the present context. The psalmist anticipates a time of vindication, when the wicked are destroyed and he is honored by God for his godly life style, e.g., '...and afterward you will receive me with honor'" (deClaissé-Walford et al. 2014:588). "The verb לְקַח (*laqakh*, 'take') here carries the nuance 'lead, guide, conduct', as in Nu 23:14, Nu 23:27–28; Jos 24:3 and Pr 24:11" (NET note).

But it should be pointed out that "the passage here, though not a clear statement of a belief in resurrection or of a bodily assumption into heaven, seems to express a confidence that the psalmist will enjoy unbroken communion with God" (Bratcher and Reyburn 1991:643)—that is, in some significant way, 'forever' (לְעוֹלָם) (v. 26)! "The man who is nearest to God upon this earth receives a foretaste of eternal felicity" (Terrien 2003:532; cf. VanGemeren 1991:482; McCann 1996:969). "Essentially it is a statement of confidence in God, a declaration of trust that God will not let death cancel the relation to him that the faithful have in life" (Mays 1994a:193). Going somewhat further, Broyles notes that "the verb in the expression 'you will take (Hb. *lqchch*) me into glory' is identical to that found in Psalm 49:15 ('But God will redeem my soul from the grave; he will surely take me to himself') and Genesis 5:24 ('Enoch walked with God...God took him away'), both of which seem to point to a divine act that transcends death" (1999:304). For further discussion of the hermeneutical possibilities in this verse, see Tate 1990:230.

[as] The "glory" of the psalmist's "destiny" (אַחַר) contrasts markedly with what is in store "afterwards" for the "wicked" (v. 17.2; cf.12.1).

[at] The merism ("in heaven"—"in earth") highlights the psalmist's personal resolve to worship the LORD and trust him completely, come what may—in contrast to his former vacillating attitude.

[au] It is possible to view this word (וְעִמְּךָ) as a foregrounded verbal hinge (with the focus on the psalmist's presence "with you"—Yahweh!), which can be construed with both cola of v. 25 (Harman 2011b:558, following Dahood 1974; cf. also Tate 1990:280). "The I-Thou dialogue in prayer reaches almost the level of identification" (Terrien 2003:533). I am also positing this central thematic concept ("[I am] with you") as marking the division of stanza F into three strophes: 21–22, 23–24, 25–26, with עִמְּךָ being on the boundary of each one.

[av] The verb could be rendered "it was failing" (i.e., "my flesh and my heart")—with reference back to the psalmist's depressed experience in v. 21 (Tate 1990:230).

[aw] Literally, "is the rocky summit of my heart and my portion" (NET note). With these traditional land- and inheritance-based metaphors, "the psalmist compares the LORD to a rocky summit where one could go for protection and to landed property, which was foundational to economic stability in ancient Israel" (NET note). This contrasts with the debilitating physical 'weakness' and/or spiritual 'failure' that the psalmist experienced (26.1) before he came to his new, God-given insight and understanding (v. 17) that has resulted in his spiritual "strengthening" (v. 26).

[ax] The psalmist strongly marks (כִּי־הִנֵּה) his closing conclusion, the psalm's final reversal, regarding the fate of the "unfaithful" (lit. "adulterous"), who are spiritually "far away" (רְחֵקֶיךָ) from God, in contrast to that of those who are "near" (קִרְבַת) Yahweh in faith and life-style—like the psalmist himself (וַאֲנִי) now (28.1)!

[ay] A chiastic structure foregrounds the destiny of the wicked: A (the ones distant from you), B (they will perish); B' (you have destroyed), A' (every fornicator). Spiritual and eternal 'death' is alienation from God (v. 27).

[az] The key words "God" (אֱלֹהִים) and "good" (טוֹב)—in reverse order—begin this psalm, thus forming a thematic inclusio.

[ba] The contrastive initial (i.e., anaphoric) pronoun (וַאֲנִי) once again highlights the psalmist's current psychological and spiritual state of mind in relation to the wicked: vv. 2.1 (negative), 22.1 (negative), 23.1 (positive), 28.1 (positive).

[bb] According to Tate, "the appearance of two divine names...is unusual... although the redundancy may serve to emphasize the object of the speaker's hope" (1990:230). It may also be significant that God's covenantal name (יְהוָה) appears here for the first time—perhaps to underscore their restored strong interpersonal relationship.

[bc] "The infinitive construct with -לְ *(lÿ)* is understood here as indicating an attendant circumstance. ["as I declare all the things you have done"]. Another

option is to take it as indicating purpose ('so that I might declare') or result ('with the result that I declare')" (NET note, words in brackets added). The psalmist's concluding declaration "I will enumerate (ספר) all your (Yahweh's) deeds" forms a topical inclusio with the psalm's opening line: "Surely God is good to Israel" (1.1). God's many deeds of deliverance certify his "goodness," not only for the psalmist, but also all those in the congregation of 'Israel' to whom he is attesting, including the "pure in heart" (1.2) of every age! The verb ספר is also found in v. 15.1 to form an inclusio around the second portion of this psalm. Terrien sees a musical implication in this verb: "The chorister will excel in his professional vocation, to proclaim in words and music the deeds of God" (2003:534). Thus the communal orality of divine worship in this seemingly introspective psalm is reinforced prominently at its beginning (v. 1) and more subtly here at its ending (cf. also VanGemeren 1991:483).

11.3 Assessment and application: Declaring all the LORD's deeds today (Psalm 73:28)

Psalm 73 is a prayer with which virtually every believer can identify and utter at least once in her/his lifetime. Certainly similar troublesome situations will arise that render the psalmist's words relevant to the contemporary observer—regarding the prosperity of the ungodly, trials being experienced by the godly, and the apparently lack of response or action on the part of their covenant Lord. But as Terrien has observed, there is during the course of this psalm a dramatic shift in outlook: "The poet of Psalm 73 began a song on the issue of theodicy [man questioning God] and ended it as a credo on the eternal presence [man venerating God]...an inquisitive essay becomes a prayer" (1978:316, cited in Tate 1990:237–238, words in brackets added).[11] From another perspective, "Theology is born out of the quest for truth and its doubts—it matures into creedal statements after the sublimity of divine possession" (Terrien 2003:535).

Following Brueggemann's lament triad of orientation—disorientation— new orientation (1995:10–15), Tate suggests that "Psalm 73 is a masterpiece of reorientation... The latter part of Psalm 73 (vv 17–28) contain three new orientations or reorientations. First, there is *reorientation toward the wicked* [vv 18–20]... The second reorientation is a *new understanding of the self* (vv 21–22)... The third orientation is that toward the *presence of God* [23–28]" (1990:238–239)—who happens to be "closer" than the believer could have ever imagined in his/her state of disorientation, and this is "good" (28.1; cf. 1.1)! "The speaker, although he had nearly slipped with the wicked, discovers that those who enter the temple [or, the sacred Scriptures!] have God as the strength of their failed heart and his nearness as their good" (Broyles

---

[11] The observation by Ross is also pertinent here: "The psalmist Asaph was careful what he said to the congregation about his questions, choosing rather to enter the sanctuary to engage God" privately as it were (2013:135).

1999:305). "For some reason, Christian faith is often understood as a reli-
gion of blind faith.... This prayer goes into those places of doubt [that we all
face in life] and, like the books of Job and Ecclesiastes, finds a path through
these times to another level of faith" (deClaissé-Walford et al. 2014:593,
word in brackets added).

     Whether or not one agrees with the preceding content summaries of
Psalm 73, one will have to admit that this poetic prayer is most significant
in terms of its *message* (both theological and personal), its *manner* (literary
style), its textual *location* (at the heart of the Psalter), and its *challenge* with
regard to communicating it in a contemporary language-culture that does
justice to the original. This would require a translation that respects and is
sensitive to the beauty of form, the depth of content, and also the meaning-
ful sound of the original text. How well do modern renditions fare in this
manifold regard? Evaluate the following samples as a concluding exercise in
applying the principles suggested in this chapter and determine the version
that seems to succeed in this communication challenge most effectively.
Then either revise the English translations to improve the text exegetically
or stylistically—or compose a completely new version that achieves a *word-
ing* as well as a *sounding* that seems more appropriate for the particular audi-
ence that you have in mind.

     The first example, from Chewa, is given simply to demonstrate how
Hebrew poetry can be matched by corresponding verse in another lan-
guage. In this case, the form approximates that which is characteris-
tic of the *ndakatulo* lyric genre of oral (now also written) poetry in
Chewa, a language of wider communication (LWC) spoken in Malawi
and Zambia. It is hoped that the more dynamic, oral-aural centered
speech style that is typical of this genre, for example, featuring the use
of ideophones, exclamations, word order shifts, and multiple deictic
"pointing," might serve to compensate for some of the rhetorical power
that is lost in transfer due to the non-equivalence of linguistic and liter-
ary forms between Hebrew and Chewa.[12] Only a portion of the *ndakatulo*
version of Psalm 73 is reproduced below, namely, its theological peak
found in verses 23–26 (a relatively literal English back-translation fol-
lows the Chewa text):

---

[12] Hatim and Mason define "compensation" as "a set of translation procedures
aimed at making up for the loss of relevant features of meaning in the source text
by reproducing the overall effect in the target language" (1997:214). De Waard
comments on the importance of such a procedure in carrying out a "functional
equivalence type of translation": "...most rhetorical features are language specific,
making any kind of formal correspondence between languages impossible. There-
fore, not the rhetorical features as such have to be rendered, but their function"
(1996:242). For a more detailed text-comparative analysis of the similarities and
differences between the Hebrew and Chewa *(ndakatulo)* poetic styles, with an
extensive application to Ps. 22, see Wendland (1993).

[23] *Koma chonsecho inu nthawi zonse ndili nanube.*
    But everything considered, you—at all times I am with you.
    Dzanja langa GWI! muligwiradi kuti ndisagwe.
    My hand TIGHTLY! you firmly grab it lest I fall.

[24] *Malangizo anu andiwongolera munjira yolungamo;*
    Your counsel leads me straight along the righteous path;
    Pomaliza pake mudzandilandira kuulemerero wanuwo.
    in the end you will receive me into your glory.

[25] *Nanga ine kopanda inu kumwamba ndidzakhala ndi yani ine?*
    As for me—without you in heaven whom will I remain with?
    Ndidzafunafunanji pansi pano? Palibiretu m'pang'ono pomwe!
    What will I search for down here below? Nothing at all, not in the least!
    Inu nokha Chauta mulipo—ndinu mumandithangata.
    You alone O God are present—you are the one who supports me.

[26] *Ha! Ngakhale ine thupi ndi moyo zingoti LEFU!*
    Ha! Although for me body and soul become completely TIRED!
    Mphambe Mulungu ndiye amandilimbitsa mtima ndithu!
    The Almighty God is the one who strengthens my heart indeed!
    Adzandisandutsa wolowa-dzina kwao mpaka MUYAYAYA!
    He will transform me into an heir at his place FOREVER!

Naturally, the Chewa text reveals some formal differences from the literal Hebrew in order to maintain an overall functional fidelity in relation to the original message. This includes, as already noted, an emphasis on stylistic forms that are effective in oral discourse. We may observe, for example, word order variations for focus and emphasis (23a, 25a: foregrounding the intimate 'you'/'I' bonding that is such an important part of this psalm's thematic resolution); ideophones and exclamations (23b, 26a: accenting the vital emotive aspect of the psalmist's new perspective on life); local figures and imagery (26b–c: highlighting the close parental ties that characterize the psalmist's relationship with his God, e.g., 'heir'—'the one entering [the] name'); the use of assonance (23b), alliteration (25b), and rhyme (23–25: rendering the text in more memorable rhythmic terms); rhetorical questions (25a–b: emphasizing the LORD's constant presence and protection in life); a traditional Chewa praise name (*Mphambe* 'Storm-Ruler', 26b: evoking the connotative context of prayerful petition). Has this vernacular version perhaps gone too far in its contemporizing? That is for a MT audience of the target group to determine.

The second example is taken from the *New Living Translation* (ParaTExt 7.4 version, 2004). Of all the contemporary versions in English, this translation seems to come the closest to the original text exegetically. See if you agree—and if not, what modifications would you suggest, including aspects of the larger structural organization (stanza units) of this psalm?

73 *A psalm of Asaph.*

1. Truly God is good to Israel,
    to those whose hearts are pure.

2. But as for me, I almost lost my footing.
    My feet were slipping, and I was almost gone.
3. For I envied the proud
    when I saw them prosper despite their wickedness.
4. They seem to live such painless lives;
    their bodies are so healthy and strong.
5. They don't have troubles like other people;
    they're not plagued with problems like everyone else.
6. They wear pride like a jeweled necklace
    and clothe themselves with cruelty.
7. These fat cats have everything
    their hearts could ever wish for!
8. They scoff and speak only evil;
    in their pride they seek to crush others.
9. They boast against the very heavens,
    and their words strut throughout the earth.
10. And so the people are dismayed and confused,
    drinking in all their words.
11. "What does God know?" they ask.
    "Does the Most High even know what's happening?"
12. Look at these wicked people—
    enjoying a life of ease while their riches multiply.
13. Did I keep my heart pure for nothing?
    Did I keep myself innocent for no reason?
14. I get nothing but trouble all day long;
    every morning brings me pain.

15. If I had really spoken this way to others,
    I would have been a traitor to your people.
16. So I tried to understand why the wicked prosper.
    But what a difficult task it is!
17. Then I went into your sanctuary, O God,
    and I finally understood the destiny of the wicked.
18. Truly, you put them on a slippery path
    and send them sliding over the cliff to destruction.
19. In an instant they are destroyed,

completely swept away by terrors.
20. When you arise, O Lord,
    you will laugh at their silly ideas
    as a person laughs at dreams in the morning.

21. Then I realized that my heart was bitter,
    and I was all torn up inside.
22. I was so foolish and ignorant—
    I must have seemed like a senseless animal to you.
23. Yet I still belong to you;
    you hold my right hand.
24. You guide me with your counsel,
    leading me to a glorious destiny.
25. Whom have I in heaven but you?
    I desire you more than anything on earth.
26. My health may fail, and my spirit may grow weak,
    but God remains the strength of my heart;
    he is mine forever.

27. Those who desert him will perish,[13]
    for you destroy those who abandon you.
28. But as for me, how good it is to be near God!
    I have made the Sovereign LORD my shelter,
    and I will tell everyone about the wonderful things you do.

Finally, we have an example of Psalm 73 from *The Voice* (2009), a translation that endeavors to accent the audio form of the text. Thus, according to the website[14] and as mentioned in 6.6 above, "*The Voice* expresses Scripture as a narrative with engaging conversations, passionate poetry, and beautiful literature. *The Voice* brings literary art to the Bible. This Bible lends itself to dramatic readings; first, because of the beauty of the language, and second, because of the unique acting-script format. It is the Good Book that reads like a good book.... By expressing the inspired text in the unique voices of the original biblical authors with all their personality, passion, grit, humor, and beauty, *The Voice* begins to recapture how the first readers would have encountered the Scripture. This results in an amplification of the voice of God so it is more clearly heard by today's readers—almost as clearly as when He first revealed His truth." Now these are some rather impressive claims. See if you agree, and again, propose

---

[13] Note that here the NLT leaves the initial marker of conclusion (כִּי־הִנֵּה) untranslated. What would you suggest?
[14] From http://www.hearthevoice.com/about-the-translation/. Accessed June 13, 2014.

corrections where you think that the voice of this English version[15] could speak more clearly, correctly, and consistently in terms of its translational frame of reference given above.

Psalm 73

1. Truly God is good to *His people,* Israel,
     to those with pure hearts.
2. *Though I know this is true,* I almost lost my footing;
     yes, my steps were on slippery ground.
3. You see, *there was a time when* I envied arrogant men
     and thought, "The wicked look pretty happy to me."

4. For they seem to live *carefree lives,* free of suffering;
     their bodies are strong and healthy.
5. They don't know trouble as we do;
     they are not plagued *with problems* as the rest of us are.
6. They've got *pearls of* pride strung around their necks;
     they clothe their bodies with violence.
7. *They have so much more than enough.*
     Their eyes bulge because they are so fat with possessions.
     They have more than their hearts could have ever imagined.
8. *There is nothing sacred, and no one is safe.*
     Vicious sarcasm drips from their lips;
     they bully and threaten to crush *their enemies.*
9. They even mock God *as if He were not above;*
     their *arrogant* tongues boast throughout the earth; *they feel invincible.*

10. Even God's people turn and are carried away by them;
     they watch and listen, yet find no fault in them.
11. *You will hear* them say, "How can the True God *possibly* know anyway?
     He's not even here.
     So how can the Most High have any knowledge *of what happens here?*"
12. Let me tell you *what I know* about the wicked:
     they are comfortably at rest while their wealth is growing *and growing.*
13. *Oh, let this not be me!* It seems I have scrubbed my heart to keep it clean
     and washed my hands in innocence.
     And for what? Nothing.
14. For all day long, I am being punished,
     each day awakening to *stern* chastisement.

---

[15] From http://www.hearthevoice.com/search-bible/. Accessed June 13, 2014.

15. If I had said *to others* these kinds of things *about the plight of God's good people,*
    then *I know* I would have betrayed the next generation.
16. Trying to solve this *mystery* on my own exhausted me;
    I couldn't bear to look at it any further.
17. So I took my questions to the True God,
    and in His sanctuary I realized *something so chilling and final:*
    their *lives have* a *deadly* end.
18. *Because* You have certainly set the wicked upon a slippery slope,
    You've set them up to slide to their destruction.
19. *And they won't see it coming.* It will happen so fast:
    first, a flash of terror, and then desolation.
20. It is like a dream from which someone awakes.
    You will wake up, Lord, and loathe what has become of them.
21. *You see,* my heart overflowed with bitterness *and cynicism;*
    I felt as if someone stabbed me in the back.
22. But I didn't know *the truth;*
    I have been acting like a stupid animal toward You.
23. But *look at this:* You are still holding my right hand;
    You have been all along.
24. *Even though I was angry and hard-hearted,* You gave me good advice;
    when it's all over, You will receive me into Your glory.
25. *For all my wanting,* I don't have anyone but You in heaven.
    There is nothing on earth that I desire other than You.
26. *I admit how* broken I am in body and spirit,
    but God is my strength, and He will be mine forever.
27. It will happen: whoever shuns You will be silenced forever;
    You will bring an end to all who refuse to be true to You.
28. But the closer I am to You, my God, the better *because life with You is good.*
    O Lord, the Eternal, You keep me safe—
    I will tell everyone what You have done.

As you re-examine the main structural breaks indicated in the preceding translation, you might ask yourself: Where do some additional stanza-strophic divisions need to be made—that is, on the basis of the earlier text analysis? Throughout the various Psalm studies of this book, we have emphasized the importance of this crucial literary-structural factor as part of our textual examination. What problem(s) might arise if this feature of the printed format is ignored or executed poorly in any published translation? You might point out an example or two—oral or written—from *The Voice* version, and then suggest how the difficulty might be remedied in the text.

11.4 Conclusion

According to the final verse of Psalm 73, "Life with God is good" the "closer" we get to him (v. 28). What better way to do this than by praying and singing the Psalter? We recall that "what is truly important about the psalms is not only that they say things about God, but...[also] that they give people the words to speak to God" (Jacobson and Jacobson 2013:174)—thus facilitating the creation or reinforcement of a personal relationship with the living God. Are there obstacles to the use of such ancient poetic worship forms in certain modern, technically "advanced" societies? Of course, but as C. Richard Wells points out, the objections cannot be sustained, not for serious believers:

> ...there are special reasons for neglect of the psalms. The language of poetry doesn't easily connect in a sound-byte culture. The psalms call for time, not tweets—time to read, ponder, pray, digest. It's easy to be too busy for the psalms. Then again, the strong emotions of the psalms make many modern people uncomfortable—which is ironic since our culture seems to feed on feelings. For pastors the psalms don't lend themselves easily to preaching and teaching.... On top of everything else, strange to say, the psalms are just so . . . well . . . God intoxicated. We are fascinated with ourselves; the psalms are fascinated with God. (2012:203–204)

The penultimate psalm of the Psalter strongly exhorts us to "Sing to the LORD a new song—his praise in the assembly of the saints" (149:1, NIV)—and the final psalm seconds this appeal to the *n*th degree (Ps. 150). It is hoped that the various studies of this book will encourage and enable all those readers who belong to the group specified as "saints" (חֲסִידִים) to *sing* God's praises—not only more intelligently, but also more enthusiastically, for it is a great "honor" (הָדָר) to do so (149:9). הַלְלוּ־יָהּ! (150:1a).

Appendix: Reviews of Four Recent Books on the Psalter

1 *Reading Psalm 145 with the Sages—A Compositional Analysis* (Lama 2013)

A description of this recent publication by a non-Western scholar is well worth including in my collection of studies in the Psalms, for the book and its manifold analysis well illustrates and confirms my own literary-structural approach to the Psalter.

Dr. Ajoy Kumar Lama was born and raised in a traditional Tibetan Buddhist family but became a Christian while studying veterinary science in India. Subsequently he did graduate studies in the USA (D.Min. from Beeson Divinity School, Ph.D. in the Old Testament from Trinity Evangelical Divinity School) and is currently serving as the General Secretary of the Council of Baptist Churches in North East India.

This book presents an edited version of the author's doctoral dissertation, consisting of six clearly defined and well-constituted chapters, six helpful appendices, and an extensive bibliography. The term "compositional" in the title has reference to the author's methodology, which situates the climactic Psalm 145 with specific intertextual reference to the Davidic psalms within the structure of Book Five of the Psalter and supplies a holistic, literary-structural analysis of the text itself. I found the phrase "with the sages" a bit misleading, however, since there is no special effort in this study to relate its contents to the Wisdom writings of the Hebrew Bible. But perhaps this expression relates rather to the many recognized scholars of the book of Psalms that Lama critically engages during the course of his wide-ranging investigation.

Chapter 1 introduces the study by considering the textual, contextual, and intertextual significance of Psalm 145. Among several reasons given, we may note that this is a (nearly) perfect acrostic psalm located in the MT at the very end of the last David collection (i.e., Pss. 138–145, which differs from the LXX position) and right before the concluding *Hallel* set (Pss. 146–150). This is the only psalm in the Psalter which explicitly states that Yahweh's kingdom is both universal and eternal (note the repetition of כָּל in vv. 9, 14, 16, 18, and לְעוֹלָם וָעֶד in vv. 1, 2, 21) (5). Lama surveys the "history of interpretation" of Psalm 145 in terms of the "major methodological criteria" of "pre-form-critical interpretation," "form critical interpretation," and "compositional critical interpretation" (7). Of particular importance in the second category is Muilenburg's approach of "rhetorical criticism," which "draws psalms scholars' attention to the rhetorical phenomena in the literary style, the structure, and the aesthetic of the psalms" (12). Under "compositional criticism" Lama overviews the work of Brevard Childs and Gerald Wilson, which led to a crucial "turning point" in Psalms studies in its emphasis upon "reading the Psalter as a book" (18). The MT's distinctive "editorial composition of Book V" (19) is noted in comparison with the "composition of the 11QPsa" Psalms scroll (21) and that of the LXX (24). Lama refutes several prominent critics of a compositional critical approach, and suggests that they often fail to fully appreciate "the literary context *(Sitz in der Literatur)* of the text," where the "emphasis is not only on the diachronic reading, but also on the synchronic reading of the Psalter" (27). The chapter concludes with "five observations" that support the significance of a "compositional analysis of Psalm 145...from its textual, contextual, and social perspective" (33).

Chapter 2 takes up a number of important "methodological considerations" (35), which provide a foundational framework for the rest of the dissertation. Lama begins with "theological assumptions," the most important being "that the final form of the Old Testament as Scripture is intrinsically theological and divinely authoritative for the believing community that receives it" (35). Lama then turns to his "hermeneutical assumptions" (38), based on Cotterell's notion of "discourse meaning," which views a text as "a communicative occurrence that meets seven standards of textuality: cohesion of grammar and syntax, coherence, intentionality, acceptability, informativity, situationality, and intertextuality" (41, further described on 46–49). Lama moves from there to Vanhoozer's "Canonical-Linguistic Approach," which promotes a "canonical reading as the 'thick description' of the text, in which the interpreter is supposed to 'read the Bible as unified communicative act, that is, as the complex, multi-leveled speech act of a single divine author'" (42). A speech-act methodology is advanced which distinguishes three types of "linguistic actions" that impinge upon a literary text: "locutionary act (actual utterance), illocutionary act (what the communicator does in utterance), and perlocutionary act (what the communicator brings about by uttering)" (43). One might quibble about these S-A definitions, but the basic concept is surely a helpful hermeneutical tool. Lama describes the method of "discourse analysis" that he will apply to Psalm 145 as an approach which "considers the lexical, syntagmatic, and paradigmatic semantics in relation to its textual context, but [which] also draws our attention to the extralinguistic context (the pragmatics of the language system) where it is intended to make sense" (45). Under "exegetical assumptions" (49–69), Lama states his position on these important issues: the possible historical context of Psalm 145, the reading ("democratization," 54–55) of "David" in the superscript, the psalm's acrostic structure, its thematic patterning in relation to other psalms, any text critical issues, and the problematic lack of a "*nun* line" in the composition. Lama's summary of "thematic patterning" in the Psalter (55–56), the literary function of the "acrostic structure" (57–58), and "text critical theory" (58–60) is very informative, and his concluding arguments in favor of including a *nun*-bicolon in the text of Psalm 145 are convincing (60–69), for in addition to being found in the LXX and other ancient texts, it completes and complements "the literary structure and the message the psalm intends to convey" (71).

Chapter 3 presents "a discourse analysis of Psalm 145" (73). After his own "translation" of the text, supplemented by detailed text-critical footnotes (74–78), Lama considers the "literary genre" of Psalm 145, concluding that it consists of a combination of subtypes: hymn of praise, thanksgiving, and wisdom (78–80)—and one might add "trust" as well (e.g., vv. 17–20). A section on the "literary structure" of the psalm comparatively summarizes the proposals of a broad selection of scholars, grouped according to whether they have adopted a "strophic structure" (81–82), a "traditional literary" arrangement (83–84), or some "thematic" outline (85–86). Lama then presents the findings of a selection of analysts who practice his preferred "rhetorical literary" approach, with respect to "key words" or *Leitwörter*. e.g., Liebreich, (87–89), a "concentric" structure, e.g., Magonet, (90), chiastic "literary symmetry", e.g., Lindars, (91–93), and a progressive intensification of themes, e.g., Kimelman, (93–99). The last-mentioned receives the greatest attention for it is merged with Lama's own proposal for the thematic-structural organization of Psalm 145, which is visually summarized in the form of a diagram on 101. While this arrangement could be criticized with respect to certain details, e.g., v. 10 viewed as being an "interlude" and not connected to either the preceding (vv. 7–9) or subsequent (vv. 11–13) stanzas),[1] the general perspective seems sound. This highlights "the central-ity of the theme of the Kingdom of God in this psalm...[and] the linear pro-gression of the theme of praise and the reign of YHWH—from the individual to the cosmic realm" (101).

The second half of Chapter 3 is devoted to a "linguistic analysis" of Psalm 145, which examines its "lexical, syntagmatic, paradigmatic, se-mantic, and...pragmatic semantics" (102). Lama begins by considering the importance and relevance of the psalm's title (תְּהִלָּה לְדָוִד) in relation to its opening two verses in particular. He concludes with a canonical per-spective: "In the absence of a political king, the post-exilic community of Israel is invited to join the historic David in praising YHWH, who has been their true King from the antiquity" (105). This leads naturally to a detailed discussion of "the Kingship of YHWH" (pp. 105–113): "Psalm 145 is the only psalm in the Psalter which designates אֱלֹהִים as the 'King' (מֶלֶךְ)" and thus promotes its central purpose: "the praise of the Great King" (106). Lama adopts Chaim Pearl's view that "YHWH is deliberately introduced as transcendent and omnipotent in the first half of the psalm (vv. 3, 4, 6, and 12) and then in the second half as immanent (vv. 8, 9, 14, 15, and 18) to balance the two natures of YHWH" (109, with a chart of related motifs on 111–112). Five verbless hymnic bicola (vv. 3, 8, 9, 13, and 17) are identified which serve as "literary markers" (or communicative clues) that "underscore the 'attributes' of YHWH as well as the perpetual nature of YHWH's Kingship" (112). Next, the key verb "bless" (בָּרַךְ) (vv. 1, 2, 10, 21) is examined with respect to its "semantic domain in the Psalter and then in Psalm 145" (114). The abundant blessings of God are described in this psalm's "language of universalism and particularism": "On the one hand, it presents YHWH's reign as open ended and cosmic in nature, which includes all humanity—on the other hand, it mentions a people group with specific characteristics: the godly ones (...v. 10), the one who calls YHWH in truth (...v. 18), the one who fears YHWH (...v. 19), and the one who loves (...v. 20)" (116). All these blessings are further reflected in the text's "language of hope": "The language of Psalm 145 is forward looking—a language of hope-ful anticipation not only for the post-exilic community but also for those who belong to the community of faith in the following generations until its full realization" (121) in YHWH's "everlasting kingdom" (v. 13). Seven summary "conclusions" resulting from "a discourse analysis of Psalm 145" bring this central chapter to a close (121–123).

---

[1] Though v. 10 might be viewed as a hinge with semantic links in both directions (e.g., "all" > v. 9; "you-sg." > v. 11), I prefer to interpret this verse as a thematic line beginning the stanza that summons all people to praise God, which includes vv. 10–13a. Verses 8–9 seem to be a tightly-knit strophe that summarizes the LORD's covenantal attributes, while the explicit mention of 'YHWH' is found in all descrip-tive stanza/strophe apertures after the initial one (i.e., vv. 3, 8, 10, 13b, 17, and 21).

Chapter 4 considers Psalm 145, "the last Davidic psalm," in relation to the Psalter's "editorial purpose" as a transitional multi-genre psalm that leads to the five concluding *hallel* psalms (125).[2] The first major section of this chapter is taken up with a detailed scholarly critique of Gerald Wilson's well-known theories concerning the final editorial shape of the Psalter,[3] with respect to these important constituent topics: "the final Wisdom Frame" (126–131); "the climax of Book V" (131–134); "the gathering of major themes," such as "the two ways of the righteous and wicked" (135–136), "the central theme of the Fourth Book" (137–139), "the 'mighty acts' of YHWH" (139–142), "the 'steadfast love' of YHWH" (142–147); and "the onset of the final *hallel* psalms" (147–153). In the second section of chapter 4, Lama considers Psalm 145 in relation to the set of final praise hymns of the Psalter, Psalms 146–150. Even though it cannot be grouped together with the latter collection, Psalm 145 "functions like *Janus* looking backward to Davidic groups of psalms, as well as forward to the final *hallel* psalms" (154). Lama provides detailed evidence to reveal "the lexical, syntactical, thematic, semantic, and pragmatic connections of each of the final *hallel* psalms (Psalms 146–150) with Psalm 145" (154) in order to suggest a plausible editorial rationale for the placement of this psalm before the concluding *hallel* corpus (154–163).

Finally, Lama provides some equally convincing reasons for his conclusion that the five *hallel* psalms function as the Psalter's "doxology," while Psalm 145 then acts as the conclusion, "the last place," rather than the "climax," of the Psalter proper (164). Among the textual evidence considered are the following elements: "inclusion-like features" (164), "lexical features" (165), "acrostic features" (166), a "thematic feature" (ידה 167), and "doxological features" (168). On the one hand, "Psalm 145 is the concluding psalm of the fifth book because Psalm 145:21 has remarkable connections with the doxologies of Books I-IV" (168). On the other hand, "numerous lexical and thematic connections between Psalm 145 and the final *hallel* psalms show...thematic continuity, patterns, and development that demands a 'thick reading' of these psalms together" (171). It is my conclusion that scholars investigating either Psalm 145 or a psalm from any of these groupings will have to take the textual evidence and argumentation that Lama has marshalled here very seriously.

Chapter 5 follows up on the description provided in the preceding chapter in relation to the theme "David in the Kingdom of God" (173). Lama's analysis follows two distinct, but ultimately interrelated pathways. First, he presents a meticulous comparative study of Psalm 145 in order to relate its "discourse meaning" to two Davidic groups of psalms (Pss. 108–110 and

---

[2] This conclusion is briefly supported by Longman (2013:226) and more fully by Snearly (2013:212–213).

[3] For example, G. B. Wilson, 1985.

138–144). The "thematic patterns emerging from this comparison...suggest reasons for the placement of this specific message in David's mouth and at the end of the Psalter" (174). Second, Lama presents a comparative speech-act (illocutionary) analysis of the "Kingdom of God" motif of Psalm 145 in relation to the "YHWH Kingship psalms of Book IV" in order to suggest why this psalm was "placed at the end of the Davidic group of psalms in the fifth book instead of Book IV" (174). After his careful textual comparison of Psalm 145 with the two sets of "Davidic psalms" (174–212), Lama concludes this section with five significant "observations," for example: "Psalm 145 provides closure to the Davidic collections of the MT," a "fuller picture of the reality of the Kingdom of God," and a "final image of David [as] a 'paradigm' for humanity to praise YHWH and stop lamenting," thus offering "hope" for all humanity in the promise of YHWH's "providential care" for all people (213–215).

Lama then turns his attention to the "YHWH Kingship psalms in Book IV" (Pss. 93, 95–99, 103) in terms of key thematic term selection and arrangement in relation to Psalm 145 (216–227). Finally, he focuses his attention once more on "the motif of the Kingdom of God" in its prominent lexical, semantic, and thematic presence within the text of Psalm 145 (228–236). The conclusions that Lama derives from his study are most insightful, for example: "It is plausible that the emphasis on the transcendence and omnipotence of YHWH in Psalm 145 is primarily intended to call attention to YHWH's immanence in the daily lives of Israel—YHWH, though invisible, is indeed their King who is much more superior and competent than all earthly kings they knew" (236). "The illocutionary intent of the message of the YHWH Kingship psalms in Book IV is apologetic (Psalms 96 and 98) and nationalistic (Psalms 97, 98, 99 and 103), whereas Psalm 145 focuses on YHWH's compassionate goodness, providential care and salvation extended to all creation" (239).

Chapter 6 presents Lama's "Conclusion" to his "compositional reading" (i.e., discourse analysis) of Psalm 145 "in relation to the YHWH Kingship psalms in Book IV, the final *hallel* psalms, and the two groups of Davidic psalms in Book V" (242). This constitutes a helpful summary of the preceding five chapters, especially certain restatements of some of the main observations of his study, for example: "The acrostic structure of Psalm 145 is not only a mnemonic device but also a literary tool to communicate its message effectively...[concerning] the universal Kingdom of God and all-inclusive praise of YHWH" (243). "Psalm 145 forms an inclusion with Psalm 107 for the fifth book,...is the last psalm for the theme of 'thanksgiving' (ידה),... [and] has doxological features" (244). "Reading the psalm together with the ten Davidic psalms (Psalms 108–10 and 138–44) provides a holistic understanding of the present reality of the Kingdom of God" (245). "Psalm 145 revives and redirects the theology of the Kingship of YHWH...by alluding to the language of YHWH Kingship psalms in Book IV...[but with] an emphasis on YHWH's providential care to all creation" (246). "The spirit of the New Testament is greatly influenced by the post-exilic psalms—this is particularly true for Psalm 145" (247).

Periodically in his discussion Lama inserts some suggestive contextual application of his study for his contemporary sociocultural setting. He ends his book on such a pertinent note: "These findings have important implications for correcting certain perceptions among people of other faiths in India, who have regarded Christianity as the religion of the western nations, and the God of the Bible as the god of the Jews and the Europeans. The compositional reading of Psalm 145, which underscores the universal Kingdom of God, counters such false social, cultural, and religious bigotry" (248).

Lama includes six appendixes that present certain background or supportive information relating to some of the major topics of his research: (Appendix 1) Gerald Wilson's proposed "order of Qumran psalms" (249– 251); (Appendix 2) Wilson's "three options for the [historical] canonization of the Psalter" (253); (Appendix 3) Magonet's "concentric structure of Psalm 145" (255, in Hebrew); (Appendix 4) a charting of the "different usage of מַלְכוּת in the Psalter" (73 occurrences, pp. 257–258); (Appendix 5) a referential chart of "the use of YHWH in Psalm 145" (pp. 259–260); and (Appendix 6) a comparative chart that sequentially displays the various "lexical connections between Psalms 103 and 145" (pp. 261–262, cf. 224, 231).

In this review I have been able only to touch upon the main topics and methods of this most comprehensive reading of Psalm 145. A. K. Lama presents us with a clearly organized, well-written, and most informative thick analysis, one that involves a variety of methodologies and perspectives on the many levels of semiotic significance that the text offers within its canonical cotextual and intertextual settings. This provides readers with a multifaceted understanding of this final "official" psalm of the Psalter (as cogently argued by the author, e.g., pp. 164–170) with respect to its distinctive structure and theme, as well as its varied formal and semantic links with other important psalms and psalm sets. This is one of those engaging and insightful biblical analyses that a person wishes he had written himself.[4] I can enthusiastically recommend this book to any student of the Psalms, whether on the undergraduate or graduate levels; in fact, I would make it required reading! *Reading Psalm 145 with the Sages* will also be of great interest to all those scholarly sages—including translators!— of the Hebrew Bible who would like a fresh perspective not only on this unique psalm text itself, but also on the composition of the Psalter as a whole.

---

[4] As already noted, Lama's excellent study clearly reflects the literary (artistic-rhetorical)—structural approach that is exemplified in the various chapters of the present volume.

2 *The Shape and Shaping of the Psalms: The Current State of Scholarship* (deClaissé-Walford, N. L. 2014)

Though not a Festschrift, this volume is dedicated to the memory of Gerald H. Wilson (d. 2005) and his seminal work on the book of Psalms, *The Editing of the Hebrew Psalter* (1985). The book consists of a Preface by the Editor[5] and sixteen essays by recognized Psalms scholars, concluding with a listing of contributors and two indexes (Ancient Sources, including textual references, and Modern Authors). Most of the relatively short, well-written essays were presented in the Book of Psalms section of the SBL 2011 Annual Meeting. The topics considered are diverse but all related in one way or another to the field of "canonical criticism,"[6] with particular reference to the structural composition of the Psalter and the hypothetical editorial process that resulted in the Masoretic edition of the Hebrew text. Wilson's foundational study is referenced many times throughout. The different chapter headings fairly well summarize the content of these essays, and my overview (not a full critical review) will consist of several salient quotes from each, along with an occasional personal comment, footnote, or evaluation.

In "The Canonical Approach to Scripture and *The Editing of the Hebrew Psalter*," Nancy L. deClaissé-Walford summarizes Gerald Wilson's main insights in relation to the distinct canonical approaches of Brevard Childs (3), James A. Sanders (4), and others (5). Wilson combined the insights of both scholars to argue that the Psalter is a unified whole that needs to be studied as such (Childs), and yet it is also the result of purposeful editorial-redactional activity (Sanders) (7). Subsequent scholars have built on these insights ("the big 'story'—the metanarrative—of the Psalter"), and now spend most of their time "focusing on the smaller units of shape, the so-called 'local narratives'" (9).

In "The Editing of the Psalter and the Ongoing Use of the Psalms: Gerald Wilson and the Question of Canon," Harry P. Nasuti surveys Wilson's central ideas and aims and observes that subsequent canonical scholars do not necessarily agree with his theories concerning the Psalter's redactional history and the intentions of its hypothetical editors (14). However, no one doubts the fact that he proposed "an important corrective to a field that had almost ignored the final form of the text in favor of the life settings of the individual psalms in ancient Israel" (18).

---

[5] She has also authored the related book *Introduction to the Psalms: A Song from Ancient Israel* (deClaissé-Walford 2004).

[6] "Canonical criticism...employs a number of traditional and nontraditional approaches to reading the text" of Psalms and is concerned with questions such as these: "How were collections of psalms and various individual psalms incorporated in the Psalter? When? By whom? For what reason?" (x-xi; all page references will be to the volume under consideration, unless noted otherwise).

In "Changing Our Way of Being Wrong: The Impact of Gerald Wilson's *The Editing of the Hebrew Psalter,*" J. Clinton McCann Jr. pays brief tribute to Wilson's importance for Psalms studies, noting that the field would have eventually "gone in the direction of [investigating the] shape and shaping" of this book, but his work greatly expedited this movement (23). While McCann does not directly state whether Wilson's theories about the Psalter's formation are correct in their more specific details (e.g., in relation to his own perspective; cf. 196), at the very least he grants that they have had "a profound impact on my way of being wrong" (24).

In "The Dynamic of Praise in the Ancient Near East, or Poetry and Politics," Erhard S. Gerstenberger, who does not agree with Wilson's theory of a "very late redactional division of the canonical collection of Psalms" (9), goes off in a somewhat different direction to explore certain aspects of hymnic praise style in the Hebrew Scriptures and in the literature of the ancient Near East (29–30). Gerstenberger comments on the perceived "power" of these panegyric forms, and concludes that for the ancients, such oral "praise oratory becomes a meaningful part of promoting world order and well-being of people and environments" (36).

In "Philosophical Perspectives on Religious Diversity as Emergent Property in the Redaction/Composition of the Psalter," Jaco Gericke applies a tripartite "emergent structure" model (46) to explore the presence of "intrareligious theological diversity" in the book of Psalms "in its format of being a redacted compositional whole" (43). The technical, literary-philosophical term "emergence" refers to "the way complex contradictions and religious diversity arise in the Psalter out of a multiplicity of relatively simple interactions between various psalms as a result of their redactional juxtaposing" (46). Gericke adopts the perspective of Wittgenstein, "who considered it the task of philosophy as clarification only, that is, to leave everything as it is" (51).

In "Let Us Cast Off Their Ropes from Us: The Editorial Significance of the Portrayal of Foreign Nations in Psalms 2 and 149," Derek E. Wittman considers the significance of "the Hebrew Psalter's second and penultimate psalms...portraying God as a royal figure" in conjunction with "references to foreign nations" (53). After an interesting study of the various literary and rhetorical relationships between these two psalms in connection with their canonical placement, Wittman concludes that while "God's kingship is of central concern" in these texts (66), as indeed throughout the Psalter, "a lasting negative impression of foreign nations" is evoked (67).[7] One wonders, however, whether the Psalter's final verse (150:6), read in conjunction with many medial texts (9:11, 22:27, 67:2, 72:17, 86:9, 98:2, 117:1, 138:4,

---

[7] A distinction between foreign peoples in general and Israel's enemies in particular needs to be made. With respect to the former, more universal category, Wittman's negative thesis is corrected by Magonet, e.g., 166–167, 174.

145:12) might not provide a contrasting, more positive perspective on foreign peoples in relation to God's wider saving plan.

In "The Message of the Asaphite Collection and Its Role in the Psalter," Christine Brown Jones discusses the "pivotal place" of these psalms (Pss. 73–83), being "located in the numeric middle of the Psalter" (71). She draws attention to the many linguistic and thematic similarities that link this set of psalms, with special reference to their "portrayal of God" on the one hand (73–76), and "the faithful" people of God, on the other (77–78). During a survey of the individual psalms in this group, the author suggests that "the role of the Davidic king is greatly diminished when compared to the psalms before and after them" (82), while "God's cosmic sovereignty as creator and God's nearness as the shepherd of Israel" is highlighted in order to strengthen the faith of his people (83).

In "Instruction, Performance, and Prayer: The Didactic Function of Psalmic Wisdom," Catherine Petrany reveals some of the many "wisdom elements [that are] scattered throughout the book of Psalms" (87), with particular attention being given to three "wisdom psalms" of different genres: "trust (Ps. 62), thanksgiving (Ps. 92), and lament (Ps. 94)" (88). Wilson pointed out the predominance of a "royal-covenantal" thematic frame in the first three Books of the Psalter in contrast to a "wisdom frame" in Books 4–5 (99). Petrany does not argue for this macrostructural perspective, but encourages interpreters rather to observe "the disparate manner in which wisdom moments appear and function in the Psalms," with each occurrence manifesting "a unique mix of content in relation to shifting modes of address" (101).

In "'Wealth and Riches Are in His House' (Ps. 112:3): Acrostic Wisdom Psalms and the Development of Antimaterialism," Phil J. Botha puts forward the argument that "Ps. 112, together with the other acrostic psalms, constitute a unified, authoritative voice against secularism, greed, and religious apostasy in the late Persian period" (105).[8] Botha makes a strong text-based case for the claim that "the alphabetic acrostic psalms in the Psalter were intended to give direction to the understanding of the book of Psalms as a whole," that is, on account of their extent ("about 12 percent of the Psalms") and, more importantly, due to their specific placement within the collection (106). A more detailed discourse analysis of Psalm 112 is presented to illustrate the prominence of the theme of wealth versus poverty in the Psalter,[9] specifically in these strategically-located acrostic psalms (111–114). Botha then carries out a precise lexical and thematic comparison to

---

[8] But the question arises: Why limit the temporal reference to a particular point in Israel's religious history?

[9] With respect to this meticulous analysis, I would disagree only with the posited midpoint, that is, between v. 6a and 6b, rather than at the beginning of the verse. This latter interpretation views the *kiy* clause of v.6a as climactic ("Indeed..."), concluding the psalm's first half, while the explicit reference to "a righteous person"

reveal the various interconnections between Psalm 112 "in the context of Wisdom writings" with specific reference to the book of Proverbs (116–118) as well as the other wisdom acrostic psalms (118–124). His conclusion is that the authors of these psalms "consciously attempted to produce wisdom intertexts...as homilies on Proverbs and the Torah proper" (125), and that the Psalter's editors situated these texts at important junctures in order to "draw a clear distinction between the righteous and the wicked...as exhortations to a certain style of [godly] living" (126).

In "perhaps YHWH Is Sleeping: 'Awake' and 'Contend' in the Book of Psalms," Karl N. Jacobson undertakes an intertextual study of selected lament psalms in order to explore the contrastive themes of divine rest and divine warfare via the imagery of awakening a sleeping God (130). An overview of the concepts of "awake" and "contend" in the Psalter prepares for a consideration of the former in Psalms 44 and 7, the latter in Psalms 74 and 43, while both "contend" and "awake" are compared in Psalm 35. Jacobson proposes that psalmic Divine Warrior imagery in the laments constitutes a judicial metaphor in which Yahweh is vigorously "called upon to speak on behalf of the psalmist" (141) against his enemies by virtue of the covenantal relationship that binds a merciful God with his faithful people.[10] In conclusion, rather than the analogy of a hymnbook to describe the Psalter, Wilson's extended metaphor is suggested: "The Psalter is a symphony with many movements, or better yet an oratorio in which a multitude of voices— singly and in concert—rise in a crescendo of praise" (143), or presumably given some hostile situation, a righteous swell of complaint instead.

In "Revisiting the Theocratic Agenda of Book 4 of the Psalter for Interpretive Premise," Sampson S. Ndoga proposes that Book 4 is organized according to a "theocratic rubric" (148). Five types of evidence are adduced in support of this hypothesis: "the way book 3 ends: Psalm 89" (150); "the way book 4 begins: Psalms 90–92" (151); "the focus on YHWH as King: Psalms 93–99" (152); "The way book 4 closes" (154); and "the thematic links of book 5" (156), for example, the close connection between Psalms 106 and 107. Ndoga's conclusion is important: "For interpretational purposes, none of the psalms in book 4 can be read in isolation from their placement within the book and within the Psalter as a whole" (158).

(tsaddiyq) marks the beginning of the second half—each half consisting of 11 lines (one half of the alphabet).

[10] I do not agree with the expression "theology of defeat" to describe the interpersonal verbal dynamics that allegedly characterizes Ps. 35—or the view that this psalm "ends with a conditional vow of praise" (142). Instead, the assertion of 35:28 is better described as a faith-based promise to proclaim Yahweh's praises after his assumed defeat of all the psalmist's enemies—a declaration that echoes vv. 10 and 18 in a manner that divides the text into three major sections: vv. 1–10, 11–18, 19–28.

A canonical approach would undoubtedly apply this hermeneutical principle to all five books of the Psalter.

In "On Reading Psalms as Liturgy: Psalms 96–99," Jonathan Magonet suggests that this set of psalms functions as "a liturgical unit" (161) due to many lexical connections (similarities as well as contrasts) between and among them, which manifest an alternating pattern of thematic focus. Thus, "Pss. 96–99 (possibly introduced by Ps. 93) form a single, coherent liturgical unit, made up of alternating hymns and 'kingship' psalms" (173). To support his case, Magonet analyzes each of these psalms, and the group as a whole according to "five elements of liturgy": an assumed historical-religious narrative framework; various lexical linkages and performative "voices;" evidence of non-verbal worshipful actions; liturgical accompaniments (e.g., musical instructions, choral insertions, congregational invocations); and indications of an occasion of worship (e.g., psalms of ascent) (162–164, 174–175). In sum, this deliberately juxtaposed cluster "celebrates and [defines] the implications of YHWH's kingship, for Israel and for the peoples of the world, with righteousness and justice being the principal feature" (176).

In "The Role of the Foe in Book 5: Reflections on the Final Composition of the Psalter," W. Dennis Tucker Jr. begins by noting that Wilson appears to have overlooked the important role of the enemies of God and the faithful in this final portion of the Psalter (179). Tucker endeavors to fill this gap by demonstrating that "book 5 operates with an anti-imperial bias, seeking to build a world absent of power, save that of YHWH alone" (190). He does this by means of a comparative lexical-thematic study of several key psalms in book 5 that feature the key term "foe" *(tsâr),* viz., Psalms 107, 108–110, as well as the subsequent collections, in which the final psalm in each set appears to reflect this same theme: 113–118, 120–134 + 135–136, 138–144/145.[11] The message then is that "while there are kings and nations who threaten the people of God, these imperial powers will be undone by the God who delivers the oppressed (Ps. 107:6, 13, 19, 28)" (186).[12]

In "Gerald Wilson and the Characterization of David in Book 5 of the Psalter," Robert E. Wallace adopts a rather different perspective (i.e., from Tucker) on the thematic core of book 5. In contrast to Wilson's view that emphasized a "sapiential framework" to the Psalter and David's diminished prominence after book 2 (193–194), Wallace argues that David and a "royal frame" are in greater or lesser focus throughout, his persona being maintained by occasional "guest appearances" in books 3–4, while in book 5

---

[11] "Ps. 145 appears to function as a conclusion to the entirety of book 5" (188).

[12] While Israel's powerful foes are clearly referenced in these passages, I can see no internal evidence for identifying them specifically with "imperial" enemies, nor is the primary function of Psalm 110 to serve as a "political text" (185). One can certainly read this theme into the psalm, but I do not think that it was understood in those terms by the majority of the faithful who made use of it in personal or corporate worship.

"David's presence is hard to ignore" (198). Wallace bases his supposition upon an analysis that utilizes psalmic superscriptions (198) to forge some significant lexical and thematic connections between the psalms and "important narrative texts of the Hebrew Scriptures...[which] allow the reader to 'narrativize' the poetic text" (194). After a thematic, David-centered survey of two sets of book 5 psalms (108–138, 139–146), Wallace concludes: "In the first half of the book, the reader glimpses what the community desires: a strong David who serves as coregent with the Almighty.... Once the divine takes a close look at David in Ps. 139, however, the reader gets a glimpse of what the community is experiencing, a 'David' surrounded by enemies, a kingship that has failed, and a community in need of YHWH as king" (205).

In "The Contribution of Gerald Wilson Toward Understanding the Book of Psalms in Light of the Psalms Scrolls," Peter W. Flint evaluates the evidence provided by "forty-five psalm manuscripts or ones that incorporate psalms" that are non-Masoretic in origin (209). Four periods of research on the psalms scrolls, including Wilson's important role in this progressive recovery process, are summarized and supplemented with an extensive bibliography. Flint concludes that "the evidence from all the psalms scrolls attests to diversity concerning the shape of the Psalter, not to uniformity in accordance with the MT-150 arrangement...[and ostensibly] three editions of the psalms were in circulation in the late Second Temple period" (225). What cannot yet be determined with certainty is temporal priority in terms of compositional age.

In "Imagining the Future of Psalms Studies," Rolf A. Jacobson attempts to overview the current "state of the study of the Psalter" and to suggest new areas of interdisciplinary research that are already contributing to our understanding.[13] Jacobson predicts that traditional form-critical, canonical, poetic, and theological approaches will continue to be developed with increasing acuity into the subject (232). Assuming that "there is an intentional canonical shape to the Psalter" (234), he proceeds to document and critique the main differences between the "European approach," which focuses on the editorial "shaping" of the Psalter and its larger as well as smaller constituents (237–239), and the practice in North America, where there is emphasis rather on the final literary "shape" of the Psalter as well as its internal constituents (240–242). Furthermore, it is safe to say that "psalms research will become increasingly more interdisciplinary," borrowing and integrating insights from postcolonial, gender-oriented, postmodern, iconographic, and reception approaches (242–243). Even more recent scholarly interests are becoming involved, such as those concerned

---

[13] The author recognizes the tenuousness of such prognosis, citing the US sports observer Yogi Berra: "It is difficult to make predictions, especially about the future" (231).

with orality, literacy, ritual theory, identity formation, and "embodiment" studies (244–245). The last-mentioned field is particularly relevant since "there is no corpus of scripture in which there is a more concentrated locus of terms and imagery drawn from the matrix of bodily referentiality than the Psalms" (244).

Whether or not one agrees with all of the inter-psalmic associations and formational hypotheses that are proposed in the various essays collected in this volume, one must conclude at the very least that "where there is smoke, there must be a fire"—somewhere. As a result of all the evidence adduced within this text and in the many other studies referenced, one cannot deny the consciously shaped corporate character of the Psalter. This is revealed by the presence of a significant number of lexical, conceptual, and thematic interconnections, which must therefore be taken into careful consideration during the analysis and interpretation of any individual psalm (or psalm set) within the whole. There is thus a substantial degree of contextually "reflected meaning" that needs to be accounted for as cognitive background and a corresponding hermeneutical frame of reference, which is the anticipated result of any given psalm's placement in a particular textual location within the larger edited collection.

Most biblical scholars realize these implications and therefore include this prominent intertextual dimension, to a greater or lesser degree, as part of their formal expositions of the Psalter—in articles, topical studies, commentaries, and so forth. Bible translators, however, often seem to be rather slow in their recognition and application of these insights. Certainly more could (should) be done to explicitly document, as part of one's translation, the principal lexical links and closely associated thematic groupings in relation to a certain psalm. This is most commonly achieved through the use of clearly relevant cross-references and, where possible, by means of expository footnotes that point out such correspondences (similarities as well as major contrasts) and their interpretive import for understanding the psalm at hand. Exact verbal reiteration, too, must always be carefully noted, and if essentially the same contextually-determined meaning is involved, this should also ideally be reflected in one's translation. Finally, as a result of the studies considered in this volume, it would be very helpful to summarize at greater length in an introduction to the Psalter some of the major findings of canonical criticism, especially with regard to the text's unified final shape, including its manifold, multi-layered literary and thematic structure (6–7).

The Shape and Shaping of the Psalter is accessible, essential reading for any student or teacher of the Psalms, as well as for all those who wish to learn more about a holistic, canonical approach to this book's composition—whether its hypothetical history (shaping) or its consequent, interconnected structure (shape).

3 *Singing the Songs of the Lord in Foreign Lands: Psalms in Contemporary Lutheran Interpretation* (Mtata et al. 2014)

The essays collected in this volume were first presented at a hermeneutics conference on the Psalms organized by the Lutheran World Federation in 2013. Most papers gave special reference to the works of Martin Luther, so it is appropriate that this conference was held in Eisenach, near Wartburg Castle. The Psalter held a prominent place in Luther's biblical studies. He presented his first lectures at the University of Wittenberg with reference to the Psalms (1512) and later observed in in his *Preface to the Psalms* (1528): "Many of the Fathers have loved and praised the book of Psalms above all other books of the Bible.... It preserves, not the trivial and ordinary things said by the [saints], but their deepest and noblest utterances, those which they used when speaking in full earnest and all urgency to God" (9; all references are to the book under review).

This book consists of an Acknowledgments page, Preface, Foreword, a brief but helpful Introduction by the three editors, sixteen essays divided into six major thematic sections (which overlap to a certain degree), and a concluding listing of the authors and their academic affiliations (the inclusion of a topical as well as a Scripture index would have been useful). "The contributions of this book underline the value of reading the Psalms and how the Psalms can contribute to our broader understanding of biblical interpretation" (15). In my content survey that follows, space allows only for a citation of the chapter headings and their authors, plus a short summary and/or a quotable quote.

3.1 Hermeneutical approaches and challenges

In "Luther's Early Interpretation of the Psalms and His Contribution to Hermeneutics," Hans-Peter Grosshans identifies "three dominant elements of interpretation" (21) in Luther's hermeneutical method: his insistence "on the historical meaning of the biblical texts" (22), "the concept of the threefold spiritual sense of the Scriptures" in relation to the Psalms "as spiritual songs" (23), and Luther's emphasis on "Christ as the *scopus* of all biblical texts" (24) in relation to his distinction between "the killing letter and the life-giving spirit" of interpretation (25). These notions are then illustrated by "Luther's interpretation of Psalm 1 of 1513" (29–32). In "'Protect Me from Those Who Are Violent' (Psalm 140): A Cry for Justice—A Song of Hope," Monica Jyotsna Melanchthon focuses on the emotions of pain and distress as expressed in/by the lament psalms in particular. She poses this question: "How can we transcribe the real problem of the 'I' in crisis into social, material, mental or physical categories—dealing with the ultimate conditions of human existence in our day and age?" (35). She applies an "intertextual reading method" (37) with reference to the sociological setting of India and gender-based violence to present a feminist perspective on the interpretation of Psalm 140 (39–53). The concluding thoughts concerning "Luther on Lament" (54–56) are instructive and relevant, especially "from the perspective of women, who experience oppression and pain far more intensely than their male counterparts" (56).

3.2 Psalms exegesis—methodologies past and present

In "Singing, Praying and Meditating the Psalms—Exegetical and Historical Remarks," Corinna Körting first lists four reasons that led Luther to stress the singing of Psalms (60–61). She then surveys research that debates the religious purposes of the Psalter, with special reference to its possible use "as a songbook for the Second Temple community" (64). She presents the case for "Psalm 150 as Closure and Goal of the Psalter" (67) and applies "a material approach" in investigating the function of "instrumental music and singing" in the Psalms (69). "Reading these [psalm] texts evokes the world of temple service with music and shouting and singing...music and sounds matter" (71). In "From Psalms to Psalter Exegesis," Frank-Lothar Hossfeld presents a compact synopsis of "the interconnection between diachrony and synchrony using three examples from the macrostructure of the Psalter" (75–76). He concludes by summarizing three aspects of Luther's hermeneutical importance to Psalms studies (77–78).

3.3 Difficult topics in Psalms and their Lutheran interpretation

In "The Topic of Violence—A Hermeneutical Challenge in Reading Psalms," Jutta Hausman investigates certain problematic aspects of the so-called imprecatory psalms, with special reference to Psalms 58 and 137 when "dealing with the experience of violence" (84). She concludes that in most cases "the topic of experienced violence [in the Psalter] is focused on the psychological terror exerted by violent language," and that "the plea for God's intervention against the enemies is often...a request to destroy the tools of speech" (87). In "Between Praise and Lament: Remarks on the Development of the Hebrew Psalms," Urmas Nõmmik develops the thesis that "praise and lament belong to the oldest cultic phenomena and literary genres in the ancient Near East and in the Bible" (103). This has reference to Israel's "Monarchic Period" (91–96) and the "Second Temple Period," where the assumption is that "many earlier lament psalms have been reworked for different settings" (98), a prominent case in point being Psalm 22 (99–102). The theological and ethical significance of the functional patterning of most lament psalms, as well as the Psalter as a whole, is that "praise at the end of the lament Psalm is an adequate answer to [human] distress and existential issues," that is, "through a certain relation to God" (103).

In "The Vengeance Psalms as a Phenomenon of Critical Justice: The Problem of Enemies in Luther's Interpretation of Psalms," Roger Marcel Wanke reflects upon the frequent appearance of "enemies" in the Psalms, whether in isolated passages or throughout a particular prayer, e.g., Psalms 12, 35, 58, 59, 69, 70, 83, 109, 137, 140. The hermeneutical perspective of "critical justice" views those psalms that cry out for justice, even harsh retribution upon the enemies, as expressing an implicit trust that God will ultimately do the right thing, even when all external circumstances seem to be pointing elsewhere (112–113). Wanke concludes with an overview of "Luther and the Vengeance Psalms" (113), with special reference to Psalm 6 (114) and Psalm 94 (115).

3.4 Psalms from the Old Testament and their reception in the New Testament

In "Psalms Outside the Biblical Psalms—The Example of Jonah," Karl-Wilhelm Niebuhr surveys the account of Jonah as it appears in the Dead Sea Scrolls (121), in Luther's "Table Talks" (124), in the Hebrew Bible (125–128, noting that the psalm of Jonah 2 consists of "a mosaic of motifs taken from biblical Psalms" [126]), in "Early Jewish Literature" (129–132), and in the "Early Synoptic Tradition" (132–134). Niebuhr concludes that the Jonah story can serve as a "test case for a biblical theology in a Christian sense" when it is interpreted with a focus upon "the confession to Jesus who died on the cross and was resurrected by God on the third day" (135). In "Interpretation of the Psalms in the New Testament—Witness to Christ and the Human Condition," Craig R. Koester uses the variable manner in which the Psalter is interpreted in the book of Acts (141–145) and John's Gospel (146–153) as a model for its hermeneutical use today. Koester concludes that, with reference to the interpretation of Psalms, "a Lutheran theology of the cross...finds God's power revealed in contexts where it would seem to be absent" (154), which has special value today when applying these biblical texts to situations of "poverty and injustice, disease and conflict, secularization and indifference...in various cultural contexts" (155). In "The Christological Reception of Psalms in Hebrews," Anni Hentschel seeks to elucidate "the interpretive program of Hebrews on the basis of its two opening chapters [which] depict the worldview of the Hebrews, [thus] providing the foundation for the author's further Christological and paraenetical reflections" (159). After a careful, but selective exegetical study (161–176), the author concludes that while "Hebrews relates the Psalms to Jesus, interpreting his life and his significance in the light of their words," nevertheless, "the Christological interpretation of Hebrews does not outdate the traditional Jewish understanding of the Psalms" (177).

3.5 Luther's interpretation of the Psalms from a contemporary perspective

In "Luther and the Psalms—How Stories Shape the Story," Vítor Westhelle surveys Luther's principles of translation with special reference to the Psalter and its perceived "Christological core" (182–188). In conclusion, Westhelle reflects upon Luther's "remarkable distinction between being holy (heilig) and being saved or blessed (selig)" (189) with reference to Aesop's fables (190). I found it rather difficult to penetrate the author's argument in this section, or indeed, to see its relevance to the essay's preceding hermeneutical discussion. In "The Psalms and Luther's Praise Inversion—Cultural Criticism as Doxology Detection," Brian Brock proceeds from the assumption that "the modern account of critical rationality [has] had an effect on how we understand language in our daily life" (192), including our hermeneutical approach to Scripture, the Psalter in particular. Brock wants to instil a more affective element into the process of interpretation, including the "tonal aspects of communication" (193). His argument is that "Luther's ethics is not one of prescription but of perception and affection," which allowed him "to deepen and theologically enrich an inversion of perception that played an important role in the ethical thinking of the earlier theological tradition" (195). After documenting Luther's so-called "doxological perception" (199) in several passages of 1 Corinthians (200–201), Brock applies this notion to Luther's approach to the Psalter in general (202–203) and to Psalm 118 in particular (204–210) in order to suggest "the power of the critical reformulation of the very questions we ask in ethical discourse that praise analysis offers to modern theology" (212). In "Theology of the Word in 'Operationes in Psalmos' (1519–1521)," L'ubomír Batka develops the argument that Luther's hermeneutical approach in this work "presents a communicative process of God's actions through the Word based on a Trinitarian structure: as an activity of God the Father, Son, and Holy Spirit on behalf of human beings realized by the power of the Word" (213). In order to properly interpret the Psalms, readers "need to be inspired with the Holy Spirit" (229) and to combine "a strong Christocentric explanation... with a clear Christology" (230).

3.6 Contextual approaches to the Psalms

In "Being ˈādām—A Contextual Reading of the Psalms Today," Madipoane Masenya *(ngwan'a Mphahlele)* advances the case that "more than any other book in the Christian Scriptures, the Psalms live in the veins of many African Christians to whose lives the Bible is central" (233). After an initial reflection on "being a human being in African South Africa" (235–236), the author applies this notion to a contemporary interpretation of Psalm 8 with special reference to a Northern Sotho/Pedi sociocultural setting and those living on the margins of the community at large (237–243). In

"The Wounds of War—Engaging the Psalms of Lament in Pastoral Care with Veterans against the Background of Martin Luther's Hermeneutics," Andrea Bieler applies Luther's insights on "the transformative power of Psalms," especially their performative "singing and reading," in relation to all manner of "troubled human beings" (246). In her discussion, Bieler explores "how working with the Psalms of lament creates an imaginative space for veterans who have to attend to the lasting psychosomatic scars left by war" (248), and she documents several case studies that illustrate this (252–256). In an interesting conclusion, the author asserts that "Psalms of lament can be a powerful resource since they open up [psychological] spaces in which veterans can borrow images in order to express their own turmoil and at the same time develop a language of hope that is geared toward trust in God and toward the work of soul repair" (259). In "Luther's Poetic Reading of Psalms," Dorothea Erbele-Küster overviews the "poetic and rhetorical analysis" that accompanies the Reformer's "appreciation of singing and music," on the one hand, and his "contextual interpretations," on the other (261). She coins the term "po/et(h)ics" to put forward the argument that "aesthetics can lead us to ethics...the poetic is intrinsically ethical" (261) and applies this to a "rereading of Psalm 27" (262–266). The author concludes with some thoughts on how "Martin Luther's readings serve as impulse for our Psalter hermeneutics from a Lutheran perspective" (267) and offers this important note regarding Bible translation: "The Psalms... should sound like songs in the mother tongue and in the language of the context" (269).

3.7 Conclusion

Undoubtedly, in a collection of such topical range and diversity by different authors, one is bound to find the occasional quarrel or quibble. While fewer in number than I had originally anticipated, I did encounter certain assertions that raised questions of an exegetical-hermeneutical, theological, and translational nature. For example, my analysis of Psalm 22 would not lead me to conclude that "it consists of several parts that do not originate from the same hand" or time period (98–99); with reference to the book of Jonah, when applying "the Lutheran distinction between Law and gospel [sic]," I would not agree that its message "obviously belongs to the gospel" (129); I cannot understand how someone can conclude that "there is definitely a gnostic element in Luther" (190); finally, I would not support the *Tetragrammaton* in the Hebrew Bible being "transliterated" [sic, "translated"] as "Eternal" (264), e.g., "Put your expectation in the Eternal" (263).

This compilation of essays provides a good overview of contemporary (LWF) Lutheran hermeneutical perspectives on the Psalter—with special reference to Luther's ongoing relevance as a commentator and, on the other hand, how the Psalms and/or Luther's take on selected texts may be used to address issues of current social concern. The essays tend to be moderate in length and well-written, by a select group of recognized authors. This book is a must for all Luther scholars; it would also serve well as a primary reference text for theological-hermeneutical courses at the seminary-graduate school level and as a secondary reference for Bible translators in training. Its modest cost should make it affordable for most libraries.

4 *The Psalms: Language for all Seasons of the Soul* (Schmutzer and Howard 2013)

This collection of well-written essays, produced by a group of recognized evangelical scholars in the field,[14] derives largely from conference papers presented in the Psalms and Hebrew Poetry section of the Evangelical Theological Society (2009–2011). The book consists of a listing of the contributors, a table of primary reference abbreviations, a brief introduction by the editors, nineteen individual studies divided into five major topical sections ("parts"), a select bibliography for Psalms studies, a subject index, and a Scripture index. The book aims to review "the enormous impact" of the Psalter upon the Christian faith and scholarship by "weaving together some [of its] primary theological, literary, and canonical themes" (15–16; all page references are to the book under review). Space limitations preclude a detailed description of contents, so in addition to the descriptive essay titles (with their authors) I am able to contribute only a brief summary and/ or a point of special interest, often in the words of the authors themselves. I relegate my occasional critical comments to the footnotes.

Part 1, "Psalms Studies in the Twenty-First Century: Where We Have Been and Where We Are Going" (17), consists of three essays that provide a broad historical and interpretative orientation to the book. Bruce K. Waltke leads off with "a personal perspective" on "Biblical Theology of the Psalms Today." He summarizes some of the main influences that have impacted his lifetime of research and writing on the Old Testament, the Psalter in particular, including the works of a number of influential scholars. As for the future, Waltke feels that "more reflection on the influence of Second Temple Judaism is needed" (27). Willem A. VanGemeren focuses on "literary analysis" when "Entering the Textual World of the Psalms" (29). He too surveys some of the principal contributors to the study of the Psalms (e.g., Kugel, Alter, Berlin) with particular attention being given to proponents and critics of a canonical-critical approach (e.g., Childs versus Longman III).[15] VanGemeren devotes the final third of his study to an appeal for more

---

[14] There may well be a reason for this, but no women are included among the authors.

[15] It would seem topically more appropriate for the paragraph on Gerald H. Wilson and his influence (40) to be juxtaposed to the canonical-critical section on Brevard Childs (30–31).

"imagination in theological interpretation" (43), namely, an "analogical imagination that invites hearers/readers of the biblical text to situate themselves within the world of the text" (45) and a metaphoric perspective that seeks out new theological patterns, paradigms, and "ways of imagining the future" (46). In "The Psalms and Faith/Tradition" (49), C. Hassell Bullock, like Waltke, summarizes "what I have especially learned about the Psalms" (50),[16] with special reference to "how they teach us to pray" (51) as well as the oft-neglected "tradition of private devotion" (54). In conclusion, Bullock rightly highlights "the musical component" of the Psalter (56) and, echoing VanGemeren, also its rich, albeit traditionally worded metaphorical dimension: "The poetry of the Psalms achieves a verbal level of iconography that more than compensates for the prescribed absence of images on the material level of ancient orthodox practice...through the word, icon is made metaphor" (59, citing Wm. P. Brown).

Part 2 of this collection, "Psalms of Praise: Expressing Our Joys" (61), includes three individual studies. Francis X. Kimmitt begins with "Psalm 46: Praise the Lord Our Help" (63).[17] After a helpful structural and semantic study of this psalm, he makes a contemporary application by reflecting on the importance of "praise and the church" (71). Next, Robert B. Chisholm Jr. surveys the topic "Suppressing Myth: Yahweh and the Sea in the Praise Psalms" (75), first in relation to the two "lament" Psalms 74 and 89 (76, cf. 84),[18] and then a selection of "psalms of praise" (78). Chisholm points out how the psalmists effectively "demythologized" (79), "transformed" (80), and "historicized the sea" (81) in their religious poetry. In the third and final essay of Part 2, Andrew J. Schmutzer examines Psalm 91 in relation to the subject of "Refuge, Protection and Their Use in the New Testament" (85).[19] In what is perhaps the most scholarly study of this book, the author employs a "multiplex" approach to set forth the "literary context" of Psalm 91 (85);

---

[16] The topical headings in this section are somewhat confusing, for example, the rather awkward general title "The Psalms' Normative Nature for Prayer and Faith" is applied specifically in close succession to "The Imprecation" and "Their Timeless Nature" (50).

[17] It might be argued that Psalm 46 is more correctly classified as a "psalm of trust," as Kimmitt himself seems to recognize: "Psalm 46 does not contain praise language typical of the hymns..." (65). What difference does it make? Genre classification affects one's interpretation of a psalm's internal functional constituents, for example, "Hymns begin with a call to worship" (68), which is not at all present in Psalm 46.

[18] Consideration of these lament psalms calls the chapter's major title into question, which specifies "praise psalms."

[19] This title too is somewhat ambiguous; one first assumes that reference is being made to God as a refuge of his people, only to discover later that the subject is really the popular apotropaic use of certain psalm verses against demonic forces which they perceived as surrounding them in life.

the "thematic sequence" of Psalms 90—92 (87); the "voice" of "Moses" (Ps. 90) in relation to Psalm 91's assumed exilic setting (88); the "didactic structure" of Psalm 91 (91); the "demon tradition" generated by verses 5–6 of Psalm 91 in the Hebrew Bible (92), "some ancient versions" (97), and the Dead Sea Scrolls (98); the use of amulets in Judaism (99); lastly, the "impact of Psalm 91 in the New Testament" (105), specifically Mt. 4:4–6 and Lk. 10:19. This is a most fascinating socio-religious investigation.

Part 3 is the largest portion of the book: "Psalms of Lament: Expressing our Sorrows and Pain" (109).[20] In " 'Severe Delight': The Paradox of Praise in Confession of Sin," Michael E. Travers employs two "penitential psalms" (51 and 32) to explore "the tensions between the sinner and his guilt on the one hand and the Lord and his forgiveness on the other" (111). In Psalm 51 the notion of confession dominates, while in Psalm 32 it is praise that takes precedence. "The juxtaposition of penitence and praise constitutes the paradox of 'severe delight' in these penitential psalms" (125). In "The Laments of Lamentations Compared to the Psalter," Walter C. Kaiser Jr. demonstrates a "shared pattern of communication" (or "genre") that links the sorrowful texts of this book to psalmic laments, both individual (e.g., Ps. 13) and corporate (e.g., Ps. 80). Kaiser succinctly surveys the literary structure and poetic features of the book of Lamentations and concludes by noting the "theological significance of the lament" composition, in which "a prayer of petition makes a call to Yahweh for help a dominant theme of this genre" (132). "The 'thou' sections of laments" are the subject of Allen P. Ross as he studies "The Bold and Earnest Prayers of the Psalmists" (135). There appear to be four levels of increasingly challenging complaint over "God's negligence," as he is boldly accused of "hiding himself" from (136), "forgetting" (138), "forsaking" (140), and worst, being "hostile" to the psalmist (141). With regard to this last category, God may appear "angry because of our sin" (141) or "not because of sin" (145), and the psalmist may sound "urgent" or even more "boldly directive" in his appeal (147). But one must always "hear" these earnest, faith-filled prayers with an ear attentive to their concern over "God's reputation [which] was being tarnished" by the psalmist's unresolved problem or predicament (149). Daniel J. Estes offers an explanation for "The Transformation of Pain into Praise in the Individual Lament Psalms" (151). This dramatic psychological change in mood is centered in the notion of "meditation," which is investigated in terms of a number of key verbs (e.g., *h-g-h* 'to groan, moan, meditate, muse') coupled with some "explicit indicators" (e.g., mention of the psalmist's "voice") (156). The typical lament psalm's inclusion of a "confession of trust" (157) is the key to a mental transformation whereby "praise" replaces "pain" as the psalmist

---

[20] One might wonder perhaps why the editors chose to go against the general thematic progression of the Psalter itself in presenting their studies of the psalms of praise before those involving the lament psalms.

contemplates different aspects of Yahweh's "character, control, care, works, word, and presence" (162). Randall X. Gauthier speculates on translation technique with reference to the Septuagint's rendering of Psalm 54 (55 in English), vv. 9 and 14–15, in relation to the theme: a God "Who Saves from Discouragement and Tempest" (165). A comparative "dialectical approach" is adopted to suggest how "translational choices provide the interpretive building blocks and constraints for which the greater discourse provides context and meaning" (166). Aspects of that "greater discourse" study include the underlying Masoretic text, a preliminary text-critical analysis, an intertextual comparison with Psalm 82(83):16, and some detailed "structural, literary, and theological observations" (175). Gauthier concludes that "Psalm 54 [LXX] is both a translation and an autonomous text, and it is the interplay between these two dimensions that provides internal guidelines for interpretation" (179).

In Part 4 we turn to "The Psalter as a Book" and "considering the canon" (181). Robert L. Cole leads off, appropriately, with "Psalms 1 and 2: The Psalter's Introduction" (183). A detailed linguistic, structural, and thematic analysis, including cross-references to Psalm 110 (188) and Psalm 3 (192) suggests that Psalms 1 and 2 form an "integrated, but independent" (185) prologue to the Psalter,[21] a coherent juxtaposition that is evidenced elsewhere in the corpus, e.g., Psalms 72–73 (195). Next, David M. Howard Jr. considers the macrotheme of "Divine and Human Kingship as Organizing Motifs in the Psalter" (197). After an overview of "the Psalter's five 'Books' " (198), Howard, like Cole (see above), zeros in on "Psalms 1–2 as the introduction to the Psalter" (200), with their four major themes serving further as "keynotes for the Psalter" (202). "A pattern of royal psalms" (204) at key junctures creates the Psalter's "macrostructure" (e.g., Pss. 72, 89), while "the return of the k/King" is featured in Book V, which "ends with a climactic crescendo of praise that also acknowledges God's kingship" (206). "The Return of the King" is also the topic of Michael K. Snearly when contemplating "Book V as a Witness to Messianic Hope in the Psalter" (209). After a sketch of the integrated "story line of the Psalter" (211), Snearly identifies "the five key words of Book V" (212), which support the major theme of kingship. Selected "evidence of Davidic hope" in the prophetic books (214) and in Chronicles (215) is referenced to show that even in postexilic times this messianic hope "was still alive" (215) and "looked for the consummation of God's kingship through his Anointed One" (217). Tremper Longman, III brings this book's series of scholarly studies to a close by examining "Psalm 150 as the Conclusion to the Psalter" under the theme "From

---

[21] Although Cole's reasoning is sound, I was not quite convinced that the evidence that he marshals would necessarily exclude the view that Pss. 1–2 are "two disparate psalms, one wisdom or perhaps Torah, and the other royal, that form a 'dual' introduction to the Psalter" (193).

Weeping to Rejoicing" (219). "Weeping" of course has reference to the
lament psalms, which predominate in the first Books of the Psalter, and in
fact normally include within themselves a "healthy turn toward praise" as
part of their structure (220). Psalm 150, "the most pure of all hymns" (221)
is examined closely with regard to "structure" (222) and "canonical setting"
(224)—in fact, "the climax of a great Doxology" (226, i.e., Pss. 146–150).
Although disagreeing with previous essayists regarding "the Psalter's over-
all structure," Longman believes that the collection's "opening and clos-
ing psalms make sense if one thinks of the book as a whole as a literary
sanctuary" (224).

Part 5 deals with "Communicating the Psalms: Bringing the Psalms into
the present day" (229). This consists of a set of four sermons (complete or
in part, and preached on different occasions) that are included to illustrate
how some of the principal themes and methods of the prior studies might
be practically incorporated into a homiletical oration. In "Psalms 16, 23:
Confidence in a Cup" (231), Mark D. Futato suggests that the purposeful
arrangement of Psalms 15–24 functions "to teach us about the true nature
of spirituality" (232). This leads to a study of how the image of a "cup" in
Psalm 16:5 and 23:5 depicts spiritual and physical blessings, respectively,
thus indicating how God takes care of all our needs (234). David A. Ridder
then considers "Psalm 84: How Lovely Is Thy Dwelling Place" (237). The
threefold structure of this psalm inspires a "sermon in three movements":
"(1) longing for the temple, (2) the experience of pilgrimage, and (3) the
reward of those who dwell in God's presence" (237).[22] In "Psalm 88: Praising
God in the Bad Times" (247), David M. Howard Jr. bravely seeks out some-
thing encouraging to say about this most morose of psalms—"the darkest
corner of the Psalter" (249). We find a glimmer of hope in the sequence of
rhetorical questions in verses 10–12, where the psalmist appeals for deliver-
ance, not for his own sake, but so that he can praise the Lord's covenantal
fidelity (251). At the very least then, *"Psalm 88 shows us that, even in the
midst of the worst circumstances, it is still possible to talk to God,* to have a
relationship with him" (252, original italics). In "Psalm 117: Everlasting
Truth for the Joy of All Peoples" (255), John Piper develops three themes
from this briefest of psalms: the reference to "all peoples" implies a mission
mandate embracing the whole world (256); the aim is to lead all people to
"praise their Creator" (258); the reason for such universal praise rests in the
everlasting faithfulness of the Lord (260). That is God's goal, and "he calls
all of us to be goers or senders" (261).

As part of the overall aim of its broad collection of studies in the Psalms,
this book is offered as a "tool...that both trained pastors and professors can

---

[22] I found one rather incongruous observation in part 3: "And being a janitor in the
house of God would be far better than being an honored guest at the *Playboy Man-
sion"* (244, my italics).

use," namely, to enrich their sermon preparation, as background material for "lay institutes in churches and seminaries," and as "a supplemental text in seminary or upper-level college courses" (16). Having benefitted from all of the studies found in this volume, I would conclude that these objectives have been admirably accomplished. In the words of several of its endorsers, this well-conceived compilation exposes readers "to the best of scholarship in the field as well as the spirituality of the Psalter itself" and "admirably draws together academic research and the life of faith;" it is, in short, "a book for 'all seasons of the soul'" (1).

References

Achtemeier, P. J. 1990. Omne verbum sonat: The New Testament and the oral environment of later Western antiquity. *Journal of Biblical Literature* 109:1, 3–27.

Agnes, M., ed. 2006. *Webster's new world college dictionary*. Fourth edition. Cleveland, OH: Wiley Publishing.

Albertz, R. 2009. Public recitation of prophetical books? The case of the first edition of Deutero-Isaiah (Isa. 40:1–52:12). In D. V. Edelman and E. Ben Zvi (eds.), *The production of prophecy: Constructing prophecy and prophets in Yehud,* 96–110. London: Equinox.

Alden, R. L. 1974. Chiastic Psalms: A study in the mechanics of Semitic poetry in Psalms 1–50. *Journal of the Evangelical Theological Society (JETS)* 17:1, 11–28.

Allen, L. C. 1983. *Psalms 101–150* (Word Biblical Commentary, Vol. 21). Waco, TX: Word Books.

Alter, R. 1981. *The art of biblical narrative.* New York: Basic Books.

Alter, R. 1985. *The art of biblical poetry.* New York: Basic Books.

Alter, R. 1987. The characteristics of ancient Hebrew poetry. In R. Alter and F. Kermode (eds.), *The literary guide to the Bible,* 611–624. Cambridge: Harvard University Press.

Alter, R. 2007. *The book of Psalms: A translation with commentary.* New York and London: W. W. Norton.

Alter, R. and E. L. Greenstein. 2012. Psalm. In Greene, 1123-1124.

Amzallag, N. 2014. The musical mode of writing of the Psalms and its significance. *Old Testament essays* 27:1, 17–40.

Anderson, B. W. 1987. The Song of Miriam poetically and theologically considered. In Follis, 285–296.

Archaeological Study Bible. 2003. Grand Rapids: Zondervan.

Associate Reformed Psalter (now known as The ARP Psalter with Bible songs). 1930 (2011). Pittsburgh: Crown and Covenant Publishers.

Attridge, H. W. 1989. *Hebrews: A commentary on the Epistle to the Hebrews* (Hermeneia). Philadelphia: Fortress Press.

Attridge, H. W. 2004. The Psalms in Hebrews. In S. Moyise and M. J. J. Menken (eds.), *The Psalms in the New Testament,* 197–212. New York: T&T Clark International.

Back, R. T. 2014. Rachel Tzvia Back discusses the art of translation after working with the poetry of Tuvia Ruebner. http://marginalia. lareviewofbooks.org/translating-poetry-act-art-preserving-essential-rachel-tzvia-back/. Accessed September 2, 2017.

Bailey, J. L. 1995. Genre analysis. In J. B. Green (ed.), *Hearing the New Testament: Strategies for interpretation,* 197–221. Grand Rapids: Eerdmans.

Bailey, N. 2013. The expression of emotion in language and in translation: Failures and successes in English translations. Paper presented at the BT 2013 Conference, Dallas, TX: SIL International.

Balentine, S. E. 1993. *Prayer in the Hebrew Bible: The drama of divine-human dialogue.* Minneapolis: Fortress Press.

Banker, J. 1987. *Semantic structure analysis of Titus.* Dallas: Summer Institute of Linguistics.

Barker, K., ed. 1985. *The NIV study Bible.* Grand Rapids: Zondervan.

Barr, J. 1973. *The Bible in the modern world.* London: SCM Press.

Barton, J. 1984. *Reading the Old Testament: Method in biblical study.* Philadelphia: Westminster.

Batka, L. 2014. Theology of the word in "Operationes in Psalmos" (1519–1521). In Mtata et al., 213–230.

Beale, G. K. 1999. *The book of Revelation* (NIGTC). Grand Rapids: Eerdmans.

Beckson, K. and A. Ganz. 1975. *Literary terms: A dictionary.* New York: Farrar, Straus and Giroux.

Beekman, J. and J. Callow. 1974. *Translating the Word of God.* Grand Rapids: Zondervan.

Beekman, J., J. Callow, and M. Kopesec. 1981. The semantic structure of written communication (pre-publication draft). Fifth edition. Dallas, TX: Summer Institute of Linguistics.

Belcher, R. P., Jr. 2008. Thanksgiving, Psalms of. In Longman and Enns, 805–808.

Beldman, D. J. H. 2012. Literary approaches and Old Testament interpretation. In C. G. Bartholomew and D. J. H. Beldman (eds.),

Hearing the Old Testament: Listening to God's address, 67–95. Grand Rapids: Eerdmans.

Bellinger W. H., Jr. 1984. *Psalmody and prophecy* (JSOT Supplement Series 27). Sheffield, UK: JSOT Press.

Bellinger, W. H., Jr. 1990. *Psalms: Reading and studying the book of praises.* Peabody, MA: Hendrickson.

Benjamin, Walter. 1923. The task of the translator. In his 1968 *Illuminations*, trans. into English, as quoted by R. T. Back.

Bergen, R. D. 1987. Text as a guide to authorial intention: An introduction to discourse criticism. *Journal of the Evangelical Theological Society* 30:3, 327–336.

Berlin, A. 1985. *The dynamics of biblical parallelism.* Bloomington: Indiana University Press.

Berlin, A. 1996. Introduction to Hebrew poetry. In L. E. Keck (ed.), *The new interpreter's Bible* (Vol. IV), 301–315. Nashville, TN: Abingdon Press.

Berlin, A. and M. Z. Brettler, eds. 2004. *The Jewish study Bible* (Jewish Publication Society). Oxford: Oxford University Press.

Berry, D. K. 1993. *The Psalms and their readers: Interpretive strategies for Psalm 18* (JSOT Supplement Series 153). Sheffield, UK: JSOT Press.

Berry, E. 2012. Poetic function. In Greene, 1056-1057.

Birch, B. C. 1985. *What does the Lord require? The Old Testament call to social witness.* Philadelphia: Westminster Press.

Blaising, C. A. and C. S. Hardin, eds. 2008. *Ancient Christian commentary on Scripture: Old Testament VII: Psalms 1–50.* Downers Grove, IL: InterVarsity.

Boerger, B. 2009. *Poet oracle English translation* [POET]: PSALMS. Dallas, TX: Self-published.

Boice, J. M. 1996. *Psalms,* Vol. 2 (Psalms 42–106). Grand Rapids: Baker Books.

Boice, J. M. n.d. *Studies in Psalms,* Vol. 2 (42–106). Philadelphia: Alliance for Confessing Evangelicals (audio tape series).

Bond, D. 2012. Biblical poetry in a postbiblical, postpoetry world. In Wells and Van Neste, 65–79.

Bowen, N. R. 2003. A fairy tale wedding? A feminist intertextual reading of Psalm 45. In Strawn and Bowen, 53–71.

Bratcher R. G. and Wm. D. Reyburn. 1991. *A translator's handbook on the book of Psalms.* New York: United Bible Societies.

Braun, J. 2002. *Music in ancient Israel/Palestine: Archaeological, written, and comparative sources.* Translated by D. Scott. Grand Rapids: Eerdmans.

Brenner, M. L. 1991. *The Song of the Sea: Ex 15:1–21 (Beihefte zur Zeitschrift für die alttestamentliche Wissenschaft* 195). Berlin and New York: De Gruyter.

Briggs, R. S. 2008. Speech-act theory. In Firth and Grant, 75–110.

Brock, B. 2014. The Psalms and Luther's praise inversion: Cultural criticism as doxological detection. In Mtata et al., 191–212.

Brogan, T. V. F. 2012. Line. In R. Greene, 801–803.

Brown, F., S. R. Driver, and C. A. Briggs. 1978. A Hebrew and English Lexicon of the Old Testament. Oxford: Clarendon Press.

Brown, J. K. 2008. Genre criticism and the Bible. In Firth and Grant, 111–150.

Brown, R. 2004. "New dimensions in communicative translation." Power Point presentation included on the CD: *Bible Translation—2003*. Dallas, TX: SIL International. Slides 1–141.

Brown, W. P., ed. 2014. *The Oxford handbook of the Psalms*. Oxford: Oxford University Press,

Broyles, C. C. 1999. *Psalms* (New International Biblical Commentary). Peabody, MA: Hendrickson.

Bruce, F. F. 1968. *The New Testament development of Old Testament themes*. Grand Rapids: Eerdmans.

Brueggeman, D. A. 2008. Psalms 4: Titles. In Longman and Enns, 613–621.

Brueggemann, W. 1987. A response to "The Song of Miriam" by Bernhard Anderson. In Follis, 297–302.

Brueggemann, W. 1994. Exodus. In L. E. Keck (ed.), *The New interpreter's Bible*, Vol. 1, 677–981. Nashville, TN: Abingdon Press.

Brueggemann, W. 1995. *The Psalms and the life of faith*. Edited by P. D. Miller. Minneapolis: Fortress.

Brueggemann, W. 2005. The Psalms as limit expressions. In D. Bland and D. Fleer (eds.), *Performing the Psalms*, 31–50. St. Louis: Chalice Press.

Buber, M., and F. Rosenzweig. 1994 (1927). *Scripture and translation*. Translated by L. Rosenwald and E. Fox. Bloomington: Indiana University Press.

Buku lopatulika [Set-apart book]. 1922. London: British and Foreign Bible Society.

Buku loyera [Holy/White book]. 1998. Blantyre: Bible Society of Malawi.

Bullock, C. H. 2001. *Encountering the book of Psalms: A literary and theological introduction*. Grand Rapids: Baker Academic.

Bullock, C. H. 2013. The Psalms and faith/tradition. In Schmutzer and Howard, 49–59.

Burgh, T. W. 2006. *Listening to the artifacts: Music culture in ancient Palestine*. New York: T & T Clark International.

Burns, J., D. Bers, and S. Tree, eds. 2011. *The music of Psalms, Proverbs and Job in the Hebrew Bible: A Revised theory of musical accents in the Hebrew Bible*. Wiesbaden: Harrassowitz.

Burton, S., R-M. Dechaine, and E. Vatikiotis-Bateson. 2012. *Linguistics for dummies*. Mississauga, Canada: John Wiley & Sons.

Calvin, J. 1840. *A commentary on the Psalms of David*, Vol. 1. Translated by J. Anderson. Oxford: Tegg.

Calvin, J. 1949. *Commentary on the book of Psalms*, Vol. 2. Translated by J. Anderson. Grand Rapids: Eerdmans.

Cassuto, U. 1967. *A commentary on the book of Exodus*. Jerusalem: Magnes.

Chadza, E. J. 1967. *Nchito ya pakamwa: Ndakatulo za m'chinyanja.* Lusaka: The Zambia Publications Bureau.

Chadza, E. J. 1970. *Tiphunzire Chichewa,* Blantyre, Malawi: Christian Literature Association.

Childs, B. S. 1974. *The book of Exodus* (OTL). Philadelphia: Westminster.

Chisholm, R. B., Jr. 2013. Suppressing myth: Yahweh and the sea in the praise psalms. In Schmutzer and Howard, 75–84.

Coats, G. N. 1969. The song of the sea. *Catholic Bible Quarterly* 31:1–17.

Coetzee, J. H. 2009. Psalm 85: Yearning for the restoration of the whole body. *Old Testament Essays* 22:554–563.

Cole, A. 1973. *Exodus* (Tyndale Old Testament Commentary). Downers Grove, IL: Inter-Varsity Press.

Cole, R. L. 2013. Psalms 1–2: The Psalter's introduction. In Schmutzer and Howard, 183–195.

Collins, C. J. 2012. Always alleluia: Reclaiming the true purpose of the Psalms in the Old Testament context. In Wells and Van Neste, 17–34.

Collins, J. J. 2004. *Introduction to the Hebrew Bible.* Minneapolis: Fortress Press.

Collins, T. 1978. *Line-forms in biblical poetry.* Rome: Biblical Institute Press.

Cook, J. A. 2008. Hebrew language. In Longman and Enns, 260–267.

Cotterell, P. 1997. Linguistics, meaning, semantics, and discourse analysis. In W. A. Gemeren (ed.), *New international dictionary of Old Testament theology and exegesis,* Vol. 1. Grand Rapids: Zondervan, 134–160.

Craghan J. F. 1985. *The Psalms: Prayers for the ups, downs, and in-betweens of life.* Wilmington: Michael Glazier.

Craigie, P. C. 1983. *Psalms 1–50* (Word Biblical Commentary, Vol. 19). Waco, TX: Word Books.

Creach, J. 2005. The Psalms and the cult. In Firth and Johnston, 119–137.

Culley, R. B. 1967. *Oral formulaic language in the biblical Psalms.* Toronto: University of Toronto Press.

Currid, J. D. 2013. *Against the gods: The polemical theology of the Old Testament.* Wheaton: Crossway.

Dahood, M. 1970. *Psalms III: 101–150.* Garden City: Doubleday.

Dahood, M. 1974. *Psalms II: 51–100.* New York: Doubleday.

Davis, E. 1992. Exploding the limits: Form and function in Psalm 22. *Journal for the Study of the Old Testament* 53:93–105.

Day, J. 1992. *Psalms* (Old Testament guides). Sheffield, UK: JSOT Press.

de Bruyn, J. 2013. A clash of space. Reaccessing spaces and speech: A cognitive-linguistic approach to Psalm 2. *Journal for Semitics* 22:193–209.

deClaissé-Walford, N. L. 2004. *Introduction to the Psalms: A song from ancient Israel.* St. Louis: Chalice Press.

deClaissé-Walford, N. L., ed. 2014. *The shape and shaping of the book of Psalms: The current state of scholarship.* Atlanta: SBL Press.

deClaissé-Walford, N. L., R. A. Jacobson, and B. LaNeel Tanner, eds. 2014. *The book of Psalms* (NICOT). Grand Rapids: Eerdmans.

de Lang, M. 2012. Historical criticism reformulated in the "Age of Imagination." *The Bible Translator* 63:3, 116–125.

de Waard, J. 1996. Hebrew rhetoric and the translator. In L. de Regt, J. de Waard, and J. P. Fokkelman (eds.), *Literary structure and rhetorical strategies in the Hebrew Bible,* 242–251. Assen, Netherlands: Van Gorcum.

de Waard, J. and E. A. Nida. 1986. *From one language to another: Functional equivalence in Bible translating.* Nashville, TN: Thomas Nelson.

Deibler, E. W., Jr. 1998. *A semantic and structural analysis of Romans.* Dallas, TX: Summer Institute of Linguistics.

Delitzsch, F. 1869. *Biblical commentary on the Psalms,* Vol. III. Grand Rapids: Eerdmans.

Dingemanse, M. 2012. Advances in the cross-linguistic study of ideophones. *Language and linguistics compass* 6:654–652.

Dobbs-Allsopp, F. W. 2002. *Lamentations.* Louisville, KY: Westminster-John Knox.

Dobbs-Allsopp, F. W. 2006. The Psalms and lyric verse. In F. L. Shultz (ed.), *The evolution of rationality: Interdisciplinary essays,* 346–379. Grand Rapids: Eerdmans.

Dobbs-Allsopp, F. W. 2014. Poetry of the Psalms. In Brown, W. P., 89–91.

Dorsey, D. A. 1999. *The literary structure of the Old Testament.* Grand Rapids: Baker Books.

Draper, J. and K. Mtata. n.d. Orality and African religions. https://www. academia.edu/1502950/Orality_Literature_and_African_Religions_ Kenneth_Mtata_and_Jonathan_A._Draper. Accessed September 2, 2017.

Driyvers, P. 1965. *The Psalms: Their structure and meaning.* New York: Herder and Herder.

DuRant, D. 2004. A conversation with Matt Redman. http://www.rzim.org/ just-thinking/a-conversation-with-matt-redman/. Accessed September 2, 2017.

Durham, J. I. 1987. *Exodus* (Word Biblical Commentary 3). Waco, TX: Word Books.

Ecclesia Bible Society. 2009. *The voice of Psalms: With reflections from the Psalms.* Nashville, TN: Thomas Nelson.

Emanuel, D. 2012. *From bards to biblical exegetes: A close reading and intertextual analysis of selected exodus Psalms.* Eugene, OR: Pickwick.

Estes, D. J. 2013. The transformation of pain into praise in the individual Lament Psalms. In Schmutzer and Howard, 151–163.

Fauconnier, G. 2007. Mental spaces. In D. Geeraerts and H. Cuyckens (eds.), *The Oxford handbook of cognitive linguistics,* 351–376. Oxford: Oxford University Press.

Finnegan, R. 1970. *Oral literature in Africa.* Oxford: Clarendon Press.

Finnegan, R. 1977. *Oral poetry: Its nature, significance, and social context.* Cambridge: Cambridge University Press.

Finnegan, R. 1992. *Oral poetry: Its nature, significance, and social context.* First Midland Book edition. Bloomington: Indiana University Press.

Firth, D. G. 2008. Asaph and sons of Korah. In Longman and Enns, 24–27.

Firth, D. G. and J. A. Grant, eds. 2008. *Words and the Word: Explorations in biblical interpretation and literary theory.* Downers Grove, IL: IVP Academic.

Firth, D. G. and P. S. Johnston, eds. 2005. *Interpreting the Psalms: Issues and approaches.* Downers Grove, IL: IVP Academic.

Fisch, H. 1988. *Poetry with a purpose: Biblical poetics and interpretation.* Bloomington: Indiana University Press.

Fitzgerald, D. 2013. Translating psalms to be sung: Encoding the poetic line. CD of the Bible Translation 2013 Conference, pp. 1–18.

Floor, S. 2013. The importance of biblical theology for Bible translation and oral Bible storying. Paper presented at the BT 2013 Conference, Dallas TX, October 14, 2013.

Fokkelman, J. P. 1998. *Major poems of the Hebrew Bible: At the interface of hermeneutics and structural analysis,* Vol. I: Ex. 15, Deut. 32, and Job 3. Assen, The Netherlands: Van Gorcum.

Follis, E. R., ed. 1987. *Directions in biblical Hebrew poetry.* Sheffield, UK: JSOT.

Ford D. F. and D. W. Hardy. 2005. *Living in praise: Worshipping and knowing God.* London: Darton, Longman and Todd.

Fox, E. 1995. *The Schocken Bible,* Vol. 1: *The five Books of Moses.* New York: Schocken Books.

Freedman, D. N. 1974. Strophe and meter in Exodus 15. In H. Bream, R. Heim, and C. Moore (eds.), *A light unto my path: Old Testament studies in honor of Jacob M. Myers,* 163–203. Philadelphia: Temple University Press.

Freedman, D. N. 1980. *Pottery, poetry, and prophecy: Studies in early Hebrew poetry* Winona Lake, IN: Eisenbrauns.

Fretheim, T. E. 1991. *Exodus* (Interpretation). Louisville, KY: John Knox.

Futato, M. D. 2008. *Interpreting the Psalms: An exegetical handbook.* Grand Rapids: Kregel Academic.

Geiger, S. 2012. Colossians 3:16—Teaching and admonishing with music. *Wisconsin Lutheran Quarterly* 109:1, 53–57.

Geller, S. A. 1979. *Parallelism in early biblical poetry* (Harvard Semitic Monographs No. 20). Missoula, MT: Scholars Press.

Geller, S. A. 1993. Hebrew prosody and poetics: Biblical. In Preminger and Brogan, 509–511.

Gericke, J. W. 2012. What is it like to be a god? A philosophical clarification of instances of divine suffering in the Psalter. *Verbum et Ecclesia* 33(1), Art. #700, 6 pages. http://dx.doi.org/10.4102/ve.v33i1.700.

Gerstenberger, E. S. 1988. *Psalms, Part 1, with an introduction to cultic poetry* (FOTL 14). Grand Rapids: Eerdmans.

Gerstenberger, E. S. 2001. *Psalms, Part 2, and Lamentations* (FOTL 15). Grand Rapids: Eerdmans.

Gerstenberger, E. S. 2014. The dynamics of praise in the ancient Near East, or poetry and politics. In deClaissé-Walford, N. L., ed. 2014, 27–39.

Gillingham, S. E. 1994. *The poems and Psalms of the Hebrew Bible.* Oxford: Oxford University Press.

Gispen, W. H. 1982. *Exodus* (Bible Student's Commentary). Grand Rapids: Zondervan.

Goldingay, J. 2006. *Psalms, Vol. 1: Psalms 1–41* (BCOT). Grand Rapids: Baker Academic.

Goldingay, J. 2007. *Psalms, Vol. 2: Psalms 42–89* (BCOT). Grand Rapids: Baker Academic.

Goldingay, J. 2008. *Psalms: Vol. 3: Psalms 90–150* (BCOT). Grand Rapids: Baker Academic.

Goodman, Wm. 2012. *Yearning for you: Psalms and the Song of Songs in conversation with rock and worship songs.* Sheffield, UK: Sheffield Phoenix Press.

Goodwin. P. 2013. *Translating the English Bible: From relevance to deconstruction.* Cambridge: James Clarke.

Grady, J. E. 2007. Metaphor. In D. Geeraerts and H. Cuyckens (eds.). *The Oxford handbook of cognitive linguistics,* 188–213. Oxford: Oxford University Press.

Grant, J. A. 2005. The Psalms and the king. In Firth and Johnston, 101–118.

Grant, J. H. 2012. How I introduced Psalm singing to my church…without getting fired! In Wells and Van Neste, 91–107.

Greene, R. (ed.). 2012. *The Princeton encyclopedia of poetry and poetics.* Fourth edition. Princeton and Oxford: Princeton University Press.

Gregg, S. 2013. *Revelation—four views: A parallel commentary* (rev. ed.). Nashville, TN: Thomas Nelson.

Grossman, E. 2010. *Why translation matters.* New Haven, CT and London: Yale University Press.

Guthrie, S. R. 2013. Love the Lord with all your voice. *Christianity Today* 57:5, 44–47.

Gutt, E-A. 1987. What is the meaning we translate? *Occasional papers in translation and textlinguistics,* no. 1:31–58.

Gwengwe. J. W. 1967. *Ndakatulo.* Nairobi and Lusaka. Oxford University Press.

Haik-Vantoura, S. (J. Wheeler, ed.). 1991. *The music of the Bible revealed: The deciphering of a millenary notation.* Second edition. North Richland Hills, TX: D. & F. Scott Publishing.

Hamlin, H. 2012. Psalms, metrical. In Greene, 1124–1125.

Harman, A. 2011a. *Psalms,* Vol. 1: *Psalms 1–72.* Fearn, UK: Mentor Books.

Harman, A. 2011b. *Psalms,* Vol. 2: *Psalms 73–150.* Fearn, UK: Mentor Books.

Hatim, B. 2013. *Teaching and researching translation.* Second edition. Applied Linguistics in Action Series. London and New York: Pearson Longman.

Hatim, B. and I. Mason. 1990. *Discourse and the translator.* London: Longman.

Hatim, B. and I. Mason. 1997. *The translator as communicator.* London: Routledge.

Hauser, A. J. 1987. Two songs of victory: A comparison of Exodus 15 and Judges 5. In Follis, 265–284.

Hausmann, J. 2014. The topic of violence—A hermeneutical challenge in reading Psalms. In Mtata et al., 81–90.

Hawkins, P. S. 2014. The Psalms in poetry. In Brown, W. P., 99–113.

Hayes, J. H. 1976. *Understanding the Psalms.* Valley Forge, PA: Judson Press.

Hilber, J. H. 2009. Psalms. In J. H. Walton (ed.), *Zondervan illustrated Bible backgrounds commentary,* 316–463. Grand Rapids: Zondervan.

Hill, C. E and M. J. Kruger. 2012. In search of the earliest text of the New Testament. In C. E. Hill and M. J. Kruger (eds.), *The early text of the New Testament,* 1–19. Oxford: Oxford University Press.

Hill, H. 2003. Communicating context in Bible translation. *Word & Deed* 2(2):1–31.

Hill, M. 2005. The challenge of acceptability of the translation by the target language community. Paper presented at OTSSA Congress on Biblical Interpretation in Africa. Pietermaritzburg, South Africa, Sept 19–23, 2005 (copy available from the author at Margaret_Hill@sil.org).

Hill, R. 2004. Contextual adjustment strategies and Bible translation. *Word and Deed* 3(1):1–25.

Hirsch, E. D. Jr. 1967. *Validity in interpretation.* New Haven, CT: Yale University Press.

Hirsch, E. D., Jr. 1976. *The aims of interpretation.* Chicago. University of Chicago Press.

Holladay, W. L. 1996. *The Psalms through three thousand years: Prayerbook of a cloud of witnesses.* Minneapolis, MN: Fortress Press.

Howard, D. M., Jr. 2013. Divine and human kingship as organizing motifs in the Psalter. In Schmutzer and Howard, 197–207.

Hrushovsky, B. 1971. Prosody, Hebrew. In *Encyclopedia Judaica,* 1200–1202. New York: Bureau of Jewish Education, Inc.

Hutchinson, J. H. 2005. The Psalms and praise. In Firth and Johnston, 85–100.

Jacobson, K. N. 2014. Perhaps YHWH is sleeping: "Awake" and "contend" in the book of Psalms. In deClaissé-Walford, N. L., ed. 2014, 129–145.

Jacobson, R. A. 2014. Imagining the future of Psalms studies. In deClaissé-Walford, N. L., ed. 2014, 231–246.

Jacobson, R. A. and K. N. Jacobson. 2013. *Invitation to the Psalms: A reader's guide for discovery and engagement.* Grand Rapids: Baker Academic.

Jacoby, M. 2013. *Deeper places: Experiencing God in the Psalms.* Grand Rapids: Baker Books.

Jakobson, R. 1960. Linguistics and poetics. In T. Sebeok (ed.), *Style in language,* 350–377. Cambridge: M.I.T. Press.

Jakobson, R. 1966. Grammatical parallelism and its Russian facet. *Language* 42:399–429.

Jakobson, R. 1972 (1960). Style in language. In R. deGeorge and F. deGeorge (eds.), *The Structuralists from Marx to Levi-Strauss,* 85–122. New York: Doubleday.

Jakobson, R. 1985. *Verbal art, verbal sign, verbal time.* Edited by K. Pomorska and S. Rudy. Minneapolis: University of Minnesota Press.

Janzen, J. G. 1992. Song of Moses, Song of Miriam: Who is seconding whom? *Catholic Biblical Quarterly* 54:211–220.

Janzen, J. G. 2003. Prayer and/as self-address: The case of Hannah. In Strawn and Bowen, 113–127.

Jenni, E. and C. Westermann. 1997. *Theological lexicon of the Old Testament,* Vol. 3. Translated by M. E. Biddle. Peabody, MA: Hendrickson.

Johnson, A. R. 1967. *Sacral kingship in ancient Israel,* second edition. Cardiff: University of Wales.

Johnson, J. W. 1993. Lyric. In Preminger and Brogan, 713–727.

Joiner, J. R. 2012. Performing the Psalms: Reclaiming the Psalms for corporate and communal worship. In Wells and Van Neste, 159–166.

Jones, C. B. 2014. The message of the Asaphite collection and its role in the Psalter. In deClaissé-Walford, N. L., ed. 2014, 71–85.

Kaiser Jr., W. C. 1994. Exodus. In K. L. Barker and J Kohlenberger III (eds.), *The NIV Bible commentary,* Vol. 1: Old Testament. Grand Rapids: Zondervan, 64–125.

Kaiser Jr. W. C. 2013. The laments of Lamentations: Compared to the Psalter. In Schmutzer and Howard, 127–133.

Keesmaat, S. C. 2004. The Psalms in Romans and Galatians. In S. Moyise and M. J. J. Menken (eds.), *The Psalms in the New Testament.* 139–161. London and New York: T&T Clark International.

Kelly, N. and J. Zetzsche. 2012. *Found in translation: How language shapes our lives and transforms the world.* New York: Penguin Perigee.

Kennedy, X. J. and D. Gioia. 2002. *An introduction to poetry.* Tenth edition. New York: Longman.

Kidner, D. 1973. *Psalms 1–72.* Downers Grove, IL: InterVarsity Press.

King, R. 2001. Two communication principles God uses with song. *Mission Frontiers* 23:2, 13.

King, P. D. 2012. *Surrounded by bitterness: Image schemas and metaphors for conceptualizing distress in Classical Hebrew.* Eugene, OR: Pickwick Publications.

Kishindo, P. J. 2003. Recurrent themes in Chichewa verse in Malawian newspapers. *Nordic Journal of African Studies* 12:3, 327–353.

Kitchen, K. A. 1966. *Ancient Orient and Old Testament.* Chicago: Inter-Varsity Press.

Kitchen, K. A. 2003. *On the reliability of the Old Testament.* Grand Rapids: Eerdmans.

Klein, Wm. W., C. L. Blomberg, and R. L. Hubbard, Jr. 1993. *Introduction to biblical interpretation.* Dallas, TX: Word Books.

Knust, J. and T. Wasserman. 2014. The biblical odes and the text of the Christian Bible: A reconsideration of the impact of liturgical singing on the transmission of the Gospel of Luke. *Journal of Biblical Literature* 133:2, 341–365.

Kofoed, J. B. 2005. Text and history: Historiography and the study of the biblical text (Diss. U Aarhus 2002). Winona Lake, IN: Eisenbrauns.

Kofoed, J. B. 2007. The role of faith in historical research: A rejoinder. *Scandinavian Journal of the Old Testament,* 21:2, 275–298.

Korpel, M. C. A. and J. C. de Moor. 1988. Fundamentals of Ugaritic and Hebrew poetry. In W. van der Meer and J. C. de Moor (eds.), *The structural analysis of biblical and Canaanite poetry,* 1–61. (JSOT Supplement Series No. 74). Sheffield, UK: JSOT Press.

Körting, C. 2014. Singing, praying, and meditating the Psalms: Exegetical and historical remarks. In Mtata et al., 59–71.

Kraus, H.-J. 1993. *Psalms 1–59* (A Continental Commentary). Translated by H. C. Oswald. Minneapolis, MN: Fortress.

Kruger, M. J. 2012. *Canon revisited: Establishing the origins and authority of the New Testament books.* Wheaton, IL: Crossway.

Kugel, J. L. 1981. *The idea of biblical poetry: Parallelism and its history.* New Haven, CT: Yale University Press.

Labuschagne, C. 2007. The Song at the Reed Sea in Exodus 15— Logotechnical analysis. http://www.labuschagne.nl/1.exod15.pdf. Accessed September 2, 2017.

Labuschagne, C. 2008. Songs, prayers, and poems in the narratives of the Hebrew Bible: A strategy for closer examination. https://www.rug.nl/research/portal/files/14437317/intro.embed.pdf. Accessed September 2, 2017.

Lama, A. K. 2013. *Reading Psalm 145 with the sages: A compositional analysis.* Carlisle, UK: Langham Monographs.

Landers, C. 2001. *Literary translation: A practical guide.* Buffalo and Toronto: Multilingual Matters.

Leach, R. 2001. http://www.selahpub.com/MusicInWorship/OnSinging Psalms.html. Accessed September 2, 2017.

Leaver, R. A. 2007. *Luther's liturgical music.* music: Principles and implications. Grand Rapids: Eerdmans.

Leeman, J. 2013. Listening to God's Word in the church. *Tabletalk* 37:1, 16–18.

Leiter, D. A. 2007. *Neglected voices: Peace in the Old Testament.* Scottsdale, PA: Herald Press.

Leonard, R. 1997. Singing the Psalms: A brief history of psalmody. http://www.laudemont.org/a-stp.htm. Accessed September 2, 2017.

Leupold, H. C. 1959. *Exposition of the Psalms.* Grand Rapids: Baker Book House.

Levine, H. J. 1995. *Sing unto God a new song: A contemporary reading of the Psalms*. Bloomington: Indiana University Press.

Levinsohn, S. C. 1983. *Pragmatics*. Cambridge: Cambridge University Press.

Lévi-Strauss, C. 1972. The structural study of myth. In R. deGeorge and F. deGeorge (eds.), *The structuralists from Marx to Lévi-Strauss*. Garden City, NY: Doubleday, 169–194.

Lewis, C. S. 1942. *A preface to Paradise Lost*. London: Oxford University Press.

Lewis, C. S. 1958. *Reflections on the Psalms*. London: Geoffrey Bles/New York: Harcourt-Brace.

Licht, J. 1986. *Storytelling in the Bible*. Second edition. Jerusalem: Magnes.

Longacre, R. E. 1989. *Joseph: A story of divine providence: A text theoretical and textlinguistic analysis of Genesis 37 and 39–48*. Winona Lake, IN: Eisenbrauns.

Longenbach, J. 2008. *The art of the poetic line*. Minneapolis, MN: Graywolf Press.

Longman, T., III. 1984. Psalm 98: A divine warrior victory song. *JETS* 27:3, 267–274.

Longman, T., III. 1988. *How to read the Psalms*. Downers Grove, IL: InterVarsity Press.

Longman, T., III.. 1993. The literature of the Old Testament. In L. Ryken and T. Longman III (eds.), *A complete literary guide to the Bible*. Grand Rapids: Zondervan, 95–107.

Longman, T., III. 2008. Psalms 2: Ancient Near Eastern backgrounds. In Longman and Enns, 593–605.

Longman, T., III. 2013. From weeping to rejoicing: Psalm 150 as the conclusion of the Psalter. In Schmutzer and Howard, 219–228.

Longman, T., III. and P. Enns, eds. 2003. *Dictionary of the Old Testament: Wisdom, poetry & writings*. Downers Grove, IL: IVP Academic.

Low, P. 2013. When songs cross linguistic borders: Translations, adaptations, and "replacement texts." *The Translator: Studies in Intercultural Communication* 19:2, 229–244.

Lund, N. W. 1930. The presence of chiasmus in the Old Testament. *The American Journal of Semitic Languages and Literatures* 46:2, 104–126.

Lunn, N. P. 2006. *Word-order variation in biblical Hebrew poetry: Differentiating pragmatics and poetics*. Bletchley, UK: Paternoster.

Luther, Martin. 1955 and 1986. Treatise on the last words of David. In Martin Luther, *Luther's works,* Vol. 15, 192. 192. Philadelphia: Concordia and Fortress Press.

Magonet, J. 1994. *A Rabbi reads the Psalms*. London: SCM Press.

Magonet, J. 2014. On reading Psalms as liturgy: Psalms 96–99. In deClaiss, N. L., ed. 2014, 161–177.

Maier, J. and V. Tollers, eds. 1979. *The Bible in its literary milieu: Contemporary essays*. Grand Rapids: Eerdmans.

Malunga, B. W. 1990. *Kuimba kwa mlakatuli.* Blantyre: CLAIM.

Masenya (Ngwan'a Mphahlele), M. 2014. Being 'ādām: A contextual reading of the Psalms today. In Mtata et al., 233–243.

Mays, J. L. 1994a. *Psalms* (Interpretation Commentary). Louisville, KY: John Knox Press.

Mays, J. L. 1994b. *The LORD reigns: A theological handbook to the Psalms.* Louisville: Westminster John Knox Press.

McCabe, R. V., Jr. 1981. *Carmen Maris Algosi:* An exegetical study of Exodus 15:1–18. Th.M. Thesis, Grace Theological Seminary.

McCann J. C., Jr. 1996. The book of Psalms. In L. E. Keck (ed.), *The new interpreter's Bible* (Vol. IV), 641–1280. Nashville, TN: Abingdon Press.

McCann J. C., Jr. 2012. Hearing the Psalter. In G. C. Bartholomew and D. J. H. Beldman (eds.), *Hearing the Old Testament: Listening for God's address,* 277–301. Grand Rapids: Eerdmans.

McCorkle, D. F. 2009. *The Davidic cipher: Unlocking the hidden music of the Psalms.* Parker, CO: Outskirts Press.

Megahan, M. L. 2013. The Biblical Hebrew concept of JOY: Cognitive lexical semantics and the meaning of Biblical Hebrew lexemes. Ph.D. Dissertation, University of Stellenbosch, South Africa.

Merwe, C. H. J. van der. 2011. The difference between הִנֵּה, הֵן and רְאֵה. In *Festschrift für Walter Groß zum 70. Geburtstag* (HERDERS BIBLISCHE STUDIEN 62), 237–258. Stuttgart: Verlag Herder.

Michalowski, P. 1996. Ancient poetics. In M. E. Vogelzang and H. L. J. Vanstiphout (eds.), *Mesopotamian Poetic Language,* 141–153. Gronigen: STYX.

Millard, A. R. 2003. Writing. In T. D. Alexander and D. W. Becker (eds.), *Dictionary of the Old Testament: Pentateuch.* Downers Grove, IL: IVP Academic, 904–911.

Miller, P. D., Jr. 1986. *Interpreting the Psalms.* Philadelphia: Fortress Press.

Miller, P. D., Jr. 1994. *They cried to the Lord: The form and theology of biblical prayer.* Minneapolis: Fortress.

Montgomery, L. 2000. Singing Psalms in the new millennium. http://npm.org/wp-content/uploads/2017/07/SingingPsalms.pdf. Accessed September 2, 2017.

Morgan, M. 2014. Singing the Psalms. In Brown, W. P., 571–582.

Morris, S. 2014. God's Word became our poetry and sang within us: Facilitating contextualisation through indigenous poetry. *Journal of Translation* 10:1–14.

Mossop, B. 2001. *Revising and editing for translators.* Manchester: St. Jerome.

Mowinckel, S., D. R. Ap-Thomas, trans. 1962. *The Psalms in Israel's worship,* Vol. 1. Oxford: Blackwell and Nashville, TN: Abingdon.

Mtata, K., K-W. Niebuhr, and M. Rose, eds. 2014. *Singing the songs of the Lord in foreign lands: Psalms in contemporary Lutheran interpretation.* Leipzig: Evangelische Verlagsanhalt.

Muilenburg, J. (1966) 1984. Liturgy on the triumphs of Yahweh. *Studia biblica et semitica. Theodoro Christiano Vriezen qui munere professoris theologiae per XXV annos functus est, ab amicis, collegis, discipulis dedicata.* Wageningen: H. Veenman. Republished in Thomas F. Best (ed.), *Hearing and speaking the Word: Selections from the Works of James Muilenburg,* 233–251. Chico, CA: Scholars Press.

Muilenburg, J. (1969) 1992. Form criticism and beyond. *Journal of Biblical Literature* 88:1–18. (Reprinted in P. R. House (ed.), *Beyond form criticism: Essays in Old Testament literary criticism,* 49–69. Winona Lake, IN: Eisenbrauns).

Mulder, J. 1972. *Studies in Psalm 45.* Nijmegen: Karmel Doddendaal.

Munday, J. 2008. *Introducing translation studies: Theories and applications.* Second edition. London and New York: Routledge.

Mvula, E. S. T. 1981. *Akoma akagonera: Ndakatulo za Amalawi.* Limbe, Malawi: Popular Publications.

Mykytiuk, L. 2013. Strengthening biblical historicity vis-a-vis minimalism, 1992–2008 (Part 2.2). *Journal of Religious and Theological Information* 12:3–4, 114–155.

Ndoga, S. S. 2014. Revisiting the theocratic agenda of Book 4 of the Psalter for interpretive premise. In deClaissé, N. L., ed. 2014, 147–159.

Nel, P. J. 1998. The theology of the Royal Psalms. *Old Testament Essays* 11:1, 71–92.

New English Translation. https://net.bible.org/#!bible/Psalms + 1. Accessed September 2, 2017.

New Living Translation (second edition). 2004. Wheaton: Tyndale House.

News24. 10 Commandments for Zambia. http://www.news24.com/ Africa/News/10-Commandments-for-Zambia-20110925. Accessed September 2, 2017.

Nida, E. A. 1964. *Toward a science of translating.* Leiden: E. J. Brill.

Nida, E. A. and C. R. Taber. 1969. *The theory and practice of translation.* Leiden: E. J. Brill.

Njoroge, J. M. 2009. *Apologetics: Why your church needs it.* Norcross, GA: RZIM Publishing.

Nord, C. 1997. *Translating as a purposeful activity: Functionalist approaches explained.* Manchester: St. Jerome.

Nordley, S. Forthcoming. Lessons from translating Exodus 15:1–18. *Journal of Translation.*

Nõmmik, U. 2014. Between praise and lament: Remarks on the development of the Hebrew Psalms. In Mtata et. al., 91–104.

O'Connor, M. P. 1980. *Hebrew verse structure.* Winona Lake, IN: Eisenbrauns.

O'Connor, M. P. 1993. Parallelism. In Preminger and Brogan, 877–878.

Okorocha, C. 2006. Psalms. In T. Adeyemo (ed.), *Africa Bible commentary,* 607–746. Nairobi: Zondervan/Word Alive.

Oliver, J. P. J. 1979. The sceptre of justice and Ps. 45:7b. *Journal of Northwest Semitic Languages* 7, 45–54.

Osborn, N. D. and H. A. Hatton. 1999. *A handbook on Exodus.* New York: United Bible Societies.

Osborne, G. R. 2006. *The hermeneutical spiral: A comprehensive introduction to biblical interpretation,* Revised and Expanded. Downers Grove, IL: IVP Academic.

Osborne, G. R. 2008. Literary theory and biblical interpretation. In Firth and Grant, 13–50.

Parrish, V. S. 2003. *A story of the Psalms: Conversation, canon, and congregation.* Collegeville, MN: Liturgical Press.

Patterson, R. D. 1985. A multiplex approach to Psalm 45. *Grace Theological Journal* 6:1, 29–48.

Patterson, R. D. 1995. The song of redemption. *Westminster Theological Journal* 57:453–461.

Patterson, R. D. 2004. Victory at sea: Prose and poetry in Exodus 14–15. *Bibliotheca Sacra* 161:42–54.

Peacock, H. 1981. *A translator's guide to selected Psalms.* London, New York, Stuttgart: United Bible Societies.

Perowne, J. J. S. 1878. *The book of Psalms.* London: George Bell & Sons.

Petersen, J. R. 2015. *The Psalms in Christian history.* Lancaster, PA: Alliance of Confessing Evangelicals.

Peterson, E. H. 1994. *The message: Psalms.* Colorado Springs: NavPress.

Peterson, E. H. 2001. *The message: The Old Testament books of Moses in contemporary language.* Colorado Springs: NavPress.

Pike, K. L. and E. G. Pike. 1977. *Grammatical analysis.* Dallas, TX: Summer Institute of Linguistics.

Piper, J. 2010. *Let the nations be glad.* Third edition. Grand Rapids: Baker.

Plass, E. M. 1959. *What Luther says: An anthology.* St. Louis: Concordia Publishing.

Popovich, A. 1976. Aspects of metatext. *Canadian Review of Comparative Literature* 3:225–235.

Preminger, A. and T. V. F. Brogan. 1993. *The new Princeton encyclopedia of poetry and poetics.* Princeton: Princeton University Press.

Räisänen, H. 2000. *Beyond New Testament theology: A story and a programme.* Second edition. London: SCM Press.

Reger, G. T. N. 2010. The song of the sea—A rhetorical-critical analysis and contextual interpretation of Ex. 15:1–21. M.A. Dissertation. Pietermaritzburg, South Africa: University of KwaZulu-Natal.

Reiss, K. 2000. *Translation criticism: The potentials and limitations (Categories and criteria for translation quality assessment).* Translated by E. Rhodes. Manchester: St. Jerome.

Ricoeur, P. 1975. Biblical hermeneutics. *Semeia* 4, 78–92.

Ross, A. P. 2013. The "thou" sections of laments: The bold and earnest prayers of the psalmists. In Schmutzer and Howard, 135–150.

Ryken, L. 1984. *How to read the Bible as literature and get more out of it.* Grand Rapids: Zondervan.

Ryken, L. 1992. *Words of delight: A literary introduction to the Bible.* Grand Rapids: Baker Books.

Ryken, L. 2009. *Understanding English Bible translation: The case for an essentially literal approach.* Wheaton: Crossway.

Ryken, L. 2012. Reclaiming the Psalms for private worship. In Wells and Van Neste, 125–138.

Ryken, L. and P. G. Ryken, eds. 2007. *The literary study Bible: ESV.* Wheaton: Crossway Bibles.

Ryken, L., J. C. Wilhoit, and T. Longman, III. 1998. *Dictionary of biblical imagery.* Downers Grove, IL: InterVarsity Press.

Sandy, D. B. and R. L. Giese, Jr. 1995. *Cracking Old Testament codes: A guide to interpreting the literary genres of the Old Testament.* Nashville, TN: Broadman and Holman.

Sanneh, L. 2003. *Whose religion is Christianity? The gospel beyond the West.* Grand Rapids and Cambridge: Eerdmans.

Scharlemann, R. P. 1987. Theological text. *Semeia* 40:5–19.

Schedewaldt, W. 1964. *Griechisches Theater.* Frankfurt am Main: n.p.

Schmutzer, A. J. and D. M. Howard, Jr., eds. 2013. *The Psalms: Language for all seasons of the soul.* Chicago: Moody Press.

Schoekel, L. A. 1988. *A manual of Hebrew poetics* (Subsidia Biblica 11). Rome: Editrice Pontificio Istituto Biblico.

Schrag, B. 1992. Translating song texts as oral composition. *Notes on Translation* 6:1, 44–62.

Schrag, B. 2013. *Creating local arts together: A manual to help communities reach their kingdom goals.* Pasadena, CA: William Carey Library.

Schuldt, J. B. 2013. A song to remember. http://odb.org/2013/01/20/a-song-to-remember/. Accessed September 2, 2017.

Searle, J. 1979. *Expression and meaning: Studies in the theory of speech acts.* Cambridge: Cambridge University Press.

Shandele, M. E. 2001. *Cimbonimboni* [Mirror]. Lusaka: Zambia Educational Publishing House.

Shreckhise, R. L. 2007. The rhetoric of the expressions in the Song by the Sea (Exodus 15, 1–18). *Scandinavian Journal of the Old Testament* 21(2):201–217.

Silberman, L. H. 1987. Introduction: Reflections on orality, aurality and perhaps more. *Semeia* 39:1–6.

Sitima, J. G. 2001. *Nthondo: Kufotokozera za ndakatulo.* Zomba, Malawi: Chancellor College.

Smalley, Wm. A. 1974. Restructuring translations of the Psalms as poetry. In M. Black and Wm. Smalley (eds.), *On language, culture, and religion: In honor of Eugene A. Nida*, 337–371. The Hague: Mouton.

Snearly, M. K. 2013. The return of the king: Book V as a witness to the messianic hope in the Psalter. In Schmutzer and Howard, 209–217.

Snyman, A. 2008. A structural-historical approach to the exegesis of the Old Testament. In Firth and Grant, 51–73.

Soanes, C. and A. Stevenson, eds. 2006. *Concise Oxford dictionary*. Eleventh edition. Oxford: Oxford University Press.

Sogaard, V. 1991. *Audio Scriptures handbook*. Reading, UK: United Bible Societies.

Spicehandler, E., E. L. Greenstein, W. van Bekkum and V. K. Shemtov. 2012. Hebrew poetry. In Greene, 601-610.

Sproul, R. C. 2012. The influence of music. In Burk Parsons (ed.), *Tabletalk* 36(9):61–62. Sanford: Ligonier Ministries.

Spurgeon, C. H. 1882. *The treasury of David*. New York: Funk & Wagnalls.

Stallman, R. C. 2008. Music, song. In Longman and Enns, 483–489.

Steiner, V. J. 2013. Celebration in song and dance: Reflections on Exodus 15:1–21. *Miqra* 12:1, 1–17. http://miqra.net/journal/miqra-12.1-winter-2013-exodus/celebration-in-song-and-dance-reflections-on-exodus-151-21. Accessed April 20, 2013.

Stendahl, K. 2008. *Meanings: The Bible as document and as guide*. Second edition. Minneapolis: Fortress Press.

Strawn, B. A. 2008. Lyric poetry. In Longman and Enns, 437–446.

Strawn, B. A. and N. R. Bowen, eds. 2003. *A God so near: Essays on Old Testament theology in honor of Patrick D. Miller*. Winona Lake, IN: Eisenbrauns.

Stuhlmueller, C. 1983. *Psalms* (Old Testament Message). Wilmington, DE: Michael Glazier.

Stutler, R. 2013. Three ways to sing the Psalms. http://www.stutler.cc/russ/sing_psalms.html. Accessed September 2, 2017.

Swanson, J. A. n.d. *A dictionary of biblical languages w/ semantic domains: Hebrew (OT)*. Logos Bible Software: Libronix Digital Library System.

Sweeney, M. A. 2008. Form criticism. In Longman and Enns, 227–241.

Tate, M. E. 1990. *Psalms 51–100* (Word Biblical Commentary, Vol. 20). Waco, TX: Word Books.

Tate, M. E. 1993. *Psalms 101–150* (Word Biblical Commentary, Vol. 21). Waco, TX: Word Books.

Tate, W. R. 1991. *Biblical interpretation: An integrated approach*. Peabody, MA: Hendrickson.

Terrien, S. 1978. *The elusive presence*. San Francisco: Harper & Row.

Terrien, S. 2003. *The Psalms: Strophic structure and theological commentary*. Grand Rapids: Eerdmans.

The NET Bible: New English translation. 2003. Biblical Studies Press (www.netbible.com).

The Psalms in verse. 1995 (republication). Uhrichsville, OH: Barbour and Company.

Towner, W. S. 2003. "Without our aid he did us make": Singing the meaning of the Psalms. In Strawn and Bowen, 17–34.

Trible, P. 1994. *Rhetorical criticism: Context, method, and the book of Jonah* (Old Testament Guides). Minneapolis: Fortress Press.

Tucker, G. M. 1971. *Form criticism and the Old Testament.* Philadelphia: Fortress.

Tucker, W. D. Jr. 2008. Psalms, book of. In Longman and Enns, 578–593.

Tucker, W. D., Jr. 2014. The role of the foe in Book 5: Reflections on the final composition of the Psalter. In deClaissé-Walford, N. L., ed. 2014, 179–191.

Turco, L. 2000. *The book of forms: A handbook of poetics.* Third edition. Hanover: University Press of New England.

Van der Merwe, C. H. J. (See Merwe, C. H. J. van der).

VanGemeren, Wm. A. 1991. Psalms. In F. E. Gaebelein (ed.), *The expositor's Bible commentary,* Vol. 5, 3–880. Grand Rapids: Zondervan.

VanGemeren, Wm. A. 1994. Psalms. In K. L. Barker and J. Kohlenberger III, eds, *NIV Bible commentary,* Vol. 1: Old Testament, 790–935. Grand Rapids: Zondervan.

VanGemeren, Wm. A. 1997a. *New international dictionary of Old Testament theology & exegesis,* Vol. 1. Grand Rapids: Zondervan.

VanGemeren, Wm. A. 1997b. *New international dictionary of Old Testament theology & exegesis,* Vol. 3. Grand Rapids: Zondervan.

VanGemeren, Wm. A. 2013. Entering the textual world of the Psalms: Literary analysis. In Schmutzer and Howard, 29–48.

Vanhoozer, K. J. 1986. The semantics of biblical literature. In D. A. Carson and J. D. Woodbridge (eds.), *Hermeneutics, authority, and canon.* Grand Rapids: Zondervan, 53–104.

Van Neste, R. 2012. Ancient songs and apostolic preaching: How the New Testament laid claim to the Psalms. In Wells and Van Neste, 35–50.

Venuti, L. 1993. Translation as cultural politics: Regimes of domestication in English. *Textual Practice* 7(2):208–223.

Van Wolde, E. 2009. *Reframing biblical studies: When language and text meet culture, cognition, and context.* Winona Lake: Eisenbrauns.

Wallace, H. N. 2009. *Psalms.* Sheffield, UK: Sheffield Phoenix Press.

Wallace, R. E. 2014. Gerald Wilson and the characterization of David in Book 5 of the Psalter. In deClaissé-Walford, N. L., ed. 2014, 193–207.

Walton, J. H., V. H. Matthews, and M. W. Chavalas. 2000. *The IVP Bible background commentary: Old Testament.* Downers Grove. IL: InterVarsity.

Wanke, R. M. 2014. The Vengeance Psalm as a phenomenon of critical justice: The problem of enemies in Luther's interpretation of Psalms. In Mtata et al., 105–117.

Watson, W. G. E. 1984. *Classical Hebrew poetry: A guide to its techniques* (JSOT Supplement Series No. 26). Sheffield, UK: JSOT Press.

Watts, J. W., 1992. *Psalm and story: Inset hymns in Hebrew narrative* (JSOT Sup 139). Sheffield, UK: Sheffield Academic Press.

Wechsler, R. 1998. *Performing without a stage: The art of literary translation.* New Haven, CT: Catbird Press.

Wedekind, K. 1975. The praise singers. *The Bible Translator 26:245–47.*

Weiser, A. 1962. *The Psalms: A commentary* (OTL). Translated by H. Hartwell. Philadelphia: Westminster.

Weissbort, D. and A. Eysteinsson, eds. 2006. *Translation—theory and practice: A historical reader.* Oxford: Oxford University Press.

Wells, C. R. 2012. Conclusion. In Wells and Van Neste, 203–206.

Wells, C. R., and R. Van Neste, eds. 2012. *Forgotten songs: Reclaiming the Psalms for Christian worship.* Nashville, TN: B&H Publishing.

Wendland, E. R. 1985. *Language, society, and Bible translation.* Cape Town: Bible Society of South Africa.

Wendland, E. R. 1990. "What is truth?" Semantic density and the language of the Johannine epistles. *Neotestamentica* 24(2):301–333.

Wendland, E. R. 1993. *Comparative discourse analysis and the translation of Psalm 22 in Chichewa, a Bantu language of South-Central Africa.* Lewiston/ Lampeter: The Edwin Mellen Press.

Wendland, E. R. 1994a. Continuity and discontinuity in Hebrew poetic design: Patterns and points of significance in the structure and setting of Psalm 30. In E. Wendland (ed.), *Discourse perspectives on Hebrew poetry in the Scriptures* (UBS Monograph Series No. 7, 28–66). Reading and New York: United Bible Societies.

Wendland, E. R. 1994b. The discourse analysis of Hebrew poetry: A procedural outline. In E. Wendland (ed.), *Discourse perspectives on Hebrew poetry in the Scriptures* (UBS Monograph Series No. 7, 1–27). Reading and New York: United Bible Societies.

Wendland, E. R. 1998. *Buku loyera: Introduction to the new Chichewa Bible translation* (Kachere Monograph). Blantyre: Christian Literature Association in Malawi (CLAIM).

Wendland, E. R. 2002 (1998). *Analyzing the Psalms: With exercises for Bible students and translators.* Second edition. Dallas, TX: SIL International.

Wendland, E. R. 2004. *Translating the literature of Scripture: A literary-rhetorical approach to Bible translation* (Publications in Translation and Textlinguistics No. 1). Dallas, TX: SIL International.

Wendland, E. R. 2007. Aspects of the principle of 'parallelism' in Hebrew poetry. *Journal of Northwest Semitic Languages* 33(1):101–124.

Wendland, E. R. 2008. *Contextual frames of reference in translation: A coursebook for Bible translators and teachers.* Manchester: St. Jerome.

Wendland, E. R. 2011. *LiFE-style translating: A workbook for Bible translators.* Second edition. Dallas, TX: SIL: International.

Wendland, E. R. 2013a. *Lovely, lively lyrics: Selected studies in Biblical Hebrew verse*. Dallas, TX: SIL International.

Wendland, E. R. 2013b. *Orality and Scripture: Composition, translation, and transmission*. Dallas, TX: SIL International.

Wendland, E. R. 2013c. 'My tongue is the stylus of a skilled scribe' (Ps. 45:2c): If so in the Scriptures, then why not also in translation? *Verbum et Ecclesia* 34:1, 1–8 (http://dx.doi.org/10.4102/ ve.v34i1.777).

Wenham, G. J. 2012a. *Psalms as Torah: Reading the biblical song ethically* (Studies in Theological Interpretation). Grand Rapids: Baker Academic.

Wenham, G. J. 2012b. *The Psalter reclaimed: Praying and praising with the Psalms*. Wheaton: Crossway.

Westermann, C. 1965. *The praise of God in the Psalms*. Richmond: John Knox.

Westermann, C. 1980. *The Psalms: Structure, content & message*. Translated by R. Gehrke. Minneapolis, MN: Augsburg Press.

Westermann, C. 1981. *Praise and lament in the Psalms*. Translated by K. R. Crim and R. N. Soulen Edinburgh: T&T Clark.

Westermann, C. 1989. *The living Psalms*. Translated by J. R. Porter. Grand Rapids: Eerdmans.

Wheeler, J. 1989a. Music of the temple. *Archaeology and Biblical Research* 2(1):12–20.

Wheeler, J. 1989b. The origin of the music of the temple. *Archaeology and Biblical Research* 2:4, 113–122.

Whybray, N. 1996. *Reading the Psalms as a book*. Sheffield, UK: Sheffield Academic Press.

Wiklander, B. 1984. *Prophecy as literature: A textlinguistic and rhetorical approach to Isaiah 2–4* (Old Testament Series 22). Gleerup: Coniectanea Biblica.

Williams, J. and A. Chesterman. 2002. *The map: A beginner's guide to doing research in translation studies*. Manchester: St. Jerome.

Wilson, G. B. 1985. *Revelation*. Durham: Evangelical Press.

Wilson, G. H. 1985. *The editing of the Hebrew Psalter*. Chico, CA: Scholars Press.

Wilson, G. H. 2005. The structure of the Psalter. In Firth and Johnston, 229–246.

Wilson, M. R. 1989. *Our father Abraham: Jewish roots of the Christian faith*. Grand Rapids: Eerdmans; Dayton: Center for Judaic-Christian Studies.

Wilt, T. L. (ed.) 2003. *Bible translation: Frames of reference*. Manchester: St. Jerome.

Wilt, T. L. 2005a. Literary functional equivalence: Some case studies. *Journal of Biblical Text Research* 10:82–116.

Wilt, T. L. 2005b. Translation principles for LiFE, inductively derived. In Philip Noss (ed.), *Current trends in Scripture translation: Definitions and identity*, 215–223. Reading: UBS.

Wilt, T. L. and E. Wendland. 2008. *Scripture frames & framing: A workbook for Bible translators.* Stellenbosch: SUN Press.

Wittman, D. E. 2014. Let us cast off their ropes from us: The editorial significance of the portrayal of foreign nations in Psalms 2 and 149. In deClaissé, N. L., ed. 2014, 53–69.

Witvliet, J. D. 2012. Words to grow into: The Psalms as formative speech. In Wells and Van Neste, 7–16.

Wolterstorff, N. 1995. *Divine discourse: Philosophical reflections on the claim that God speaks.* Cambridge: Cambridge University Press.

Wright, N. T. 2013a. Saving the Psalms (Interview by Andrew Byers). *Christianity Today* 57(7):79.

Wright, N. T. 2013b. *The case for the Psalms: Why they are essential.* New York: Harper One.

Zevit, Z. 1990. Roman Jakobson, psycholinguistics, and biblical poetry. *Journal of Biblical Literature* 109(3):385–401.

Zogbo, L. and E. Wendland. 2000. *Hebrew poetry in the Bible: A guide for understanding and for translating.* New York: United Bible Societies.

Index

SIL International Publications
Additional Releases in the
Publications in Translation and Textlinguistics Series

7. **Prophetic rhetoric: Case studies in text analysis and translation.** Second edition, by Ernst R. Wendland, 2014, 719 pp., ISBN: 978-1-55671-345-3

6. **Orality and the Scriptures: Composition, translation, and transmission,** by Ernst R. Wendland, 2013, 405 pp., ISBN 978-1-55671-298-2

5. **Lovely, lively lyrics: Selected studies in Biblical Hebrew verse,** by Ernst R. Wendland, 2013, 461 pp., ISBN 978-1-55671-327-9

4. **LiFE-style translating: A workbook for Bible translators.** Second edition, by Ernst R. Wendland, 2011, 509 pp., ISBN 978-155671-243-2

3. **The development of textlinguistics in the writings of Robert Longacre,** by Shin Ja Hwang, 2010, 423 pp., ISBN 978-1-55671-246-3

2. **Artistic and rhetorical patterns in Quechua legendary texts,** by Ågot Bergli, 2010, 304 pp., ISBN 978-1-55671-244-9

1. **Translating the literature of Scripture: A literary-rhetorical approach to Bible translation,** by Ernst R. Wendland, 2004, 509 pp., ISBN 978-1-55671-152-7

SIL International Publications
7500 W. Camp Wisdom Road
Dallas, TX 75236-5629 USA

General inquiry: publications_intl@sil.org
Pending order inquiry: sales_intl@sil.org
www.sil.org/resources/publications

About the Author

Ernst R. Wendland earned a B.A. in Classics and Biblical Languages from Northwestern College (Wisconsin), an M.A. in Linguistics and a Ph.D. in African Languages and Literature from the University of Wisconsin, and a Master of Sacred Theology in exegetical theology from Wisconsin Lutheran Seminary. Wendland has lived in Zambia since 1962 and been an instructor at the Lutheran Bible Institute and Seminary (Lusaka, Zambia) since 1968. A former United Bible Societies translation consultant, he serves as Professor Extraordinary in the Centre for Bible Interpretation and Translation in Africa (CEBITA) within the Department of Ancient Studies at the University of Stellenbosch, South Africa, as a dissertation examiner in Zambian languages for the University of Zambia's Department of Literature and Languages, and as adjunct professor in theology and translation at the Asia Lutheran Seminary, Hong Kong. His research interests include structural, stylistic, and rhetorical studies in biblical texts and the Bantu languages of south central Africa.

Recent books

2017. *Survey of translation studies: From the perspective of Bible translation theory and practice.* Fourth edition. Academia.edu/11318453/: CEBITA, Stellenbosch University.

2016. de Regt, Lénart J. and Ernst R. Wendland. *A handbook on Numbers (UBS Handbook Series).* Miami: United Bible Societies.

2015. *The dramatic genius of Julius Chongo: Selected Nyanja radio tales, with English translations.* Academia.edu/11866659/: CEBITA, Stellenbosch University.

2014. *Prophetic rhetoric: Case studies in text analysis and translation.* Dallas: SIL International.

2013. *Lovely, lively lyrics: Selected studies in Biblical Hebrew verse.* Dallas: SIL International.

2013. *Orality and the Scriptures: Composition, translation, and transmission.* Dallas: SIL International.

Academic website

https://sun.academia.edu/EWENDLAND

CPSIA information can be obtained
at www.ICGtesting.com
Printed in the USA
LVOW08s2349120917
548450LV00011BB/73/P